GERMANY'S AIMS IN THE
FIRST WORLD WAR

GERMANY'S AIMS
IN THE FIRST
WORLD WAR

By

FRITZ FISCHER

With Introductions by
HAJO HOLBORN
YALE UNIVERSITY
and
JAMES JOLL
LONDON SCHOOL OF ECONOMICS AND POLITICAL SCIENCE

W · W · NORTON & COMPANY · INC · NEW YORK

CONTENTS

v

CONTENTS

Part Three: 1918

Maps

ILLUSTRATIONS

INTRODUCTION TO THE
AMERICAN EDITION

STUDENTS of history as well as the general reading public in recent years have given greatly increased attention to the history of World War I, the war that ushered in the age in which we live. The war started over European conflicts and for the first three years was fought chiefly by European powers, although Russia was more than a European power and the British overseas dominions early came to the assistance of the mother country. Moreover, final victory or defeat even in the years 1914–16 would have decided the fate not only of Europe but of the Middle East and Africa as well.

By 1917 the European powers found themselves incapable of breaking the military stalemate that had lasted since the fall of 1914. Only the entry of the United States, which turned the war into a global war, made the full defeat of Germany possible. In the same year, 1917, the Bolsheviks seized power in Russia and at the very moment when democracy seemed about to become the universal form of government the foundations of the first totalitarian state were laid. Ever since the struggle between democracy and totalitarianism has been the major conflict of our time.

Another significant aspect of World War I was the transformation of war itself. Whereas the European wars of the nineteenth century had been fought only by armies, all the human and material resources of the belligerent nations were mobilized in the long war of 1914–18. It became what Ludendorff first called a 'total war'. Owing to the blockade and the limitation of her reserves this process went farthest in Germany. The German economy ultimately was converted into a government-directed economy which could be characterized as either war socialism or state capitalism. At the same time Germany, which after the summer of 1917 was under a virtual military dictatorship, went further than any other nation in the control of public opinion and individual expression. This wartime system of economic and ideological control was easily revived and extended by National Socialism. Thus World War I created a model for the fascist version of totalitarianism as well.

With this book on German war aims policy in World War I Professor Fritz Fischer has made a significant contribution to the understanding of the events of World War I which left a deep mark on the history of the subsequent thirty years. Through long labor he has collected from the archives of West Germany and Austria a tremendous range of mostly unpublished material, which serves as the solid basis of his work. It does not seem likely that future students of the German war aims will be able to cull any important additional information from official records. New material may appear from private sources and some actually has come to light since the German edition of this book was published in 1961, but it has only confirmed some of Fischer's judgments.

Fischer's historical studies of German war aims policy in 1914–18 have brought him into conflict with ideas still rampant in Germany after the collapse of 1945. While the Nazi period and Hitler's guilt for starting World War II have generally been condemned by German historians, the rise of National Socialism has been declared by many of them an ephemeral event within German history, chiefly caused by the Versailles Treaty, the run-away inflation of the early 1920s, and the great depression after 1930. In their view imperial Germany conducted legitimate policies: Emperor William II's big words meant very little, since he always wished for peace at heart and his ministers disregarded his annexationist schemes. Besides World War I was started by a series of errors for which not only Germany but all the great powers were to be criticized.

These opinions were almost universally held in Germany before 1933, and they were expressed again after 1945, particularly by the older generation. Fritz Fischer was the first German historian who recognized the need for a critical review of German history during World War I, when the official sources became available. In a sober and solidly documented narrative he relates the history of Germany's wartime policies. Although he does not intend to write the history of Germany's part in the origins of the war, he gives at the beginning a brief and probably somewhat oversimplified glimpse of the forces behind German imperialism before 1914. He then treats more fully the policies of the German government in the July crisis of 1914, proving beyond any reasonable doubt that the chancellor, Bethmann Hollweg, was determined to use the Austro-Serbian conflict to break the 'encirclement' of Germany–by which he meant the cohesion of the Triple Entente–at any price, even that of a great war. Fischer places the chief responsibility for the start of the war squarely on the shoulders of the imperial German government.

Outside of Germany this has been the predominant view among historians for some time. First presented by Bernadotte Schmitt and Pierre Renouvin it originally had to contend with opinions which came closer to the German position that all the great powers or at least Russia, Austria-Hungary and Germany–in that order–were to blame for the conflict. The two-volume work of the Italian Luigi Albertini on the origins of World War I, translated into English in 1952, did much to crystallize the judgment of the non-German historians around the conviction that the chief responsibility for plunging Europe into war rested with the German government. Fritz Fischer's treatment, while adding some interesting new details, conforms in general to Albertini's narrative.

The real theme of Professor Fischer's book, however, is the war aims policy of imperial Germany. While it has been customary to describe the civilian government as relatively moderate and the military men as the proponents of a wild annexationism, with the popular forces standing on either side, Fischer offers a very different picture. He shows how the civilian government, and that meant in the first place Chancellor von Bethmann Hollweg, was in deep sympathy with the general intent to fight the war in order to make Germany a 'world power', equal to Britain and Russia. Bethmann Hollweg never questioned the need for drastic changes of the political map of Europe and the Europe-dominated Africa. In the days when complete victory in France seemed within the grasp of the German army he put together the first systematic program of German war aims. This program of September 9, 1914, remained the archetypal plan of all German policies till the end of the war. Temporary adjustments were made when the prospects of victory dimmed. But it was characteristic of the German government leaders that, even in 1915, when they tried hard to make a separate peace with Russia, they were not prepared to give up all conquest made in the east.

The war aims included the creation of a big *Mitteleuropa* under the full military and economic control of the German Empire and made unassailable by annexations in the west and east as well as the establishment of a ring of satellite states. In the west, Belgium was to be made a German dependency and the iron-rich French Lorraine to be annexed. In the east, Lithuania and Courland were to be brought under German dominion, a large section of Central Poland was to be annexed, and the remainder of Poland, together with Austrian Galicia, was to form a Polish state that, in spite of some political ties with Austria-Hungary, would be economically and militarily dominated by Germany. Rumania, too, was to be held in economic servitude. It was assumed that the Netherlands and the Scandinavian countries would feel compelled to join the mighty trade bloc that would arise from the war. In addition the German government intended to acquire most of Central Africa from coast to coast.

Critics of Fischer's book have questioned that Bethmann Hollweg considered the September program a realistic or even desirable political goal. And it is true that in private the chancellor occasionally expressed his doubts whether such extravagant aims could be reached with the means at Germany's disposal and even whether the German people would not morally suffer were they to wield such great power. Yet he was not only convinced that by historic circumstances Germany was forced to expand but he also believed that he had no choice as chancellor but to conduct a policy that represented the ideas and longings of the ruling powers in Germany. He himself called it the 'policy of the diagonal' between the competing political forces. These forces, however, were very uneven in strength. The military, which already in peacetime had had an overweening influence on the state created by Bismarck, gained in the war a firm hold on all war policies, particularly the formulation of war aims. But the generals did not have to impose their policies on an unwilling people. On the contrary, in some respects they were led on by the propaganda of the big interest groups, among which the iron and coal industrialists became the most active and rabid proponents of annexationist demands. Yet annexations were desired also by the liberals, not excluding those who in 1918–19 were among the leading builders of the Weimar Republic. Even the Social Democratic party, which was the largest German party after 1912, did not prove altogether immune to the temptation of imperialism. Although the Social Democrats had always espoused anti-militarism and pacifism without rejecting national defense–some of the minor leaders and functionaries of the party became ardent annexationists. What was still more serious, the official party leadership conspicuously failed to fight the annexationism of the government. This led to the split of the Social Democratic party, and although the secessionist Independent Socialists represented only a minority of the old party, on the issue of war aims the mass of party followers in the country was probably in sympathy with the Independents.

Thus the great majority of the German people, led by its ruling classes, indulged in wild dreams about the overwhelming strength that Germany had to acquire as the result of the war. Wisely Professor Fischer does not confine his narrative to the policies of the German government, which in 1917 practically fell into the hands of the army, but also deals with the powerful desires for conquest held by the non-proletarian classes. Particularly the role of the industrialists and bankers, whose counsel the government liked to follow and who more than any other group fomented the domestic propaganda for expansionist war aims, has never before been so clearly elucidated.

In their war aims policies, as set forth in Professor Fischer's book, the Germans displayed a shocking disregard for the rights of other nations, especially of the small states. Even the contemptuous treatment that Germany's major ally, Austria-Hungary, received was completely motivated by the sentiment that Germany as the strongest power on the Continent could claim immunity from the laws which would prevent her from firmly establishing herself as a world power like Britain, Russia or the United States. Social Darwinism served as the justification for this untrammeled pursuit of power politics. The superiority of the German race over the Slav and Latin races was generally declared to be a proven fact of history.

Professor Fischer also shows us the full scope of the German activities launched at the beginning of the war with the intention of subverting the enemy governments. The attempts to make the Mohammedans rise against their British, French and Italian colonial masters failed, as did the support of the Irish revolution. The greatest result this German policy of subversion achieved was in Russia. Originally directed upon making the non-Russian nationalities revolt against the Russian Tsardom the German operations did not produce a strong response. But when the Germans proceeded to back social revolution as well, the effect was world-shaking. By transporting Lenin from Switzerland to Russia and by giving further help to the Bolsheviks Germany was able to end the war in the east and to realize her maximum program of conquest through the peace treaties of Brest-Litovsk with the Ukraine and the Soviet Union as well as through the subsequent treaty with Rumania at Bucharest. Conquest it must be called, since none of the new states was to be free to develop its own national statehood. The Baltic states were to become German satellites; Rumania was reduced to an economic colony; and the future fate of Poland was supposed to follow similar lines.

The eastern peace treaties of 1918 refute the assertions of some German critics of Fischer who argue that the governmental memoranda used by him were only meant as material for internal discussion and that the aims sketched out in the documents were never absolute demands but rather starting points for bargaining and compromise. With relentless zeal the maximum aims were pressed by the Germans at the conference of Brest-Litovsk in spite of the fact that the imposition of such an oppressive peace necessitated the retention of one million German soldiers in the east. If at least a substantial part of these troops had been transferred to the west, the spring offensive of 1918, Ludendorff's greatest venture, would have stood a better chance of success.

There is nothing to support another assertion occasionally made by German writers. They suggest that the treaties of Brest-Litovsk and Bucharest were products of the war emergency and would have been modified if all the powers together had drafted the final peace settlement. Yet assuming for a moment that Germany had won the war in the west, why should we expect the German rulers thereafter to have cut their cherished gains in the east? Clearly, they simply would have added western acquisitions to their eastern grabs. For no other reason did Ludendorff take the big gamble to attack in the west, although he knew that in the case of failure the strength of the Allied armies, steadily growing through the arrival of American troops, would become overwhelming. Thus the political war aims of Germany contributed to her ultimate military defeat.

While Professor Fischer demonstrates the continuity of the German war aims program during World War I, he abstains from raising the question to what extent was there a continuity between German war aims of World War I and World War II. Yet any reader will ask this question. And there can be no doubt that the events of 1914–18 had a profound influence on Adolf Hitler. His program of conquest in the east stemmed directly from World War I. His aims in the west were a revised version of those in World War I. When England refused to make peace in 1940, the World War I plan for a German Central-African empire was revived.

At the same time, there were also great differences. Although in discussing the annexation of a 'Polish frontier strip' some officials advocated the removal of the Polish and Jewish population, such advice did not prevail in the councils of imperial Germany. The project of settling many Germans in the eastern territories was popular within the government and among the public, but was to be accomplished by peaceful means. Hitler's extermination of the Jews, the annihilation of the intelligentsia of the subjugated peoples and the expulsion of indigenous population from regions earmarked for German settlement had no precedents in the plans of the older German nationalists. The leaders in World War I were made overbold by their greatly exaggerated belief in German might, and in their thirst for power and riches they began to disregard Christian and humane sentiments. But they were unprepared to part with all restraining moral values of the past. Hitler for that reason scorned the nationalism of the old ruling classes. His was a Social Darwinism stripped of all cultural connotations and moral inhibitions. Barbarism was to him the desired, since most effective, method of achieving German domination.

Yet although a distinction must be drawn between the German leaders of World War I and World War II, it is clear that the old-type German nationalists were not people who would uncompromisingly stand up against National Socialism. On the contrary, they were easily susceptible to persuasion, the more so since in the period of his rise to power Hitler gave them the impression that his policies would broadly conform to the old ideals. We have Hitler's testimony that in the first years after the end of World War I Germans were willing to look back on German war policies with critical eyes. In *Mein Kampf* he reports that when he began his public speaking and directed his thunder against the shameful Treaty of Versailles people in the audience would interject 'and Brest-Litovsk?' But German nationalists of all persuasions soon made the German people forget the calamitous history of World War I. They even succeeded in convincing many Germans that Germany would have won the war or at least come out of it unharmed if she had not been 'stabbed in the back' by the leftist revolutionaries at home and had not trusted Wilson's promises of a just peace.

The suppression of critical appraisals of German history during World War I greatly assisted the spread of the nationalist legends and lies on which National Socialism fed. Hegel was wrong when he said that if a historical tragedy was repeated at all it would go on stage as a comedy. World War II was an even greater tragedy than World War I, and the two wars were closely related. It is one of the great merits of Professor Fischer's book to have brought this connection clearly to light. I believe that his main thesis will eventually be generally accepted also in Germany, though over some subordinate questions the historians on both sides of the Atlantic may conduct learned debates. For a long time to come Professor Fischer's massive presentation will not only be the chief source on German foreign policy in World War I but also an invaluable introduction to the history of our own age.

HAJO HOLBORN

Yale University

INTRODUCTION TO THE ENGLISH EDITION

ALTHOUGH the period since 1945 has been dominated by the problems left by the Second World War, more and more people, both among historians and the general public, have come to see the First World War as the crucial event in the first half of the twentieth century. The searing experience of the trenches, the mood of the belligerents—so different from that of the Second World War—and above all the political consequences—the Russian Revolution, America's emergence as a world power, the break-up of the Hapsburg Monarchy, the establishment of the Weimar Republic—all contributed to the circumstances in which the Second World War had its origins.

In the years between the wars, research into the origins of the First World War was dominated by the desire to establish where the responsibility for its outbreak lay. The insertion by the Allies in the Treaty of Versailles of the notorious Article 231, by which Germany was made to accept responsibility for the 'war imposed . . . by the aggression of Germany and her allies', caused the German government to publish a large collection of documents from the archives of the Foreign Ministry in order to rebut the charge. Other governments followed their example, and historians of all nationalities contributed to the discussion of 'war guilt', putting forward rival interpretations, some accusing the Germans, some the Austrians, some blaming France's desire to avenge the defeat of 1870 or Russia's desire to expand in the Balkans, while others pointed to the harm done by Britain's hesitation to commit herself, and others again simply saw the war as a result of 'international anarchy' or of an unrestricted arms race.

However, most of these studies stop short with the actual outbreak of war in August, 1914, and it is typical of the preoccupation with war guilt that the great collections of published documents on foreign policy—the German *Grosse Politik der Europäischen Cabinette*, the *Documents diplomatiques français* and the *Documents on British Foreign Policy*—all stop in 1914; and where the series have been continued for the inter-war years, they have started again in 1919, so that we have been without much first-hand archival material for the war years themselves. Consequently, the diplomacy of the war and the ends of wartime policy, as opposed to the military history of the war, have been somewhat neglected. The German defeat of 1945, however, and the capture by the Allies of much of the German government archives, led to these becoming available for study, although they are scattered between various centres in west and east Germany, while some still remain in the United States. Professor Fischer's book is a pioneering attempt to utilise this material for the period of the First World War, and he has undertaken a major piece of research both in the west and east German archives in order to produce *Germany's Aims in the First World War*.

It is an important book for several reasons. First of all, it links the development of German war aims during the war with the general climate of opinion among Germany's rulers in the years before the war, and shows how the hopes of annexing territory on both Germany's western and eastern frontiers were the logical result of ideas which had been widely discussed for some years before 1914, ideas which the initial victories of August and September, 1914, seemed to be about to enable the German government to put into practice. Secondly, the book shows the tenacity with which the German leaders clung to these initial aims, so that in spite of a growing demand by some sections of German opinion for a 'peace without annexations', it was impossible for Germany to envisage a peace based on a return to the *status quo* of 1914. This in turn leads to a re-assessment of the character of Theobald von Bethmann Hollweg, the Imperial Chancellor until the summer of 1917. Professor Fischer's demonstration that Bethmann was, as early as September, 1914, committed to a programme of widespread annexation has come as a shock to many people, for whom the Chancellor seemed to be a moderate and liberal figure attempting to stand out against the extreme demands of the militarists and ultra-nationalists. There is, no doubt, still room for argument about Fischer's interpretation, but the very fact of challenging a hitherto accepted view has already led to the production of much new evidence about the personality and actions of Bethmann Hollweg. This is only one example of the way in which the book has opened up a new and fruitful discussion.

In general, indeed, the great merit of Professor Fischer's work has been to re-open questions which many had regarded as closed, by the discovery of a vast quantity of new evidence and by using it to suggest an interpretation of German policies which raises once more – though this was doubtless not the author's original intention – the whole question of German responsibility for the war. As a result, the book has been in Germany the centre of one of the most violent academic controversies of recent years. In Britain, perhaps, the evidence which Fischer produces of the extent and intransigence of Germany's annexationist aims in east and west will seem less surprising and shocking than it did to many Germans; but there is enough in this book to suggest that the time has come for a re-assessment of the nature of the war aims of all the belligerent countries and not of Germany alone.

Some of Professor Fischer's German critics have accused him of producing an indictment of Germany, without indicting the other belligerent governments, who were, it is alleged, as much affected by the spirit of the age of imperialism as the Germans, and whose aims in the First World War were as aggressive and insatiable as those of Germany. This is an unfair charge against Fischer, who has already, by the volume and depth of his work in the German archives, done all the research that a single historian could humanly be expected to do; and he has placed us all in his debt. But the charge does suggest one way in which his book may be as influential, even if not as controversial, in Britain as it has been in Germany. The British government has recently opened all the British archives down to the fall of the coalition government in October, 1922, so the way is now open for a detailed account of the development of the war aims of at least one of the major belligerent powers besides Germany. It is to be hoped that British historians will be fired by Professor Fischer's scholarly example to undertake in comparable detail a study of Britain's aims in the First World War.

That the subject of war aims in the First World War is still a sensitive one is shown by the controversy and even personal hostility aroused in Germany by this book. One can understand why those Germans who are prepared to accept Hitler's responsibility for the Second World War and even, to some extent, the Germans' responsibility for Hitler, find it hard to reopen the whole question of war guilt in the First World War and resent any suggestion that the aims of the Kaiser's government differed little from those of Hitler a quarter of a century later. It may be that such a suggestion is implicit in Fischer's work, even though it is not his main theme. Would a study of British war aims raise equally embarrassing questions? Perhaps not, if only because we already know what was actually done by the Allies in the peace settlement of 1919 and therefore presumably know the worst. Yet, in some recent historical works based on private papers—on the origins of British intervention in Russia or on the political ideas of Lord Milner, for example—many of the high moral attitudes of the wartime British government look somewhat hollow. Even if Fischer's work reinforces the belief that the German leaders bear the greatest weight of responsibility for the outbreak and prolongation of the First World War, it therefore imposes all the more strongly on British historians the duty of looking again at the record of the British government.

Germany's Aims in the First World War suggests a new way of studying the period 1914–18, and its reception in Germany suggests that we all have still much to learn about looking at the history of the first quarter of the twentieth century through fresh eyes and without the prejudices of a generation ago. It also suggests that statesmen often base their decisions less on long-term plans than on the instinctive promptings of ideas and beliefs already current in the society which formed them, that they have a stock of reactions on which they fall back and to which they cling stubbornly when faced with political or strategical emergencies. Professor Fischer has studied in detail how German policy in the First World War was formed and how, once formulated, it destroyed the freedom of action of those such as Bethmann Hollweg, who had originally decided on it. The attention and controversy which Fischer's book has aroused is based on more than a discussion of his specific evidence and conclusions, for it raises questions about the nature of international politics and of the causes of war as well as about the way in which political and strategic aims are decided. Thus this work of detailed and specialised scholarship acquires a more general interest and relevance.

London School of Economics   JAMES JOLL
   and Political Science

AUTHOR'S FOREWORD

In the 1920s the theme of this book was the subject of acute political controversy in Germany. Today, in the perspective created by the Second World War and in the completely different political conditions prevailing in Europe, it has become history and can be made the object of dispassionate consideration. This book is therefore neither an indictment nor a defence. It is not for the historian to accuse or defend. His duty is to establish facts and to marshal them in the sequence of cause and effect. In so far as this leads him to recognise ideas, ambitions and decisions of individuals as factors in the formation of political causation, he must seek to explain and 'understand' them, without reprobation or excuse. He must avoid over-simplifying and thus distorting his picture by placing on a single 'scapegoat' the blame for some development which later turned out to be disastrous. It would, for example, be too simple to represent the German Emperor as solely responsible for German policy before the First World War, or Ludendorff during it, just as Hitler is now commonly charged with the sole responsibility for 'the doom of Germany' in the 1930s and 1940s. The truth is that ideological motives, religious or traditional, institutions and social structures, old and new and (not least) material factors, produce a complex of forces among which the role of the individual can be important, but only as one of a multitude of other factors which condition it and without which it could not act at all. This is no less true of the moderating elements, than of the active. For example: Bethmann Hollweg's freedom of action was so limited by the structure of the Reich, especially by the position occupied by the armed forces and by the great power enjoyed by the crown, that in spite of his position as Chancellor, he was not able to put through the policy which he held to be necessary, either at home or abroad. Yet the traditional picture of 'the philosopher in the Chancellor's chair' is quite mistaken, since it denies to Bethmann's policy its own power-political aims.

The material on the theme of this book is so enormous that the introductory chapter cannot attempt to do more than sketch in brief outline how a consciousness of strength, an urge for expansion and a need for security combined to mould the policy of Wilhelm II's Germany; an exhaustive description of Germany's policy before the war would require a book in itself. In the other direction this book contains pointers to fields wider than its own, for it indicates certain mental attitudes and aspirations which were active in German policy during the First World War and remained operative later. Seen from this angle, it may serve as a contribution towards the problem of the continuity of German policy from the First World War to the Second.

Some may regret the absence of continued reference to the war aims of Germany's enemies. But, firstly, the British, French and Russian archives have not yet been opened to the public for the period after 1914; secondly, the war aims of each of these states would require a separate book. Investigation of certain special aspects, such as 'annexationism' (all great powers had 'annexationist' policies in the age of imperialism) would not contribute much to an understanding of the motives and aims of that German imperialism whose late start and thrustfulness and insistent moral claims to a 'place in the sun' made it specially vexatious in the eyes of other powers and so shook Europe, and the world, to their foundations. But the meaning and purpose of this book is to show that the age of imperialism did not end, as most historians make out, in 1914, but reached its first climax in Germany's colossal effort to weld continental 'Mitteleuropa' into a force which would place Germany on equal terms with the established and the potential world powers: the British Empire, Russia and the United States.

This book grew, in the first instance, out of seminars held in 1955–6 on the history of the First World War. Adequate examination of the source-material became possible only when the German archives, confiscated by the Allies at the end of the last war, were made available to researchers, first in microfilm and then in the original after their return to Germany. From 1957 to 1960 I carried out extensive studies in the archives in Bonn (the political archives of the *Auswärtiges Amt*), Coblenz (*Bundesarchiv*), Potsdam (German central archives, including the material of the former *Reichsarchiv*, especially of the Imperial Chancellery, the Imperial 'offices' and the Commercial Department of the *Auswärtiges Amt*, Merseburg (German central archives, including the material of the former Prussian secret state archives), and Vienna (Austrian state archives and *Haus-, Hof- und Staatsarchiv*). Other information and assistance has come from the state archives in Munich and Stuttgart, and the Public Record Office in London. I have therefore been able to base most of this work on archival material (I hope soon to be able to supplement the narrative with a volume of documents). I wish to express my thanks to the directors and staffs of these bodies for their generous collaboration and friendly assistance. I am particularly indebted to the Joachim-Jungius Society of Hamburg and, especially, to the *Deutsche Forschungsgemeinschaft* for material assistance afforded me from 1957, which has made these studies possible and, most of all, secured for me the help of Fräulein Dr. Lilli Lewerenz.

Dr. Lewerenz and Dr. Imanuel Geiss, who have dealt with particular aspects of German war aims policy in the First World War in their dissertations, have helped me to examine the archives and assess the extensive material in them. I owe especial thanks to my Assistent, Herr Helmut Böhme, for his untiring and selfless support, both in preparing economic-historical preliminary studies and in my seminar, and to Herr Joachim Pragal for help in checking notes and reading proofs.

Hamburg, October 1, 1961   FRITZ FISCHER

FOREWORD TO THE SECOND (GERMAN) EDITION

THIS second edition of my book was quickly called for, and contains no changes apart from the correction of certain slips. I am obliged to the readers who have been kind enough to point these out. The fruits of further research must wait till they can be included in the form of a supplement.

Some critics have complained that this book treats German policy before the war, at its outbreak and during its course too much in isolation: that it does not set it sufficiently in the general context of the age of imperialism, and so fails to bring out its true relationship to the trends and objectives followed by the other European and world powers. I must recall and emphasise what I wrote on this point in the foreword to the first edition. I must also point out that my whole purpose has been to establish the bases for an understanding of German policy in the war, for which it was necessary to concentrate on the special conditions of Germany's political, social and economic life. Essentially, German war aims were not merely an answer to the enemy's war aims, as made known in the course of the war, nor the product of the war situation created by the 'beleaguered fortress' and the blockade; they are explicable only in the light of factors operating since 1890 or even earlier – naval policy, the 'policy of bases', colonial, eastern, Balkan and European economic policies, and the general political situation which – primarily as an effect of Germany's own policy – produced after 1904 and 1907 the attempt to overthrow Germany by 'encircling' her.

It may further be recalled that the Entente's war aims (the roots of which themselves go back to the pre-war situations of the respective powers and to their permanent policy objectives) were made known in broad outline before the end of the war in the answer of the Entente powers to Wilson's offer of mediation, and through the Soviets' action in publishing the Allied secret treaties after Lenin's seizure of power. Furthermore these aims, reduced in some directions, extended in others, were transmuted into historic reality in the peace treaties which concluded the war. It will be for scholars of the future, when the archives of these powers are opened, to trace the origin and development of their war aims. Viewed in this light, the present book is simply a contribution towards a general appreciation of the war aims policies of all the belligerents.

Hamburg, May 1, 1962   F. F.

FOREWORD TO THE THIRD (GERMAN) EDITION

FOR this edition Chapters 1 and 2 have been re-written and substantially enlarged on the basis of new material which has become available since this book was first written. The remainder of the book has been revised and enlarged in places.

Hamburg, June 28, 1964   F. F.

FOREWORD TO THIS EDITION

THE text here presented has been reduced, by the author himself, by about one third, in order to make it easier for an English-speaking audience. The structure and substance of the original have not been altered. The book is based almost exclusively on documentary material from various archives. To save space about eight hundred source references have been omitted, as has the catalogue, twenty-two pages long, of the archival files used; the archives themselves are, however, listed. Readers in need of the detailed references can obtain them from the German edition.

                                                                 F. F.

LIST OF THE PRINCIPAL PERSONAGES
AND THE POSITIONS HELD BY THEM IN THE
YEARS COVERED BY THIS BOOK

All offices are German unless otherwise stated

BACHMANN, Admiral Gustav, Chief of the Naval Staff, 1915–16

BADEN, Prince Max of, Imperial Chancellor, 1918

BALLIN, Albert, General Director of the Hamburg-America Steamship Company

BARTENWERFFER, General Paul von, Chief of the Political Division of the General Staff

BERCHTOLD, Count Leopold, Austro-Hungarian Ambassador at St. Petersburg, 1906–11; Foreign Minister, 1912–15

BERNSTORFF, Count Johann von, Ambassador at Washington, 1908–17; at Constantinople, 1917–18

BESELER, General Hans von, Governor-General in Poland

BETHMANN HOLLWEG, Theobald von, Minister for the Interior, 1907–9; Imperial Chancellor, 1909–17

BISSING, General Moritz Ferdinand von, Governor-General in Belgium

BRATIANU, Jon, Rumanian Prime Minister and Minister for War, 1914–18

BROCKDORFF-RANTZAU, Count Ulrich von, Minister at Copenhagen, 1912–19

BÜLOW, Prince Bernhard von, Ambassador at Rome, 1893–97 and 1914–15; Foreign Minister, 1897–1900; Imperial Chancellor, 1900–9

BURIAN, Baron Stephen von, Austro-Hungarian Minister for Finance, 1903–12; Hungarian Minister at Vienna, 1912–15; Austro-Hungarian Foreign Minister, 1915–16 and 1918

BUSSCHE-HADDENHAUSEN, Baron Hilmar von dem, Ambassador at Bucharest; Under-Secretary, Foreign Office

CAPELLE, Admiral Eduard von, Under-Secretary for the Navy 1914–15; Navy Minister, 1916–18

CAPRIVI, General Leo von, Imperial Chancellor, 1890–94

CLAM-MARTINITZ, Count Heinrich von, Austrian Prime Minister, 1916–18

CLASS, Heinrich, publicist and leader of the *Alldeutsche Verband* (Pan-German Association)

CONRAD VON HÖTZENDORF, Baron Franz, Chief of the Austro-Hungarian General Staff, 1906–11 and 1912–17

CZERNIN V. U. Z. CHUDENITZ, Count Ottokar von, Austro-Hungarian Minister at Bucharest, 1913–16; Foreign Minister, 1916–18

DELBRÜCK, Clemens von, Minister for the Interior, 1909–16

DERNBURG, Bernhard, Director of the Darmstädter Bank; Minister for the Colonies, 1907–10

DUISBERG, Carl, President of I. G. Farbenindustrie

FALKENHAYN, General Erich von, Prussian Minister for War, 1913–15; Chief of the General Staff, 1914–16; C.-in-C. IX Army (Rumania), 1916–17; C.-in-C. X Army (Lithuania), 1918–19

GIERS, N. K., Russian Foreign Minister, 1892–95

GOLTZ, Baron K. von der, Field-Marshal in charge of the Turkish army, 1909–11

GORCHAKOV, A. M., Russian Foreign Minister, 1856–82

GROENER, General Wilhelm, Chief Quartermaster-General, 1918

GWINNER, Arthur von, Director of the Deutsche Bank, 1894–1919

HELFFERICH, Karl, Director of the Deutsche Bank; Finance Minister, 1915–16; Minister for the Interior, 1916–17; Ambassador at Moscow, 1918

HERTLING, Count Georg, Bavarian Prime Minister and Foreign Minister, 1912–17; Imperial Chancellor, 1917–18

HINDENBURG, Field-Marshal Paul von, C.-in-C. VIII Army (Eastern Front), 1914–15; Chief of the General Staff, 1916–18

HINTZE, Admiral Paul von, Ambassador at Mexico City, 1911–14; Peking, 1914–15; Christiania, 1915–18; Foreign Minister, 1918

HOHENLOHE-LANGENBURG, Prince Gottfried zu, Austro-Hungarian Ambassador at Berlin, 1914–18

HOHENLOHE-SCHILLINGSFÜRST, Prince Clodwig zu, Imperial Chancellor, 1894–1900

HOLSTEIN, Baron Friedrich von, Foreign Office, 1880–1906

HOLTZENDORFF, Admiral Henning von, Chief of the Naval Staff, 1916–18

HOYOS, Count A., Permanent Head of the Austro-Hungarian Foreign Office

PRINCIPAL PERSONAGES

HUGENBERG, Alfred, Director of Krupps

IONESCU, Take, Rumanian Minister for the Interior, 1912–14

IZVOLSKI, Alexander, Russian Foreign Minister, 1906–10; Ambassador at Paris, 1910–17

JAGOW, Gottlieb von, Foreign Minister, 1913–16

KIDERLEN-WÄCHTER, Alfred von, German Minister at Bucharest, 1899–1910; Foreign Minister, 1910–12

KIRDORF, Emil, Director of Gelsenkirchener Bergwerksgesellschaft and promoter of the Coal Syndicate of Rheinland-Westphalia

KÜHLMANN, Richard von, Counsellor of embassy at London (1908–14) and Constantinople (1914–15); Minister at The Hague, 1915–16; Ambassador at Constantinople, 1916–17; Minister for Foreign Affairs, 1917–18

LERCHENFELD-KÖFERING, Count Hugo von, Bavarian Minister at Berlin, 1880–1919

LICHNOWSKY, Prince Karl von, Ambassador at London, 1912–14

LIMAN VON SANDERS, General Otto, Chief of German Military Mission to Turkey, 1913–14

LUDENDORFF, General Erich, Chief of Staff, VIII Army (Eastern Front), 1914–15; Chief Quartermaster-General, 1916–18

LYNCKER, General Baron Moritz von, Chief of the Emperor's Military Cabinet, 1908–18

MICHAELIS, Georg, Under-Secretary, Prussian Ministry of Finance, 1909–17; Food Minister, 1917; Imperial Chancellor, 1917; President of Pomerania, 1918–19

MOLTKE, General Helmuth von, Chief of the General Staff of the Army, 1906–14

MÜLLER, Admiral Georg von, Chief of the Emperor's Naval Cabinet, 1909–18

PASIC, Nicholas, Serbian Prime Minister and Minister for Foreign Affairs, 1906–18

PAYER, Friedrich von, Vice-Chancellor, 1917–18

POHL, Admiral Hugo von, Chief of the Naval Staff, 1913–15; Commander-in-Chief, High Seas Fleet, 1915–16

POURTALÈS, Count Friedrich von, Ambassador at St. Petersburg, 1907–14

RATHENAU, Walther, Director (1890) and President (1915) of the Allgemeine Elektrizitätsgesellschaft; Director of the Berliner

Handelsgesellschaft; Chief of the Raw Materials Department of the Ministry for War

RÖCHLING, Karl, Saar industrialist, President of Röchlingsche Eisen-und Stahlwerke

ROEDERN, Count Siegfried von, Minister for Alsace-Lorraine, 1914–16; Finance Minister, 1916–18

ROMBERG, Baron Gisbert von, Minister at Berne

SAZONOV, S. D., Russian Minister for Foreign Affairs, 1910–16

SCHLIEFFEN, General von, Chief of the General Staff of the Army, 1892–1906

SCHOEN, Baron Wilhelm von, Ambassador at Paris, 1910–14

SIEMENS, Karl Friedrich von, President of the Siemens group of companies in the electrical industry

SOLF, Wilhelm, Minister for the Colonies, 1911–18

STINNES, Hugo, President of the Stinnes coal and shipping enterprises

STOLYPIN, P. A., Russian Prime Minister, 1906–11

STUMM, Wilhelm von, Foreign Office, 1911–16

STÜRGKH, Count K., Austrian Prime Minister, 1911–16

SZÖGYÉNY-MARICH, Count Laszlo von, Austro-Hungarian Ambassador at Berlin, 1892–1914

THYSSEN, August, President of Thyssen & Co. and other iron and steel companies

TIRPITZ, Alfred von, Navy Minister, 1897–1916

TISZA, Count Stephen, Hungarian Prime Minister, 1903–5 and 1913–17

TSCHIRSCHKY UND BÖGENDORFF, Heinrich von, Ambassador at Vienna, 1907–16

WALLRAF, Max, Minister for the Interior, 1917–18

WANGENHEIM, Baron Hans von, Ambassador at Constantinople, 1912–15

WARBURG, Max, Head of the Warburg bank

WIEDFELDT, Otto, Director of Krupps

ZIMMERMANN, Arthur, Under-Secretary for Foreign Affairs, 1911–16; Foreign Minister, 1916–17

Introduction

1

GERMAN IMPERIALISM

FROM GREAT POWER POLICY TO WORLD POWER POLICY

THE German Empire created by Bismarck in 1871 was a partnership between the Prussian military and authoritarian state and the leading circles of the new industrial and commercial liberal bourgeoisie. It is true that, as a new nation state, it was one of a whole series of such entities which came into existence between 1789 and our own day; yet it occupied a position of special importance in the history of nations. The Germans were the only people who did not create their state from below by invoking the forces of democracy against the old ruling groups, but 'accepted it gratefully' at the hands of those groups in a defensive struggle against democracy. The Prussian state, the power and prestige of the Prussian crown, the constitution which made the Prussian king German Emperor and the Prussian Prime Minister Chancellor of the Reich, the composition of the Prussian Diet (a Lower House elected on a restricted franchise and an overwhelmingly feudal Upper House), the bureaucracy, the schools, the universities, the established Protestant churches and not least the armed forces, directly subordinated as they were to the kings of Prussia, Bavaria, Saxony, etc.–all these were factors which guaranteed the predominance of the conservative elements against the pressure of the rising forces of democratic liberalism and later of democratic socialism.

Prussia and the Reich

The 'Holy Roman Empire of the German Nation' which succumbed to Napoleon in 1806 consisted of more than three hundred principalities and Free Cities. In the German Confederation (*Deutscher Bund*) created to succeed it by the Congress of Vienna, and presided over by the new Austrian Empire, this number was reduced to about thirty, amalgamating the smaller units into 'secondary states'. This federation never satisfied the German people, who tried in the revolution of 1848 to create 'unity and liberty' from below under the inspiration of west European ideas and on the model of the American federal constitution. But the liberal bourgeoisie was defeated by its own weaknesses and by its own dread of red revolution, which drove

3

it into alliance with the princes. Another reason for the failure to achieve national unification lay in the rivalry between the two leading states in the federation, the Austrian Empire which sought to defend its position by the 'Grossdeutsch solution', and the rising economic and military power of the kingdom of Prussia, with its 'Kleindeutsch solution'. The struggle for hegemony in Germany between the Catholic Hapsburgs and the Protestant Hohenzollerns was won by Prussia, under Bismarck's guidance, in the war of 1866 against a majority of the German states. Prussia then broke up the federation, excluded Austria from the future Germany, and extended its own power position by annexing the duchy of Schleswig-Holstein (detached from Denmark in an enterprise conducted jointly with Austria as recently as 1864), the kingdom of Hanover, the electoral principality of Hesse-Cassel, the duchy of Hesse-Nassau and the Free City of Frankfurt-am-Main, and by founding the North German Federation (Norddeutscher Bund) in 1867. This unification was thus created from above, but it was accepted by the majority of the liberal bourgeoisie, even though it meant the renunciation of democracy and parliamentary life in the Western sense.

Our description of Germany's war aims policy between 1914 and 1918 will show that the efforts to create a 'Mitteleuropa' (like the Dual Alliance between the new German Empire and Austria-Hungary, which was formed in 1879 and lasted until 1918) were in a certain sense attempts to undo the decision of 1866 (subject, indeed, to Prussia's retaining hegemony over Austria). After breaking France's resistance to the incorporation of south Germany and annexing Alsace-Lorraine in 1870–1, Bismarck took advantage of the power position achieved in 1866 to incorporate south Germany in the new Reich, with the king of Prussia as German Emperor. This empire was a federation, composed of twenty-four member states: four kingdoms (Prussia—with five-eighths of the total area—Bavaria, Württemberg and Mecklenburg-Schwerin), six duchies, six principalities and three Free Cities (Hamburg, Bremen and Lübeck).

The federal element, which Bismarck utilised in order to attract the south German states of Bavaria, Württemberg, Baden and Hesse to Prussia and north Germany, undoubtedly helped the survival and development of the variety of German cultural life, as evidenced for example by the operas, theatres, concert halls, academies and museums of Munich, Stuttgart, Dresden, Weimar and Hamburg; but politically federalism counted for little in the decisions which were taken by the German Empire under Prussian leadership with Berlin, itself a cultural centre of the first rank, as capital both of Prussia and of the Reich. The representation of the federal states in the Federal Council (*Bundesrat*) – in which Prussia was the most strongly represented state – had little effect on the policies of the Imperial Chancellor.

Under the imperial constitution the Emperor appointed and dismissed the Chancellor at his discretion. The Chancellor, who was the only imperial official, was politically 'responsible' to the Reichstag, before which he had to defend imperial policy; it had, however, no influence over his appointment, and he could not be a member of it. The Reichstag, as the national representative body, had the power to accept or reject the budget, and a voice in imperial legislation. The Chancellor had therefore to collect enough support among the parties to give him a majority; if he failed to do so, he had to dissolve the Reichstag and seek his majority at the polls. Foreign and military policy and decisions over war and peace were expressly reserved as prerogatives of the crown, which exercised them through the Chancellor. There was no imperial ministry responsible to the Reichstag, which could neither appoint a ministry, nor force it to resign by outvoting it, nor was there any collective Cabinet responsibility; the heads of the imperial ministries or 'offices' (*Ämter*), who were known as Secretaries of State, were subordinate to the Chancellor, and were appointed and dismissed by the Emperor on his advice.

Another factor which strengthened the position of the crown and was calculated to restrict the Chancellor's power to determine policy was that the Prussian army (in time of war, also the armies of the other federal states) and the imperial navy were under the direct authority of the monarch. He exercised this authority through his military and naval cabinets (for questions of personnel) and through the general and naval staffs; the Chancellor had no voice in these questions, nor was there any co-ordinating machinery (the person of the monarch excepted) whereby the political aspects of military decisions could be given their proper weight. The Prussian Minister of War (who also represented the armies of the other federal states *vis-à-vis* the Reichstag) and the Secretary of State of the imperial Naval Office were concerned only with the recruiting and equipment of the armed forces, and with sponsoring the vote for them in the Reichstag; that body's influence over the army and the navy was limited to the indirect control which it enjoyed through its right to be consulted over the budget, but this right was restricted by the fact the vote was not annual, but was given for seven years at a time from 1874 to 1893 and for five years after 1893.

Another factor limiting the Chancellor's freedom of action was that (as a rule) he doubled his office with that of Prussian Prime

5

Minister. In the latter capacity, however, he was only *primus inter pares* among the Prussian Ministers of State, who, like himself, were appointed and dismissed by the king, independently of parliament. This gave the Prussian state ministry considerable influence over the formation of Reich policy; the more so, since the restricted franchise ensured the preponderance of the conservative element in both Chambers of the Prussian Diet, while in the Reich the franchise was general, direct, secret and equal. The effects of the industrial revolution thus showed themselves in the growth of social democracy and of democratic and liberal groups, and this in turn widened the breach between political sentiment in the Reich and in its biggest individual state, Prussia.

Bismarck had expressly set himself to keep west European parliamentarism from establishing itself in the Reich or in its component states, and he was very successful in doing so. From 1867 to 1878 he conducted his internal and economic policy in partnership with the moderate, or 'National', Liberals, known as 'the Party of the Founders of the Empire'. A radical change took place in 1878–9. Firstly, Bismarck abandoned free trade in favour of a 'national' policy of protective tariffs on the American-Russo-French model for heavy industry and large-scale agriculture. Secondly, he began to relax the *Kulturkampf* which he had conducted since 1871 against the Catholic church and the Catholic party or Zentrum, and to draw that party over to support of the Prusso-German state by an accommodation with Pope Leo XIII and a new economic policy. Thirdly, in 1878 he opened his campaign against the Social Democrats (described by him as 'the party of subversion') by emergency legislation directed against them, a course which he maintained until his fall in March, 1890. Under the policy of protection the old ideological parties—Conservatives, Liberals, Catholics—changed increasingly into bodies representing economic interests; the old landed aristocracy allied itself with the new industrial 'aristocracy' against the opposition camp of Liberals and Social Democrats.

After the liquidation of the *Kulturkampf* the three parties of the right (German Conservatives, Free Conservatives and National Liberals) and the Zentrum, while not formally combining in a cartel, jointly represented the dominant forces, economic, political and social, in the new Germany, although it was not the Reichstag which made them dominant. The pull of this concentration of power, combined with an economic prosperity which had been steadily increasing since 1890 and the international nimbus and the growing power of the Empire, was so powerful inside Germany that by the close of the epoch even the two parties which had originally consti-

tuted the opposition, the left-wing Liberals and the Social Democrats, had come to accept the existing order, as August 4, 1914, and
and even November 9, 1918, were to prove beyond cavil.

From Bismarck to Wilhelm II

The foundation of the German Empire greatly enhanced the
national consciousness of the Germans. This new German self-consciousness was, in contrast to that of 1848, conservative and dynastic.
After 1878 the liberal element in the German national movement
was overshadowed by the dynastic and military elements. The popular consciousness regarded the foundation of the Empire itself, almost
exclusively, as the fruit of three 'victorious wars'. The national festi-
vals, the anniversary of Sedan symbolising victory over France, and
the Emperor's birthday (he was born on January 27, 1859) were
living expressions of this unreserved acceptance of the Empire.

One other factor, beside the military, coloured the nature of the
new German national consciousness. In the '70s the campaign
against liberalism and socialism led to the mobilisation of the *petite
bourgeoisie* under the slogan (an old one, but re-furbished) of 'throne
and altar'. This was the class which had been hardest hit by the new
industrial developments, and was now hoping for help, especially
help from the state, in its struggle to compete with the new big business. This mass feeling linked up with an anti-Semitism which was at
first religious, then racial, and the fusion brought into being an entirely new kind of nationalism, which from 1890 onwards gave a
wishful and emotional content to *völkisch* and racial conceptions
which did not stop at the frontiers of the Prusso-German dynastic
state. In 1881 the Union of German Students came into being as a
part of this anti-Semitic movement, of which it soon became the most
important mouthpiece. Founded with the purpose of providing the
students' associations with an overall organisation and firing academic youth with the new German nationalism, and exerting considerable influence on the older rival student associations, corps and
fraternities, it soon became a big factor in inclining the students'
mentality towards the new dynastic-military, conservative and *völkisch* nationalism. The de-liberalisation of the Prussian bureaucracy
and the nationalist spirit of the German Lutheran church are trace-
able to the same source.

The men of this generation which grew up in the late Bismarckian
era were also convinced devotees of the 'world policy' devoted to
securing for Germany a 'place in the sun', which the young Emperor
had been quick to announce as his programme. It was the accession
of Wilhelm II in July, 1888, that really unleashed the conservative-

7

dynastic forces at home; those calling for pushful expansion abroad got their heads after the dismissal of Bismarck in March, 1890. This is not the place for yet another appreciation of the Emperor's character, but he was beyond question in many ways a typical product of his age. While entirely imbued with the concept that Monarchy came of Divine Grace, he was a 'modern' king who sought contact with savants, merchants and technicians and, like the British Prince of Wales (afterwards King Edward VII), 'covered' the world as 'the first commercial traveller' of his people. Wilhelm II's insistence that Germany must not yield place to England coloured both his own political creed and the ideas of the great majority of his ministers and Secretaries of State.

In the centre of his political plans stood the construction of a great fleet. This, it seemed, was the only way of catching up with Britain as a world power and getting recognised by the other world powers as an equal. The fleet, combined with economic power, was to furnish the basis to support Germany's claim for a revision of the colonial *status quo*; for her late entry into the colonial race having left her with what was, in her view, less than her fair share of its prizes, she proposed to use these means to obtain a position consonant with her claims and appropriate to her economic, military and cultural potential. From the 1870s on a redistribution of territory was going on in Africa and Asia which led to an extension of the colonial empires, and in this redistribution Germany participated ever more actively as the transformation of her own structure proceeded. When the Sino-Japanese War of 1895, the Spanish-American of 1898 and the Boer War of 1899–1902 seemed to prove beyond all question the importance of sea-power as a *sine qua non* of world power, the goal of the creation of a strong navy as the expression of Germany's claims was adopted by industry and popularised by new forms of mass propaganda until it became axiomatic for the whole German people.

In the course of discussions on the navy estimates leading representatives of Germany's intellectual life – its university professors – shaped the conscious new German nationalism. The most prominent representatives of German academic thought, Gustav Schmoller, Hans Delbrück, Max Sering, Dietrich Schäfer, Max Lenz, Otto Hintze, Erich Marcks, Alfred Hettner, Friedrich Ratzel – to name only a few – announced in unison that the age of apparently peaceful competition between states was gone for ever; equally dead was the limitation of the great powers to the European state system. Yet they were only the mouthpieces of the decisive forces in the German Reich who saw in 'neo-mercantilism' and 'imperialism' the governing forces of the new age.

As early as 1890, when Caprivi, Bismarck's successor in the chancellorship from 1890 to 1894, was working for the establishment of
a central European economic system linking the German Reich
closely with its neighbours, Schmoller had written an article in support of this policy, in which these new ideas found expression. He
drew a picture of the new system of world states and the role of Germany in it, in words which anticipated one of the main aims of
German policy in 1914:

> He who is perceptive enough to realise that the course of world history in
> the twentieth century will be determined by the competition between the
> Russian, English, American, and perhaps the Chinese world empires, and
> by their aspirations to reduce all the other, smaller, states to dependence on
> them, will also see in a central European customs federation the nucleus of
> something which may save from destruction not only the political independ-
> ence of those states, but Europe's higher, ancient culture itself.[1]

What Schmoller, at whose feet a whole generation of future economists, administrators and diplomats had sat, taught primarily in
respect of economics was repeated by no less prominent historians
in respect of Germany's power position and cultural heritage. They
saw the expansion of national states into world states as determined,
not only by economic interests, but most of all by the 'will to power'.
They saw Germany fulfilling her 'world mission' by virtue of that
'fitting share of the world power which human nature and higher
Providence assign to the civilised peoples' which her army and navy
would ensure for her. Against the 'cultural monopoly of the Anglo-
Saxons' (Britain and America) and the 'Russo-Muscovite world' the
German professors called for a policy which should make Germany's
special cultural and political heritage safe and thereby guarantee
at once the multiplicity and individuality of all peoples and the
balance of power in a new world system of states.[2]

A second, basic element operated at an early stage alongside these
innermost 'motive forces' of German world expansion. Only ten
years after the launching of Germany's claim to world power status,
Paul Rohrbach, in his widely-read book *Deutschland unter den Weltvöl-
kern* raised the question whether the new German world power's
European basis was broad enough and secure enough to achieve and
hold an overseas empire (the objective taking shape was a German

---

[1] G. Schmoller, *Ges. Aufsätze*, p. 20 ff.

[2] Hans Delbrück, *Preuss. Jahrbücher*, Vol. 149, August 1912, cit. Annelise Thimme,
Hans Delbrück als Kritiker der Wilhelminischen Epoche (Düsseldorf, 1935), pp. 111 ff.;
Otto Hintze, *Der Sinn des Krieges* in *Deutschland und der Weltkrieg* (Leipzig and
Berlin, 1915), p. 685; cf. id., *Deutschland und das Weltmachtsystem* (Leipzig and
Berlin), pp. 3 ff.

Central Africa). European objectives were added to the colonial. Rudolf Kjellén, whose geo-political-biological picture of *Die Grossmächte der Erden* was to exercise so powerful an influence on German thought, called for a federation of Europe under German leadership as a basis for Germany's colonial empire, and this idea was fully endorsed by wide circles in the political and academic worlds before 1914.

But the emergence of such ideas from the world of theory into the world of practice also antedates the war. Attempts to counteract the high American protective tariffs led to the formation of economic associations which attempted to lay the foundations of an economic unification of Central Europe.[1] The conferences of the Central European Economic Union (*Mitteleuropäischer Wirtschaftsverein*) were at first limited to Germany and Austria-Hungary. It was, however, intended from the first to bring in similar associations and schools in France, Holland, Belgium, Switzerland and (Hungary indeed objecting) Rumania, and up to a point this was done. Special importance was given to this movement in Germany by the participation of all important groups of German industry, both heavy industry and finishing industries, and of the leading banking, shipping and agricultural interests. The object as defined by Max Schinkel, director of Germany's second biggest bank, the Disconto-Gesellschaft, was to secure for Germany that 'broader basis in Europe' which was recognised to be 'necessary for laying the economic foundations of German world policy'.

The German-Austrian Economic Association (*Deutsch-Oesterreichischer Wirtschaftsverband*) founded shortly before the war marked in one respect a retreat from the European objectives of the Central European Economic Union, but in another it marked an advance, urging as it did, much more intensively, the 'concentration' of the German and Austro-Hungarian markets. Influential German personalities were represented in this body.[2]

In 1912 Walther Rathenau,[3] the leading personality in the Allgemeine Elektrizitätsgesellschaft (A.E.G.), told Bethmann Hollweg that German policy should be directed towards the creation of a central European customs union, and secured the Chancellor's

---

[1] Cf. Henry Cord Meyer, *Mitteleuropa in German Thought and Action 1815–1945* (The Hague, 1955), extensive bibliography. Meyer, who was not able to utilise the German archives for the war period, seriously underestimates the importance of these movements.

[2] Paasche (Vice-President of the Reichstag), Stresemann, Friedrichs (President of the *Bund der Industriellen*), Lehmann (President of the *Verband der sächsischen Industrie* in the *Bund der Industriellen*), Steinthal (Director of the Deutsche Bank).

[3] See below pp. 10–11, 16, 28–9, 101; cf. also 'Mitteleuropa', pp. 249 ff.

agreement. In 1913 Rathenau again set out these ideas in a memorandum to the Chancellor. On August 1, 1914, the day Germany declared war on Russia, he again formulated his ideas in a memorandum which was destined to have a decisive effect on the policy of the German government during the World War. What made this possible had been, not least, the radical transformation which had taken place in the social, economic and political structure of Germany in the previous generation. The fundamental changes in economic conditions, the wide-spread prosperity, the rapid growth of the population, the swift expansion in all branches of economic life, combined to create a general conviction, which was reinforced by nation-wide propaganda, that Germany's frontiers had become too narrow for her, but that the ring of powers round her would never consent to their extension. The diplomatic campaign to 'split the Entente' by peaceful means cannot be understood without a glance at these structural changes.

Economic Expansion and World Power Aspirations

Germany's claim to world power was based on her consciousness of being a 'young', growing and rising nation. Her population had risen from about 41 millions in 1871 to about 68 millions in 1915, while that of France, with a larger area, had remained almost stationary, reaching only 40 millions in 1915. Moreover, more than one-third of the population of Germany was under fifteen years of age, and this gave the national consciousness a dynamic element which further reinforced the demand for *Lebensraum*, markets and industrial expansion. Although emigration had been high (1·3 million persons emigrated between 1881 and 1890), the population figures for 1910 were nevertheless far more favourable than, for example, those of France: an excess of births over deaths of 800,000 (8·9 per 1,000 against 3·4 per 1,000 in France), while the expectation of life was increasing and infant mortality on the decline. With increasing industrialisation, internal migration was beginning to replace migration overseas and immigrants were beginning to come in from Austria, Italy, Russian Poland and other European countries. Germany was developing more and more into a highly industrialised exporting country, and the problem of finding markets and raw materials to support her population was growing increasingly urgent. Industrialisation had concentrated the population in certain areas – the Ruhr, Saxony, Silesia, Berlin, the Rhine-Main area – and had within a few years totally transformed the face of the country: the numbers living in large towns had doubled and the occupational distribution of the population had changed radically.[1] This industrialisation and concentration of the population in a few centres had been accompanied by a shift from east to west, the results of which included a severe and growing shortage of agricultural labour in eastern Germany.

Wage and price levels were generally stable; slumps occurred, but the long-term economic trend was upward, and in spite of a chronic shortage of capital the national income was rising, as evidenced by rising real incomes and increased savings and investment.[2]

The increased wealth of all classes of society, combined with the stability of the currency, generated a feeling of security and strengthened the popular belief that continued growth would develop in an expansion which seemed almost predetermined by the laws of economics. Contemporaries pointed proudly to the national figures for imports and exports as proof of Germany's industrial development: between 1887 and 1912 the former had risen by 243·8 per cent (from 3,100 to 10,000 million marks), the latter by 185·4 per cent (from 3,100 to 8,900 million).

The balance of trade had thus become unfavourable, and the restoration of a favourable balance had consequently become one of the essential tasks of German economic policy. No other country could show an increase in imports over this period comparable to Germany's 243 per cent. Britain's figure was 108·7 per cent, America's 136·9 per cent, France's only 95 per cent. On the other hand, the increase in American exports during the quarter century (208·6 per cent) had exceeded Germany's. The total increase in foreign trade had, however, been far the highest in Germany (13,400 million marks, or 214·7 per cent); America's figure was 173·3 per cent, Britain's 113·1 per cent, France's 98·1 per cent.

There was, however, another factor of importance for Germany's world trading policy. In 1913 she was still leading in exchanges with the European states, but the direction of her trade had undergone a disquieting change since 1880. In that year 80 per cent of her exports had gone to Britain, France and south-east Europe, and 77 per cent had come from European countries. In 1913 the share of Europe in her imports and exports had gone down by 30 per cent; overseas countries, the tropics and above all South America, were supplying an increasing proportion of her raw materials.

The world-wide activities of Germany's entrepreneurs were

[1] In 1870 50 per cent of the population was employed in agriculture; in 1913 only 33 per cent, against over 50 per cent employed in commerce and industry.

[2] 21,500 million in 1896; 40,000 million in 1912. See the calculations in Karl Helfferich, *Deutschlands Volkswohlstand 1888–1913* (Berlin, 1913), pp. 92 ff.

strongly supported by an official policy aptly described as one of 'neo-mercantilism'.[1] It had become axiomatic that the state should support economic enterprise, both at home and abroad; in nationalising the postal, telegraphic and railway services the state had already made itself into an important factor in Germany's economic life, and its social legislation, its protective tariff policy and its system of export premiums had laid the foundations of Germany's economic expansion, and therewith of the transformation of her economic structure. The foundation of a Reichsbank to act as a central clearing house for the German money market had made it possible for the state to collaborate with the private banks in supplying the country, short of capital as it was, with such ample resources that it was able to venture on big, politically important enterprises.

This advance was based on the expansion of the interlinked complex of the great iron, steel and mining industries. The production of coal, iron and steel in the great centres of the Ruhr, Lorraine and Upper Silesia had increased since the 1870s with a rapidity unparalleled elsewhere in Europe. The 5,000 million marks of the French war indemnity (which had begun the process), large orders for armaments, and above all the big expansion of communications within and beyond Germany's frontiers had enabled the Reich to increase its coal production by 800 per cent, while England's had only doubled. At the same time German enterprise had entered the continental market in a big way; the mining industry, protected by the 1879 tariff, had now found secure outlets for its products in France, Belgium, Holland, Switzerland, Italy and Austria-Hungary. The growth of Germany's coal production, which was exceeded only by that of America (which rose in the quarter century before 1912 by 336·6 per cent against Germany's 218·1 per cent and Britain's 72·6 per cent), was accompanied by an even more spectacular growth in her iron and steel production: the production of raw iron rose from 4·0 million tons in 1887 to 15·5, an increase of 387 per cent. The figure for America was comparable (368·5 per cent), but Britain—and that was the decisive thing in German eyes—was able in that time to raise her production of iron ore only by 30·6 per cent (from 7·6 to 10 million tons). The development of Germany's steel production was unparalleled anywhere in the world. Tomas's new processes and Siemens' and Martin's inventions enabled the production of steel to rise by 1,335 per cent, from 0·9 million tons in 1886 to 13·6 millions. The estimated value of the production of Germany's mines

---

[1] Cf. Wilhelm Treue, *Wirtschafts und Sozialgeschichte Deutschlands im 19. Jahrhundert*, in Bruno Gebhardt, *Handbuch der deutschen Geschichte*, 8th ed. (Stuttgart, 1960), pp. 403 ff., heading '*Neumerkantilismus*'.

coal, ores and salt) rose from 700 million marks in 1886 to 2,000 million in 1912. At the same time Germany was becoming increasingly dependent on imports for her raw materials; these rose from 5·7 million marks in 1872 to 161·3 millions in 1910.

While the expansion of her heavy industry was the foundation on which the economic transformation of Germany rested, a number of entirely new industries also came into being: the chemical, electrical and optical industries and others. The new discoveries in aniline chemistry enabled the chemical industry, within a few decades, to outdistance all its European competitors; its exports in 1913 were of the value of some 125 million marks – an important item in Germany's trading figures. With its 150,000 employees, concentrated in a few mammoth enterprises, whose leading firms – Bayer, Hoechst and Ludwigshafen – had formed a cartel in 1904 (followed in 1916 by their fusion in I. G. Farben), the chemical industry was a typical example of the new, highly concentrated form of enterprise. The electrical industry was also concentrated in a few hands. Its connections with the big banks were particularly close. Equipped with patented inventions, less localised of its nature than heavy industry, it was by 1910 exporting to the tune of over 125 million marks and had a payroll of over 107,000 persons, most of them in Berlin. The optical industry, with 60 million marks, was smaller, but hardly inferior in the value of its production.

The textile industry, the only one to escape such high concentration, had maintained a steady growth since 1870. Its chief centres were Saxony, northern Bavaria, Württemberg and the lower Rhineland. The tendency towards intensification and mechanisation, characteristic of all German industry, was here particularly marked. While the number of persons employed in it hardly altered, its production rose tenfold in the quarter century: from 37,500 tons in 1878 to 370,000 in 1905.

The advance of the heavy and electrical industries would, however, not have been possible without the simultaneous development of communications and the rationalisation of trade and business, of which the concentration of the banks is the most striking example. In 1870 the German capital market was entirely in the hands of the private merchant bankers. By 1913 a complete change had come about; the world of German credit was dominated by the four 'D Banks' – the Deutsche Bank, the Disconto-Gesellschaft, the Dresdner Bank and the Bank für Handel and Industrie, commonly called the Darmstädter Bank. On the eve of the World War these huge institutions, each of which was represented on the boards of the main industries, controlled 65 per cent of the capital resources of all

Germany's credit institutions, thus typifying the advanced degree of concentration which the German economy had achieved.[1]

Amalgamations, foundation of subsidiary branches and so on, had enabled the joint-stock banks, in partnership with the old private banking houses of Rothschild, Bleichröder, Warburg, etc., to go into business abroad. The Deutsche Bank, for example, financed the construction of the Anatolian Railway and the St. Gotthard road, and floated a number of issues in both North and South America. The great banks succeeded in establishing themselves securely in the main bourses and the chief centres of world trade – London, Paris, Brussels, New York, Vienna, and Madrid. By founding foreign subsidiaries, such as the Banca Generale Romana, the Brasilian Bank, the German East African Bank, the German–Asiatic Bank, etc., they secured the financing of the Otavi Mining and Railway company in South-West Africa, the Baghdad Railway in Asia Minor, the Shantung Railroad and Mining Company in China, the New Guinea Company, oil enterprises in Rumania and Iraq, the Tientsin–Puckow Railway and the Venezuela Railway. Combination between the banks enabled them to act as issuing houses for a large number of loans in Germany, both Reich and Federal, and also in Austria-Hungary, Turkey, Russia, Finland, Norway, Sweden, Italy, Switzerland, the Argentine, Brazil and China.

To free herself from dependence on British ships for moving the increasing volume of her merchandise, and to enable her to bring her exports, financed by her own capital, to their markets abroad without British middle-men, Germany had to have her own merchant marine. Its construction was accompanied by the expansion of the great ports of Bremen and Hamburg. Here, too, the trend towards concentration was apparent: in the Hapag and the Norddeutscher Lloyd, the biggest of many shipping companies which sprang into existence within a few years, Germany possessed for the first time merchant lines of international calibre.[2] They began their careers, and first grew rich, by carrying emigrants; when this traffic ebbed away, they turned their interest to regular passenger and freight services, for which the demand was growing as Germany's exports increasingly took the form of specialised finished products. Movement through the German ports had grown by 300 per cent in 25 years, from 9·8 to 29·6 million tons incoming, and from 7·8 to 21·1 millions outgoing – figures which, it is true, still lagged far behind the

---

[1] W. Strauss, *Die Konzentrationsbewegung im Deutschen Bankgewerbe* (Berlin, 1928), p. 18; H. Weber, *Der Bankplatz Berlin* (Cologne, 1957), pp. 47 ff.

[2] 1881, registered tonnage 1·8 million (nearly all sailing vessels); 1913, 3·1 million (all steam)

British. The banks were also closely involved in the construction of the merchant fleet, as was a swiftly developing German dock industry (Howald, Blohm and Voss, Bremen Vulkan, Schichau-Danzig), which in its turn made possible the construction of a German navy.

The introduction of the 1879 tariff marked also the real beginning of the cartels; it was the protection of the new tariffs which made possible the creation of cartels capable of resisting both domestic and foreign competition. So the door was opened to a new type of entrepreneur, like Emil Kirdorf, who did not own the business managed by him, but was usually the 'employee' of a new combine founded by one of the big banks. The ideal of these men was the systematic expansion of the giant concern as the most efficient economic form, and they therefore took advantage of every opportunity to combine the small mines and furnaces into productive, solid and profitable mixed enterprises, whose products were marketed by arrangement through syndicates. Men like Hugo Stinnes and August Thyssen, personally more ruthless and more familiar with the niceties of capital management than the older generation represented by Krupp, Stumm, Vögler and Röchling, built up their great combines on the 'vertical' plan. The leading positions alike in heavy industry, in banking and in commerce came to be filled by men of essentially 'patriotic' outlook. This new class, which largely moulded public opinion and exercised an increasing influence on government policy, was a characteristic phenomenon of the new Germany. The more it succeeded in introducing the principles of neo-mercantilism into German policy, the greater its influence became. Bankers such as Gwinner, Helfferich and Stauss (Deutsche Bank), Solmssen (Disconto-Gesellschaft), Nathan and Gutmann (Dresdner Bank), Rathenau (Berliner Handelsgesellschaft), Schinckel (Norddeutsche Bank) or Dernburg (Darmstädter Bank, afterwards Secretary of State in the Reich Colonial Office); industrialists such as Carl Friedrich von Siemens, Emil and Walther Rathenau (electric industry), Carl Duisberg (chemical industry), and the heavy industrialists mentioned above; the leading dock-owners, etc., etc., formed a group of entrepreneurs characteristic of the Germany of the day, whose assimilation with the older leading classes of society was facilitated by the ennoblement of many of them. The close relationship in which Ballin and Warburg stood to the Emperor is well known; no less significant was the position of a Gwinner, made a member of the *Herrenhaus* at the Emperor's own wish in recognition of his services in connection with the Baghdad Railway, or the intimate relationship in which, for example, Gwinner, Rathenau and Helfferich stood to Bethmann Hollweg.

Besides using their personal influence on many domestic issues – not least against the workers' associations – the employers combined in new pressure groups to influence foreign policy. Bueck and Roetger, the Secretaries of the heavy industrialists' powerful association, the *Centralverband Deutscher Industrieller* (General Federation of German Industrialists), Stresemann as a 'syndic' of the *Bund der Industriellen* (Industrialists' Association), Voss as Secretary of the *Verein der Deutschen Berg und Eisenhüttenleutte* (Union of German Mining and Ironworks Owners), Riesser as President of the Bankers' Association – to name only a few – exemplify the close connection which existed between business interests and government policy. A glance at the list of deputies in the Reichstag – even more, in the Prussian House of Deputies – belonging to the Conservative, Free Conservative, National Liberal and Zentrum parties will show how high a percentage of them were so intimately connected by business interest with agriculture, industry, commerce, etc., as to make a distinction between business and politics almost unreal (the officers of the business associations, for example, nearly always sat in parliament, usually as National Liberals).

The link between business and politics grew progressively closer in the opening years of the new century, as the basic political outlook of the leading industrialists, bankers and officers of the employers' associations came to conform more closely with that of the intellectual bourgeoisie, the higher bureaucracy and army and navy officers. The spiritual 'nationalisation' of the German employer class, however, tended to aggravate political crises. Furthermore, Germany began to measure power by the yardstick of steel production, to regard Britain as an 'ageing state', and to expect that the moulding of the future economic and political shape of the world would lie with the U.S.A. and Germany alone.

As early as 1900 George von Siemens, senior director of Germany's biggest bank, the Deutsche Bank, published in the *Nation* an article 'On the National Importance of the Bourse', the significance of which as a programme was at once recognised, and its ideas endorsed, by leading bankers and industrialists. Arguing from the experience of the German money market on the London and Paris exchanges, Siemens pleaded for the establishment of a strong German bourse. Should war break out, as he thought only too probable in view of the existing tension, Germany would need to place her economy on a footing of self-sufficiency, for which purpose a bourse was essential.

Economic calculation, emotions and straining after world power interacted mutually in a crescendo of crises and in controversies over Germany's claims and over what were felt to be the rights usurped by Britain, France or Russia in the Near or the Far East. Their outward and visible sign was the widespread support given to the Emperor's and Tirpitz's naval programme. The chorus was led by the Navy League (*Flottenverein*). In its origin a purely business creation, founded by the *Centralverband Deutscher Industrieller*, whose first reaction to a naval programme was the thought that it would provide them with safe orders for years ahead, the League developed into the first great example of state-controlled propaganda.[1] The presidents of the Prussian provinces and the princes of the non-Prussian states were its patrons; its members included the senior bureaucracy and junior civil servants, such as teachers. Provincial and local school councils carried its ideas into every village; public opinion in return influenced the political parties. At least up to 1908 it was thus a 'state association' which united industry and state service in devotion to the same patriotic cause. The retirement of the agitator in chief, General Keim, who had overstepped the limits envisaged by Tirpitz and given the campaign too much of an anti-government flavour, did not alter the League's character. The only result was that it now came under state control, being placed under the direction of the Reich Naval Office. General Keim became co-founder, with General Litzmann, and agitator in chief of the *Wehrverein* (Defence Association), a body founded in 1912 to call for expansion of the long neglected land forces on a scale equal to that now planned for the navy. The popular appeal of the *Wehrverein* soon exceeded that of the Navy League itself.

A German navy would, as the Navy League convinced the nation, protect German shipping, force Britain to regard Germany as an equal, a desirable ally and a friend, and thus become a symbol of Germany's claim to world power. At the same time it was one of the reasons for the hostility between Britain and Germany, although it would be an over-simplification to regard it as the only decisive factor in the relationship between the two countries. For the navy itself was unimaginable without the backing of Germany's economic power and without the pressure exercised by wide economic circles for a status of recognised partnership overseas and leadership in Europe. Often as the possibilities of worldwide expansion were discussed, they did not at that time really exist. And mutual consultation on plans – even governmental plans – relating to trade and business penetration was becoming regular: the discussions over Near and Far Eastern ores, oil and railways provide examples.

As the volume of Germany's production grew, the narrowness of the basis of her raw materials market became increasingly apparent,

[1] Cf. Jonathan Sternberg.

and as she penetrated more deeply into world markets, this narrowness became increasingly irksome. Devices such as the purchase of mines, obtaining concessions or shares in them, undercutting, and squeezing foreign rivals out of markets, enabled German interests to penetrate and establish themselves in the great minette field of Longwy–Briey and the iron ore deposits of Normandy. German industry reached out from Saxony across Bohemia and linked up the main industrial centre of Austria-Hungary with that of central Germany. At the same time, this penetration of German commerce into the still mainly agricultural economy of the Dual Monarchy made the latter increasingly dependent on German capital. And Austria-Hungary herself was only a bridge to south-eastern Europe, where German 'commercialisation', as Conrad called it, steadily won ground against its Austro-Hungarian, French, British and Belgian competitors. The biggest of all the enterprises in this field was the Steaua Romana: here the big banks, led by the Disconto-Gesellschaft, succeeded in establishing an oil company, almost entirely financed by German capital, whose production was to go exclusively to continental consumers. This enterprise was to be linked with a consumers' organisation covering France, Belgium, Holland, Russia, Austria-Hungary and Germany, and to form a counterweight to the giant Standard Oil and Royal Dutch Shell companies. German industry, under the state-encouraged patronage of the great banks, participated in the construction of the Anatolian and Baghdad Railways and so paved the way to increasing investment in Turkey itself. In eastern and south-eastern Europe the chief advances were those made by the industry of Upper Silesia, which concentrated on these markets, as it could not venture overseas. At the same time, lack of native steel refineries drove heavy industry to penetrate the deposits of Krivoi Rog and Tchiaturi in the Ukraine and the Caucasus, and the banks tried to finance these plans through links with Russian banks – the more so since, in spite of French competition, big profits could be made out of Russia's need for armaments.

An economy organised on the most modern lines, regularly introducing every modern innovation and invention, fed by a network of technical academies organised exclusively to serve it, and manned by a disciplined, industrious and thrifty population – this was one side of the picture. In contrast to it, the organisation of the army, with a conservative leadership and methods which retarded not only democratisation but even the technical modernisation of its own weapons, constituted a glaring anachronism.[1]

[1] The strength of the army was hardly raised up to 1912; machine guns were introduced late and in insufficient numbers, the intelligence service was too small; the

Economic expansion was the basis of Germany's political world diplomacy, which vacillated in its methods between rapprochment and conciliation at one moment, aggressive insistence on Germany's claims the next, but never wavered in its ultimate objective, the expansion of Germany's power.

The Diplomacy of World Policy

Even in Bismarck's day, for all his elaborate system of alliances, there were signs that Germany's policy was leading her into isolation. She took the first step along this path when in 1879 she opted for alliance with that great question-mark, Austria-Hungary. In the 1880s it proved impossible to establish close relations with any one of the three other great powers, notwithstanding the achievement of a tolerable *modus vivendi* with Britain under Disraeli and Salisbury in spite of differences over colonial questions, and notwithstanding the reinsurance treaties which, in the days of Gorchakov (1856–82) and Giers (1882–95), preserved a contractual relationship with Russia which, though rendered fragile by the increasing hostility of Russian public opinion, survived successive Balkan crises. This development was accentuated by the 'new course' of the 1890s. First Russia was estranged, then Britain, and the Russo-French military alliance of 1893 wrought a radical change in Germany's position in Europe. From 1897 onward, the year in which Bülow became Foreign Secretary (from 1900 to 1909 he was Chancellor) and Tirpitz Secretary of State in the Reich Naval Office, Germany's pursuit of a 'world policy' led straight to an isolation which was made inevitable by her over-insistence on the principle of a 'free hand' and her over-assessment of her own strength.

The very first steps taken by her in the Far East, the lease of Kiaochow in 1897 and the attempt made in 1898, after first acquiring some of the Samoan islands, to establish a fortified base in the Philippines, led to sharp clashes with Britain, Russia, Japan and the U.S.A. Her Middle Eastern policy of these years was even more disquieting to Russia and Britain. Wilhelm II's tour and his speech in Damascus in November, 1898, in which he assumed the role of protector of three hundred million Mohammedans, were bound to sound like challenges to both Russia and Britain, with their numerous Mohammedan subjects; and they were in fact so taken, much more seriously

air arm (unlike that of France) was neglected, even for reconnaisance purposes; motorisation was insufficient; the cavalry arm was too large; cavalry regiments were brigaded together with insufficient artillery, development of tanks and anti-tank weapons in the war was belated.

than they had been meant. Similarly, the Baghdad Railway project, the concession for which was renewed in 1899, could not fail to rouse the mistrust of Britain and Russia. This mistrust was enhanced by Germany's attempts to establish coaling and trading stations in Aden, Yemen and on the south Persian coast, on the sea-route to India. Similarly, her efforts to secure concessions for borings for oil and irrigation works in Iraq trespassed on a zone of British interests. The threat to British and Russian interests presented by Germany's economic invasion of the Middle East seemed the more serious because in the same years Germany undertook the task of propping up Ottoman power, first delegating von der Goltz to reorganise the Turkish army (1886–95 and 1909–13) and then sending Liman von Sanders in the crisis of 1913.

The advance of German economic interests in the shipping, railways, ports and mines of East and South-West Africa, and particularly in the Boer Republic in the 1890s, led to friction with Britain: the 'Kruger telegram' of 1896 was peculiarly resented. This worldwide search for acquisitions could not but lead to friction between Germany and the established powers of the world, but the immediate cause of her clash with Britain was her claim to possess her own battle fleet. The construction of this fleet cut across the feelers for an alliance which were put out between 1898 and 1901, and was one of the factors – Germany's over-rigid attitude towards the alliance being another (she believed that the differences between Britain and Russia were irreconcilable, and thought that she could steer a course between the two) – which made Britain decide finally after 1901 to seek other partners. Britain's immediate reaction was to assure herself of Japan through the alliance of 1902, proceeding to approaches to France in 1903 and the establishment of the Entente in 1904.

In this situation of growing isolation, the counter-moves undertaken by Germany showed that at least Holstein, the most influential member of the Foreign Ministry, and Schlieffen, Chief of the General Staff from 1892 to 1906, were ready, if necessary, to detach France from the Entente by force. When the Emperor and Bülow renounced the appeal to arms on which the Schlieffen Plan was based, they did so chiefly in the hope of being able to establish a continental bloc, consisting of Germany, Russia and France, by peaceful means; when the Emperor met the Tsar at Bjoerkoë in July, 1905, he believed that he had achieved this aim. The measure of the excitement engendered in Germany by the Russian revolution, particularly the bloody repression of the workers' rising in Moscow in December, 1905, and by the war scare of that year, may be judged from the Emperor's famous New Year letter to Bülow, written in a sort of attempt to clear himself after his 'flabby' attitude during the crisis. Making a characteristic nexus between domestic and foreign events, he instructed the Chancellor, 'now that the Christmas candles have been re-lit': 'Shoot down, behead and eliminate the Socialists first, if need be, by a blood-bath, then war abroad. But not before, and not à tempo.'[1]

In this letter the Emperor was expressing what had been his pet idea since the end of the 1890s, that if she engaged in a major war, Germany must first conclude an alliance with Turkey and then revolutionise the Islamic world.

Disappointment over the course and results of the Algeciras Conference, which Germany had engineered in the hope of obtaining American support, caused her to determine never again to accept a conference as a method of resolving an international dispute. She had hoped to be able to play Britain and America off against one another at Algeciras. This hope proved illusory. Yet thereafter, up to the World War, German policy held fast to its old dogmas, entirely misinterpreting the effects of the events in the Philippines in 1898 (the clash between the American fleet and a German naval squadron); of the Venezuelan incident of 1902, when Britain and Germany carried through a joint blockade in defence of their interests (which American opinion resented more from Germany than Britain); and above all, of Britain's retreat from the West Indies in 1901, thanks to which America was able to make Colombia her satellite and to undertake the construction of the Panama Canal single-handed.

The Algeciras Conference revealed not only how few Germany's friends were, but how unreliable. Italy ranged herself on the side of the Entente, Austria's support was lukewarm. And just at this juncture 'encirclement' became a reality. Defeated by Japan in the war of 1904–5 and shaken by revolution, Russia switched her attention from the Far East back to Europe. She was thereby brought increasingly into conflict with Austria-Hungary, and also with Germany, while at the same time an understanding between Britain and Russia became possible. A delimitation of their respective spheres of influence in Afghanistan, Tibet and Persia (this last amounting to a diplomatic partition of that country) led to the Anglo-Russian Entente of 1907, after which the Russo-French military alliance and the Anglo-French Entente hardened into the Triple Entente. One of the factors which attracted Russia to this rapprochement was the fear of German designs on the Baltic coast (which were in fact partly realised during the First World War), while for Britain it was another

[1] Cf. Bülow, *Denkwürdigkeiten*, Col. II (Berlin, 1930), p. 198.

answer to Germany's attempts to gain a footing in Persia and India via Turkey.

The 'encirclement' in turn brought Germany into increased dependence on the policy of her ally, Austria-Hungary. This dependence became evident in her reactions to Austria's policy in the Bosnian annexation crisis of 1908. Both the Chancellor, Bülow, and the Emperor (whom he had purposely kept in the dark until the last moment) at first disapproved strongly. The Emperor felt that 'the Eastern policy which he had been following for twenty years' had been completely ruined, and that Britain had outbid him in support of Turkey. Bülow hoped that a strong and demonstrative stand by Germany would at once cover her Austrian ally and keep the link with Turkey from snapping, and this hope proved justified, partly owing to Russia's reasonableness (although she drew closer than ever to her partners in the Entente), partly owing to the retreat of the Young Turk leaders, especially those in the army. Britain's popularity in Turkey soon passed, and the young German-trained officers accepted Germany's proposal of a financial indemnity for the cession of Bosnia-Herzegovina and responded again to Germany's advances.

Germany had been prepared – or so she had asserted – to enforce with arms a solution in the Balkans favourable to Austria-Hungary, rather than expose her ally to the danger of a humiliation *à la* Algeciras.

At the same time, Germany was trying to expand her continental power by diplomatic action, using Austria-Hungary as a bridge to Turkey. With the conclusion of the Franco-German colonial agreement of February 9, 1909, and the visit of the Tsar and Sazonov (Izvolski's successor as Foreign Minister) to Potsdam on November 3–4, 1910, her old goal of a constitutional bloc seemed on the point of realisation: the Tsar promised to loosen his ties with the Entente on the basis that Germany would similarly relax her links with Austria, and to withdraw the opposition which Russia had so long maintained to the construction of the Baghdad Railway; Germany in return recognised northern Persia as a Russian zone of influence and agreed to pay for the construction of branch lines running from the Baghdad Railway into Persia. The German–French agreement, which buried the Algeciras controversy in many respects, cleared Germany's path towards her goal of a large and continuous colonial empire.[1] But hopes of a continental understanding in east and west

---

[1] France received a free hand in North Morocco; Germany was left confined to South Morocco, but was to receive French help for the construction of a railway line from the Cameroons to East Africa across the French and Belgian Congos.

perished at Agadir in 1911 in the second Moroccan crisis, although Germany attempted to use the problems raised by France's advance in Morocco to bring about a continental bloc via the colonial problem.

The negotiations carried on in the summer of 1911 between Kiderlen-Wächter, Secretary of State in the Foreign Ministry, and the French Ambassador in Berlin, Jules Cambon, were at first directed towards reaching a delimitation of interests in Morocco itself; later, however, Kiderlen-Wächter's demand for the cession of the whole of the French Congo as 'compensation' for Germany's *désintéressement* in Morocco, revealed one of the essential objectives of Germany's diplomacy: to acquire a continuous colonial empire in central Africa. Behind this stood the even more far-reaching ambition of breaking-up, or at least weakening, the Entente Cordiale by means of a Franco-German 'settlement'. Britain parried this danger by a public intervention in favour of France in the shape of Lloyd George's famous Mansion House speech, and by initiating with France military conversations of great importance; whereupon, in the autumn, Germany yielded and contented herself with the 'prestige success' of an addition (of small intrinsic value) to her possessions in the Cameroons. Britain had saved France from the humiliation of a 'settlement' with Germany involving French sacrifice which had threatened to undermine the solidarity of the Triple Entente and to replace the British policy of balance by a German hegemony in Europe.

The strong reactions of public opinion to the crisis, the sharpness of the language used by statesmen, and above all the new prominence of the part played by the military, differentiated these later exchanges markedly from the transactions of the first years of German world policy. The German policy of 'compensation', of those abrupt and seemingly endless demands which had so irritated all the powers except Germany's own allies and had done so much to draw them together against her—this was now at an end. Up to 1911 Germany had not succeeded in adopting Britain's policy of concluding compromises with her competitors, for she had equated moderation with an inferiority incompatible with the world power status which was her aim. Such a policy was inevitably rejected by a generation of politicians who had grown up in revolt against Bismarck's doctrine that Germany was a 'saturated power', regarded the expansion of Germany as the supreme object of their policy, and were now occupying the leading positions in the imperial Chancellery, the Foreign Ministry and the Prussian ministries.

England the Enemy

The second Morocco crisis was worked up by propaganda and press campaigns by the Foreign Ministry, in a quiet way from the crises of 1905–6 and 1908–9, which were more purely diplomatic; a much wider appeal was made to the national feelings of the masses. The effect on German opinion was therefore even greater. All the deeper was the disappointment at the results of the negotiations, when instead of receiving the French Congo as the corner-stone of the future great, continuous colonial empire in Africa, Germany was fobbed off with the meagre strips of land on the Congo and Ubangi. Germany had felt confident of worsting France, and her wrath at this failure was directed primarily against Britain, whose support had alone saved France from defeat. Both sides were ready to fight. A jotting by the Chief of the German General Staff, which is instinct equally with excitement and disappointment, shows how feeling was running in Germany after the interruption of the diplomatic negotiations in mid-August, 1911 (when, on the other side, military conversations were going on between the British, French and Russians). Moltke, Chief of the German General Staff from 1906 to 1914, wrote:

> I am thoroughly fed up with this wretched Morocco business. If we slink out of this affair *again*, as in 1906, with our tail between our legs, if we cannot pluck up the courage to make an energetic demand which we are prepared *to enforce with the sword*, then I despair of the future of the German Reich. Then I shall go.[1]

Germany's leading economic and political circles were no less embittered against France and Britain. They feared that the threat of a war on three fronts would find them unprepared, militarily and financially, and that weakness would force them to give way.

All this disappointment – from which the Emperor, who was openly attacked in the Pan-German Press for his weakness, was not exempt, and which actually led to proceedings being started against Kiderlen-Wächter – vented itself in the stormy Reichstag debates of November, 1911. The Conservative leader, von Heydebrand und der Lasa, said in open debate: 'Now we know where to find our enemy.' Germany experienced a sort of national revolution, an 'awakening', fanned by the 'pressure groups' of the Navy League, the Colonial League, the *Alldeutscher Verband* (Pan-German Association), and the latest and very effective recruit to their numbers, the *Wehrverein*. The state had failed to give a 'strong answer' in July; then, said the

---

[1] Hellmuth von Moltke, *Erinnerungen*, p. 303, cit. Hermann Oncken, *Deutschland und die Vorgeschichte des Weltkrieges*, Vol. 2, p. 705 (Leipzig, 1933); italics the present author's.

Reichstag, that answer shall come from us: Germany shall be stronger than before; she shall arm at sea against Britain, and on land against France and Russia. Compared with this emotion-born cry for more armaments everywhere, Bethmann Hollweg's merely tactical manoeuvre has little significance. Tirpitz promptly answered the Reichstag's demand by bringing forward a supplementary naval estimate. The Chancellor got the Ministry of War to produce in its turn a supplementary army vote, hoping thereby to delay the passage of the navy vote. The promotion of Ludendorff to a position of direct influence on the General Staff[1] must also be viewed in the light of the altered mood of the nation. This excitement, these calls for more arms, were greatly stimulated by unfavourable comments on the German army by British and French observers at the summer manoeuvres of 1911: they found it backward, both in tactics and equipment, thereby putting a finger on one of imperial Germany's weak spots.[2]

In France, meanwhile, the appointment of Poincaré as Prime Minister had brought with it a sort of national renaissance. In Britain, however, reactions were divided. Opposition groups in the Commons and the City disliked a too exclusive association with France and advocated an understanding with Germany. German diplomacy snatched at the possibility of substituting alliance with Britain against the Continent for the continental bloc against Britain. As early as the summer of 1911 von Kühlmann, then the most active of the German diplomats in London working for an agreement with Britain, maintained that it would be possible to effect a radical transformation of Anglo-German relations. On June 6 he wrote to Berlin that Germany had the choice between two alternatives: either naval expansion and breach with Britain, or an armaments programme confined to the land forces, leaving the navy law unchanged, with the possibility of a far-reaching colonial agreement on Angola and the Congo basin. Two leaders of the business world, the Emperor's and Bethmann Hollweg's friend Ballin, and Cassel, a naturalised British subject of German origin in close relations with official circles in England, then took the initiative which led to the famous Haldane Mission.

The objects and course of this enterprise are less interesting for us in their historical aspect as one more unsuccessful attempt at an

---

[1] Cf. Gerhard Ritter, 'Staatskunst und Kriegshandwerk. Das Problem des "Militarismus"' in *Deutschland*, Vol. 2 (Munich, 1960), pp. 273 ff. Moltke–Ludendorff memorandum of December 21, 1912, full of long, purely political considerations.

[2] Cf. Oncken, op. cit., p. 713. Similar views were expressed in *The Times* and *France Militaire*.

Anglo-German *rapprochement*, than for the light which they throw on Germany's continental aims. Of the trilogy of the naval question, political agreement and colonial understanding, the Germans from the first attached the greatest importance to the political settlement, whereas for Haldane all else was subsidiary to the naval discussions. Yet on the eve of Haldane's arrival the Emperor had announced the new supplementary naval vote in a speech from the throne, thus heavily prejudicing the success of the discussions before they had so much as started. To add to the difficulties, the Emperor and Tirpitz conducted the naval discussions with Haldane alone, in Bethmann Hollweg's absence, and both were determined on principle to refuse any concession; in the following weeks they showed the greatest displeasure at British criticisms and counter-measures.[1]

While not prepared to meet Britain over the question of the naval arms race, the Germans asked her to assume most extensive engagements when they came to discuss the political settlement. Both Bethmann Hollweg, as the man technically responsible for the policy of the Reich, and the Emperor himself, persistently rejected Britain's offer of neutrality in the event of an *unprovoked* attack on Germany, demanding (in addition to a sufficiently imposing colonial empire) an assurance of neutrality defined by Kiderlen-Wächter in the following terms: Should either of the contracting parties *become involved* in war with one or more Powers, the other contracting party pledges itself to observe at least benevolent neutrality, and to use its influence to secure the localisation of the conflict.'[2]

The contractual assurance which Germany asked of Britain would have given Germany a free hand *vis-à-vis* France, since it would have obliged Britain to stand aside from a continental war, even if provoked by Germany; not to mention that so far-reaching a promise would have endangered her own Ententes, which were less precise in their wording. But the essential object for Britain was – as Haldane emphasised in his very first conversation with Bethmann Hollweg on February 8 and Sir Arthur Nicolson repeated later in a very acute *aide mémoire* – precisely to prevent France from being crushed by the power of Germany. Bethmann Hollweg refused to modify his

---

[1] Wilhelm II on March 5: 'My patience and that of the German people is exhausted.'

[2] Bethmann Hollweg's draft for an Anglo–German agreement, submitted by him to Haldane on February 10, 1912 (*Grosse Politik*, Vol. 31, pp. 116 ff.). According to Bethmann Hollweg's notes (ibid., pp. 117 ff.), Haldane thought that the draft went too far, as Britain could not bind herself for the case of an attack by Germany on France; in particular, there would then be a danger of the French ports falling into German hands. Nicolson writes: 'If the Germans once had British neutrality in their pockets, peace would not last long' (*British Docs.*, Vol. VII, p. 734). Haldane's diary for February 2 is reprinted in *B.D.*, VII, p. 506.

neutrality formula even although Haldane offered him the Belgian Congo and Angola—he spoke of a 'belt' running across Africa—with Zanzibar and Pemba, besides concessions over the Baghdad Railway.

It emerges in these conversations that two objectives possessed an especial importance for Germany: firstly, the colonial settlement offered by Britain, which would have meant a German 'Mittelafrika', and secondly, a German-dominated 'Mitteleuropa', the outline of which formed the object, at this very juncture, of repeated conversations between the Emperor, Bethmann Hollweg and the author of the idea, Walther Rathenau. The ideas were still indeterminate; sometimes peaceful methods were envisaged, sometimes force, as fear of Russia or resentment against America predominated. Two days after the Haldane Mission, the Emperor expounded to Rathenau his ideas for an economic unification of the Continent as a defensive measure against the American reprisals policy of high tariffs. 'His plan' was for a 'United States of Europe against America'. He thought that this would not be disagreeable to the British, and that they would come into it. 'Five States (counting in France) can achieve something' (that is to say the Triple Alliance, France and Britain against America).[1] The Emperor was against running after Britain for her favours, and in no case was he prepared to sacrifice the naval programme (which had been laid before the Reichstag on February 19 and passed by it on May 19). 'But a last attempt is to be made: England is to be offered an alliance, coupled with the inclusion of France in 'Mitteleuropa'. Here lie the roots of the ideas pursued by Bethmann Hollweg in July and August, 1914.

It must remain an open question whether the inspiration was transmitted by the Emperor to Rathenau, or vice versa (the ideas of both men undoubtedly owed much to Bernhardi's book—to which we shall return—which had appeared at the beginning of 1912). In any case, Rathenau expounded these ideas shortly afterwards (on July 25, 1912) to Bethmann Hollweg in Hohenfinow, and found the Chancellor in general agreement with them. The Chancellor was just back from a tour in Russia, which had reassured him as to the immediate position but had filled him with the deepest anxiety, even fear, for the future, as Russia's power grew. He saw Russia's 'wealth of natural resources and of crude physical man-power' as the bases for the development of 'an expansive and gigantic industrial power' which might one day crush Germany. Germany could resist

---

[1] Cf. Walther Rathenau, *Tagebuch 1907–1922* (reproduced in MS. form), pp. 86 ff., 100 ff.; F. Fischer, *Weltpolitik, Weltmachtsstreben und deutsche Kriegsziele*, *Hist. Zeitschrift 199-2*, October, 1965, pp. 322 f., 324 ff., and Egmont Zechlin, *Deutschland zwischen Krieg und Wirtschaftskrieg*, ibid., pp. 399 ff.

this power only by an expansion of her bases, which must include expansion to the west. Rathenau's report on the conversation, at the end of July, ran:

> I developed my ideas: 1. Economics. Customs union with Austria, Switzerland, Italy, Belgium, Netherlands, etc., with simultaneous closer association. 2. Foreign Policy. Key to it: the Franco-German conflict, on which all nations grow fat. Key: England. Disarmament impossible today. Begin by increasing tension – though dangerous – also undermine England's position in Mediterranean. Then alliance. Object: Mittelafrika, Asia Minor.

All the general points of German world policy figure in association in this conversation – Mitteleuropa, Mittelafrika, Asia Minor. We must note above all the appearance, in July, 1912, of the two cardinal aims which figured two years later in Bethmann Hollweg's September Programme of 1914: Mitteleuropa and Mittelafrika.

The Inevitable War

Germany's obstinate insistence on a policy directed towards securing British neutrality and a free hand for herself on the Continent shows once more that her leaders were at this time regarding war with France and Russia as extremely likely, if not imminent, and sometimes even as inevitable. Important evidence to this effect comes from Germany's ally, Austria-Hungary.

Germany had initiated the new armaments race when, on May 10, 1912, the Reichstag had agreed to the increases in the land forces (first asked for in the previous autumn, these were relatively modest: the figure was raised from 595,000 men to 622,000), and on May 15 had adopted the Navy Bill round which so much discussion had turned during the Haldane Mission. The new Austro-Hungarian Foreign Minister, Count Berchtold,[1] paid his inaugural visit to Berlin on May 24–6. During the second Morocco crisis Austria had shown even more awareness than at Algeciras of Germany's increasing hostility to Britain and France, and had disappointed Germany by the reserve of her attitude. Austria's interests lying elsewhere, Berchtold showed himself very sensitive to the anti-Western atmosphere in Berlin. Emphatic as were the assurances lavished on him in Berlin, and duly noted by him, of the accord between the foreign policies of Germany and Austria-Hungary, unspoken differences yet remained. 'Firstly, there are the efforts *to bring Britain, by diplomatic means,* into a precarious situation calculated to make her more amenable to Germany's overtures for a *rapprochement.*'

To this end, Germany was encouraging Italy's Mediterranean

---

[1] *Oesterreich–Ungarns Aussenpolitik*, IV, No. 3540, p. 185.

policy in a manner which ignored Austria's interests completely. Another point was: 'that all the calculations of German foreign policy were directed from beginning to end towards the eventuality of a clash with France, an eventuality on which German diplomacy is directing practically its entire talents for combination,' yet one which Vienna found unpalatable in view of the absence of any substantial conflict of interests between Austria-Hungary and France.

These tacit reservations in Austro-Hungarian policy constituted a complication for Germany's policy, which looked primarily westward because of Germany's naval rivalry with Britain and her antagonism towards France which was partly emotional. For, firstly, in Germany's plans France was the first object of attack in a major war. Secondly, France, as the financier of Russia and the Balkan League, was, from the economic-political point of view, the kernel of all anti-German combinations. Thirdly, France was beginning to take advantage of Germany's weakness in capital coverage to shoulder her out even of Greece and Turkey. For this reason the conviction was taking ever deeper root in Germany, after the unsatisfactory outcomes of the Morocco crisis and the Haldane Mission, and the revelation of unconfessed differences between Germany and Austria-Hungary, that a great 'settling of accounts' was sooner or later inevitable.

This was why Germany had been negotiating in Rome since the end of 1911 to get the Triple Alliance renewed ahead of the specified date. Germany wanted to give Italy a twofold role in the anticipated conflict with France and Russia. Italian divisions were to relieve the German army in its first encounter with the French by pinning down French forces on the Alpine front (further agreement was reached in 1912 that in the event of war three Italian corps were to be sent to Alsace). Secondly, Germany hoped, by strengthening Italy's position in the Mediterranean, to put pressure on Britain to approach the Triple Alliance, and thus to secure British neutrality.

Austria's primary interests, unlike Germany's, lay in the southeast. Since the annexation of Bosnia-Herzegovina in 1908–9 the Southern Slav movement had grown into a steadily increasing threat to the existence of the Monarchy–the more so, since Russia's policy was, in accordance with the tradition which made Russia the protector of the Slav world, using the movement to further her own imperialistic aims. Berchtold himself reported in his notes on his visit to Berlin that the German Chancellor had informed him of the recent conclusion (of which he had learnt through secret sources) of a Balkan League between Serbia, Bulgaria, Greece and Montenegro. Germany had not, apparently, seen much cause for uneasiness in this development. Yet that same autumn saw the outbreak of war between the Balkan League and Turkey over the League's demand for 'autonomy' for Macedonia (then still under Turkish sovereignty).

The unexpected victories of the Balkan states of Bulgaria, Serbia and Greece over Turkey in the First Balkan War of 1912, following Italy's success in Tripoli a year before, created an impression, especially in Paris, that German armaments and strategy had suffered a considerable reverse, for the Turkish army had been trained by German officers and equipped by German firms. People talked of 'Creuzot's victory over Krupp'. This strengthened the war spirit in Poincaré's France. The Turkish débâcle also had its effects in Russia, the patron of the Balkan League. Serbia, whose self-confidence had risen correspondingly, demanded an outlet to the Adriatic. Austria-Hungary was prepared to agree to territorial gains for Serbia but she was not prepared to agree to Serbian access to the Adriatic and she also demanded the constitution of an 'independent' Albania. The war against Turkey threatened to develop into a war between Serbia and Austria-Hungary, with the danger that the two groups of great powers might be drawn into a European war.

In this tense situation Germany and Britain succeeded in working together. Both wanted a peaceful settlement of the crisis and worked to this end at the Conference of Ambassadors which met in London in December, 1912. This new *rapprochement* between Britain and Germany – the initiative for which had come from Grey in October – combined with memories of the Haldane Mission, revived Bethmann Hollweg's hopes of a possible European policy based on the assumption of British neutrality. He was convinced that if war broke out with Russia over the Balkan question, this would mean war with France; yet, as he wrote on December 18, the day after the opening of the London Conference, there seemed to him to be 'many indications which made it at least doubtful whether England would intervene actively if the *provocation* appeared to come directly from Russia and France'. He thought that if Germany avoided any suspicion of provocation, Britain might content herself with 'an intervention, at first diplomatic, in favour of France after her defeat'. This calculation shows how little Bethmann Hollweg's ideas changed between 1912 and July, 1914, when he was primarily interested, not in saving the peace, but in saddling Russia with the responsibility for the war, because his policy was based on the theory that Britain could be kept out of a continental war if Russia was made to appear the aggressor. This would have the advantage for Germany – an invaluable one after her experience of Austria's doubtful loyalty during

31

the two Morocco crises (where the issues had concerned Germany alone)—that in such a case Austria could be counted on with certainty to stand by Germany.

Just as in July, 1914, so now, the idea that Germany would thus be able to crush France without Britain's intervention was contradicted by Lichnowsky, who had been promoted in November, 1912 to charge of the embassy in London. In view of the possibility of conflict between Austria-Hungary and Serbia, and of the danger of the development of a European conflagration, Grey had told Haldane to repeat expressly that British policy, 'being concerned to maintain some balance between the groups of Powers, could under no circumstances tolerate France being crushed'; and a few days later (December 9), when Grey was expressing disquiet over Bethmann Hollweg's words about 'loyalty to allies' and 'fighting' in his Reichstag speech, Lichnowsky formulated Grey's ideas as follows: 'Britain's policy towards us is one of peace and friendship, but no British government would regard a further weakening of France as compatible with the vital interests of the country.'

The British people would under all circumstances guard itself against seeing France collapse a second time, as in 1870, and then finding itself face to face with a single, over-mighty power dominating the Continent. A little later he wrote: 'England cannot and will not find herself afterwards facing a unitary continental group under the leadership of a single power.'

The Emperor's marginal notes to these reports and the consequences which he afterwards drew from them show that Wilhelm expected from the first to find Britain on the side of France and Russia if war came; yet he was ready to face a conflict, even against this combination. His comment on the maintenance of the balance was: 'will change'; on the warning that Britain would never tolerate France being crushed: 'she will have to.' The Emperor regarded the coming war as 'the last battle between Teutons and Slavs', one which would 'find the Anglo-Saxons on the side of the Slavs and the Gauls'. Out of 'envy' and 'hate' England 'wanted to forbid other Powers to defend their interests ... with the sword'. Haldane's conversation with Lichnowsky tore away every veil of uncertainty from before the Emperor's eyes.

England will undoubtedly stand behind France and Russia against Germany out of hatred and envy. The imminent struggle for existence which the Germanic peoples of Europe (Austria, Germany) will have to fight out against the Slavs (Russians) and their Latin (Gallic) supporters finds the Anglo-Saxons on the side of the Slavs. Reason: petty envy, fear of our growing big.

Other marginal comments by the Emperor on reports on the Ambassadors' Conference make it abundantly clear that Wilhelm II saw no possibility whatever of finding, through the diplomatic machinery of a conference, a lasting solution for the antagonism between Germany on the one hand and France and Russia on the other – an antagonism which had grown only more obvious during the laborious efforts to localise the Balkan Wars.

Chapter 2 of the Great Migrations, he wrote, is over. Now comes Chapter 3, the Germanic peoples' fight for their existence against Russo-Gallia. No further conference can smooth this over, for it is not a question of high politics, but one of *race* . . . for what is at issue is whether the Germanic race is to be or not to be in Europe.

The Emperor's conviction that the political conflicts of the day are only the surface symptoms of a fundamental inter-racial conflict was shared by Helmuth von Moltke, the Chief of the German General Staff. When Austria-Hungary mobilised in the winter of 1912–13 to prevent Serbia from expanding to the Adriatic (also sending certain units to her frontier with Russia in Galicia), Moltke, on February 10, 1913, writing to his Austrian opposite number, Conrad, who was urging a preventive war, warned him against such a step *at that juncture*, because it would infallibly lead to world war; and a 'war of nations' could be waged only if the governments could count on the full understanding of their peoples. Quarrels over the frontier between Serbia and the new state of Albania would not produce this understanding. Nevertheless, Moltke

remains convinced that a European war is bound to come sooner or later, and then it will, in the last resort, be a struggle between *Teuton and Slav*. It is the duty of all states who uphold the banner of German spiritual culture to prepare for this conflict. *But the attack must come from the Slavs.* Those who see this struggle approaching will be clear that it will call for the concentration of all forces, the utilisation of all possibilities, and above all, complete understanding on the part of the people for the world-historic development.

The Emperor always combined the idea of the inevitable racial war with the feeling that the British were on the wrong side in it. So he wrote on May 15, 1913: 'Policy against Germany (Teutons) with Slavs and Gallics absolutely impossible in the long run for Anglo-Saxons.'

At that time the Emperor was hoping that Britain would collaborate with Germany in the defence of Turkey (against Russian and Bulgarian aspirations) or in a partition of Turkish territory between them. The main point for him was that the partition 'must not be made without us. I take Mesopotamia, Alexandretta, Mersina. Sensible Turks are already awaiting their fate with resignation.'

On the same February 10, 1913, on which Moltke warned Conrad against a preventive war on the grounds that such a step would lead to an inopportune world war, Bethmann Hollweg sent Berchtold a warning to the same effect, giving his own reasons for the 'not yet'. There were some signs, he said, of an impending change of course in Britain's policy, and this must be given time to take shape.

I should regard it as an error of incalculable magnitude to bring about a solution involving force at a moment when there is a possibility – if only a remote one – that we may be able to wage the conflict [sc., the great continental war] under conditions much more favourable to us.

Moltke, as we have seen, had thought it necessary to prepare the people psychologically for the all-important conflict. During the war scare of December, 1912 the Emperor had given instructions for a press campaign to mobilise opinion in his own country.

Welcome occasion for such preparation was provided by the centenary celebrations in 1913 to commemorate the 1813–15 wars of liberation against Napoleon. These celebrations opened in March and reached their end and culmination in October in the dedication of the memorial perpetuating the memory of the 'Battle of the Peoples' outside Leipzig. In June of the same year came the celebrations of the Emperor's twenty-five years on the throne, all of which were designed to demonstrate Germany's military power and preparedness. The feelings animating very wide nationalist circles in Germany found their most faithful expression in General Friedrich von Bernhardi's *Deutschland und der nächste Krieg* (Germany and the next war), which appeared in 1912 and ran through five editions by the end of the year. This book is generally dismissed by German historians as the eccentric outpourings of an undisciplined pan-German with little relationship to the plans either of the general staff or of the government, but the author's summing up of his arguments and conclusions under the heading 'World Power or Decline' epitomised the intentions of official Germany with great precision. In his view three things were necessary for Germany's advance to a position of world power:

(i) The elimination of France (*die Ausschaltung Frankreichs*): France must be 'completely brought to the ground, so that she shall never again be able to obstruct our path' – a formula which recurred almost verbatim in the September Programme drawn up by Bethmann Hollweg a few weeks after the outbreak of war.

(ii) Foundation of a Central European federation under German leadership. Bernhardi's expectation that the smaller states ('the weaker neighbours') would seek the protection of German arms and 'attachment to Germany' was shared by leading circles in Germany during the war. The German government attempted officially, after 1914, to realise his demand for a 'Mitteleuropa'.

(iii) The development of Germany as a world power through the acquisition of new colonies. Bernhardi agreed with the German professors, economists and political leaders in seeing the future no longer in terms of the old European system of states, but in a new system of world states, in which the balance depended on real factors. But for him, as for them, world power was at the same time a cultural mission. In the same December, 1912, in which the Emperor ordered the psychological preparation of the nation, he instructed the Foreign Ministry that recognition of the coming life and death struggle of the Teutons against Gauls and Slavs must be made 'the basis of our policy', and allies for it must be recruited wherever they could be found. 'We must conclude a military agreement with Bulgaria ... Turks, also with Rumania. We must also conclude such an agreement with Japan. Any power which can be got is good enough to help us.'

This idea, together with the addition of the promotion of revolutions, recurred eighteen months later in Moltke's programme of action for the outbreak of war on August 4, 1914.

Finally, a third impulse emerged from the Balkan crisis of 1912–13. Negotiations were still going on when a demand arose for a further expansion of the armed forces. This expansion was realised in the big increases in the army effected in the spring of 1913.

Impressions acquired during the First Balkan War in the autumn of 1912 had led the general staff, where Ludendorff's voice was now the decisive one on such questions, to call for an increase in Germany's standing active army (then numbering 622,000 men) by 50 per cent, out of which three new army corps were to be formed.[1] The National Liberals, who were profoundly mistrustful of Bethmann Hollweg's government, and feared that the planned army increases might turn out to be too small, convoked a special session of their party committee for February 9, 1913, where the party's hatred of Bethmann Hollweg vented itself in the adoption of a maxim almost revolutionary in tone: that the Reichstag must fulfil those duties in respect of foreign policy and defence which the government was neglecting. The politicians who took the Ludendorff line and called

---

[1] G. Ritter, op. cit., especially pp. 272 ff.; also G. Howe, 'Das Heer von 1911–1914', in *Weltmachtsstreben und Flottenbau*, ed. W. Schüssler (Witten/Ruhr, 1956), pp. 115 ff.

for the complete utilisation of Germany's man-power potential did not, however, win the day. The conservative elements in the Ministry of War, who argued the need for a qualitatively high cadre–and were anxious to preserve the aristocratic character of the officer corps–themselves cut down the number, so that the increase which the Chancellor asked the Reichstag to sanction in the spring of 1913 was only 117,000 rank and file and just under 19,000 officers and N.C.O.s–in all, a fraction under 136,000 men. This was the largest army estimate in German history. It was accepted by a majority composed of the right in the Reichstag. It took months of negotiation before the requisite expenditure, including over 1,000 million marks for non-recurrent items, could be voted, and it was finally accepted by a majority in which the centre of gravity had shifted leftward and included the Social Democrats. 132,000 men were voted, of whom 72,000 were called up on October 1, 1913; the remainder were to be called up in a second batch in the autumn of 1914. The actual peace strength of the German army in 1913–14 was thus 694,000 men, to which must be added 72,000 in the navy. In relation to war the peacetime figures were less important than the fact that the German army, unlike the French, was able to put fully trained reserve formations into the field from the first day of war– there were 13 German reserve corps on the western front alone–and was thus numerically superior to the French, at least at the outset of war.

These big increases evoked counter-measures from Germany's neighbours. The Reichstag was still in session when France announced the introduction of three years' military service, which brought her an increase by 1914 of 160,000 men against Germany's additional 72,000. The peacetime strength of the Russian army, which had been under reorganisation with French financial help, had been 1,500,000 since 1906, twice that of the German and 300,000 more than the German and Austrian together (the Austrian figure was 450,000). Moreover, the Russian army had still not reached its full target of over 2 millions; this was to be attained only in 1917. The reorganisations in progress were bound in the near future to increase still further the superiority of the armies of Germany's and Austria's two continental neighbours over their own.

While this race was going on, and in the now sure expectation of a war on two fronts, Moltke had worked out a revised operational plan, based on Schlieffen's (the last edition of which Schlieffen had passed to Moltke shortly before his death), which now concentrated the full weight of operations on the western front, so that after 1913 no plans were made for an advance in the east.

This situation was communicated to the party leaders in the Reichstag in April, 1913, in the strictly confidential preliminary negotiations on the military estimates. In the course of them the Secretary of State, von Jagow, justified the army increases by adducing the expectation of 'the coming world war', and told the party leaders (the representatives of the military departments who were in attendance supplying the necessary details) that even in the event of war breaking out with Russia over the conflicts in the Balkans, the first phase would be fought in France, where the decisive offensive would take place. When the Social Democrats ventured to ask whether this would not involve violation of Belgium's neutrality, the Chancellor deliberately evaded the question, although the German plan for the western offensive provided for precisely that (the only modification to Schlieffen's plan made by Moltke had been to cut out the violation of the neutrality of the Netherlands).

This concentration on the west made Germany's plans entirely dependent on the Austro-Hungarian army, which would have to hold the first Russian thrust until the German army had won its anticipated victory in the west and could turn east. On May 12, 1914, when the allies were holding their last staff talks, Conrad asked Moltke how long it would be after the outbreak of the anticipated war on two fronts against France and Russia before Germany would be able to send strong forces against Russia—in other words, how long the Austro-Hungarian armies would have to meet Russia's main forces unaided. Moltke's reply was: 'We hope to be finished with France in six weeks after the commencement of operations, or at least to have got so far that we can transfer our main forces to the east.'[1]

The general staff's calculations were based on the assumption that the six divisions of the Belgian army (who were contemptuously described as 'chocolate soldiers') would not offer any serious resistance. In order to make sure, Wilhelm II had tried repeatedly, through dynastic channels, to secure from Belgium an assurance of her passivity, if not an alliance. As early as the 1904 crisis the Emperor had asked Leopold II for an alliance and permission for German forces to march across Belgium, offering in return the restoration of the Duchy of Burgundy at the expense of France; Leopold had, however, refused. In November, 1913, the Emperor invited Leopold's successor, King Albert, to Berlin[2] in another attempt to gain Belgium's co-operation. He dilated on France's irreconcilable hostility to Germany

---

[1] Conrad, *Aus meiner Dienstzeit*, III, p. 674.

[2] Bülow, *Denkwürdigkeiten*, II, pp. 82–5; Emile Cammaerts, *Albert of Belgium* (New York, 1935), pp. 108 ff.; Beyens, *Deux Années à Berlin, 1912–1914* (Paris, 1931), Vol. II, pp. 38–43; R. Poincaré, *Memoirs*.

and on her repeated provocative acts, and asserted that war was not only inevitable but imminent—nearer than the Belgian king thought. France's introduction of three years' military service was an unfriendly act, and all France was filled with thirst for *revanche*. King Albert made no concessions. It is a matter of controversy what part the British Expeditionary Force (of four to six divisions) played in the German General Staff's calculations. On the one hand, the soldiers rated the effectiveness of Britain's military contribution low, and thought they would be able 'to deal with it *en passant*'; they also hoped to conclude the war on land fast enough to make a blockade ineffective. The civilians, on the other hand, thought that Britain's entry into the war might have serious consequences and were anxious to keep her neutral, at least for a time. The continuance of the conversations with London on colonial and Near Eastern questions was one of the means by which they hoped to achieve this end.

World Policy Without War

The last attempt made by Germany before the war to conduct an expansive 'world policy' by acquiring a continuous colonial empire in central Africa had shown her that her objectives were not to be attained without a fundamental re-grouping of the contractual and sentimental relations between France, Britain and Russia. The Haldane Mission constituted another attempt to force Britain out of the hostile alliance, and although the naval and political conversations failed, those on the colonial question were carried further in negotiations for the revision of the treaty of August 30, 1898, between Britain and Germany on a 'partition' of the Portuguese colonies.[1] That treaty, although concluded within the framework of the general efforts to reach a *rapprochement* which marked that period, had yet, as Britain saw it, been extracted from her as compensation for possible increases of her own power, and Germany's frequent threats ultimately to turn to France and Russia had finally resulted in estrangement and mutal offence when Britain—disloyally, as the Germans thought—concluded with Portugal the secret Treaty of Windsor which confirmed the ancient Anglo-Portuguese alliance and thus in practice excluded any partition—which could in any case only have taken place in the event of a Portuguese financial collapse. The negotiations, which opened in 1912, ended on October 21, 1913, with the initialling of a final draft of a revised agreement in the same form as that of 1898, providing that the customs receipts from the colony of Mozambique south of latitude 16 and of Angola east of longitude 20 should be applied to the service of British loans to

[1] *Grosse Politik*, Vols. 14, 31, 37·1, and *British Docs.*, Vol. X.

Portugal and those from the rest of those colonies to the service of German loans (in the event of a subsequent occupation of Mozambique the port of that name would thus have gone to Germany). Britain further declared herself uninterested in the islands of S. Thomé and Principe. As in 1898, speculation on bankruptcy by Portugal was uncertain; moreover, the two powers in any case pledged one another to joint acting, which meant that the implication of the agreement would depend on the state of Anglo-German relations. The British government, which was uninterested in the question and only carried on the negotiations *pro forma* in order to show the opposition that relations with Germany were not being neglected, wanted the new treaty abolished, together with the old treaty and the Treaty of Windsor; the German government was against this course, fearing with Jagow that the German public would feel that Germany had been over-reached. Stumm, then Head of the Political Section of the Foreign Ministry, pointed out Germany was not assured of her railway concession from Benguela in southern Angola to Katanga in the Belgian Congo because the part of Angola assigned by the treaty to Britain came between the part of Angola assigned to Germany and Katanga. Britain, for her part, found herself subjected to increasing remonstrations from France for having permitted Germany further access to the Congo basin without consulting Paris, and Grey consequently lost interest in seeing agreement reached. The German government, on the other hand, which feared that publication of the agreement might endanger the Chancellor's own position, wanted it signed as soon as possible, and when it failed to secure this, told the British government, in extremely sharp terms, that it regarded itself as 'morally bound' by the initialled text—a declaration which Grey ostentatiously left unanswered. Bethmann Hollweg's readiness to make concessions, and his simultaneous insistence on this question and on that of the Baghdad Railway, were characteristic of his political conceptions and of the hopes that, as late as the spring of 1914, he pinned on keeping the contact with Britain unbroken. On July 28, 1914, itself, when the crisis was at its height, Lichnowsky received instructions authorising him to continue the Angola negotiations (Britain was to 'push through' Portugal's consent to the German concession for a railway to run up-country from Benguela).

After the negotiations over the Portuguese colonies, the Anglo-German conversations were chiefly concerned with attempts to reach a settlement in the Near East.[1] Turkey's first railway concession to

[1] There is a voluminous literature on the Railway question. See, *inter alia,* Edward Mead Earle, *Turkey, the Great Powers and the Baghdad Railway, 1923;* John

Germany had been granted, and a beginning made with the construction of a railway starting from Constantinople and planned to run to Baghdad, while Bismarck was still in office. The concession to extend the line to Baghdad was granted in 1899, and in 1903 a supplementary agreement authorised the construction of a further line from Baghdad to a point on the Persian Gulf. This extension touched the British zone of interest in Kuwait, and objections from Britain now added to those already coming from Russia against plotting the line so far north in Anatolia. It was only in 1910, on the occasion of the Tsar's visit to Potsdam, that Russia could be detached from this hostile complication, but there was no similar *détente* with Britain, who had not only increased her influence in Turkey after the Young Turk revolution but had also secured recognition of her interest in Mesopotamia and the Persian Gulf, and a concession to carry out irrigation works between the Euphrates and the Tigris for which Germany had already submitted designs.

On top of all this, British capital began in 1909 to take an intensive interest in the Mesopotamian oilfields. There had been moves in this direction as early as 1901; the Deutsche Bank had also asked for oil concessions as security for Germany's loans for the construction of the Baghdad Railway. As Germany's second bank, the Disconto-Gesellschaft, had just secured large oil concessions in Rumania, with better marketing prospects, the Deutsche Bank did not take up the concessions received by it in 1903 for making borings, nor the option which it had secured in 1904 on Baghdad–Mosul oil with the prospect of a four years' nonopoly. Up to 1909 German concessions confronted British capital. Sir Ernest Cassel then founded the National Bank of Turkey, the chief purpose of which was to establish a concern uniting the two interests, and a new phase of the struggle for Turkish oil opened. After prolonged negotiations with the great oil companies, Cassel achieved his objective in 1912 in the shape of the Turkish Petrol Company. The real political significance of this manoeuvre became apparent in 1913. The Anglo-Persian Oil Company, with the official support of the British government, took over both Cassel's share and the greater part of the holding of the Royal Dutch–Shell, which, after the resignation of its agent

B. Wolf, *Diplomatic History of the Baghdad Railway* (New York, 1936), 2nd ed. (Northampton, 1947). On the general complex of questions see also W. W. Gottlieb, *Studies in Secret Diplomacy* (Cambridge, 1958). Bethmann Hollweg to Lichnowsky, April 24, 1913, *Grosse Politik*, 37, Nos. 14, 731; this contains also the second memorandum from the Deutsche Bank to the Foreign Ministry, signed by Gwinner and dated May 3, 1913. On the oil question, Stephen Hensley Longrigg, *Oil in the Middle East, its Discovery and Development*, 1st ed., 1954, 2nd ed., 1955; see also *British Docs.*, XII, Nos. 139, 140, Parker, August 19–20, 1913, on British oil interests, in conversation with Kühlmann.

Gulbenkian, and a sharp conflict with the Deutsche Bank, sided with Britain. The Deutsche Bank was thus isolated. At the same time the extension of the Baghdad Railway became dependent on whether the British government (which in 1914 had officially become a participant in the Anglo-Persian Oil Company) gave its consent to an increase in the Turkish tariff duties, on which again the guarantee of the railway loans depended. As, however, Britain could not induce Turkey to transfer the Deutsche Bank's concession to herself, a compromise was reached by founding a new concern, in which British influence was preponderant. The credit for this agreement must go primarily to the German government. Although the treaty was disadvantageous to Germany, Bethmann Hollweg, on Kühlmann's advice, persuaded the Deutsche Bank to accept it as a matter of policy.

In the negotiations which went on from May, 1913 onward, Britain's chief interest, both strategic and economic, was to prevent the Baghdad Railway from being extended farther south than Basra. Germany gave way on this point, stipulating that Britain should pay for making the Shatt el Arab navigable, in order to allow the movement of goods from the terminus of the railway to the Persian Gulf; in return a new British company, connected with the Indian Navigation Company, was founded, and was given the monopoly of shipping on the Tigris and the Euphrates. The Deutsche Bank was represented on this company's board of directors. The agreement was highly advantageous to Britain, and Ballin, Director of the Hamburg–America Line, protested against it, but vainly.

The agreements on the railway, the ports on the Persian Gulf and the irrigation of Mesopotamia show how strongly Germany was endeavouring to reach an understanding–and ultimately an 'alliance'–with Britain, even at the cost of sacrifice. In these fields Germany was unmistakably willing to play the junior partner to Britain as a world power. German public opinion, on the other hand, in the knowledge of the nation's power and economic potential, was not prepared to accept such a position: it claimed nothing short of fully independent status, equal to England's, America's and Russia's.

The Crisis of German Imperialism

The signature of the Treaty of Bucharest in August, 1913, concluding the Second Balkan War, seemed to initiate a period of general *détente*. The German Emperor sent an open telegram to King Carol of Rumania, the author of the peace, welcoming it with an enthusiasm which was due in considerable part to the fact that it had, thanks to Wilhelm's support, brought his other Balkan friend, King

Constantine of Greece, a gain in the shape of the long-desired port of Kavalla. The Danubian Monarchy, however, unlike Germany, regarded this peace as by no means a basis for further developments of the Balkan question but rather as a set-back for the Monarchy, bringing as it did gains in territory and prestige to the Monarchy's adversary in chief, Serbia. Berchtold accordingly immediately set about trying to get the dispositions laid down at Bucharest revised. Austria, in contradistinction to Germany, wanted to bring about the formation of a bloc consisting of Bulgaria, Austria-Hungary and Albania, which would force Serbia to come to terms with Austria. Germany's aims were not, at bottom, any different, but Wilhelm attached special weight to an understanding between Greece, Turkey, Rumania and Germany. These latent tensions grew more acute when, as an effect of the Second Balkan War, the great powers began to increase their armies and to resume their rivalry for influence over the Balkan states and Turkey in the now familiar form of loans (armament and other) to governments, carrying with them orders for industries in the greater states. In the autumn of 1913 Germany lost to France, which was able to mobilise massive capital resources in support of her political moves, much of the ground which she had acquired in the course of decades in Rumania, Greece, Serbia and Turkey. Since, however, Germany's capital coverage had become extremely thin in 1913, and the Reich was no longer able herself to produce all the loans for which the Balkans were asking, she was increasingly forced to take precautions to prevent Austria-Hungary from slipping over into the Entente camp. The danger became very real at the end of the year, when both Turkey and Austria-Hungary began looking round the western money-markets and enlisting Entente capital for their policies. On top of this, Britain concluded the 'Dock Agreement' with Turkey, which secured her the construction of the vessels (both civilian and military) in which Turkey was investing, with repairs and coastal fortifications. This agreement horrified the German dockyard and munitions industries, for it signalled an obvious decline of Germany's economic and political influence in Turkey. Germany's nervousness was enhanced when she lost orders in Rumania to Italy, for here again, as earlier in Greece, the discrepancy between Germany's pretensions and her resources had become glaring. And although it was only a relatively small number of specialist firms in Germany that were directly affected— for example, the Deutsche Bank and Philipp Holzmann for railway construction, or the Dresdner Bank, Krupp, the Rheinische Waffenfabrike and Mauser-Rottwell for armaments orders—yet the interests of these firms were regarded by the Foreign Ministry, and still more by the Emperor, as so essential to the Reich that the Ministry often acted as their agent and the Emperor himself personally intervened on their behalf.

Disappointment over the situation in the Balkans and Turkey, the tension between Austria-Hungary and Serbia over the Southern Slav question in Bosnia-Herzegovina, and further tension between Austria-Hungary and Rumania, forced Austria and Germany apart. Encircled by the Entente, Germany saw her isolation becoming more and more total. The consequence was that when, in October 1913, the Austro-Serbian conflict threatened once again to lead to active hostilities–this time over Serbia's thrust to the Adriatic–Zimmermann, whose voice was the decisive one in the Foreign Ministry, tried to prevent a European conflagration from breaking out *at that moment* by giving Austria stronger support. He sent several telegrams to Vienna, London and Belgrade saying that Germany was taking 'a firm attitude', and publicly announced that the establishment of a viable Albania was a vital interest of her ally, Austria. He hoped that these gestures, like Germany's invocation of her 'shining armour' in 1909, would bring Austria back into close association with Germany, and he hoped too that Russia would not at that juncture want to see another conflict between the Slav brothers, Serbia and Bulgaria, and that she was still unprepared for war–as was Germany herself. At the same time the Emperor, whose Near Eastern policy was becoming an increasing danger to the solidity of the Triple Alliance, was taken firmly in hand by the military during the September manoeuvres in Silesia, and 'urgently counselled' to give up his dynastic policy. Wilhelm yielded. Germany backed Austria's ultimatum to Serbia of October 16. When the Emperor met Conrad at the unveiling of the memorial to the 'Battle of the Peoples' in Leipzig, he told him–reversing what Moltke had said in the previous spring–'I shall march with you'; and he again assured this Austrian advocate of a preventive war that Germany would march against Russia too, if she tried to intervene in an Austro-Serbian conflict. This event, however, was precisely what Germany hoped to avoid by stressing the German–Austrian alliance. The Emperor adjured Conrad:

The others are not ready, they will do nothing to stop you. You must be in Belgrade within a few days. I was always in favour of peace; but that has its limits. I have read a lot about war, and know what it means. But in the end situations arise in which a great power can no longer stand aside; it must grasp the sword.[1]

[1] Conrad III, pp. 469 f., see also *Grosse Politik*, Vol. 36, I, pp. 387 fn., October 18, 1913.

A few days later, Wilhelm met the Austrian heir to the throne, Franz Ferdinand, in Konopischt. Here the Emperor was back on his old Near Eastern line, for he knew that Franz Ferdinand had opposed, although vainly, the despatch of the ultimatum to Serbia on October 16. Franz Ferdinand was against the policy of the military and the court party, the Hungarians and the clericals, and wanted to take the wind out of the sails of the Southern Slav movement by reforming the internal structure of the Monarchy, not by force. The monarch and the heir to the throne were thus able to reach an understanding on 'the final aims of the policy followed by both realms' and to register 'complete identity of their policies'. Wilhelm here completely ignored the problem of Bulgaria; he only emphasised that 'in view of the danger of all Slav elements in the Balkans combining' it was necessary 'to reach a relationship of confidence and intimacy with the non-Slavonic Balkan States', viz. Rumania and Greece. Serbia would then have to adhere willy-nilly. The principle would apply: 'and wouldst thou not freely, I must thee compel.[1] The Emperor had thus reverted to his old list of priorities, disregarding the hopes of Austria, which Berchtold in particular was pinning strongly on Bulgaria.

A few days later Wilhelm visited Berchtold in Vienna. On that occasion he depicted Germany's policy entirely in the light of the conflict between her and Russia, declaring that since the accession of Alexander III Germany 'had had to reckon with a power which is hostile to us, bent on our destruction, and one in which quite other elements than the Emperor are in control'. 'War between East and West,' he told Berchtold, 'was bound to come sooner or later,' for this was an open challenge to the leading Slav Power 'in a world-historical process of the order of the Great Migrations.' For that reason Serbia must be completely subordinated to the Monarchy, or incorporated in it, no matter how: 'If His Majesty the Emperor Franz Joseph expresses a wish, the Serbian government must conform, and if it does not do so, Belgrade will be bombarded and occupied until His Majesty's wish is fulfilled.' Wilhelm assured the Austrian minister that in the coming life-and-death struggle, 'I shall stand behind you, and am prepared to draw the sword whenever your moves make it necessary'. At the end of the conversation, Berchtold said that the Emperor's utterances could be summed up in the words: 'Whatever comes from the Foreign Ministry in Vienna will be taken by him (Wilhelm) as an order.'[2] Berchtold had thereby

[1] Report in private letter from Szögyény to Berchtold, November 4, 1913; *Oe.U. Aussenpolitik*, Vol. VII, No. 89341.

[2] Berchtold's report dated October 28, 1915 on conversation with Wilhelm II on October 26, 1913, *Oe.U. Aussenpolitik*, Vol. VII, No. 8934.

got what he wanted: Germany's unconditional support for Austria's policy. Germany too had achieved her purpose: 1913 had passed without a world conflagration, the Triple Alliance seemed to have recovered its solidity, and the Emperor has not yet been forced to give up his hope of a league of the non-Slavonic peoples of the Balkans under German patronage.

Thus in October and November, 1913, Germany believed that she had re-attached Austria to herself quite firmly by her *fortissimo* protestations of Nibelung loyalty, and after the conclusion of the Treaty of Bucharest in the latter month, she fondly believed that she had secured Turkey, Rumania and Greece for allies. Yet at the end of the year it became apparent that all the financial resources which she could muster were still insufficient to produce the loans which the Balkan states demanded as a kind of guarantee of their political and economic support. In December the embattled capital of the Paris market met and unhorsed Wilhelm II's Hohenzollern dynastic policy. The plainest proof of this was given by the king of the Hellenes' journey to Berlin and Paris. In Berlin he was presented with a field-marshal's baton, but Germany's money-bags were empty. In Paris he had no recourse but to accept a French loan on the usual conditions, drawing a veil over his Berlin speeches, in which he had attributed the victories of the Greek troops to the training which they had received from German instructors. At the same time the Prime Ministers of Serbia (Pasic), Greece (Venizelos) and Rumania (Take Ionescu) met, either *en route* for Petersburg or in conference in Bucharest, to conclude a new Balkan League which was both anti-Austrian and anti-German.

The autumn's moves included Germany's last attempt to stop Turkey, completely exhausted as she was by the two Balkan Wars and in crying need of money, from moving over into the Western camp, by securing an influence over her army with the help of Enver Pasha, who had been trained in German military academies. The appointment of the German General Liman von Sanders to be the new Instructor General to the Turkish army and commander of the Constantinople Army Corps failed, however, to bring Germany the increased influence for which she had looked; it came rather within a hair's breadth of provoking war.[1] Germany hoped that even this crisis would turn to her advantage: she hoped to be able to make capital out of the Anglo-Russian tension and thus detach Britain from France and Russia. But this hope, too, proved unfounded. In the end Britain made common cause with France and Russia against

[1] *Grosse Politik* 38, c. CCXC.

Germany. Isolated, Germany had to retreat, and it was only with great difficulty that she succeeded in saving her face by getting Liman von Sanders appointed a Turkish field-marshal, with functions limited to those of military adviser.

If Germany's intentions, as made apparent in the Liman von Sanders affair, entailed a risk of war, the new tone of German policy and the change which had come over her methods since October 13 were even more marked in the case of Major Kübel's mission to Turkey.[1] This was a characteristic example of what was possible under the German constitution. Kübel was sent to Turkey under orders from the general staff, issued without the knowledge of the Imperial Chancellor, the Foreign Office, or even the German ambassador in Constantinople, with the mission of adapting the Turkish railway system to the demands of war within six months. The major's exceedingly brusque behaviour, which was always defended by the no less high-handed Liman von Sanders, was strongly resented both by the Turkish government and the Deutsche Bank, the financial power behind the Baghdad Railway Company. The last bastion of German influence in Turkey was threatened. Bethmann Hollweg's reaction expressed by him directly to the Emperor, was correspondingly vigorous. He insisted that the mission of Liman and his subordinate was 'not an end in itself, but a means to an end'; for what advantage would Germany have from a reorganised Turkish army if Turkey herself were lost politically? 'We have no inducement to whet the Turkish sabres for the benefit of France or Russia'—and the behaviour of the German officers had made this a very real danger. The Emperor thought that German influence in Turkey was at that juncture 'already as good as nil'. The Turks 'had set their course for Russo-French waters, where there is money. . . . We can't keep Turkey moored up to us, because we have no money.' And he repeated, once again: 'they're no longer moored up to us.' The German ambassador was being told lies, the Young Turk government was definitely approaching the Entente.

In fact Turkey received a large state loan from France in the spring of 1914.[2] Germany had no longer been able to satisfy all the Turkish demands, so that the whole transaction went to France, which received enormous concessions most clearly detrimental to German interests.

In May, 1914, while the German–Turkish military and financial negotiations were in progress, a sharp difference broke out between the most important German business groups interested in the Near

[1] Hallgarten, Imp II.
[2] *Grosse Politik*, 37, c. CCLXXXVI.

East, with Krupp and the Dresdner Bank on the one side and the Deutsche Bank and the Baghdad Railway on the other. Krupp asked for a loan of 120 million marks, to be raised on the Berlin market, for its armaments transactions. Such a loan, however, would have overloaded the market with Turkish paper and have threatened the stability of Baghdad Railway stock. Furthermore, over and above purely economic considerations, the security of the Baghdad Railway was being increasingly threatened by the Anglo-German negotiations, which were coming more and more to revolve round tariffs, indirect taxes and concessions (the guarantees for the interest loan), again with the immediate effect of making the placing of the Baghdad Railway's stock more difficult. The grave disquiet with which the big banks, particularly the Deutsche Bank, were viewing the situation in the early summer of 1914 is reflected in a handwritten note attached by Helfferich to a memorandum by the Deutsche Bank. On May 29, 1914, he wrote for Zimmerman's attention:

As things are going, everything is at stake for Baghdad. . . . Not one man on our board can take the responsibility of going one step further with the advances for the construction of the Baghdad Railway without certain prospect that a Baghdad loan will come in the very near future. If the market is upset for us by Bulgarian or Turkish armaments loans we shall have to shut up shop.

The bankers' sensation of threatening catastrophe could not have been expressed more clearly and openly, for a stoppage of work on the railway, with which they threatened the government, would not only have dealt a devastating blow to German prestige in Turkey: it would have ruined the strategic plans which depended on the completion of the railway, and would have made Major Kübel's mission purposeless. German imperialism found itself caught in a painful dilemma between the armaments deal, which had become essential to the overgrown heavy industry, and the railway deal, on which the prestige and the real influence of Germany in Turkey depended. The Foreign Ministry decided in favour of the Deutsche Bank. It took over the loan alone, Krupp's got a share, the Dresdner Bank had to withdraw. Once more, with the greatest difficulty, Germany's economic expansion in the East had–apparently–been assured. On June 13, 1914, just a fortnight before Sarajevo, Gwinner, the Chairman of Directors of the Deutsche Bank, wrote to his Emperor:

We felt obliged to undertake this sacrifice [sc., of making big uncovered advances for the continuation and acceleration of the construction] because it was all-important to show our strength to the Powers which are unfriendly to the railway, and because to halt construction, which would have been the right thing to do from the purely business and financial point of view, would have been interpreted by our enemies as meaning that Germany's financial resources were insufficient to carry through this great work.

In 1914 Germany also took pains, on grounds of policy and prestige, to arrange with the Disconto-Gesellschaft to satisfy Bulgaria's wishes for a loan.

In spite of these successes, however, Germany's position in the Balkans was endangered, as were the prime objectives of her imperial aspirations in the Near East. Against Germany's success in Bulgaria had to be set gains by France and Russia in Serbia, Rumania and Greece. Her success in Turkey was more than outweighed by the British 'Dock Agreement'. Now the more Germany's enterprises ran aground and the more her cards got over-trumped in the international imperialist game between the powers, the louder grew the cry that she should break out from the threatened encirclement before it was complete; and this demand was further stimulated by the internal tensions which had come completely to dominate German public opinion since the Zabern incident. The Emperor, who had hesitated in 1905–6 and 1911, himself thought that the moment had now arrived which, ever since 1907, he had described as the critical point in Franco-German relations: he minuted a despatch on the threat of French competition in the Near East:

> Envy, envy, envy; everyone is envious of us. But the Gauls, in particular, must be taught quite plainly that they are not to presume that the Entente with Britain allows them to amuse themselves by trying to unseat us in the Near East. *These are vital interests*, the defence of which is all-important. *I will fight for them, if need be.*

Whether, in spite of his big words, the Emperor would really fight if things became serious was doubted by many, not least by the army. Who knew whether the monarch would not 'swallow his words', as Moltke put it, once again, and Germany slink away from another conflict with her tail between her legs? Since, however, both general staffs, the Austrian under Conrad and the German under Moltke, expected an international crisis in 1914–'probability of war'–it became a question of supreme importance to know what attitude the imperial master would take up and how Germany's plans for the advance in the west could be co-ordinated with Austria-Hungary's interests in the Balkans. The work of the general staff therefore early concentrated on the question whether Russia would 'strike', as Conrad thought very probable when the Duma received the news of the Liman von Sanders mission with such great excitement.[1] The pos-

[1] Conrad, III, p. 670.

sibility did not displease him, for the earlier Russia struck, the better would the position be for the Central Powers, since 'our situation is not improving'. Moltke agreed with him when the two men met on May 12, 1914, for the last time before the outbreak of war. He too admitted 'that any delay reduces our chances, for we cannot compete with Russia when it is a question of masses'. The soldier, unlike the Chancellor, held the possibility of a settlement with Britain to be illusory; he was convinced that if a major conflagration came, Britain would side with France and Russia – as the emperor put it, that the Anglo-Saxons would side with the Gauls and the Slavs. He therefore told Conrad, with a dig at his government's illusions, that *'unfortunately, our people are still expecting a declaration from England that she will not join in.* England will never make that declaration'. Nevertheless, twenty-five days before Sarajevo, the Emperor was still fully supporting Bethmann Hollweg's policy: he instructed the Chancellor that in his handling of the press feuds with Russia and France, the tension between Austria-Hungary, Serbia and Rumania, the Tsar's proposed visit to King Carol in Constantza, and not least the general situation in the Balkans and Turkey, he must *'clarify our relations with England'*. For 'chapter three of the Balkan War will soon open, and in it we shall all be concerned. Hence Russia's and France's colossal preparations for war.'.

As late as March, 1914, when Conrad, in conversation with Tschirschky, had asked his regular question whether it would not be better for the Central Powers for the great Teuton–Slav conflict to come sooner rather than later, the ambassador had answered that this was certainly so, but 'there are two highly-placed obstacles: your Archduke Franz Ferdinand and my Emperor'. Conrad agreed completely with Tschirschky; he took the same view of the policy of both Germany and Austria as dictated 'on the highest levels'. He regretted the attitude which had so often allowed the possibility of warlike action to pass unutilised, or had insisted on yielding. He also concurred when the ambassador went on to say that these two men, the Archduke and the Emperor Wilhelm, 'would only decide for war under compulsion and if faced with a *fait accompli*; it would have to be a situation in which there was no alternative but to 'strike'.' 'I replied,' wrote Conrad, 'that in view of the Franco-Russo-Austro-Hungarian-Anglo and German imperial policies, which in 1910–12 had increasingly chosen the Balkans as the object of their political activity, complications were always threatening in the Balkans which could create such a situation.[1]

'Such a situation' came into being with the Sarajevo assassination.

[1] Id., p. 597.

GERMANY
AND THE OUTBREAK OF WAR

THE MISCALCULATION ON BRITISH NEUTRALITY

IN spite of all the surface calm, the feeling, or conviction, that a great European conflict could not be long postponed had become general in Europe. Germany found herself, as Moltke put it, 'in a condition of hopeless isolation which was growing ever more hopeless'. Her confidence in the invincibility of her military strength had been deeply shaken by the increases in the French and Russian armies (of which the latter would in 1917 reach its maximum peacetime strength of 2,200,000 men),[1] and the idea of a 'preventive war' was acquiring an increasing appeal, especially in military circles. 'We are ready, and the sooner it comes, the better for us,' said Moltke on June 1, 1914.[2] At about the same time, Moltke asked Jagow to precipitate a preventive war as soon as possible. Jagow refused, but admitted later that he had never wholly excluded the idea of a preventive war and that Moltke's words had influenced him during the crisis of July–August 1914.[3] Another element of danger was the fact that Conservative circles had come, especially since the Reichstag elections of 1912, to regard war as a 'tempering of the nation' and calculated to strengthen the Prusso-German state. Bethmann Hollweg, who in December, 1913, had already rejected the suggestion passed on to him by the crown prince, and emanating from the pan-Germans, that a *coup d'état* should be carried out against the Social Democrats,[4] spoke out again just six months later against these specu-

[1] Gerhard Ritter, *Staatskunst und Kriegshandwerk*, Vol. 2. *Die Hauptmächte Europas und das Wilhelminische Reich (1890–1914)* (Munich, 1960), p. 279. Ritter's quotation repeats Moltke's political arguments in his memorandum to the Chancellor (Rk) of 1911 and December 1912; Moltke went over his second memorandum with Ludendorff. The total strength of the Russian army was to stand at 1·8 millions in the summer of 1917, and at 2·2 millions in the winter, it being proposed that the first classes of reservists should regularly be kept with the colours.

[2] Eckardstein, *Lebenserinnerungen*, Vol. 3 (Leipzig, 1921), p. 184.

[3] H. Pogge-v. Strandmann and Imanuel Geiss, *Die Erforderlichkeit des Unmöglichen*, Hamburger Studien zur neueren Geschichte, No. 2 (Frankfurt, 1965), p. 66. A recent find makes it clear that even Bethmann Hollweg, at least in February, 1918, thought in his enforced retirement that 'in a certain sense' the war was a 'preventive war', since his generals had urged him that success would no longer be likely two years later. Cf. Wolfgang Steglich, *Die Friedenspolitik der Mittelmächte 1917–18*, Vol. I (Wiesbaden, 1964), p. 418, n. 3.

[4] Cf. Pogge and Geiss, op. cit., pp. 18–26.

lations on the internal political consequences of a war. He told Lerchenfield, the Bavarian minister, at the beginning of June, 1914, that:

There were still circles in the Reich which looked to war to bring about an improvement, in the conservative sense, of internal conditions in Germany. He thought that the effects would be the exact opposite; a world war, with its incalculable consequences, would greatly increase the power of Social Democracy, because it had preached peace, and would bring down many a throne.[1]

A month later the Chancellor agreed on foreign-political and military grounds to take the risk of a great war, while recognising – unlike the Conservatives – that the war could not be carried on without the co-operation of Social Democracy.

Sarajevo, the Hoyos Mission and Germany's Blank Cheque

The news of the murder of the heir to the Austro-Hungarian throne evoked indignation and consternation throughout Europe, but there was no feeling that it must inevitably lead to a European crisis. The reactions were mixed in the Monarchy itself. There was genuine mourning; but a close observer could not fail to note that wide circles in the Monarchy felt undisguised relief at the death of the man who meant to put through some sort of trialist or federalist reorganisation of the Monarchy favourable to its Slavonic elements. Besides the Germans and Magyars, who had felt their dominating positions threatened by Franz Ferdinand, and besides the Emperor Franz Joseph, who had never forgiven his nephew his morganatic marriage, there was also a third group in the Monarchy who welcomed the archduke's death, because they saw in it an opportunity to settle accounts once and for all with Serbia by a war in which Germany would be behind them. The spokesman of this group was Baron Conrad von Hötzendorf, Chief of the Austro-Hungarian General Staff.

Although since 1912 Conrad had described the idea of a military reckoning with Serbia as a *va banque* gamble, if it had to be risked without the support of Rumania – on which he had counted confidently in 1905 – and with a stronger Russia, only a few days after the murder he thought that the conflict with Serbia, bad as its prospects were, could no longer be avoided, and immediately the news reached him he told the Austro-Hungarian Foreign Minister, Berchtold, that Austria should mobilise; she should 'cut through the knot', or her

[1] *Bayrische Dokumente zum Kriegsausbruch und zum Versailler Schuldspruch*, 3rd ed., Munich, 1925, No. 1: Lerchenfeld to Hertling, June 4, 1914. For the July crisis see also the collection of documents edited by Imanuel Geiss, *Julikrise und Kriegsausbruch 1914*, 2 vols. (Hanover, 1963–4).

prestige would be gone for ever and her position among the great powers be irretrievably lost.[1] But even this thruster, when he tried to persuade the hesitant diplomats, Berchtold and his assistant, Forgach, to adopt the military solution, was not willing to risk war without a firm promise of help from Germany. The Emperor was for taking the risk. Tisza, the Hungarian Prime Minister, was more doubtful than Berchtold himself; the political situation was un-favourable, Russia too strong, public opinion unprepared. The final decision thus depended on Germany's attitude. Both the German ambassador in Vienna, von Tschirschky, and Zimmermann, the Under-Secretary of State in the Foreign Ministry (Jagow, his chief, was away on his honeymoon) were at first very reserved and coun-selled moderation.[2]

But this policy of hesitancy was abruptly altered by Wilhelm II, who was outraged that the ambassador should take so much upon himself. By July 4 the Emperor was all for 'settling accounts with Serbia'. 'Tschirschky will be so good as to drop this nonsense. We must finish with the Serbs, *quickly*.'[3] With his famous words 'now or never' the Emperor laid down the general course of Germany's policy for the next weeks. From that hour Tschirschky and Zimmermann were among the most decided advocates of a hard policy towards Serbia.

This reversal of attitude came as no surprise to Austria-Hungary. On July 1 the German publicist Victor Naumann,[4] a confidant of the German Foreign Ministry, had been in Vienna and had talked to Count Hoyos, the permanent head of the Austro-Hungarian Foreign Ministry, to whom he had given an illuminating sketch of the mentality then prevailing in leading political circles of Germany. The conversation was afterwards officially described as having been purely private; what made it so important was that Germany's ac-tual behaviour in the July crisis exactly confirmed Naumann's pro-phecies. The heads of the services thought the Triple Alliance 'not strong enough at present', but the adherents of the idea of a preven-tive war were growing steadily, both in the army and navy, and in the

---

[1] Id., p. 293.

[2] *German Documents on the Outbreak of the War* (*DD*), ed. Count Max Montgelas and Walter Schücking, Vol. 1, Doc. No. 7, Tschirschky to Rk., June 30; on Zimmermann's attitude cf. Luigi Albertini, *The Origins of the War of 1914*, Vol 2, *The Crisis of July 1914* (London, etc., 1953), p. 137.

[3] Marginal notes by the Emperor on Tschirschky's report, cf. n. 3, *DD*.

[4] Victor Naumann was a friend of the then Prime Minister of Bavaria, Hertling, for whom he often made semi-official journeys to the Court in Vienna; *Oesterreich–Ungarns Aussenpolitik, Von der bosnischen Krise 1908 bis zum Kriegsausbruch 1914* (quoted as OeU), ed. Ludwig Bittner and Hans Uebersberger, Vol. VIII, Vienna and Leipzig, 1930, Doc. No. 9966, Note by Hoyos.

Foreign Ministry. This 'idea' was also supported by a second consideration. It was hoped that the Anglo-German settlement in Africa had 'made it certain that Britain would not intervene in a European war'. Naumann openly counselled military action against Serbia. The Triple Alliance was strong, Britain would be neutral. The Foreign Ministry, as he knew from von Stumm, would certainly not oppose it, and–the fourth favourable factor–the Emperor would not shrink from war, as he had in the Moroccan crises. Moreover, public opinion would force the Foreign Ministry to let things take their course.

On July 4 the Austrian Foreign Ministry had been unofficially informed by Tschirschky, through an *homme de confiance* of the German embassy, that 'Germany would support the Monarchy through thick and thin, whatever action it decided to take against Serbia. The sooner Austria-Hungary struck, the better.'

Since Conrad's plans for war against Serbia were dependent on Germany's support, the first essential for Vienna was to secure official information on Germany's definitive intentions. Count Hoyos was sent to Berlin to obtain this. On July 5 he handed Szögyény, the Austro-Hungarian ambassador in Berlin, two documents: a memorandum, compiled by Tisza, on the situation of the Monarchy, coupled with a proposal that advantage should be taken of the Serbian question to attach Bulgaria to the Triple Alliance, and a letter in Franz Joseph's own hand to the effect that the only way of saving the Monarchy from being swallowed up in the 'Pan-Slav flood' was 'to eliminate Serbia, which at present constitutes the corner-stone of pan-Slav policy', as a political power-factor in the Balkans. Szögyény handed the two documents to the Emperor the same day. At first the Emperor evaded taking a decision, but after lunch, to which he had invited Szögyény in the Neues Palais in Potsdam, he authorised him to inform his monarch that Austria-Hungary could 'count on Germany's full support' even in the case of 'grave European complications'; Germany, 'loyal as ever to her ally', would stand by Austria even should the Serbian conflict lead to war between Austria and Russia. Wilhelm even told the ambassador that if Vienna should decide on military action against Serbia, she ought to march at once. He thought that he could himself dispel Austria's anxieties about Rumania's attitude by a personal intervention with King Carol. At the same time he told Szögyény what had been the chief consideration that had made it so easy for him to decide to support Austria-Hungary: 'In any case, as things stood today, Russia was not at all ready for war, and would certainly think long before appealing to arms.'

53

This was, as we shall see, one of the basic assumptions of German policy in these weeks: that Russia and France were still militarily weak enough to enable Germany to weather the crisis, however it developed.

When the audience was over, Szögyény was able on the same day to pass this 'blank cheque' of the German Emperor to Vienna, and to report that Wilhelm II 'would regret it if we (Austria-Hungary) let this present chance, which was so favourable for us, go by without utilising it'. The Emperor had indeed made the reservation, which the constitution imposed on him, that he must get the Imperial Chancellor's consent, but he had had no doubt, as he had expressly emphasised, that Bethmann Hollweg 'would entirely agree with him'.

This was exactly what happened. Bethmann Hollweg and Zimmermann were summoned to Potsdam the same afternoon, and to them the Emperor unfolded the same train of thought as he had to Szögyény;[1] and, as Wilhelm expected, Bethmann Hollweg, who did not yet know the exact text of the Austrian memorandum, agreed completely with his imperial master. The Minister of War, von Falkenhayn, the Adjutant General, von Plessen, the Head of the Military Cabinet, von Lyncker, Captain Zenker of the naval staff, and Admiral von Capelle, representing von Tirpitz, were now successively called into the presence, and the question of 'preparatory measures for war' was discussed with them on the evening of the 5th and the following morning, so as 'to cover every case' before the Emperor left for Kiel to start his regular North Sea cruise. The question 'whether the army was ready for any eventuality' was answered by von Falkenhayn with 'a curt affirmative'. On July 17 Major-General Count Waldersee, Quartermaster General in the general staff, who was then in the country, wrote to von Jagow in strict confidence: 'I can move at a moment's notice. We in the general staff are *ready*; there is nothing more for us to do at this juncture.'[2] For the same reason Helmuth Count von Moltke, Chief of the General Staff, who had been informed by von Falkenhayn of the consultation of July 5 and by Lieutenant-Colonel Tappen of the Potsdam decision, found it unnecessary to leave Karlsbad.[3] How strongly the Emperor's decision had been influenced by his faith in the strength of Germany's military forces is shown by what he said on July 6 to

[1] Albertini, op. cit., pp. 140 ff., also Bernadotte Schmidt, *The Coming of the War, 1914*, Vol. 1 (London and New York, 1930), p. 296; Alfred von Wegerer, *Der Ausbruch des Weltkrieges, 1914*, Vol. 1 (Hamburg, 1939), p. 132.

[2] *DD*, I, No. 74 (author's italics).

[3] S. B. Fay, *The Origins of the World War*, Vol. II, *After Sarajevo*, 2nd ed. (New York, 1930), p. 117; Wegerer, op. cit., p. 132.

Capelle and Lieutenant-General Bertrab of the general staff: France and Russia were not ready for war; he did not believe in a general war, but thought that now the army had been brought up to its present strength, and with Germany's superiority in heavy artillery, he could regard the outcome of a war with confidence (the campaign in the west was expected to last 5–6 weeks). So, too, Waldersee said: 'The plans for mobilisation had been duly completed on March 31, 1914; the army was ready, as always.'

'In order,' as he said himself, 'not to alarm world opinion', the Emperor, after making all necessary dispositions, left for his North Sea cruise. He did so in full awareness of the import of the assurances which he had given to Austria. Shortly after, when he was in the company of Krupp von Bohlen and Halbach, with whom he was on terms of intimacy, he assured him that:

> He would declare war at once, if Russia mobilised. This time people would see that he was not 'falling out'. The Emperor's repeated protestations that in this case no one would ever again be able to reproach him with indecision were almost comic to hear.

To understand the Emperor's insistence, we must remember the criticisms of his attitude made by the military during the Morocco crisis of 1911, and the *Alldeutsche* threat that if he again showed weakness, he would be deposed and replaced by the Crown Prince.

While his imperial master was boarding the train for Kiel, Bethmann Hollweg, with Zimmermann in attendance, formally confirmed to Hoyos and Szögyény the Emperor's decision of the previous day. This gave constitutional cover to the 'blank cheque'. The Chancellor left it to Austria to take the final decision but, like Wilhelm II, advised her to act at once, without informing Italy and Rumania; and like the Emperor, he justified his course by appeal to the favourable international situation. Szögyény had been prepared for this communication by the Emperor; Hoyos by Zimmermann, with whom he had talked on the 5th. Hoyos had wanted military action against Serbia '*sans crier garde*', and Zimmermann had given him to understand that if Austria acted against Serbia at once, Russia and France would keep clear of the conflict. Any doubts or hesitations in Austria were removed when, on the 7th, Hoyos brought back Germany's unconditional promise to stand by Austria even if 'measures against Serbia [which, Hoyos reported, Germany advised] should bring about the big war'.[1] The conditions for Conrad's plan were fulfilled.

[1] Conrad, *Aus meiner Dienstzeit 1906–1918*, Vol. 4 (Vienna, 1923), p. 42; cf. also *DD*, I, No. 18, Tschirschky to AA, July 7.

A shift in the Hungarian Prime Minister's Austro-Hungarian policy came at a meeting of the Ministerial Council on July 7. All the participants except Tisza, who was still opposed to it, agreed on the necessity of war against Serbia, either by a direct attack without previous warning or by the presentation of an ultimatum with unacceptable demands which would equally lead to war.[1] How strongly the decisions of the Council were influenced by the attitude of the Emperor and the German military is apparent from the answer given to Tisza by the Austrian Prime Minister, Count Stürgkh, who feared that 'a policy of hesitation and weakness' would lose Austria Germany's support thereafter. When reporting to Franz Joseph two days later, Berchtold advised the ultimatum procedure, which would avoid 'the odium of attacking Serbia without warning, put her in the wrong,' and thus make it much easier for Rumania and Britain to preserve 'at least [sic] neutrality.' That he counted on the possibility of war with France and Russia is shown by the 'long debate on the relative forces and the probable course of a European [sic] war' which we know from Hoyos' report and Conrad's notes to have taken place, although it was regarded as 'not suitable for minuting'.

Tisza, who on July 8 had still objected that an attack by Austria on Serbia would lead to 'intervention by Russia and consequently world [sic] war', had, like Franz Joseph, been convinced by Germany's 'unconditional attitude' that 'the Monarchy had to reach an energetic conclusion'. (When Tschirschky reported this, Wilhelm II added 'certainly'.) On the 14th Tschirschky was able to report that Tisza himself, the one opponent of war with 'Serbia', had now agreed to a note 'which would almost certainly be rejected [doubly underlined by Wilhelm II] and should result in war'.[2] So the first decision had been taken. That Germany faced the prospect of a general conflagration with open eyes emerges further from an instruction drafted by Radowitz, a Counsellor in the Foreign Ministry, as early as July 7 and sent by Jagow to Lichnowsky in London on the 14th.[3] Jagow warned the ambassador of the possibility of 'general complications'; Germany wished to localise the Austro-Serbian conflict, but not to prevent it. On the contrary, Lichnowsky was instructed to mobilise the British press against Serbia, although he must be careful not to give the impression 'that we were egging Austria on to war'. This epitomised German policy after the Hoyos mission. When Tschirschky had reported on July 10 that Berchtold was

---

[1] What Tisza said was: 'It was not Germany's business to tell us whether we should go ahead now against Serbia, or not.'

[2] *DD*, No. 49, Tschirschky to Bethmann Hollweg.

[3] *DD*, I, No. 36.

now in favour of 'unacceptable demands', but that her 'chief care' would now be how to put these demands, the Emperor commented: 'They had time enough for that', and further made a suggestion which he thought bound to succeed: 'Evacuation of the Sanjak! Then the cat is among the pigeons at once!'[1]

German Pressure on Vienna

The mouthpiece in Vienna of Germany's pressure was her ambassador, Tschirschky, who from July 7 onwards was holding almost daily discussions with the Ballhausplatz on the proposed action against Serbia. Tschirschky also attended the most important conferences between the Austrians, so that Vienna's decisions were taken, literally, under his eyes.

After Austria had made up her mind to solve the Serbian question by war, Tschirschky called on Berchtold on July 8 to give him another message from the Emperor, who wanted it 'stated most emphatically that Berlin expected the Monarchy to act against Serbia, and that Germany would not understand it if . . . the present opportunity were allowed to go by . . . without a blow struck.'

As Berchtold reported, Tschirschky confirmed Stürgkh's fears that hesitation by the Monarchy would destroy her value as an ally in Germany's eyes. There was an implicit threat in his words when he told Berchtold 'that if we compromised or bargained with Serbia, Germany would interpret this as a confession of weakness, which could not be without effect on our position in the Triple Alliance and on Germany's future policy'. Tschirschky's influence can already be traced in Berchtold's audience with the Emperor Franz Joseph on July 9, for the Emperor consented to the minister's proposed action on the ground that he feared 'that a weak attitude would discredit our position in Germany's eyes'.[2]

On July 11 Tschirschky, as he told Jagow in a strictly confidential private letter, 'again took the occasion to discuss with Berchtold what action was to be taken against Serbia, chiefly in order to assure the minister once again, emphatically, that speedy action was called for'.[3]

The report by Berchtold on his interview with Tschirschky is supplemented and confirmed by a letter of July 12 from Szögyény. If it were possible a priori to think that Berchtold had invented his story of Tschirschky's pressure – the archives contain no telegram from

[1] DD, I, No. 29, Tschirschky to Chancellor. Continuation of Emperor's marginal note: Austria must get the Sanjak at once, without fail, to prevent Serbia and Montenegro joining up and Serbia reaching the sea.

[2] Hugo Hantsch, Graf Berchtold (Graz, 1963), Vol. II, p. 589.

[3] DD, I, No. 349.

Tschirschky confirming it–this suggestion would have to be dismissed in the light of the Emperor's marginal notes and Szögyény's despatch. Szögyény fully confirmed Tschirschky's attitude. Germany, he wrote, Emperor and Chancellor alike, were pressing most vigorously for Austria to take immediate military action against Serbia. Szögyény believed that this 'absolute' insistence on war against Serbia was based on the two considerations already mentioned: firstly, that Russia and France 'were not yet ready' and, secondly, that Britain

will not at this juncture intervene in a war which breaks out over a Balkan state, *even if this should lead to a conflict with Russia, possibly also France.* . . . Not only have Anglo-German relations so improved that Germany feels that she need no longer fear a directly hostile attitude by Britain, but above all, Britain at this moment is anything but anxious for war, and has no wish whatever to pull the chestnuts out of the fire for Serbia, or in the last instance, for Russia.

Szögyény accordingly summarised his own views and those of Berlin in the following conclusion: 'In general, then, it appears from all this that the political constellation is as favourable for us as it could possibly be.' On the 13th Tschirschky was able to report: 'Minister [Berchtold] is now himself convinced that immediate action called for.'[1] Wilhelm II received this communication (which he again underlined doubly) with obvious relief.

The other way in which Germany was exerting pressure on Austria was by insisting that the ultimatum to Serbia should be couched in terms so strong as to make acceptance impossible; here too the Emperor had given the cue on July 6, and here again his lieutenants followed his lead. As early as July 12 Germany was informed of the contents of the Austrian note, and agreed that it should be delivered about July 25, after Poincaré had left Petersburg.[2] 'What a pity!' was the Emperor's comment on the lateness of the date.

Yet although Tisza had consented to military action–he expressly emphasised that it was Germany's attitude that had decided him–Vienna was still uncertain how sharp to make her demands on Serbia. The Austrians had decided to make the ultimatum unacceptable, yet when Berchtold talked on July 17 to Prince Stolberg, Counsellor at the German embassy, he spoke as though it was not yet quite certain whether Serbia would not after all accept the

---

[1] *DD*, I, No. 40, Tschirschky to Foreign Ministry.

[2] *DD*, I, No. 34a (1927 ed.), Tschirschky to Chancellor, July 11, marked out by Bethmann Hollweg, July 12. Cf. also Schoen, Bavarian Chargé d'Affaires, to Hertling, July 18, *DD*, IV, App. IV, No. 2, Zimmermann's account of demands of the Austrian note, *DD*, I, No. 49, Tschirschky to Chancellor, July 14.

ultimatum. Stolberg reported to Bethmann Hollweg that he had had difficulty in concealing his displeasure at this hint that Austria might weaken. His report continued:

If Austria really wants to clear up her relationship with Serbia once and for all, which Tisza himself in his recent speech called 'indispensable', then it would pass comprehension why such demands were not being made as would make the breach unavoidable. If the action simply peters out, once again, and ends with a so-called diplomatic success, the belief which is already widely held here that the Monarchy is no longer capable of vigorous action will be dangerously strengthened. The consequences, internal and external, which would result from this, inside Austria and abroad, are obvious.[1]

Jagow expressed the same train of thought the next day in a long private letter to Lichnowsky.[2] He was trying to answer the indirect warning which Grey had had conveyed to Lichnowsky on July 9, that Britain would never take the side of an aggressor, by explaining why Germany thought sharp action by Austria against Serbia indispensable. First, he argued, war against Serbia was the Monarchy's last chance of 'political rehabilitation', for the Monarchy already 'hardly counted any more as a real great power'. 'This decline in Austria's power position,' he went on, 'has also greatly weakened our group of allies'; this was why he did not want, under any circumstances, to stop Austria from acting. He did not want to force a preventive war, but should war come, he would not 'jib at the post', since Germany was militarily ready and Russia 'fundamentally was not'. The struggle between Teuton and Slav was bound to come (a thought which often reappeared in Jagow's utterances at critical junctures during the war); which being so, the present was the best moment for Germany, for 'in a few years Russia . . . will be ready. Then she will crush us on land by weight of numbers, and she will have her Baltic fleet and her strategic railways ready. Our group meanwhile is getting steadily weaker.'

The argument that Germany was ready, while Russia was not yet ready to strike, was especially emphasised by 'German industrialists who specialise in armaments manufacture'. Beyens, the Belgian ambassador in Berlin, reported that Krupp had assured him that 'the Russian artillery was far from being either good or complete, while the German had never been better'.

The Emperor, Bethmann Hollweg, Jagow and Zimmermann were all convinced of Germany's military superiority; so was the general

[1] *DD*, I, No. 87, Stolberg to Jagow, July 18 (private letter).
[2] *DD*, I, No. 72.

staff.[1] Count Lerchenfeld, the Bavarian minister in Berlin, reported at the end of July that Moltke had said that 'a moment so favourable from the military point of view might never occur again'.[2] The reasons given by Lerchenfeld—which, he wrote, were by no means to be dismissed as 'gossip between underlings'—were the familiar ones: superiority of German artillery and infantry rifle, insufficient training of the French army owing to the transition from the two to three years' term of service, the harvest in, and the training of the German first-line classes complete.[3] For these reasons the politicians—Jagow, for example—could face the possibility of a European war with confidence: 'If the conflict cannot be localised, and Russia attacks Austria-Hungary, this gives the *casus foederis*.'[4]

If we study the documents and the political moves, Jagow's letter of July 18 to Lichnowsky puts Germany's attitude, and also the reasons for it, in a nutshell. It is impossible to speak seriously either of Germany's being 'towed along in Austria's wake' or of her being 'coerced'. From the Emperor's first intervention in the Serbian question on July 4 to July 18, German policy followed an unbroken line, as nothing proves better than the constant assurances by Vienna that Berlin could rely on Austria-Hungary's willingness to fight—that there was 'no question' of indecision or hesitation. But Germany's own aims were even plainer: if France proved too weak, militarily and financially, to support Russia, Bethmann Hollweg—so he hinted to Count Roedern, Secretary of State for Alsace-Lorraine and later of the German Treasury, on July 16—hoped at least to be able to divide France from Russia. Germany did not care so much what happened over Serbia; the central objective of her diplomacy in these weeks was to split the Entente, and this Bethmann Hollweg meant to enforce at any price, with or without war. In any case the Serbian crisis would bring about a re-grouping of continental power relationships in a sense favourable to Germany and without intervention by Britain. The conflict must be localised, the great powers should 'watch without acting', and Germany hoped to bring about a new grouping of forces in both the Balkans and the Mediterranean.[5]

[1] As early as July 12 Moltke had discussed the question of 'quick action' with Conrad. Cf. Conrad, op. cit., III, pp. 669 ff.

[2] *DD*, IV, App. IV, No. 27 (private letter from Lerchenfeld to Hertling, 317).

[3] G. Ritter, *Staatskunst*, Vol. II, p. 381, n. II.   [4] *DD*, I, No. 72, cf. n. 23.

[5] Id., I, No. 58; on localisation of the conflict, cf. *DD*, I, No. 44, Jagow to Flotow (Rome) and Chargé d'Affaires in Bucharest, July 14; cf. also *Documents Diplomatiques Français*, Ser. III, Vol. X, No. 538, Jules Cambon, report from Berlin on article in *N.A.Z.*, July 19; also *BD*, XI, No. 77, reporting that Jagow had himself said that he had drafted the article. Note also the 'intentionally moderate' tone of the article. 'Please take care that this is not falsely interpreted as a retreat by Germany from her earlier decision' (to Tschirschky).

The German government, as Jagow informed Jules Cambon and Bronewski, the French ambassador and Russian chargé d'affaires in Berlin, on July 21, had no official information on Austria's aims or on its note.[1] The Foreign Ministry, however, 'entirely agreed that Austria must take advantage of the favourable moment, even at the risk of further complications', but both Jagow and Zimmermann, in obvious displeasure at Austria's weakness, doubted 'whether Vienna would nerve herself to act'. Zimmermann went so far as to transfer the description of 'the sick man of Europe' from Turkey to Austria.

Berchtold confirmed the 'nervousness' of the German statesmen. 'Already,' he wrote,[2] 'Berlin is beginning to get nervous.' Reports were trickling through that Austria had hesitated too long before acting, and Zimmermann thought that 'he had gathered the impression that Vienna, timid and undecided as it always was, was almost sorry' (!) that Germany was not pressing caution and moderation on her. Berchtold was pressing for action now. Conrad was urging 'haste', and the Minister of War, Baron von Krobatin, said that 'everything was ready for mobilisation'. The reason for haste was to prevent Serbia from 'smelling a rat' and 'herself volunteering compensation, perhaps under pressure from France and Russia'. If that happened, then as Germany saw it, Austria-Hungary's reason for war against Serbia would vanish; but with it Germany would lose her minimum objective of a diplomatic victory, a major political success.

The Austrian Ultimatum to Serbia

After prolonged internal argument, the Austro-Hungarian Ministerial Council in Vienna decided on the final text of the ultimatum on July 19 and fixed the 23rd as the day for its delivery; both the Austrians and the Germans thought it prudent to wait until Poincaré and Viviani had left Petersburg, and thus prevent the French and Russians from agreeing immediately on their counter-measures.[3] So active was the part played by Germany in the events of these days, so strong her influence over Austria-Hungary's policy, that Jagow actually had the time of the note's delivery on the 23rd put back an hour in order to make quite sure that the ship carrying the French statesmen had left Petersburg. The text of the note (the substance

---

[1] Albertini, op. cit., pp. 191 ff., letter from Cambon to Poincaré in Petersburg, July 22. From the *Doc. Dip. Fr.*, 3.X.551 and id., 3.X.555.

[2] Cf. n. 15, Schoen to Hertling.

[3] Jagow writes: 'Let Austria postpone presenting the note by one hour, to make certain that the Frenchmen have left.'

of which had been communicated to Germany on July 12) was conveyed by Tschirschky to the Foreign Ministry on the 22nd.[1] If, as is
often suggested, the Chancellor, Jagow or Zimmermann had found
its wording too strong, they had time enough (from the evening of
the 22nd to 6 p.m. on the 23rd) to protest against its presentation in
that form. On the contrary: as late as July 18 Count Hoyos had reassured Prince Stolberg that the demands contained in the ultimatum 'were *really* such as to make it *really* impossible' for the Serbian government to accept them with honour. As late as the 21st July
Jagow had again assured Szögyény that Germany would stand behind Austria 'unreservedly and with all her power'.[2] When he said
that it was 'vitally necessary' for Germany to know what Austria's
plans for Serbia were, this was not out of any qualms about Austria's
intentions, but because she wished, as Jagow put it to Tschirschky
on the 17th, 'to avoid giving any impression that we were wanting
to impede Austria's actions, or to prescribe certain limitations or ends
to her'.

Now Germany waited for the presentation of the ultimatum.

The day before this was due, the purpose of the travelling about,
of the 'holiday spirit' of the military and political leaders of both
Germany and Austria-Hungary, and of the efforts to keep the 'Sarajevo spirit' alive, without, as Berchtold said, 'making other powers
begin thinking about mediation', became very plain. Vienna thought
this the best way of keeping the Serbian action isolated. Germany,
too, as Schoen, the Bavarian chargé d'affaires, told Munich (while
passing on the three chief points of the ultimatum) wanted to make
it look as though she was not a party to, or even informed about,
what Vienna was doing. This despatch, however, also traced out
clearly the line which Germany in fact followed:

> In the interest of localising the war, the government will, as soon as the
> Austrian note has been presented in Belgrade, initiate diplomatic action
> directed to the great powers. She will point to the absence of the Emperor on
> his North Sea cruise, and of the Chief of the General Staff and the Prussian
> Minister of War on holiday, as evidence [sic] that Austria's action has come
> as a surprise to her as much as to the other powers.[3]

As early as July 21 Bethmann Hollweg and Jagow opened the
official moves to localise the conflict with a circular despatch.[4] Even

---

[1] Id., I, No. 106, Tschirschky to Chancellor, July 21; text of the note, id., IV,
Annexe I.

[2] For Jagow's letter to Tschirschky, id., I, No. 61.

[3] Cf. n. 15, Schoen to Hertling.

[4] Id., I, No. 100, Chancellor to the Ambassadors in Petersburg, Paris and
London.

before the ultimatum had been presented, Berlin was instructing its embassies in Petersburg, Paris and London to support Austria's action, and was undisguisedly threatening the European powers with a major conflict if the Serbian question were not confined to Serbia and Austria. Austria's attitude, which had not yet been announced (it was only the *Norddeutsche Allgemeine Zeitung's* communiqué of the 19th which revealed to France the possibility of a major conflict), was 'regarded as equitable and moderate', and Jagow now brought the whole discussion between Germany and Austria, including the underlying purposes, before the international forum in the following words:

> If the Austro-Hungarian government is not going to abdicate for ever as a great power, she has no choice but to enforce acceptance by the Serbian government of her demands by strong pressure and, if necessary, by resort to military measures. The choice of methods must be left to her.

On the 23rd, however, Jagow realised that this despatch was not easy to reconcile with the story that Germany had been 'surprised' by Austria's action. A second despatch, drafted by Stumm, was hurriedly sent after the first instructing the ambassadors not to make their *démarches* until the text of the ultimatum had been published: 'otherwise the impression might be given that we had had foreknowledge of it'.[1] The despatch required the great powers to abstain from any intervention in the Austro-Serbian conflict, even threatening 'incalculable consequences' if the warning were disregarded. This demand by Germany for a free hand for Austria surprised and displeased Grey, who did not believe that a war could be localised.[2] In Germany, on the other hand, the conviction that Britain would stand aside from a European conflict was so firmly rooted that when Pourtalès, the German ambassador in Petersburg, reported Sazonov having told him that Britain would disapprove deeply of Austria's conduct,[3] the Emperor wrote in the margin: 'He's wrong'; and on Sazonov's warning that he must 'reckon with Europe' in case of an attack on Serbia he commented: 'No! Russia, yes!'

Yet, as innumerable documents show, Germany knew that Russia would never allow Austria-Hungary to act in the Balkans unopposed. She took the risk of war with open eyes. This is confirmed by the preparations taken by Germany when the ultimatum was presented to Serbia. Jagow, for example, asked for the exact itinerary of the imperial yacht, because:

[1] Id., I, No. 126, Jagow to Lichnowsky; the corresponding letter from Jagow to Lucius, July 23; id., I, No. 123.

[2] *BD*, XI, No. 100 and minutes by Crowe, Nicolson and Grey.

[3] *DD*, I, No. 120, Pourtalès to Chancellor, July 21.

Since we want to localise the conflict between Austria and Serbia, we must not have the world alarmed by His Majesty's returning prematurely; on the other hand, His Majesty must be within reach, in case unpredictable developments should force us to take important decisions, such as mobilisation. His Majesty might perhaps spend the last days of his cruise in the Baltic.[1]

On July 20 the Directors General of the Hapag and the Norddeutscher Lloyd were, on the Emperor's suggestion and with the Chancellor's consent, given warning by Jagow of the impending ultimatum, so that they could take measures for the protection of their vessels in foreign waters. On the same day the Emperor ordered the concentration of the fleet.[2]

Even before that 6 p.m. of July 23, 1914, when Baron Giesl, the Austrian minister in Belgrade, presented the ultimatum, the coming of war was assumed. On July 18 Count Hoyos had 'comforted' Prince Stolberg with the assurance 'that the demands [contained in the ultimatum] were *really* such as to make it *really* impossible for a state with any self-respect and dignity to accept them'.[3]

Thus only unconditional acceptance by Serbia of the ultimatum could have averted war, and on July 22 Vienna asked Berlin how the declaration of war was to be effected, as Austria wanted her own answer to the rejection to consist of the rupture of diplomatic relations and the recall of her minister. She suggested that Germany might transmit the declaration of war. Jagow refused, saying that it would look too much 'as though we had been egging Austria on to make war'.[4]

The 'No' to British Mediation

The publication of the Austro-Hungarian ultimatum to Serbia evoked worldwide consternation except in Germany, where it was, in general, approved. The suspicion was often expressed that Germany was behind Austria's action, or at least privy to it. This suspicion was, as the German documents prove, completely justified, but Zimmermann denied it, as planned, in a telegram sent on the 24th to the German embassies in Paris, London and Petersburg. He asserted that Germany 'had exercised no influence on the contents of the note' and had had 'no more opportunity than any other power to take up any attitude towards it before its publication'.[5] The

[1] D. tel., I, No. 67, Jagow to Wedel (Minister *a latere* to the Emperor) July 18; id., No. 80, Wedel to Foreign Ministry, July 19, also n. 4 to No. 80.

[2] Id., No. 82, Müller to Jagow.

[3] Id., No. 87, cf. n. 22 (author's italics).

[4] Id., No. 142, Jagow to Tschirschky, July 24.

Id., No. 153.

previous day Jagow had informed the Emperor that Grey had made his first attempt at mediation, suggesting to Lichnowsky that Britain should urge Russia to influence Serbia, and Germany to influence Austria-Hungary.[1] The minutes with which the Emperor studded Lichnowsky's despatch, which Jagow forwarded to him, show what he wanted quite clearly. His pent-up rage vented itself: Britain's 'condescending orders' were to be rejected, and so was Grey's proposal that Vienna should retract any 'impossible demands'. 'Am I to do that? Wouldn't think of it! What does he mean by "impossible"? These fellows [the Serbs] have been intriguing and murdering, and they must be taken down a peg.' He gave emphatic backing to the instructions from the Foreign Ministry which Jagow had sent to Lichnowsky 'for guidance in your conversations'. These show once more the consistency and purposefulness of German policy in July 1914. The ambassador was told that 'we did not know what Austria was going to demand, but regarded the question as *an internal affair of Austria-Hungary, in which we had no standing to intervene*'.

As Sazonov had prophesied, the effect of the ultimatum on London was 'absolutely annihilating'. Lichnowsky reported that Britain believed that Germany, for all her protestations of innocence, was at least 'morally an accomplice', and he went on to warn: 'If we do not join in the mediation, all faith here in us and in our love of peace will be finally shattered.'[2] Germany, however, made no more than a pretence of supporting the vigorous action for mediation now initiated by Britain; indeed, in order to prevent the possibility of mediation, she actually sabotaged the proposals put forward by Britain between July 24 and the declaration of war. Her actions, and her motives, can be clearly followed, day by day, in the despatches.

As early as July 24 Grey, alarmed by the provocative tone of the Austrian note and the shortness of the time limit, again warned Lichnowsky of the danger that 'European war *à quatre*'—meaning, said Lichnowsky, Russia, Austria-Hungary, Germany and France—would break out if Austria crossed Serbia's frontiers. At the same time he suggested mediation by the four powers not directly affected—Britain, France, Germany and Italy—in the event of 'dangerous tension between Russia and Austria'.[3] Jagow, however, passed on Grey's request for an extension of the time limit so late that it reached Vienna only after the ultimatum had expired. Moreover,

---

[1] Id., No. 121, July 23.

[2] Id., No. 163, Lichnowsky to Foreign Ministry, July 25.

[3] Id., No. 157, Lichnowsky to Foreign Ministry; No. 164, Jagow to Lichnowsky, July 25; No. 171, Jagow to Lichnowsky, July 25.

he passed it on without comment, which in diplomatic parlance was tantamount to asking that it should be rejected.

Grey initiated his second attempt at mediation on July 25 with his old proposal that Berlin should intervene in Vienna to say that it found Serbia's answer satisfactory.[1] Again the proposal was passed on without comment, although on the 25th Lichnowsky sent three urgent messages advising Germany to give Austria 'the hint'. This is not surprising: the Germans were furious with Berchtold for having received the Russian chargé d'affaires on the 24th. 'Quite superfluous,' commented the Emperor: 'will give an impression of weakness. Austria ... has ... taken the step, now it can't be sort of reconsidered retrospectively.'

Meanwhile, Petersburg had announced in an official communiqué that it could not remain 'uninterested' if Austria annexed Serbian territory. The French and Russian ambassadors gave it as their personal opinions that Grey's proposal for four-power mediation in London was unacceptable, because the first step must be to mediate between Austria-Hungary and Serbia and thus prevent a local war.[2] Germany accepted this latter proposal, not least in order to prevent the 'satisfactory line to England' from getting cut, especially at a moment when Britain, France and Russia were not yet working as one; Grey had stressed that he distinguished 'sharply' between the Austro-Serbian and the Austro-Russian conflicts and did not wish to interfere in the Austro-Serbian affair. The British proposal thus meant 'localising' the conflict, as Germany wished, and it was accordingly answered affirmatively by Jagow late the same evening.[3] On the 26th, however, Bethmann Hollweg, while not revoking the consent, threatened that Germany would mobilise if the reports of alleged call-up of Russian reservists were confirmed.[4] But the deeper reason for Germany's agreement, and for her policy–again announced by the Emperor–of 'localising the conflict' can be found in the documents of the Foreign Ministry and of the Austrian embassy in Berlin. Germany's undoubted object was to thrust Russia far back. Tschirschky had reported on the 24th that Austria wanted 'no alteration in the existing power relationships in the Balkans'.[5] The Emperor marked this report 'weak', and his notes on it reveal what

---

[1] Id., No. 186, Lichnowsky to Foreign Ministry, July 25; Lichnowsky's three telegrams, Nos. 163, 165 and 179. Tschirschky's despatch on call of the Russian Chargé d'Affaires, No. 155.

[2] Wegerer, op. cit., pp. 335 ff.

[3] DD, I, No. 192, Jagow to Foreign Ministry, July 25.

[4] Id., No. 199, Bethmann Hollweg to Lichnowsky, July 26.

[5] Id., No. 155, Tschirschky to Foreign Ministry, July 24.

were the objects which Germany was following in the Serbian question: the alteration of the Balkan power relationships, he wrote, 'has got to come. Austria must become predominant in the Balkans . . . at Russia's expense'. Szögyény confirmed that Germany's policy was to 'localise the conflict', but that she was aware that localisation might prove impossible, and was prepared to risk the consequences. 'Here', he reported, 'it is generally taken for granted that if Serbia rejects our demands, *we shall at once reply by declaring war* and opening military operations. We are advised . . . to confront the world with a *fait accompli*.'[1] On the 25th Giesl left Belgrade; Serbia's answer had thus not been that demanded by Austria. On the same day Franz Joseph signed the order mobilising eight army corps. The 28th was given as the first day of mobilisation. Tisza, too, in an audience with Franz Joseph, gave full support to the German pressure; hesitation would 'greatly impair belief in the Monarchy's energy and capacity for action, in the eyes of both friend and foe'.

On the 28th Lichnowsky transmitted yet another (the fourth) offer of mediation, this time from King George V as well as Grey. He reported that 'since publication of Austrian demands no-one here believes any more in the possibility . . . of localising conflict'; Britain proposed a conference of ambassadors, 'Britain and Germany working together, with France and Italy brought in . . . to secure Austria full satisfaction . . . since Serbia would be more easily induced to yield to pressure from the Powers and to submit to their united will, than to Austria's threats.' Grey and the Under-Secretaries, Nicolson and Tyrell, saw in this procedure 'the only possibility of avoiding general war'. 'The absolute condition for success of the conference and for maintenance of peace' was, however, 'absence of any military dispositions'.[2]

If Serbia's territory was violated, Lichnowsky reported, 'world war could not be averted'. Britain's disapproval of the line being followed by Germany was equally unambiguous. 'Localisation of the conflict, as hoped for by Berlin, was quite out of the question, and not to be considered as practical politics.' Lichnowsky urgently advised the Foreign Ministry 'to let our policy be determined singly and solely by the necessity of sparing the German people a struggle in which it has nothing to gain and everything to lose'. In spite of these warnings, when Goschen, the British ambassador in Berlin, officially presented the proposal for a conference, Jagow rejected it. Even before this, Bethmann Hollweg had given a formal refusal in

[1] Author's italics.

[2] Id., I, Nos. 201, 218, 238, all telegrams from Lichnowsky to Foreign Ministry, July 26.

writing, on the ground that Germany 'could not bring Austria's dealings with Serbia before a European tribunal'.[1] The Chancellor was not prepared to listen to Lichnowsky's representations, nor to follow Britain's change of course (meaning the dropping of the distinction between the Austro-Serbian and Austro-Russian conflicts). His replies to London continued to take, as sole basis, the British proposals for localising the conflict. At the same time, a circular despatch issued by him reaffirmed Germany's attitude that the conflict concerned only Austria-Hungary and Serbia.

The day before, Berchtold had told Austria's representatives to take the same line, and had added that if localisation should prove impossible, Austria-Hungary was reckoning 'with gratitude' that Germany 'will support us if a struggle against another adversary is forced on us'. Again on the 26th, Moltke had drafted a demand to Belgium to allow the passage of German troops in the event of 'the imminent war against France and Russia',[2] thereby proving plainly that Germany knew that war between Austria and Russia would immediately produce a continental war. Finally, on the 27th Grey sent an urgent appeal to Berlin to use its influence on Vienna to accept Serbia's answer as satisfactory, for only so could London, on its side, exercise a moderating influence on Petersburg.[3] Lichnowsky reported that if war should after all break out, 'it would no longer be possible to count on British sympathy or British support'. Grey had said plainly that the key of the situation lay in Berlin; if Berlin was sincere in wanting peace, Austria could be prevented from following 'a foolhardy policy'.[4] Three hours later Lichnowsky repeated urgently that Grey was convinced that the maintenance of peace depended on Berlin. In London there was a steadily growing impression that 'the whole Serbian question was developing into a trial of strength between Triple Alliance and Triple Entente'. If Austria-Hungary tried to beat Serbia into submission, Britain, said Lichnowsky, 'would most certainly side with France and Russia' (the contents of

[1] Id., No. 234, circular instruction by Bethmann to Ambassadors in Paris, London, Petersburg, July 26, not sent off; id., No. 248, Bethmann Hollweg to Lichnowsky, July 27; also No. 247, B.H. to Schoen, July 27; Berchtold's circular, OeU, VIII, No. 10714.

[2] DD, II, No. 376, Jagow to Minister in Brussels, July 29. The demand was addressed in Moltke's draft to the Belgian government; it was recast by Stumm and given the form of a communication from Jagow to the minister, who was to wait for special instructions before presenting it (No. 375). Cf. also Albertini, op. cit., p. 487, also on July 26, when Moltke returned from Carlsbad.

[3] Id., I, No. 258, Lichnowsky to Foreign Ministry, July 27; id., No. 265, id. to id., July 27.

[4] This was also the opinion of the acting French Foreign Minister, Bienvenu-Martin; Doc. Fr., III, II, No. 20 (circular instructions by B.–M., No. 2), August 24.

this telegram were not shown either to Tschirschky or to the Emperor). Reports came in from Russia that Sazonov was being 'more conciliatory', trying 'to find a bridge . . . to satisfy . . . Austrian demands'.[1] Pourtalès reported, however, that the maintenance of the Balkan balance of power was a vital interest of Russia. Rome, too, reported the British proposals for mediation,[2] and von Schoen telegraphed from Paris that France was ready to negotiate.[3] The Quai d'Orsay would probably be ready to use its influence in Petersburg if Germany was prepared 'to counsel moderation in Vienna, since Serbia had fulfilled nearly every point'.

The Austro-Hungarian Declaration of War on Serbia

All these appeals and warnings failed to move Berlin to put any pressure on Vienna to avoid the local conflict. On the contrary, that same day–July 27–Berchtold, urged thereto by Germany, laid the declaration of war before Franz Joseph for his signature. He explained that, Serbia having answered as she had, the Entente might yet succeed in getting their proposals for mediation adopted 'unless a clear situation was created by a declaration of war'. Tschirschky reported to Berlin that the declaration of war would go off to Belgrade on July 28, or the 29th at the latest, 'chiefly in order to eliminate any possibility of intervention'.[4]

This message reveals another feature of German policy in the July crisis. Not only did Germany consistently reject any attempt at mediation not calculated to 'localise' the conflict, but while Grey and Sazonov were trying to gain time, Germany was pressing Austria to act quickly. As early as July 14 Vienna had intimated that it wanted to stop short of the irrevocable. In Berchtold's and Franz Joseph's eyes the ultimatum did not necessarily mean war, and Count Mensdorff, the Austrian ambassador in London, seemed not disinclined to accept Grey's offer of mediation. Germany, however, as she had stated *expressis verbis* on July 25, was pressing for a *fait accompli* to prevent other powers from intervening. When it received Tschirschky's report, the Wilhelmstrasse saw its goal achieved. The Chancellor accordingly adopted an attitude of reserve towards British pressure and showed no inclination to put quick and explicit pressure on Austria. It was only shortly before midnight that he

[1] *DD*, I, No. 217, Pourtales to Foreign Ministry, July 26.
[2] Id., No. 249, Flotow to id., July 27.
[3] Id., No. 241, Schoen to id., July 26.
[4] Id., I, No. 257, Tschirschky to Foreign Ministry, July 27. Bethmann Hollweg transmits contents of Lichnowsky's telegram No. 238 to Tschirschky, No. 277.

passed on to Vienna the telegrams received that afternoon from London.

And before they were passed on Jagow had prepared the ground in another conversation with Szögyény. Again, as on July 18, he explained how Vienna was to interpret Germany's apparent change of course; again he confirmed the consistency and purposefulness of Germany's policy. Szögyény reported that, 'in order to avoid any misunderstanding', Jagow had twice emphasised that:

the German government assured Austria in the most binding fashion that it in no way identifies itself with the proposals [sc., the British proposals] which may very shortly be brought to Your Excellency's notice by the German government; it is, on the contrary, *decidedly* opposed to consideration of them, and is only passing them on out of deference to the British request.[1]

The Secretary of State himself was 'absolutely against taking account of the British wish'. At the same time, however, deference to Britain's wish was given as the pretext for the apparent acceptance. When explaining his point of view Jagow was more explicit still:

The German government's point of view was that it was at the moment of the highest importance to prevent Britain from making common cause with Russia and France. We must therefore avoid any action which might cut the line, which so far had worked so well, between Germany and Britain.

Bethmann Hollweg confirmed Jagow's point of view when passing on to Tschirschky, late on the evening of the 27th, Lichnowsky's telegram on his interview with Grey:

As we have already [sic] rejected one British proposal for a conference, it is not possible for us to refuse this suggestion also *a limine*. If we rejected every attempt at mediation the whole world would hold us responsible for the conflagration and represent us as the real warmongers. *That would also make our position impossible here in Germany, where we have got to appear as though the war had been forced on us.* Our position is the more difficult because Serbia seems to have given way very extensively. We cannot therefore reject the role of mediator; we have to pass on the British proposal to Vienna for consideration, especially since London and Paris are continuously using their influence on Petersburg.[2]

Bethmann Hollweg's and Jagow's point of view explains why the British telegram was passed on to Vienna so belatedly, and why the

---

[1] Author's italics.

[2] Id., I, No. 272, Bethmann Hollweg to Tschirschky (author's italics); with last sentence cf. No. 258, Lichnowsky to Foreign Ministry, July 27.

last sentence was – characteristically – suppressed: it might conceivably have given the Austrian government another, eleventh hour, chance of escaping out of the German stranglehold: 'Also, the whole world here is convinced, and I hear the same from my colleagues, that the key to the situation lies in Berlin, and that if Berlin seriously wants peace, it will prevent Vienna from following a foolhardy policy'.

But London was sent the completely untruthful message that: 'We have immediately initiated mediation in Vienna in the sense desired by Sir Edward Grey'.[1]

The duplicity thus shown by the Chancellor in respect of Britain's grave warnings proves that in the night of July 27–8 he was no longer trying to avoid a continental war, but only to manoeuvre Germany into the most favourable position possible. If this aspect of Germany's policy had not emerged clearly enough from the judgment passed on the Anglo-German conversations by Bethmann Hollweg in his commentary when he forwarded Lichnowsky's telegram to Tschirschky,[2] it is made still more plain from the fact that the Chancellor simultaneously forwarded to the Emperor the text of the British offer, with an exposé of Germany's attitude identical with that which had gone to Vienna. Although he wrote that he had 'followed the Emperor's orders' in transmitting the British offer, he had in fact distorted the Emperor's intentions in his treatment of Grey's proposal: on returning from his North Sea cruise on the afternoon of July 27 and on reading Bethmann Hollweg's report that Germany had rejected the conference of ambassadors, Wilhelm had given orders that Grey's next proposal – for direct influence on Vienna – was to be accepted.[3]

It was only on the 28th that the Emperor read Serbia's answer to the ultimatum, although the Serbian chargé d'affaires had handed it to the Foreign Ministry at noon on the 27th.[4] The Emperor's comment confirmed Germany's policy once again: '*But* that eliminates any reason for war'. Wilhelm's 'halt in Belgrade' was issued independently of Grey's similar proposal. Since, however, he, unlike the Chancellor, was unaware that Austria's declaration of war on Serbia was imminent, he passed this proposal on to Jagow without

[1] Id., No. 278, Bethmann Hollweg to Lichnowsky, July 27.

[2] See *DD*, I, No. 277, Chancellor to Tschirschky, July 27; *DD*, II, No. 283, id. to Emperor, July 27; also No. 278, id. to Lichnowsky, July 27, 1914.

[3] Grey's latest proposal reached the Foreign Ministry at 4.37 p.m., 3½ hours after the Emperor's return to Potsdam at 1 p.m. (No. 258, n. 2.)

[4] *PD*, II, No. 293, Emperor to Jagow, July 28; cf. also the Emperor's marginal notes at the end of the Serbian answer to the Austrian ultimatum, *DD*, I, No. 271 (author's italics).

much urgency. His opinion was: 'The few reservations which Serbia has made with respect to certain points can in my opinion surely be cleared up by negotiation.' This was the moment dreaded by the Foreign Ministry and by the military, the danger-hour which might see the monarch's weak nerve give way at the last moment, as it had in 1906 and 1911, before the certainty of war. Accordingly, he was now deliberately deceived. There is no other explanation for the fact that the Chancellor passed on this new suggestion too, belatedly, without urgency, and in distorted form. The only condition laid down by the Emperor in his 'halt in Belgrade' was that Austria 'had to have a guarantee that the promises were carried out'. He thought this could be found in a '*temporary* occupation of parts of Serbia'. In contradiction to this, Bethmann Hollweg emphasised to Tschirschky that the occupation must be the means of compelling '*complete fulfilment* by the Serbian government of the Austrian demands'. But the real falsification of the Emperor's proposals lay in Bethmann Hollweg's express insistence to Tschirschky

> You must most carefully avoid giving any impression that we want *to hold Austria back*. We are concerned only to find a *modus* to enable the realisation of Austria-Hungary's aim *without at the same time unleashing a world war*, and *should this after all prove unavoidable, to improve as far as possible the conditions under which it is to be waged.*[1]

'The War Guilt is Russia's'

This addendum of July 28 reveals on the one hand the motives behind Germany's actions and on the other the Chancellor's conscious risk of a world war. For he himself explained what he meant by 'favourable conditions': firstly, Russia must be made to appear to blame for the outbreak of war, and secondly, Britain must be kept neutral. Bethmann Hollweg believed himself to have found the key to this problem in the 'policy of localisation'. As early as July 26 he had expounded Germany's governing ideas very clearly both to the Emperor and to Pourtalès, Lichnowsky and Schoen, in the words: 'Since Count Berchtold has assured Russia that Austria is not aiming at any territorial extensions in Serbia . . . the maintenance of European peace depends exclusively on Russia.'[2] Germany's attitude must be 'calm', for only if attacked could Germany count on British neutrality and carry public opinion at home with her, the chief need being to get the Social Democrats' support for war. From this point

[1] Id., II, No. 223 (or 323???), Chancellor to Tschirschky (author's italics).

[2] Id., I, Nos. 197, 198, 200, Bethmann Hollweg to Emperor, Pourtalès, Lichnowsky and Schoen; cf. also No. 214, Jagow to Chargé d'Affaires in Bucharest, July 26. Marginal note by the Emperor: 'Calm is the citizen's first duty! Calm, always calm! A quiet mobilisation is something new.'

on the idea of making 'Russia alone responsible for any extension of the conflict and disturbance of the European peace' appears with increasing frequence in the German documents. Jagow tried to influence the attitude of Italy, Rumania and Bulgaria in the event of a conflagration by asserting that both Germany and Britain were continually at pains to 'keep the conflict localised' and that only Russia could begin the war.[1]

The Chancellor took up this line of argument again in a memorandum sent by him on July 28, *qua* Prussian Prime Minister, to the Prussian legations at the German Courts. Again he defended Austria's conduct and underlined his policy of localising the conflict. Just as Jagow, for example, writing to Bucharest on July 26, had alluded to the 'obvious consequences' should Russia move against Austria, so Bethmann Hollweg ended his memorandum with the following passage:

> Meanwhile should, contrary to our hopes, an intervention by Russia spread the conflagration, then we should be bound under our alliance to support our neighbour with the whole might of the Reich. Only under compulsion would we resort to the sword, but if we did so, it would be in calm assurance that we were guiltless of the sufferings which war might bring to the peoples of Europe. . . . Russia alone must bear the responsibility if a European war breaks out.[2]

Finally, the Chancellor drafted a telegram from the Emperor to the Tsar which reveals more clearly still his intention of saddling Russia with the odium of a 'European conflagration'. 'If,' he told the Emperor, 'War should come after all, such a telegram would make Russia's guilt glaringly plain'.[3]

At 11 a.m. on July 28 Austria presented her declaration of war on Serbia. It was not until the afternoon that Tschirschky appeared with the Emperor's 'halt in Belgrade'. Berchtold rejected any intervention as too late.[4] At the same time, however, tension had arisen between Vienna and Berlin. On July 27 Jagow had realised that Austria could not begin hostilities 'in practice' until August 12. The German government found this delay regrettable, and in his

[1] Id., No. 214, Jagow to Chargé d'Affaires in Bucharest, July 26.

[2] *DD*, II, No. 307; *DD*, I, No. 214, Jagow to Chargé d'Affaires in Bucharest.

[3] Id., II, No. 308, Bethmann Hollweg to the Emperor, July 28; English text of the telegram, *DD*, II, No. 335, Emperor to Tsar; cf. the addition appended by B.H. to a second draft of a telegram from the Emperor to the Tsar, July 30: 'As this telegram, too, will be a document of the greatest importance for world history, I would most respectfully recommend Your Majesty not to indicate in it that Your Majesty's role of mediator is at an end until Vienna's decision is announced' (the Chancellor knew that this would be negative). *DD*, II, No. 408, Chancellor to Emperor.

[4] Id., II, Nos. 311 and 313, Tschirschky to Foreign Ministry, July 28.

73

telegram to Tschirschky of July 28, quoted above, Bethmann Hollweg explained the motives of German policy, which was not so much concerned to prevent a European war, as to avoid Austria getting herself saddled, out of weakness and (as Lerchenfeld reported to Munich) political stupidity, with the odium of having herself provoked the war:

The Imperial government is thus put into the extraordinarily difficult position of being exposed during the intervening period to the other Powers' proposals for mediation and conferences, and if it continues to maintain its previous reserve towards such proposals, the odium of having provoked a world war will in the end recoil on it, even in the eyes of the German people. But a successful war on three fronts (viz., in Serbia, Russia and France) cannot be initiated and carried on on such a basis. It is imperative that the responsibility for any extension of the conflict to Powers not directly concerned should under all circumstances fall on Russia alone.[1]

The Chancellor held unwaveringly to his line: 'localisation' of the conflict; should this prove impossible, then Russia must be branded as the aggressor, thus to assure Britain's neutrality. The first object was achieved: from the outbreak of the war to the present day, the chief responsibility for it had been ascribed to Russia. The hope of British neutrality was to prove a great illusion.

In spite of all Lichnowsky's warnings, the German government continued to count confidently on British neutrality in a European conflict. It also hoped that neither Italy nor Rumania would be able to intervene actively against Germany. With Austria-Hungary's declaration of war, however, the diplomatic manoeuvrings reached the critical stage when the event would show whether the confident attitude of Germany's diplomacy and the threat of her 'gleaming sword' would again tip the balance and secure localisation of the conflict, as in 1908–9. The question whether localisation was possible was raised on the afternoon of July 28, when Conrad asked whether mobilisation was to be carried through against Serbia alone, or also against Russia; for he needed to know which the fronts were to be by the fifth day of mobilisation, or all the troop trains would be sent towards Serbia. The 'automatic operation of the war machine' now began to show its effects in Germany, as well as Austria-Hungary. Simultaneously with a call from Szögyény, bringing Conrad's request for pressure on Russia (Berchtold already thought it essential for both Austria and Germany to answer Russia's partial mobilisation by general mobilisation), the Chancellor received a memorandum from the general staff in which Moltke gave a clear and unambiguous

[1] Id., No. 323, cf. n. 72; on Jagow, *OeU*, VIII, No. 10792, Szögyény to Vienna, July 27.

analysis of the mechanics of mobilisation and alliances and explained that they must inevitably lead to world war.[1] Moltke emphasised particularly the causal nexus linking Austria's intervention against Serbia via Russian partial mobilisation to Austrian, Russian and German general mobilisations, which would then inevitably draw in France, the first objective of German military strategy. The general staff's appreciation of the military position caused the Foreign Ministry to revise its view of the importance of Russia's partial mobilisation (which the day before Jagow had not regarded as a cause for German mobilisation).[2] Up to this point Bethmann Hollweg had rejected as premature Austria's request for far-reaching military counter-measures, but under this pressure from Moltke and Conrad he addressed Petersburg in almost ultimatum terms, although the day before, Pourtalès had reported Sazonov as entirely ready to come an astonishingly long way to meet Austria's standpoint, which would have made possible some relaxation of the diplomatic tension.[3] It was technically necessary for the military to get a clear picture of Russia's attitude, but Bethmann Hollweg's sharp tone was also clearly in line with the whole of German diplomacy during the July crisis. So long as England remained out–and it was hoped that a declaration of war by Russia would ensure this–the Chancellor was not in the least afraid of putting the Triple Alliance to the test of a European war.

As pendant to his strong attitude towards Russia, Bethmann Hollweg made every effort to appear in British eyes as the ardent searcher after peace. In two further interviews with Falkenhayn and Moltke, in the morning and the late evening of July 29,[4] on each occasion before meeting the British ambassador, he succeeded in getting the proclamation of a state of emergency, for which the Prussian Minister of War was pressing, postponed, arguing that Germany must wait until Russia began general mobilisation; for unless the blame for 'the whole shlemozzle' could be pushed on to Russia, it was vain to hope for Britain's neutrality. If, however, Russia were saddled with the war guilt, Britain could not take her side. The generals, nevertheless, although still bound by the

[1] Conrad, Vol. IV, pp. 137 ff., General Staff's memorandum, DD, II, No. 349, Grand General Staff to Chancellor, July 29.

[2] See Albertini, op. cit., II, pp. 481 ff.

[3] DD, II, Nos. 342 and 380, Bethmann Hollweg to Pourtales, July 29. Continuance of Russian mobilisation measures would force Germany also to mobilise 'so that it would then hardly be possible to avoid a European war'. Pourtales' letter, DD, II, No. 282, July 27, arrived at the Foreign Ministry 4.36 a.m., July 28.

[4] Cf. also Albertini, op. cit., pp. 490 ff., n. 1 to p. 491, DD, IV, Annexe IVa, No. 2, 1917 ed.; cf. also Hans v. Zwehl, Erich von Falkenhayn, General der Infanterie (Berlin, 1926), pp. 56 ff.

imperial 'halt!', yet decided to send to the German minister in Brussels the demand (drafted on July 26) to allow the passage of German armies through Belgium.

In his morning conversation with Goschen on this day of July 29[1] Bethmann Hollweg again emphasised Germany's will for peace, and informed the ambassador in the strictest confidence of the Emperor's note to Vienna (Halt in Belgrade), again trying to give the impression that he was putting the brake on hard in Vienna, which, as we have seen, was in reality far from being the case. In the afternoon the Emperor consulted successively the Chancellor, Bethmann Hollweg, the Minister of War, von Falkenhayn, the Chief of the General Staff, von Moltke, the Head of the Military Cabinet, von Lyncker (4.40 p.m.), Grand Admiral Prince Henry (6.10 p.m.), the Secretary of State for the Navy, von Tirpitz, the Chief of the Naval Staff, von Pohl, and the Head of the Naval Cabinet, von Müller (7.15 p.m.). The conversations seemed to confirm Germany's hopes of British neutrality, for Prince Henry was able to report that George V ('Georgy') would remain neutral.[2] The word of a king which the Emperor accepted, although von Tirpitz had doubts, brought the conversation round to France, Belgium and Holland. The Emperor emphasised that Germany wanted no territorial annexations from France, although his reasons reflected unspoken first war aims: Germany only wanted guarantees which should enable her to 'prevent' further wars. Wilhelm built so largely on King George's reported word that (with Tirpitz's strong support) he rejected the proposal made by Bethmann Hollweg (who hoped to make the offer a sort of reward to Britain for her neutrality) for a naval agreement with Britain.

In his evening conversation with von Falkenhayn and von Moltke the Chancellor again insisted that Germany must wait until Russia ordered general mobilisation or attacked Austria. For partial mobilisation did not create a *casus foederis*, it did not necessarily involve war. Germany must wait for total mobilisation, because only thereafter would both German and British public opinion support Germany's attitude in 'the imminent war with Russia and France' (as the ultimatum to Belgium had already put it).

Germany concentrated her hopes ever more on getting Britain's promise of neutrality made contractual—as she had already tried to do on the occasion of the Haldane Mission. In the famous conversation vetween Bethmann Hollweg and Goschen late in the night

---

[1] *BD*, XI, No. 264, telegram from Goschen to Grey, July 29.

[2] *DD*, II, No. 374, Prince Henry to Emperor, July 28; on the 'Crown Council', Albertini, op. cit., pp. 494 ff.

of July 29–30[1] the Chancellor tried to pin Britain down by holding out prospects of a general agreement on neutrality. He assured Goschen: 'We can assure the British Cabinet—*provided we are certain of their neutrality*—that even in case of a victorious war we shall not seek any territorial advantage in Europe at the expense of France'—a promise which, however, when Goschen raised the point, he refused to extend to France's colonies. Further, he declared himself ready to respect the neutrality and integrity of Holland, provided Germany's enemies would do the same. In speaking of Belgium, however, he betrayed Germany's intention of violating her neutrality by giving only the obscure assurance (which also agreed *verbatim* with the ultimatum) that Belgium's integrity (he did not mention her sovereignty) should not be impaired after the war 'provided Belgium does not take sides against us'—provided, that is, Belgium did not resist Germany's illegal violation of her territory.

The British immediately grasped the decisive importance of this conversation. Now, Grey for the first time recognised Germany's intention of drawing the maximum political advantage from the Serbian conflict, even at the risk of European war. That on top of this Germany proposed to march through Belgium, Bethmann Hollweg had already admitted. Grey called the German offer 'infamous'.[2] Similarly, Eyre Crowe, his right-hand man in the Foreign Ministry, concluded that Germany had practically made up her mind 'to go to war'. What had held her back hitherto had only been the fear that Britain would come to the help of France and Belgium. At the same time, however, the interview had revealed Germany's intentions; wrapped up as they had been, they could be recognised simply as the first stages of those German war aims which revealed themselves nakedly soon after the outbreak of the war: French colonies, in continuation of the policy of the second Morocco crisis of 1911; in respect of France herself Germany was binding herself only if Britain should remain neutral in a continental war (when she would make this sacrifice). In that case she would renounce annexations at the expense of France; but the implied converse of this observance was that if Britain entered the war, Germany, if victorious, would claim a free hand to annex French territory. The same reservation

---

[1] *DD*, II, No. 373, Chancellor's notes for his interview with Goschen; cf. also Goschen's report to Grey, checked for accuracy by Bethmann Hollweg, *BD*, XI, No. 293. Jagow's draft for the declaration to Goschen originally included an offer of a naval agreement in return for assurance of Britain's neutrality in the crisis at issue; this offer, however, had to be cancelled owing to objections by the Emperor. Cf. Albertini, op. cit., pp. 506 ff.

[2] *BD*, XI, No. 303, Grey to Goschen; for Crowe, see his minute on the despatch from Goschen to Grey, id., No. 293.

had been made also in respect of Belgium. Since Belgium resisted, Germany afterwards claimed a free hand there also; this reservation was already implicit in Bethmann Hollweg's words.

The position had been clarified. Germany had revealed her aims to Britain in the hope that the attempts made by both sides to reach a political settlement would now bear fruit. The conversation also marked the high watermark of Germany's 'policy of localisation'; the despatch in which Goschen reported the conversation, the verbal accuracy of which he got the Chancellor to check immediately afterwards, showed no sign of compromise either in tone or in substance. It was only after the British ambassador, who, as he said himself, had hardly been able to repress his astonishment but had raised no objections, had left the room, that Bethmann Hollweg received Lichnowsky's telegram,[1] which had arrived earlier but had only now been deciphered. Its contents for the first time shook the whole structure of Bethmann Hollweg's diplomacy, the corner-stone of which had been the hope of British neutrality.

The Collapse of Bethmann Hollweg's Policy

Lichnowsky reported that Grey had again repeated with extreme earnestness his proposal for four-power mediation, and had emphasised that Britain, as a neutral power, was prepared, if Germany helped her, to mediate between Austria-Hungary on the one side and Serbia and Russia on the other, but that the moment France was drawn into the war, Britain would *not* be able to stand aside. This upset the calculation on the basis of which Germany had urged Austria to take military action against Serbia and believed herself capable of regarding the prospect of European war 'with equanimity' in the confident hope that Britain would after all remain neutral if the responsibility for the war were laid on Russia. Now the situation suddenly became threatening. Only three days before Jagow had confidently told Jules Cambon, who thought that Britain would intervene immediately: 'You have your information, we have ours; we are certain of British neutrality.'[2] The Germans, Bethmann Hollweg most of all, were surprised, even shattered, by Lichnowsky's report, and they grew unsure of themselves. The foundation of their policy during the crisis had collapsed. Britain would not remain neutral if France were 'drawn into' the war. The telegram sent to Tschirschky at 3 a.m. on the 30th to inform him of Lichnowsky's message[3] described the new situation:

[1] *DD*, II, No. 368, Lichnowsky to Foreign Ministry, July 29.

[2] Cf. Albertini, op. cit., p. 520, following Raymond Recouly, *Les heures tragiques d'avant-guerre* (Paris, 1922), p. 23.

[3] *DD*, II, No. 395, Chancellor to Tschirschky, sent 2.55 a.m.

If, therefore, Austria should reject all mediation, we are faced with a conflagration in which Britain would be against us, Italy and Rumania in all probability not with us. We should be two Great Powers against four. With Britain an enemy, the weight of the operations would fall on Germany. . . . Under these circumstances we must urgently and emphatically suggest to the Vienna cabinet acceptance of mediation under the present honourable conditions. The responsibility falling on us and Austria for the consequences which would ensue in case of refusal would be uncommonly heavy.

Only five minutes later Bethmann Hollweg sent a telegram to Vienna[1] in which he summoned his ally even more energetically to stop 'refusing any exchange of views with Russia'. 'We are prepared,' he went on, 'to fulfil our duty as allies, but must refuse to allow Vienna to draw us into a world conflagration frivolously and without regard to our advice.'

These two documents, composed simultaneously and despatched to Vienna in the small hours, are used, together with Bethmann Hollweg's address to the Prussian Ministry of State on the afternoon of the same July 30,[2] to prove the peaceable nature of Germany's policy and to show the 'absolutely desperate efforts' made by Bethmann Hollweg to make Vienna retreat. But the significant thing about them is not so much Bethmann Hollweg's urgent attempt to get Vienna to accept the British proposals as the fact that they find no parallel among the documents of the night of July 20–30 or of July 30 itself. The first despatches to go out after the arrival of the news from London, they are the products of the shock born of the unexpected information about Britain's attitude.

As late as 11.5 p.m. on the 29th Bethmann Hollweg, completely consistently with his previous policy of 'localisation', had summoned Russia in almost ultimatum terms 'not to provoke any warlike conflict with Austria'. At 12.30 a.m. he informed Vienna of Russia's partial mobilisation and added: 'To avert a general catastrophe, or'– and this shows clearly the tactics consistently followed by German civilian policy, uninfluenced by the Emperor or the general staff– '*in any case* to put Russia in the wrong, we must urgently wish Vienna to begin and continue conversations [with Russia] in accordance with telegram 174.[3] The deductions drawn by the Chancellor from the 'Russian mobilisation' are astonishing, for telegram 174 was that sent by Jagow to Tschirschky on the 28th, which gave Vienna its first information of the British proposals for mediation, but with the

[1] Id., No. 396, id. to id., sent 3 a.m.

[2] Id., No. 456, minutes of session of Prussian Ministry of State, July 30.

[3] Id., No. 380, Chancellor to Pourtalès, July 29; No. 385, id. to Tschirschky July 29 (author's italics).

characteristic addition: 'You must avoid most carefully giving any impression that we want to hold Austria back.' Up to the morning of July 30 Berlin had followed its policy of absolutely pressing action on Austria. It was only after 12.30 a.m. that Bethmann Hollweg saw Lichnowsky's report from London; this he sent on to Vienna at 2.55 a.m. with the first urgent warning. This telegram, however, also explains what the German 'advice' for the prevention of the 'world conflagration' really came to. Austria-Hungary was thus not being at all 'tough' (*pace* Gerhard Ritter) or obstinate, nor set on war, and Germany was not being dragged in her wake. Furthermore, Austria-Hungary had involved herself so deeply in the crisis that neither Berchtold nor Tisza thought it possible for her, as a great power, to give way now to German pressure which, moreover, was not applied with the whole weight available to Germany. Moreover, Vienna had, as the discussions went on, grown ever more convinced that the way to strengthen the structure of the Monarchy was by way of a war covered by Germany.

But this is not the only circumstance revealing the exceptional character of the documents; there are also the warnings given in the course of July 30. For the very next documents show plainly that what chiefly concerned Bethmann Hollweg was not so much to save the peace as such as to shift the responsibility and guilt for the war on to Russia. But the essential point was that although the premises of Bethmann Hollweg's policy, his conditions for undertaking war, as laid down by him on July 5 and 6, had collapsed, he could not steel himself to change his policy, to talk unambiguously to Vienna and to force it to obey him. A declaration to this effect, combined with a threat to leave Austria alone if she disregarded it, could have saved the Reich from the catastrophe of a war waged under conditions which had become so unfavourable. But nothing was done. On the contrary, the old policy was resumed in the course of the 30th.

This emerges clearly from the record of the meeting of the Prussian Ministry of State on July 30, to which Bethmann Hollweg reported on the situation. His main preoccupation was again 'to *represent* Russia as the guilty party', and this, he thought, would be most easily achieved if Vienna accepted Germany's suggestion, namely, to assure Petersburg that she meant only to occupy parts of Serbia temporarily, as guarantee for the satisfaction of her demands. But it also emerges clearly why Bethmann Hollweg was still continuing to insist on Russia's 'war guilt'. Previously his chief motive had been to secure Britain's neutrality – a hope which, he now remarked bitterly, had practically disappeared; the second factor in his 'mission' as Chancellor (second to the *rapprochement* with Britain) now came increasingly into the foreground. If the declaration of war came from Russia, he said, there was 'nothing to fear' from the Social Democrats. 'There will be no question of a general or partial strike, or of sabotage.' The British intervention had shifted the emphasis in his motives, no more. This appears plainly in the despatch sent that evening to Vienna and in its cancellation, which also affected indirectly the German move taken in the course of the night.

If [the Chancellor wired to Tschirschky on the evening of July 30] Vienna . . . refuses . . . to give way at all, it will hardly be possible to place the blame on Russia for the outbreak of the European conflagration [not to prevent the war, but to place the blame on Russia]. H.M. has, on the request of the Tsar, undertaken to intervene in Vienna, because he could not refuse without awakening an irrefutable suspicion that we wanted war.[1]

Alluding to Britain's attempts to mediate in Paris and Petersburg, he went on:

If these efforts of Britain's meet with success, while Vienna refuses everything, Vienna will prove that it is set on having a war, into which we are dragged, while Russia remains free of guilt. This puts us in a quite impossible position in the eyes of our own people. We can therefore only urgently recommend Vienna to accept Grey's proposal, which safeguards its position in every way.

The telegram stresses once again the cardinal importance of British neutrality, of Russian war guilt and of national solidarity as the factors governing German policy. Yet Germany's peaceful protestations to Britain were purely tactical, as is made plain by the fate of a telegram from King George to Prince Henry[2] suggesting cooperation between Germany and Britain to save the peace. This telegram arrived just before midnight (11.8 p.m.) on July 30. Vague as was the glimmer of hope which it offered that Britain might remain neutral, it was enough for Bethmann Hollweg to cancel his demand that Vienna should 'accept Grey's proposal' only twelve minutes later (11.20 p.m.). At the same time the Chancellor completely lifted such pressure–and it had been weak enough–as he had been putting on Vienna. No proof could be plainer of the tactical nature of Germany's 'peace moves'. Comparison with the instructions sent to Tschirschky[3] makes this more glaring still. Telegram No. 200 called on Vienna to accept mediation, since otherwise Russia 'would bear no blame'. Telegram No. 201, sent by Jagow in

[1] Id., No. 441.

[2] Id., No. 452, July 30.

[3] Tel. 200, cf. n. 93; Tel. 201, *DD*, II, No. 442, Jagow to Tschirschky, July 30; Tel. 202, No. 450, Chancellor to id., July 30; Tel. 203, No. 464, id. to id., July 31; Tel. 404, No. 479, id. to id., July 31.

the same hour, rejected Austria's proposal for a joint *démarche* in Paris and Petersburg on the ground that Germany 'could not take the same step again'. Telegram No. 202 cancelled telegram No. 200. Telegram no. 203 explained telegram No. 202, and telegram No. 204 on July 31 demanded Austria's 'immediate participation in the war against Russia'.

Besides explaining the cancellation telegram by King George's message, Bethmann Hollweg had also drafted, although not yet sent, a military explanation[1] which ran: 'I have cancelled execution of instructions in No. 200, because the General Staff has just informed me that military measures by our neighbours, especially in the east, compel speedy decision if we are not to be taken by surprise.' This alluded to the military considerations which became more and more prominent on July 30 and acquired great cogency when the news of Russia's partial mobilisation arrived.

The Beginning of World War

That the two demands sent to Vienna—for tactical reasons, and by no means in any 'desperate endeavour to save the peace'—to accept the British proposals constitute an isolated episode, a hesitation in view of Britain's attitude, appears more plainly than ever if we turn to the steps initiated by Moltke when the news of Russia's partial mobilisation against Austria-Hungary arrived. As late as July 29, Moltke and Falkenhayn postponed the proclamation of a 'state of imminent war', in obedience to the Emperor's orders and out of deference to Bethmann Hollweg's hopes of British neutrality, but on the morning of July 30 all such considerations were swept aside when the Foreign Ministry (presumably Zimmermann) passed on to the general staff the Emperor's marginal notes on Pourtalès' report that Russia had ordered partial mobilisation.[2] Wilhelm's comment on Sazonov's announcement that Russia was 'mobilising against Austria' was: 'Then I must mobilise too', and he went on: 'Then he [sc., Tsar Nicholas II] is taking on himself the guilt' (for a European war). . . . 'I regard my attempted mediation as having failed.' In such theatrical wise did Wilhelm II lay down what on another occasion he called 'his office of mediator', an office which he had in reality never assumed. The Chancellor thereupon informed the Emperor 'that any explanation given by Vienna to Petersburg on the purpose and extent of Austria's measures against Serbia

---

[1] *DD*, II, No. 451, draft for a telegram (not despatched) from Chancellor to Tschirschky, July 30.

[2] Id., No. 399; Chancellor communicates to Emperor Pourtalès' despatch of July 29 (No. 343) (arr. 2.52 p.m.). Both were handed to the Emperor at 7 a.m. on July 30 and returned by him the same day with his minutes on the covering letter.

[which he urged Berchtold to give] could only make Russia's guilt heavier and prove it more clearly to the whole world'.[1] Thus did Bethmann Hollweg again interpret to the Emperor on July 30 the governing principles of his policy.

But the noonday hours of July 30 are important in other respects also. During these hours the Emperor received further information both on the Russian partial mobilisation and on Britain's attitude,[2] the latter supported by a report from the naval attaché in London that 'the British fleet will launch an *instant and immediate attack on us at sea* if it comes to war between us and France'.[3] This report caused the Emperor extraordinary consternation and disillusionment. He and Prince Henry had just been concocting an answer to King George, based on his first message that 'we shall try all we can to keep out of this and to remain neutral'.[4] He had hoped very long that Britain would remain neutral, but when the despatches reached him – very, very belatedly – the situation changed. Their effect on Bethmann Hollweg was to cause temporary hesitations and retreats; on the Emperor it was the opposite. His naked hatred of 'perfidious Albion', of 'that filthy cur, Grey', of 'that filthy nation of grocers' vented itself with elemental violence. 'England drops the mask the moment she thinks we are safely in the corral and done for, so to speak.' He now discovered who was the real war criminal, for Russia would never have been able to begin the war without England's support. 'England alone is responsible for war and peace, not we any more!' The Emperor's marginal notes grow more and more sweeping.[5] Germany is encircled; the war of annihilation has been concerted; Germany is to go under; all this is purposeful 'anti-German world policy'; 'and there have been people,' he writes in sarcastic allusion to the Chancellor, 'who have believed it possible to win over or appease England by one petty concession or another!!! And we have put our heads into the noose and have even introduced the slow march in our naval programme in the pathetic hope that this would placate England!!!' Wilhelm II felt himself betrayed and double-crossed. 'Edward VII dead is stronger than I am alive.' At the same

[1] Id., No. 407, Chancellor to Emperor, July 30.

[2] Ibid. On the 30th the Chancellor sends the Emperor Lichnowsky's report of July 29 (No. 368). It returns the same day, covered with the Emperor's comments.

[3] The Emperor's marginal notes on the document referred to n. 88. On the extent of the mobilisation cf. *DD*, II, No. 410, Pourtalès to Foreign Ministry, July 30, arr. 11.50 a.m.

[4] *DD*, II, No. 374, July 28, Prince Henry to Emperor on his conversation with King George.

[5] Marginal notes on Lichnowsky's despatch (cf. n. 87) and Pourtalès' report No. 401, July 30.

time, however—and this is the further and historic importance of Grey's warning and of Pourtalès' reports—his long-harboured idea turned into the conscious purpose of destroying the British Empire by unleashing revolution in the Mohammedan world.

Even before it broke out the war had ceased to be one of the traditional wars between cabinets. On July 28 Bethmann Hollweg had offered Turkey definitive terms for an alliance guaranteeing Turkey's territorial integrity *vis-à-vis* Russia if Turkey would place her army under German military command in case of war and would further bind herself to take Germany's side if Russia entered the war as a belligerent.[1] The Austro-Serbian conflict was treated as 'localised', but the whole crisis viewed in the light of general war. On July 30 the negotiations were resumed more intensively with the aim of making Turkey the base for a war of revolution in the grand style against Britain.[2] The results of this turn of policy were the surprisingly quick conclusion of a German–Turkish alliance on August 2 and the despatch of the German cruisers *Goeben* and *Breslau* to Constantinople. On July 30 and 31 preparations began to stir up revolt in the Caucasus and especially Poland, and thus to initiate the revolution against the conservative imperial power of the Romanovs which ended in the revolutionising of east-central Europe. The strategy of 'utilising to the full all means of harming the enemy' which Germany, in Moltke's words, felt herself 'entitled to adopt without any reservation', was consistently executed. On August 2 Moltke sketched out to Bethmann Hollweg the outlines of Germany's plans for revolution: Turkey was to be made the basis of operations in India, Egypt and Persia, Japan was to be supported and induced to ally herself with Germany in return for recognition of the Far East as a Japanese sphere of interest, the Union of South Africa was to be subverted and Scandinavia neutralised, if not drawn into alliance with the Central Powers; similarly, the situation in the Balkans, Belgium and Italy was to be clarified without delay.[3]

On August 5 Moltke reported to the Chancellor that the plans for insurrection in Poland had been laid, and after further allusion to 'India, Egypt and also the Caucasus' (already touched on on August 2) he extended the revolutionary activity to North America. 'Feeling in America,' he reported, 'is friendly to us; perhaps the United States may be induced to turn their navy against Britain if Canada is held out to them as the prize of victory.'[4]

[1] *DD*, II, No. 320, Chancellor to Wangenheim.
[2] Id. Nos. 405 and 411, Wangenheim to Foreign Ministry.
[3] *DD*, III, No. 662, Moltke to id.
[4] *DD*, IV, No. 876, id. to id.

First, however, the Emperor's attitude had enabled the military to begin action in Prussia and Germany. Since Russia's partial mobilisation did not yet constitute, in German eyes, sufficient ground for Germany to initiate general mobilisation, Moltke pressed Austria-Hungary to adopt instant general mobilisation without, however, declaring war on Russia, since the *casus foederis* for Germany would only arise if Russia declared war[1] – and if Russia declared war, Moltke still believed that Britain would keep out. When, then, at 11.50 a telegram from Pourtalès revealed the *extent* of Russian partial mobilisation, the military were alerted. Nevertheless, when Bethmann Hollweg met Falkenhayn and Tirpitz at noon on the 30th, he succeeded once again in securing postponement of the proclamation of 'imminent threat of war' on grounds of internal policy. Moltke, however, who had attended the meeting uninvited, now took independent action. He sent an urgent warning to Conrad[2] to mobilise immediately against Russia (letting the dispositions against Serbia take second place) and to announce as his reason the Russian proclamation of partial mobilisation ('thus,' according to Ritter, 'making Russia appear the aggressor'). Only 'so would the *casus foederis* for Germany arise'. Britain's latest step to preserve the peace must be rejected. 'To last out a European war' was 'the last means of preserving Austria-Hungary'. 'Germany will come in under all circumstances.' In the evening Moltke repeated his demands and sent the assurance that 'Germany would mobilise'. Szögyény reported that 'till recently, all authoritative circles here had regarded the possibility of a European conflict with the most complete calm'. Since July 30 signs of nervousness had become apparent, but the reason was not nervousness over the outbreak of a European war, but 'anxiety lest Italy might fail to fulfil her obligations towards her partners in the Triple Alliance in the event of a general conflict'. It was only because Berlin and Vienna 'absolutely needed Italy if they were to be safe in entering a general conflict' that Germany was repeatedly pressing Vienna – as Moltke did twice on the 30th – to go to the limit in meeting Italy over the question of compensation.

At 9 p.m. on the 30th Bethmann Hollweg and Jagow yielded to Moltke's and Falkenhayn's insistence that the 'state of imminent war' must be proclaimed by noon on the next day at the latest. At midnight, only three hours after the evening meeting, Moltke had

[1] Conrad, op. cit., pp. 151 ff. Tel. Captain Fleishmann to Moltke, cf. Ritter, op. cit., pp. 319 ff., cf. Wegerer, op. cit., II, pp. 113 ff.; *DD*, II, No. 410, Pourtalès to Foreign Ministry, July 30.

[2] Conrad, op. cit., pp. 152 ff.; Tel. from Austro-Hungarian Military Attaché in Berlin, Baron Bienerth, to Conrad, July 30, midday; Tel. from Moltke to Conrad, July 30, evening, arr. 7.45 a.m., July 31.

his adjutant, von Haeften, draft the Emperor's proclamation to his people, his army and his navy.[1] At 9 a.m. on July 31 it was agreed that the order for the measures of mobilisation consequent on this proclamation should be issued if Russia's general mobilisation was confirmed.

The report of Russia's general mobilisation was confirmed at noon on July 31. In the afternoon the Emperor, speaking from a balcony of the Palace, proclaimed a 'state of imminent threat of war', declaring that 'they are pressing the sword into our hand', Bethmann Hollweg's courage in waiting for Russia to order general mobilisation had thus reaped its reward: the German people was ready for war in the conviction that it had been gratuitously assailed. Sazonov had put this trump into his hand. By making Russia appear the guilty party, Bethmann Hollweg had also been able to eliminate the possibility of opposition from the Social Democrats. On the 31st Lerchenfeld reported to Munich, sarcastically but with relief, that the Social Democrats had 'in duty bound, demonstrated in favour of peace', but were now 'keeping quite quiet'.[2] This was also the purpose of giving Russia twelve hours' notice in the ultimatum, and of the postponement until August 1 (made possible by the perfection of her dispositions) of Germany's general mobilisation.

At the very last hour it again appeared possible that Bethmann Hollweg's policy might bear fruit and Britain remain neutral. On August 1, after the order for mobilisation had been signed, an offer arrived from London to guarantee France's neutrality.[3] This seemed to hold out the prospect of war on a single front. The Emperor accepted the offer and ordered Moltke 'to hold up the advance westward'. There followed the famous scene which exposed the utter helplessness of Germany's military rigidity. Moltke protested against the Emperor's order, saying that the only up-to-date plan of campaign (the famous Schlieffen Plan, revised by him in 1913) provided for attack only against France. Nevertheless the Emperor ordered that the advance, which had already begun – patrols had penetrated into Luxemburg – was to be halted. Moltke was beside himself at the possibility of France remaining neutral and said that if the advance into France did not take place, he could 'undertake no responsibility for the war'. 'Now,' he remarked bitterly, as we know from the recollections of the Head of the Naval Cabinet, 'it only remains for Russia to back out, too.' After sharp argument, the Chancellor and

[1] Wegerer, op. cit., II, p. 122.

[2] *DD*, IV, Annexe IV, No. 27, Lerchenfeld to Hertling, July 31 (private letter).

[3] Georg Alexander von Müller, *Regierte der Kaiser? Tagebuchaufzeichnungen*, ed. Walter Görlitz (Berlin and Frankfurt, 1959), p. 38.

the Chief of the General Staff ended by agreeing that the advance would have to go on 'for technical reasons'. Britain's offer had come too late. Yet the illusion persisted and even gathered strength. A second telegram from Lichnowsky on the same day suggested a possibility that Britain might remain neutral even in a war between Germany and both Russia and France.[1] 'What a fabulous turn of events,' reported Müller 'the Emperor was delighted, and called for champagne', as was his habit later, during the war, to celebrate real or imagined victories. Bethmann Hollweg's policy seemed to have succeeded. Germany could engage Russia and France at her ease. But these hopes were to prove short-lived.

The subsequent disillusionment served to inflame still further Germany's hatred of Britain, which now became almost unbounded. On the other hand, it cleared the way for the westward advance as foreseen in the Schlieffen Plan. Italy having declared neutrality, the Germans began the World War in the face of the most unfavourable possible grouping of the powers. The declaration of war on Russia on August 1 and on France on August 3, punctilious as they were from the bureaucratic point of view and devastating as were their effects on opinion elsewhere in the world, nevertheless only marked the formal end of the complex process which had led up to them. In this respect, too, it is characteristic that Austria-Hungary's declarations of war on Russia and on the Western Powers followed only a week later, under German pressure, and that Germany's declaration of war had long since started on its journey when the Tsar telegraphed again to express confidence that peace could still be preserved in spite of the mobilisations. The violation of Belgium's neutrality enabled the British government to win over parliament and people for immediate entry into the war, a decision politically motivated by the often expressed determination not to allow Germany to overthrow France and leave Britain to face alone a continent dominated by Germany.

Who Was 'Guilty'?

There is no question but that the conflict of military and political interests, of resentment and ideas, which found expression in the July crisis, left no government of any of the European powers quite free of some measure of responsibility—greater or smaller—for the outbreak of the war in one respect or another. It is, however, not the purpose of this work to enter into the familiar controversy, on which whole libraries have been written, over the question of war guilt, to

[1] Id., p. 39; cf. also *DD*, III, No. 570, Lichnowsky to Foreign Ministry, August 1.

discuss exhaustively the responsibility of the individual statesmen and soldiers of all the European powers concerned, or to pass final judgment on them. We are concerned solely with the German leaders' objectives and with the policy actually followed by them in the July crisis, and that only in so far as their policy throws light on the postulates and origins of Germany's war aims.

It must be repeated: given the tenseness of the world situation in 1914–a condition for which Germany's world policy, which had already led to three dangerous crises (those of 1905, 1908 and 1911), was in no small measure responsible–any limited or local war in Europe directly involving one great power must inevitably carry with it the imminent danger of a general war. As Germany willed and coveted the Austro-Serbian war and, in her confidence in her military superiority, deliberately faced the risk of a conflict with Russia and France, her leaders must bear a substantial share of the historical responsibility for the outbreak of general war in 1914. This responsibility is not diminished by the fact that at the last moment Germany tried to arrest the march of destiny, for her efforts to influence Vienna were due exclusively to the threat of British intervention and, even so, they were half-hearted, belated and immediately revoked.

It is true that German politicians and publicists, and with them the entire German propaganda machine during the war and German historiography after the war–particularly after Versailles–have invariably maintained that the war was forced on Germany, or at least (adopting Lloyd George's dictum, made for political reasons, that 'we all stumbled into the war') that Germany's share of the responsibility was no greater than that of the other participants. But confidential exchanges between Germany and Austria, and between the responsible figures in Germany itself, untinged by any propagandist intent, throw a revealing spotlight on the real responsibility.

A few weeks after the outbreak of war, during the crises on the Marne and in Galicia, the Austrians asked urgently for German help against the superior Russian armies facing them. It was refused. Count Tisza then advised Berchtold to tell the Germans: 'That we took our decision to go to war on the strength of the express statements both of the German Emperor and of the German Imperial Chancellor that they regarded the moment as suitable and would be glad if we showed ourselves in earnest.'

Just three years later, on August 14, 1917, at the climax of a heated debate whether the war should be continued in the interest of Germany's war aims, Austria-Hungary's Foreign Minister, Count

Czernin, told his German interlocutors excitedly: 'It was not Austria alone that began the war then.' Characteristically, the official German minutes in the Imperial Chancellery left Czernin's next sentence incomplete and passed over the retorts of the German statesmen, Michaelis, Kühlmann and Helfferich, but the minutes of the Army High Command (the OHL) gave the sentence in full: 'Germany demanded that the ultimatum to Serbia should be drawn up in those sharp terms.'[1]

In February, 1918, again, Czernin asked Berchtold if he would object if he (Czernin) published a letter written by him to Tisza shortly before the outbreak of war, which showed: 'what strong efforts Germany was making at that time to hold us to a hard line, and how our alliance might have been in danger if we had given way'.[2]

There is other evidence to confirm that the Central Powers in no way 'slid into war'. Josef Baernreither, an Austrian politician who was entirely well disposed towards the Reich and was a leading champion of the Mitteleuropa idea during the war, made the following entry on the July crisis in his diary for December, 1914:

> The Germans were afraid that we would refuse to go with them if the war broke out over some question remote from us. At Algeciras we were still 'seconds': later, not even that; in the Morocco crisis we did not stand by Germany firmly. But war was bound to come, as things had developed, through the faults of German and Austro-Hungarian diplomacy. So when the Sarajevo murder took place, Germany seized her opportunity and made an Austrian grievance her signal for action. That is the history of the war.[3]

Finally, on October 8, 1919, Czernin telegraphed to Karl H. von Wiegand (the Berlin correspondent of the *Herald and Examiner*) the following reply to questions addressed to him by Wiegand:

> Repeated conversations and interviews I had with Ambassador von Tschirschky could create no other impression than that his [the German] government expected warlike action on our part against Serbia. Especially a conversation I had with him during the early half of July convinced me that if we did not show this time that we were in earnest, then on the next occasion Berlin not only would not support us, but would in fact 'orient' itself in some other direction.
>
> What that would have meant for us, in view of the ethnographical composition of the Dual Monarchy and the territorial aspirations of our neighbour states, need not be explained.
>
> Tschirschky was informed about the material points in the ultimatum to

---

[1] Müller, op. cit., p. 245 (entry of December 31, 1916).

[2] Hantsch, op. cit., II, p. 811.

[3] From Baernreither's papers preserved in the Vienna Staatsarchiv.

Serbia before the final editing of the note and the textual contents were given to him two days before the Belgrade *démarche*.[1]

Baernreither was confirmed in his view of the nature of the July crisis by a conversation which he had in November, 1915, with Otto Hoetzsch of Berlin, the historian of eastern Europe, leader-writer for the *Kreuzzeitung* and later German National deputy in the Reichstag. 'Then' (sc., after July 5, 1914), runs the entry in Baernreither's diary, 'the Emperor went off to Norway, knowing certainly that war would break out. Germany had arranged all this very cleverly, and had shown alertness and judgment in picking an occasion when she was certain of Austria's support in waging a war the inevitability of which had been becoming apparent for years past.'

A week later Hoetzsch's Berlin colleague, the economist Jastrow, confirmed the correctness of Hoetzsch's view to Baernreither.

Arthur von Gwinner, Director of the Deutsche Bank, again confirmed most clearly the will to risk war which existed in Germany, especially in the Foreign Ministry, in a conversation which he had on the July crisis at the end of August, 1914, with von Capelle, the Under-Secretary of State in the Reich Naval Office. He, too, stressed the factor of Austria's unreliability:

> The only reason why Lichnowsky was not informed was because here [in the Wilhelmstrasse] they were determined to force a conflict. When Capelle asked who had been the man behind this pressure, Gwinner answered, 'Herr von Stumm, in the Foreign Office, for example.' When Capelle expressed some doubt, he went on: 'Perhaps it was a whole group. They worked systematically to get Austria committed inextricably, as the first step, so as to be sure of her. The whole plan of campaign against Serbia was arranged in advance to make a conflict inevitable.'[2]

This grave statement was published as early as 1926 by no less a man than Grand Admiral von Tirpitz, in his *Deutsche Ohnmachtspolitik* (Germany's Policy of Weakness), but it has, so far as the author knows, passed unnoticed.

Admiral Müller, commenting in his diary on the Entente's answer of December 31, 1916, to the German peace offer—a document which ascribed to Germany a substantial share of the guilt for the World War—wrote that it 'contained certain bitter truths on our doings at the outbreak of the war'.[3]

Finally Albert Ballin, Bethmann Hollweg's and Jagow's intimate

[1] Joseph Goricar and Beecher Stowe, *The Inside Story of Austro-German Intrigue* (New York, 1920), pp. 300 ff.

[2] Alfred von Tirpitz, *Deutsche Ohnmachtspolitik im Weltkriege* (Berlin, 1926), pp. 65 ff.

[3] Müller, op. cit., p. 245 (entry of December 31, 1916).

political confidant (he was sent to London by Jagow at the beginning of the crisis of July, 1914, in an attempt to secure Britain's neutrality, and was summoned to Berlin in the middle of 1915 to help draft Germany's note to the United States which was to decide on peace or war with America but was not received by Jagow after all), wrote at that date to the Secretary of State, out of his intimate knowledge of what had been done in July, 1914:

> I make every allowance for a man who is heavily incriminated, as Your Excellency is, and has to bear the frightful responsibility for having staged this war (*für die Inscenierung dieses Krieges*) which is costing Germany generations of splendid men and setting her back 100 years.[1]

The official documents afford ample proofs that during the July crisis the Emperor, the German military leaders and the Foreign Ministry were pressing Austria-Hungary to strike against Serbia without delay, or alternatively agreed to the despatch of an ultimatum to Serbia couched in such sharp terms as to make war between the two countries more than probable, and that in doing so they deliberately took the risk of a continental war against Russia and France. But the decisive point is that, as we now know – although for a long time it was not admitted – these groups were not alone. On July 5 and 6 the Imperial Chancellor, Bethmann Hollweg, the man in whom the constitution vested the sole responsibility, decided to take the risk and even over-trumped the Emperor when he threatened to weaken. That this was no 'tragic doom', no 'ineluctable destiny', but a deliberate decision of policy emerges beyond doubt from the diary of his private secretary, Kurt Riezler, who recorded in it his conversations with the Chancellor in the critical days (and, indeed, over many years). These diaries have not yet been published,[2] but the extracts from them which have seen the light furnish irrefutable proof that during the July crisis Bethmann Hollweg was ready for war. More than this. Riezler's entry for the evening of July 8, after Bethmann Hollweg's return to Hohenfinow (where Rathenau was also stopping) shows what advance calculations the leaders of Germany were making in respect of the situation produced by the Sarajevo murder. According to his secretary, the Chancellor said: 'If war doesn't come, if the Tsar doesn't want it or France panics and advises peace, we have still achieved this much, that we have manoeuvred the Entente into disintegration over this move.'

In other words, Bethmann Hollweg reckoned with a major general

---

[1] Ballin to Jagow, Foreign Ministry, *Weltkrieg*, No. 18 (secret).

[2] The diaries have not yet been made available to the public. They are being prepared for publication by K. D. Erdmann, who has quoted a few extracts from them in a lecture. See *Geschichte in Wissenschaft und Unterricht*, 1964.

war as the result of Austria's swift punitive action against Serbia. If, however, Russia and France were again to draw back (as in 1909 and 1911)–which he at first regarded as the less probable eventuality–then at least Germany would have achieved a signal diplomatic victory: she would have split Russia from France and isolated both without war. But war was what he expected, and how he expected its course to run we learn from his predecessor in the Chancellorship, Bülow, who had a long discussion with him at the beginning of August. Bethmann Hollweg told Bülow that he was reckoning with 'a war lasting three, or at the most, four months . . . a violent, but short storm'. Then, he went on, revealing his innermost wishes, it would 'in spite of the war, indeed, through it', be possible to establish a friendly relationship with England, and through England with France. He hoped to bring about 'a grouping of Germany, England and France against the Russia colossus which threatens the civilisation of Europe'.

Bethmann Hollweg himself often hinted darkly during the war how closely Germany had been involved in the beginning of the war. He was less concerned with the 'staging' of it than to register the spirit of the German leaders who had made it possible for the war to be begun even after the premises for it had collapsed. The following bitter words are taken from his address to the Central Committee of the Reichstag at the beginning of October, 1916, during the sharp debate on the initiation of unlimited submarine warfare; they outline Germany's real 'guilt', her constant over-estimation of her own powers, and her misjudgment of realities:

> Since the outbreak of the war we have not always avoided the danger of underestimating the strength of our enemies. The extraordinary development of the last twenty years seduced wide circles into over-estimating our own forces, mighty as they are, in comparing them with those of the rest of the world . . . in our rejoicing over our own progress (we have) not paid sufficient regard to conditions in other countries.[1]

The July crisis must not be regarded in isolation. It appears in its true light only when seen as a link between Germany's 'world policy', as followed since the mid-1890s, and her war aims policy after August, 1914.

[1] Records of the Budget Committee of the Reichstag, Vol. XVI.

Part One

1914–1916

3

IN EXPECTATION OF A BLITZ VICTORY

FROM BETHMANN HOLLWEG TO CLASS

WITH the outbreak of the World War the general staff's plan for a war on two fronts–prepared years previously–immediately came into operation. The deployment of the German army was based on the Schlieffen Plan, which reckoned with the Russian army's mobilisation being slow and therefore allowed at first for only a delaying action with weak German forces in the east, leaving the Austrians to bear the main weight of the operations on that front. In the west the mass of the German expeditionary force was to march through Belgium and annihilate the French army and British expeditionary force, if present, in a super-Cannae within a few weeks. After France had been eliminated as a military power and Britain, if she had intervened, been driven out of the Continent, the general staff planned to transfer the German army to the east, where it would combine with the Austro-Hungarian army in advances from East Prussia and Galicia and inflict an equally decisive defeat on the Russian army in Poland.[1] So within a few months the Central Powers would be left dominating the Continent as undisputed victors.

Successful execution of these plans would have left Belgium and Poland at Germany's mercy after a few months, with France and Russia forced to accept her terms. When the campaign seemed to be working out according to plan, the outline of the problem of the fate of these countries–in other words, Germany's war aims–began to take shape.

Pre-war Imperialism and War Aims

In the fantastic national upsurge of August, 1914, considerations of war aims at first hardly entered into the consciousness of the mass of the German people. When, on August 4, the Reichstag met in solemn session in the White Hall of the royal palace in Berlin, and the Emperor, in his speech from the throne, uttered his famous words: 'It is no lust of conquest that inspires us', he was beyond

[1] Gerhard Ritter, *Der Schlieffen Plan* (Munich, 1956, the latest and most exhaustive study of this complex of problems); id. in the *Herzfeld Festschrift*, 1957; in November, 1912, Moltke reckoned on beating France in *'four to five weeks'* (Ritter, p. 541, n. 38).

95

doubt voicing the feelings of the overwhelming majority of the German people. The popular enthusiasm which erupted in patriotic songs in streets and squares was rooted in a sincere feeling of having been made victims of a long-planned 'encirclement' and deliberate assault by jealous enemies–as the Chancellor said often enough on later occasions. Both public opinion and the government's official utterances strongly stressed the defensive character of the war; and up to the end of the war, and after it, all official commentaries explaining Germany's attitude during the war took this line. The German official version of the First World War as a purely defensive struggle has proved so enduring that it has largely determined the picture of German war aims, not only from 1914 to 1918, but down to our own days.

By adopting the slogan of a war of defence, the government seemed to have renounced in advance all conquests. But it was only a few weeks before the slogan changed from 'war of self-defence' to the necessity–in view of the possibility of a second war–of acquiring 'safeguards' and 'guarantees' for the future of the German Empire before arms could safely be laid down. This led to a determination to achieve decisive victory and to dictate the peace terms to the enemy. On that same August 4 on which the Reichstag listened to the Emperor's speech from the throne, the *Militärwochenblatt* struck the key-note for the future in the following passage: 'Russia has forced war on us unscrupulously for the sake of –Serbia! The hour of reckoning, which could not long have been postponed, has struck. . . . If God in His grace should grant us the victory, then . . . *vae victis*!'[1]

A week later, when the First Foot Guards left for the front, the Emperor swore not again to sheathe the sword until he could dictate the peace.[2] In exactly the same way, the king of Bavaria, Ludwig III, promised to carry on the war 'until the enemy accepts the conditions which we dictate to him'.

The Party Truce and War Aims

The German government could not openly proclaim its desire to make profit out of the war, or at least to keep a free hand for the eventuality of ultimate victory; it had to present itself both to world public opinion and to its own people in an attitude consonant with its solemn announcement that its war was one of self-defence. This was particularly necessary in dealing with the Social Democrats

[1] *Militärwochenblatt*, August 4, 1914, col. 2301 f.
[2] *Deutscher Geschichtskalender*, ed. von Wippermann and Purlitz, 1914, Vol. 2, August 11, 1914; cf. *Der Europäische Krieg in aktenmässiger Darstellung*, Vol. 1, (Leipzig, 1914), p. 132.

who had been the strongest party in the Reichstag since 1912, and with the Socialist Trade Unions, which constituted the biggest political mass organisation in imperial Germany. Without the Social Democrats and the workers controlled by it the war could not be carried on. This was why the mobilisation of anti-Tsarist emotion among the Social Democrats was essential for the establishment of the national united front of August 4, 1914. In fact, even before war broke out, Bethmann Hollweg was able to report with satisfaction to the Prussian Ministry of State, on July 30, that feeling was 'generally good', and that

he believed himself entitled to conclude from his conversations with the deputy Südekum that there was no reason to fear any particular trouble from the Social Democrats or their party leaders. There would be no question of a general strike or of partial strikes or of sabotage.[1]

The Conservatives, at least, who had at that time to be counted as a government party, were from the first firmly resolved not to exclude conquests by war.[2] The Social Democrats, who, by virtue of their special position in imperial Germany, were the one party capable of speaking up in the Reichstag, proposed on August 4 to include in their statement, to be read out by Hugo Haase (President of the party and of its parliamentary representatives), a passage to the effect that the Social Democrats would oppose any attempt to make a war of conquest out of the conflict. Laborious negotiations followed, and Count Westarp, the spokesman for the Conservatives, forced the Social Democrats to revise their attitude by threatening that if they made such a declaration, he would answer Haase's speech with another which, in the nature of things, could only be directed against the 'impossible and internationally detrimental passage' about the war of conquest. The Social Democrat deputies retreated and contented themselves with a vague remark that peace must be restored after the security of Germany's frontiers against foreign enemies had been established. The episode contained the germs of all those future tensions within the Social Democratic party which the collaboration between their right wing and the Chancellor afterwards brought to an open split.

It was the Social Democrats' retreat over the war aims question that made possible the inter-party truce of August 4 and also saved the Chancellor from the need to define his attitude on the question of annexations at that date.

[1] *DD*, II, No. 456, p. 178, Minutes of the session.
[2] Kuno Graf v. Westarp, *Konservative Politik in Kaiserreich* (Berlin, 1935), Vol. II, pp. 1 f.; letter from Westarp to Heydebrand und der Lasa, August 6, 1914.

Consideration for the German workers, and for international opinion, led Bethmann Hollweg to veto an official debate on war aims at the end of 1914, although very far-reaching war aims for Germany had been publicly formulated in the ebullience of the first weeks of war. Bethmann Hollweg's public reticence has been generally interpreted by historians as indicating that he had himself no war aims in mind.[1] The real reason, however, why he wanted no public debate on war aims was that he thought that its political effects, both internal and international, would be harmful. He said as much himself in confidence, for example in a letter which he wrote in March, 1916, to the Munich historian, Erich Marcks. Marcks, as spokesman for the 'national circles', had urged the Chancellor to allow a public debate on war aims. Bethmann Hollweg's answer[2] is extremely characteristic of his attitude. Pressed to define 'positive' war aims, he answered: '. . . I understand that many circles should entertain this wish, and I share it. I, too, am anxious for the moment when it will be possible to give a lead in this sense, to define concrete aims.' He ended: 'The moment when the end can be foreseen, or the direction from which it comes, the time to speak will have arrived.' He admitted that any public statement made by him on war aims could only mask or hint at his real intentions. He wrote to Marcks:

> I have thrown open to debate the great middle-European idea which will determine our future, I have alluded to our great tasks in the east, but for the rest I could not in my speeches go beyond securing our frontiers against every danger, blocking the invasion-gates of Belgium and Poland. My allusions assumed the inclusion of Belgium and Poland within the sphere of power of Mitteleuropa, which is assuredly no small aim. . . . We are keeping all the cards in our hand hidden from the enemy's eyes.[3]

The Genesis of the September Programme

If the Chancellor spoke in March, 1916 of his own war aims, the basis for these must be sought in his war aims programme of September, 1914. For, quite contrary to what he said after his dismisal

[1] Cf. also Werner Conze, *Die Zeit Wilhelms II* in *Deutsche Geschichte im Ueberblick, ein Handbuch*, ed. Petter Rassow (Stuttgart, 1953), p. 605. So also the latest general account by Karl Dietrich Erdmann, *Die Zeit des Weltkrieges* in Bruno Gebhardt, *Handbuch der deutschen Geschichte*, 8th revised edition, ed. H. Grundmann, Vol. IV, p. 42, where Bethmann Hollweg's attitude is described as wavering and unsystematic. The same view is argued by Martin Göhring, *Bismarcks Erben 1890–1945, Deutschlands Weg von Wilhelm II bis Adolf Hitler*, 2nd enlarged ed. (Wiesbaden, 1959), p. 112.

[2] Statement to Admiral Pohl who conveyed it to Jagow on September 5, 1914, cf. E. Zechlin, 'Deutschland zwischen Kabinettskrieg und Wirtschaftskrieg', *Histor. Zeitschr.* 199/2, October, 1965, p. 376.

[3] Ebenda, pp. 377, 383.

and in his memoirs, Bethmann Hollweg occupied himself in the very first weeks of the war with the question of the future extension of Germany's power.

The Chancellor showed that he completely shared the expectations and illusions of the military chiefs when, in explaining the possible uses of the German fleet in the first days of September, he 'repeatedly' stressed that he intended to keep the fleet up to strength 'in order that England should not in the end be in a position to deprive us of the fruits of victory over France and Russia'. He spoke these words on September 5, one day before the opening of Joffre's counter-offensive, at the height of the optimism about the outcome of the war. (The victory at Tannenberg in the east was won on August 27. On August 31 Jagow judged 'our successes' in the west to be so consider-able that from Luxembourg he informed the German ambassador in Rome via Zimmermann in Berlin that the time for discussing compensations and concessions to Italy had passed; Italy had backed the wrong horse.)

Drafts of the Emperor's proclamation to the French people, dated September 6 and prepared in French by the Chancellor's personal assistants at General Headquarters—Kurt Riezler, Gerhard von Mutius and Wilhelm von Radowitz—provide proof of the general expectation that the decisive victory over France was at hand. In a war, the proclamation ran, into which Germany had been forced by the coalition policies of the Triple Entente, the issue between Germany and France was now settled; France, or rather northern France, was occupied and would remain occupied so long as 'your allies, and especially England, continue the war—and so prevent your government from concluding a just peace'. (The London agreement whereby the three Entente powers engaged themselves not to conclude a separate peace had been signed on the previous day.)

The fact that the publication of this proclamation was prevented by the battle of the Marne does not affect its historical significance in assessing German expectations before the turning point in what Moltke called 'this brilliantly initiated campaign'.[1]

According to the view expressed by Bethmann Hollweg to Bülow shortly after the outbreak of war, the defeat of the French army was to be followed immediately by a separate peace with France and the offer of a Defence and Aid Pact; France would be 'spared' in order that she might 'do battle with us', that is to say, fight on the German side—against Britain? against Russia? Such were the calculations between the Emperor, Bethmann Hollweg, Jagow, Tirpitz and

[1] Hellmuth v. Moltke, *Erinnerungen usw. 1877–1916* (Stuttgart 1922), pp. 385 ff.

others at headquarters between August 19 and September 10. France, if she was to be won for this programme, would have to be compensated for the projected loss of the ores of Longwy–Briey by receiving, after the partition of Belgium, the Walloon southern half of that country, that is to say, a large part of industrial Belgium. On October 20 Delbrück, Secretary of State in the Reich Interior Office, endorsed such a solution as a 'reasonable compromise'. Further, at the end of October, Delbrück, still anticipating an imminent German victory (since the whole nation, including senior civil servants, had been deceived about the seriousness of the setback on the Marne), drew up lists of persons suitable for administrative employment in the military government to be established in France.

These plans had further purposes: either, on the one hand, to secure the withdrawal of England from the war as a consequence of the fall of France (and the expected collapse of Russia), or alternatively, should England remain stubborn, to secure the use of the coasts of France for the prosecution of the war against Britain, particularly with submarines and in the air. On September 5 the Württemberg plenipotentiary, General von Gravenitz, reported in the following terms to his Prime Minister von Weizsäcker, from General Headquarters, on the basis of a number of conversations with leading military and civilian personages: The Chancellor, like everybody else, was proceeding from the assumption that England and Japan must be defeated; but it was clear to the more thoughtful among them that Germany's existing naval strength was insufficient for this purpose and that the German fleet needed to be substantially increased–specifically with French and Belgian finance. There must therefore be an interim peace with France after the complete destruction of French power. Further, the German fleet must be so reinforced with the help of French and Belgian levies–either for the current war or a second one–that it would be able to lay siege to Britain and so enable Germany to compel England to recognize the situation created by Germany on the Continent, east and west.[1]

On September 6, the day on which Joffre's order of the day unleashed the allied counter-offensive on the Marne, the Chancellor wrote: 'We must persevere until Germany's future security is fully guaranteed.' On the next day Moltke referred in a proclamation to a peace 'which in the foreseeable future could be disturbed by no foe'.[2]

What the Chancellor meant when he referred to Germany's

---

[1] E. Zechlin, *Probleme des Kriegskalküls und der Kriegsbeendigung im Ersten Weltkrieg,* Gesch. in Wissenschaft u. Unterricht, 1965, p. 75 (from the papers of Carl v. Weizsäcker).

[2] *Amtliche Kriegsdepeschen nach Berichten von Wolffs Telegraphenbüro,* WTB, 1, p. 117.

'security' can be discovered in the 'preliminary principles' for an armistice with France which he sent to Delbrück on September 9 when the collapse of France seemed imminent. This September Programme should be understood not merely as an examination of the means to the end of defeating Britain (as some German historians have interpreted it—since it was first published in the first edition of this book); it was also a statement of war aims because its general principles, if carried into effect, would have permanently changed the face of Europe.

The kernel of this September Programme consists of the Mitteleuropa idea with its claim to German hegemony. This idea had taken root even before the war among a party of German bankers and industrialists, and took shape on the outbreak of war as a war aim which was meant as a more moderate alternative to the *Alldeutsch* programme of conquest, and one which seemed economically both necessary and attainable. Memoranda and letters from Walther Rathenau and Arthur von Gwinner had confirmed Bethmann Hollweg in these ideas, which he had discussed with Delbrück in mid-August, 1914; before he left Berlin for General Headquarters at Coblenz. Rathenau, who had been entrusted in the same month with the organisation of the Department for military raw materials in the War Ministry and thus put in a position of key importance for the further conduct of the war, had submitted to the Chancellor a lengthy memorandum[1] recapitulating the ideas already brought forward by him in 1911 and 1913. As he argued it, only a Germany reinforced by 'Mitteleuropa' would be in a position to maintain herself as an equal world power between the world powers of Britain and the United States on the one side and Russia on the other. The road to this he saw in a compromise with France on the one hand, and on the other, in a complete Customs Union between Germany and Austria-Hungary. He saw in the war a possibility of bringing about this 'essential objective', if necessary by force. It is true that Delbrück, who in conversation with Bethmann Hollweg at the beginning of August had agreed in principle with the general aim of Mitteleuropa and now, too, welcomed warmly the definition of these ideas in the Chancellor's programme, was against the idea of forcible incorporation of other areas in Germany's economic sphere.

Bethmann Hollweg appeared deeply impressed by Rathenau's

[1] Bethmann Hollweg thought this memorandum so important that he had it circulated throughout the Department. Another letter from Rathenau to Bethmann Hollweg, dated September 7, 1914, reproduced in *Walther Rathenau, ein preussischer Europäer, Briefe*, ed. M. von Eynern (Berlin 1955), pp. 118 ff. See also Erich Kollmann, *Walther Rathenau in German Foreign Policy*, in *Journal of Modern History*, Vol. XXIV, No. 1, pp. 127 ff.

general idea, the basis of which, customs and economic union between Germany and Austria-Hungary as nucleus of a wider Central
European unity, he took over complete; and, unlike Delbrück, Bethmann Hollweg was convinced that neither the narrower nor the
wider objective could be achieved unless Germany resolved herself
'to throw her political preponderance into the scales'.

Arthur von Gwinner, senior Director of the Deutsche Bank, who
was also on friendly terms with Bethmann Hollweg, had similar
ideas. When the 'Wednesday Club', an association of leading men
from the spheres of politics, economics and cultural life, held its first
wartime meeting in Berlin on September 2, he argued against
'blindly following a policy of annexations', pleading rather for a less
conspicuous but all the more effective course, namely that of 'establishing Germany's economic domination' (in Europe). The Under-
Secretary of State, Zimmermann, thought his ideas so important
that he at once sent a copy of the speech to the Chancellor and Jagow
in Coblenz, where it arrived in time to be utilised in the September
war aims programme.

Besides the comprehensive, mainly economic, Mitteleuropa
programme (which in this version included Continental Western Europe) and another plan–which took concrete form as early as this–
for thrusting Russia back, the rounding off and expansion of
Germany's colonial possessions in Africa were also the subject of
discussion as early as August. At the end of the month Jagow was considering the bases for peace terms with France and Belgium, and
asked Solf,[1] the Secretary of State in the Reich Colonial Office, to
submit concrete proposals for colonial acquisitions. Solf's memorandum on the 'partition of the African possessions of France, Belgium
and Portugal' presupposed that Germany did not intend to expand
her frontiers in Europe to any great extent, but that she did mean
substantially to enlarge her colonial empire in Africa. Linking his
proposals with the pre-war Anglo-German conversations on the partition of Portugal's colonial possessions, Solf suggested that Portugal, although neutral, should cede to Germany Angola and the northern half of Mozambique as far as the Primera Islands, therewith
making the acquisition of a continuous colonial empire in Central
Africa one of official Germany's war aims. Besides the Portuguese
colonies, this empire was to include the Belgian Congo and French
Equatorial Africa as far north as Lake Chad, Togoland enlarged by
Dahomey and in the north by a slice of Senegambia up to Timbuctoo, thus making the course of the Niger the northern frontier. Solf

---

[1] On Solf, see Eberhard von Vietsch, *Wilhelm Solf, Botschafter zwischen den Zeiten*
(Tübingen, 1961).

gave the arguments for his proposals in detail, accompanied by detailed maps (see map, p. 596). The most important economic objectives in this plan were possession of the Katanga mines, control of the railway between Katanga and the Atlantic coast, and the safeguarding of the ports of Portuguese Angola.

The whole basis of this conception was the expectation that the defeat of France was imminent. Solf did not share the widely-held sanguine belief that Britain would soon be forced to her knees, and accordingly he made no proposals at this stage for the annexation of British colonies. He did, however, explain what he would demand of Britain, should she too be defeated, recommending *inter alia* the acquisition of the wealthy Nigeria as a link between Germany's prospective western possessions of Togoland–Timbuctoo and the eastern areas round Lake Chad, the new empire being thus completely rounded off.

Although the objectives enumerated in Solf's memorandum are considerable enough, he intended the effects of his proposals to lean towards moderation. His concentration on Africa was intended to divert the nation from wanting to annex large areas in Europe by emphasising the attractions of an autarchic economic area, guaranteed by enlarged colonial possessions, as a basis for world power status. Mittelafrika acquired a significance similar to Mitteleuropa. Bethmann Hollweg included the plan of creating a 'continuous central African colonial empire' in his September programme, and this ambitious overseas programme continued thereafter to hold a permanent place among Germany's war aims.

Bethmann Hollweg's September Programme

Expecting as he did that peace negotiations would be opening shortly, Bethmann Hollweg described his programme of September 9 as 'provisional notes on the direction of our policy on the conclusion of peace.'[1]

The 'general aim of the war' was, for him, 'security for the German Reich in west and east for all imaginable time. For this purpose France must be so weakened as to make her revival as a great power impossible for all time. Russia must be thrust back as far as possible from Germany's eastern frontier and her domination over the non-Russian vassal peoples broken.'

The objectives in the east epitomised in the lapidary last sentence of this introduction were not yet set out in detail in the programme itself, since peace with Russia was not yet regarded as imminent, but this does not mean that they had not yet assumed concrete form. The

[1] DZA Potsdam, Rk, Gr. Hq. 21, No. 2476.

detailed enumeration of 'individual war aims' was confined to the continental west, where alone the conclusion of peace seemed within grasp. They ran as follows:

1. *France.* The military to decide whether we should demand cession of Belfort and western slopes of the Vosges, razing of fortresses and cession of coastal strip from Dunkirk to Boulogne.

The ore-field of Briey, which is necessary for the supply of ore for our industry, to be ceded in any case.

Further, a war indemnity, to be paid in instalments; it must be high enough to prevent France from spending any considerable sums on armaments in the next 15–20 years.

Furthermore: a commercial treaty which makes France economically dependent on Germany, secures the French market for our exports and makes it possible to exclude British commerce from France. This treaty must secure for us financial and industrial freedom of movement in France in such fashion that German enterprises can no longer receive different treatment from French.

2. *Belgium.* Liége and Verviers to be attached to Prussia, a frontier strip of the province of Luxemburg to Luxemburg.

Question whether Antwerp, with a corridor to Liége, should also be annexed remains open.

At any rate Belgium, even if allowed to continue to exist as a state, must be reduced to a vassal state, must allow us to occupy any militarily important ports, must place her coast at our disposal in military respects, must become economically a German province. Given such a solution, which offers the advantages of annexation without its inescapable domestic political disadvantages, French Flanders with Dunkirk, Calais and Boulogne, where most of the population is Flemish, can without danger be attached to this unaltered Belgium. The competent quarters will have to judge the military value of this position against England.

3. *Luxemburg.* Will become a German federal state and will receive a strip of the present Belgian province of Luxemburg and perhaps the corner of Longwy.

4. We must create a *central European economic association* through common customs treaties, to include France, Belgium, Holland, Denmark, Austria-Hungary, Poland [sic], and perhaps Italy, Sweden and Norway. This association will not have any common constitutional supreme authority and all its members will be formally equal, but in practice will be under German leadership and must stabilise Germany's economic dominance over Mitteleuropa.

5. *The question of colonial acquisitions*, where the first aim is the creation of a continuous Central African colonial empire, will be considered later, as will that of the aims to be realised *vis-à-vis* Russia.

6. A short provisional formula suitable for a possible preliminary peace to be found for a basis for the economic agreements to be concluded with France and Belgium.

7. *Holland.* It will have to be considered by what means and methods Holland can be brought into closer relationship with the German Empire.

In view of the Dutch character, this closer relationship must leave them free of any feeling of compulsion, must alter nothing in the Dutch way of life, and must also subject them to no new military obligations. Holland, then, must be left independent in externals, but be made internally dependent on us. Possibly one might consider an offensive and defensive alliance, to cover the colonies; in any case a close customs association, perhaps the cession of Antwerp to Holland in return for the right to keep a German garrison in the fortress of Antwerp and at the mouth of the Scheldt.

In retrospect it is easy to recognise in the Chancellor's war aims objectives of pre-war German economic ambitions in Belgium, Luxembourg and Lorraine, now directly incorporated in official policy but intensified by the Mitteleuropa idea and given an anti-British twist. These economic motives overshadowed the strategic and maritime aims which were designed finally to break the ring round 'Fortress Germany', at the same time eliminating the two western great powers as future military opponents of Germany.

The realisation of this programme would have brought about a complete revolution in the political and economic power-relationships in Europe. After eliminating France as a great power, excluding British influence from the Continent and thrusting Russia back, Germany purposed to establish her own hegemony over Europe. If we concede that it is a statesman's duty, even in the midst of armed conflict, to conceive and to set before himself a dispassionate and imaginative picture of the world at peace, again, we cannot but ask ourselves uneasily whether Bethmann Hollweg's picture could have provided an adequate foundation for an enduring peace in Europe. The realisation of his programme would have broken the coalition of the three Entente powers, but if their association had seemed irksome even in time of peace, what replaced it would have been an order so restricting the positions of the three great powers—Britain, France and Russia—and the freedom of manoeuvre of the smaller nations of Europe, as infallibly to lay up a store of terrible explosive material for new conflicts; especially as the federative element was to be subordinated to Prusso-Germany's claim to lead and dominate.

Bethmann Hollweg himself saw—he wrote as much to Delbrück on September 16, only a week after drawing up the programme, and while the effects of the check on the Marne were still unclear—that the formation of a great central European economic unit under German leadership 'could not be brought about on the basis of agreement on common interests . . . but only under the pressure of political superiority, should we be in the position to dictate peace terms'.

The last part of this sentence shows that the Chancellor was already influenced by the reverse on the Marne. Nevertheless the special significance of the September Programme for the history of the development of Germany's intentions during the First World War lies in two points. First, it was no isolated inspiration of the Chancellor's: it represents the ideas of leading economic, political–and also military–circles. Secondly, the main ideas set forth in it remained, as we shall see, the essential basis of Germany's war aims right up to the end of the war, although modified from time to time to fit changing situations.

Finally, the Chancellor's ideas, far-reaching as they look to us today, were yet conceived as a programme of moderation, a check on the wave of annexationist feeling which had swept over all Germany after the military successes of August and September, and which was most significantly expressed in Class's memorandum.

Class's September Programme

At its first wartime session, on August 28, 1914, the Executive Committee of the *Alldeutscher Verband* laid down the principles of a pan-German war aims programme. These were printed at the beginning of September, over the signature of Justizrat Class, President of the *Verband*, and under the title of *Memorandum on German War Aims*.[1] Class agreed with Bethmann Hollweg on the Chancellor's central idea of a Mitteleuropa.

It is [he writes] an absolutely imperative demand, and widely accepted as such, that Mitteleuropa, inclusive of those areas to be acquired by the German Reich and Austria-Hungary as prizes of victory, must form one great, united economic unit. The Netherlands and Switzerland, the three Scandinavian States and Finland, Italy, Rumania and Bulgaria will attach themselves to this nucleus gradually and of compulsive necessity, without need of the least pressure from the nucleus-States. If one includes the dependencies and colonies of these States, the result will be a vast economic unit capable of asserting and maintaining its economic–political independence against any other in the world.

He thought that the aim of weakening the enemy economically could be achieved by imposing a war indemnity so high as to prevent it from becoming dangerous to Germany for many years.

In respect of direct annexations, east and west, Class went beyond Bethmann Hollweg. Like him, he wanted a grip maintained on Belgium, if only as a means of pressure on Britain; also Longwy-Briey and the French Channel coast to be detached from France; Class

[1] See Werner Kruck, *Geschichte des Alldeutschen Verbandes 1894–1944* (Wiesbaden, 1954), pp. 71 ff. Class's memorandum was later printed, with small alterations, as a pamphlet under the title *Zum deutschen Kriegsziel* (Munich, 1917).

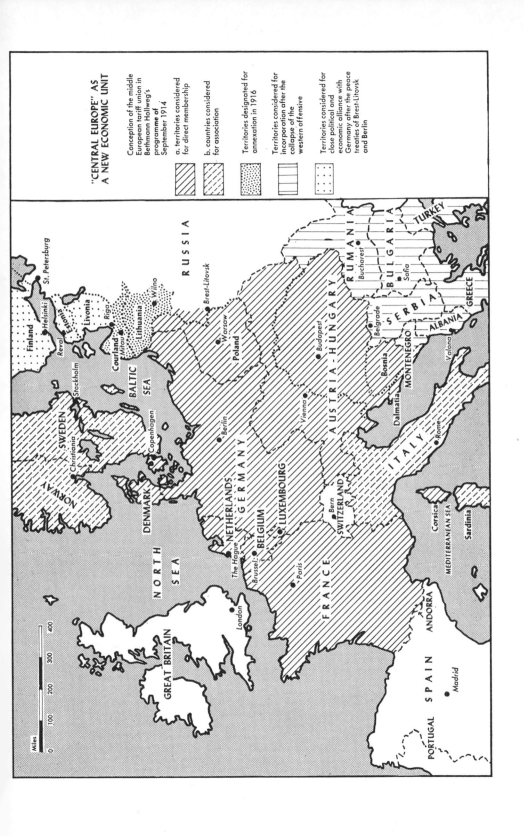

"CENTRAL EUROPE" AS
A NEW ECONOMIC UNIT

Conception of the middle
European tariff union in
Bethmann Hollweg's
programme of
September 1914

a. territories considered
for direct membership

b. countries considered
for association

Territories designated for
annexation in 1916

Territories considered for
incorporation after the
collapse of the
western offensive

Territories considered for
close political and
economic alliance with
Germany after the peace
treaties of Brest-Litovsk
and Berlin

wanted the ceded area to extend beyond Boulogne, down to the Somme. Class demanded not only Belfort, but the whole line of fortresses from there to Verdun, and also suggested making France cede Toulon to Germany as a fortified port – a proposal which Bethmann Hollweg, as we know his intentions, rejected as absurd – as he did another, brought forward by the pan-Germans, that Germany should annex Petersburg.

As regards the east, Class wrote that 'Russia's face must be forcibly turned back to the east and her frontiers must be reduced, approximately, to those of Peter the Great'. The territorial acquisitions which he demanded in the east, for strategic security and as fields of colonisation, were the Polish frontier districts, the Russian government of Lithuania and the Baltic Provinces. Official plans drawn up from December 1914 onwards, first with respect to the Polish Frontier strip and later to Lithuania and Courland, were along the same lines, if less extensive. Although Bethmann Hollweg always remained opposed to incorporating Livonia and Estonia (unless it should prove possible to detach Finland from Russia), yet by initiating his policy of border states he adopted a course which had in effect the same aim in a different form: the weakening of Russia and 'security' for Germany.

The Demands of German Industry

Class's ideas were endorsed by Krupp (who, it is true, retreated after the battle of the Marne to Bethmann Hollweg's somewhat more moderate line)[1] and also by Hugo Stinnes, who went still further and demanded the detachment from France of the iron and coal fields of Normandy. It was Stinnes who secured general acceptance of Class's ideas at a meeting of Germany's economic leaders convoked jointly by Class and Hugenberg in October, 1914, out of which there later developed the famous memorandum of the Six Economic Associations of March and May, 1915.

A long memorandum drawn up at the beginning of September, 1914 by the busy Zentrum politician, Matthias Erzberger, who had connections with the Disconto-Gesellschaft and was an *homme de confiance* of the Thyssen combine, also favoured big annexations in both east and west. Erzberger summarised Germany's principal aims in the war under three headings:

1. 'Elimination of the intolerable tutelage exercised by Britain over Germany in all questions of world politics.'

---

[1] On the following section cf. Kruck, op. cit. On Krupp's war aims programme, see Siegfried Boelcke, *Krupp und die Hohenzollern* (Berlin, 1956), pp. 147 ff. On Stinnes' programme, see below, p. 229.

2. 'Shattering the Russian colossus.'
3. Elimination of weak, 'allegedly neutral states' on Germany's frontiers.

To achieve these aims, Erzberger (in complete agreement with Bethmann Hollweg) demanded German military supreme control over Belgium and the French Channel coast from Calais to Boulogne; annexation of the whole minette field of Longwy-Briey; liberation of the non-Russian peoples 'from the Muscovite yoke' under German military supreme control; and the establishment of a kingdom of Poland under German sovereignty. Austria-Hungary was to expand in the Ukraine, Rumania and Bessarabia. He, too, dreamt of the creation of a great German central Africa from Dar-es-Salaam to Senegambia, to incorporate the Belgian and French Congos, Nigeria (from Britain), Dahomey and the African west coast (from France); he was in complete accord with Solf's official proposals. He also made detailed proposals for the imposition of a war indemnity high enough to cover all Germany's war damage and expenditure, and in addition to pay off the Reich's entire internal debt. But high as he pitched these requirements, Erzberger still regarded them as only 'the minimum which all sections of the German people should demand on the conclusion of peace'.

More extreme still was a memorandum by August Thyssen, which Erzberger conveyed to the government on September 9, 1914. This document demanded the incorporation of Belgium and the French departments of Nord and Pas-de-Calais with Dunkirk, Calais and Boulogne, the department of Meurthe-et-Moselle with the French belt of fortresses and the Meuse, and—in the south—the departments of Vosges and Haute-Saône with Belfort. In the east Thyssen wanted the Baltic provinces and perhaps the Don basin with Odessa, the Crimea, the Lvov area and the Caucasus. He justified his demands by the need to secure Germany's future reserves of raw materials. He was especially interested in the minette ores of Longwy-Briey, the Belgian coalfields, the iron of the Don basin and the manganese ore of the Caucasus. He too pleaded for a central European customs union. Thyssen's far-reaching dreams culminated in the idea of acquiring a land-bridge across south Russia, Asia Minor and Persia, whence to deal the decisive blow against the British Empire—the real enemy in this war—in India and Egypt. Only so did Thyssen see Germany's rise to world power status assured, and doubly so if her increased economic strength, as compared with her remaining competitor, Britain, was fed by new markets in a German central African colonial empire which included the French and Belgian Congos and Morocco.

Although Thyssen's plans, with their pan-German colouring and extensive demands for annexations, differed perceptibly from Bethmann Hollweg's ideas, and although the relationship between the two men was later to become one of open hostility, yet in respect of first aims their intentions coincided.

The important point, however, is that Thyssen was one of the most powerful industrialists, whose voice the government could not easily ignore.

The Government's Western War Aims

The heart's desire of the *Centralverband deutscher Industrieller* (i.e., in the first instance, the heavy industry of the Rhineland) – that the basis of Germany's supply of raw material should be extended through incorporation of the adjacent ore-fields of France and Belgium – harmonised with the Chancellor's aim of bringing those areas into direct or indirect dependence on Germany. One of the most specific German war aims during the First World War was the acquisition of the ore-field of Longwy–Briey. As early as August 26, 1914, Bethmann Hollweg had instructed Delbrück to ascertain the extent of the ore deposits of French Lorraine and of the participation of German capital in them.[1] Even before Delbrück's answer had come in, or the Chancellor's own programme of September 9 had been worked out, Freiherr von Dallwitz, Governor of the Reichslande (Alsace and Lorraine), forwarded to him the proposals of the leading Saar industrialist, Röchling. Röchling wanted the annexation of as much as possible of the Longwy–Briey basin, and Dallwitz extended this programme by demanding further the annexation of the western slopes of the Vosges and Belfort. On September 9, the day on which he sent his war aims programme to Delbrück, Bethmann Hollweg wrote to Dallwitz, who was a personal friend of his, thanking him for sending Röchling's proposals and assuring him that 'they seem to me very noteworthy and coincide with my own ideas'. The Chancellor also 'entirely agreed' with Dallwitz's own suggestions for advancing the frontier of Alsace-Lorraine in the Vosges and at Belfort. In fact, he incorporated this suggestion in his own programme.

In the following weeks Bethmann devoted further intensive study to the question of Germany's future frontier with France. On October 22 he wrote to Delbrück that it would be desirable to effect the

---

[1] See also Volkmann, 'Die Annexionsfragen des Weltkrieges' in *Das Werk des Untersuchungsausschusses der Verfassunggebenden Nationalversammlung und des deutschen Reichstages 1919–30*, series 4, Abt. II, Vol. 12 (Berlin, 1929), p. 35; Dallwitz's and Röchling's memoranda are also summarised shortly, ibid., p. 36.

incorporation of the Briey basin and 'the transference into German hands of its ore reserves', so as to make the French and Belgian industries dependent for their ore on Germany and thereby substantially weaken their competitive power. A litttle later, on November 17, he sent Delbrück his documentation on Longwy–Briey, including Thyssen's and Röchling's memoranda. He instructed Delbrück to prepare for the anticipated conclusion of peace with France, on the one hand, the 'maximum which we could wish for' and on the other, the 'minimum, being the least which we must secure'.[1]

The plans for the west were complicated by a bizarre idea of the Emperor's, repeatedly put forward by him in the hectic atmosphere of victory prevailing at General Headquarters before the reverse on the Marne–that the areas to be annexed from Belgium and France should be cleared (in the pan-German phraseology, 'made free of human beings') and then settled with 'deserving N.C.O.s and men'. The Chancellor's attitude towards this idea of the Emperor's is particularly instructive, for it led to a very concrete idea which was tenaciously pursued throughout the whole war, especially in the East:

I must admit [he writes to his deputy] that this idea is in many respects beguiling, but its execution will encounter many practical difficulties. Nevertheless, one might consider whether a formula might not be found in the preliminary peace imposing such an expropriation, up to a certain point, on the conquered state.

Finally, the Chancellor ordered 'the preparation of a draft' whereby the French government, on ceding Longwy–Briey to Germany, was to transfer the iron-works there to German ownership.

The second major specific German aim in the west was Belgium, and for this the Chancellor had settled his general line on September 9: Belgium was to be degraded to the status of a 'vassal state' of Germany. Since immediately after the battle of the Marne he was still counting on a German victory, and consequently on an early peace in the west, he gave Zimmermann in Berlin, on October 18, strictly secret instructions to examine in detail, with Delbrück, 'the possibilities . . . of a solution of the Belgian question'. 'The first of these,' he wrote, 'would be the restoration of Belgium as a tributary state, as far as possible independent in name, but in practice at our disposal, both militarily and economically.'

Zimmermann and Delbrück were instructed to examine the legal problems involved in such a solution, and to submit proposals from

[1] Volkmann, op. cit., p. 36. The Chancellor had already given a similar commission to Dallwitz on September 9, 1914.

their departments. The Chancellor was interested in 'finding forms which allow economic penetration without executive control and give us control of the coasts, fortresses and transport systems against the eventuality of further wars'. This last sentence touched on Belgium's key position in relation to Britain and at the same time brought out the strategic aspects of the Belgian coasts in the event of another war.

Zimmermann and Delbrück submitted a joint opinion on December 31. It contained a detailed programme for the military and economic control of Belgium as required by the Chancellor, but added a warning on the domestic and foreign political consequences for Germany.[1] Bethmann Hollweg, however, while rejecting as 'Utopian' extreme demands such as the direct annexation of all Belgium, was not to be deterred from his basic idea of establishing at least an indirect military and economic domination of the country.

The most important instrument for securing this indirect domination, after the economic and military provisions, was the Flemish policy. As early as September 2, 1914, Bethmann Hollweg wrote to the head of the civilian administration attached to the Governor-General of Belgium drawing his attention to the importance of the Flemish movement as a handle for securing political influence in Belgium, and as a possible basis for an understanding with Holland. On December 16 the Chancellor sent a detailed memorandum to the newly-appointed Governor-General of Belgium, General von Bissing, with 'definite and clear general principles for a German-Flemish policy', culminating in a plan for turning Ghent University into a purely Flemish university. Thereby Bethmann Hollweg indicated a course for German policy in Belgium which he himself followed very actively throughout the whole war. He was supported in this by von Bissing personally, and by the head of his Political Department, von Lancken, both of whom advocated and consistently endeavoured to bring about a long-term relationship between the two countries rather than a short-term exploitation of Belgium for war purposes.[2]

For a military opinion the Chancellor wrote on January 8, 1915, from Supreme Headquarters where he was then staying, to von Tirpitz, asking him for his views on the future of Belgium. He especially begged him, when making his proposals, to take into account not only the standpoint of his own department, but also 'quite generally,

[1] Id., pp. 193 ff.
[2] Cf. on this Tilt Frh. von Wilmowsky, *Rückblickend möchte ich sagen* . . . (Oldenburg and Hamburg, 1961), pp. 81 f.

that of Germany's future world power position'.[1] This is the first occasion, at least as recorded in the documents, when the man responsible for the policy of the Reich mentioned the programme of 'a future world power status' for Germany and, as his instructions to Tirpitz prove, was prepared to draw the consequences in framing his war aims policy.

Knowing Tirpitz's strongly anti-British feelings, we can readily understand that he joyfully adopted Bethmann Hollweg's slogan of Germany's 'world power position', which depended in his view on an impregnable German position on the Channel opposite England. He therefore wanted possession of the Belgian coast, with Antwerp, as a base, and the incorporation of Belgium in the German Empire 'no matter what the domestic difficulties'. This attitude *already* went beyond Bethmann Hollweg's ideas on Belgium, but Tirpitz went further still when he made Germany's world power status the criterion of a successful or unsuccessful war: 'If we fail to keep secure the possibilities of development offered in Belgium, I should regard the war, considered in relation to Germany's world power status, as lost; with Belgium, as won.'

In other words: Belgium had become the kernel of Germany's war aims policy in the west. Only thus we can explain how it came about that the leaders of Germany, while constantly changing their views on the possible forms under which Belgium could be drawn into the German sphere of interest, were never, up to the autumn of 1918 able to decide to relinquish it altogether.

The Government's Eastern War Aims

As for the west, so for the east, specific war aims emerged out of discussions in government circles during the very first months of the war. There are two threads in Germany's aspirations in the east: military–strategic and demographic–political considerations, which produced the aim of limited, direct annexations, while another school of thought aimed at weakening Russia generally by loosening its structure and dominating it economically, as a source of raw materials and as a market.

The course of military operations made Poland the first and most immediate object to enter the field of vision of German eastern policy, and thenceforward it occupies in that field a central position similar to that of Belgium in the West. It is true that the Polish problem was

[1] On November 15, 1914, Tirpitz told Falkenhayn in the course of a conversation on the employment of the fleet 'that we [the navy] had at first counted on the army's capturing Calais and the Channel ports very quickly'. Alfred von Tirpitz, *Deutsche Ohnmachtspolitik im Weltkriege, Politische Dokumente* (Hamburg and Berlin, 1926), p. 166.

complicated by domestic political factors connected with the Polish element in Prussia and, abroad, by the need to consider Germany's ally, Austria-Hungary.

The breach with Russia forced Germany to consider the possibility of detaching Congress Poland from Russia–a prospect which Bismarck had regarded, a generation earlier (when a preventive war against Russia was being discussed), as the disagreeable but unavoidable consequence of such an operation.[1] In 1906 Bethmann Hollweg, then still Secretary of State in the Reich Ministry of the Interior, had expressed to the Emperor views similar to Bismarck's but he had not regarded the restoration of an independent Polish state as undesirable–in which respect Bülow had disagreed with him strongly.[2] Bismarck in his day had envisaged connecting Poland, if detached from Russia, with the Danubian Monarchy under an Austrian archduke as king. The Austrians proposed the same course in the 'Austro-Polish solution' suggested by them only a fortnight after the outbreak of war; as compensation for the acquisition by themselves of Congress Poland, they offered their German ally 'frontier rectifications'.[3] On the German side, the Emperor had himself as early as July 31, 1914, a day before Germany declared war on Russia, given the German–Polish magnate Count Hutten-Czapski (a personal acquaintance of his) a non-binding assurance that the Polish state should be restored when Russia was defeated.[4] The imperial promise may have been vague, but the Imperial Chancellor confirmed it on the same day and five weeks later the idea of thrusting Russia back behind a chain of buffer states and including a Poland detached from Russia in Mitteleuropa appeared as the kernel of Bethmann Hollweg's war aims policy in the East. As another pointer in the same direction we may note that immediately on the outbreak of war this same Hutten-Czapski, who was a lieutenant-colonel in the Prussian army, was attached to the general staff in charge of Polish and Ukrainian questions. His first commission was to foment insurrection in Congress Poland by means which included the raising of a Polish Legion–the counterpart to Pilsudski's in Galicia–and the dissemination among the Poles of leaflets and cartoons to awaken sympathy for the Central Powers.

[1] Cf. on this Hermann Oncken, 'Preussen und Polen im 19. Jahrhundert', in *Deutschland und Polen, Beiträge zu ihrer geschichtlichen Entwicklung*, ed. Albert Brackmann (Berlin, 1933), pp. 231 f.

[2] Bernhard Fürst von Bülow, *Denkwürdigkeiten*, Vol. 2 (Berlin, 1930), pp. 245 f.

[3] The idea was born at the Congress of Vienna in 1813, when the 'Kingdom of Poland' was created within the Russian Empire.

[4] Graf Bogdan von Hutten-Czapski, *60 Jahre Politik und Gesellschaft*, Vol. 2 (Berlin, 1936), pp. 145 f.; also for next paragraphs.

A month later Hutten-Czapski was relieved of this commission but only, it would appear, because his sympathies were too strongly nationalist. After this the Imperial Chancellery was the planning centre for Germany's Polish policy. Bethmann Hollweg's closest collaborator, his Under-Secretary in the Chancellery, Arnold von Wahnschaffe, who, like Zimmermann, had stopped behind in Berlin, now became the key figure in this policy.

One of the most active 'eastern experts' was the former German consul-general in Warsaw, Freiherr von Rechenberg, who had pleaded for a re-orientation of Germany's Polish policy as early as Caprivi's chancellorship in 1890–4. On August 27, 1914, Wahnschaffe gave him formal instructions to draw up a memorandum on the future of Congress Poland.

Rechenberg assumed that Germany did not propose to make territorial acquisitions in Russian Poland, but that it would be essential for her to possess an eastern frontier more secure than her existing one. He proposed to combine these two requisites by inciting Congress Poland to revolt and constitute a new Polish state, which would then be united with Galicia and incorporated in the Habsburg monarchy as a new crown-land. He recommended that the new kingdom should consist of the ten 'governments' of Congress Poland, with Suwalki in the north, and also the western parts of the governments of Grodno, including the cities of Brest-Litovsk and Grodno; it should further extend northward through the western parts of the governments of Kovno and Courland to the southernmost tip of the Gulf of Riga, thus possessing an independent outlet to the sea. The eastern frontier of the new Poland would protect the eastern frontier of Germany–this idea, and the frontier proposed, obviously influenced Bethmann Hollweg's thinking, although the idea of extending Poland north-eastward was afterwards discarded in favour of other policies, first that of annexation to Germany herself, later that of establishing border states in the north-east.

In further correspondence with Wahnschaffe, Rechenberg mooted the idea of deporting some of the Poles of Posen and West Prussia and settling them in the new Polish state. Wahnschaffe asked whether there would be enough suitable land for them; Rechenberg said there was–on the Russian crown domains, the Tsar's estates and those which had been granted to Russian officers and officials. The idea of moving Prussian Poles to Congress Poland evolved in the course of the next months into the plan to establish the so-called Polish 'Frontier Strip' to 'secure' Germany's eastern frontier if Poland should be attached to Austria-Hungary, or become independent, or possibly be restored to Russia. The 'Frontier Strip', which was to run approximately along the Warthe–Narew line up to and including Suwalki, was now in its turn to be 'cleared' by deporting part of its Polish population and all its Jews.[1]

The motives behind the idea of the 'Frontier Strip" were very various: to get strategic security and facilitate the defence of the eastern provinces; to round off the Upper Silesian industrial area; to separate the Prussian Poles from their countrymen in a future Polish state by a Germanised 'frontier wall' and thus to isolate them; to acquire free land on which to settle Germans from Germany proper (*das Altreich*–the Old Territories) as well as families of German Russians brought back from Russia, especially from the Volga. This last consideration pointed to a transformation of the old Prusso-German patriotism into a neo-German racialist nationalism which, by withdrawing the outposts of 'Deutschtum', threatened to disrupt Eastern Europe's old political and ethnic frontiers.

While discussing the 'Frontier Strip' programme, the Chancellor had already hinted at his plans for limited annexation and deportation in a conversation with the Bavarian Prime Minister, Count Hertling, on December 2, 1914. On December 6, when paying his first visit to Hindenburg's Headquarters in Posen, he asked the field-marshal to state what modifications of Germany's eastern frontiers he thought desirable. Hindenburg afterwards denied in his memoirs that he had discussed questions of annexations with the Chancellor, but in fact he sent Bethmann Hollweg his view of the optimum frontier, with a detailed map, as early as December 11, receiving the Chancellor's grateful thanks two days later.

The 'Frontier Strip' project, which was a limited one compared with the policy based on the non-Russian nationalities and the creation of border states, is only to be understood with reference to the decision (taken by the Chancellor under the impact of the difficult general situation in late November and early December) to beat a political retreat on the eastern flank and seek a separate peace with Russia which would not, he hoped, be impeded by annexations on so limited a scale. But preoccupation with the idea of a 'Frontier Strip' idea made it necessary to clarify its extent and internal structure.

On the Chancellor's instructions Wahnschaffe had asked in the autumn and winter of 1914–15 for written appreciations from a whole series of senior administrative officials in the Prussian eastern provinces. The most vigorous advocate of a policy of annexations and colonisation proved to be Friedrich von Schwerin, *Regierungspräsident* of Frankfurt an der Oder. Schwerin belonged to the inner

---

[1] On the Polish frontier strip, see Imanuel Geiss, *Der polnische Grenzstreifen 1914–1918* (Hamburg and Lübeck, 1960).

circle of the high Prussian bureaucracy, but with his strong bent for politics and his 'völkisch' mentality he represented rather a type of German practical politician more characteristic of a later age. He was commissioned by the Imperial Chancellery some time around the turn of the year 1914–15 to work out for Bethmann Hollweg the principles to govern Germany's policy of annexations and settlement in the East. He submitted his first report to the Chancellor on March 25, 1915, and a second, still more detailed, on December 31. His central proposals were for the annexation of the Polish 'Frontier Strip' and of the provinces of Lithuania and Courland, in which he proposed to carry through an extensive settlement scheme with colonists from the interior of Germany and from Russia. The wealth of material in his memoranda made Schwerin the Chancellor's adviser-in-chief on problems of annexation and colonisation in the east. Further important suggestions were contributed in September, 1915, by his collaborator, Max Sering, the leading agrarian expert at Berlin University, in a report on an official journey made by him through the recently conquered territories in the east.

War Indemnity

Besides territorial and political war aims, a third aim of German policy emerged from the official discussions on the amount of the war indemnity to be imposed on the enemy: the aim of weakening Germany's neighbours by syphoning off as much as possible of their financial resources and transferring to them the burden of Germany's war expenditure.

As early as the end of August, 1914, the Chancellor invited Helfferich, the Director of the Deutsche Bank, to General Headquarters to discuss this problem, and on August 26 he instructed Delbrück to calculate 'how high a war indemnity France and Belgium would be able to pay'. On August 28, when the war had been in progress for only five weeks, Rathenau proposed demanding from France the sum of forty thousand million gold francs. In his war aims programme of September 9 the Chancellor laid down the general principle that the indemnity to be paid by France to Germany must be so high as to prohibit her from spending any considerable sums on armaments during the next eighteen to twenty years.

In order to gain a survey of the economic possibilities the Chancellor, in the middle of October, instructed Zimmermann and Delbrück to get in touch with the heads of the principal Berlin joint-stock banks, the Deutsche Bank, the Disconto-Gesellschaft, the Dresdner Bank, the Darmstädter Bank and the Berliner Handelsgesellschaft, and with the heads of the trusted private banking houses of Mendelssohn, Bleichröder and Warburg. He asked the banks for opinions in writing on war indemnities, expressly emphasising that the experts 'were not to confine themselves to naming large figures, but were to concern themselves primarily with the modalities of payment and with the security for it'. Bethmann Hollweg also considered the idea of requiring 'the transference to German hands of the British, French and Belgian-owned railway, harbour and mining concessions in the Near and Far East' in lieu of cash payments. New here, as compared with the September Programme, is Bethmann Hollweg's idea of imposing heavy financial demands on Belgium, Britain and Russia, as well as France: a logical expansion of the idea of crippling the enemy powers for the long term. The banks at once produced the required memoranda with detailed estimates of the financial capacities of the enemy powers and of the possibilities of exploiting them.

No 'Premature' Peace

Both German public opinion and Germany's leaders were fully resolved to overthrow all their enemies and dictate peace to them. Consequently, Germany could not think of making peace with only one enemy so long as the others were still undefeated and so long as Germany could still hope for total victory.

So much is apparent from Germany's reactions to the first attempt to mediate peace. When the battle of the Marne was at its height, President Wilson, expecting France's early military collapse, made tentative enquiries through Gerard, his ambassador in Berlin, on the possibility of Germany consenting to conclude peace with France on the basis of the territorial *status quo ante* in Europe, Germany being free to ask what war indemnity she liked from France and to take any French colonies she pleased. This was on September 9, the day on which Bethmann Hollweg drew up his war aims programme. Zimmermann rejected the approaches brusquely, answering:

Germany was completely determined to see the war followed by a lasting peace. This wish would certainly not be satisfied, as things stood at present, by a treaty on the pattern offered here; it presupposes rather a settlement of accounts, not with France alone, but also with Britain and Russia. Otherwise we should have . . . to reckon in a few years with another war with the Entente Powers, and this the German people was determined to avoid, after its present enormous effort.

In considering what weight to attach to Zimmermann's reference to 'the people' we must, of course, remember the extraordinary excitement of those weeks: he was also, presumably, paying some

deference to the American turn of mind. Nevertheless, his further remarks show how greatly things had changed in Germany since Bismarck's day, when foreign policy had been conducted without any
regard to the internal political position, and how strongly the German government now felt itself constrained by public opinion, by
the parties and the associations. It was to those great forces that the
Under-Secretary of State alluded when he went on to say that the
government 'simply would not dare, in the interest of its own existence, to entertain his, the ambassador's, doubtless friendlily-meant
suggestions'. Even had it so wished, the government could not at that
stage have survived had it renounced war aims in Europe.

Bethmann Hollweg accordingly completely approved Zimmermann's provisional reply, and on September 12 sent him instructions in this sense for his official answer:

We did not want the war; it was forced on us. Even if we defeat France,
Russia and England will still be in the field against us. . . . If we now
accepted an offer of mediation from America, this would only be interpreted
by our enemies as a sign of weakness, and not understood by our people. For
the people, which has made such sacrifices, wants guarantees for our security
and tranquillity.

Reports of attempted mediation by German–American banking
circles had been exploited by the anti-German press with the suggestion that the German government had initiated these moves. The
Chancellor energetically repudiated these rumours by declarations
in the German press, using to the public the same phraseology that
he had found for his answer to the American ambassador: he spoke
of 'safeguards' and 'guarantees', 'which the people must have for its
security and its future', 'to be protected against fresh wanton assaults
by its enemies' – the word 'future' extending the demand beyond the
formula used hitherto.

In the slogan 'guarantees' Bethmann Hollweg had found the word
by which he continued thereafter to attempt to reconcile, at home
and abroad, offensive war aims with the allegedly defensive character of the war. However the military situation changed, he and his
successors, Michaelis and Hertling, regularly used this slogan, in
constantly varying forms, to reject any return to the *status quo*.

The result of the battle of the Marne did not cause either the
Chancellor or the German people, from whom its military implications were concealed, to revise their war aims. Prince Hohenlohe,
the Austro-Hungarian Ambassador in Berlin, drew from a multitude
of observations the definite general impression that Germany was
solved 'to thrash France and England as soundly as possible', and
'Russia as soundly as the enemies in the west, or even more so'.

4

THE PROMOTION OF REVOLUTION

MEANS AND ENDS

WHILE the German armies were trying to overrun France in their first onset, the German government, in collaboration with the general staff, was working out a far-reaching programme of revolution which was directed equally against the British Empire and imperial Russia, although in the upshot it achieved immediate successes only in Russia, where it helped to set in motion a train of events of world-historical moment. These activities began immediately on the outbreak of war. They were at first a means of strategic warfare; they were intended, on the one hand, to delay the Russian deployment on Germany's eastern frontier and keep part of the Russian armies tied down by internal unrest, and on the other hand, to draw off part of the British fleet to overseas stations and make it difficult for France to raise recruits in her colonies.

The promotion of revolution as a means of warfare was an aspect of the war aim of breaking up the British and the Russian empires. The most vulnerable points of France and Britain seemed to be among their coloured colonial subjects, while Russia offered fields for subversion among her non-Russian peoples. The German authorities were determined from the first to exploit the weaknesses of the enemy coalition. But the promotion of independence of large parts of the British Empire, such as Egypt and India, was itself a German war aim in the wider sense, since Germany's rise to world power was thought to be dependent on the disintegration of the British Empire. So the Emperor asserted in a handwritten letter to the Emir of Afghanistan, drafted for him by Zimmermann:

It has long been . . . my wish to see *the Mohammedan nations independent* and to achieve for their states the maximum of free development. I am therefore *not only* immediately concerned to help the Mohammedan peoples in their struggle for independence, but I will support them in the future through My Imperial Government. . . . The community of interests which exists to-day between the German people and the Mohammedans will continue in being after the end of the war.[1]

[1] The countries described by the Emperor as 'groaning under the yoke of Britain and Russia' are Afghanistan, India, Baluchistan and Russia in Asia.

The Emperor as Revolutionary

The anti-British programme had its forerunners in ideas which had developed during the two decades of German world policy, and in pet ideas of the Emperor himself.

The Emperor–inspired by Max von Oppenheim's theories of the importance in world politics of the pan-Islamic movement–had already proclaimed himself the protector of over three hundred million Mohammedans in his famous Damascus speech of November, 1898. This claim must be seen in the light of Oppenheim's picture of the revolutionary possibilities which Islam would offer in the event of war with France, Russia and the British Empire. That Wilhelm accepted this picture is proved by the fact that he returned to it in two critical situations when war seemed imminent, in 1906 and 1908. 'The British', he wrote, 'had better realise that war with Germany means the loss of India, and therewith the World War'.[1]

At the decisive moment, on July 29, 1914 (before, that is, the outbreak of war), when a new crisis was blowing up–one which this time really did end in war–the Emperor at once reverted to this idea. A telegram had arrived from Constantinople expressing the unanimous wish of the German military mission and of General Liman von Sanders to return to Germany in the event of war; the Emperor wrote in the margin: 'Must stay there and also foment war and revolt against England. Doesn't he yet know of the intended alliance, under which he is to be Commander in Chief?!'

A day later, on July 30, the Emperor expressed his plan for general revolution against Britain in the east even more drastically in a marginal note to a telegram from Pourtalès, the German ambassador in Petersburg:

England must . . . have the mask of Christian peaceableness torn publicly off her face. . . . Our consuls in Turkey and India, agents, etc., must inflame the whole Mohammedan world to wild revolt against this hateful, lying, conscienceless people of hagglers; for if we are to be bled to death, at least England shall lose India.[2]

The hopes of revolutionising the Islamic world were by no means only private ideas of the Emperor's; they had behind them the whole weight of Germany's official policy–the continuation 'by other means' of the Eastern policy initiated in the mid-1890s. The German–Turkish alliance of August 2, 1914, was concluded with an eye to the unleashing of a pan-Islamic movement, which was to lead

[1] Bülow, *Denkwürdigkeiten*, Vol. I, pp. 197 f.; cf. also Hermann Oncken, *Das Deutsche Reich und die Vorgeschichte des Weltkrieges* (Leipzig, 1933), Vol. II, p. 619, n. 3.

[2] *DD*, II, No. 401, pp. 130 ff.

off with a 'Holy War'–which was in fact proclaimed by the Sultan-Caliph after Germany had brought Turkey into the war.

Turkey thereby acquired an important dual role in Germany's war strategy. Guardian of the Straits, with the duty of severing communications between Russia in the Black Sea and the western allies, and of exercising a constant threat against Russia's southern flank, she was also meant to act as a springboard from which Germany should attack Britain at her two most vulnerable points, India and Egypt.

The Agents of the Programme of Revolution

The subversive enterprises were directed from the Foreign Ministry, in collaboration with the Political Section in the reserve (*stellvertretende*) general staff. After Bethmann Hollweg and Jagow the most important figure in the Berlin Headquarters was the dynamic Under-Secretary of State, Zimmermann, whose conviction that Germany must bring down Britain and Russia simultaneously in the war made him the moving spirit of Germany's initiatives in East and West.

Zimmermann's career is typical of the generation which the years round 1910 brought into leading positions in Germany. He was born in 1864 in Marggrabowa, hard on the East Prussian frontier. His impressionable student years were those of the 1880s which were so important for the formation of German nationalism; he was only two years younger than Schwerin,[1] a man of ideas very similar to his own, who made his first mark at that time in connection with the foundation of the *Verein Deutscher Studenten* at Berlin University. After completing his legal studies he entered the foreign service and in 1897–1902, the years which saw the hectic beginnings of German 'world policy', was serving in various consulates in the Far East. At that time Bülow had lent him to Admiral Tirpitz, to help strengthen Germany's position in the Far East, where he duly imbibed the strongly emotional anti-British atmosphere of the German overseas and naval policy of those years. From 1905 on he was employed in the Political Department of the Foreign Ministry, becoming head of the department in 1910. The next year he was promoted Under-Secretary of State. The true source of his political influence was, however, the circumstance that during the first months of the war he was alone in Berlin, while the Chancellor and Jagow were at the Supreme Headquarters. More important still, Zimmermann, of all the civilians in high places, was the man best trusted by the Emperor, who found his abrupt and unconciliatory manner more sympathetic than the ways of either Bethmann Hollweg or Jagow, with neither of

[1] Cf., pp. 125 ff., 187 ff.

whom did he ever feel intimate. So it came about that on the Emperor's rare visits to Potsdam in 1915 and 1916 Zimmermann, although still only Under-Secretary, was summoned sooner and more often to the Neues Palais for intimate political consultations than his superiors, the Chancellor or the Secretary of State.

His opposite number was the head of the Political Section in the reserve general staff, Rudolf Nadolny,[1] another East Prussian. He was a member of the Foreign Ministry whom von Falkenhayn had invited to fill this post at the outbreak of war, and was a man of similar metal to Zimmermann, if somewhat more obliging. For work on the Islamic world Resident Minister (retired) Freiherr Max von Oppenheim was recalled to the Foreign Ministry on August 2, 1914, immediately war broke out. Oppenheim, who had worked in the East as diplomat and scholar, was by his whole career[2] predestined to take a leading part in Germany's revolutionary activities in the Near East. As early as July 5, 1898, when attaché at the German consulate-general in Cairo, he had written a long memorandum on the possibilities of mobilising the pan-Islamic movement in the interest of Germany's then embryonic eastern policy. A short account of his own revolutionary activities, which he had included in his documents, had inspired the Emperor to his Damascus speech. Oppenheim maintained that Islam was experiencing 'a renaissance of power and vitality' which was producing repercussions in Russia-in-Asia and in north-western India. Islam was turning against the alliance between Christendom and European colonial policy and meant to shake off the Christian domination over Mohammedan countries. He drew attention to the pan-Islamic idea which was transcending all national distinctions and uniting all Arabs to the religious fraternity of the Senussi with its potent influence in North Africa and

[1] Rudolf Nadolny, *Mein Beitrag* (Wiesbaden, 1955), contains a short account of the author's activities as revolutionary, pp. 39 ff.

[2] It was only a little while after his entry into the Prussian State Service in 1883 that Oppenheim began his extensive travels through the Islamic countries of the Mediterranean, Spain and Morocco. Further explorations took him from the Atlantic to the Ganges (1891, Syria and Mesopotamia; 1894–6, Constantinople and Asia Minor). He studied Arabic and Islam in Cairo. In 1896 the German government put him in charge of an expedition to the Lake Chad area, to secure it for Germany. From 1896–1910 he served as Attaché to the Consulate-General in Cairo. After resigning from the Foreign Service he carried out further explorations and excavations of the Hittite city of Tel Halaf. On August 2, 1914, he was recalled to the Foreign Ministry, where he started and directed the 'Information Service for the East'. In 1915 he was sent to Constantinople (information from the Political Archive of the Foreign Ministry). Cf. also Ulrich Gehrke, *Persien in der deutschen Orientpolitik während des I Weltkrieges* (Hamburg dissertation) in *Darstellungen zur Auswärtigen Politik*, Vol. I, ed. Herbert Krüger (Stuttgart, 1960), Vol. II, p. 11, n. 13. According to this work, Oppenheim knew the Arabic parts of the Turkish Empire well, but not Persia, Afghanistan or India, so that 'the German government . . . was certainly not adequately and reliably advised on those countries'.

Arabia, and finally to the Jehad or Holy War. 'Even today its proclamation, after the Mohammedan people had been properly prepared,
would have incalculable effects.'

It was Oppenheim who, in another long memorandum of September, 1914, gave definite shape and direction to the plans for the
various enterprises. Taking up his ideas of 1898, he recommended
the Holy War and pan-Islamic propaganda as the most effective
weapons for revolutionising the Islamic world, and as a first step he
proposed that expeditionary forces should be sent to Persia and
Egypt. These proposals were taken so seriously that on December 12,
1914, Zimmermann ordered that all telegrams dealing with the revolutionary programme in the East should be shown to Oppenheim.

Oppenheim's colleague and the most important propagandist of
Germany's eastern policy was Ernst Jäckh, at that time professor of
Turkish History at Berlin University and an active publicist of
Liberal tendencies.[1] Among other activities he had worked with
Matthias Erzberger in the *Nachrichtenstelle für Auslandsdienst* (Information Office for Foreign Countries), set up at the outset of war to
expand Germany's propaganda activities abroad. As a member of
Bethmann Hollweg's circle of intimates, Jäckh enjoyed the advantage, both before and during the war, of being allowed on occasions
to expound his ideas to the Emperor. At the beginning of 1915 he
submitted a long report on Germany's subversive activities in the
East to date. He was several times sent on special missions to Constantinople, which was the most important advanced post for the
revolutionising of the Near East and Africa, and also of the Caucasus
and south Russia.

The experienced ambassador in Constantinople, Freiherr von
Wangenheim, was entirely in accord with the line of imperial world
policy, as represented by Zimmermann. Wangenheim's personal
conduct of his office in Constantinople has often been criticised as
too easy-going, but he strongly supported the revolutionary activities; indeed, he complained with point and emphasis that they
ought to have been better prepared before war broke out. His greatest personal achievement in the field was to discover the German–
Russian revolutionary Alexander Helphand, who wrote under the
pseudonym of Parvus. Wangeheim had him sent to Berlin and put
on the job of 'undermining' Russia.

Very important for the Russian field, especially the Ukraine, was
the Baltic German Paul Rohrbach, a friend of Jäckh and Friedrich

---

[1] See Ernst Jäckh, *Der goldene Pflug, Lebensernte eines Weltbürgers* (Stuttgart, 1954);
this work, however, contains no mention of the author's role as a leading revolutionary.

Naumann. Hans Delbrück, the editor of the *Preussische Jahrbücher*, who began in the mid 1890s to take an increasing interest in German–Russian relationships,[1] had commissioned the young Rohrbach to make a systematic tour of Russia and the Near East and to report his own observations on internal conditions in the Tsarist Empire. These impressions engendered in Rohrbach views which made him, with Theodor Schiemann, Johannes Haller and other Baltic Germans living in the Reich, a leading exponent of the idea of dismembering Russia by forcing her back to the frontiers which were hers before Peter the Great, and thus permanently weakening her. He regarded the Ukraine, being the richest part of Russia, as the best jumping-off point for a policy of border states.

Here too the official policy of the German Reich was even more important than the propagandist activities of Rohrbach and his friends. The most active worker in the Russian field, with Zimmermann, was the minister Diego von Bergen.[2] He was chiefly concerned with mobilising Russian revolutionaries belonging to the radical wing of the Socialists in Russia itself.

Another important figure was the relatively youthful legation secretary von Wesendonck,[3] the promoter-in-chief of revolution among the peoples of the border areas of the Russian Empire. No better testimony can be paid to the grand scale of his activities, and the high importance which was attached to them, than the fact that the Baltic Baron Uexküll, whom the Foreign Ministry had comissioned to organise the 'League of Russia's Foreign Peoples',[4] said in a letter of thanks which he wrote to Wesendonck on May 8, 1916, that the German Reich ought to erect two monuments in recognition of his services: one on the northernmost point of Finland, the other on the southernmost point of the Caucasus.

Hardly less important than these men in the Wilhelmstrasse were three of the Reich's Heads of Missions in neutral countries: Freiherr von Romberg in Berne, Count Brockdorff-Rantzau in Copenhagen

[1] See Paul Rohrbach, *Um des Teufels Handschrift* (Hamburg, 1953), pp. 18 ff.; cf. also the reports in the *Preussische Jahrbücher*, 1896–7; also in book form as *In Turan und Armenien auf den Pfaden russischer Weltpolitik* (Berlin, 1897).

[2] Diego von Bergen (1872–1943) entered the Foreign Ministry at the age of 23 from the university. After a year as Secretary of Legation in Pekin and three years in Brussels he worked from 1906 to 1911 under the German Minister to the Vatican. He was then recalled to the Foreign Ministry where he was employed from 1911 to 1919. From 1919 to 1943 he was Minister to the Vatican.

[3] Otto Günther von Wesendonck (1885–1933) entered the Foreign Service in 1908. After short spells in London, Brussels, Constantinople and Tangiers, he left the state service in 1914 in consequence of having married a Portuguese wife. On the outbreak of war he was re-employed in the Political Department of the Foreign Ministry.

[4] See *infra* (pp. 145 f.).

and Freiherr Lucius von Stoedten in Stockholm. Their missions, with the embassy in Constantinople, constituted the nerve-centres of the network of informers and agents with which Germany covered the whole Russian Empire, and they devoted a large part of their energies to furthering Germany's programme of revolution. These diplomats expressed their views on important questions in extensive despatches which not infrequently influenced headquarters in Berlin by suggesting courses which were in fact adopted later.

The Islamic World

Berlin entertained great hopes of provoking a large-scale revolution in India.[1] As early as August 2, Moltke had written to the Foreign Ministry putting forward an idea which, embittered by Britain's declaration of war, he repeated on August 5, very sharply, in a memorandum from the general staff to the Foreign Ministry: 'Revolution in India and Egypt, and also in the Caucasus . . . is of the highest importance. The treaty with Turkey will make it possible for the Foreign Office to realise this idea and to awaken the fanaticism of Islam'.

Agents, especially Indian students, were sent to their homes to help kindle revolution, and contact was established with Indian princes. The signal for the revolution was to be given by an invasion by the Emir of Afghanistan, who was said to be passionately desirous of marching into India.[2] A series of expeditions was sent to Persia to make contact with the Emir[3] In Persia, the northern half of which was under Russian occupation and the southern under British, and which had declared official neutrality, the legal position of the German expeditions was particularly dubious and their freedom of movement consequently limited. The isolated parties of Germans were unable to achieve their objective of making contact with Afghanistan, still less of drawing it into war with India and thereby initiating revolution against the British rule there.

During the whole war Germany tried to secure Persia as an ally and to induce her to enter the war by extending the Holy War to the Shiites, from their spiritual centre in Baghdad. These efforts were at their most intensive in the autumn and winter of 1915, when the

[1] Oppenheim had already suggested the basic idea on August 18, 1914, in a memorandum to the Chancellor: 'It will not be until the Turks enter Egypt and the fires of revolt flame up in India that England will be ripe for destruction.'

[2] The first memorandum on this subject was written by Reichenau to the Foreign Ministry on August 24, 1914, after the arrival of the Swedish explorer Sven Hedin. Cf. also Gehrke, op. cit., I, 23.

[3] Gehrke, op. cit., I, pp. 21 ff.; von Niedermayer, Klein, Wassmuss and Hetig were among the emissaries. See Werner Otto von Hentig, *Mein Leben eine Dienstreise* (Göttingen, 1962).

German government was pressing Persia to conclude a formal treaty, under which she should pledge herself to attack Britain and Russia with all her available forces, and over and above this 'to win over the neighbouring states of Afghanistan, Bokhara and Khiva' (the two last-named being Islamic territories under Russian rulè). In return, Germany declared herself ready to give an 'assurance' that in the event of a favourable issue to the war, she would support the independence and sovereignty of Persia, and promised to supply her with officers, arms and munitions and with a loan of thirty million marks. Persia was not, however, prepared to accept so vague an assurance; the Shah and his Prime Minister demanded instead a full 'guarantee of the territorial integrity and political independence of Persia'.

Wangenheim strongly recommended acceding to these wishes in the form of a collective guarantee by Germany, Austria-Hungary and Turkey. No such treaty was, however, ever concluded, although Germany, working in collusion with the nationalist party, used every possible means of influencing the government, parliament and press of the deeply divided country under the slogan of guaranteeing the liberation of the peoples from the Russo-British yoke.

In spite of all these efforts Germany was unable to secure Persia's entry into the war. Nevertheless she achieved a position of great influence in Teheran, strong enough to keep Persia neutral.

Besides his diplomatic and propagandist activities, the German chargé d'affaires in Teheran organised certain adventurous enterprises with the help of German and Austrian prisoners of war to foment unrest in the interior of Russia and to blow the bridges of the Trans-Siberian Railway.[1] More systematic attempts were made to sabotage the oil wells and installations of the Anglo-Persian Oil Company in Abadan from across the neighbouring Turkish frontier, when they were either to be taken over by Germany, as Ballin had proposed and the Army High Command (*Oberste Heeresleitung – OHL*) and the Foreign Ministry agreed at the end of 1914, or at least rendered useless. All these enterprises had to be abandoned when the Turkish and German forces, after initial successes, were driven out of Baghdad by superior British and Indian forces.

A German–Turkish operation against the Suez Canal, which was months in the preparing and was regarded in Berlin with extravagant hopes as 'a mortal blow against Britain's position', came nearer to succeeding. The first task given to Turkey had been to take the offensive in the Caucasus, in order to relieve the Russian pressure on Austria-Hungary. But the Germans thought it even more important that Turkey should undertake an offensive against the Suez Canal,

[1] Cf. Gehrke, op. cit., I, pp. 137 f.

if only in the form of a 'raid' by 20,000 or 30,000 Turkish troops, supported by German money, arms and war material, which should start a rebellion in Egypt against British rule. Even Berlin thought a rebellion unlikely in default of some such external stimulus. If, however, the Turks appeared on the Canal, Jäckh, for example, prophesied in January, 1915, that they would 'be joined by 70,000 Arab nomads'.

In preparation for the German undertaking in Egypt, the German embassy in Constantinople had been in touch since the beginning of August, 1914 with the Khedive of Egypt, at whose disposal it had placed 4 million gold francs. The object of the operation, as defined by Zimmermann on August 25 in his instructions to Wangenheim, was 'the destruction of British rule in Egypt'. As a first stop Zimmermann recommended the despatch of agents to incite the populations and native armies in Egypt and the Sudan against Britain by means which included spreading reports that the Sultan-Caliph would be joining the war against Britain in the near future. The German plan of campaign included liquidating the British corps of officers in the Egyptian army and, above all, blocking the Suez Canal, and demolishing locks and waterworks, telegraph offices, railway bridges, barracks, port installations, etc., in Suez, Port Said and Alexandria.

When the Turks objected to the military difficulties of the operation, Zimmermann, in Berlin, urged them at least to send mule and camel detachments against the Suez Canal; for the revolt in Egypt had to be brought about 'under all circumstances'. The Foreign Ministry gave Turkey £100,000 to induce her to act, and further financial support was promised when the operation was set on foot. Subsidiary difficulties were caused by the rivalry between Liman von Sanders and Enver Pasha, and between the latter and the Khedive, over the question of who should be in command of the operation. The Egyptians regarded the prospect of Turkish troops entering their country with mixed feelings, fearing to find British rule succeeded by a return to the old subjection to Turkey.[1]

The revolt in Egypt never broke out, because the British transferred the native army to the Sudan and sent British and Indian units to the Suez Canal; these then repelled the two attempts made by the Germans and Turks to capture the Canal.

The next field of action for German policy was Arabia. German operations here were to be based on Damascus, with forward stations in Jiddah and Medina. For this purpose new German consulates

---

[1] The German troops were commanded by the Bavarian Lt.-Col. Kress von Kressenstein, who was afterwards General Commanding the German expedition to the Caucasus.

were established in these cities, with the further task of winning over the Arab tribal chiefs, whose allegiance to the Sultan-Caliph was only loose and often uncertain, and also to penetrate across the Red Sea into the Anglo-Egyptian Sudan. The Germans devoted special pains to wooing the Sherif of Mecca, the spiritual overlord and guardian of the Holy places of Islam, and they succeeded for a while, but only for a while, in persuading him to take over propaganda for Germany in Mecca and Medina.

The political situation in Arabia was particularly complicated, because the two most powerful tribal chiefs, Ibn Saud, the founder later of the present kingdom of Saudi Arabia, and Ibn Reshid, were at permanent feud with one another. Under German and Turkish influence, Ibn Saud did at first offer an armistice; later, however, he went right over into the British camp. The Germans and Turks were successfully opposed here by the legendary 'Lawrence of Arabia'. British military successes at Baghdad and the circumstance that Britain, unlike Germany, was able to promise the Arabs complete independence, explain why British policy was more effective than German in Arabia.

In the hope of supporting the German operations conducted from Palestine against the Suez Canal and Egypt an attempt was made to incite the Senussi to invade Egypt from Libya. This was Enver Pasha's particular pet idea, and he sent agents to the Senussi to work them up. But the plan of mobilising the Senussi gave rise to a series of political complications. They had been the backbone of the resistance to the conquest of their country by Italy in 1911, and in 1914 there was still much tension between them and their new colonial masters. Austria-Hungary, in particular, therefore feared that instigation of the Senussi might prove the last straw in driving Italy, whose neutrality was already wavering, into the arms of the Entente. Germany and Turkey tried to dispel these fears, and believed themselves in a position to guarantee that if the Senussi rose in a Holy War, they would turn their arms only against Britain. Turkish and German agents, some of whom had most adventurous experiences in reaching Libya, wooed the Senussi for months but failed to persuade them to intervene effectively, even after Italy's entry into the war in 1915 had removed the necessity of considering her feelings.

The Germans also planned to reach out beyond Egypt, and to raise the Anglo-Egyptian Sudan against British rule. The reports on the preparations for this expedition show that it was to have advanced from the Sudan into central Africa, accompanied by German colonial administrators. For this purpose Jagow sent the German explorer, Leo Frobenius, to Abyssinia. He instructed the German minister 'to use every means to induce Abyssinia to intervene against England'. The minister was authorised to promise the Abyssinian government Germany's support for territorial acquisitions in the region of the Blue Nile; the imperial government would regard favourably any extension of Abyssinian power in this direction, provided it was done without injuring Italy's colonial territories or spheres of influence. The possibility of bringing Abyssinia into the war on the German side to help raise the Sudan collapsed with the failure of the plans to promote revolution in Egypt, but the plans show that the German government was aiming at establishing a bridge to carry German influence from the Near East to the goal of 'German Central Africa'.

Germany's revolutionary activities covered the whole of North Africa as far as Casablanca and were thus directed also against the French colonial empire, where it was hoped to raise the Arabs and Berbers against France. The brothers Mannesmann in the German consulate in Tripoli made use of their existing business connections to make contact with the Senussi and also with the east Algerian Kaid, Mohammed Brali, whose influence was considerable in the border regions between Tripolitania and Algeria. The Kaid agreed to the German plan, the aim of which was that French troops should be tied down by operations undertaken by him on the Mediterranean coast. The German government hoped that here, as in Egypt, a rebellion once started would spread to other tribes.

The pre-conditions for German agitation were more favourable in north-western Africa, and in particular in the coastal areas, than in any other part of the Islamic world, for here the traditional resistance of the tribes to French colonial rule was already stiffened by awakening aspirations for national self-determination. 'The Mohammedans of Algiers and Tunisia,' wrote Oppenheim, 'are filled with hatred against France and long for liberation.' He, and with him the Foreign Ministry, concluded that West Africa as a whole was now ripe for revolution. The event proved that these hopes were premature.

In Morocco too German policy was able to link up with old connections dating from before the war. The Germans' earlier attempts to enlist the help of native princes against France's penetration of Morocco had created personal relationships which were revived and intensified when war began. As before the war, the German consulate-General in Barcelona was the central clearing station for German shipments of arms to Morocco. Similarly, Madrid was the centre of the German agitation which used Spanish Morocco as a jumping-off place for raising French Morocco. Another way of weakening France's position in North Africa was to instigate desertions from the French Foreign Legion; in August, 1914, the Emperor issued an amnesty to all returned legionnaires.

A survey of the campaign to raise the Islamic world, from Lahore to Casablanca, at the beginning of the war leaves a divided impression. On the one hand there are grandiose ideas, circulating in categories and dimensions of world policy and universal history. The vehicles of these ideas are the official political organs of the Reich, working in close collaboration with the general staff. Behind them there stood also private interests, whose pre-war connections were now skilfully utilised by the government: associations, newspapers, individuals; the *Verband Deutscher Handlungsgehilfen* (Society of German Commercial Staff), the *Kölnische Volkszeitung*, the *Welt am Montag*, the brothers Mannesmann, Emil Kirdorf, Regendanz, the liaison man between the Imperial Colonial Office and the banks, the chief mover behind the scenes of policy in Morocco, and the busy Paul Rohrbach. On the other hand, the actual means and persons employed in the field bore no relation whatever to the high-flown expectations, either as regards the immediate aim of relieving the military position of the Central Powers or the long-term aim of effecting a fundamental change in the power-relations of the world: they were totally inadequate, and the effect produced by them was practically nil.[1] As in the conduct of the campaign in Europe, so here, Germany greatly over-estimated her own and her allies' potential strength, and fatally underestimated the enemy's power of resistance.

Ireland

Germany's subversive activities include also an attempt to create difficulties for England on her doorstep through an armed rising in Ireland. Here, too, Germany could build on a situation of traditional conflict which in the years before the war had reached the verge of open rebellion. The initiative came this time from German–Americans and the pan-German consul-general in New York, Falcke. The German ambassador in Washington, Count Bernstorff, raised objections to Falcke's proposals, since he feared that such an attempt would give the politically and culturally dominant English element in the United States its chance to prejudice the United States against Germany. In spite of these warnings, the German government had

[1] How almost naïve were the ideas with which the German statesmen approached the task of promoting revolution is shown, for example, by Jagow's instructions of November, 1914, which contain the words: 'bearer of these instructions, Herr Leo Frobenius, has orders to collaborate with Turkey in raising the Sudan in revolt. It would be very valuable if the Abyssinian government would give this enterprise active support.'

Sir Roger Casement brought from New York to Germany, where he raised the hopes of both the political and the military authorities in the prospects of a rising in Ireland. The circumstances of Casement's landing from a German submarine on the coast of Ireland, his arrest and execution, are as familiar as is the history of the Easter Rebellion in Dublin. It is, however, important for our purposes to note that here too Germany greatly over-estimated her strength. The attempt to revolutionise Ireland is a also a particularly clear example of the nexus between methods of warfare and war aims; on the one hand, Germany's western front was to be relieved by an attack on England's base and on the other, the British Empire was to be weakened by the detachment of one of its members. The Germans were attempting to utilise the crisis of the world war to help existing national aspirations to fruition in their own right

The Nationalities in the Russian Empire

Favourable fields for Germany's subversive activities in Russia were offered by the national movements of the non-Russian peoples from Finland to the Caucasus and by the aggravated social problem created by rapid industrialisation. Both social and the national grievances had found explosive vent in the revolution of 1905–6 and both had since continued to work in inseparable combination. The failure of the Russian revolution had further produced a great wave of emigration, which had spread all over Europe. When world war broke out the German government could at once turn to the Russian émigrés as agents for revolutionising Russia.

The Foreign Ministry had begun its preparations for the 'liberation' of Poland at the end of July, even before the outbreak of actual hostilities. As early as August 5, 1914, Jagow told the German ambassador in Vienna that 'our troops are carrying in their pockets proclamations for the liberation of Poland'. On August 3 Zimmermann telegraphed instructions to the German embassy in Constantinople that the Caucasus was to be raised against Russia. At the same juncture the Foreign Ministry was thinking of producing revolution among the Letts of Courland, but the general staff rejected the idea as militarily undesirable. On August 6 the Chancellor instructed the German minister in Stockholm, von Reichenau, to investigate a revolt in neighbouring Finland, promising the Finns 'an autonomous buffer State (Republic)'. Thus by August 6, only a week after the declaration of war, Germany's plans for revolutionising the East from Finland to the Black Sea had been laid.

It was in this connection that the Chancellor first sketched out his idea of Germany's New Order in the East, a month before his September Programme. The 'principles' for the leaflets to be circulated in Finland were, according to Bethmann Hollweg's instructions, to describe Germany's war aims in the East openly as 'liberation and security for the peoples subjugated by Russia, Russian despotism to be thrown back on Moscow'. The Ukrainian question also made its appearance at the beginning of August. Revolution was openly acknowledged as a means of warfare and as an aim of war, a fact admitted at the time by the leading German statesmen themselves. Instructions of August 11, 1914, from the Chancellor to the German embassy in Vienna, drafted by Jagow, are revealing on this point. They define the aims of German policy in the following words:

> To produce revolution, not only in Poland but also in the Ukraine, seems to us very important:
> 1. As a means of warfare against Russia,
> 2. Because should the war end favourably for us the creation of several buffer states between Russia and Germany and Austria-Hungary would be desirable as a means of relieving the pressure of the Russian colossus on western Europe and thrusting Russia back to the east, as far as possible.
> 3. Because, in Rumania's view, the recovery of Bessarabia for Rumania would only be profitable and lasting if it were protected by the formation of other non-Russian states.

It was thus not only at Brest-Litovsk in 1918, not only after its alleged capitulation before the Third Army High Command under Ludendorff and the pan-Germans, that the German government first conceived the idea of creating an independent Ukrainian state; as early as the second week of the war it had declared the detachment of the Ukraine from Russia to be an official object of German policy, and it preserved this long-term aim for the eventuality of a German dictated peace. In the further diplomatic exchanges between Berlin and Vienna in connection with the attempts to induce Turkey, Bulgaria and Rumania to enter the war, all three states were told that it was a war aim of the two Central Powers to force back Russia's frontiers. Berchtold told the Bulgarian government on October 17, 1914, and the Turkish at the beginning of November: 'Our main aim in this war is to weaken Russia enduringly, and for that reason we should, in the event of our victory, welcome the establishment of an independent Ukrainian State'. On both occasions the German Foreign Ministry associated itself with the Austro-Hungarian step by parallel *démarches* in Sofia and Constantinople.

The German government could count on widespread approval in Germany for its plans to detach the peripheral non-Russian peoples from the Tsarist Empire. The *Alldeutsch* circles close to them were as much in favour of these plans as, for different reasons, were the parties of the Centre and the groups on the left – Social Democracy's anti-Tsarist complex had been an important element in its decision not to oppose the war. The extension of German influence far into Russia was a central feature of the *Alldeutsch* programme, although it laid more weight on direct annexations than did the Liberals. The extensive memorandum drawn up by the Zentrum politician, Matthias Erzberger, in September, 1914, had contained, besides far-reaching aims for the West and a Mitteleuropa programme, the following war aim for the East: 'Liberation of the non-Russian peoples from the Muscovite yoke and establishment of internal self-government for each people. All this under German military supremacy, perhaps also with a Customs Union.'

Erzberger's final aim was 'to cut Russia off from both the Baltic and the Black Sea'. Helmut von Gerlach, later a leading pacifist, wrote an article in the *Welt am Montag* of August 17, 1914, 'Necessity knows no Law' (*Not kennt kein Gebot*), calling for the liberation of the non-Russian peoples, the Finns, Estonians, Letts, etc., down to the Mohammedan peoples of Russian-Asia, by promoting revolution in Russia and the Islamic world.

The Caucasus

The most distant of all the objects of German agitation were the Turkomans beyond the Caspian, who were to be subverted from Teheran.[1] Here the Germans had at first little success, but after the Bolshevik revolution of October, 1917, these areas detached themselves temporarily from Russia and anti-Bolshevik groups in them sought German support.

In the Caucasus area the Turks tried to influence the Mohammedan tribes, while the Germans addressed their agitation in the first instance to the Christian Georgians, among whom the revolution of 1905 had evoked revolts and separatist movements aimed at recovering old lost freedoms. As recently as 1912 there had been sporadic outbreaks of unrest in Georgia; Theodor Schiemann had pointed to them as indications of Russia's internal weakness, but had over-estimated their importance. The suppression of the revolution had driven a number of Georgian political leaders into exile. All of them saw in the outbreak of world war their people's chance to recover its independence. They early found support from Germany and – much more hesitantly – from Turkey. Georgian émigrés of the most various schools of thought formed joint political committees in Berlin, to which Armenians later adhered. Prince Machabelli,

[1] See Gehrke, op. cit., I, pp. 136 ff. There is much archival material.

Tseretelli, the brothers Kereselice and others helped in this work, some of them sacrificing their private fortunes to it. German policy enlisted their national ambitions in its service, and as time went on the Georgians became increasingly dependent on Germany.

The Georgians asked for a binding promise that an independent Georgian state should be recognised if the war ended in victory, and the German government was prepared to give this assurance. But the Turks refused, because the creation of an independent Georgian state would have blocked their own planned expansion and annexations in the Caucasus; moreover, the Georgians, as a Christian people, would have posed a problem similar to that posed by the Armenians on both sides of the Turkish frontier. German diplomacy, however, put such strong pressure on the Turks that in the summer of 1915 they too gave the guarantee for which the Georgians asked, although in a somewhat non-committal form.[1]

The plans of the Georgian émigrés were set out in a memorandum drawn up by Prince Machabelli in September, 1914. His plan envisaged a neutral Caucasian Federation, with Georgia a kingdom under a west European prince, the Armenian and Tatar districts under a Mohammedan prince, while the so-called mountain peoples were to be under a ruler chosen by themselves. Machabelli's idea of a tripartite federative state was in fact realised, although in a different shape, after the Russian February revolution.

Besides the Committee in Berlin, a secret Committee of Action was constituted in Tiflis, composed of representatives of the three major Georgian parties, the Social Democrats, the Federalists and the Nationalists. The Azerbaijanians, although non-Christians, joined this committee. On German initiative a Georgian Legion was formed in Trebizond, on Turkish soil, under a German captain, Count von der Schulenberg, but after endless friction with the Turks it had to be disbanded. It never numbered many members.

The revolutionary movement in the Caucasus, like that in Turkey, depended in the last instance on a successful advance by the Turks. But the Turkish offensive in the Caucasus broke down in the autumn of 1914. The Germans could thus in the end do no more than take some individual agents, including Machabelli, in submarines and set them on shore near Batum. The country being occupied by Russian troops and under strict control, the agents understandably found the local populace, which had had experience enough of the pains of unsuccessful revolution, little inclined to rise in arms.

Although Germany's endeavours to stir up revolution in the

[1] The document in question, which was filed in the German embassy, was signed, not by the Grand Vizier or Foreign Minister, but by a subordinate official.

Caucasus did not achieve their immediate purpose, they were not without effect. The activities of the Georgian émigrés, especially of Prince Machabelli, awakened interest in Georgia, both in German political and military circles and among the public, especially since there were German industrial groups with material interests in the background. When autonomous states came into being in the Caucasus in 1917 and 1918, the Germans' earlier political contacts had prepared them to enter into closer political relationships.

The Ukraine

The Ukraine[1] was another area in which the German and Austro-Hungarian general staffs had planned and prepared to start a revolt. These plans were influenced by the expectation that after the anticipated speedy victory in the west the main theatre of war would be transferred to south Russia. Here, too, the rising was conditional on the armies of the Central Powers really advancing into the Ukraine.

The organisation of the Ukrainian revolutionary movement was at first in the hands of the Ruthene National Committee in Austrian Galicia, which was supported by the German consul-general in Lemberg, Heinze.[2] On his suggestion, the German ambassador in Vienna, Tschirschy, sent von Levicky, the head of the National Committee, to Berlin at the end of August, and he persuaded the Chancellor and the Foreign Office to support him.[3] The great Polish landlords of Galicia, however, put Berchtold against the German–Ukrainian connection and against any revolutionary activity in the Ukraine. Although criticising the Germans for being too conservative, he feared lest a focus of anarchy should come into being in south Russia which might have detrimental effects on the Monarchy. It was in view of this Polish opposition a matter of some importance that the Ukrainian Archbishop in Lemberg supported the Ukraine activities from 1914 to 1917–18 in the hope of being able to detach the 30 million Greek-Orthodox Ukrainians from Moscow and bring them into the Uniate Church.

The second and decisive phase of Germany's revolutionary activities in the Ukraine began in August, 1914, with the arrival of a group

[1] On this subject, again, the archival material is very extensive. On the literature on the subject see Hans Beyer, *Die Mittelmächte und die Ukraine* (Munich, 1936); for the first years of the war, recent work based on the Austrian archives, Helga Grebing, 'Oesterreich–Ungarn und die "Ukrainische Aktion", 1914–1918; Zur oesterreichisch–ungarischen Ukrainepolitik im ersten Weltkriege', in *Jahrbücher für Geschichte Osteuropas*, Vol. 7, Heft 3, pp. 270 ff.

[2] On this, besides the archives, see also Bogdan Fr. S. Graf von Hutten-Czapski, *Sechzig Jahre Politik und Gesellschaft*, Vol. II, pp. 145 ff.

[3] See Beyer, op. cit., pp. 1 ff.

of Socialist émigrés from the Ukraine, some of whom had left their homes only on the outbreak of war. They formed a 'League for the Liberation of the Ukraine'[1] which was encouraged by Heinze, by the Foreign Office and also by Levicky's group and was given regular financial support by the Reich. The objective of the League was an independent Ukraine of democratic-socialist character. The group criticised German propaganda, holding it, for example, to be completely futile to hope to win over the Ukrainian peasants by leaflets in the pedantic German style recalling the long-past days of greatness when the Ukraine was independent under its Hetmans and grand princes. Instead, the Ukrainian Socialists concentrated their propaganda on the agrarian question in the conviction that the only way of mobilising the Ukrainian peasants was to promise them land.

At this point the mutual interaction of the national and the social revolutionary motifs begins to become apparent; but the element of social revolution made the Austro-Hungarian government increasingly reserved towards the League, out of consideration for the Polish landed magnates of Galicia and also in view of the prospective annexation of Congress Poland. The promotion of revolution in the Ukraine thus became a purely German enterprise. The League, which was now financially entirely dependent on Germany, established agencies under the aegis of the German embassies in Constantinople and Bucharest, from which centres they sent agents into the Black Sea ports from Odessa to Rostov and tried to undermine the morale of the Russian fleet. In Constantinople Wangenheim was assisted by Helphand, who in his exposé of March, 1915, had designated the national movements in Russia, especially the Ukrainian, as the weapon to pierce the armour of the Tsarist Empire, and had submitted detailed proposals for action. From 1915 on, increasingly important work was done by the German minister in Berne, Romberg, who had discovered and recruited for the German service a particularly serviceable Ukrainian Socialist named Stepankowski, who played an important role in Germany's Ukrainian policy in 1917.

Another method of promoting revolution in the Ukraine was to segregate Ukrainian prisoners of war in the German P.O.W. camps and have them indoctrinated by special German commissions with the purpose of making them the torch-bearers of a Ukrainian independence movement. Similarly, and with the same purpose, Polish, Georgian, Mohammedan and Finnish prisoners of war were segregated from the Russian. *Regierungspräsident* Schwerin formed a

[1] On this, besides the archives, in detail, Grebing, op. cit., pp. 267 ff.

137

special staff for dealing with the Ukrainians and succeeded in winning many of them for the German cause.[1]

Owing to the Austrian defeat in Galicia, German propaganda and subversive activity never produced a revolution in the Ukraine, and its real importance, again, lies in its effects on German public opinion. Thanks largely to Paul Rohrbach's work, an ever-increasing flood of German publications on the Ukraine began to appear in 1915–16, and in them the economic aspects of the question were given increasing prominence. A man as influential as Albert Ballin called for an offensive against Kiev in the summer of 1916, saying that Kiev was generally regarded as 'the economic heart' of Russia. Both the German government and German public opinion were thus ready to exploit the favourable situation which arose out of the February revolution of 1917.

Poland

Germany's campaign of subversion in Poland could build on a living tradition of national risings which had manifested themselves in a series of rebellions in the nineteenth century, and more recently in the unrest accompanying the revolution of 1905–6. Bismarck's idea that in the event of a German–Russian war Russian Poland should be incited to rise and should be reinstated as an independent state, was a two-edged sword for Prussia's Ostmark policy, for the appearance of a new Polish state could not but have its effect on the millions of Poles in the eastern provinces of Prussia.[2] The situation in Austria was rather different. Here the Crown land of Galicia presented an analogous problem. The Poles of Galicia, however, unlike the Poles of Prussia or Russia, enjoyed cultural and political security and had a big voice in the government and parliament of their state. Vienna was therefore readier to consider promoting revolution in Russian Poland, the more so since it could hope to bring the areas detached from Russia into the framework of the Dual Monarchy. This situation explains why it was only with half a heart that Berlin embarked on the revolutionising of Congress Poland and the restoration of Polish sovereignty.

Even before the final breach with Russia in July, 1914, Germany had decided that, if war broke out, Congress Poland must be incited to revolt and be reinstated as a state. The evidence now available

[1] From the end of 1917 on the Supreme Command begins to intervene actively; it sent the Foreign Ministry a screed on propaganda in the East 'requesting that the Finnish, Estonian, Livonian, Ukrainian and Rumanian press be taken in hand forthwith'. A 'real position of hegemony' was especially necessary in the Ukraine.

[2] On this see also Oncken, *Preussen und Polen im XIX Jahrhundert*, pp. 224 ff.

forces us to give more credence than was previously customary to Hutten-Czapski's assertion that on July 31, 1914, not only the Emperor (this is admitted) but also the Imperial Chancellor promised him that Poland should be restored after a German victory.[1] Germany's intention of promoting revolution in Congress Poland is confirmed by the fact (already mentioned) that with the approval of the German government agreements along these lines were concluded between the German and Austro-Hungarian general staffs at the end of July, 1914.[2]

On August 5 the Foreign Ministry decided to secure the consent of the Holy See for the Polish clergy to use their influence on the population of Congress Poland. The Prussian minister to the Vatican, von Mühlberg, was instructed to secure the co-operation of the Vatican in the sense that the Holy See should make it clear to the Poles 'that the Allied armies were working for the liberation of Poland and must therefore be supported by all Poles, including the Polish clergy', since Catholic Austria-Hungary was fighting also against 'the Orthodox Church, which was violating the rights of the Catholic Church in Poland'. In order to mobilise further religious emotions in the service of the German cause, Erzberger had thousands of leaflets distributed in Congress Poland bearing a coloured print of the Emperor Wilhelm II and Pope Benedict XV side by side; also a grandiose picture of German troops driving Russians back, while the Polish people surges forward in brightly-clad masses, bearing church banners blessed by the Madonna.[3] The appeal to the Polish clergy proved, however, ineffectual. The overwhelming majority of the Poles, including their clergy, remained partisans of the Entente, and in some frontier districts whence the Russian officials had fled in panic, Polish priests themselves took charge of the mobilisation of the men called up for service.[4] Furthermore, the presence of Russian troops, at first 400,000 of them, later a million, put any idea of a rising out of court. The Germans deceived themselves in supposing that the Poles were longing to be liberated by Germany. In reality the neo-Slav movement, with its doctrine of pan-Slav solidarity, had weakened the traditional hostility between Russian and Pole. The

[1] Cf. Hutten–Czapski, op. cit., Vol. II, pp. 145 and 295, with his letter of November 5, 1916, to the Emperor, reminding him of his assurance of July 31, 1914.

[2] Westarp, *Konservative Politik*, Vol. II, p. 1: 'I knew that revolution would break out today among the Poles of Russia.'

[3] Reichenau reported from Stockholm on October 31, 1914, that Russian papers showed a tendency to suggest that the Emperor's reason was affected. They based this on his alleged dream that the Holy Virgin had appeared to him in a vision and charged him to liberate her home in Czenstochau.

[4] Friedrich Schinkel, *Polen, Preussen und Deutschland* (Breslau, 1931), p. 225.

industrialisation of Congress Poland was having the same effect, since the interests of influential Polish economic circles, especially those of the textile industry, were now bound up with the great Russian market. The dominant political tendency among the Poles, represented by the National Democrats, was oriented towards democratic western Europe, and was therefore pro-Entente. Finally, Prussia's Ostmark policy had done its bit towards filling the Poles with mistrust of Germany.

All these reasons make it understandable that the rousing proclamation issued on August 17, 1914, by the Russian Commander in Chief, the Grand Duke Nikolai Nikolaievitch should have made a considerable impression on wide Polish circles. The proclamation promised the Poles the unification of *all* Polish-inhabited territories, including Prussian Poland and Austrian Galicia, under the Russian sceptre, but with far-reaching autonomy.[1] Against this, the Central Powers had no more to offer than, at the most, the resurrection of Congress Poland.

In Galicia there had been enough anti-Russian feeling to admit the formation of Pilsudski's famous Polish Legion. Since, however, the Legion, in collaboration with an underground Polish 'National Government' in Warsaw, put forward far-reaching political demands for a future Polish state, it was incorporated in the Austro-Hungarian army and so gagged politically.[2] It is less well known that in the first weeks of the war an attempt was made to raise a Polish Legion in Germany, but the negotiations, which were carried on between representatives of the Polish 'Sharp-shooters'' organisations on the one hand, and on the other hand the Reserve General Staff in Berlin and Hindenburg's IX Corps in Posen, led to no result. The central German authorities concerned, which included the War Office and the Reich Interior Office, were prepared to allow the Polish organisations to enlist voluntary recruits, but not to conscript them, since this would have been tantamount to conceding them sovereign rights. Even at this stage Delbrück raised political objections. When he read in various reports that meetings of Sharp-shooters had been demanding Posen and West Prussia for the future Polish state, he made energetic protests which resulted in the disbandment of the Polish organisation and the cancellation of its agreement with the military authorities. This went through the more easily because the Sharp-shooters had been criticising Germany over the Kalisch incident (Kalisch, a town on the Russo-Polish border,

[1] Schulthess, *Geschichtskalender*, Jg. 1914, p. 848.

[2] The latest comprehensive account of Pilsudski's mission in 1914, Conze, *Polnische Nation und deutsche Politik im Ersten Weltkrieg* (Cologne, 1958), pp. 53 f.

was destroyed by German troops in the first days of war), while Austria had meanwhile protested in Berlin against the activities and agitation of the Polish Legion. At the beginning of November the few, half-trained formations of the German Polish Legion were taken to Cracow and there put under Austro-Hungarian military command. All further agitation in the Polish territories occupied by German troops was forbidden and the agreement between the Sharp-shooters and the military authorities was again cancelled.

By the beginning of December, 1914, Germany's brief flirtation with Polish revolutionary and democratic nationalism was already over. The Poles' ambitions with regard to Posen and West Prussia had touched Prussian political self-consciousness on the raw. It was only after the establishment of the two governments general in Warsaw and Lublin, that is, of a German and an Austro-Hungarian military administration, that the ideas mooted vaguely in the autumn of 1914 took concrete shape in a decision to create a Polish army and to incorporate it, and with it a new Polish state, in a German-controlled central European system.

The Jews

In August, 1914, the optimistic eye of the Germans – of Consul-General Heinze, for instance, to judge from his reports – classed the Zionist movement with the Polish and Ukrainian as the third 'strongest movement against Tsarism'. The Jews of Russia were counted as a quasi-German element, if only on account of their Yiddish speech; on the other hand, they were a minority living under a special dispensation, confined to a strip along the western frontier of Russia, and in the two decades before the World War had frequently been the victims of the notorious pogroms whereby the Tsarist regime had sought to divert attention from its own internal difficulties.

In the days which brought the outbreak of war all German Jewry, including the Zionists (who formed only a minority), were a prey to national excitement. The Cologne Judiciary Councillor Max Bodenheimer,[1] one of the founders of the 'Zionist Association for Germany', approached the military authorities in the Rhineland with a proposal for a proclamation to the Jews of Russia. Through Hutten-Czapski's mediation he was put in touch with Diego von Bergen, the Foreign Ministry's specialist for revolutions, who was himself thinking along similar lines. On August 17 official consent was secured for

[1] Egmont Zechlin, *Friedensbestrebungen und Revolutionierungsversuche, 3, Die Allianz mit dem Judentum, Beilage zu 'Das Parlament'*, January 21, 1961, pp. 342 ff., following archives and memoirs.

the foundation of a 'Committee for the Liberation of the Jews of Russia', the Presidency of which was assumed by the Berlin sociologist, Professor Franz Oppenheimer, with Bodenheimer as Vice-Chairman. The Committee was approved by the Central Committee of the International Zionist League in Berlin, under Professor Otto Warburg, and soon came to enjoy the support of Germany's non-Zionist Jews as well. This development filled the German government with most sanguine hopes.[1]

On August 17 an appeal to the Jews of Russia, signed by the Supreme Command of the German and Austrian armies, called on them to rise in arms, promising them 'equal civic rights for all, free exercise of their religion and their civil callings and free choice of residence within any territory occupied in future by the Central Powers'. In this as in other leaflets as, for example, those distributed by the Jewish Committees in Galicia, the Jews were adjured in burning words to avenge themselves for the pogroms: 'Jews of Russia! Rise! Spring to arms! Help hunt the Moskal [sc., the Russian] out of the West, out of Poland, Lithuania, White Russia, Volhynia and Podolia! Freedom is coming from Europe . . .!'

The Committee of Liberation seems to have been less interested in persuading their co-religionists in Russia to rise than in pinning down the governments of the Central Powers to public definition of the future rights of the Jews in 'the Russian West'; for only so would the sympathies of those Jews be definitively acquired for the Central Powers. Bodenheimer went further still: he wanted a multinational buffer state created between Germany and Russia, with the political and economic leadership in it shared between the Jews and Germans. This idea of a German–Jewish alliance against the Slavs, particularly against the Poles, was, however, not supported in German governmental circles, which did not want to anticipate too far the territorial readjustment of these areas.

Nor did it prove possible to secure the support of the Zionist movement as a whole for the plans of the Liberation Committee. After the military reverses of the autumn of 1914 the Executive Committee of the World Zionist Organisation in Copenhagen pronounced in favour of strict neutrality, and forced all Zionist members to resign from the Committee of Liberation; the latter then transformed itself into a relief organisation for the Jews of the occupied territories. Attempts to secure the support of American Jewry for the objectives of the Committee also proved unsuccessful, the anti-Semitism preva-

[1] A report submitted to the Imperial Chancellor on August 20, 1914, sees in the Zionist movement 'an invaluable instrument for our intelligence service and our agitation abroad . . . particularly for the territory of the Russian Empire.'

lent in the Reich proving a deterrent. The Jews in the occupied territories themselves were disappointed by the attitude towards them
adopted by the German military and civilian authorities, which did
not answer to the expectations awakened by the proclamation. Still
hoping for internal reforms, they remained as loyal to the Russian
state as did the Jews of central and western Europe to their own
countries of residence; the more so since Socialist ideas had struck
deep roots among the east European Zionists, which made collaboration difficult with a state whose persecution of the Socialists was
still fresh in the memory.

An example of the early German hopes may be quoted from September, 1914. The German consul in Bucharest got into touch with
Jewish agents who promised to produce 'a rising in Bessarabia within ten days and later a general revolution against Russia'. The consul had already paid out 50,000 marks in gold for the preparations
for the rising and promised two million more if the enterprise succeeded. Zimmermann, in the name of the Foreign Ministry, expressly approved and endorsed the promise that Germany would support
the emancipation of the Jews in Russia.

Here, too, Germany's hopes proved deceptive, but the Central
Powers' inflammatory proclamations and incitements to revolution
had tragic consequences for the Jews of Russia. The Russian government and the militant right-wing circles which had been reponsible
for the pogroms before the war, found in these events justification for
their hatred of the Jews, whom they now more than ever regarded as
enemies of Russia. There were fresh excesses against Jews and official
measures which resulted in terrible sufferings for the victims. It is a
fact that the refugee movements and mass deportations increased
Russia's internal difficulties and thus made the country still more
ripe for revolution.

Lithuania and the Baltic

Contrary to its policy in Poland and Finland, the German government did not try to promote revolution in Lithuania or among the
Baltic peoples. In Lithuania the Germans did not expect to find
national self-consciousness, and it was only during the war that they
realised how strongly developed it was, and that the Lithuanian
national movement possessed a class of intellectual leaders and extensive connections abroad, especially in the United States. In so far
as German policy concerned itself with Courland, Livonia and
Estonia at the outset of the war, no revolution seemed necessary,
since Germany already possessed a leading class in the shape of the
Baltic Germans, through whom it could carry out whatever policy

it wished. And the presence of this ruling class of Baltic Germans made it impossible from the German point of view to promote evolution among the Letts and Estonians, because their inflamed national feelings, which politically were oriented westward, would in the last resort have turned against the Germans themselves and brought the downfall of the Baltic Germans. Moreover, parts at least of Courland and Lithuania were at an early stage under consideration as suitable areas for direct annexation to Germany.

Finland

The geographical situation of Finland, like that of the Ukraine and Georgia, excluded annexation to Germany. There were therefore no reasons against inciting it to revolt against Russia, and this was in fact the object pursued by the Germans from the first days of the war. A suitable starting point for Germany's efforts was offered by the Grand Duchy's constitutional status within the Tsarist Empire, which had been so bitterly disputed in and after the revolution of 1905. To this was added the existence of a relatively large body of émigrés, based principally in Sweden. At the beginning of August, 1914, the German government began collecting these émigrés to serve as liaison officers with Finland; they were supported through the legations in Stockholm, Copenhagen and Berne, and were further advised by Swedish diplomats and princes of the Church, such as the Swedish minister in Berlin, Count Taube, and the Archbishop of Upsala. On August 6 Bethmann Hollweg instructed the German minister in Stockholm to begin preliminary preparations for a rising in Finland; among other things, he was to establish contact with the Swedish party there. Proclamations were to be distributed among the Finns, holding out to them the prospect of an autonomous state as their reward if they rose, although the German government was not yet prepared to give undertakings binding in international law.

The Finnish negotiators said that they could not rise unless Germany landed troops in Finland, or Sweden entered the war against Russia, an object which German diplomacy for years tried vainly to bring about. The Finns then pointed out that given their shortage of leaders, organisation and arms, any rising in their country must inevitably be crushed. So Germany could only wait and prepare for action in the future.

Finnish and Estonian socialists (Zilliakus and Kesküla) had early imported a new element into Germany's revolutionary activities. They said that the revolution could not succeed unless supported by the German Social Democrats, and in fact German Social Democrats were soon taking a hand in the revolutionising of Russia. Further more, the leading Finnish patriots regarded revolution in Finland as only one link in the chain of the liberation of the non-Russian nationalities as a whole – confirming the Germans' own view on this point. The Finn Wetterhoff, for example, concluded a regular treaty with the Georgian Committee, and the most important of these Finns, a lawyer named Castrén, pronounced the mission of this war against Russia to be the liberation from Russian rule of the Poles, Finns, Lithuanians, Mohammedans, Armenians, Jews, Estonians and Letts.

The most positive result achieved by these revolutionary preparations was the formation of a 'Finnish Legion' of Finnish volunteers, whose numbers, like those of all the similar enterprises, remained extremely modest. This was the 'Finnish Chasseur Battalion' which later achieved such fame, although it did not see action until the spring of 1918. In the spring of 1917 Zimmermann strongly pressed the Finnish Committee in Stockholm to seize the occasion of the February revolution to strike, but the Finns continued to back. It was only the October revolution that brought them full independence – soon jeopardised once more by civil war and only assured in the spring of 1918, in a sense favourable to German interests, by the intervention of German troops.

A general survey of the whole range of these revolutionising policies within Russia shows that all Germany's attempts to mobilise the nationalities had only a relatively minor effect. Their historical significance is that they reveal Germany's overall war aim in the East, which was to weaken Russia by liberating the non-Russian peoples and so to construct a position of power for Germany herself. The clearest proof is to be found in a little-known event of the early summer of 1916. At that period Germany was still courting the favour of opinion in the U.S.A. and the neutral world, and also of Liberals in the Entente countries, who were becoming powerfully impressed by the new slogan of the 'right of national self-determination'. German propaganda immediately picked up this effective slogan. Wessendonck, who was the Foreign Ministry's propagandist in chief on national questions, and some of his assistants (notably the two Baltic Germans von Uexküll and von der Ropp)[1] brought into being the so-called 'League of Russia's Foreign Peoples'. The purpose of this body was to co-ordinate the propaganda of the committees of the different nationalities, all of which were by now more or less dependent on Germany, and to get them to make a public proclamation. After complex negotiations, and after long hesitation, the Foreign

[1] See on this Friedrich von der Ropp, *Zwischen Gestern und Morgen* (Stuttgart, 1961), pp. 83 ff.

Ministry decided that the most effective form for such a demonstration would be to issue an appeal to Wilson as 'the foremost champion of humanity and justice'. In it the representatives of the different peoples arraigned the Russian government before the whole civilised world and begged for 'help and protection from destruction'. This appeal appeared simultaneously in Stockholm and Lausanne, under the careful direction of the Berlin headquarters, with the object of presenting Germany as the protector of the rights of the 'oppressed peoples'.

The Radical Socialists as
Agents of Revolution

The mobilisation of the Russian revolutionary socialists brought Germany even bigger gains against Russia than the mobilisation of the nationalities. With the aid of the disintegrating impact of socialist activities Germany brought about Russia's defection from the war in November, 1917, and the conclusion of a separate peace on Germany's terms.

As in her national agitation, so in her social, Germany was able to take advantage of internal tensions in the Russian political and social system. The chief sources of these were the still unsolved agrarian question and the social grievances produced by over-rapid industrialisation under the prevailing form of society, which had resulted in the development of a radical workers' movement.[1] The collapse of the revolution of 1905 and the subsequent reaction had produced a large emigration of Russian revolutionaries, now scattered over all Europe and even America, for whom the outbreak of the First World War meant the possibility of a return to political life. From the first days of the war the German government harnessed the energies of these émigrés in its own service, at first with the limited purpose of weakening Russian military pressure on the Central Powers by stirring up internal unrest in the Tsarist Empire. Soon, however, the military objectives developed into political aims. Again there were two stages. In the first, revolution was fostered as a means of pressure on Tsarist Russia to conclude a separate peace with Germany along lines desired by Germany; in the second, after the first had repeatedly failed, the object of revolution was the overthrow of the Tsarist regime and the elimination of Russia as a world power.

[1] We assume the reader's knowledge of the inner purposes and outward course of the revolutions of 1905–6 and 1917, and therefore confine ourselves to certain aspects of them particularly connected with our theme. For general works, see G. von Rauch, *Geschichte des bolschewistischen Russland* (Wiesbaden, 1955) and Osker Anweiler, *Die Entwicklung des Rätegedankens in Russland* (Leyden, 1958).

Surprisingly, it was not Germany but Austria-Hungary which first suggested the possibility of using the Russian revolutionaries for the purposes of the Central Powers. At the beginning of August, 1914, as Tschirschky reported to Berlin on August 6, the Austrians had 'advised all Russian revolutionaries in Switzerland to return to Russia via Austria'. Romberg, in Berne, sent a long report to the Foreign Ministry at the beginning of October pointing out the presence of numerous Russian revolutionaries in Switzerland and their potential usefulness for Germany's purposes. On December 26 the German minister in Bucharest, von dem Bussche, reported on the beginning of a Russian revolutionary movement. He further recommended letting German Socialists collaborate, whereupon the Foreign Ministry sent Südekum, the Reichstag deputy, to Bucharest at the beginning of January, 1915, where he negotiated with Russian revolutionaries. Finally, on January 8, 1915, Wangenheim, in Constantinople, drew the attention of the Foreign Ministry to Parvus Helphand, the key figure in the complex ramifications of the revolutionising of Russia. Helphand was at that time employed by the Turkish government as a financial expert. He had recommended himself to the German embassy in the following words:

Russian democracy could only achieve its goals through the complete destruction of Tsarism and the dismemberment of Russia into smaller states. Germany, for her part, would not achieve full success unless she succeeded in starting a major revolution in Russia. The Russian danger would, however, continue even after the war so long as the Russian Empire was not dismembered into its component parts. The interests of the German government were identical with those of the Russian revolutionaries.

Helphand's idea of dismembering and weakening Russia accorded with Bethmann Hollweg's thinking in August–September, 1914. The new element was a combination of social with national revolution.

Zimmermann, and after him Bethmann Hollweg and Jagow, at once took up Wangenheim's suggestion of using Helphand. The Chancellor sent his special confidant, Kurt Riezler, from General Headquarters to get in touch with Helphand, whom the Foreign Ministry had meanwhile had brought to Berlin.[1] Helphand then made his suggestions and set out his ideas fully in a long memorandum which he submitted to the Foreign Ministry at the beginning of March, 1915. In this memorandum he recommended organising a political mass strike in Russia under the slogan 'freedom and peace'. The focal point of revolution was, he said, Petersburg with its munition factories, docks and railway works. He further advised

[1] See Z. A. B. Zeman, *Germany and the Revolution in Russia 1915–1918*. Documents from the Archives of the German Foreign Ministry, p. 2.

calling a conference of all Russian Socialists, preferably in neutral Switzerland, the special object of which should be to get all Socialist groups in Russia, radical and moderate alike, to combine in 'initiating an energetic campaign against absolutism'. He thought such a unification possible, because the leader of the radicals, Lenin, had himself raised the possibility of co-operation. In his view the ideological influence of German Social Democracy was strongest among the moderate wing of the Russian Socialists, the Mensheviks. He therefore believed that the authority of leading German and Austrian Social Democrats could win the Mensheviks for unification. By following this method he hoped also to exercise a strong propagandist effect on public opinion in Briain and France. He furthermore assumed that it would be possible to get the support of the Social Revolutionaries, if not for a mass strike, at least for influencing the peasants.

Helphand made detailed proposals for making contact with the representatives of the strike movement which had never quite died out since 1905 and for provoking strikes in the Black Sea ports, the Black Sea Fleet, the Baku oilfields and the mining districts of the Donetz and the Urals. The poverty of the population made it impossible to carry these operations through smoothly without ample financial support. Helphand thought it particularly important to revolutionise Siberia, because its representatives in the Duma were Socialists. He said that it was purely a question of money to contrive the escape of the political deportees to Russia in Europe, and thus to secure thousands of 'highly efficient agitators'. Their return would, he thought, produce an effect on the Socialist party centres and drive them into the United Front. An extensive press campaign should be initiated, especially with the help of Socialist papers in neutral countries, to support revolutionary activity in Russia. He attached great importance to agitation in North America, where the numerous Jews and Slavs formed an element which was very susceptible to anti-Tsarist propaganda. If the millions of immigrants from Russia were roused, American public opinion would undoubtedly be affected. The agitation abroad must in his view inevitably be reflected in Russia; at the least it would provoke reprisals by the government against the Socialist movement which would inflame the masses still further against Tsarism and finally force the government to employ the army against the people.

In the Ukrainian movement, Helphand thought, the agrarian unrest would chime in with the demand for autonomy, because the peasants would demand the division of the big estates, most of which were owned by nobles from Great Russia, and this again could only be achieved through the formation of an independent Ukraine. Peasant unrest in Great Russia would follow, and must in its turn bring the Social Revolutionaries into action. Helphand believed that the risings in Central Russia would give the signal for a general rising in Finland, for which preparations should be made with the help of the Finnish Social Democrats. The Finnish rising of 1905 had shown that the Russian government had had to employ a whole Russian army there for two years to put it down. Before this, however, the Finns could render invaluable service in providing information, and above all in keeping contact with Russian revolutionaries in Petersburg. For the revolution in the Caucasus Helphand insisted that the Turkish government must explain clearly to the Mohammedans the necessity of co-operating with their Christian neighbours, the Armenians and Georgians, in the fight against Tsarism; he was not blind to the difficulties of stimulating the Mohammedans into action.

After a general glance at the position of the Russian Social Democrats, who professed themselves loyal to the Russian state but opposed to autocracy and Tsarist imperialism, Helphand finally summarised his ideas in a single pregnant sentence:

In this way the united armies and the revolutionary movement in Russia will shatter the immense Russian centralisation represented by the Tsarist Empire, which will remain a danger to world peace so long as it exists, and will bring down the central fortress of political reaction in Europe.

Helphand's expositions must have impressed the German government deeply. Immediately after his first visit to Berlin the Foreign Ministry gave him two million marks, and in the course of the winter of 1915–16 another 20 million roubles, with which, as instructed by the government, he built up an extensive organisation, with headquarters in Copenhagen, for revolutionising Russia.[1]

It is easy to see that Helphand, with his objective of disintegrating the Russian Empire, was thinking in principle along the same lines as the Chancellor, with his programme of peripheral states (although the Chancellor did not, of course, agree with the ideological aspects of Helphand's programme). But there were two weaknesses in Helphand's scheme of things: he reckoned on an earlier outbreak of the revolution than was in fact possible, and he deluded himself into believing that he could win over the Mensheviks to his programme. In reality the Menshevik 'Social Patriots' such as Axelrod, Alexinski, Deutsch and Plekhanov, were no more ready than their German opposite numbers, Scheidemann, Ebert, David and Noske, to renounce

[1] For the financial arrangements, see Zeman, op. cit., pp. 2 f.

their positive support of the war, much less overthrow their own government in the middle of a war. Just as Helphand and the German Social Democrats saw in Russian Tsardom the stronghold of reaction, which it was their task to destroy, so the moderate Socialists of Russia regarded the German Empire as the reactionary enemy of all progress, and put out all their strength to overcome this reactionary enemy with the help of Tsarist Russia, in alliance with the democratic West.

The weaknesses of Helphand's ideas were recognised by another social revolutionary, the Estonian Kesküla, with whom Romberg had been in contact since February, 1915. Kesküla had already pointed out in an earlier conversation that only the extreme wing of the Russian Socialists, i.e., the Bolsheviks, wanted a German victory, while his impression of the Mensheviks was 'that they saw their chief purpose to be to split the German Social Democrats and win them over for peace, so that indirectly they were doing the work of the Russian government'.[1] Kesküla, who had been working on similar enterprises in Stockholm since the autumn of 1914, tried to influence his fellow-countrymen in Estonia and at the same time to enlist the co-operation of all the non-Russian nationalities, especially the Ukrainians.[2]

The decisive point, however, was that in September, 1915, Kesküla definitely changed the course of Germany's revolutionary policy towards Russia, for from that date the Foreign Ministry, on his advice, put all its money on the Left Radicals, i.e., Lenin and his friends in order to play them off against the Russian 'Social Patriots'. It can only have been through Kesküla that the German government learned that the Russian Mensheviks were receiving large sums of money from their own government to keep the Russian workers loyal. Kesküla consequently advised the German government to come quickly to the financial help of the Left Radicals in Russia before 'Social Patriotic currents' could get the upper hand among the Russian workers. In this connection he emphasised the especial importance of Lenin, who was the only man who would in his view be ready to conclude a separate peace with Germany in the event of a successful revolution. In September, 1915, he actually succeeded in getting from Lenin a formal programme which gave the conditions under which the Bolsheviks would be ready to conclude peace with

---

[1] On this, besides the archives, see also Zeman, op. cit., pp. 6 ff., and Werner Hahlweg, *Lenins Rückkehr nach Russland*, in *Studien zur Geschichte Osteuropas*, Vol. IV (Leyden, 1957), pp. 40 ff.

[2] See Michael Futrell, 'Alexander Keskuela', in *St. Antony's Papers, No. 12, Soviet Affairs No. 3* (London, 1962), pp. 21–32.

Germany after their own victory in Russia.[1] Lenin said that the most important of these points—apart from the domestic political aims of a republic, confiscation of the big estates, the eight-hour day, full autonomy for the nationalities—was No. 5 in which he declared himself ready to offer peace without considering the Entente. Germany would have to renounce annexations and a war indemnity, but Kesküla remarked that this condition would not exclude detaching territories inhabited by the nationalities and forming them into buffer states between Russia and Germany. He was, of course, himself an Estonian and a Social Patriot.

The question of annexations and or buffer states was, however, the heart of Germany's war aims programme for the east. Romberg himself had left open whether any importance ought to be attached to Lenin's conditions, as transmitted by Kesküla, especially since Lenin, according to Kesküla, was still sceptical about the prospects of an early revolution in Russia. Nevertheless, Romberg recommended calculated indiscretions about Lenin's programme and, in general, a link with Russian 'democracy' in order to influence French public opinion and make it readier for peace. The German government did not adopt this idea, but it did agree to the proposed unreserved support of the Russian radicals. Lenin's conditions have an extraordinary historical importance over and above this consideration because his programme must have made it clear to the German government beyond all possibility of error that even the one group which was ready to make a separate peace with Germany in the event of Russia's military defeat and a successful revolution still insisted on Russia's territorial integrity and the renunciation by Germany of a war indemnity. The German government were bound from now on to conclude that the other groups, which still supported their country's struggle, must be even less ready to conclude a pact with Germany if required to accept conditions which even a Lenin rejected.

As early as August, 1915, von Brockdorff-Rantzau, in Copenhagen, had submitted a long report on Helphand and his organisation, and had recommended unreserved support for Helphand. At the beginning of December, 1915, when the German advance in the east had just ended and annexationist feeling was running high, Brockdorff-Rantzau had again urged on his government most emphatically the importance of a radical upheaval in Russia if Germany was to achieve her war aims. He had come to this conclusion because he had been unable to see an early prospect of peace with either Britain or Russia. In expressing this view he was answering

[1] Zeman, op. cit., p. 6.

151

objections by the Emperor who, during discussions in the previous summer about revolution in Finland, had expressed scruples about attacking the Tsar's throne. A year later, when Germany was again hoping for a separate peace with Russia, the Emperor again urged his government to appeal to the Tsar in the name of the solidarity of the imperial powers against the 'lawyer-governments of the West'. In contrast Brockdorff-Rantzau, in a long memorandum of December 6, 1915, openly advocated the overthrow of the monarchic order in Russia. 'It would,' he wrote, 'be a disastrous error if we continued now to attach serious weight to our traditional relationships with Russia, that is, with the Romanov dynasty.'

In his view the House of Romanov had 'sacrificed by its gross ingratitude' the traditional friendship which Germany had shown it during the Russo-Japanese War. For him Germany's very existence was at stake in the war; unless she succeeded in pulling one of her enemies out of the ring of the Entente, it would end in her exhaustion and her collapse. He saw in this extreme device of the revolutionising of Russia the only way of escaping the threatening danger: 'but victory, and as its price, the first place in the world, are ours if we succeed in revolutionising Russia in time and therewith smashing the coalition'.

Peace once concluded, he thought that the inner political collapse of Russia would be of little interest to Germany and might not even prove undesirable. He therefore proposed 'to make use of the veteran revolutionary Helphand before it was too late'. He thought that Germany's relationship with the new Republican Russia would be one 'which our grandchildren would one day regard as our traditional policy' when 'the German people, under the leadership of the House of Hohenzollern' had 'found its way to lasting friendship with the Russian people'. And he went on: 'This aim will not be reached until the Tsarist Empire as it stands today has been overthrown.' He summarised his calculations in a moving passage:

> The stakes are certainly high and success not absolutely certain; nor am I at all blind to the consequences which this step may entail for our own political life. If we have the military resources to force a final decision in our favour, that would certainly be preferable; but if not, I am convinced that we have no alternative but to try this solution, because our existence as a Great Power is at stake—perhaps more than that.

In these words Brockdorff-Rantzau puts with unique clearness what he thought the revolution was to do: it was to eliminate Russia if Germany's military power proved insufficient to achieve victory over the enemy unaided. As Wilson later appealed to the German people directly over the heads of the Emperor and his government, so Brockdorff-Rantzau envisaged a Russian people liberated from the Tsarist dynasty in a Russia which, territorially diminished by the creation of the new border states, would renounce dreams of great power status and live as Germany's modest and peaceable neighbour. The German aristocrat's view accorded with that of the Estonian revolutionary Kesküla who, when recommending Lenin in July, 1915, to the German government as the man to destroy Tsarist Russia, had warned his audience against the danger of a great modernised Russia, whose extensive natural resources would soon put it ahead of Germany, militarily and economically.[1] It is one of the ironies of history that the same Lenin whom the German government used to weaken Russia should have proved the man who, after sweeping aside her feudal and bourgeois social structure, transformed Russia into an industrialised and centralised state and laid the foundations of its present world power status, thus bringing to pass the very danger which Kesküla foresaw if the Germans failed to revolutionise Russia with the help of the Bolsheviks.

Brockdorff-Rantzau's strong support and Helphand's own conversations in Berlin with Zimmermann and Helfferich succeeded in so thoroughly convincing the Foreign Ministry and the Treasury of the importance of Helphand's work that he was allotted an allowance of forty million marks for work up to January, 1918 (though in fact by that date only twenty-five millions had actually been handed over).[2]

In 1915–16 the revolutionary work was carried on only by a relatively restricted number of agents, many of whom did not even know one another and were often not even aware that the German government

[1] See W. Hahlweg, op. cit., pp. 8 f.

[2] The famous 'Kaiser's millions for Lenin' of which so much has been heard must be reduced to their proper proportions. Accounts made up to January 30, 1918, show that Germany had up to that date authorised or spent 382 millions on the special account for propaganda and special activities. Of this roughly 11 million had been spent on Erzberger's propaganda campaign, 10 million each on propaganda in the U.S.A., Spain and Italy, 47 million in Rumania, and so on. 38 millions had been authorised for general propaganda, and 6·5 actually spent; for operations in Morocco the figures are 14·8 and 12·4; for Persia, 36·2 and 31·8; for Afghanistan, 5·2 and 4·8. The 40,580,997 marks for Russia make up about 10 per cent of the total expended. On January 1, 1918, about 14·5 million marks had not yet been spent, but the expenditure up to July 1, 1918, on German propaganda in Russia amounted to about 3 million marks monthly. Shortly before his murder the ambassador Count Mirbach asked from Moscow for a further round sum of 40 million marks, and this was allowed him, to counterbalance the money being spent by the Entente. Of these 40 millions, only 6 or at the most 9 (two or three monthly quotas) had been sent and used by the end of the war. The 40 or 80 million marks spent in the service of German policy in Russia should also be compared with the 6,000 million roubles which Russia had to pay Germany under the Treaty of Brest-Litovsk.

was behind Helphand's organisation.[1] At this stage eight persons were working in the Copenhagen headquarters and ten more were regularly travelling round Russia. The organisation maintained close touch with the Russian revolutionaries in Switzerland, such as Kesküla and Lenin, and with the Russian émigrés in Scandinavia, and sought to influence Russians returning from the U.S.A. and Canada. Newspapers and pamphlets were also distributed among the Russian people, and especially the army. Quite early the organisation tried to influence the Russian recruits, and great hopes were reposed in the students entering the Corps of Officers, since they had already been infected with revolutionary ideas at the university.

It was only the outbreak of the February revolution that enabled the German government to harvest the fruits of their long preparations. The climax and at the same time the most effective move in the whole campaign was the despatch of Lenin to Russia in the spring of 1917. Germany could count as indirect successes the October revolution and Russia's defection from the ranks of her enemies, and the Peace of Brest-Litovsk seemed to her to bring her a long step nearer attainment of her war aims in the East.

[1] For further details of Germany's activities, see the author's article in *H.Z.*, 188/2, October 1959, pp. 301 ff.

5

POPULAR PRESSURES

PUBLICISTS, SOCIETIES, PARTIES AND PRINCES

THE outbreak of the World War and the popular excitement which this produced evoked stronger demands than ever before that Germany should make her weight felt in the world. Two decades of German 'world policy' had generated and fostered in the German people a conviction that it was called, and entitled, to the status of a world power. A whole school of historians, the neo-Rankeists, had developed the theory of the rising system of world states, in which Germany would take her place as an equal, as she had in the old European state system.[1] Beside the German historians stood an innumerable phalanx of publicists of the most various dispensations, who proclaimed the 'German war'[2] as Germany's occasion to rise from a great power to a world power. This idea first took shape in August, 1914, and then in the face of the difficulties which began to emerge in the winter of 1914–15 hardened into a fixed determination to fight the war through until the goal was reached.

The 'Ideas of 1914'

Behind this blend of national emotion and very purposeful political thought stood an intellectual movement, the product of German professors–both humanists and economists–who felt themselves called to provide the war with a positive philosophy. In the 'Ideas of 1914',[3] under which name this movement has gone down to history, the war was no longer merely a defensive struggle which Germany had to wage against the ring of enemies who had fallen on her, but something more than this: a higher, predestinate necessity rooted in

[1] Ludwig Dehio, *Deutschland und die Weltpolitik im 20. Jahrundert* (Munich, 1955; as *Germany and World Politics in the Twentieth Century*, London and New York, 1959).

[2] *Der Deutsche Krieg, Politische Flugschriften*, ed. Ernst Jäckh (Stuttgart and Berlin, 1914 ff.).

[3] The expression comes from Rudolf Kjellén, 'Die Ideen von 1914', in *Zwischen Krieg und Frieden* (Leipzig, 1914), p. 29. Cf. Klaus Schwabe, *Die deutschen Professoren und die politischen Grundfragen des Ersten Weltkrieges* (Diss. Freiburg, 1958), pp. 34 ff. Cf. also *Deutsche Reden in schwerer Zeit* (Berlin, 1914), with contributions by Wilamo-witz–Moellendorff, Roethe, von Gierke, Delbrück, von Harnack, Sering and others; also *Deutschland und der Weltkrieg*, ed. O. Hintze, F. Meinecke, H. Oncken, H. Schumacher (Leipzig and Berlin, September, 1914).

the antithesis between the German spirit, German culture, German political forms, and the life and forms of her alien enemies. The disappointed hate-love towards Britain in particular swung round to unalloyed hatred of the British Empire. Britain, branded as the author of 'encirclement', became the progenitor of all utilitarian, egotistical, purely mercenary powers; the Anglo-Saxon 'shopkeepers' spirit' was contrasted with German 'heroism'. Meinecke talked of the lying phraseology of idealism which was used to mask a pure power policy, and of the danger to the development of any free personality presented by the 'uniformalised, mechanical' Anglo-Saxon type of humanity. Britain was the old people, now abdicating its place in world history, Germany the young nation, strong, upsurging, only now fulfilling itself. The war was being waged to help this natural process to consummation. Germany would win the victory, not through fortune on the battlefield, but because she represented a higher culture fighting in the service of human history. The war became invested with a sort of religious nimbus; it appeared, not as a fight of one nation against another, most certainly not as a test of technical and economic potentials, but in the terms of Hegel and Ranke, as a struggle between contending moral forces.[1]

This philosophic interpretation of the war—which had nothing to do with any realistic political thought—helped to mobilise German public opinion and released unsuspected reserves of force, precisely because of its non-rational, emotional appeal. This background explains both the war enthusiasm of the two first years of war and the 'nation's' claim to world power, with which the political and intellectual leaders of Germany identified themselves.

The Propagandists of Germany's Claim to World Power Status

The *Alldeutschen* were the group which shouted the loudest for German 'world policy', but their interest for us lies less in their crass demands (the general tenor of these is familiar and we have already touched on it in connection with the memorandum of their most important representative, Class) than in the influence exercised by their ideas in Germany. A large number of the 25,000 members of the *Alldeutscher Verband* occupied influential positions in political and

[1] Ideas like this were expressed sharply and in a politically effective form in the appeal drawn up by Ulrich von Wilamowitz–Moellendorff, which was first signed, at the beginning of October, 1914, by 93 leading German savants, and later, thanks to energetic propaganda by Dietrich Schäfer, collected about 4,000 signatures, i.e., those of nearly every German professor. This 'Declaration of the 93' was inevitably taken abroad as proof of the German intellectual classes' support of militarism (Clemenceau, for instance, called it 'Germany's greatest crime') and was still arousing indignation, above all in America, after the war. See M. Lenz, op. cit.

social life, and besides their own members, whose numbers were after all not inconsiderable, they had many sympathisers in the state services, the army, the navy, business, journalism and intellectual circles. The fact that ideas which are commonly regarded as specifically *Alldeutsch* were in general currency in the German Empire and can be traced in the very wording of the official language used by diplomats, civil servants and politicians, shows how extensive was their ideological and political influence and how impossible it is to dismiss them as an uninfluential clique of political fanatics.

This influence can be found among personalities and groups which called themselves liberals, strongly repudiated the name of *Alldeutsch* and yet in their political demands agreed very largely with the aims of the *Alldeutschen*. They took as their slogan 'the German idea in the world', as Paul Rohrbach had put it in 1913 in the title of his widely read book, but they linked this 'idea' closely with Germany's claim to world power status. Many of them openly confessed to a faith in German 'imperialism', while others reserved the word 'imperialism' to designate the policy of the enemy powers, while themselves going almost as far in practice.

If these views were expressed before the war in many variants, in war they led directly to an open profession of German imperialism. For example the editor of *Der Panther* (founded in 1912 in commemoration of the 'panther-leap' to Agadir) wrote in January, 1915:

> If the hour to realise German imperialism had perhaps then not yet struck, yet it was time to speak the word which should prepare the way before it. The ship's [sc., the *Panther's*] part was to fight for Germany's rights and her greatness, the periodical's to enter the lists for liberalism and imperialism. Both defenders of the German spirit were at bottom pursuing the same goal, but by different means and with different words, each in its own sphere. . . . What had then to be left for the future has become today a bloody and yet splendid actuality.[1]

An attempt to find an objective interpretation of the same phenomenon was made in 1916 by the historian Justus Hashagen in an article entitled 'German Imperialism'[2] in *Das Grössere Deutschland*, a periodical founded shortly before the war by Rohrbach and Jäckh with the purpose of giving systematic support to the idea of German world policy. Hashagen wrote that German imperialism had 'been only a modest plant' compared with the efforts of other nations to achieve world power; only the beginning of the World War had brought with it 'Germany's emergence to self-consciousness as a

[1] Axel Ripke, 'Das Erbe von Agadir', in *Der Panther*, 1915, No. 1, pp. 1 f.

[2] Justus Hashagen, 'Deutscher Imperialismus', in *Das grössere Deutschland*, 1916, pp. 673 ff.

world power'. He pointed beyond the Mitteleuropa project (which at that time was being widely discussed as a way of broadening the basis of Germany's power in Europe) and put forward colonial and Far Eastern policies as lasting 'aims of Germany's road to world power'.

An anonymous writer in the respected liberal–conservative organ *Die Grenzboten* signing himself 'Darius' (probably the editor himself, Georg Cleinow) went a step further still. 'Darius' confessed that 'he had long been a devotee of the German imperialist idea', and that 'the outbreak of the war and its course to date had given him great satisfaction'.[1] He regarded Germany's world policy before the war as the real cause of the World War and concluded that the mighty event of war must force every German to 'become conscious of the aim' to achieve which the war is being waged – 'the entry of Germany into the ranks of the great imperialist nations, and the realisation of the demands due to her as a world power'.

What few of us hitherto desired, what slept in the subconsciousness of many, what our statesmen made only occasional efforts to achieve, by peaceful means, what our enemies feared in secret, that the events of these days hammer indelibly into the brain of every German: this war is being waged to make Germany greater and mightier than she was; for there is only the choice between this and sinking back into the condition of a second-class Power, there is no third way, no possibility now of halting on the line where we stand. . . . Germany a World Power: that is the theoretical demand.

The editor of *Neues Deutschland*, the Free Conservative Adolf Grabowsky, saw the springs of German imperialism in the industrialisation and growth of the population by 30 millions since 1871.[2] The frontiers of the German Reich were wide enough for 'a satiated State'. But:

For one of the greatest industrial and trading States these narrow frontiers have gradually become fetters. For a State and a people which is consciously following imperialist aims, aiming, that is, to found a world empire and to take a great place among the world empires by the propagation of its culture and its language, by the might of arms and by trading connections, by possessions and settlements in far parts of the globe – for an imperialist-minded people this basis has become too narrow. . . .[3]

'Beyond any doubt,' wrote Grabowsky, 'Germany's own home is

[1] 'Darius', 'Ziele des Krieges', in *Die Grenzboten*, 74th year, No. 6, February 10, 1915, pp. 161 ff.

[2] Adolf Grabowsky, 'Die neue Weltmacht', in *Das neue Deutschland*, 4th war number, October 28, 1914.

[3] Id., 'Der innere Imperialismus', ibid., 8th war number, February 27, 1915, pp. 217 ff.

too limited an economic territory for a world power', and he consequently drew the conclusion that 'cost what it may, we must extend
our continental territory in this war':

> Nothing is more urgent today than that the will to conquer the world
> should take hold of the whole German people. Only then shall we raise our-
> selves from a half-unconscious World Power to a clearly conscious and thus
> an imperialist Power. Only then shall we be able to challenge England.[1]

These are but a few voices picked from a great choir of their likes.
A special study of Germany's periodical and daily press could produce innumerable variants on the same theme. This small selection,
however, is typical of the thinking in wide circles of the politically
leading classes of Germany.

What the *Alldeutschen* and the wing of the Liberals who openly
called themselves imperialist were saying clearly and unambiguously was repeated in substance, if in a different style, by the representatives of another group, perhaps best described as 'Government–Liberal'. This group occasionally polemised against *Alldeutsch*
exaggerations, but they too in fact propagated the theses of Germany's broader continental basis and of her claim to world power
status–theses whose realisation would, in view of their final aims,
have amounted in practice to the same as those described above. This
group included professors, publicists, business men and administrators, all more or less adherents of Bethmann Hollweg.[2] Many representatives of this school used *Das Grössere Deutschland* as their mouthpiece or, after 1916, a new journal *Deutsche Politik*, founded when
Das Grössere Deutschland came too strongly under *Alldeutsch* influence.
This group made its appeals to the wider public through *Der
Deutsche Krieg* (the German War), the series of pamphlets whose first
number was written by Jäckh's friend Rohrbach under the explana-
tory title: '*Warum es der deutsche Krieg ist*' (Why it is the German war).[3]
The central idea of this essay was that war would bring about
Germany's rise to world power status and would therefore go
down to history as the 'German war'. In 1915 the geographer Alfred

---

[1] Id., 'Deutscher Glaube', ibid., 6th war number, December 22, 1914.

[2] The best-known names are: Adolf von Harnack, Ernst Troeltsch, Friedrich
Meinecke, Hans Delbrück, Hermann Oncken, Max and Alfred Weber, Schulze-
Gaevernitz, Max Sering, Karl Lamprecht, Erich Marcks, Friedrich Naumann,
Paul Rohrback, Ernst Jäckh, Albert Warburg, Georg Solmssen, Karl Helfferich,
Franz Urbig, Bernhard Bernburg, Carl Duisberg and Robert Bosch. Bethmann
Hollweg's closest collaborators, Clemens von Delbrück, Wahnschaffe and Jagow,
were also associated with this circle.

[3] Paul Rohrbach, 'Warum es der deutsche Krieg ist', in *Der Deutsche Krieg*,
No. 1, October, 1914.

Hettner described 'the aims of our world policy' in the following words:

> The English regard themselves as a chosen people and believe themselves entitled to rule the seas and the world; but we deny them this right and make ourselves their equals. The Russians, too, claim a right to extend their empire ever further, but we challenge their right, too, with our own.[1]

The Germans had a right to maintain that their culture was the equal and the superior of the British and the French: 'We want to be the educators of the world, to carry our culture out into the world. The German Idea shall heal the world.' The great aim was clear to him: 'Germany . . . cannot live from the crumbs which fall from the World Powers' tables; she must be a World Power herself, the peer of the others'.

Paul Rohrbach reverted over and over again in his *Deutsche Politik* to the idea of the three world nations, the English, the Russians and the Americans, and added proudly: 'The fourth nation – that is ourselves.'[2] When we remember that Rathenau had inspired Bethmann Hollweg with this idea in August and September, 1914, we see how widely this Hegelian concept had spread. Ernst Jäckh, like Paul Rohrbach and Friedrich Naumann, proclaimed the kernel of the new world power to be 'German Mitteleuropa' from Spitzbergen to the Persian Gulf.[3]

The economist and Progressive deputy, Schulze-Gaevernitz, likewise regarded the purpose of the war to be Germany's rise to world power status and the final assurance of that status by the broadening of her basis in a Mitteleuropa. After Bethmann Hollweg's Reichstag speech of April 5, 1916, in which the Chancellor announced as his aim the detachment from Russia of the non-Russian peoples under her rule (her 'Western territories'), Gaevernitz wrote as follows of the proposed new German settlements on the Baltic and in Lithuania and of the bases of the new world power:

> Hemmed in between World Powers on the west and the east, we can see only one way out: Mitteleuropa. . . . This Mitteleuropa, in close alliance with the Balkans, Turkey and Greece – the East Mediterranean Power-to-be – would constitute a political and economic World Power capable of exerting pressure on Africa overland via Suez. If we harvest this result from the war, the war . . . is not lost for us, but won.[4]

[1] Alfred Hettner, 'Die Ziele unserer Weltpolitik', ibid., No. 64, p. 28.

[2] P. Rohrbach, 'Das Kriegsziel im Schützengraben', in *Deutsche Politik*, 1st year, No. 6, February 4, 1916.

[3] Ernst Jäckh, 'Mitteleuropa als Organismus', ibid., p. 1065.

[4] Von Schulze-Gaevernitz, 'An der Schwelle des Dritten Kriegsjahres', ibid., 1st year, No. 36, June 1, 1916.

Hans Delbrück took up the same position:

> The whole German people is imbued with the feeling that we, who were first pent in, then gratuitously attacked by a coalition of enemies partly envious, partly revengeful, can and must use our victory to secure our political future and to set out national future on so broad a basis that we can remain at least the equals of the other world peoples.[1]

When Delbrück was trying in July, 1917, to define a 'German peace' which avoided the extremes of Scheidemann's 'peace of conciliation' and Hindenburg's pure 'peace of power' in a 'peace of the national future', he rejected 'the narrow idea that Germany could retreat into the oyster shell of a well-secured continental position' and insisted that the German people, as a world people, also had tasks to fulfil overseas. The German African Empire envisaged by him was in all important points identical with that in Solf's programme of August, 1914, enlarged by linking territories acquired from Britain:

> The greater our victory, the greater must our colonial empire be. . . . If our victory is great enough, we may hope to unite under our rule the whole of Central Africa, besides our former South-West: Senegambia, Sierra Leone, the Gold Coast, Dahomey, populous Nigeria with the port of Lagos, the fertile islands of San Thomé and Principe, the French and Belgian Congos, Angola–a land of the future–with its excellent ports, the orefields of Katanga, Northern Rhodesia, Nyasaland, Mozambique with Delagoa Bay, Madagascar, German East Africa, Zanzibar, Uganda, then, on the Azores, the great, highly-developed port of Ponta Delgada, a most important and frequented coaling station, and Horta, one of the most important centres of the transatlantic cable.[2]

Delbrück, whose vision extended so far overseas–thus carrying farther an important line of Germany's pre-war policy–held consistently throughout the war to the idea that Germany must broaden her continental basis. Even when in 1917 he abandoned the idea of expansion in the west because he did not wish peace to break down over Germany's claim to Belgium, he made no such renunciation in the east. In August, 1915, he took Bethmann Hollweg's Reichstag speech of August 19 as a text to demand the liberation of the Poles and, above all, of the Germans of Courland,[3] and as late as May 27, 1918, when the expansion of German power was at its zenith after

---

[1] Hans Delbrück, 'Die Differenzen über die Kriegsziele hüben und drüben', in *Krieg und Politik*, Vol. 1, p. 143, first appeared September, 1914, in *Preussische Jahrbücher*.

[2] Id., 'Versöhnungsfriede, Machtfriede, Deutscher Friede', ibid., p. 220, first appeared June, 1917.

[3] Id., 'Die Rede des Reichskanzlers und die Zukunft Polens', ibid., p. 134, first appeared August, 1915.

Brest-Litovsk, he was able to say: 'The vast access of power which Germany has gained in the East, and which will always constitute our real reward of this war . . . is the shattering of the Great Power of Russia.'[1]

'The New Germany' and World Power Status

Two examples illustrate how deep were the roots struck in the thought, not of publicists alone but also of men playing a direct part in the moulding of the government's political will, by the idea that Germany was destined to world power status: the long memorandum produced by Schwerin in March, 1915, on Bethmann Hollweg's instructions on the creation of new areas for settlement on Germany's eastern frontiers,[2] and the report submitted by Geheimrat Sering on his journey, undertaken under instructions from the government, through the newly-conquered territories of the north-east. Both reports decisively influenced Germany's eastern policy during the war.

Schwerin and Sering collaborated closely, the one as President, the other as Vice-President, in the *Gesellschaft zur Forderung der inneren Kolonization* (Society for the Promotion of Internal Colonization) founded by the former. The terms of reference of both men had been to examine the possibilities of settlement and annexation in the new eastern territories, and to clarify the theoretical bases for those operations, but both quite deliberately set out far-reaching recommendations within the wider framework of the establishment and defence of Germany's world power status.

Schwerin begins with the fundamental proposition:

When we come to the question of the aims of the war and of the future development and shape of the German Reich, then, with all deference to the reserve which it has been necessary to maintain initially, two considerations are clearly dominant: that of achieving military security for our World Power position, or more accurately, that of obtaining a broader basis for a secured World Power position, and that of the future economic expansion of our conditions. In other words, power and wealth for the German people are the obvious war aims for the broad masses.

As antidotes to the dangers of one-sided industrialisation and urbanisation, with their detrimental effects on natural increase, he wishes to balance the annexation of Belgium by providing the *Herrenvolk* with more room for settlement on the land in the east, where a prolific peasant population would keep the German stock from decline. Internal colonisation and housing reform were not sufficient. These

[1] Id., 'Die erneuerte Kriegszielerörterung', ibid., Vol. 3, pp. 67 f., first appeared April 26, 1918.

[2] Cf. also Geiss, *Grenzstreifen*, p. 83 and above, pp. 126 f.

considerations led to a fundamental demand to make use of the unique opportunity presented by the war to expand the area of German settlement in the east:

> The German people, the greatest colonising people of the world, must be mobilised again for a great operation of colonisation, it must be given wider frontiers within which it can live a full life. The overseas territories suitable for colonisation by Germans have already been distributed, and cannot be acquired as prizes of victory in this war, so that an attempt must be made to acquire new land for settlement contiguous with the present Germany.

We can already catch the overtones of the idea of *Lebensraum*, even though Schwerin did not use the word. He too saw the broadened base on which Germany's world power must be founded in a Mittel-europa under German leadership, including, besides Austria-Hungary and Turkey, a Polish 'protectorate'.

Even more fundamental and more universal in their world-historical outlook were the 'general considerations' advanced by Sering in September, 1915, in his official report to the government in Berlin on 'the conquered territories of the North-East'. He adopted the picture of the three rival world powers, to which Germany must add herself as a fourth and an equal. He saw one basis for modern world power in the possession of extensive tropical and sub-tropical colonial territories as sources of raw materials and markets for domestic industries. But more important yet was the 'home', 'the true seat of the people's strength', for which extensive areas in the temperate zone were needed in order to secure the nation's food supply, and above all, 'because they permit the breeding of healthy human beings'. In contrast to Germany, the established world powers – the U.S.A., Russia and the British Empire (the last-named in its 'white settlers' colonies') – possessed sufficient spaces for the settlement of their white populations. In Sering's view the growth of these three 'giant empires' had exposed the older great powers to the threat of degradation to 'secondary power' status (here we catch echoes of Tocqueville, Seeley and Kjellén). If Germany wished to escape this danger, her only remedy was to raise herself into the ranks of the world powers; but this, said Sering, could be done only by broadening the area of German settlement and its economic basis. This could be done – and here Sering agreed with wide circles of *völkisch* pan-Germans – only in one direction: in the Slavonic east. Germany's expansion in the east would at the same time have the advantage of weakening one of the existing world powers – Russia – so materially as to diminish decisively its numerical superiority over the Central Powers. Sering, like his friend Schwerin, regarded the economic unification of Mitteleuropa as an indispensable counterpart to the territorial enlargement of Germany. As Schwerin saw in the war the last possibility of German expansion into the eastern territories, so in Sering's eyes the issue in the war was whether Germany could compass her rise to world power status through her eastward expansion.

The present war, unleashed by the Europe-based giant empires against the Central Powers, will decide whether the latter, and the countries of Central Europe as a whole, can continue to exist at the side of the giants as their equals, or not. They can do so only if the map is altered very radically in their favour.

Hegemony in Europe and its Economic Basis

The reverse on the Marne and the costly attempts made after it to fight a way through to the Channel coast past Ypres and Arras, the Austrians' heavy defeat in Galicia and the alternation of defeat with victory in north Poland, together with the beginnings of acute shortages of munitions and trained reserves at the end of November, 1914, added up to a considerable deterioration of the military situation of the Central Powers, as compared with their position in August, 1914. But as already mentioned, the press policy of the Army High Command and the government had concealed from the German public the full importance of the military reverses in east and west. Furthermore, the fortunate partial successes of Tannenberg and the sinking of three old British armoured cruisers by the U9 obscured from the public mind the critical military situation. The German propaganda over Tannenberg and the U9 had, however, far-reaching political and psychological consequences: the victory of Tannenberg gave birth to the Hindenburg myth, the sinking of the three British vessels to faith in the decisive effectiveness of the submarine weapon. Both events helped to strengthen the over-valuation of the military factor as opposed to the political, which was already a Prusso-German tradition.

In mid-November, 1914, both the military and the political authorities of the Reich realised that Germany's position was serious. There followed the first tentative peace feelers towards Britain and Russia. A separate peace with either meant, however, scaling down Germany's war aims on the front which seemed to offer a possibility of peace. Rumours of these attempts soon filtered through to the German public and produced a wave of fear of a separate peace with its presumable consequences. There was widespread nervousness at the possibility that the government might conclude a 'premature' peace which spared one enemy. Bethmann Hollweg himself, certain diplomats, and certain pro-British business men, especially if of

Jewish origin, were widely accused of wanting to conclude a 'cheap' or 'rotten' peace.

Leading figures in west German industry, with Hugo Stinnes playing an active part, had their demands formulated by the Bonn economist, Professor Schumacher, and presented to the Chancellor through his personal secretary, Legation Councillor Kurt Riezler. In this programme the industrialists demanded the annexation of Belgium or at least economic domination over it, the acquisition for Germany of the ore-field of Longwy–Briey, and considerable territorial gains in the east.

A further step towards the systematisation of national war aims was effected by the foundation of the *Kriegsausschuss der deutschen Industrie* (War Committee of German Industry). The main purpose of this was originally to co-ordinate and mobilise German industry for the war effort, but very soon the discussion of war aims became one of its leading activities. A sub-committee, which included Stresemann, was founded for the discussion of the subject. Thenceforward the great industrial associations intervened quite formally in war aims policy.

On December 8, 1914, two days after his visit to Hindenburg in Poland, Bethmann Hollweg received in Berlin the representatives of the two biggest German employers' associations, Landrat (retired) Roetger, Syndic of the *Centralverband deutscher Industrieller* and the National Liberal deputy Stresemann, second President of the *Bund der Industriellen*.[1] Roetger was representing the organised heavy industry, Stresemann the finishing industry. They not only put forward, in the names of their associations, the familiar demands in the west (Belgium, Longwy–Briey, Belfort), but also demanded extensive annexations in the east, especially Poland and Courland but also further afield, and the establishment of a central European customs union. The Chancellor, according to Stresemann's notes, 'signified his broad agreement'; and today, now that we know the documents, particularly Bethmann Hollweg's September programme, we need not regard this remark either as an exaggeration on Stresemann's part or as mere political tactics on the Chancellor's, even if we concede that Bethmann Hollweg may not have agreed completely about Estonia.[2] The Chancellor certainly had war aims, but in view of the uncertain military situation in the late autumn of 1914

[1] Paul R. Sweet, 'Leaders and Policies, Germany in the Winter 1914–5', in *Journal*, Vol. 16, October, 1956, pp. 244 ff.

[2] Egmont Zechlin, supplement to *Das Parlament*, June 21, 1961: *Die Allianz mit dem Judentum*, pp. 341 ff. Reprint of Stresemann's notes on his interview with the Chancellor on December 8, 1914, from *Nachlass Stresemann, politischer Schriftwechsel*, Vol. 139 AA, in: id., ibid., supplement of June 14, 1961, appendix, p. 335.

he wished to avoid any public discussion of them, and he was therefore trying to damp down the public agitation on war aims which had found such explosive vent in the first months of the war. He did so out of consideration both for enemy and for neutral opinion, not least in view of possible peace feelers which he did not wish to see upset, and also with an eye to the Socialist workers of his own country who were only prepared to support a war of self-defence.

These were the reasons for the government's ban on any public discussion of war aims, and for the official action taken against the *Alldeutsch* leader, Class, and his famous memorandum on war aims, nearly two thousand copies of which had been circulated in December, 1914. In the event, the government's intervention produced exactly the opposite effect from that which the Chancellor had hoped for. His action caused a big public sensation, and the courts before which the Class case came took the side of the *Alldeutsch* leader, so that in the spring of 1915 the government was forced to release him from police supervision. The prohibition of public discussion of war aims gave the *Alldeutscher Verband* the leading role in that very discussion, and its extensive connections enabled it to mobilise on its side the Prussian House of Deputies, in which, thanks to the restricted franchise, the supporters of the war aims movement were in an overwhelming majority. At the beginning of February, 1915, they put through the reinforced Budget Commission of the House a resolution asking for immediate permission to debate war aims. The government itself underlined the political importance of this debate when it found itself forced to publish an article in the *N.A.Z.* of February 21, 1915, defending itself against the charge of having no war aims. The wording and reasoning of this article (*Das Kriegsziel* — The War Aim) point unmistakably to Bethmann Hollweg's personal authorship. The author feared that the solidarity of the nation and the alliance with Austria-Hungary would be jeopardised if the government permitted public discussion of war aims at that juncture. He emphasised the fundamental unity of the supreme authorities of 'sword and pen', and declared that the one and only essential at the moment was to achieve military victory. 'Then,' he wrote, in remarkable agreement with the Chancellor's letter of March, 1916, to Erich Marcks,[1] 'the government will disclose its peace aims without hesitation, and a free people will be able to speak freely.'

But it proved not so easy to put off the big employers' associations. On March 10, 1915, they submitted their petition for a public discussion of war aims to the Reichstag and appended their famous

[1] See above, p. 98.

memorandum on the war aims question.[1] The pre-history of this is a most characteristic example of the decisive influence exercised by the *Alldeutschen* on German business circles. Alfred Hugenberg, a foundation member of the *Alldeutscher Verband* and at that time a director of Krupps, had invited leading members of the trade associations to a meeting in Berlin. There Class gave a lecture setting out the ideas of his memorandum on Germany's war aims. Hugo Stinnes supported Class's demands, in principle, in the name of the *Centralverband deutscher Industrieller*. He was followed by Friedrichs, speaking for the *Bund deutscher Industrieller*, von Wangenheim for the *Bund der Landwirte*, and many others, including Kirdorf, Beukenberg and von Borsig. The meeting appointed Hugenberg, Class and the National Liberal deputy, Ernst Hirsch, Syndic of the Essen Chamber of Commerce, to draft a joint statement. The outcome of this was the memorandum of the Five Trade Associations of March 10, 1915, which was submitted to the Reichstag and expanded on May 20 into the famous Address of the Six Trade Associations.

After the industrialists' move of March 10 the government felt compelled to reply to the suggestions that it was thinking of peace with a further declaration in the *N.A.Z.* of April 24 stating categorically that 'no reasonable human being could suppose that Germany would sacrifice the advantages of her favourable military situation by concluding a premature peace with any of her enemies'.[2] In spite of this reassuring statement from the government, the representatives of the associations thought it prudent to re-submit their representations of March 10, this time to the Chancellor direct.[3] The memorandum of May 20, 1915, was signed by the bodies afterwards known to history as the 'Six Associations': the *Centralverband Deutscher Industrieller*, the *Bund der Industriellen*, the *Bund der Landwirte*, the *Deutscher Bauernbund*, the *Reichsdeutscher Mittelstandsverband* and the *Christliche Deutsche Bauernvereine;* the *Hansabund*, representing commerce, adhered to it later. These associations represented all Germany's business interests. The memorandum demanded a colonial empire sufficient for all Germany's economic interests, 'security' in the fields of tariff and commercial policy, 'an adequately guaranteed war indemnity', and further, as 'chief aim', territorial acquisitions in east and west. The associations called for military and economic domination of Belgium; the population of Belgium was not,

[1] Entry of March 10, 1915, in Grumbach, *Das annexionistische Deutschland* (Lausanne, 1917), pp. 124 ff.; for what follows, Kruck, op. cit., pp. 76 f.

[2] For this article, see Schulthess, *Europäischer Geschichtlicher Kalender*, 1915.

[3] See also the petition of May 5, 1915, from the *Alldeutscher Verband*, *Gegen Sonderfrieden mit Russland, solange Landerwerb nicht gesichert.*

however, to be granted political rights within the German Reich. They claimed the Belgian and French Channel coasts in order to secure 'the outlet to the Atlantic which is vitally necessary for our future sea power' and also as a means of exerting pressure on England. Besides strategic frontier rectifications, such as Belfort and Verdun, they demanded (as Stinnes had done in September, 1914) the annexation of the ore-fields of Longwy–Briey and the coalfields of the department of the Nord and the Pas de Calais. In these areas, too, the local populations were to be deprived of all political rights, and the local 'economic power-factors, including the large and medium estates', were to be transferred to German ownership. The programme of annexations in the east was governed by the idea of supplying an 'agrarian' counterweight in the east to the proposed increases of the industrial elements in the west. The minimum proposals envisaged the acquisition of parts of the Baltic provinces and of areas southward of them; these would also give better protection to the frontier.

Parallel with this address, leading figures of west German industry made a second attempt to get round the official ban on the discussion of war aims. On May 12 a group of industrialists led by Hugenberg and including, among others, Stinnes, Kirdorf and Thyssen, and certain prominent academic economists, jointly submitted a detailed statement of their war aims[1] to General Gayl, commanding the military forces in the Ruhr area. The programme was broadly identical with that of the Six Associations; new elements in it were the idea of acquiring the Ukraine for Germany (a plan only seriously taken up in 1917–18), an explicit demand for the annexation of the entire Baltic coast, and a detailed examination of the position of Austria-Hungary in connection with the problem of Mitteleuropa.

Hugenberg's and Kirdorf's remarks also showed the interaction between war aims and the presumed social and domestic consequences of a so-called 'peace of renunciation'. It was necessary, so Hugenberg argued, to pitch war aims high, for only so would the entire nation, including the so-called 'enemies of the Reich'–the Social Democrats and the Ultramontanes–accept the sacrifices entailed by the war. In a polemic against Bethmann Hollweg, Hugenberg criticised the Chancellor for having allowed a specially privileged position to the leaders of the 'parties hostile to the State', especially the Social Democrats and trade unions leaders, thereby enabling them to recover that influence over the masses which

[1] Besides the archival material, see also Boelcke, *Krupp*, pp. 143 ff. On the treatment of the Baltic and Polish problems in these memoranda see the accounts in Lilli Lewerenz, *Die deutsche Politik im Baltikum 1914–1918* (Diss., Hamburg, 1958), pp. 105 f., and Geiss, op. cit., pp. 48 ff.

had slipped from their hands in August, 1914. In his view the democratisation of Germany–by which he meant that the trade unions
would dominate economic life and thus weaken the Reich–would
bring the end of its national existence. It was possible, and also necessary, to use the war to eliminate France for ever, and Russia for
many decades, as England's allies.

Schumacher, the economist, admitted the impossibility of inflict-
ing the same mortal blow on Russia as could be dealt to the smaller
France. He therefore recommended that Germany should be 'moderate' in her claims on Russia and not touch real Great Russian territory. For all this theoretical modesty, however, the frontier proposed
by him involved very considerable annexations: it was to run in the
north-east from Narva across Lake Peipus to Dünaburg and Vilna.
Hugenberg went further and asked also for Brest-Litovsk, as Hindenburg did eighteen months later. Hugenberg divided the territories
to be annexed by Germany into a *Kulturland*, which was to be settled
intensively with Germans, and a *Vorland*, a sort of glacis on which the
future wars against Russia were to be fought out. Like his friend
Schwerin and like Sering, Hugenberg envisaged the connection between the new territories and the German Reich as such a close one
that he gave them the name of 'New East Germany'.[1]

The southward extension of the new 'frontier wall' by the creation
of the Polish 'Frontier Strip' was discussed in detail by Professors
Bernhard and Wegener, whose joint memorandum on the subject
had been ready in outline on August 18, 1914. The new frontier was
to follow approximately the line of the Narew, Vistula and Warthe
rivers, and to take in the valuable coal and iron fields of Dombrowa,
east of Upper Silesia. The Poles were to be moved north-eastward
out of the 'Frontier Strip'. The purpose of the strip was strategic, but
after it had been Germanised it was to form a wall between the Poles
of the eastern provinces of Prussia and a new Polish state.

Especially noteworthy are the views of Krupp von Bohlen und
Halbach. A little later he rejected the most extreme demands of the
trade associations and of his director, Hugenberg, but his own war
aims programme, which he had put into writing in November, 1914,
when he had 'given it to Secretary of State von Jagow and to some
other friends of mine in the government', differed little from the programme of the associations except on the point of expansion in the
north-east, and agreed closely with what Bethmann Hollweg was
wanting in September, 1914.[2] Krupp expressly rejected any Peace
Congress, i.e., any general peace negotiations; he was convinced

[1] See above, pp. 116 ff. and 162 ff.
[2] Boelcke, op. cit., pp. 149 ff.

that 'to use the words of His Majesty the Emperor and King, the peace can and must be dictated to the enemy'. For him *Deutschtum* constituted the heart of Europe, round which he wanted to build a firm economic combination in the form of Mitteleuropa, which was to include in particular Austria-Hungary, Holland, Switzerland and the Scandinavian states. Like Bethmann Hollweg and Class in 1914, he wanted to see France finally eliminated as a great power. Further, he asked for the annexation of French territory along the line of the Moselle and the Meuse, primarily on industrial grounds: 'A France lacking any considerable reserves of iron and coal can no longer present an economic danger on the world market, or a political danger in the council of the great powers'.

Krupp saw the real enemy in Britain, and for that reason demanded military domination over Belgium and perhaps military control of the north coast of France. Like Tirpitz, he believed that the establishment of Germany's power on the Channel could compel Britain to give Germany her friendship:

Here we should be lying at the very marrow of England's world power, a position – perhaps the only one – which could bring us England's lasting friendship. For only if we are able to hurt England badly at any moment will she really leave us unmolested, perhaps even become our 'friend', in so far as England is capable of friendship at all.

In the east Krupp regarded the re-establishment of an independent Poland as axiomatic. He conceived the new Poland as a 'buffer state' and wanted 'a firm bolt drawn' against it through the establishment of the Germanised 'Frontier Strip', to prevent it from 'lusting after' territories which had formerly been Polish but were now Prussian.

Germany's power-position in the world was to be rounded off by an 'internally secure' and militarily defensible colonial empire in Africa and by a string of naval bases and coaling stations forming a 'bridge of Africa'. This would ensure Germany markets for her industries and raw materials, and the expansion of Germany's cultural influence in the world. 'If these aims are achieved, German culture and civilisation will direct the progress of humanity; to fight and to conquer for such a goal is worth the price of noble blood'.

Such far-reaching war aims, voiced by the trade associations, gave rise to suspicions that the driving force behind Germany's war aims policy was merely one of material interests. It was largely in order to counter this reproach that in the early summer of 1915 the war aims movement mobilised the academic circles of the German middle classes.[1] Here, again, it was Class of the *Alldeutscher Verband* who, un-

[1] Westarp, op. cit., Vol. II, pp. 166 ff.

seen, pulled the wires. The two men who took the most active parts in organising this new demonstration were the Berlin theologian Reinhold Seeberg and the Bremen merchant Andreas Gildemeister; the latter was chiefly responsible for drafting the address. Kirdorf provided the link with the industrial world. The so-called 'Intellectuals' Address' agreed in substance with the proposals of the Six Trade Associations, but emphasised more strongly the idea of using colonisation in the east as a safety valve to relieve social pressure in the interior. To this was added the *völkisch* idea, as repeatedly put forward by Paul Rohrbach, Sering and others, of parrying the growth of the Slav and Russian masses by 'decomposing' Russia, by erecting a Germanised 'frontier wall' in the east and by an active population policy, a course for which the east offered a unique possibility.[1]

The Address was soon ready and was presented to the Chancellor on July 8, 1915;[2] it was signed by 1,347 persons from all walks of German public life. Professors provided much the largest contingent, with 352 signatures; but the signatories also included numerous business men, parliamentarians, schoolmasters, clergymen and artists.

A later product of the Intellectuals' Address was the 'Independent Committee for a German Peace' (*Unabhängiger Ausschuss für einen deutschen Frieden*) which afterwards played so important a part in the German war aims movement under the leadership of the Berlin historian, Dietrich Schäfer. On November 15, 1915, this committee published another address which demanded the incorporation of Longwy–Briey in the west and the detachment of the Baltic provinces from Russia in the east. It was presented to the Chancellor by Seeberg in July, 1916, when the committee was officially founded.

The Chancellor had resented the Address of the Six Associations, the representations to General Gayl and the Intellectuals' Address as troublesome interferences with the prerogatives of the government; he regarded them, for the reasons of foreign and domestic policy mentioned above, as inopportune, if not actually harmful. His reaction towards them had accordingly been cool and reserved. The event proved him completely right, for both the Associations' and the Intellectuals' Addresses soon became known in enemy and neutral countries, where they were regarded unfavourably as expressions of Germany's desire for domination. A commentary on the two addresses drawn up by friends of Bethmann Hollweg's shows,

[1] So Oberregierungsrat Stumpfe of the Ministry of Agriculture wrote (under the pseudonym of Ekkehart Ostmann): 'in the national struggle the important point is the production of human material.' Cf. M. Kranz, *Neu Polen* (Munich, 1915), p. 69. Friedrich Naumann wrote in the same vein in connection with his 'policy of more men', 'Mitteleuropa needs children, children, children' (*Mitteleuropa*, p. 186).

[2] For further details, see Grumbach, op. cit., p. 140.

however, on close analysis, that the customary view of those circles as 'anti-annexationist' is totally mistaken; their aims were entirely positive, and corresponded with those of the September Programme. The only point on which this essay, which was composed in the summer of 1915 by Georg Bernhard of the *Vossische Zeitung*, takes a stand is on the principle of rejecting 'the incorporation or association of independent peoples accustomed to independence'. But the strong criticisms directed by the right against this circle, the most prominent representatives of which were Adolf von Harnack and Hans Delbrück, are unfounded, so far as essentials go. The 'liberal' formula only rejected the annexation of the *whole* of Belgium, or the *whole* of Poland, because the populations of those countries were accustomed to independence. But it allowed a free hand for partial annexations in Belgium or for other forms of dominating that country, and for the expansion of German power in the east. This interpretation is no piece of over-acute hindsight; the sentence was interpreted in this sense in the same year of 1915 by Harnack himself to a perturbed fellow-Balt:

If [he said] you read and interpret the paper from this angle, you will find that on the point of annexations, nothing is excluded except the naked annexation of the Belgian State. Neither the annexation of parts of Belgium, nor a disposition under which Belgium would become partially or entirely dependent on us, is excluded.[1]

This is exactly Bethmann Hollweg's line of establishing at least a partial domination over Belgium. As early as August, 1915, Delbrück explained what was meant by 'a free hand in the east': annexation of the Baltic provinces, Suwalki and Kowno. The weight of this statement is only increased by Delbrück's emphasis and proud insistence on the continuity of his ideas before the war and now: 'Old ideals rise up in our minds, the liberation of the ancient German colonial territory from the Muscovite yoke! Decades ago I got as far as this in a political reverie in these annals.[2]

Finally, in the spring of 1917, only three weeks before the outbreak of the Russian revolution, Friedrich Meinecke, with Karl Friedrich von Siemens and the National Liberal Eugen Schiffer, handed the Chancellor a mass petition with over 20,000 signatures calling for the annexation of the Baltic provinces and their settlement with Germans.[3] The principle of annexations, for the purpose of rounding off

[1] Memorandum by Broedrich-Kurmahlen, *Das neue Ostland*, privately printed (Charlottenburg, 1915).

[2] Delbrück, *Rede des Reichskanzlers*, l.c., pp. 129 ff.

[3] The mass petitions were presented to the Chancellor on March 31, 1917. On that occasion Schiffer made a speech commenting on them; see Lewerenz, op. cit., p. 117.

and extending their Mitteleuropa, was thus by no means foreign to the Liberal circle round Delbrück, Harnack and Naumann,[1] even if it is true that especially before 1917 they attached less importance to direct annexations and were chiefly concerned with extending Germany's power in east Europe and overseas.

The Reichstag and the Parliamentary War Aims Majority

The parliamentary counterpart of the extra-parliamentary war aims movement was the inter-party War Aims Majority. Officially it comprised all the bourgeois parties, but unofficially it extended to a considerable proportion of the Social Democrats, who used the cover of the 'truce' to abstain from opposing the government's policy, and whose right and centre wings tacitly or expressly endorsed Bethmann Hollweg's 'moderate' war aims. The War Aims Majority continued in being during the whole of the war; even the new Peace Resolution Majority of July 19, 1917, constituted only a temporary deviation from the persistent main line.

The basic annexationist mentality of the Conservative party was always quite undisguised. If inner political considerations sometimes prompted it to adopt an attitude of reserve on the war aims movement after the Chancellor had made some declaration which satisfied it, it remained a firm member of the War Aims Majority, and one which was constantly in search of more power. Its spokesman on these questions was Count Westarp. In October, 1915, the Party Committee adopted a resolution to carry on the war until 'the foundations of the German future' were secured. Among these the Conservatives 'naturally' included 'territorial extensions'. Being mainly an agrarian party, they worked for annexations in Poland, the Baltic provinces and Lithuania, where they hoped to find land for settlement and recruiting grounds for agricultural labour. But they also advocated the establishment of some form of German domination over Belgium.[2]

Their immediate neighbours were the Free Conservatives, representing the higher bureaucracy and a fraction of the great landed proprietors of the rank of the Silesian magnates. At the beginning of

[1] Delbrück, *Der definitive Friede mit Russland und unser Verhältnis zu den Randvölkern, Preussische Jahrbücher 1918*, Vol. 172, p. 133. Relatively realistic as he was, he was sober enough to recognise that Germany could not win the Poles for his 'Mitteleuropa' if at the same time she made them her enemies by annexations and deportations. Similarly, he wanted *after* the peace of Brest-Litovsk to apply national self-determination honestly in the Baltic provinces, even if the result went against Germany.

[2] Text of the Resolution in Grumbach, op. cit., p. 40; cf. also Hans Booms, *Die deutsch-konservative Partei* (Düsseldorf, 1934), pp. 126 ff.

December, 1915, this party adopted a resolution similar to that adopted two months before by the German Conservatives.[1] They demanded that the 'heavy sacrifices in blood and gold' should not prove vain:

> They [sc., the sacrifices] call for the peace aim of a Germany fortified in her whole power position, considerably extended beyond her existing frontiers by the retention of as much as possible of the territories now under occupation and compensated for her financial expenditure.

The preponderance of the annexationist elements among the National Liberals is quite indisputable. As they had previously been the 'party of the foundation and the maintenance of the Reich', so now they felt themselves to be the party of its extension.[2] In the middle of May, 1915, their Executive Committee and representatives of its land and provincial organisations had met in Berlin to discuss the political situation. The report of the meeting recorded that it had expressed its fixed resolve 'to carry on the war to its victorious end', and further:

> the meeting unanimously demanded that the full political fruit be gathered of the mighty successes of our incomparable army and our heroic navy. In particular, the territory in the west which is necessary for securing and strengthening our power position by water and land must be attached to the Reich politically, militarily and economically. In the east Germany must acquire not only strategically improved frontiers, but also new land for settlement.

With these words the party laid down the line to which it adhered down to the late summer of 1918.

The discussions on war aims brought together, in co-operation, the centre and the right wings of the party, which before the war had been openly hostile to one another. The right was dominated by the Rhineland–Westphalian heavy industry; its leader was the *Alldeutsch* Syndic of the Essen Chamber of Commerce, Hirsch, and its other prominent spokesmen included two members of the Prussian Chamber of Deputies, Fuhrmann and Bacmeister, both members of the Supreme Committee of the *Alldeutscher Verband*. The reconciliation within the party was demonstratively expressed on June 18, 1915, when Bassermann and Stresemann spoke in an internal party meeting of the central organisations of the Rhineland and Westphalia. Stresemann said: 'We must become strong, and we must weaken our opponents so ruthlessly, that no enemy will ever again dare attack

[1] Text in Grumbach, op. cit., p. 39.

[2] See the annual report of the National Liberal Party in Duisburg for 1915, in Grumbach, op. cit., pp. 38 f.; ibid. for the following paragraph.

us. For this, frontier alterations in east and west are absolutely necessary.'

Bassermann had already said in the first winter of the war: 'But in the east barriers must be set up to prevent the Russian flood from overwhelming the German world. Germany, Austria-Hungary and Turkey must be made safe against this.[1]

The will to power which inspired the National Liberals found expression, in the west, in the demand for the annexation of Antwerp and Calais. Stresemann stuck to his Belgian war aims to the last, and also expressly called for the annexation of the Longwy–Briey basin.

The Bassermann–Stresemann–Hirsch group represented the great majority of the party. The opposition to them consisted of a small group which also wanted Germany's power and frontiers extended, but on a moderate scale. Their leader was Schiffer, the *spiritus rector* of Delbrück's Wednesday evening parties, in which their ideas were developed in close association with Rohrbach and Jäckh. This circle wanted colonial acquisitions and the addition to the Reich of the 'old German' Baltic lands. Apart from all the rest stood von Richthofen, who throughout took such a pessimistic view of Germany's military prospects that he thought a peace based on the *status quo* would be a success. He was later joined by Prince Schönaich-Carolath.

The Zentrum was another active component of the War Aims Majority in the Reichstag. When the party leaders of the majority discussed the question with the Chancellor on May 13, 1915, the Zentrum's leader, Spahn, had confessedly spoken as the mouthpiece of the Trade Associations. He was also the spokesman for the majority when the Reichstag met in full session, and it was he who on December 2, 1914, and March 10, 1915, read out the joint declaration of all the bourgeois parties in which they disassociated themselves from the views of the Social Democrats.[2] He also spoke in the name of all other parties on the Social Democrats' interpellation on war aims of December 9, 1915. The Executive Committee of the Zentrum, meeting at Frankfurt am Main on October 24–25, 1915, adopted a resolution which called in general terms for increased protection for Germany in east and west.[3] The object must be to 'deter' the enemy from 'attacking Germany again' and the increased protection had further to assure 'economic provision for our growing population'. In other words, the Zentrum was expressing here, in

---

[1] The Resolution of the Central Executive Committee of the National Liberal Party, August 15, 1915, in *Wippermanns deutsche Geschichtskalender*, 1915, Vol. 2, p. 305.

[2] An account in Westarp, op. cit., pp. 51 f.   [3] Grumbach, op. cit., p. 35.

very cautious phraseology, the then widely current view that Germany needed wider frontiers both for her strategic security and for the livelihood of her growing population. By his championship of the Trade Associations Spahn had given these generalities concrete shape, and Erzberger followed him with a whole string of remarks offstage, often even when taking diplomatic soundings as a semi-official official spokesman for the government. On September 2, 1914, Erzberger had sent the Chancellor a confidential letter with his views on what might be Germany's war aims, saying: 'It is our urgent duty so to utilise the consequences of victory that Germany's military supremacy on the Continent shall be assured for all time.'

During the first three years of the war the great majority of the Zentrum party was united on the question of war aims; in principle, it favoured annexations. Nevertheless, we can distinguish two trends. Spahn was the leader of the extreme wing, whose organ was the *Kölnische Zeitung*; Erzberger belonged to this group until 1916. The organ of the moderates was the *Germania*.

The left-wing liberals of the Progressive People's Party[1] were less extreme and open in their official pronouncements than the other bourgeois parties, and it should be remarked that they did not attend the meeting between the other big bourgeois parties and the Chancellor on May 13, 1915. In the course of the war, nevertheless, a number of their leading deputies gave more or less whole-hearted support to various war aims, including annexations in one form or another. Among these was their most important speaker, Friedrich Naumann, who at the end of 1914 spoke in favour of partitioning Belgium, Germany to take the Flemish parts and France the Walloon, and in December, 1915, advocated making Germany master of Congress Poland and other frontier districts in the interest of Mitteleuropa.[2]

In the first years of the war the group of Progressives adhered consistently to the War Aims Majority. The Central Committee of the party defined its views on December 5, 1915. It protested against 'the presumptuous claims of our enemies to prescribe to us the conditions of peace, in spite of their defeats', and was convinced that 'the conditions of peace must give Germany, not restoration of the *status quo ante bellum*, if that, but rather lasting protection against foreign attacks and permanent increase of its power, its well-being

---

[1] See Hermann Ostfeld, *Die Haltung der Reichstagsfraktion der Fortschrittlichen Volkspartei zu den Annexionsund Friedensfragen in den Jahren 1914 bis 1918* (Diss. Würzburg, 1933).

[2] Cf. also Lie. Gottfried Traub, editor of the *Eiserne Blätter* as supplement to Naumann's *Hilfe*; strong propagandist for annexionism, joined the Vaterlandspartei in 1917.

and, in so far as its security seems to demand it, also of its territory.[1]

The maximum expression of the German Reichstag's annexationist ambitions and at the same time, a sort of codification of them, was contained in the famous Declaration of all the bourgeois parties, including the Progressives, of December 9, 1915. It was an answer to an interpellation by the Social Democrats against annexations. Spahn read out the majority's resolution, and argued the case for it:

> Let our enemies conspire again to persevere with the war; in complete unity and quiet determination we await the hour which shall make possible peace negotiations in which Germany's military, economic, financial and political interests must be permanently guaranteed to their full extent and by all means, including the necessary territorial acquisitions.

What makes this resolution especially important is that before it the Chancellor had held two secret meetings (on November 29 and December 2) with the leaders of the bourgeois parties, at which the procedure and the division of roles in the Reichstag had been carefully discussed. The 'conducting of the Reichstag' of which the Chancellor spoke on this occasion really meant that the parties of the majority submitted a resolution which expressed more exactly certain things at which the Chancellor felt himself unable, for obvious political reasons, to do more than hint. And in the division the Social Democrats, for whom Scheidemann spoke,[2] were assigned the part of a well-tempered opposition, to open a safety valve for the workers' strong opposition to annexations.

The Social Democrats' various interpellations and declarations of protest have earned the majority Socialists the reputation of having been the opponents on principle of annexation. This is technically true as regards their official statements, but behind these a considerable number of their leaders accepted 'moderate war aims', at least tacitly, and not a few, especially of their right-wing members, endorsed them actively. In the autumn of 1914 the Party Committee was, indeed, at pains to allow no annexationist sentiments to be voiced in the party press, but this was not because it, or the majority of the party, was against war aims on principle, but for reasons similar to Bethmann Hollweg's own.

The Berlin Police President, von Jagow, confirmed that the 'anti-annexationist shindy' was Karl Liebknecht's doing; the majority of the party leaders, he reported in 1915, could easily be brought to accept annexations in Flanders and Poland. A number of utterances by leading representatives of the right wing of the Social Democrats

[1] Schulthess, *Europäische Geschichtskalender*, 1915, Vol. 1, p. 378.
[2] See on this, Philipp Scheidemann, *Der Zusammenbruch* (Berlin, 1921), pp. 30 ff.

which filtered through to the public during the war confirm the accuracy of this report. In particular, the groups connected with the *Sozialistische Monatshefte* and with the new periodical *Die Glocke* (The Bell) founded by Parvus Helphand with financial support from the government favoured annexations more or less openly. Noske, and later, August Winnig.[1] were leading advocates of the policy of annexing Courland and settling it with Germans.

Their anti-Tsarist feelings made it easier for the Socialists to accept frontier rectifications in the east than in the west. Otto Landsberg, for example, asked at a meeting of the Social Democrat deputies of the Reichstag: 'If the annexation of the Narew line were required in the interest of Germany's better defensibility in the East, ought any German to object?'[2]

But, as Georg Ledebour replied, the annexation of the Narew line would have entailed annexing Suwalki and Polish territory across the Vistula; and he added bitterly: 'So it has come to this, that the spokesmen of the majority among us venture in private to approve annexationist plans of the most pernicious kind, while in public the majority leaders protest that they, too, are against annexations.'

It was only after the outbreak of the Russian February revolution that Scheidemann, under the pressure of feelings among the workers, adopted the Russian formula of 'no annexations and no indemnities' and gave it such currency that it became thereafter the definition of a 'peace of renunciation'. From the summer of 1917 onward, when Germany's military situation was growing so threatening, Scheidemann used the new formula with intent as a 'protective formula' in order to save for Germany at least a peace on the basis of the *status quo*.[3] The Majority Socialists made many protests against annexationist ambitions; but their policy amounted in practice to tolerating them, for they never dared put their protests in such vigorous form as to entail political consequences.

In the face of the massive front of the War Aims Majority and the lukewarm attitude of the Social Democrats, the decided opposition on grounds of principle which came from the few bourgeois groups of pacifist leanings and from the little squadron of left-wing radicals was practically negligible. Their protests, in so far as the strict censorship allowed them to reach the public at all, exercised not the slightest effect either on public opinion or on government policy. The censorship gagged most of them effectively, and the most radical

---

[1] On Winnig's activities in the Baltic provinces see his notes, *Am Ausgang der deutschen Ostpolitik* (Berlin, 1921), pp. 5 ff.

[2] Grumbach, op. cit., p. 112.

[3] See below, pp. 328 ff.

representative of the left-wing Opposition, Karl Liebknecht, was in prison after May, 1916.

The German States:
Particular Interests and Annexationist Policies

Besides the pressure of public opinion, of the Trade Associations and of the parliamentary War Aims Majority for the establishment of an enlarged Germany as a world power, another not inconsiderable factor influencing the decisions of the government was the war aims policies of the German federal states.

The active intervention of the German princes in the war aims question was in no small measure dictated by fear of the 'unitary wave' which had manifested itself in the enthusiasm of the first weeks of war and would presumably rise higher still in the event of a victorious outcome to the war. They saw in territorial enlargement of their own states the only way of securing the dynastic and particularist principle against the preponderant forces of political and national unit and against the prospective territorial enlargement of Prussia.

Immediately the war broke out, the king of Bavaria, Ludwig III, put in his country's claims: 'Partition of the *Reichsland* of Alsace-Lorraine, Belgium must disappear and the mouth of the Rhine become German.'[1] This demand, which was registered on August 15, 1914, was stimulated by the successes of Rupprecht of Bavaria's army in Lorraine. Next Ludwig III told the general headquarters in Coblenz that the incorporation of the whole of Alsace in his kingdom was a Bavarian war aim, no less important to her than opening the Rhine to the ocean was to the economic life of south Germany. But Ludwig III was not alone; the victorious advance of the German armies fired Wilhelm III of Württemberg and the Grand Duke Friedrich II of Baden to demand compensation for the blood and material which the war was costing them. They were therefore very reserved towards the Bavarian plans, and expressed 'the utmost doubts' about the incorporation of Alsace in Bavaria. Although the Bavarian Prime Minister, Count Hertling, tried to tone down his monarch's demands in view of the objections of the other states, he did no more than put them in a more flexible form. These questions were, however, trivial for Bavaria compared with Prussia's claim to Alsace-Lorraine, which the military, the professors and the higher bureaucracy were pressing on the ground that only Prussia could

[1] Karl Heinz Janssen, *Macht und Verblendung, Die Kriegsziele der Bundesstaaten (1914–1918)* (Diss. Freiburg, 1957), pp. 13 ff. (August 15, 1914); for Wilhelm II of Württemberg, p. 22; Ludwig III and Erzberger, 1914, p. 32.

undertake both the Germanisation and the defence of this frontier area. Since, however, Bavaria had announced her plans so early it was difficult to adopt the Emperor's proposed solution of overriding her and incorporating Alsace-Lorraine in Prussia. The result of the consequent deliberations was the so-called Dallwitz Plan, evolved by the Governor of the Reichslande, in the hope of satisfying both parties. This so-called 'Alsatian–Belgian combination' envisaged partitioning Alsace-Lorraine between Prussia, Bavaria and Baden, Prussia to have Lorraine (with Longwy–Briey) and the western approaches to the Vosges from Belfort to Charleville with an outlet via Strasburg, while Bavaria would receive the north of Alsace, and Baden the south. This would have assured Prussia's object of keeping the defence of the Reich in her hands.[1]

In order to create a basis for Bavaria's claim to Alsace, the Bavarian government endeavoured – as it did throughout the war – to divert Prussia's interest to Belgium, and later to Courland and Lithuania, and to put pressure in this sense on the Emperor, the Chancellor and the general staff, or to encourage ambitions directed towards the annexation of those areas.[2]

Framed in the expectation of swift victory, Bavaria's aims were re-stated by Ludwig III on November 28, 1914, at the time of the deep gloom which followed the reverses on the Marne and at Ypres. Bethmann Hollweg had written on November 15 strongly criticising 'Utopias' in the field of war aims and defining his own aims as 'what is useful and what is possible'. He considered it possible to 'establish Germany on the North Sea coast, assume some form of military guardianship over Belgium, and create close economic relationships with that country'; but he rejected the annexation of Belgium on social grounds and for reasons of internal policy.[3] The king of Bavaria, however, was not prepared to renounce his hopes, and feared that the Chancellor might conclude a 'premature' peace. On November 28 he therefore gave Hertling the following instructions for negotiations in Berlin:

1. We must hold on until a result has been achieved proportionate to the vast sacrifices and the potent *élan* of the German people.

2. The Reichsland must be partitioned with due regard for Bavaria's interests.

3. Belgium must not continue to exist as an independent state; it must be attached to some German state; if not to Prussia, then to Bavaria.[4]

[1] Ibid., Dallwitz's compromise suggestion of October 31, 1914, pp. 33 f.

[2] Ibid., Hertling's proposal to make Belgium 'a Prussian Crown Colony on the English model', p. 53.

[3] Ibid., Bethmann Hollweg to Hertling, p. 26.

[4] Ibid., p. 27.

The essence of Bavaria's position was her determination to maintain her demands on Alsace-Lorraine, irrespective of the form or the extent of the increases in Prussia's power. But Bavaria could achieve her object only through an agreement with Prussia which would override the objections of the other secondary states to Bavaria's demands. The objective of the largest possible annexations in Alsace-Lorraine, combined with the wish to obtain a safe outlet to the sea, and the consequent need for agreement with Prussia, governed Bavaria's war aims policy, the most ambitious expression of which is to be found in the Crown Prince Rupprecht's exposé of the spring of 1915. This is in answer to a memorandum by von Bissing, the Governor-General of Belgium, on the Belgian question. Von Bissing's proposals were very much in the line of Bethmann Hollweg's own ideas: they envisaged an association of Belgium with Germany which should be economic and military rather than explicitly constitutional. Rupprecht went further, in respect both of territorial and of constitutional changes. Holland, enlarged by the Flemish areas of Belgium and northern France, and Luxemburg, enlarged by the south-eastern portion of the Belgian province of the same name, were to enter the Reich as new federal states. Prussia would receive the other areas of northern France, Walloon Belgium with Liége and Namur, and the salient of Holland round Maastricht, while the rest of Lorraine (Longwy–Briey), with Alsace, was to be partitioned. This exposé is one of a series of endeavours by Bavaria to encourage Prussia's renunciation of her aspirations in Alsace. Rupprecht was expressly aiming at breaking Prussia's hegemony in the Reich by substituting for it a sort of trialist structure resting on Prussia, Bavaria and Holland.

Although Rupprecht himself doubted as early as the end of 1915 the possibility of a German peace of victory, Bavaria's war aims policy in respect of Alsace and her policy of 'combinations', either with Belgium (possibly through a separate peace in the east) or with Courland–Lithuania as Prussian acquisitions or spheres of interest,[1] continued in being throughout the war, as did Baden's and Württemberg's (for Alsace, Mömpelgard and Hohenzollern)[2] and Saxony's (in the east), and constituted a factor in favour of annexations in the formulation of Germany's war aims policy.

These demands by the bigger dynasties were chiefly dictated by particularist interests; they contrast with the aims of some of the smaller, pan-German-minded princes, who were more interested to

[1] Ibid., pp. 171 ff.

[2] Hohenzollern: originally a small enclave in Hemberg; Mömpelgard, a medieval Württemberg hereditary fief, the present Montbéliard, in Burgundy.

see Germany established as a world power through hegemony in Europe and empire overseas. The Grand Duke of Oldenburg, Friedrich August, thought that the way to establish Germany's power in Europe would be to split France into two–a Republic in the north and a Bourbon kingdom in the south–and make it into a vassal state of Germany. He tried to get the support of Ludwig III of Bavaria for these plans. Prince John Albert of Mecklenburg, President of the German Colonial Association and in 1917 Honorary President of the *Vaterlandspartei*, composed a memorandum in the spring of 1915[1] polemising against the idea of 'a rotten, soft-hearted compromise' and demanding the broadening of Germany's base by big annexations in east and west: Germany's future western frontier should run west of the fortresses of Belfort, Épinal, Toul, Verdun, Charleville, Hirson, Cambrai and Arras, and reach the Channel south of Boulogne, while her eastern frontier should at least take in parts of Lithuania and run across Congress Poland to give easy connections between east Prussia and Galicia. The ancient duchies of Courland, Livonia and Estonia–possibly also the Ukraine–should be ruled by native princes and attached to the German Reich–a variant on the border states policy. The special feature of Albrecht's memorandum was the proposal that the native population should be deported from these advanced frontiers and replaced by German settlers, ex-soldiers or expellees or '*Volksdeutsche* from the interior of Russia', not only in the east, as suggested by Schwerin, Bethmann Hollweg and others, but also in the west.

On Belgium, Albrecht wrote, after first strongly advocating the deportation of its population to France:

> If we wish to reincorporate this ancient German *Kulturland* in any form, in whole or in part, in Germany, we must act consistently and not take over with it the alien, degenerate Walloon population, but leave them to their friends, the English and French, for their use, and in compensation.

Like the Grand Duke of Oldenburg, the Prince of Mecklenburg also tried to win the king of Bavaria to his side. Crown Prince Rupprecht, to whom he sent a copy of his memorandum, rejected the idea of general expropriation in the west and favoured only nationalisation of large mines and the parcelling of the big estates among peasant colonists.

The princes justified their war aims programmes by appeals to feeling in the people and the army, as the government and the

---

[1] Janssen, op. cit., pp. 59 ff., and ns. 191 and 192; Johann Albrecht von Mecklenburg, as President of the Colonial Association, demanded *inter alia* also a continuous German colonial empire in Central Africa. Britain and France were to be expelled from the African Continent altogether.

Supreme Command did in September and November, 1914. They saw in their demands a contribution of their own to the strengthening of the nation's will to conquer. Under the constitution, the sovereignty of the Reich resided in the princes, and it offered them a possibility – a very limited one, it is true – to influence the formation of government policy through the Federal Council (*Bundesrat*) or its Foreign Affairs Committee. The latter body was convoked fairly often during the war,[1] but its deliberations showed plainly the overwhelming strength of the position of the imperial Chancellor, coupled as the post was with the Prime Ministry of the largest German state, Prussia. The assemblage of plenipotentiaries of the Federal Council showed itself, on the whole, receptive. The Chancellor reported important decisions to it, but this was often done only at very short notice; moreover, it was Bethmann Hollweg's way neither to inform his audiences fully when the situation was serious, as it was at the turn of 1914–15, nor to keep them abreast of his frequently changing plans. As in the Reichstag, so in the Federal Council, although rather less pronouncedly, the annexationists like Bavaria and Saxony were stronger than the moderates like Württemberg, whose Prime Minister, Freiherr von Weizsäcker, took up an attitude of reserve over the question of annexations, as he did later over that of submarine warfare.

The essential unity of the nation in respect of war aims was not materially modified by differences between the states, especially since the largest of them, Prussia, was entirely bent on expanding its own power.

---

[1] Ernst Deuerlein, *Der Bundesratausschuss für die auswärtigen Angelegenheiten 1870–1918* (Regensburg, 1955); an account based on the Bavarian, Württemberg and Baden archives.

6

THE WAR AIMS POLICY OF THE REICH'S LEADERS, 1915

FROM DEPRESSION TO THE CLAIM FOR HEGEMONY

A CAMPAIGN which, according to the original calculations, should have been successfully concluded in two months, having failed, Germany was, as Falkenhayn at once recognised,[1] faced with the threat of a war of exhaustion for which she was neither armed nor economically prepared, and in which there was no guarantee of final victory. The German general staff saw no way to meet this danger except by concentrating all the nation's available troops on one front, and this, it seemed, could be achieved only by the tactical device of concluding a separate peace on the other–which meant temporarily shelving war aims in one direction. Emotional factors–it was the government itself that had accused Britain of breach of faith and had pilloried her as the author of encirclement–economic needs and military calculations led to the conclusion that it was best to give up many ambitions in the east in favour of forcing a decision and making sure of the war aims in the west.

The Situation After the Failure of the Blitzkrieg: East or West?

It was Tirpitz, with his strong anti-British prejudice, who suggested to Falkenhayn that Germany should try for a separate peace with Russia.[2] In view of the heavy losses of the German troops in Flanders and the great difficulties in the east, Falkenhayn at once took up this idea. He expounded his ideas in a long conversation with the Chancellor,[3] who thought them so important that he at once passed them on to the Foreign Ministry in Berlin.

In substance [he wrote], Falkenhayn had said to him that so long as Russia, France and Britain held together, it would be impossible for us to

[1] E. von Falkenhayn, *Die Oberste Heeresleitung, 1914–1916* (Berlin, 1920), pp. 20 f.

[2] A. von Tirpitz, *Deutsche Ohnmachtspolitik im Weltkriege* (Hamburg, 1926), p. 167, note by Tirpitz on his conversation with Falkenhayn of November 15, 1914; cf. also p. 161, Hopmann to Capelle, November 10, 1914; Jagow agrees with Tirpitz' view.

[3] Besides the archives, see also the description in Paul R. Sweet, op. cit., pp. 229 ff.

defeat our enemies decisively enough to get a decent peace. It was more likely that we should ourselves slowly become exhausted. Either Russia or France must be chiselled off. If we succeed in what must be our first aim, to get Russia to make peace, then we could so crush France and Britain that we could dictate the peace, even if the Japanese came across the seas to France and if England sent a stream of new reinforcements into the field. It could, however, be safely assumed that if Russia made peace, France would give up too. Then, if England did not submit to us completely, we could defeat her by using our Belgian bases to blockade her, even if it took months.

From Falkenhayn's estimate that victory against three enemies was no longer a military possibility, Bethmann Hollweg drew the similar conclusion that only a political move could bring the war to a successful conclusion for Germany.

The attempt to crush France in the first phase of the war having failed, and judging from the way that our military operations are going in the west in this second phase, I too must doubt whether the military defeat of our enemies is any longer possible so long as the Triple Entente holds together.

Bethmann Hollweg therefore agreed in advocating a separate peace with Russia; and he defined its purpose unambiguously and precisely:

Then we could, if we thought it right, even reject any peace offer that might come from France, and if the fortune of arms favoured us, so force France to her knees that she had to accept any peace that we liked, and at the same time, if the navy lives up to its promises, also impose our will on England. . . . Thus for the price of having our relations with Russia remain in essentials what they were before the war, we could create what conditions we liked in the west. At the same time, this would end the Triple Entente.

The difficulties of the general situation had thus led the Chancellor to renounce his original eastern programme of August and September, 1914, in favour of a separate peace with Russia for the sake of winning the war on one front and securing what were for him 'the more vital war aims'.

But although Bethmann Hollweg agreed with Falkenhayn in principle on the desirability of a separate peace with Russia, there was an important difference between the Chancellor's and the soldier's ideas: Bethmann Hollweg rejected Falkenhayn's suggestion of 'sending Russia an invitation'; he preferred to wait for feelers to come from Russia. His political experience told him that the consequences at home and abroad would be disastrous if it became known that Germany was making a peace offer. Further, he had at that time more confidence than Falkenhayn in Germany's powers of endurance; he therefore kept the aims which he had laid down in September, 1914, unmodified for the west, and in the east he retained what he regarded as irrenounceable safeguards. The dominant anti-British tone perceptible in Falkenhayn's reference to the 'demand of popular feeling' that England must be crushed was reinforced by the Emperor's assent to the idea of a separate understanding with Russia. The policy here initiated by Tirpitz, Falkenhayn, Bethmann Hollweg and Wilhelm II represented a deviation from the original war aims which was bound to bring Germany into conflict with the aims of her allies, Austria-Hungary and Turkey, for whom Russia was the chief enemy.

The first reaction of the Foreign Ministry was to point out this effect on Germany's allies. The utmost caution must be observed, said Jagow, in telling the allies anything about Germany's intentions, since there was a danger that Austria-Hungary might relax her military efforts and 'leave Germany stuck in the west'; Turkey, the newly-acquired ally, might also 'not keep up the struggle against England'. Jagow's demand that Germany must always keep a 'free hand' towards Austria-Hungary is to be understood as an allusion to the possibility of using Galicia, most of which was then in Russian occupation, as a bargaining counter in possible negotiations for a separate peace.

The anti-British line of Germany's policy is shown even more clearly in her rejection of a second American offer of mediation which arrived just when General Headquarters was discussing the possibility of a separate peace with Russia. Through his confidante, Colonel House, President Wilson had got in touch with the Austro-Hungarian ambassador in Washington, Dumba. Berchtold informed Berlin of this step on November 10, adding that in his opinion the Central Powers ought not to reject on principle an offer of mediation, since they must 'avoid the appearance of being engaged in an ordinary war of conquest'. They should declare themselves ready to end the war that had been 'forced on them' on condition that the peace 'genuinely secured' their most important vital interests and brought them the necessary 'compensation' for their heavy sacrifices. He thought that an exposé of 'our relatively moderate aims' would make a favourable impression on public opinion in America. He thought 'that the two imperial powers should first agree on what war aims were to be their final targets' before answering America.

Characteristically, Jagow's reply left this concrete proposal for the mutual determination of war aims completely unanswered, and was very sharply negative towards Wilson's offer. He too thought that it would be inopportune to reject the offer of mediation *a limine*, because the Central Powers had to avoid the appearance of being 'on principle for carrying on the war *à outrance*', but he did not at all want a peace mediated by America. As America was trying to mediate peace with England only, for the sake of its commercial interests, the result could be nothing but a 'rotten peace' and so 'the indefinite prolongation of a latent state of war'. England was for him the most obstinate of enemies, and mediation 'was unlikely to lead to acceptable results' with her. Jagow absolutely refused to consider Wilson's proposal for bringing the war to its end by means of an international peace congress, since Germany and her allies could not be certain of securing their demands at such a meeting.

Wilson's proposals, however, were not confined to the direct mediation of peace: they included the ideas of a League of Nations and of the assurance of peace through an international order which should prevent future wars. Jagow drew a contrast between this 'unpractical *Schwärmerei* for peace' and the principles of a 'realistic politician' and rejected the most important of Wilson's practical proposals, that is to make peace possible by renouncing 'substantial or vital territorial accessions' which 'inflicted lasting damage on national interests or self-esteem and thus necessarily created new desires for *revanche*'. Such a renunciation in the interests of world peace would have meant giving up war aims which the German government regarded as necessary for the security of the Reich; and for this it was not yet prepared in November, 1914, in spite of Germany's reverses.

Both courses – understanding in the east with Russia or in the west with Britain – were categorically rejected by Zimmermann, the 'strong man' in the Foreign Ministry, in a long memorandum dated November 27. For the alternatives of concentrating against either Russia or Britain he substituted a 'both'. He rejected any idea of a separate peace with Russia out of consideration for Austria-Hungary and Turkey. It would, he argued, give a fresh impulse to the independence movements of the Slavonic elements in the Dual Monarchy, because Russia would certainly interpret such a peace as a victory and would resume her pan-Slav agitation; the disintegration of the Monarchy would be accelerated and Germany would lose her ally. The effects of a separate peace with Russia would be equally disadvantageous for Turkey. As Russia was Turkey's main enemy, Turkey would regard the peace as a 'betrayal', and might 'fail us in the struggle against England'. Zimmermann was determined to prosecute the battle against Britain 'to the bitter end' (like Falkenhayn, he appealed on this point to 'popular feeling') and for this purpose Germany needed Turkey with her army of 800,000, her navy and her moral power to fanaticise the Islamic peoples of Asia and Africa by proclaiming the Holy War. Moreover, if Russia was not seriously weakened, she would after the war endanger Germany's vital economic interests in the east, where she would resume her old policies and trespass on Germany's fields of activity throughout Asia Minor.

Zimmermann conjured up the spectre of a huge over-powerful Slavonic empire (comprising the Slavs of the Balkans and the Danubian Monarchy) whose pressure Germany would be unable to withstand. If accounts were not settled with Russia *in this war*, any peace which Germany might buy, perhaps by sacrificing Austrian East Galicia, would only be an armistice which must inevitably be followed within a few years by another war. He therefore argued with the utmost force that Britain *and* Russia must be crushed simultaneously; a separate peace with Russia would not make the decision in the west any easier, but on the contrary would imperil it by the effects on Germany's allies and the neutrals. He proposed holding the western front defensively for a while, concentrating all forces in the east and enforcing a decision there. The occupation of Poland and the clearing of Galicia would, he hoped, win over neutrals – Bulgaria, Rumania, perhaps Sweden – and would make possible the success of the revolutionary activities which he was directing in the interior of Russia. He therefore advised strongly against a separate peace with Russia; a separate peace with France might, on the other hand, be considered as a tactical move. He thought that the war was unpopular in France and that France was weakening to such a degree that Germany could count on a peace which would be not only decent, but lasting.

Only if Germany's military resources should prove insufficient for this plan, should she consider joining her allies in concluding a separate peace with Russia, but the initiative must in any case come from Russia. Zimmermann thought that such an 'invitation' could certainly be elicited from Russia by crushing Serbia, and he therefore wanted every available man concentrated against that state. Germany would then have to grant Russia 'equitable peace conditions, for example, the territorial *status quo vis-à-vis* us and our allies' and concede 'a moderate war indemnity', in return for which she would get the benefit of being able to turn all her forces against the west; the Austro-Hungarian army could be used against France; Turkey's road to Egypt would be free; Italy and Rumania would remain at least neutral. Thus a temporary renunciation in the east would enable Germany to achieve her aims in the west.

Bethmann Hollweg's Conception:
a Separate Peace in the East and Peace with Victory in the West

Meanwhile on November 24–at the right moment–a fresh offer of mediation had been received at General Headquarters. Albert Ballin had reported to the Emperor on conversations which he had had with his friend, Etatsrat Andersen, Director of the Danish East Asiatic Line in Copenhagen. Andersen, perhaps on Ballin's suggestion, had persuaded King Christian of Denmark to try to initiate peace talks between the belligerent powers. Now Andersen asked in King Christian's name: 'Whether H.M. the Emperor would agree to the King asking the king of England and the Russian Tsar to allow him to approach H.M. the Emperor with the offer of a mediation for peace.'

King Christian promised to make it appear as though the approaches to London and Petersburg were being made entirely on his own initiative, without the Emperor's foreknowledge.

This move, coming as it did at the moment when Germany's military fortunes stood at their lowest ebb, for the first time forced the Chancellor clearly to face the question of Germany's war aims. As in his conversations with Falkenhayn six days earlier, Bethmann Hollweg laid down that Germany must not take any initiative towards a peace offer, because any such step would be interpreted as a sign of weakness, with disastrous consequences at home and abroad. Unlike the soldiers, he therefore recommended to the Emperor that he should put off answering King Christian 'until the decision had been reached in the east'; he should rather wait for a peace offer to come from Russia. If, however, such an offer were to come, perhaps through the Dowager Tsarina, who was a Danish princess, then the answers should be: 'Germany was waging a war of defence, and consequently was ready at any time to examine any peace proposals reaching her which guaranteed her full compensation and security against further attacks from three enemies.'

In respect of 'security against further attacks' Bethmann Hollweg reverted to the idea which he had formulated during the discussions on Wilson's first offer of mediation, that it was impossible to return to the *status quo*. Here his character reveals itself. Gloomy as the military situation was, he had the nerve to wait until a military success should bring the Russians to offer peace. Although he felt that the conclusion of a separate peace with one side (in this case Russia) was a compelling necessity, he was still not prepared to go back to the *status quo*, but held fast to his aim of 'safeguards'. Here again, as with the first peace feelers after the failure of the original plan of campaign the dilemma of his war aims policy is apparent: on the one hand he wanted a separate peace because in his view Germany's military potential was no longer sufficient to achieve simultaneous victory on all sides; on the other, he demanded even of the antagonist with whom he hoped to conclude the separate peace annexations, if only moderate ones, and multifarious indirect 'safeguards' such as he regarded as essential for the security and future power-position of Germany. So we find him up to the last constantly on the lookout for the possibilities of a separate peace, yet always attaching to them conditions such as no opponent could accept short of complete defeat. It must further be remembered that he regarded negotiations for a *separate* peace, while rejecting a general peace, as a tactical step to disrupt the enemy coalition, defeat the remaining enemies decisively, and thus bring into being an entirely new constellation of the powers. Bethmann Hollweg had before his eyes a very definite vision of Germany's power-position, before he was pushed into a particular path by the military, the pressure groups of the Trade Associations, the parties, or public opinion. It is, however, characteristic of him that he never gave up his own conception; even in quite secret conversations he always used vague, nebulous and innocent terms to describe his war aims, in order to satisfy the insistent, soothe the hesitant and retain for himself as free a hand as possible.

In December, 1914, he again defined his minimum programme, this time to Hertling. In contrast to the party which wished to annex Belgium, he confined himself to a less crude, more easily acceptable form of domination through economic, military and political ties and had the modalities worked out in detail by the military authorities, the Reich offices and the Prussian ministries. In order to secure his aim and to secure Longwy–Briey, he was prepared to rest content in the east with a strip along the frontier. In a conversation at headquarters on December 6, he asked Hindenburg to define the acquisitions which he thought necessary for the security of Germany's frontiers–a request with which Hindenburg complied (with maps attached) on December 11. Thus thinking about a separate peace was the midwife of the so-called Polish 'Frontier Strip', the direct annexation of which had several purposes: the military advantage of gaining possession of the Polish frontier fortresses, the acquisition of land for settlement and (in Upper Silesia) of industrial areas and raw materials, and above all, the cutting off of the Polish population of Posen and west Prussia from that of a possible future Polish state by moving out the local Poles and Jews and bringing in Germans in their place, especially 'repatriates' from Russia. Poland had not yet been conquered, and its future was still open; but the Polish question, like the Belgian, continued to occupy Bethmann Hollweg. The day after his visit to Posen he talked about it to the Austrian ambassador, Hohenlohe, in his typically veiled and negative phraseology. 'In principle,' Hohenlohe reported, 'Germany's basic ideas on Poland . . . that is, not to permit the creation of an independent Polish State and not to claim any large territorial accessions for herself . . . have not changed'. In the same conversation, in which Wilson's second offer of mediation and Andersen's proposal were discussed, Bethmann Hollweg refused, as had Jagow, to work out the 'joint peace programme' for which Hohenlohe had asked, pointing out that Austria-Hungary and Germany had agreed not to allow a general Peace Conference to follow victory, but to settle all relevant questions *à deux*. Bethmann Hollweg's evasiveness on this point initiated a conflict between Austria-Hungary and Germany on the definition of war aims which went on till the end of the war. At the very first conversation on Poland Germany reserved a free hand to substitute a Germano-Polish for an Austro-Polish solution.

A day later, on December 8, Bethmann Hollweg received the leaders of the great industrial associations, Stresemann and Roetger, and spoke to them so affably that they believed him 'on the whole' in agreement with their demands.

These privy conversations between statesmen, military authorities, federal states, allies and trade associations were accompanied by a wave of hatred against 'the arch-enemy England' which culminated in a sort of hypnotic determination, which seized more or less the entire population of Germany, to force England to her knees by blockade or invasion. The Austrian diplomats, who were afraid that Germany might betray them for the sake of her western aims, saw that Germany might change her aims, and pressed her repeatedly and strongly to treat Russia as the enemy *par excellence* (which she was, of course, for Austria and Turkey) and to weaken her permanently. They feared, not without reason, that Germany might buy her separate peace at their expense, perhaps by allowing Russia to retain East Galicia. They therefore worked with might and main against such a separate peace, hoping to find an ally in Zimmermann, who, according to Hohenlohe, 'played a far more dominant role in foreign policy than his position suggested'. Conrad interpreted Bethmann Hollweg's and Jagow's secret intentions accurately when he expressed the view that the Germans no longer believed their troops to possess enough striking power to end the war on both fronts by military victory, and that what they wanted was therefore to make sure of what they had won in Belgium, and in the east simply to create a situation in which they could negotiate with Russia. Berchtold, for his part, described Germany's policy as inelastic, pointing out the contradiction between her new Russian and her old eastern policy and, like Zimmermann, conjuring up the danger presented by an unweakened Russia to the continued existence of Austria-Hungary as a great power, with all the consequences for the Slavonic Balkans and the east. Hohenlohe, too, demanded the crushing of Serbia, as indispensable for the maintenance of Austria-Hungary's position in the south-east.

In spite of Austrian counter-pressure, Bethmann Hollweg continued to look for feelers for a separate peace with Russia through the most various channels—for example, through Count Witte, the former Russian Minister of Finance, who was reputed pro-German. Witte died in March, 1915, but the Chancellor tried to get the Grand Duchess of Baden to influence the Tsarina through her brother the Grand Duke of Hesse; he tried Russian business men, or politically influential individuals such as Kolyshko, the former Under-Secretary of State in the Russian Ministry of Finance, who had married a German and was now living in Stockholm. It always transpired that the Russians were frightened of the Germans' economic and financial demands—in which respect, as Nobel said (and the Austrians concurred), German policy was largely determined by the bankers[1]—and of exorbitant German territorial demands on the Baltic and in Poland, extending perhaps to Warsaw itself.

The most important of the projects was still the Andersen mission. Andersen himself was personally interested in a compromise with Britain, and King Christian duly sent him to London. But his conversations, had they had a positive outcome, would have been a step towards a general peace, whereas Bethmann Hollweg was interested only in a separate peace as a tactical method of disrupting the coalition, and although Russia (as he wrote to Ballin on January 26, 1915) was not yet 'ripe', she was, in spite of the difficulties with Austria-Hungary and Turkey, the only partner with which a separate peace was possible.

Andersen's first visit to Petersburg was in March, at a moment when German diplomacy was trying to keep Italy out of the war by putting strong pressure on Austria to cede the South Tyrol. Andersen got a categorical 'no' from the Tsar, who was not going to play his allies false and feared Britain's revenge if Russia were isolated; but he was encouraged to keep the threads unbroken and to come

[1] Pallavicini commented to Forgach on January 1, 1915: 'there are no real statesmen there (sc., in Berlin), that becomes more and more obvious; instead, the big industrialists and bankers play the leading role.'

back again in about six weeks. On his return he was summoned to report personally to the Chancellor and the Emperor. The continuity of Bethmann Hollweg's policy emerges clearly from the notes which he gave to the Emperor for his conversation with Andersen:

The war which we are carrying on is a defensive one which has been forced on us, not one of conquest. Furthermore, our situation in the east is so favourable that it is not for us to make peace offers. We must have a peace which secures us permanently. This security can come only from a peace which is felt and recognised by the German people to recompense it in full for the enormous sacrifices which it has made.

At the same time (March and April, 1915) the Chancellor was engaged in argument with the War Aims Majority in the Reichstag and with the Trade Associations, who had been made uneasy by rumours of a separate peace and by the announcement of internal reforms. He wrote to the Conservative leader, Count Westarp, on April 25, in an attempt to moderate the emotions and enlighten the minds of the parties and the Associations.[1] He dissociated himself from the extreme demands of the *Alldeutschen*, insisted that even if the enemy were totally defeated he proposed to champion a policy of 'relative moderation, in the spirit of Bismarck', and defined what he regarded as the necessary safeguards for German interests in Belgium:

If we are to achieve a lasting peace, Belgium must at least be rendered incapable of harming us. We must have military, political and economic guarantees against Britain or France using Belgium against us in future political conflicts. Those guarantees presuppose at least Belgium's military and economic dependence on Germany.

That the Chancellor's aims were by no means so modest as the *Alldeutschen* were complaining is shown by what he said in a long conversation with the leaders of the bourgeois parties in the Reichstag (the Progressives excepted) on May 15.[2] Taking the speech from the throne of August 4, 1914, as his text, he protested that Germany had not gone out for conquest either before the war or since it had broken out. Germany's action in marching through Belgium had, however, created bitterness 'unprecedented in world history'. He was convinced that even before the war Belgium had had an 'understanding' with Britain and France, and he therefore repeated his demand of April 25: 'We must, assuming that the military situation allows it, render Belgium harmless, prevent it from becoming an English and

[1] Printed in Westarp, op. cit., pp. 48 f.; cf. also Westarp's impression of Bethmann Hollweg's ideas about Belgium: 'But it is more important that B. (Bethmann Hollweg) has at last announced his opinion about Belgium. In my view, in a way to which there can be no more objections (!), and I see in this progress and success.' Letter from Westarp to Heydebrand und der Lasa, April 25, 1915, ibid., pp. 49 f.

[2] A short report, Westarp, op. cit., pp. 51 f.

French dependency, militarily, economically or politically; how, is another question. Not a vassal State of England, but of ourselves.'

On military requirements Bethmann Hollweg said, interestingly, that the military were asking for smaller annexations than he himself. Hindenburg, he alleged, wanted only to annex Liége, nothing more; he himself would not stop at that if the military situation allowed more. Falkenhayn wanted, in addition, a right to occupy the whole country, including the Flanders coast. For the Chancellor it 'went without saying' that Germany would 'make Belgium economically profitable'; he had in mind a customs union, but also attached importance to the question of railway tariffs. The port of Antwerp was enough for him, and he held the optimistic view that Antwerp was not a 'prize of war' for the British. He expressed his Flemish policy in the formula: 'A counter must be found to Frenchifying influences.'

The Chancellor described his war aims against France concisely. He wanted 'to weaken France, whether she resents it or not'. For this purpose he spoke of a war indemnity and annexations and 'whatever the General Staff thinks right', although he said that Falkenhayn did not yet want to commit himself. He himself, on the other hand, had very definite and consistent ideas: he wanted 'in any case to take Briey from France', to rectify the frontier in the Vosges and if possible also to annex Belfort, even if this should 'raise difficulties'.

As regards Russia he took the same view as Spahn, that military considerations were even more important in the east than in the west. He thought that Germany's economic interests could be safeguarded by 'a good, very long-term commercial treaty'. He said that 'the sections which we need for military reasons' were not very big, but 'included some land for settlement'.

He hoped to be able to keep Italy and Rumania out of the war, for otherwise Russia 'might be too much for us'. He warned his audience against underestimating Russia, which still possessed 'a large and superior army', but yet spoke of 'perhaps bringing Russia down in the course of this summer', although he was cautious enough to add that 'it was difficult to make prophecies'.

In essence what the Chancellor said on May 13 was a repetition of his September programme. We can therefore well understand that the leaders of the 'national' parties went away, as Westarp reported, 'satisfied'.

On May 23, a few days after this interview, the situation was overcast by the entry of Italy into the war. This event drove the Chancellor, who felt the need to counteract the effect on German morale, to publish his war aims to the world in a speech in the Reichstag on

May 28 which was delivered with passion, instinct with 'righteous anger', and described by contemporaries as 'splendid, powerful, steel-sharp'.

The greater the danger [he said] which we have to face from the ring of enemies round us . . . the more necessary is it for us to hold out until we have fought for and achieved all possible real guarantees and safeguards that none of our enemies will again dare appeal to arms, alone or in company.[1]

Thunderous applause greeted the Chancellor, and hosts of deputies, it was reported, breathed again and blessed the hour 'which had made the Chancellor so hard'.

The first cracking of the Russian front, which began with the German advances into Lithuania and Courland and the breaks-through at Gorlice and Tarnow, and led on to the great offensive in the east, induced Bethmann Hollweg, true to his conviction that a secure separate peace could be obtained only from a winning position, to regard the situation in May as favourable for renewed feelers for a separate peace with Russia; and Austria-Hungary, hard pressed by Italy, now consented.[2] Both Sazonov, however, in a speech to the Duma, and the Tsar in a telegram to the king of Denmark, had brusquely rejected any idea of a separate peace or armistice; the counter-influence of Britain was clearly at work. Bethmann Hollweg's interpretation was that the Tsar would never act without previously consulting his allies. But such a course would presuppose Germany's willingness to conclude peace with all her enemies on the basis of the existing military situation; and even supposing that these enemies were ready to negotiate, after Italy's entry into the war, 'such a peace could, at the best, be only on the basis of the *status quo*'. It was, said the Chancellor, for the military to decide whether Germany must accept such a peace. On the same day Falkenhayn again pleaded for a separate peace 'on the ground of our military successes', but he at once withdrew his proposal on learning of the Tsar's refusal.

At this juncture when the armies of the Central Powers were advancing together in the east and policy in Belgium was being energetically prosecuted, Bethmann Hollweg further clarified his main aim in respect of Germany's future position in a reconstructed Europe. On June 5 the Mitteleuropa plan was discussed at a great

[1] Friedrich Thimme, *Bethmann Hollwegs Kriegsreden* (Stuttgart and Berlin, 1919), p. 35.

[2] An undated letter from Jagow to Wangenheim, expresses the view that the peace feelers must be kept in German hands, against the possibility of a *rapprochement* between Austria-Hungary and Russia. All the documents show the Austrians consenting to the peace feelers, and in favour of meeting Russia on the question of the Straits.

Conference of State. Bethmann Hollweg found the leading figures in the Prusso-German higher bureaucracy little enamoured of his plan for a German–Austro-Hungarian customs union as the kernel of a European customs alliance. The Chancellor, however, stuck to his plan in the face of all objections, being most strongly supported by Helfferich, now Secretary of State of the Reich Treasury, while Delbrück, of the Interior, saw economic disadvantages in the proposals but accepted the Chancellor's overriding political considerations.

Meanwhile the German troops were advancing in the east. Przemysl was re-taken on June 3, Lemberg fell on June 22, and the great offensive from the Baltic to the San and the Bug opened on July 1. Bethmann Hollweg, in spite of the Tsar's refusal, redoubled his efforts to secure a separate peace with Russia, one of his devices being to bribe deputies of the Duma. On June 25 he urgently begged Andersen to make a second journey to Petersburg, and assured him that he could tell the Tsar that Germany was ready 'to conclude with Russia a peace which should safeguard the future of us both, preserve our neighbourly interests and rights, and take Russia's natural interests into full account'. It is against this background that we must judge Bethmann Hollweg's much commented opposition to the agitation of the Schiemann school in the general staff, particularly against their idea of annexing not only Courland, but also Riga and the whole Baltic coast. Bethmann Hollweg thought these plans justified, at the utmost, only if 'Sweden could be brought to co-operate and Finland too detached from the Russian Empire'[1]–a striking proof that the Chancellor's grand ideas of September, 1914, had not yet been finally set aside. He asked that no further Russian territory east of Warsaw should be occupied, for fear of driving the Russians to 'a struggle of desperation', and that nothing should be said 'by highest quarters in Germany' which might give the impression that Russia's military strength was broken or nearing collapse.

Bethmann Hollweg's efforts to achieve a separate peace with Russia reached a fresh peak at the beginning of July, 1915. Following up a suggestion from the German ambassador in Constantinople, he tried to show the Russians that Britain and France could not secure for them their principal war aim of free passage through the Dardanelles, but that German help could. As part of Germany's efforts to make Russia 'ripe for peace', Jagow had put strong pressure on Turkey to agree officially on April 18 to terms which granted

[1] On the Andersen mission and Germany's offer to Sweden of an alliance, see also W. M. Carlgren, *Neutralität oder Allianz, Deutschlands Beziehungen zu Schweden in den Anfangsjahren des ersten Weltkrieges*, Acta Universitatis Stockholmiensis, No. 6 (Upsala, 1962), pp. 84 ff. and 102 ff.

Russia 'a claim to economic and military co-use' of the Straits; Turkey asked in return for the cancellation of the famous 'Capitulations' which restricted her sovereignty over the Straits.

While he was assuring the Russians through such channels as Fritz Warburg and the Grand Duke of Hesse that Germany's territorial demands were only modest, Bethmann Hollweg was trying also to turn the Tsar's mind towards peace by pointing out the danger which would threaten his throne from revolution if the war went on. He did not go so far as Conrad von Hoetzendorf who, when Galicia had been cleared and the fall of Warsaw was imminent, proposed offering Russia not only a separate peace but an alliance, but he described that moment as the most favourable one for a separate peace, if one was ever to be achieved at all. On this occasion he also explained why he was pursuing the idea of a separate peace with Russia with such unexampled tenacity, in spite of the Tsar's repeated 'Nos': he was convinced that this was the easiest way to solve the remaining problems 'in the west, south and south-east'—in Belgium, the Balkans and the east. He thought that the prospect for such a peace would be endangered 'if we had already disposed unilaterally of big Russian territories', obviously meaning all Poland and the Baltic provinces.

A common factor in all these efforts to achieve a separate peace is that they were all tactical methods of assuring the war aims in the west, and were themselves dependent on 'safeguards and gurantees'. Bethmann Hollweg's view of these guarantees at the very moment when he was readiest to reach an understanding with Russia is shown by the fact that on July 13 a conference was held to settle the dimensions and character of the Polish 'Frontier Strip'. The dimensions may have been modest by Russian standards of size, but they would have perceptibly weakened Russia's position in Europe, and they would have placed Poland under German military domination since the frontier, which was to take in the fortress of Modlin, would have run almost under the gates of Warsaw. For Germany, the strip would have meant enlarging Prussian territory by an area twice as large as Alsace-Loraine, not counting the possible detachment from Russia of territory in Courland and Lithuania.

On August 3, however, the Tsar's third 'No' arrived and shattered all Germany's hopes of a separate peace. When Andersen called personally on Bethmann Hollweg and Ballin in Berlin on August 9, 1915, he told them that Russia did not regard herself as beaten, since Russians did not think of either Courland or Poland as real Russia, and Russia's great depth made her still perfectly capable of lasting out the war.

197

The Tsar's 'No' and the Advance in the East:
East and West again

The big success of the offensive in the east–the great fortresses fell on August 4, 1915, and Warsaw the following day–had kept alive German and Austrian hopes that Russia would sue for peace. But when Russia failed to make any overtures, Bethmann Hollweg gave up his long cherished hopes of a separate peace and reverted to the idea of forcing Russia back and weakening her. He always however, kept in view two parallel eastern policies: the larger solution of forcing Russia back by the creation of border states after promoting revolution through defeating the Russians in the field; and the lesser solution, in favour at times of military deadlock, when the general situation became menacing and the military called on the diplomats for help. In August, 1915, the factors in favour of the larger solution re-asserted themselves.

The shift from a policy of separate peace to one of a dictated peace was made in obedience to careful considerations which the Chancellor expounded to Falkenhayn on the eve of the fall of Warsaw. Should Russia after all show herself ready to conclude a separate peace (of which there were no immediate signs), then she should be given a 'cheap' peace; that is, she should be allowed to retain Poland 'except for the strategic frontier rectifications which we must have'. But should peace be forced on her by military and revolutionary actions, then there were two possible ways of dealing with Poland: 'either an autonomous Polish kingdom is brought into being, linked with us or with Austria-Hungary by an alliance and a military convention, or the larger part of Congress Poland is amalagamated with Galicia as a State under Austrian rule'. Here the eastern border states policy is taken up again, and it is striking that the highest official in the German Reich puts the Germano-Polish solution as the first of several possibilities.

A report by Bethmann Hollweg to the Emperor on August 11, written under the influence of Brockdorff-Rantzau's reports from Copenhagen on the success of Helphand's revolutionary enterprises in Russia, shows the same line of thought:

> Should the military developments and events in Russia itself make it possible *to thrust the Muscovite Empire back eastward, detaching its western portions,* then our liberation from this nightmare in the east would certainly be a worthwhile goal, worth the great sacrifices and extraordinary exertions of this war.

The Austrian ambassador, Hohenlohe, at once sensed the shift in the German government's aims. He saw in 'the absolutely fantastic military successes of these days' what would be 'most likely the last chance' to force Russia to make peace. The Central Powers, he told the Chancellor, had already advanced a long step towards their goal of breaking Russia's influence in Europe by winning Poland and the Baltic provinces. In respect of border policy Hohenlohe went even further, suggesting that East Galicia and the Bukovina might be combined, perhaps with a frontier strip of Russian territory, into a new Ukrainian crown-land within the Dual Monarchy, which would then constitute a nucleus round which an autonomous Ukraine under Austrian influence might take shape when Russia disintegrated. The aim of forcing Russia back seemed to the Austrian so vitally important to the Central Powers that Hohenlohe wanted Germany to reach an understanding with Britain which would have entailed the renunciation of Germany's war aims in the west.

Various factors, not least among them revelations (believed to be the work of the British ambassador in Petersburg) about his negotiations with Russia, made Bethmann Hollweg take steps 'to keep the nation in good humour' and to assuage the mistrust of the great economic interests and the majority parties in parliament. His speech, which was called 'an achievement of the very first order' and greeted with 'prolonged and tempestuous cheers and applause', was uncompromising in tone and grandiose in its treatment of the problems of both east and west. 'Gentlemen, we shall carry on the fight until those peoples demand peace of the real guilty parties, until the path is free for a new Europe, liberated from French intrigues, from Muscovite lust of conquest and from English tutelage.'

Bethmann Hollweg said openly that this forcing back of the other powers would, as he saw it, lead to the supremacy of Germany as the 'power of order', and meant a breach with the past.

A new thing must come! If Europe is ever to achieve peace, this can come only through Germany's occupying a strong and unassailable position (Hear, hear!). . . . The English policy of the Balance of Power must disappear. . . . Germany must so extend her position, so fortify and reinforce it, that the other powers lose the taste for any more policies of encirclement.

This same speech contained the Chancellor's first open reference to the 'liberation' of Poland from the Russian yoke. 'We, with our allies, have liberated almost all Galicia and Poland, we have liberated Lithuania and Courland from the Russians . . . Ivangorod, Warsaw and Kovno have fallen.' The occupation of the eastern frontier of Congress Poland, effected on that day, marked the beginning of a development which would abolish the old antagonisms between Poles and Germans.

Yet Bethmann Hollweg was clinging to his aims both in east and west. He made this clear in his Reichstag speech of August 19.

This interpretation of the occupation of Poland created a political fact only to be understood in the context of the idea of forcing Russia back; in other words, of Bethmann Hollweg's 'larger solution'.

But this speech was not directed exclusively, nor even primarily, to the east. The greater part of it consisted of a passionately bitter indictment of Britain, whose friendship Germany had always sought and never found (in the Haldane Mission of 1912 and at the outbreak of war). The Chancellor was particularly critical of Britain's refusal to promise 'unconditional' neutrality in the event of a war in which Germany should become 'involved'. This speech was naturally taken as 'a flaming indictment of England' and its effects were compared with those of Lissauer's 'Hymn of Hate' and Mackensen's letter describing England as the real author of the world conflagration (Russia and France being only accessories). German opinion still looked on Britain as 'the most audacious, the slyest and the most dangerous enemy'.

The 'liberation of Poland, Courland and Lithuania', of which the Chancellor has spoken, had begun to emerge as a fixed aim of German policy with the creation of the General Government of Warsaw on July 25 and the initial steps in the organisation of an 'Administrative District Oberost'; negotiations with Austria on these points had been begun six days before the speech. Poland was now being treated as war booty and was to be attached to Austria-Hungary, a solution to which the Chancellor appears to have agreed provided always that it did not jeopardise the position of the Germans in the Danubian Monarchy. Burian suggested that Germany might take the Baltic provinces as a sort of compensation for Austria's acquisition, and asked Bethmann Hollweg if he was still against annexing them. 'Bethmann Hollweg said no, and agreed that the two questions hung together, strategically and economically.' Thus the new eastern frontier, as demanded by Rechenberg back in August, 1914, took shape – far beyond the areas so far singled out for annexation as the so-called 'Frontier Strip'. The potential dangers, and also the extent, of Germany's ambitions, were already visible in the demand for German leadership in the Dual Monarchy as a guarantee of political and military reliability, and in the special economic and strategic conditions stipulated in return for leaving the new Polish kingdom to Austria-Hungary (land for the Poles expatriated from the 'Frontier Strip', maintenance of the economic *status quo* in Poland).

While in July the tactical move of a separate peace with Russia had taken first place, now, a few weeks later, the establishment of

Germany's position in Europe by means of the creation of an eastern bastion had become the dominant motif of German policy.

Mitteleuropa as the Basis for Germany's World Power Status

The development of the political aims of Germany's leaders entered a new phase at the end of August, 1915, when the Chief of the General Staff, in an appreciation of the general situation, expressed with exceptional clarity the conclusion that 'after the battles of the last four weeks Russia was so weakened that she could not become a serious danger to us within an appreciable period'.[1] He was, however worried that the Western Powers had not done more to relieve the pressure on Russia; he concluded that they would pin their hopes on a 'methodically conducted war of exhaustion' against Germany. He therefore turned once more to the politicians for help; he wanted the formation of a 'Central European Federation', i.e., Germany, Austria-Hungary, Bulgaria and Turkey should conclude a long-term offensive and defensive alliance which should have economic and cultural, as well as military, aspects. Falkenhayn saw in this Central European Federation the psychological and political means of destroying Britain's hopes of a war of successful attrition, particularly if other states, such as Sweden and Switzerland and perhaps also Greece, could be attached to it; the Polish question would also be easier to solve within this larger framework.

The exchanges between the Chief of Staff and the Chancellor on the questions thus raised reveal the basic views of the two men on the inter-relation of political, economic, cultural and psychological factors. Bethmann Hollweg flatly rejected Falkenhayn's plan (although the Emperor had already approved it) as not calculated either to weaken the enemy's military power, or to strengthen that of Germany, Austria-Hungary and the Ottoman Empire. The resources of these three Empires were already fully at the disposal of the Supreme Command, and there seemed to be no prospect of the adherence of small Balkan states (except Bulgaria, already attached) to the 'German–Austrian–Turkish bloc'; the adherence of the Scandinavian states and Holland would expose them to British pressure, unless Sweden entered the war actively on Germany's side.

The Chancellor's objections to Falkenhayn's plan did not, however, mean that he had given up his own Mitteleuropa idea, which he had advanced as a war aim in September, 1914. But he saw no

[1] This estimate of Russia's strength proved itself a year later, in August, 1916, to have been a very serious underestimate of the enemy, as Bethmann Hollweg himself admitted to the Federal Council.

practical advantage to be got at that moment from such a defensive and offensive alliance, and he also feared that the creation of a Central European Federation in wartime would jeopardise Germany's essential trade with the neutrals.[1] He regarded it, however, as axiomatic that Germany's future programme must be 'to detach the Balkan states from Russian influence and to bring them and the Germanic countries of the Continent nearer to us by political and economic ties'. In contrast to Falkenhayn, for whom, as he said himself, 'Mitteleuropa was solely a means of warfare', Mitteleuropa was for Bethmann Hollweg *the* aim of German policy–but one to be achieved as a result of the war.

At the end of August, as we saw, Falkenhayn had believed Russia to be 'so weakened that she could not again become a serious danger within an appreciable period'. Yet only a week later he was fearing a Russian offensive in the following spring. He therefore wanted the mobilisation of all possible resources, and he asked the Chancellor to win over the Polish population for the German cause and to make use of the 'army manpower' in it, because man-power was the department in which Germany would first feel her supplies running short. But it was not only to obtain Polish recruits, but also on account of the political and moral gain benefits to be extracted from Poland turning against Russia, that Falkenhayn asked for 'a decision to be taken on the future of Poland'. Bethmann Hollweg, however, had doubts on the score of international law and was not convinced that Germany's war effort would gain much by drawing on the Poles.

The idea of forcing Russia back and weakening her was taken up with great energy by Jagow. Just as Zimmermann was the moving spirit among the top Germans for the 'world programme', so Jagow seems to have been the prime champion of an eastern policy, which was rooted in obsessions about the magnitude of the Russian danger and Russia's non-European racial and cultural nature. The influence of Schwerin and Sering on Jagow's ideas is unmistakable, and he expressly referred to both men as 'experts'. Thus on September 2 he wrote in a long memorandum on the Polish question (which the Emperor fully approved):

Hitherto the giant Russian Empire, with its inexhaustible human material, its possibilities of economic recovery, its expansive tendencies, has brooded over Western Europe like a nightmare. In spite of the veneer of Western civilisation given it by Peter the Great and the German dynasty

[1] Paul R. Sweet, 'Germany, Austria, Hungary and Mitteleuropa, August 1915–August 1916', in *Festschrift für Heinrich Benedikt*, ed. H. Hantsch and Novotny (Vienna, 1957), p. 182.

which followed him, its basically Byzantine–Oriental culture separates it from the Latin culture of the West, and the Russian race, part Slav, part Mongol, is foreign to the Germanic–Latin peoples of the West.

He went on to argue that pan-Slavism, as a protest against western Europe, undermined 'the traditional friendship of the dynasty' (a view which calls in question the effectiveness of all Bethmann Hollweg's attempts to achieve peace through dynastic connections). The Reinsurance Treaty was only 'an outcrop of earlier conditions'; since its day Russia had been arming steadily (the Emperor added, 'with French money'), 'and we should not have been able to keep up with her armaments much longer'.

Now that war had come after a century and a half of peace, Poland must be made into a buffer state; its inhabitants were admittedly Slavs but without Russians' Mongol strain, and they were divided from the Orthodox Russians by their Catholic and Protestant religions. Now 'the forcing back of the Russian nightmare eastward at least to the Mitau–Bug line must be regarded as a desirable war aim.'

Under no circumstances must Russia have a 'road to invade Germany, such as the deep salient of Congress Poland had constituted for Prussia–Germany; moreover, Courland can only be detached from Russia if Poland is also detached'. To restore Poland to Russia seemed therefore impossible, even if it was perhaps the simplest way of solving the Polish problem.

Like Bethmann Hollweg, Jagow saw several possible solutions for this problem. A completely independent Poland seemed to him not possible, since it could not offer military guarantees that it would constitute 'a useful buffer State between Russia and Germany'; it would rather see-saw between the two, be a focus of *irredenta*, and inevitably seek an 'outlet to the sea', viz., Danzig. The annexation of Poland would be a national disaster, since it would bring millions of alien subjects into the German state, but even the formation of an autonomous state under German suzerainty would have only disadvantages, apart from the solitary advantage of bringing the fortresses into German hands.

The only solution was therefore an autonomous Poland under Austrian suzerainty. Jagow would, however, make this concession conditional on the safeguarding of the preponderant influence of the Germans in the Dual Monarchy; whether the best way of securing this safeguard was through the so-called 'sub-Dualism',[1] he would

[1] Burian told Bethmann Hollweg at their meeting on August 14, 1915: 'the Dualist structure of the Monarchy (that is, its division into a Transleithanian, or Hungarian, and a Cisleithanian, or Austro–Bohemian half) makes it impossible to

not discuss. With eighteen million Poles, he calculated, a Trialist form was bound to emerge; the disintegration of the state could only be delayed, not prevented. The German Lands of Austria would then fall to Germany; the German element in them must preserve its strength and vitality against that day; in particular, the Czech element must be forced back. The Great German Empire of the future would thus consist of Prussia–Germany plus Austrian Cis–Leithania; Hungary would be independent, and the independent Poland that would then emerge would probably seek to lean on Germany.

Besides securing this fundamental condition of strengthening the influence of the Germans over the general policy of the Monarchy – as against the anti-German tendencies in the church, the higher aristocracy and the traditionalist 'Austrian' civil service – the securing of Germany's economic and military interests in the future Poland would constitute the first step towards the German–Polish solution. Jagow calculated that Poland would remain a separate customs area from Austria-Hungary, in order to safeguard Germany's exports to it, which constituted three-quarters of German exports to Russia; he repeated the demand that Poland must cede a frontier strip and settle on her own territory the Poles and Jews expatriated from the area ceded. The Emperor, however, expressly insisted that the Austro-Polish solution must be conditional on the prior conclusion of a military convention with Austria-Hungary giving Germany:

predominant influence over the reorganisation and improvement of the Austrian army, and also joint control over the Vistula line and fortresses, which, lying as they do in front of West Prussia, Posen and Silesia, are, after all, a purely Prussian interest, not an Austrian one, and will, it is to be hoped, be made the screen for our eastern frontier.

This meant a further direct infringement of Austria's sovereignty over the Poland which was to be allotted to her.

Such reflections by the highest personages in Germany betray a change of attitude towards Austria-Hungary, of whose military strength, economic powers of resistance and political cohesion Germany held the lowest opinion; Germany was proposing to organise and penetrate Austria, in order to keep Germany's only partner in the world in existence, strengthen her and bind her to Germany.

The Polish plans led to the idea of extending the advanced frontier northward to the Baltic provinces, which were to be attached to

add thereto a third, equal State entity, therefore no so-called Trialism.' The only possibility would be 'institutions lying entirely within the framework of the existing Dualism' for a 'Polish Kingdom of Austria' which 'should receive very extensive autonomy'.

Germany in one form or another. Jagow emerges as the real author of the north-eastern policy usually ascribed exclusively to Generals Ludendorff and Hindenburg. The generals long clung to the aim of direct annexation, while Bethmann Hollweg and Jagow, characteristically, preferred forms of indirect rule. Jagow himself appreciated the arguments in favour of annexing and Germanising these areas – sentimental reminiscences of the old State of the Teutonic Knights, and safeguards for the national culture of the local German landowners and burghers – but he thought that the same objects could be assured by the constitution of an autonomous duchy under a German prince, closely attached to Germany in respect of defence and tariffs and presumably also communications. He was already referring to the Baltic provinces as a whole, but was so far thinking only of Lithuania and Courland, with the 'possible inclusion', as he put it, of Riga.

Bethmann Hollweg, who had forwarded Jagow's memorandum to Falkenhayn on September 11 with a covering note,[1] accepted Jagow's proposal to attach Poland to Austria in a relationship something like that of Croatia to Hungary as 'the least disadvantageous solution . . . provided that Austria fulfils the conditions which we must lay down in our own political, economic and military interests'. The inclusion of Poland must not weaken the influence of the German element in Austrian public affairs, but rather strengthen it; economically, the *status quo* must not be altered to Germany's disadvantage; on the military conditions, the importance of which the Chancellor described as 'primary', he asked Falkenhayn for his opinion. At this point the Polish question became involved in Bethmann Hollweg's planning with his aim to establish close links between Germany and the Austro-Hungarian Monarchy as a whole; these links again he envisaged as threefold: 'as in the political and economic fields, so, above all, in the military.'[2]

It was now Falkenhayn's turn to oppose a close military association of Austria-Hungary with Germany, because he regarded Austria as 'a corpse' and its army as 'slack' and 'slipshod'. An Austria

[1] Sweet, op. cit., p. 190.

[2] To support his thesis of a close connection between Austria-Hungary and Germany, Bethmann Hollweg adduced a 'Memorandum from Austria-Hungary' the initiator in chief of which was the Viennese historian, Heinrich Friedjung Friedjung represented a circle in Austria which was 'strongly nationalist, without being German Nationalist in the party sense of the term, and on the other side, in favour of social reform, and yet not socialist'. The central pages of the memorandum examined the possibilities of a closer connection between the two allies. It is characteristic that it made a sharp distinction between political points of view (a twenty-five years offensive and defensive alliance), military (more complete integration of the two armies) and economic (customs and economic union). The memorandum was printed in Leipzig, for private circulation only. Cf. Sweet, op. cit., pp. 184 ff

strengthened by the conquests conceded by Germany and by a military convention with Germany would, he feared, 'renounce our friendship and fight against us in the next war', so that Germany would very soon have to 'wage a struggle for hegemony' with her. Bethmann Hollweg, however, stood by his own line; he was backed by the Prussian Minister for War.[1]

On October 13 and 15 Bethmann Hollweg and Falkenhayn fought out their differences over the Central European Federation and over Jagow's ideas in two long discussions,[2] in which the Chancellor, in face of the most various objections, pressed his idea of a Europe re-shaped on the basis of a close economic, political and military alliance between Germany and Austria-Hungary, safeguarded in the west by a Belgium similarly linked to them and safeguarded in the east by a Poland similarly linked and by a new north-eastern frontier. Neither Falkenhayn's misgivings about the military convention nor the resistance of the pressure groups (the Economic Committee) and the ministries affected (the Reich Interior Office and the Prussian Ministry of Commerce) availed to make him renounce his political vision.[3]

Bethmann Hollweg insisted on early consideration of the Polish question in view of the forthcoming visit of the Austro-Hungarian Foreign Minister, Baron Burian, who was due in Berlin on November 11. On October 30 Falkenhayn at last abandoned his opposition to the military convention,[4] but by this time Jagow had developed his ideas; he now regarded the Polish question as secondary to the wider European problem, which necessitated 'chaining the Monarchy' as closely as possible to Germany.

It is [he wrote] to be assumed that now that the clash between the Germanic and the Slav worlds has come, the pan-Slav tendencies in Russia will develop more sharply than ever, the traditional dynastic connections which formerly existed between us and Petersburg will be finally buried, and Russia will be our enemy in the future too. We should consider whether the forcing back of the semi-Asiatic Muscovite Empire behind the Bug is not an imperious necessity now that the development of history has enabled us, as the representatives of Western culture, to press forward against the Slavs from the Elbe to the Oder and the Vistula.

[1] Bethmann Hollweg reported his conditions for an Austro-Polish solution as follows:
  1. Extensive frontier rectifications (Kovno, Grodno, Ostrolenka, Plosk, Warthe line).
  2. Lithuania and Courland as compensation for Austria's territorial acquisitions, and on annexionist grounds.
  3. A Military Convention. . . .
[2] Cf. n. 15; also, Sweet, op. cit., pp. 192 ff.
[3] Ibid., p. 209.   [4] Ibid., p. 194.

Poland must perforce be left to the Danubian Monarchy, because in view of the lasting hostility of all other European great powers towards Germany, and her threatened isolation, 'whether we like it or not, this war will leave us bound more indissolubly than ever to our Austro-Hungarian allies'; and because Germany needed Austria 'as a bridge to the Balkans and Turkey'.

In agreement on this point with Falkenhayn, Jagow pleaded for a tighter alliance, perhaps 'a general defensive alliance, such as Prince Bismarck wanted'. Such a political alliance demanded the close economic unification of the two Empires, and would provide the basis for concrete military agreements.[1]

If Jagow's exposé had cast a side-glance at the Balkans and the east, the German ambassador in Vienna thought that Germany's eastern policy must govern the whole Austro-Hungarian problem. He opposed the idea of a Trialist construction of the Monarchy because this would lead to its disintegration, which would in turn inevitably obstruct the aims of Germany's eastern policy 'for which we need an empire on the Danube closely linked to us, as a bridge'. The cession of Poland to Austria would bind the Austro-Hungarian state to Germany:

> So long as we have not definitively ceded Poland to Austria we have kept in our hand the trumps to force Austria to give us the military and economic guarantees which we need to keep the whole Monarchy, including Poland, at our side. I continue to regard it as imperative that we should make certain of these guarantees before we give a definitive solution to the Polish question.

Until these guarantees had been secured, Germany could not give up Poland without risking the further loss of Austria-Hungary. In addition to a military convention with Austria-Hungary–how Germany conceived this convention is shown by Falkenhayn's draft of the same date, October 29–she needed special safeguards for her military influence in Poland, 'especially on the future Polish–Russian frontier'. Finally, the ambassador implored Bethmann Hollweg to be firm in the forthcoming conversations with Burian; he repeated once again, as often before, 'that only through the closest military and economic union shall we achieve *a permanent chaining of the Monarchy to ourselves* and at the same time a strengthening of the German element in Austria.'[2]

Jagow's concurring opinion, conveyed on November 6, that

---

[1] The decisive consideration here is the guarantee of the supremacy of the German element in Austria over the Slav–Clerical influences, which would be still further strengthened by the addition of Poland; which is why Jagow would prefer Trialism (which was also resisted by Tisza) to sub-Dualism.

[2] Author's italics.

Germany should not relinquish the parts of Russian Poland occupied by her 'before we have received from the Austro-Hungarian government the guarantees in the economic and military field necessary to keep the Monarchy at our side in the future also' shows how the idea of Mitteleuropa was dominating German high policy in November, 1915.[1] Against this background Friedrich Naumann's book, *Mitteleuropa*, which caused such a sensation at the time, appears merely as a remarkable, but yet thoroughly unrealistic, flight of fantasy.

Guarantees and Safeguards in the East: Austria-Hungary as the Germanic Eastern March

Bethmann Hollweg's wrestling match with Falkenhayn, the discussions on Poland set afoot by Jagow with his long memorandum, and not least Prussian resistance to the Austro-Polish solution – all these factors influenced the preparations for the conference between Bethmann Hollweg and Burian which was to take place in Berlin on November 11 and was 'to clear up' besides general questions 'the Austro-Polish solution, as the chief problem at present of the Mitteleuropa plan'. Burian, who had come to Berlin in the hope of gaining Germany's consent to the Austro-Polish solution, found himself disappointed. Bethmann Hollweg met him with aims in both west and east which, as he said, were 'veiled' and 'masked' to a high degree, but none the less highly 'realistic' and 'definite' and, above all, exactly tuned to Germany's position in 1915.

The conference saw a powerful effort by the Germans to impose their Mitteleuropa Plan on Austria-Hungary. It is extremely interesting to compare the reports on it from the two sides. Bethmann Hollweg insisted that their partnership of destiny in the war called for the establishment of an intimate connection between the two Empires through 'the extension of contractual obligations in political, economic and military respects', so that this relationship 'should be apparent also to our enemies as a lasting factor of international policy, with which they must reckon'. The German Imperial Chancellor's report is very laconic, but Burian's much more extensive account shows that Bethmann Hollweg referred back to Bismarck's plans of 1878–9 for a permanent institutional connection between the two Empires, and that he argued the case for establishing such a connection to meet the lasting threat from the Entente powers which would continue permanently hostile even after defeat: it was 'only through the formation of an invincible Central European bloc'

[1] On this cf. also Ludendorff's remarks: Hans Delbrück, *Ludendorffs Selbstporträt* (Berlin, 1922), p. 71. For the confidential relationship between Ludendorff and Zimmermann, see Conze, *Polnische Nation*, p. 87.

that Germany could avert a renewed attack from her three enemies, and at the same time 'open up all the possibilities for development of an assured period of peace'. Besides political and military matters the Chancellor, said Burian, had also gone deeply into the question of the economic integration of the two powers, which was to be protected against the outer world by a unified tariff system, while internally their economic development could be better fostered 'through the mutual and complementary development of their productive resources'.[1]

According to Bethmann Hollweg, Burian agreed 'completely' with his proposals, only pointing out, in view of the military tasks envisaged, Austria-Hungary's weaker financial resources. Burian's version shows that while he agreed with the general idea, he made reservations in the political and military fields, while in the economic he was much more sceptical on the possibilties of getting the tariff proposals accepted, especially by the neutrals such as the U.S.A and Switzerland.

It is especially striking that Burian expressly mentions (and the German report does not) that the two statesmen agreed 'in the event of victory to limit our war aims strictly to the essential interests of our states'. Both of them (and this was the feeling at the end of 1915) were expecting the course of military operations to influence the enemy towards peace; both were against themselves taking any steps in that direction.

Bethmann Hollweg, with Burian, rejected alike the Trialist solution, a proposal for 'sub-Dualism' which had come from the Austrian Prime Minister, Count Stürgkh, and partition of Poland between Germany and Austria-Hungary; but the pressure of German public opinion made it impossible for him to drop his demands for safeguarding the position of the Germans in Austria, which seemed to him the only way to guarantee that the Monarchy would continue to exist at all. With internal and external difficulties in the way of the annexation of Belgium already beginning to appear, German opinion would not allow Austria alone to secure an important territorial acquisition as a prize of victory, while Germany emerged with no territorial gains or only small ones. With extreme annoyance, Burian saw that this threat jeopardised the Austro-Polish solution,

---

[1] According to Burian, the Chancellor also immediately made a suggestion that the new block, with its new tariffs, could compel recognition from the other powers, whose treaties with Germany, which were based on the m.f.n. principle, he wanted retained. At the peace negotiations demands were to be addressed to France and Britain to abolish the preferences between the metropolitan countries and their colonies. They would presumably refuse, and after this he hoped that the recognition of the new German–Austrian system would meet with no difficulties.

which he had thought safe; for the conditions laid down by Germany as indispensable if she were to let Austria have Poland would make Germany the real mistress of Austro-Poland. Bethmann Hollweg demanded: (i) strategic frontier rectifications ('besides the rectifications necessary to improve her frontier in the Government of Sulwaki and area adjacent to Courland and Lithuania, also certain areas of our Poland which brought Germany great economic advantage'); (ii) very numerous and far-reaching guarantees which would make the transport system on which the Polish economy was based absolutely dependent on Germany. There were also the familiar demands for land on which to settle the deportees from the German Frontier Strip; freedom of emigration for Polish labour; Burian at once divined Germany's hidden intention of keeping Poland economically entirely at her own disposal, while saddling Austria with the social and political problems entailed by the assumption of sovereignty over the country; and he hinted at doubts whether Austria wanted to take Poland at all.

Burian thought that 'the Chancellor regarded the questions coming under the heading of Belgium and the Baltic provinces as even more unclear and veiled than that of Poland'. He saw that Germany was renouncing direct annexation of Belgium, but wanted to create 'institutions' and provide for 'interventions' which would leave Belgium with only 'the appearance of independence'. He saw that Germany wanted here too to exploit the economic resources of the country without burdening herself with the political problems and disadvantages of incorporation: a real 'squaring of the circle'. He thought that the Germans' very express and obvious desire to obtain compensation in the east was the immediate political result of their fear of emerging empty-handed in the west.

A fourth question raised was that of the Balkans. Germany's treatment of this problem reflected exactly her policy of that autumn, which was to assure her own hegemony by establishing a preponderant influence over Austria-Hungary. In the Balkans, said Burian, the German government did acknowledge in general terms Austria-Hungary's right to give her own interests priority, but when it came to details, 'special German wishes or reservations cropped up everywhere'. Now that the successful campaign in Serbia had realised 'Germany's main aim in the South-East, the link with Bulgaria and Turkey', Bethmann Hollweg pressed for a separate peace with Serbia, and before Burian had time to comment in detail on the problems of that area, asked whether it would not be best to unite Serbia with Montenegro and make peace quickly on that basis.

Burian on his side, in his endeavour to save Poland for Austria, tried to overcome the Imperial Chancellor's aversion from large territorial acquisitions and to egg him on by saying 'that consideration for the security of our common eastern frontier should not be overridden in the northern sector by the possibility of a future danger' of fresh Russian expansion.

Bethmann Hollweg ended this thorough exchange of views after the successes in the east in 'high satisfaction' at having 'reached complete agreement on the essentials'. Burian, as he himself wrote, 'could only profess a similar satisfaction, but not altogether feel it'. He had been treated to eloquent assurances of his ally's loyalty, but these academic assurance had 'always been accompanied by more or less undisguised notice of very far-reaching claims, reserve on all concrete questions, remarks that it was still too early to take a decision since everything depended on the issue of the war which was still uncertain'. The real significance of the discussions is that the Monarchy had itself become a war aim, because under the proposed close relationship with Germany it had to fit itself into the larger unit dominated by Germany. The *pro memoria* written by Jagow two days after the meeting and sent by him to the government in Vienna as a basis for further discussions showed what was the role assigned to Austria.

This document constitutes the official communication to Austria-Hungary of Germany's Mitteleuropa programme, to which Germany supposed herself already to have received the Monarchy's assent. It was to be realised 'formally and materially' through long-term political, economic and military treaties, valid perhaps for thirty years. Jagow's conviction that the war was the decisive struggle between Teuton and Slav was made the basis for political argument and action; it also permitted the German Secretary of State for Foreign Affairs to intervene deeply in the internal affairs of the Monarchy and its own self-interpretation. He repeated the demand for guarantees for the maintenance of the leadership of the German element in Cis–Leithania 'to prevent any further Slavisation of Austria and to restore to the German element that leading position which is due to it in the interest of Austria as the Germanic Eastern March'. Only thus would the German–Austro-Hungarian Treaty of October 7, 1879, be revived and restored, the treaty which, for Jagow, rested on the predominance of the Magyars in the Hungarian half of the Monarchy and of the Germans in the Austrian half. The military agreements and conversations were to be left to the military authorities (as Falkenhayn had indicated, they should come only after the conclusion of the political and economic treaties), and the purpose of the economic connection, as established by 'a customs treaty with mutual preferential treatment', was described as 'leading to the fusion of the whole area in an economic unit'. Even more far-reaching was the proposal to recast the treaty relations between the two states. As a basis for further negotiations the German government wanted 'a mutual guarantee of each partner's territory on the basis of the coming peace treaties and appropriate extension of the *casus foederis*'. In other words, a mutual guarantee of future acquisitions and new possessions was to be given while the war was still in progress.

While agreeing in principle to all three points, the Austro-Hungarian government repudiated the suggestion that the Monarchy was being progressively Slavised and assured Germany that Austria-Hungary's reliability as an ally did not rest only on the predominance of her Magyars and Germans. Austria was not simply, as Jagow had suggested, a 'Germanic Eastern March', and her Slavs were not basically Germanophobe.

This exchange of notes closed the conference of November 11, and the next steps towards extending the alliance were left to the departmental ministries, beginning with the economic specialists, who from January, 1916, onward held repeated conversations on the basis of the *pro memorias* on economic policy already exchanged.

At this stage the idea of a separate peace in the east had retreated far into the background. Bethmann Hollweg had indeed again told Burian that 'if Russia were to offer us a separate peace *soon*, and if the general situation were such as to make acceptance desirable, it must involve restoring Poland'; but the Emperor, partly in his disappointment over Russia, partly in an access of confidence in victory, had noted: 'No intention of this! This is all over! *Now I don't consent to it.*' Too much German blood had been spilled 'to allow it just to be given back, even under a separate peace with Russia'.

A suggestion by Hohenlohe that the Central Powers might advance peace proposals at once produced a serious clash between Bethmann Hollweg and Falkenhayn. The general accused the Chancellor of himself wanting to make a peace offer for reasons of domestic politics. Falkenhayn's deep pessimism is shown by his attitude at the close of this year which had brought so many successes but yet also such heavy losses and no final decision. He refused to accept that a readiness for peace and a determination to carry on were alternatives before Germany. 'In reality,' he wrote, 'we have not got this choice; we are forced to tread the latter path to the end for good or ill, whether we will or not'; for this was no war 'of the type we used to know', but a struggle for existence; any talk of peace could only weaken the will to hold out, and was not justified by the military situation. Bethmann Hollweg had equally few illusions over the general situation, but in contrast to the almost fatalistic mood of the soldier, he saw possibilities in diplomacy. He did not want to advance peace proposals of his own, but he wanted 'to support inclinations towards peace which may show themselves among our enemies . . . and thus to renounce no weapon which might aid the military effort to weaken the enemy'. These remarks throw light on Bethmann Hollweg's peace feelers and reveal them as an integral part of Germany's will to victory.

In the course of the various peace soundings, Bethmann Hollweg's war aims had taken very definite shape. This was made clear in his second big Reichstag speech, on December 9, 1915. To the thunderous applause of the bourgeois parties, he described Germany's demands for a peace in the following words:

> I cannot say what guarantees the Imperial Government will demand in – for example – the Belgian question, what power-bases it will hold necessary for these guarantees. But one thing our enemies must tell themselves: the longer, the more bitterly, they carry on this war against us, the bigger the guarantees will become which we find necessary. . . . Neither in the east nor the west can we allow our enemies of today to hold gateways through which they can threaten us again tomorrow more sharply than before.

This wording had been chosen after elaborate prior conversations with the leaders of the War Aims Majority, which had resulted in an agreement in principle between the Chancellor and the parties that, in order to keep up public morale, the speech should contain as precise a definition as possible of Germany's war aims. While Bassermann and Spahn wanted the words 'territorial acquisitions' to come into the speech (as they did in the declaration afterwards made by Spahn as spokesman for the War Aims Majority), the Chancellor preferred the word 'glacis'. Spahn objected that this left out the economic implications. Finally the Chancellor opted for Jagow's suggestion of 'gateways' (*Einfallstore*), which sounded defensive, and repeated the flexible formula of 'guarantees'.

His phraseology was, indeed, deliberately vague, because at that very moment separate negotiations with Belgium were on foot, the detailed examination of which will show that Germany's war aims were taking very definite shape in the west as well as in the east. The Chancellor's aims relating to Belgium played an especially important part in Bethmann Hollweg's general scheme, as was apparent when Colonel House, President Wilson's friend and special emissary, visited him in Berlin at the end of January, 1916. This renewed offer of mediation, coming from the greatest neutral power, obviously offered unique opportunities for skilful diplomacy. Bethmann Hollweg began by saying that a condition for lasting peace was that Germany must in future be safe from threat, either from Poland or from Belgium; he was also asking for compensation for northern France, which France would have to pay. House's primary interest was naturally in a settlement between Germany and Britain. To this Bethmann Hollweg answered, as he had often done on other occasions, that from the day he became Chancellor he had dreamed of an understanding with Britain adhered to by America, a triple alliance which would have guaranteed the peace of the world; this had been a long-term objective compared with which he had thought the breach of Belgian neutrality a small thing. House assured him that Britain trusted him, Jagow, Zimmermann and Solf, but mistrusted the military party. Bethmann Hollweg replied 'with the greatest decision, that no one and nothing stands between me and the Emperor'.[1] In saying this, the Chancellor described his own position and his policy much more accurately than he tried to make out in his retrospective account, for the aims of the Emperor (who soon after backed the Chancellor publicly by dismissing Tirpitz) and of the military party (whom Bethmann Hollweg omitted to mention) differed from his own only in their methods, not in their general tenor; Bethmann Hollweg was indeed the man who, when Emperor and generals wavered, once he had conceived his general scheme of 'safeguards and guarantees', held to it, flexibly but yet clearly and steadfastly.

[1] According to the account which Riezler later gave to the board of enquiry, Bethmann Hollweg asserted at this time that in the event of peace negotiations he could secure the Emperor's assent to any terms, even against the opposition of the Supreme Command. This statement at any rate shows that the Chancellor had not definitely renounced all the demands involved in German war aims. (See W. Steglich. *Friedenspolitik*, p. 4 f., n. 20.)

7

THE WAR AIMS POLICY OF THE
REICH'S LEADERS, 1916

FEELERS FOR A SEPARATE PEACE IN WEST AND EAST

In the course of the negotiations with Belgium, Bethmann Holl-weg, on New Year's Day, 1916, again formulated Germany's war aims policy towards that country. By this stage of the war he had ceased to believe in the possibility of a dictated peace which would allow Germany 'to do whatever she pleased with Belgium'; the most that he thought could be achieved would be 'a definite treaty with political, military and economic safeguards; whether or no we annex Liége is a question for later consideration'. Von Bissing asked, rather hesitantly, whether Bethmann Hollweg believed that, if Germany based her position in Belgium on a treaty of this kind, she could strengthen it by vigorous promotion of the Flemish movement. Bethmann Hollweg said 'yes', and proposed the formation of a 'Flamand Committee' to support Germany's administrative efforts in this direction, thereby extending the policy initiated by him in 1914. He did not want this done secretly, but publicly; he wanted the world to see Germany as 'the benefactor of the Flemish'. He was against a 'Kingdom of Flanders', which he did not think would prove viable, except possibly in a personal union with Holland.

This was the background against which the German government opened negotiations for a separate peace with the king of the Belgians, in the hope of anticipating the general conclusion of peace by creating a *fait accompli*, viz., Germany's indirect domination of Belgium. These efforts advanced beyond the feeler stage to that of genuine negotiations.

Guarantees and Safeguards in the West:
a Separate Peace with Belgium through King Albert

In August, 1914, after the fall of Liége, the German government had made offers to Belgium but King Albert had rejected them as unacceptable[1] on the grounds that a voluntary submission to the German occupying power would have been tantamount to the

[1] Hans W. Gatzke, *Germany's Drive to the West* (Baltimore, 1950), pp. 8 f.

abandonment of neutrality. The initiative for the new negotiations came from Erzberger in the summer of 1915. Hertling took up the suggestion, largely in the interests of Bavaria's own war aims policy, and passed it on to Bethmann Hollweg on August 11 (the day on which the Chancellor was advocating the 'larger solution' in Russia to the Emperor), at the same time advising the use of the dynastic connections of the House of Wittelsbach with King Albert. The Chancellor welcomed the chance and asked Hertling to find a suitable intermediary. Hertling had already given the Chancellor the name of Princess Sophie, the Belgian queen's sister, and the idea of entrusting this delicate diplomatic mission to her husband, Count Törring-Jettenbach, was obvious.

Törring must soon have been able to establish contact with Belgium in the capacity of emissary of the German government. Between the end of November, 1915, and February, 1916, he had in all four secret meetings in Zürich with the king of the Belgians' agent, Professor Waxweiler. We have sufficiently full accounts of these meetings from his reports to Jagow. The first meeting was on November 24–25. Törring had received strict orders from Berlin to maintain an attitude of reserve, to make no proposals himself and above all not to reveal in any way the official origin of his mission. Waxweiler gave him a letter from King Albert repudiating emphatically and at length the German accusation, which Germany had tried to support by publishing selected Belgian documents, that Belgium had not preserved a neutral attitude before the war. The letter protested eloquently that it was Belgium's right and her moral duty to defend her neutrality against attack from any quarter; it was for this reason, and not as an ally of the Entente, that her army was confronting Germany in the field.

With King Albert maintaining the principle of neutrality so vigorously, the incompatibility of the two points of view was bound to emerge as soon as the German negotiators offered Belgium an understanding based on Germany's official war aims towards Belgium. This became apparent at the first Zürich meeting. The king's attitude being as described, Törring concentrated his arguments against the principle of neutrality. Pointing to the case of Greece, he tried to persuade Waxweiler that 'the maintenance of the principle of neutrality was not desirable for small associations; it was even harmful'. Törring described these, even at this early stage, with extraordinary frankness: a German occupation force and free passage for German troops, control of the Belgian railways, the adherence of Belgium to the German customs union. He actually allowed it to be understood that Germany wished to annex certain strategically important points in Belgium, offering Belgium compensation on the Belgo-French frontier: the corner of the Meuse north of Charleville, the Maubeuge salient, and perhaps something in French Flanders.

Waxweiler rejected Germany's 'suggestions' categorically and continued to insist on the neutrality, sovereignty and territorial integrity of Belgium as pre-conditions for any future profitable development of the relations between the two countries. He did agree that an 'improvement' of Belgium's frontier against France was theoretically desirable, but he doubted whether his king would consent to such a 'transaction', any more than he would to ceding the Congo to Germany. Nevertheless, the first contact left Törring with the impression that, reserved as the king had been, it might be possible to break his resistance in respect of neutrality, and that Germany should concentrate on that point in the future.

The second meeting took place on November 29, and to it Törring, who meanwhile had been in Berlin, brought formal German proposals, as communicated to him by Jagow or Bethmann Hollweg. Waxweiler, for his part, had obviously received instructions to be more accommodating towards the German agent. In any case the two men were able, after exhaustive discussion of details, to agree on a French text which was meant to serve as a basis for further discussions. This text began with a sort of preamble laying down the following principles:

Germany will not annex Belgium. Germany will never conclude any sort of peace whatever without receiving guarantees against attack from England and France. These guarantees must come in Belgium. Whatever shape they take, they will respect the full internal autonomy of the Kingdom and will not entail any interference in the administration of the country.

The detailed wishes put forward by Germany as a basis for an understanding were:

(i) Belgium to renounce neutrality.

(ii) The right of passage for German troops.

(iii) The right to occupy certain designated points of strategic importance to Germany's defence.

(iv) Germany to participate in the administration of strategically important Belgian railway lines (a possible form might be the creation of a joint stock company in which Germany held a majority of the shares).

(v) Belgium to enter into an economic understanding (*entente économique*) with Germany

(vi) The cession of certain frontier districts to Germany. Compensation for Belgium not excluded.

Waxweiler's readiness to join in working out these points strengthened Törring's hopes of getting rid of Belgium's neutrality. He now thought that Waxweiler's insistence on neutrality at the first meeting had been due to Belgian fears of 'far-reaching and decisive demands' which would expose Belgium to the danger 'of finding herself completely subjected to Germany's will'. Törring's statement that Germany would not annex the whole Belgian state had produced in Waxweiler 'a certain relief and satisfaction'. Whether the German interpreted the Belgian's feelings truly, or whether he exaggerated them out of wishful thinking, it remains a fact that he qualified very heavily Germany's renunciation of the annexation, to which he had given so much prominence. According to his own account to the Foreign Ministry, all he had said was that 'Germany had no intention of incorporating Belgium provided that for the rest Belgium fulfilled the other demands which Germany felt compelled to make, and which were now known, if only in rough outline'. This blend of apparent conciliation and veiled threats, which had begun with the demand addressed to Belgium on the outbreak of the war, continued to characterise German policy: her renunciation of annexation was only to bind her if Belgium submitted to Germany's other demands, which added up to 'the economic conquest of Belgium' and aimed at reducing her to political and military vassaldom.

If to Waxweiler Törring had spoken only of the 'rough outlines' of Germany's demands, he himself made suggestions for the clarification of two essential points. He wanted to get the German military to explain more exactly to the Foreign Ministry what they needed in respect of transit for troops and garrisons. Further, he recommended that Belgium should not be asked to pay Germany a war indemnity, but should herself be given an indemnity 'at the expense of our enemies'. While approving in principle Germany's policy towards Belgium, Törring advised that Germany should exercise her authority in a skilful and elastic fashion, so that 'in future every Belgian should be obliged to say that Belgium was better off under the new regime than before'. In sum, the Germans must have felt after this second meeting between Törring and Waxweiler that they had advanced a considerable step towards their goal of inducing King Albert to renounce neutrality, especially since Waxweiler, for his part, had mentioned as desirable compensation for the prospective local annexations by Germany certain definite territorial acquisitions at the expense of France and Holland: the line of the Meuse north of Charleville, areas round Maubeuge, Roubaix and Tourcoing, and the Dutch territory on the left of the mouth of the Scheldt.

After this first indirect indication of yielding on Belgium's part, the third interview between Törring and Waxweiler, which took place on January 5 and 6, 1916, marked the peak of Belgium's real or apparent readiness to meet Germany. Waxweiler brought with him a holograph letter from the king to Törring which was expressly marked as being for Bethmann Hollweg's eyes, and also formal Belgian counter-proposals to the exposé jointly drawn up by the two agents on November 25. These proposals show even more plainly than the king's letter a readiness on Belgium's part *'to give up the principle of Belgian neutrality'* and, as Törring put it, 'to effect *a rapprochement with Germany* in a form which spared the feelings of the Belgian people'.

To account for this far-reaching step, which was at variance with the whole political tradition of his country, the king pointed to the experience of August, 1914, which had proved that the neutral status – imposed on Belgium (against her will) when she was created in 1829–30 – had not availed to keep her out of wars between the great powers. Destiny would therefore force her to another solution (*disposition*). However, his oath to the Constitution and his conscience as man and king forbade him to agree to any settlement which did not leave intact Belgian's full sovereignty and internal self-government, or which in any way bore the stamp of vassaldom (*témoignage quelconque d'inféodation*), if not only to offend Belgian national feeling and thus imperil the Monarchy. Finally, he defined once more, in a single sentence, his extreme limit of concessions: 'The moment that Germany admits that any guarantees for her western frontier shall avoid infringing either Belgium's political and economic independence, or her territorial integrity, the disquiet of which you [sc., Törring] speak could vanish.'

In a sort of attempt to save his face, King Albert wrote that a German–Belgian understanding could be achieved only by means of a defensive agreement between equal partners. He accordingly urged the Germans to spare the feelings of his people by renouncing a right of occupation and contenting themselves with occupying instead Givet, Maubeuge and possibly Condé, which lay on French soil hard against the frontier of Belgium. He was ready to give the Germans the control of the railways leading to these places.

The Belgians further offered to stop using the fortresses of Liége, Namur and Antwerp, stationing only small garrisons in them. Co-operation would thus result on the basis that 'the military defence of the southern half of the Kingdom would, in a way, be made Germany's special charge', while the defence of its northern half was 'primarily the duty of the Belgian army'. The Belgians disliked the idea of a direct customs union, but signified their willingness to revise their existing tariff and also to introduce 'legislative reforms in the field of protective labour legislation' within a certain period.

In the notes with which Törring accompanied the Belgian proposals, when forwarding them to the Foreign Ministry, he suggested certain ways in which they could be further turned to Germany's advantage; he also thought that Germany would be able to secure control over the defensive dispositions on the North Sea coast within the framework of the future defensive agreement. He further reported that Waxweiler, allegedly acting without special instructions, had suggested a partition of the Belgian Congo, Germany to purchase a share of it.

The touchstone, as it were, of Germany's war aims policy, and especially of the extent of her aims, must be whether she would content herself with gaining Belgium as an equal partner, on the basis of Waxweiler's proposals, or whether her intentions went further. The answer to this question is given by the official German reply to the Belgian proposals, brought by Törring to his fourth meeting with Waxweiler on February 25. It was designed to serve as a basis for further negotiations for a separate peace between Germany and Belgium, and it reveals Germany's intentions towards Belgium unmistakably, especially to those aware of the secret deliberations which had gone on over her war aims. The document shows quite plainly that Germany was not content with the principle of an alliance between equals. What she intended was the subordination of Belgium, in practice rather than in law, with the help of 'real guarantees' (to which Bethmann Hollweg recurred again and again) in the political, economic and military fields, just as she proposed to do with Poland and (under the slogan of Mitteleuropa) with Austria-Hungary. The official attitude is expressed in a letter from Törring to Waxweiler, which deserves to be reproduced in full as an example of how the two elements–efforts to reach a separate peace and war aims policy–interacted:

The Government of the Reich welcomes the decision of H.M. King Albert of Belgium to abolish Belgium's neutral status. The renunciation of this principle is and remains the precondition for the profitable continuation of the negotiations now in progress between Germany and Belgium.

The *full autonomy* of Belgium in all her internal affairs is to be left to her and guaranteed.

As regards the preservation of Belgium's *present territorial integrity*, the answer to this question depends entirely on whether and how far Belgium agrees to adopt a *rapprochement* with Germany which meets the wishes of the

Government of the Reich, as expressed in the course of these dispositions. This applies both to Belgium's European and to her colonial territory.

Military defence is in the future to be left for the most part to Germany. Belgium will therefore have to confine herself to *maintaining a militia* for the preservation of internal order. The existing fortresses *will be abandoned.* Germany demands *free transit* and a *facultative right of occupation.* The *practical* exercise of this right depends on the form taken by the relationship between Germany and Belgium. The assurance can be given that it will be used sparingly as circumstances allow. The Government of the Reich must under all circumstances insist on being able to establish *a base on the Belgian coast.* For the protection of this . . . [illegible passage] including the Zeebrugge–Port of Brüges–Ostende triangle. A long-term lease might possibly be considered here. The Belgian suggestion that Germany might take certain places on French territory, such as Givet, Maubeuge, Condé, as military bases, is rejected as insufficient.

On grounds of military security Germany demands *a right of control over the main Belgian railways* and the *port installations of Antwerp* in the form of creation of a share company and gratis transfer of 60 per cent of the shares to the German Reich.

Acquisition of the Dutch territory on the left bank of the mouth of the Scheldt cannot at present be considered.

Germany desires *the closest possible customs association* between Belgium and Germany. The detailed practical arrangements are left for later agreement.

Note has been taken of the declaration of January 5 under which Belgium declared herself prepared to introduce legislative reforms in the field of protective labour legislation, and a binding declaration to this effect will have to be included in the final Peace Treaty.

The German memorandum went beyond the Belgian proposals in every respect. In the internal arrangements only a few details are new, but more important is the principle (again a parallel to Germany's policy in Poland) of making Germany's conditions on the two most important points–the territorial status in Europe and Africa, and the exercise of the right of occupation–dependent on the closeness of Belgium's *rapprochement* with Germany. But the special interest of this document lies in its official character.

It had, indeed, no immediate political results, for Törring in the end did not hand it to Waxweiler, whose attitude on February 25 and 26 had been such as to make Törring feel that it would be wiser to keep Germany's detailed demands to himself. The inadequacy of a purely dynastic approach towards a separate peace had in the meantime made itself painfully plain to the German government. Indiscretions, the source of which is not apparent from the German documents, had produced uneasiness, both in Belgian public opinion and in Entente circles. The Entente had reacted against the threat of a separate peace between Germany and Belgium in two ways: first in

a note to Belgium, dated February 14,[1] to which the Belgian government had returned on the same day a reply which, as Törring told
Waxweiler as soon as they met on February 25, had 'made a painful
impression' on Germany; secondly, by sending Lord Curzon on a
special mission to King Albert on February 15. Waxweiler had, it is
true, denied any connection between these happenings and the peace
feelers, and had also denied that the leakage could have come from
the Belgian side, since only the king, the queen and he himself knew of
the conversations–not the Belgian government, not even the Foreign
Minister, Beyens. Törring, however, disbelieved him, threatened to
break off the negotiations, and then actually did so. The formal German conditions were therefore never handed over, presumably because Törring was afraid that Germany would be compromised still
further if such far-reaching demands became known. The negotiations with King Albert, which had begun so promisingly, had thus
broken down, and it was hardly more than a diplomatic formality
when Törring and Waxweiler agreed (although only provisionally) to
meet again at the beginning of May. The meeting never took place.[2]

In retrospect one must ask what were King Albert's motives. Had
Germany's recent successes–the conquest of Poland, Lithuania,
Courland and Serbia–and the expectation of a great German offensive in the west, so impressed him that he saw the only salvation of
his country in friendship with Germany? And it had been only the
counter-pressure of the Entente and of his own people that had driven
him to drop his plan? Or had he entered on the negotiations only in
order to discover what were Germany's intentions towards Belgium
and then recovered freedom of action by means of a calculated in-
discretion? Either way he would have been playing a double game,
either towards his own government, or towards the Germans. Whatever the truth may be, it lies hidden in the Belgian archives, but it is
in any case of only secondary importance for the history of Germany's war aims policy. In spite of their disappointing experiences
with the Tsar and the king of the Belgians, the German leaders still
retained such faith in the efficacy of dynastic connections that they
made a later attempt to achieve their war aims in Belgium through
private negotiations with King Albert. In April, 1916, an offer
reached Berlin from the Vatican to mediate between Germany and
Belgium on the basis of respect for Belgium's territorial integrity.

[1] A. de Ridder, *La Belgique et la Guerre, IV., Histoire diplomatique* (Brussels, 1925),
pp. 198 ff.

[2] The Germans' hopes during these negotiations were so fantastic that Törring
actually suggested that King Albert might surrender himself as a prisoner of war–a
proposal which, indeed, only provoked Waxweiler to laughter.

Törring thought that it was impossible for Germany to reject this offer, but she must not allow the Holy See to do more than inspire the negotiations and set them going. For the rest the Foreign Ministry, as before, refused to go beyond a vague assurance that Belgium would be allowed to continue in existence and in enjoyment of her internal autonomy, provided she gave Germany adequate guarantees against renewed attack.

In the course of these negotiations Germany told the Pope on June 10, 1916, through Erzberger, that she 'consented in principle to peace negotiations conducted through His Holiness'. In another conversation four days later Erzberger informed the Pope's private secretary, 'speaking not under explicit official instructions but as the result of many conversations which I have had with the Imperial Chancellor, the Secretary of State, von Jagow, and other persons in authority in the Foreign Ministry', what he thought he could say was 'the view of competent official circles here' on the bases for a mediation by the Pope which would be acceptable to Germany. Belgium seemed to him the point at which 'His Holiness could set in train his action for bringing peace about'; a separate peace between Germany and Belgium could lead to similar moves towards Germany's other enemies.

The only possible basis for a separate peace with Belgium would be a middle way which excluded both annexation pure and simple, and also the *status quo*. In Erzberger's view Belgium must: (i) retain her territorial integrity undiminished (even though military circles were demanding annexation of the Meuse line or at least Liége); and (ii) retain her complete sovereignty; King Albert must be allowed to return and 'the right of maintaining missions to foreign Powers must not be taken from her'. Internally, she must indeed agree to partition into a French and a Flemish administrative area. The German military government had secured for the Flemish the use of their mother-tongue in education, the press, administration, etc., and Germany could no longer allow the Flemish to be Gallicised by the Walloons. The Pope was told (the same argument was used in connection with Germany's policy in Poland and Lithuania) that 'the Flemish are reliable Catholics, while most of the Walloons are Freemasons and Social Democrats and are eternally drawn to the atheistic French Republic'; (iii) 'Belgium is completely free in the conduct of her internal administration; in particular, the regulation of religious and educational questions is left entirely to Belgium's discretion.'

Belgium's true future position of a German 'vassal state' was nakedly revealed in the 'German counter-demands'. These were:

  (i) Belgium concludes a defensive and offensive alliance with Germany, valid for all time. . . .

 (ii) Belgium concludes a customs union with Germany, like Luxemburg. . . .

(iii) The Belgian railways enter the Prusso-Hessian railway system. All existing railway lines in Belgium, private or state, can easily be combined in one share company working in closest conjunction with the Prussian railway management. . . .

(iv) Germany receives the right of unimpeded transit through Belgium in the event of another war, and Belgium pledges herself to dismantle her existing fortresses, and will not need to keep up an army.

 (v) A special agreement will have to be concluded on Belgium's colonial possessions in the Congo; it will not matter very much whether the Congo belongs to Belgium or passes to Germany, for if the other proposals are carried through, the tariff and economic union in Africa will have to be carried through exactly like that between Germany and Belgium.

All these conditions, Erzberger emphasised, could bring nothing but great economic advantage to the Belgian people, and on this basis the two peoples could become 'intimate friends'. Germany would indeed have to insist on 'the right of transit and occupation', and in particular on the right to make use of the Belgian coast for the duration of the war, until the decision had been reached against England.

Erzberger pointed out that 'a frightful outcry would arise in the widest German circles if this treaty were concluded, because it would be regarded as insufficient from the German point of view'.

He himself thought these conditions, and also those for France, 'extremely moderate'. The latter were:

  (i) Better frontier in the Vosges . . . (on the western slopes).

 (ii) The ore deposits of Briey and Longwy behind Metz, partly for the protection of the existing deposits, partly to ensure Germany's future.

(iii) War indemnity.

(iv) A German colonial empire [viz., partly at the cost of France, which must also consent to the other changes of colonial ownership].

The instructions sent by the Foreign Ministry to von Romberg, the minister in Bern, for the peace feelers at that time in progress with French politicians show that what Erzberger told Mgr. Gerlach represented the views of the German government.

A Separate Peace with France Through the Radical Socialists

If Germany's wishes in her secret negotiations with Belgium were directed chiefly towards isolating and detaching her, the feature of the sounding of French groups which began a little later was that, apart from certain annexations, they were subordinated to the larger aim of prising France out of the enemy coalition and, by eliminating her from its ranks, influencing decisively the subsequent course of the war against Britain.

After eighteen months of propaganda in France things had so far progressed that at the end of May, 1916, 'a prominent member of the French Radical Socialist Party which, with the United Socialists, forms the majority in the French parliament', got into direct touch with a German confidant via Romberg, and proposed 'the conclusion of a separate peace and the inauguration of a lasting understanding between the two countries if his party should come into office'. The conditions were that France must receive certain compensation for 'the service which she would be rendering Germany by breaking up the enemy coalition'. Romberg thought this possibility a very serious one; he saw in it a unique opportunity to reach an understanding with France, because it was only with this opposition party that such a turn could be given to the course of events. But Germany would have to go a long way to meet France.

This course, however, was blocked by the attitude of the general staff.[1] Falkenhayn demanded as a *conditio sine qua non* for peace with France the cession of Belfort with the adjacent heights of Douaumont for the protection of Longwy–Briey, and Bethmann Hollweg submitted to the demands of the military and even went beyond strategic considerations in his instructions to Romberg, which were 'not to let the thread snap, but to give no assurances in the sense of the proposals made to us'.

To these instructions, a characteristic example of Bethmann Hollweg's eternal attempts to square the circle,[2] Romberg replied in despair that they were 'practically asking the impossible of him'. If he revealed the Army Command's demands to the French, they would produce a rupture of the contacts no less surely than if he confined himself to 'general phraseology'. This view would be confirmed by Hoffmann, head of the Swiss Department in the Foreign Ministry, and by the experienced minister in Paris. At least 'apparent concessions' should be made; he thought it possible that Germany might get 'the plateau of Briey and a considerable war indemnity in return for trivial frontier adjustments in favour of France in Alsace and perhaps an exchange deal in Africa', but this was the maximum that could be asked of France without wrecking everything. He urgently

[1] For Belfort cf. also Bethmann Hollweg's programme of September 9, 1914.

[2] Romberg himself used this phrase to describe Bethmann Hollweg's manoeuvrings.

pressed upon the Chancellor the possibilities which a separate peace with France would open up:

> When I consider on the one hand the enormous advantages of a separate peace with France, ensuring us as it would, at one blow, victory and the attainment of extensive war aims, the saving of innumerable lives and many billions of money and an immediate end to the distress under which our people is suffering, and on the other hand, the military and economic dangers to which we are exposed by carrying on the war under like conditions and by the maintenance of the enemy coalition after it, then I am obliged, in spite of the negative attitude of our Supreme Army Command, to beg Your Excellency to give my proposal renewed careful consideration.

On a visit to Berlin Romberg had gathered the impression that even military circles and the parliamentary right would not be against this view, because their war aim in chief was, after all, 'to disrupt the enemy coalition, and even more, to settle accounts thoroughly with England'. Heavy would be the responsibility of the man who impeded this aim 'by an all too intransigent attitude towards France based simply on military considerations', and who 'besides prolonging the war indefinitely, exposed [Germany] to the danger of another Congress of Vienna'. Hardly any diplomat had yet ventured to address such language to the Imperial Chancellor.

Bethmann Hollweg replied through Jagow that Germany was ready to discuss the proposals. But what Romberg regarded as the utmost limit was for Jagow the most obvious pre-condition for any undertaking, namely, Longwy–Briey with its strategical approaches which, though they need not include the city of Verdun, must include certain heights which commanded the plateau militarily. It was no longer sufficient for France simply to leave the war; if, 'in view of the military situation' – this was written on June 8, while the battle of Verdun was still in progress and, three weeks before the opening of the Allied offensive on the Somme – Germany decided to conclude a separate peace with France on such a basis, the purpose of such a peace would only be to break up the enemy coalition and, beyond that, to 'inaugurate a future lasting understanding with France'. Only a separate peace which meant the first step towards a Franco-German alliance against Britain was any use to Germany. If this was not achieved, any assurances proffered would become null and void. Then Germany would have no other course 'but to seek the realisation of our war aims by crushing France completely and making our losses good at her expense'. If Germany had to count on the continuance of the Anglo-French coalition after the war, she had no other course than to weaken one of the two powers of the coalition as far as possible, and that one, as things stood, would be France.

A separate peace on Germany's terms was not only a tactical war-move but, at the same time and primarily, was meant to lay the foundation of a new constellation of the powers. As the separate peace with Russia was to blow up the bridges between Russia and France and Britain, so the separate peace with France was to blow up the bridge between France and Britain.

The soundings on this basis led to no result, while 'the Austrian defeat [in Russia] and later the entry of Rumania into the war, com-bined with the successes on the Somme and at Verdun'–so Romberg reported on November 27, 1916–weakened the pro-peace feelings which had been active in France in May and June. Nevertheless, the Foreign Ministry refused to revise its directives and continued to demand 'substantial accessions of territory' as a condition for peace conversations, while Romberg declared it impossible to trans-mit them, for France was 'not nearly ripe for such a communica-tion'. In the same despatch he passed on a suggestion by the Papal representative in Switzerland, Mgr. Marchetti, that the Central Powers should choose the zenith of their military successes, perhaps their entry into Bucharest, to announce a peace offer through the neutrals, the core of which should be a declaration that they were prepared 'to restore the *status quo*' in Belgium and France and to re-instate Serbia in her sovereignty 'without any reservations relating to guarantees or to territorial cessions, even if only in the form of frontier rectifications based on mutual exchanges of territory'. This was also the substance of the answer to Erzberger's letter to Gerlach of June, 1916.

The soundings of the French Radical Socialists had therefore pro-duced no result. Nevertheless, in spite of Romberg's and Marchetti's warnings, the new Secretary of State, Zimmermann, repeated on December 12, 1916, the day of the publication of the German 'peace offer', almost exactly the same conditions as those of the summer for conversations with another French group interested in peace, the Conservatives. Like his predecessor, Jagow, he laid down as mini-mum demands the cession of the Briey basin, colonial concessions and a war indemnity, 'which might be disguised in some way and thus made acceptable to French vanity'. 'These points are the least which the military situation and the heavy sacrifices of our people justify us in demanding.' This 'least', but without indemnity and without the French Congo–although the Foreign Ministry took him to task for this–was what the ever-busy Erzberger had already de-manded in the course of feelers for a separate peace with France; in his draft both countries were to recognise and mutually guarantee for ever the frontier of August 1, 1914, with the single exception of a small territorial exchange: 'France receives the Canton of Château Salins, Germany receives the Districts of Briey and Longwy, without payment, after the removal of the present French population.'

Erzberger regarded this offer, which was to be transmitted through the Pope, Spain or another neutral power, as so modest that its publication would tend to unify feeling in his own country and create division in the enemy camp. Like the top officials, he thought that the separate peace might perhaps be extended into a continental peace if France would agree to mediate with Russia and Italy; Britain, however, must be conquered.

The peace feelers towards France brought no result. They show, however, what Germany understood by a separate peace, and how stubbornly she held to the war aims which she regarded as 'vital'.

A Continental Bloc:
Separate Peace with Russia through Japan

In January, 1915, the Germanophile Japanese minister in Stockholm, Ushida, had told his Austrian colleague that Japan wanted to re-orient her foreign political relationships when her alliance with Britain expired in 1921.[1] The instructions sent to the German minister, von Lucius, in the spring and summer were to answer this revelation by trying, if possible, to slow down or stop Japan's deliveries of war materials to Russia; more ambitious moves were not then envisaged. These were set on foot only in July, 1915, by Albert Ballin, who had been told by Bethmann Hollweg that Russia was ready for peace and was only fighting on under joint pressure from Britain and Japan. Another Japanese hint in November, 1915, stimulated the feelers and led Fritz Warburg (brother of the well-known banker, Max), who was at that time attached to the German legation in Stockholm as a financial expert, to seek a meeting with Ushida. At this stage Zimmermann, then still Under-Secretary in the Foreign Ministry, was not yet prepared to accept Japan's demand for the cession of Tsingtao.

One move came from the German side, from Tirpitz, whose hostility to Britain had led him as early as August, 1915, to suggest to the Imperial Chancellor an alliance between Germany, Russia and Japan, to be directed against Britain and, in view of the tension then existing between Japan and the U.S.A., ultimately against the latter

[1] Erwin Hölzle, 'Deutschland und die Wegscheide des ersten Weltkrieges', in *Geschichtliche Kräfte und Entscheidungen, Festschrift zum 65. Geburtstage von Otto Becker* (Wiesbaden, 1954), p. 272.

too.[1] Stinnes took up this idea in the spring of 1916, when he had occasion to talk to the Japanese minister in Stockholm. Von Lucius insinuated himself into the conversations on April 1 and 'speaking as a private individual' gave the Japanese to understand that in spite of the war no insuperable differences existed between Germany and Japan. Although Lucius and Stinnes were careful not to voice any 'wishes' for a separate peace, they yet expressed their 'private opinions' 'that the only way of taking the first step towards peace would be if the Tokyo government could induce Petersburg to send a competent person to Stockholm who could make contact with German and Japanese personalities, at first without any official instructions'.

In April Ushida expressly rejected the idea of a separate peace between Germany on the one side and Russia and Japan on the other as incompatible with the London Agreement of September 5, 1914, and the Anglo-Japanese Treaty, which had still five years to run. In another conversation, however, on May 7, he told Stinnes – not yet speaking with his government's authorisation – that the alliance with Britain presented no obstacle to the opening of early conversations for an alliance between Germany, Russia and Japan. All he asked as price for an early peace with Germany was the cession of Germany's Pacific islands and Kiaochow.

The moving spirit in the conversations so far had been Stinnes, who was pressing for an alliance with Russia in order to assure Germany's aims in the west and thus safeguard his own business interests. Jagow opposed this strongly; a long private letter sent by him on May 8, 1916, to the minister, simultaneously with telegraphed directions for his further negotiations, contains the following passage: 'This lad Stinnes is a pusher, who is trying to force our policy into his own spheres of interest. Therefore, alliance with Russia, in order to get us completely at cross-purposes with the West.'

For tactical reasons Jagow did not want to refuse outright an alliance with Russia, and he therefore gave Lucius a free hand to 'flirt' with the idea; but the most that he wanted was a treaty of neutrality between Germany and Russia. Jagow thought what Ushida had said so important that he took it as a text for an exposition on his ideas on the constellation of the powers during and after the war, and at the same time for an analysis of Japan's motives in taking this step. Jagow wanted to be sure of keeping a free hand for negotiations in both directions, and he therefore wanted Stinnes 'discarded'.

He explained his rejection of the suggested alliance with Russia by

[1] Alfred von Tirpitz, *Erinnerungen*, 5th ed. (Berlin, 1927), p. 499. The date of the letter is August 24.

saying that that country was so weakened by internal dislocations that she would be merely an impotent ally, and Germany had enough of those. A treaty of neutrality with Russia, on the other hand, would paralyse France and force her to seek an understanding with Germany. He expected still less from an alliance with Japan, since it would drag Germany into the Japanese–American field of tension in the Far East.

I am not one of those who want an alliance with Russia *à tout prix*, only in order to bring about a *finis Britanniae*. Russia is the weaker partner, and to bring England down is not so easy as the gentlemen think. But Germany cannot frame her ends exclusively to meet the interests of heavy industry.

Jagow, like the Emperor and the Chancellor, was only prepared to cede Germany's possessions in the Far East to Japan 'if Japan gets to work in Petersburg at once and procures us peace with Russia without delay'. At the back of this haste was the wish to forestall the imminent Russian offensive by a separate peace.

That these negotiations were not merely casual, and that they awakened great hopes in the highest quarters in Germany, is shown by the activity which they provoked not only in the Foreign Ministry, but also in the departmental ministries. Tirpitz' successor as Secretary of State for the Navy, Admiral von Capelle, agreed to the cessions in the Far East; if they ensured both peace with Japan and 'an advantageous separate peace with Russia', he saw in them 'such a big chance . . . of ending the whole war favourably to ourselves, as to outweigh the disadvantages of the cessions'.

A few days later Germany's hopes broke down. On May 17, 1916, the Japanese government disavowed Ushida and returned a flat refusal to the German feelers for a separate peace. Tokyo was ready to enter into peace negotiations with Germany only if it was allowed simultaneously to inform the Entente Powers of Japan's readiness to make peace. But this step by Japan would again involve Germany in the danger of a general peace, which would have made the realisation of her war aims doubtful, if not quite impossible. When Lucius reported Japan's refusal, the Emperor, whose temperamental and drastic way of expressing himself betrayed Germany's intentions much more openly than the diplomatic phrases of Bethmann Hollweg and Jagow, minuted in the margin: 'As soon as no separate peace can be made, the whole swindle ceases to matter. The game's not worth the candle. We don't need them [sc., the Japanese] as go-betweens for a general peace.'

Beside the immediate aim of the separate peace, which was to prise Japan and, through Japanese mediation, Russia away from the enemy coalition, Germany hoped to use it as a basis for re-shaping the constellation of the powers after the war. This intention had become apparent in the conversations between Lucius and Ushida. Even if Lucius, like Jagow, thought a treaty of neutrality sufficient, because such treaties usually developed into alliances, yet if Stinnes is to be believed, the idea of an alliance had been discussed with Bethmann Hollweg and Helfferich and presumably also with Zimmermann.

The conditions were drawn up in two drafts compiled in the Foreign Ministry, a short one on May 8 and a very detailed one on May 17; the shorter confined itself to the conditions for Japan's mediation for a separate peace with Russia, while the second adopted these conditions as the starting-point but expanded them into a second phase which was concerned with Britain and France and was distinguished sharply from the first. In the latter, the Swedish Foreign Minister, Wallenberg, was designated for the chief part. The decisive point, however, is, that on May 17, when the feelers seemed nearest to success, the conditions for a treaty with Japan and Russia were supplemented by conditions for peace with Britain and France and by a detailed scheme for future alliances and secret treaties directed primarily against Britain. If these drafts are considered in the light of the actions and plans of the German government relating to the conditions of possible peace settlements in east and west, that is, of the ideology of Germany's war aims policy, it cannot be doubted that they outline aims which the German government had in mind for its negotiations with Japan and Russia.

The breakdown of the negotiations (taken in conjunction with the fact that Japan had meanwhile achieved both a concession from England over China and an agreement with Russia) was not the result of any German decision to opt for the west, as opposed to the east. It was not that Germany had decided to accept American mediation and a renunciation of aims against Britain and to reject Russo-Japanese mediation and thrust the Muscovite empire back, but rather that Germany was determined to seek a separate peace in the east only so long as it was certain that the peace treaties would not be concluded simultaneously.[1] Germany 'abhorred' negotiations for a general peace, she was interested only in a sequence which first neutralised the east, a step which, as the draft said, would bring about 'the paralysis of France' and consequently the isolation of Britain and her readiness to make peace. In order to give Japan an honourable escape from her alliance with the Entente, Germany commissioned her in the draft to bring about a general peace after

[1] This is the view taken by Hölzle, op. cit., pp. 278 ff.

the understanding between Germany, Russia and Japan had been reached. Japan undertook, as Kemnitz, the drafting official in the Foreign Ministry, put it, 'to use her influence to secure the acceptance by the western powers of . . . the minimum demands of the Central Powers'; if the western powers rejected these demands, the Central Powers were left with a completely free hand towards Japan's former allies, to whom Japan was to give no sort of support. This is a foretaste of the formula of Brest-Litovsk.

In the first version, drafted on May 8 for the immediate negotiations, Germany offered Japan – with the consent of the Reich Naval Office – 'cession of Tsingtao and the German possessions in the Pacific now in Japanese occupation' and Germany's consent to the establishment of a Japanese protectorate over China, except those areas falling within the Russian sphere of interests. In return Japan was to mediate peace with Russia on the following basis:

a. Russia cedes Poland, Lithuania and Courland and agrees that Persian Kurdistan, Luristan and Khuistan shall go to Turkey. She disinterests herself in the Balkans. She consents to the abolition of the Capitulations in Turkey.
b. Russia receives that part of Turkish Armenia conquered by her, the rest of Persia, East Turkestan, Kukunor, Dzungaria, Outer Mongolia, North Manchuria, Kensu, Shensi. She receives the right of passage for single ships of war through the Straits.

Japan herself was to safeguard existing German economic enterprises in China and guarantee most favoured nation treatment for German commerce; she was to recognise that the Dutch East Indies were not a Japanese sphere of interest. She was to conclude a defensive treaty with Germany against Britain and France at the end of the war, or at the latest on the expiration of the Anglo-Japanese alliance. The specific details relating to Russia show that the idea of forcing Russia back, both from Germany's eastern frontier – where the provisions were exactly the same as those demanded by Bethmann Hollweg three weeks earlier in his negotiations with Burian – and from the Balkans, constituted a fixed element in Germany's war aims policy, even when she was trying to reach a settlement with Russia.

The revised draft of May 17, produced in a period of intensive diplomatic activity, made a serious attempt to meet Russia, which was offered compensation in the shape of further territory (in addition to part of Turkish Armenia) belonging to Germany's allies, viz., those parts of East Galicia then in Russian occupation; indeed: 'if needs be, we must agree to the cession of the whole of East Gali-

cia, with Lemberg, and the Ruthene part of the Bukovina, the Rumanian part of which will then go to Rumania.' For the rest, the
draft reproduces its predecessor's 'demands on Russia' for Courland,
Lithuania and Poland. Germany herself renounced, 'if needs be',
the annexation of Courland and Lithuania, but claimed 'the territory west of the general line Niemen–Grodno–Brest-Litovsk–the
Upper Bug, including the two towns named'. 'Details' (over Poland)
were 'to be settled between Germany and Austria-Hungary.' Here
we find a reappearance of the idea, which had been in Germany's
mind since the end of 1914, of population transfers to be effected by
transferring Poles out of the 'Prussian Eastern March' (with its old
and new frontiers) eastward into the new Poland and importing into
the land thus made available 'German–Russian repatriates and
other German colonists'–thus promoting 'the Germanisation of the
Prussian Eastern March' and 'clearing up as far as possible the
intermingling of Germans and Poles'. The Serbian question was
to be reserved for separate negotiation between Austria-Hungary
and Bulgaria only. Montenegro was to conclude a defensive and
offensive alliance with Austria-Hungary and enter the Austro-
Hungarian free trade area–provisions exactly in accordance
with Germany's and Austria-Hungary's general Balkan policy in
the war. Russia was to be forced out of Turkey as well as out of the
Balkans; she was to renounce railway concessions acquired by her
in the northern zone of Anatolia, and the renunciation was to be
perpetual and to apply equally to private entrepreneurs. The promise to allow Russia a 'right of passage for single ships of war through
the Straits' showed that Germany had accepted the Japanese minister's demand that Russian aspirations be given some satisfaction on
this point. Britain was to be excluded from Persia, and Germany to
acquire an extension of her sphere of interest in Asia by way of Turkey together with guarantees for future discoveries of oil, while (in
the second draft) Turkey would annex three provinces and Russia
receive the rest of Persia and Afghanistan as her sphere of interest.
Germany expressly recognised Russia's sphere of interest in China,
and also Japan's further ceding to Japan her rights in Shantung
acquired under the Kiaochow Treaty. Germany's future commercial relations with Russia and Japan were to be based on the most
favoured nation principle, with the reservation that it was not to
affect the Mitteleuropa preferential tariffs between Germany and
Austria-Hungary.

Taking account of Germany's tactical interest in making the peace
treaties consecutive, the draft first laid down the respective contributions to be made by Germany, Japan and Russia to their mutual

understanding, leaving the exact delimitation of spheres of interest in the Balkans, Poland and the Far East for bilateral negotiation, while the conditions designed to form the basis for an understanding with France and Britain appeared at a second stage, in the form of appendices, dealing with Germany's western aims and her colonial aims, which were to be rounded off by embracing Portugal.

This draft brings out sharply and clearly the power-position at which Germany was aiming in the east, the west and overseas. France and Britain were to be required to accept the incorporation of Luxemburg in the German Reich, and the cession to Luxemburg of the adjacent Belgian area of Arlon. Britain was to agree to a radical transformation of Belgium: 'Belgium as far as the Meuse, with Liège and Namur' to go to Germany; the greater part of Wallonia (the Menin–Namur–Givet triangle) to France as 'a contribution by Germany'; the new frontier to run from Givet to Rocroi, east of the Meuse, and thence south-eastward to Etain and Nomeny. France would thus cede the Longwy–Briey deposits with a strategic glacis. The mainly Flemish part of Belgium, enlarged by French Flanders down to Gravelin, would become a nominally independent 'Duchy of Flanders', in close association with Germany and connected with it territorially through Limburg, which was to be acquired from Holland by exchange. It was to accede to the German customs union and conclude a defensive and offensive treaty with Germany, which 'receives the right to maintain garrisons in Antwerp, Zeebrugge and Dunkirk'. In place of the narrow pass at Liége, Germany would thus be assured of a broad access route with a twofold railway connection via Roermund and Maastricht and a waterway, still to be constructed, capable of taking large vessels from the industrial district of the Rhineland to Antwerp, 'thus giving the Rhine a German mouth'– an idea which Bethmann Hollweg had personally advocated in the winter of 1914–15. It was even hoped to persuade Holland to cede it to Flanders (in exchange for other territory) the south bank of the Scheldt, thus adding Antwerp to the list of naval ports.

'Germany receives the Belgian Congo' ('if necessary, the Belgian Congo is to be left to Flanders'). Similarly, France was to cede the French Congo and French Somaliland with Obok and Djibouti ('if necessary, Somaliland can be renounced'); in return she would receive Togo.[1] Likewise Britain would receive Germany's possessions in the South Seas and Germany would recognise the annexation of Egypt by Britain; in return, however, Britain must endorse both the continental and the overseas arrangements. 'England cedes

[1] Erzberger, in his memorandum of August 10, 1916, had also proposed ceding Togo to France.

to Germany the district of Yola (on the west coast of the Cameroons), Wallfish Bay, Zanzibar and Pemba, British Somaliland, Socotra and the Chushan Islands (in the Indian Ocean, with a good harbour). (If necessary, Somaliland and Socotra can be renounced.) England cedes to Turkey the Sinai Peninsula up to about longitude 33°. The Reich demanded of Portugal, on which it had shortly before (on March 9, 1916) declared war, the cession of either Madeira or the Cape Verde Islands for 'coaling and cable stations on the way to Africa and South America'; also of São Thomé and Principe and that part of Angola lying south of 14 degrees latitude and east of 18 degrees longitude 'to link up German South-West with the former colony of Belgian Congo' ('if necessary' this could be renounced). Here once more, as in 1914 and again in November, 1916, 1917 and 1918, the claim to a Central African colonial empire was staked out.

The 'Alliances and Treaties of Neutrality' outlined in the second part of the draft looked forward to the fundamental changes and new alliances which were to follow the war. They comprised a system of secret agreements, based on the mutual understanding between Germany, Russia and Japan, and designed to give Germany security against Britain and France–but also, *le cas échéant*, against Austria-Hungary and Russia. Germany's protection against the West lay in the undertaking that, if she were 'attacked' by Britain (after 1921, when the Anglo-Japanese Alliance has expired, if she 'becomes involved in war' with Britain–this provision to be kept secret from Austria-Hungary) she would receive armed assistance from Russia and Japan. If Germany were attacked by France alone, Russia would remain neutral. In the east, if Germany or Austria-Hungary were attacked by Russia, Japan would give armed assistance. These ideas reflect at least one shape of the future world power position aimed at by Germany, seen entirely from the angle of an anticipated second war with Britain, which both the soldiers and the diplomats so often declared during the war to be inevitable. The realignment along the Germany–Japan axis had been suggested by Moltke to the Chancellor on August 2, 1914, in his improvised programme of a world war against Britain,[1] and reappeared in altered form a year later in the attempt made by Zimmermann, after the U.S.A.'s breach with Germany but before her adherence to the Entente, to draw Japan over to Germany's side and into the war against the U.S.A. and Britain. In this plan Zimmermann was hoping to exploit the latent hostility between Japan and Britain masked by the Alliance, and the open antagonism between Japan and the U.S.A.

Further conversations conducted after May 17, one in Stockholm

[1] Cf. above, p. 84.

between Stinnes and Kolyshko (the latter in contact with the Russian Prime Minister, Stürmer, who took a gloomy view of Russia's situation and wanted peace) and another between Fritz Warburg and two Duma deputies, were only non-committal in character. Germany had learnt meanwhile that the Japanese had informed Russia (and thus her allies) of the conversations with Germany, and Jagow therefore ruled that any further correspondence between Kolyshko and Stürmer was pointless 'before clarification of [Russia's] readiness for a separate agreement'. Finally, on June 25, after the Brusilov offensive had opened, Zimmermann ruled that 'for the present' any step by Germany 'to bring about the understanding with Russia (and also with Japan) would be dangerous'.

In the course of conversations with Kolyshko Stinnes had agreed 'to get Germany's counter-proposals' out of Berlin. What these would have been appears not only from Kemnitz's draft, analysed above, but also from Erzberger's letter to Gerlach of a bare month later in connection with the French and Belgian peace feelers. These demands show once more the consistency of Germany's war aims:

  (i) The Russian Baltic provinces of Courland and Estonia [sic] must be included in the German Baltic provinces.
 (ii) Lithuania, whose population is entirely Catholic, must also be detached from Russia, perhaps made into a German Duchy or attached to Prussia as a province.
(iii) Poland to become a sovereign State: details to be agreed between Germany and Austria-Hungary.

Further, Russia would have to pay an adequate war indemnity and leave the Balkans to Germany and Austria-Hungary as their sphere of interest, to be partitioned between them by agreement.

These aims were retained unmodified throughout the great crisis of the summer of 1916, as is shown by the war aims programmes drawn up in the late autumn for the peace negotiations then anticipated.

An 'Independent' Poland: Discussions with Austria-Hungary

Symptoms of a change in Germany's attitude towards the Germano-Polish solution were apparent in December, 1915, and January, 1916, and after Falkenhayn had expressed his wishes, the change found clear expression in instructions sent by Jagow to Tschirschky on February 16, 1916.[1] Jagow began by saying that

[1] On the gradual change in Germany's policy, and Falkenhayn's attitude, see Conze, op. cit., pp. 143 ff.

236

Germany 'had not yet taken up a binding attitude on the future of Poland'; she admitted the possibility of its being attached to Austria-Hungary, subject to conditions of an economic, political and military character. He now remarked, with unconcealed ill-humour, that Austria was refusing to regard the Monarchy as simply 'a Germanic Eastern March'. As Austria-Hungary had not yet given the guarantees demanded by Germany for the Austro-Polish solution,[1] Jagow adopted Falkanhayn's line and said that Germany must now direct her policy towards the foundation of a Polish state closely associated with herself. Tschirschky was expressly instructed to prepare the Austrians tactfully for the new solution.

Soon afterwards, Bethmann Hollweg instructed the Governor-General – the parallel with his Flemish policy is exact – to stimulate a pro-German movement among the Poles in order to prepare them for their new relationship with Germany; in particular, Austrian propaganda was to be neutralised.[2] Beseler rejected these instructions as incompatible with the position of the German occupying forces and with Prussian–German traditions. The Poles were fundamentally anti-German and there could be little hope of changing their feelings, nor need German policy depend on the change; the association with Germany could never be other than 'forced on' them. Only after many delays, and the opening of the Brusilov offensive, did the German occupying forces at last, in June, recognise Studnicki's pro-German group,[3] the 'Polish State Club' (*Klub des polnischen Staatswesens*), but it always remained unimportant. Thus although the German civilian administration made repeated efforts to get Poland treated differently from a conquered country – whatever the demands of the military – and in spite of the re-opening of the University of Warsaw in November, 1915 (a move on which Bethmann Hollweg pinned a great hopes, as he did on his plan for a Flemish university in Ghent), no effective pro-German movement ever came into being in Poland.

During the same period the Foreign Ministry was trying to harness the national feeling of the Tsar's non-Russian subjects in the service of Germany's war aims through its creation, the 'League of Russia's Foreign Peoples'.[4] It was also hoped that this agitation might 'help conciliate certain influential circles in England and America which were unfavourably disposed towards Russia'.

[1] Id., pp. 146 f.   [2] Ibid.

[3] Id., pp. 180 ff.; see also Werner Basler, *Deutschlands Annexionspolitik in Polen und im Baltikum, 1914–1918* (Berlin, 1962), pp. 137 ff.

[4] The groups represented on March 3 were Jews, Mohammedans, Georgians, Poles, Baltic Germans, Finns, Ukrainians. White Russians, Lithuanians, Letts, Estonians and Rumanians were represented at later meetings.

Germany's eastern policy was in reality aimed at direct annexations and the establishment of vassal states, but the Chancellor used the 'liberation' theme of the League to disguise it with trimmings of idealism in his Reichstag speech of April 5, 1916. There had been a debate on peace aims in the British House of Commons on February 23, and Asquith had sharply attacked Bethmann Hollweg for certain of his pronouncements, especially on Belgium. He had demanded the complete restoration of Belgium, adequate security for France against attack, and the safeguarding of the rights of the smaller nationalities of Europe and the destruction of the 'military domination' of Prussia. Answering Asquith on April 5, when Serbia had been crushed, the Western Powers' enterprise in the Dardanelles had failed, Russian and Italian offensives had been halted and the assault on Verdun was promising to develop favourably, Bethmann Hollweg for the first time named names, where in December, 1915, he had confined himself to vague allusions: Belgium, Courland, Poland and Lithuania. Invoking the principle of nationality, to which Asquith himself had appealed, he declared that Germany would not voluntarily consent 'to hand back to the rule of reactionary Russia those peoples living between the Baltic and the Volhynian marshes – Poles, Lithuanians, Balts or Letts – liberated by her or her allies.' He said also that Germany would not 'yield up the lands occupied by her in the west, on which the blood of her people has been spilled, without complete security for our future'. And in his characteristically negative and circuitous way of describing his own aims, he went on: 'We shall secure for ourselves effective guarantees that Belgium does not become an Anglo-French vassal State, is not built up, militarily and economically, into an advance post against Germany. Here, too, there is no *status quo ante.*'

Bethmann Hollweg further introduced an entirely new element into the Belgian problem, in alluding publicly, for the first time, to the Flemish policy initiated by him eighteen months earlier. He said that Germany 'could not allow the long-repressed Flemish people to be abandoned again to denationalisation (*Verwelschung*), but would assure it a healthy development, appropriate to its rich gifts, on the basis of its own native language and individuality'.

By comparison with the war aims of the Entente powers, which were threatening Germany with 'annihilation, dismemberment of the Reich' and the destruction of its military and economic power, and whose motives were 'lust of conquest, lust of revenge, jealousy of their competitors on the world market', Bethmann Hollweg regarded Germany's war aims, as formulated by himself, as moderate and conducive to peace.

The German press, as exemplified by the *Kreuzzeitung* and the *Vorwärts*, interpreted the Chancellor's speech as an avowal of decided annexationism, something along the lines of the previous demands of the six great Trade Associations, and the spokesmen for the parties in the Reichstag debate, with the exception of Haase,[1] at least endorsed his demands, especially in respect of Belgium (this was the line taken by Stresemann, Spahn, von Payer and Count Westarp). Even the main speaker for the Social Democrats, Scheidemann, approved the liberation of the Poles from the Tsarist yoke and the encouragement of the Flemish, and regarded a return to the *status quo* as impossible.

That the Chancellor's speech was no mere propagandist attempt to keep up war feeling among the German people but an expression of his very real aims, was proved when the German–Austrian conversations were resumed later in the month. Burian had expressed an urgent wish to meet Bethmann Hollweg again, and a few days before the meeting he transmitted through Hohenlohe a re-statement of Austria-Hungary's aims: an autonomous Poland, minus frontier rectifications in favour of Germany, but including the government of Cholm and parts of Volhynia, and within the Austrian customs zone. He had modified this document in instructions sent to the ambassador on April 8; he now wanted Germany to limit her 'Frontier Strip' to Suwalki and to compensate herself in Courland, Grodno and Vilna for her exclusion from Poland.[2] Austria had thus again put forward her claim to Poland in precise form; and thus now encountered German aims which were, on that very account, themselves formulated even more precisely, and were incompatible with Austria's.

If Germany's intentions had been to some extent 'veiled' in the conversations of November, 1915, Bethmann Hollweg now confronted Burian with a naked statement of his claims in Poland, which were closely bound up with all the other problems of Mitteleuropa and the east. Germany felt the re-orientation of her policy to be so fundamental that when Burian's visit was announced, Bethmann Hollweg felt impelled to give the Emperor a detailed account of the new ideas and to secure his monarch's backing (this was on April 10). He passed in review the familiar three possible solutions:

(i) The Austro-Polish solution, subject to the cession of a 'Frontier Strip' contiguous with Germany, and including Modlin (which would put

[1] Haase's group had split off from the Social Democrats in April, 1916, to form the *Sozialistische Arbeitsgemeinschaft*. This constituted itself as the Independent Socialist Party of Germany (*Unabhängige Sozialistische Partei Deutschlands*, U.S.P.D.) in April, 1917.

[2] Conze, op. cit., p. 148.

Warsaw within range of German guns). This solution, however, seemed to him tantamount to a Fourth Partition of Poland, and would have saddled Germany with two and a half million Poles and 'second-rate' Jews.

(ii) A partition of Poland between Austria-Germany and Germany on the basis of the frontiers of the zones of occupation, after which Germany should set up a 'Grand Duchy of Warsaw'.

(iii) The plan of making all Congress Poland into an autonomous unit in safe dependence on Germany.

Bethmann far preferred (ii) or (iii), provided they could be combined with a complete guarantee of the security of Germany's eastern frontier, although he realised clearly that both would meet very sharp opposition in Vienna, especially from the Emperor Franz Joseph. 'Perhaps,' he said hopefully, 'the blow might be softened if we proposed an Archduke as Prince of the new autonomous State', and he suggested the Archduke Karl Stefan, who was thought to be pro-German.

The Emperor agreed to this programme, and on April 14–15 Bethmann Hollweg expounded it to Burian, who had arrived in Berlin. The Austrian heard him with extreme displeasure, and the meeting, not unnaturally, ended in complete disagreement; and yet Burian was perhaps not yet wholly aware of Germany's final intentions, which were, as Jagow had told the Emperor, to establish an autonomous Poland, including Galicia, under German suzerainty. We know from Burian that Bethmann Hollweg put the case for the German solution not only on grounds of military security, which 'naturally' required that 'the new buffer State should be completely subject to the military authority of Germany', but primarily on economic grounds, which necessitated the incorporation of the little Polish state in the great German economic system. For the rest, Burian interpreted Germany as intending that the state should be 'independent, under its own monarch, and enjoy full freedom of national self-expression'. He reasoned that Bethmann Hollweg was trying in this way to escape 'the odium of an annexation of Poland', for the age was no longer one for annexations, but one in which smaller states had to nestle up against the great powers.

Germany, he thought, could not allow her ally to acquire rich lands and thus to emerge from the war strengthened, while Germany herself got only vague and uncertain 'safeguards' in Belgium and at the best a frontier rectification on the Baltic in Lithuania. Burian indignantly rejected Bethmann Hollweg's demands and his arguments in favour of them, above all his suggestion that these were no annexations. He said that 'this militarily and economically fettered

Poland, gripped in Germany's powerful fist, would soon be very little different from direct German territory'. But above all, this solution would be intolerable for the Austro-Hungarian Monarchy, because the Poles of the Monarchy would never forgive it 'for having handed over the majority of their nation to the hated Prussianisation', and their fear of Germanisation and of lasting partition would drive them into the arms of Russia as their only resort. He drew up a balance sheet, contrasting Austria's 'frontier rectifications' at the expense of the 'small and poor countries' of Serbia and Montenegro with Germany's acquisitions in Courland and Lithuania (147,000 square kilometres) and her domination of Poland (127,000 square kilometres), besides the political and economic advantages which Germany was securing in Belgium. Bethmann Hollweg retorted (on the second day) that Germany wanted to incorporate in the Reich only the provinces of Suwalki, Courland and Kovno, with parts of those of Grodno and Vilno, in all some 60,000 square kilometres with about three million inhabitants, 'while the rest would, as far as possible, be incorporated in the proposed buffer State'. If we include the Polish 'Frontier Strip' of about 30,000 square kilometres (the area of Alsace-Lorraine was only 14,000), this would have meant direct annexations by Germany of areas amounting to 90,000 square kilometres with 5–6 million inhabitants, as much as the present Austria, while the rest of Poland, with about 95,000 square kilometres more, would come under indirect German rule; in all, an area of about the size of the present Czechoslovakia.

Bethmann Hollweg had been and was fortified in his new attitude by the views and actions of von Beseler, who was disquieted by the failure of the negotiations between the allies–which would be especially dangerous in any peace negotiations–and wrote to the Chancellor strongly urging the creation of what he called 'a Polish national State', to include Austrian Galicia, in the closest association with Germany, as 'a final settlement of conditions on the Eastern March'. This state would have to be 'in the closest political, military and economic association with the future Central European federation'.

Burian maintained his standpoint in an *aide-mémoire* of June 6, although on June 3 Germany had made proposals to meet his objections, including the offer of the crown of the new Poland to the Archduke Karl Stefan. Then the issue was decided by the collapse of the Austrian front under the impact of Brusilov's offensive at the beginning of June. Writing to Tschirschky on June 19, Jagow made only brief reference to Germany's former objections to the Austro-Polish solution; Austria had been defeated again, again German blood had had to hold the front. 'The facts speak so plainly that even Baron Burian will be unable to ignore them. We, however, must draw the consequences from them.'

While German public opinion had at first shown little interest in the Polish question, which it regarded rather as a Prussian concern, now, as the Austrian ambassador observed, both the 'agrarians' and the 'industrialists' began to show 'an ever-increasing interest . . . in acquiring this land of rich resources' which appeared 'ever more tempting and potentially profitable'. Similar interest was shown by the Reich Interior Office and the Prussian economic ministries. Germany's interest, wrote the ambassador, was always concentrated on the economically most valuable parts of Congress Poland, Warsaw, Lodz, Radom, Petrikom, Kielce, the Dombrowa basin, and if the country were partitioned, Germany was certain to claim the industrial areas and coalfields west of the Vistula; the recently mooted idea of a condominium found little favour with the German public, which in general was interested only in economic questions. Whatever form the Polish state took, Germany meant to assure herself the real domination over it by tariffs, provisions for unimpeded transit of goods to Russia, measures securing for herself the supply of Poland's raw materials, and the assimilation to her own systems of the Polish railways and inland waterways 'under the exclusive hegemony of German capital'. Besides control over the railways, roads, waterways and postal and telegraph services, the Germans hoped to retain exclusive military control.

That the ambassador's observations exactly reflected Germany's intentions before the April conversations, and still more so after them, is proved by two instructions to Tschirschky, of May 29 and June 19 respectively, both drafted by Jagow and signed by the Chancellor, to the effect that the Polish question was to be kept a live issue, even although the April conference had failed to bring a decision, and that he was to press unyieldingly for the German solution. Rejecting most categorically 'annexation by Austria', Jagow repeated the familiar demands and arguments from his own, Bethmann Hollweg's and Beseler's arsenals. He concluded by laying down that when Europe was re-shaped after the war, 'a situation must be created which, by all human calculation, assures our future'.

That this spacious political thinking was inspired far less by a wish for peaceful co-existence with 'the Polish nation' than by a single-minded intention to secure Germany's power-position against any threat from Russia, emerges particularly clearly from Jagow's second set of instructions. After Austria's latest defeat, he wrote, it was impossible to leave the defence of Germany's eastern frontier in the hands of the Austrian state. Thus military and economic objectives combined in the minds of Germany's leaders to make them claim the whole of Poland–a mere means to an end–from their allies.

All these long-term considerations were soon overshadowed by the army question. The collapse of the Austrian front in July and the near-exhaustion of Austria's human material caused both Conrad and Falkenhayn to revert to the idea of drawing recruits from the reservoir of Poland's human masses. But Polish divisions could not be raised unless Poland was made 'a State of some kind or other', as Falkenhayn put it. Beseler saw this very clearly; he thought a regular army raised by compulsory service preferable to the enlistment of volunteers, and hoped that the Austrians would make their zone of occupation available for this. Germany was not able to realise this aim immediately. Negotiations took place in Vienna on August 11 and 12,[1] and Bethmann Hollweg was forced by Burian's opposition to agree to a compromise which, at least nominally, constituted 'agreement by both parties that an independent Kingdom of Poland should be established with a hereditary Monarchy and Constitutional institutions'. An announcement to this effect 'was to be made at the earliest possible moment by the two allied Monarchs, while the constitution of the State itself would have to be reserved for a later juncture, after the conclusion of the war'. In respect of foreign policy, Poland was 'to be attached to the alliance of the two Empires . . . Poland cannot conduct a foreign policy *of her own*'. The sole concession to Germany's wishes was that Burian promised to support the principle that the control over and supreme command of the Polish army should 'be unitary, and shall fall to Germany', while the conclusion of the necessary military convention with Poland should be 'conducted by the two Central Powers'. The two Empires were to enjoy equal rights in the economic field, especially in respect of the share capital in the future Polish railway company. Thus the supremacy of Germany was replaced by a sort of condominium, in which Germany enjoyed a certain preference only in respect of the army.

[1] Erich Ludendorff, *Urkunden der Obersten Heeresleitung über ihre Tätigkeit 1916–1918*, 4th ed. (Berlin), pp. 298 ff. Writing to Andrian on August 24, 1916, Burian emphasises strongly that 'what was accepted was not the German plan, which was designed to bring Poland into complete dependence on Germany, but my counter-proposal, which aimed at ensuring the maximum of independence for the Polish State'. Its sovereignty was 'in essence' to be unlimited, except by a Military Convention to be concluded with Germany and Austria. Germany, on the other hand, wanted 'to make Poland also completely dependent on her economically by including her in the German customs district', against which Burian meant to insist on the creation of a separate Polish customs area and complete parity between Germany and Austria *vis-à-vis* Poland.

In reality, however, the Vienna agreement was only a tactical concession to Burian. Only a week later Bethmann Hollweg revealed his real intentions on Poland to the Prussian Ministry of State: 'After allowance for a strategic frontier rectification [this was the 'Frontier Strip'] Poland could be granted autonomy in the form of the closest possible association, military, political and economic, of the future Polish State with Germany.'

The final fate of the future state would necessarily depend on the development of the relationship between the two allies, and in fact Germany secured for herself the preponderant influence in Poland in May, 1917.

OHL 3 Takes Over

A few days after Germany's bid to gain control of Poland had suffered this check, the general situation changed. The Austrian collapse, the failure of the peace feelers in the West, and reports of internal difficulties and war-weariness in Russia (Stürmer had taken over the Ministry of Foreign Affairs from Sazonov on July 23, and the Grand Duke Nicolai Nicolaievitch was rumoured to have made a peace offer to Enver Pasha) decided Bethmann Hollweg again to concentrate all political and military forces on seeking a decision of the war in the east. The Emperor, similarly, thought that after Germany's defensive actions in east and west had ended in the expected successes, 'Russia would get sick of going on with the war' and 'Germany would be able to make a separate peace with her'. He was anxious that this should not be impeded by the publication of plans about Poland. He had now adopted completely Bethmann Hollweg's old point of view: 'to tackle Russia militarily, so as to push her out of the coalition, which would probably drag France after her, and we should get a free hand against England.'

Two weeks earlier Bethmann Hollweg, after engaging in a regular conspiracy against Falkenhayn,[1] had succeeded in getting the boycott on the popular hero, Hindenburg, and his collaborator, Ludendorff, lifted and the supreme command on the eastern front transferred *de facto* to them.

While, however, Bethmann Hollweg allied himself with the rising stars of these two soldiers, the Emperor had continued to back Falkenhayn, in whose sincere acceptance of the new 'Eastern Idea' he believed; it was only Rumania's entry into the war, which had caught Falkenhayn unprepared, that led to Falkenhayn's dismissal and the transference of the supreme command of the armies in the

---

[1] K. H. Janssen, *Der Wechsel in der Obersten Heeresleitung 1916, Vjh. f. Ztgesch.*, 1959, pp. 337 ff., especially pp. 360 ff.

field to the General Officer Commanding in the East and his Chief of General Staff.

With the appointment of Hindenburg and Ludendorff, and the fading away once more of a separate peace owing to Rumania's entry into the war, the question of raising Polish troops came up again. On September 2 von Beseler struck a 'tactical alliance'[1] with Hindenburg and Ludendorff, under which the soldiers persuaded von Beseler to drop his plan for a military service law and a regular army (which presupposed a state) and confine himself to voluntary recruiting; they also demanded that Austria hand over her administrative zone to Prussia–Germany as a precondition for the creation of a Polish volunteer army. This the Chancellor failed to achieve. On November 5 when, after much opposition within Germany, especially Prussia, had been overcome, the Manifesto of the two Emperors at last appeared, it still proclaimed the new Poland 'an independent State' 'in association with the two Allied Powers'. As the Poles had taken no active part in this act, and as the future conditions of the state seemed quite uncertain – above all, 'the more exact determination of its frontiers' was 'reserved' – the hopes that the Proclamation would bring immediate results in the form of Polish soldiers were disappointed; instead of three divisions, only 370 volunteers came in, 350 of them Jews.

The maintenance of Germany's war aims had a part in the changes in the army command.[2] The operative dispositions taken by Falkenhayn showed that, although he agreed with the Emperor, he was not really prepared to seek a decision in the east; he wanted to continue his tactics of wearing down the enemy by offensives in the west. Bethmann Hollweg, on the other hand, shared the Emperor's view that 'the decision lay in the east, more than ever'. Beside what the army might effect, he also had certain hopes of the Stürmer system, and reported to the Emperor that the method recommended by him of using non-official middlemen, Jews, etc., for peace soundings in Petersburg had been regularly employed and should be continued. He accordingly told the Ministry of State on August 19 that:

he was not in the fortunate position of being able to opt between east and west, he had to take the first opportunity of splitting the Entente which presented itself. He had tried every possible way to reach a separate peace with Russia, but without success. Naturally, he would continue these attempts to split the Entente.

His best hopes were of Russia, which, according to information received from Stockholm, could not stand another winter campaign.

[1] Conze, op. cit., pp. 169 ff.

[2] Janssen, op. cit., pp. 365 ff.; he quotes Steglich, but comes to other conclusions.

Hindenburg and Ludendorff were for Bethmann the Men of the East, who would seek and enforce the decision there. In the Rumanian crisis the Hindenburg myth was the only way of stabilising public opinion, without which no aim could be achieved, of appeasing the masses and strengthening their will to hold out until an acceptable peace could be obtained. Furthermore, Bethmann Hollweg could hope that the fall of Falkenhayn would restore the intimacy of his own personal relations with the Emperor. The Zimmermann–Ludendorff connection helped to get the change made and provided an early indication of the community of views between the Foreign Ministry and the new men at the head of the army.

They were one, above all, in the aim of advancing Germany's power-position in east and west and in asserting her status as a world power. Ludendorff's policy was harder in method, less elastic, more inconsiderate and more imperious than that of Bethmann Hollweg, Jagow and Zimmermann, of Helfferich or later of Kühlmann, but basically it did not differ so much as the accepted tradition has it from Germany's intentions as they had been conceived in September, 1914. Colonel Hoffmann, his staff officer, had an extraordinarily low opinion of Hindenburg–'a wretched fellow, this great military genius and idol of the people . . . no one in history ever became so famous at the cost of so little intellectual and physical exertion'.[1] Yet with his steady nerves, which never failed him except perhaps that once, in March, 1915 (when Germany was at her lowest), he was the man to surmount every crisis unshaken, the indispensable man for this war and for that other war which might perhaps soon follow, however little understanding he might have of the statesmen's intricate Mitteleuropa plans and of their devices for exercising indirect control. Ludendorff, charged with energy, greedy for power but also highly nervous, the technician of total war, represented a populist-national, imperial, but always military way of thinking, to which he subordinated all interest in economics or expansion. And neither of them stood alone. Although Bethmann Hollweg talked in the Ministry of State of the masses who were ready to fight for their fatherland but not for a programme of expansion, yet he himself stood for a programme of expansion, which Erzberger had just conveyed to the Pope as the German's government's moderate programme. It would have been decisively rejected, as inadequate, had the Chancellor announced it openly, by an equally broad bourgeois mass and by influential business circles. But neither the Chancellor nor the army leaders of the north-east, bound as they were by their repute, could stand out against the feeling of the nation.

[1] See Janssen, op. cit., p. 348 and p. 366, n. 147.

8

THE OBJECTIVES
OF WAR AIMS POLICY, I

VASSAL STATES, A GERMANIC NORTH-EAST
AND ECONOMIC INTEGRATION

IF the utterances, public and private, of the leading German statesmen are reviewed in chronological order, they show Germany's war
aims policy, in spite of its fluctuations and its dependence on the
military situation, to be essentially self-contained and consistent, and
this impression is confirmed if we examine Germany's plans
and political activities in the areas which were under her control and
were early marked down for permanent incorporation in her power-
sphere.

Mitteleuropa as a New World Economic Unit on a par
with America, Russia and the British Empire

In August, 1914, when the waves of annexationism – the desire to
seize territory adjacent to Germany on any side – were running high,
Bethmann Hollweg launched the idea of Mitteleuropa. The core of
this community was to consist of a German–Austro-Hungarian customs union, to which the medium and small states of the continent
of Europe were to adhere. Bethmann Hollweg pursued his idea un-
deviatingly throughout his whole chancellorship, in the face of all
opposition from officialdom in the Reich and in Prussia, and also of
certain economic interests. Kühlmann and Hertling followed it with
no less determination even after the progress of the war had ruled
out the possibility of including France in the west and the idea of a
'German Eastern Empire' was threatening to overshadow the idea of
Mitteleuropa.

The idea had been conceived before the war by Walther Rathenau and Arthur von Gwinner. Bethmann Hollweg adopted it. At the
beginning of September, 1914, it was subjected to detailed examination by Delbrück, the Secretary of State in the Reich Interior Office,
and Johannes, head of the department of the Foreign Ministry in
charge of commercial policy.

Delbrück wanted to take as the starting-point the attempts made
by Prussia and Austria in 1833 to equalise their tariffs, and he found

in the Austro-Prussian Commercial Treaty of 1853 the model to be followed in a re-statement of the economic relationship between Germany and Austria. Unlike Caprivi's treaty of 1890–4 and Bülow's of 1904–6, which were due to expire in 1916 and which were based on the most favoured nation principle, the treaty of 1853 established a sort of tariff community between the *Zollverein* and Austria which was protected against the rest of the world by differential tariffs, while internally there were only low tariffs between the two units. Delbrück thought this the right solution of the problem. He found no new ideas in Rathenau's proposals, except that Rathenau wanted the far-reaching reorganisation of the economic relationship between Germany and Austria-Hungary put through during the war, in 'a hand's turn', and Delbrück thought this over-precipitate. The Chancellor, however, in thanking Rathenau on September 14, assured him that 'the matter was in hand'. Meanwhile, the Chancellor had sent his September Programme to Delbrück with instructions to prepare the ground for a Central European Economic Union at first with Austria-Hungary, possibly also with France. In his answer to these instructions, dated September 13, Delbrück defined his idea of the future Continental Europe:

> Where hitherto we have tried to protect our national production by high duties and tariff treaties with all European States, in future the free play of forces is to reign in most respects throughout the great area *from the Pyrenees to Memel, from the Black Sea to the North Sea, from the Mediterranean to the Baltic*. . . . The assumptions on which our economic policy formerly rested no longer exist; we are no longer fighting for the mastery in the internal market but for *mastery in the world market* and it is only a Europe which forms a single customs unit that can meet with sufficient power the over-mighty productive resources of the transatlantic world; we ought to thank God that the war is causing us, and enabling us, to abandon an economic system which is already beginning to pass the zenith of its success.

The documents, which are numerous, show that Bethmann Hollweg's September Programme did not stand by itself. Besides Delbrück's first commentary, the memorandum produced by Johannes in September, 1914, showed that numerous discussions on the problems involved took place in the following months. Johannes started from the assumption, which most persons discussing the question took as axiomatic, that Germany would be driven out of the British market, both metropolitan and overseas, because Britain would go over to imperial preference. Germany must therefore find a substitute in Europe in the shape of an economic unit dominated by herself. While, however, this aim was desirable 'in itself', there were

serious arguments against it, which Johannes stressed strongly: firstly, German agriculture had to be considered – it would suffer if exposed to unrestricted competition from Austria-Hungary; furthermore, industrial conditions had developed differently, and taken
different forms, in the two empires, and the backing of the curren-
cies was different. Johannes feared that Germany might lose through
the establishment of a free trade area, particularly since she was not
sure of securing the leadership in it. The question of the machinery
involved in a Customs Parliament and Customs Federal Council –
the precedent of the German–Luxemburg union could not, he
thought, be applied between two great powers – appeared to him, as
it did later to the Prussian ministries in particular, the great obstacle
to a Mitteleuropa; for in such a German–Austrian Customs Parliament Prussia might lose her preponderant influence. On top of all this
came the problem of getting the neutrals, especially the U.S.A., and
the enemy states, England, France and Russia, to agree to the Union.[1]

After the first discussions at General Headquarters between Bethmann Hollweg, Jagow and Delbrück, Delbrück took over all further
work on the subject. He agreed with the Chancellor's view that these
questions of 're-shaping of the economic conditions of Central Europe'
should be discussed in strict secrecy with the departmental ministries
concerned, the representatives of business being initiated as little and
as late as possible, lest the 'great cause' be endangered by individual
interests. The conversations with the ministries began in the middle
of October. Belgium and Austria-Hungary were treated as being on
the same footing, and the object of including France was always kept
in mind.

The possible solutions to emerge were: (i) complete customs union –
favoured by Bethmann Hollweg, Helfferich and Falkenhausen;
(ii) a Customs Federation with low internal tariffs but high protection against other countries – supported chiefly by Delbrück; and
(iii) expansion of commercial treaties and perhaps co-operation in
questions of commercial policy – the course favoured by Schoenebeck, Havenstein and Sydow and supported by the great majority of
the representatives of the Prussian departmental ministries. An overwhelming majority of the leading personalities, including Schoenebeck, rejected a Customs Union or Customs Federation on the
grounds that Germany, with her worldwide industrial connections,
would lose by being confined to the leadership of Europe (where her

[1] At the beginning of September, before the battle of the Marne, all the weight
of the Mitteleuropa plans was in the west. France, too, was to be included in the
central European Customs Federation. Bethmann Hollweg long kept this possibility in view; it was analysed and pursued as an objective in all top-level memoranda.

industrial potential in any case ensured her predominance), since the European markets could not adequately replace overseas markets as outlets for German industry. But even the opponents of a customs union agreed that after the war Germany would be facing an economically unified world. Schoenebeck, however, hoped that if Germany renounced the extension of her economic autonomy, America for example would make a similar renunciation. They also argued that it was unwise for Germany to commit herself to Austria-Hungary 'for better, for worse'; but they were entirely in favour of the unification of Europe, as Müller of the Reich Interior Office put it, 'including Switzerland, the Netherlands, the Scandinavian States, Belgium, France, even Spain and Portugal, and via Austria-Hungary, also Rumania, Bulgaria and Turkey'. And here the 'Noes' joined hands with the 'Ayes', whose final aim was the 'United States of Europe' but who supported the union with Austria-Hungary as a first step. Among the principal points put forward was the probability of an economic conflict with the world powers after the war. Lusensky,[1] a director in the Prussian Ministry for Trade and Industry, argued that the advantage of the customs union of the European states lay in the unification *vis-à-vis* the outer world of states 'whose individual trade potentialities are growing ever more unfavourable by comparison with the great world economic areas (the U.S.A., the British Empire, Russia) in a global organisation on a par with the others.' Similarly von Falkenhausen, representing the Ministry of Agriculture, State Lands and Forestries, regarded the aim and task of German commercial policy as being:

To match the great, closed economic bodies of the United States, the British and the Russian Empires with an equally solid economic bloc representing all European States, or at least those of central Europe, under German leadership, with the twofold purpose: (1) of assuring the members of this whole, and particularly Germany, the mastery of the European market, and (2) of being able to lead the entire economic strength of allied Europe into the field, as a unified force, in the struggle with those world powers over the conditions of the admission of each to the markets of the others.

Even Delbrück, who on the tariff question favoured the middle line of a Customs Federation, regarded Mitteleuropa as a sort of compensation for the expected loss of overseas markets, and concluded: 'the unrestricted opening of the Austro-Hungarian economic territory will then undoubtedly be of great advantage to our industry'. He went still further: 'The Central European States can only count for anything against the three established World Powers if they

[1] Lusinsky had worked under Caprivi on the German–Austrian negotiations in 1890.

can face the struggle no longer separated but united by firm economic and institutional [sic] ties.'

His assistant, von Schoenebeck, wrote:

Difficulties of procedure should not make us forget the 'great final aim' of creating a great central European economic unit to enable us to hold our place in the economic struggle for existence of the peoples and to save us from sinking into economic impotence against the ever-increasing solidarity and power of the economic World Powers, Great Britain with her colonies, the United States, Russia, and Japan with China.

The supporters of a Customs Federation – who appealed to the example of Chamberlain's idea of imperial preference – hoped further 'to reduce the political differences inside the continent of Europe to tolerable dimensions through the creation of common economic interests'.

The debates on the economic arguments for a customs union and the almost unanimous rejection of the idea by the planners in the ministries caused Bethmann Hollweg to give formal orders to Jagow and Delbrück on February 11, 1915, to submit as soon as possible definite proposals for the organisation of a Customs Federation. The Reich and Prussian ministries still proved unable to agree on aims and organisation, and Delbrück himself reported that no decision would ever come out of debates in committee: it would have to be taken by 'the statesman responsible'.

In spite of the rejection by the overwhelming majority of the ministries of his plan for 'the elimination of customs barriers in Central Europe', and in spite of the objections of a number of organisations representing business interests, Bethmann Hollweg refused to drop his Mitteleuropa. Although only Helfferich, of the Secretaries of State, supported him, he held to his idea and to his aim of September, 1914, of at least trying to achieve, as a first step, 'uniform minimum tariffs for the whole economic area against the products of other countries and low preferential tariffs for trade between its members'. He insisted that the plan should be continuously studied and perfected at home, and he pressed on Austria-Hungary cautiously, but tenaciously and purposefully.

What were the motives and intentions which made this allegedly irresolute man pursue his plan with such unwavering fixity? As in September, 1914, so now his decision was again determined by an essentially political vision. He dreamed of imposing the Customs Federation with Austria-Hungary (or other states) on France and Russia when peace was concluded with them, even at the risk of a tariff war with America. The union, so he thought, had to be,

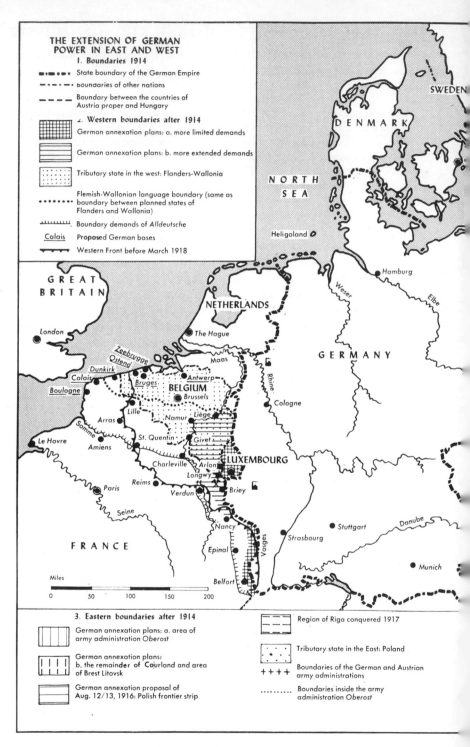

THE EXTENSION OF GERMAN
POWER IN EAST AND WEST

1. Boundaries 1914

▪━▪━▪ State boundary of the German Empire

━▪━▪━ boundaries of other nations

━ ━ ━ Boundary between the countries of
Austria proper and Hungary

2. Western boundaries after 1914

German annexation plans: a. more limited demands

German annexation plans: b. more extended demands

Tributary state in the west: Flanders-Wallonia

●●●●● Flemish-Wallonian language boundary (same as
boundary between planned states of
Flanders and Wallonia)

⊥⊥⊥⊥⊥ Boundary demands of *Alldeutsche*

Calais Proposed German bases

━▼━▼ Western Front before March 1918

SWEDEN

DENMARK

NORTH
SEA

Heligoland

Hamburg

Weser

Elbe

GREAT
BRITAIN

NETHERLANDS

London

The Hague

GERMANY

Zeebrugge

Ostend

Dunkirk

Maas

Rhine

Calais

Bruges

Antwerp

Cologne

Boulogne

BELGIUM

Brussels

Lille

Namur

Liège

Arras

Somme

St. Quentin

Givet

LUXEMBOURG

Le Havre

Amiens

Charleville

Arlon

Longwy

Paris

Reims

Briey

Verdun

Seine

Nancy

Danube

FRANCE

Strasbourg

Stuttgart

Epinal

Vosges

Miles

Belfort

Munich

0   50   100   150   200

3. Eastern boundaries after 1914

German annexation plans: a. area of
army administration Oberost

German annexation plans:
b. the remainder of Courland and area
of Brest Litovsk

German annexation proposal of
Aug. 12/13, 1916: Polish frontier strip

Region of Riga conquered 1917

Tributary state in the East: Poland

++++ Boundaries of the German and Austrian
army administrations

●●●●● Boundaries inside the army
administration Oberost

252

Estonia

Dago

Moon

Ezel

Livonia

BALTIC SEA

Courland

Riga

Libau

Mitau

Dwinsk (Dünaburg)

Lithuania

Niemen

Königsberg

Kovno

Wilno

Smorgon

Wilno-Suwalki

Minsk

Suwalki

Grodno

Grodno

Nowogródek

R U S S I A

Bialistok

Thorn

Narew

Byalistok

Lomza

Bialowieza

Warthe

Vistula

Bug

Bielsk

Pruzany

Pinsk

Plock

Bresk Litovsk

Berlin

Oder

German Army Administration

Warsaw

Siedlce

Kalisz

Warsaw

Łódź

Piotrców

Radom

Kowel

Dubno

esden

Breslau

Austrian Army Administration

Lublin

Chelm

Kielce

Lublin

Brody

Bedzin

Tarnogrod

Prague

Krakow

Lemberg (Lwow)

A U S T R I A - H U N G A R Y

Kamenets-Podolsk

Hotin

Czernowitz

R U M A N I A

Vienna

⦿⦿⦿⦿⦿⦿⦿ Proposal of OHL
for a wider frontier strip

▪▫▪▫▪▫ East boundary of the kingdom of Lithuania,
recognized March 23, 1918

⠿⠿⠿ Boundary of the Ukrainian People's Republic
proclaimed July 16, 1917

⨯⨯⨯⨯ Boundary of the Ukrainian *Hetmanship*
1918/1919

▲▲▲▲ Eastern Front, December 1917

⚒ Mineral deposits

🔒 Industrial centres

⬟ Fortresses

because without Austria-Hungary Germany would be unable to hold
her own in Europe and the world; unless she possessed this link, unless she could build up a central European bloc, Germany would become dependent on Britain (America) or Russia and would be unable to maintain herself as an independent power. The threefold
link, military, political and economic, was the means of saving the
integrity of Austria-Hungary; further, the economic penetration and
the relationships established thereby were the guarantee that, should
Austria-Hungary disintegrate, Germany's interests in the successor
states would be safeguarded and organic links between them and
Germany maintained. Finally, this economic-military penetration
was also a cultural mission, like 'the hallmark' of a 'World People'.

> The old Reich still lives on today. All South-Eastern Europe is a cultural
> colony stretched before our doors. . . . The task of policy is to make room –
> including physical room – for German values. The strongest protection for
> England is not her fleet, but the cultural cohesion represented by the Anglo-
> Saxon world. Our task is to create a similar cultural cohesion.

The differences over the Mitteleuropa question were threshed out
once again between the chancellery and the ministries in June, 1915,
when Helfferich again supported the Chancellor on political grounds.
In the great state conferences of the autumn and winter of 1915,
which were attended by all the leading heads of departments of the
Reich and Prussia, the decision for or against a Customs Federation
with Austria was no longer debated; only the tactics of the approach
to Austria. The proper purpose of these conferences was to regulate
the Polish question; but the extension of the customs union to Scandinavia, Switzerland, the Balkans and France was also discussed,
and the aim of an autarchic economic territory of 'Germany' reaffirmed. Helfferich again explained his attitude on the customs
union in a memorandum submitted after the conference: 'The Customs Federation must aim at *amalgamating* [author's italics] the
whole territory of the Contracting Parties into an economic unity.'
Helfferich thought the security of a long-term alliance especially important; Germany needed 'to give German industry decades of occupation in Austria-Hungary . . . to set German capital working there'.
Thus prepared, Berlin in November, 1915, proposed to the Austrians a Customs Federation with mutual tariff preference which
would not be enjoyed by third states unless they adhered to the Federation. The Federation was to receive international recognition
under the peace treaty. Special value was attached to the establishment of efficient railway traffic with Russia (Poland) and the east (the
Balkans) and to linking up the navigable waterways; these proposals

were governed by plans elaborated by Breitenbach, the Prussian Minister of Public Works, for 'a direct German–Austro-Hungarian–Bulgarian railway connection' and for taking over the Polish railways. 'Heavy political weapons and the whole weight of the Reich's authority in the world' were–as Delbrück had demanded as the preconditions of any agreement on tariffs–brought to bear on Austria to make her accept the objects of Mitteleuropa in the solution of the Austro-Polish question. On this point also Germany was trying to create a *fait accompli* which even an international Peace Conference would be unable to undo. Bethmann Hollweg's anxiety to reinforce the German-Austrian military and political alliance then under discussion with a customs union appears clearly in the conversations which he now held with the Secretaries of State (Naumann, Bassermann, Schiffer, and Roland Lücke, the Director of the Deutsche Bank, were invited to attend these meetings, but were given only a broad outline of what was going on, and were not consulted).

At the end of November Germany's aims were finally formulated in a set of 'principles for the negotiation of the Customs Federation with Austria-Hungary';

> The economic-political unification of Germany with Austria-Hungary is a political necessity. . . . The negotiations are thus to be carried on, without prejudice to any reservation imposed by tactical necessity, with the firm determination to reach an agreement which fulfils *the political objective* in as complete a form as possible.

The agenda for the negotiations, which opened in Salzburg, was to cover: mutual grant of preferential tariffs (three-quarters of the minimum tariff) while most favoured nation, normal or even punitive tariffs were to be imposed on neutrals; no commercial-political activities to be undertaken without Germany's consent; the 'Principles' specifically named the Balkan states, Turkey, Scandinavia, Belgium, Holland, Poland and also France as part of the free trade area. Getting the desired preferential tariffs imposed in the free trade area dominated by Germany was, the 'Principles' said, 'simply a question of power'. 'If,' they concluded, 'we fail now to secure the possibility of an economic-political unification of central Europe, the opportunity will not recur for generations.'

In November, 1915, the German government sent a delegation to Vienna, headed by Richter, Under-Secretary of State in the Reich Interior Office, and Tschirschky, to clarify the general bases of the economic *rapprochement* in oral conversations. The further progress of the Mitteleuropa plan was, however, always dependent on the Polish problem. Deadlocks between Berlin and Vienna over the Polish question always resulted in similar deadlocks in the Mitteleuropa negotiations.

By the end of 1916, thanks largely to a renewal of internal friction on the subject, not only had the Germans achieved nothing positive in this field, but Naumann's agitation had evoked lively reactions from the Entente. The Paris Economic Conference gave the answer to the threatened exclusion of Britain, France and Russia from the central European market. If the Central Powers carried through their economic unification at the expense of the commercial interests of other states, the Entente powers would carry on hostilities in the shape of a trade and tariff war even after the conclusion of peace. This worldwide opposition presented Germany with the choice either of renouncing Mitteleuropa or of pressing it forward in all seriousness. Bethmann Hollweg and his successors opted for the latter course, although in the internal negotiations the dangers to Germany's world trade were never forgotten, and efforts were consequently made to meet reactions by giving the central European economic alliance a certain elasticity of form.

Mitteleuropa, in the form of a purely economic arrangement, but one so designed as to combine the efficacy of a customs union with the less conspicuous organisation of a customs treaty without institutional superstructure, had become a German war aim, and it held that place until the summer of 1918. The construction of an economic unit on the basis of reduced internal tariffs, protected against competition from outside by most favoured nation clause as the maximum concession, would have enabled the German economic potential to dominate Europe without any clear definition of power-relationships. Bethmann Hollweg, Helfferich and the Foreign Ministry saw this clearly, and tried constantly to effect it, and they were soon joined by the Old Prussians when Prussia's influence was assured by by the substitution of a Federation for a Union. Lentze, the Prussian Minister of Finance, revised his earlier standpoint and described the Customs Federation as the great aim of German policy.

If [he wrote] the negotiations are carried on in no petty spirit, but generously, keeping the *national* (*völkisch*) and *political* aims in view and without shrinking from momentary sacrifices, the Customs Federation can be achieved before the opening of the peace negotiations. The demand of the hour, which may be the hour of destiny, is that the Customs Federation come into being, and that it do so quickly.[1]

Roedern, Secretary of State in the Reich Treasury, who at first had regarded both a customs union and a customs federation as 'jumps in the dark', underwent a similar conversion.

[1] Author's italics.

Longwy–Briey, the Prime Aim of German Heavy Industry

As we have seen, Bethmann Hollweg's September Programme laid down as a war aim (in the interest of 'security for the German Reich') that 'France must be so weakened that she never again recovers as a great power', and to this end the Chancellor wanted a substantial war indemnity, a commercial treaty which should secure the French market for Germany's exports and exclude British commerce, perhaps some strategic frontier rectifications, and 'in any case' the cession of the ore-field of Longwy–Briey 'as necessary for the supplies to our industry'.

The centre of the French iron-mining industry was taken in August, 1914, and a civilian administration for it set up under the Governor of Metz. The mines themselves were put under a special 'Imperial Protective Administration', with an industrial 'adviser', which organised the resumption of production. At the end of 1916 the civilian administration was militarised, and placed directly under the Supreme Army Command.

Even during the war it was often asserted that it was only the uninterrupted exploitation of these mines that had enabled Germany to meet the demand for arms and munitions – which was far higher than had been anticipated – and carry on the war. This is probably no exaggeration. The view in Germany was that in this particular respect, and in general, the possession or non-possession of these ore deposits, the richest in Europe outside Sweden, was decisive for the power-potential in iron and steel, and consequently, in an industrial age, also for the real political and military power on the continent of Europe.

A glance at the innumerable memoranda, appreciations, statistics and research papers prepared by the German ministries, particularly the Ministry of the Interior (in obedience to Bethmann Hollweg's orders to Delbrück of August 26, 1914), or presented to the government, or compiled at its behest, by the experts of Germany's heavy and mining industries (the documentation would fill several volumes) gives the following picture: Germany's total reserves of iron ore in 1914 amounted to 2,300 million tons, of which 1,777 million were in the minette areas of German Luxemburg, the rest being in the Siegerland, the district of Lahn-Dill and Peine-Salzgitter.[1] The

[1] Given a maximum annual production of 40 million tons, the German–Lorraine and Luxemburg district would have a life of 45 years, the Siegerland one of 42 years, with a production of 2·7 million tons, Lahn-Dill and Peine would last for 56 and 135 years respectively; but their production was relatively insignificant.

257

total iron ore reserves of France, on the other hand, were reckoned at 8,200 million tons; in other words, three times as large as Germany's. Of these, 4,722 million tons were in Normandy, but only a 'minute' part of these enormous deposits was being worked.[1] The German memoranda maintained that the ironfields of Normandy could 'with the utmost ease' be made to produce as much as the French minette districts. The total reserves of Longwy–Briey were put at 2,775 million tons of high-quality ore,[2] 2,000 millions of them in the minette basin of Briey alone. While the figures of the reserves seemed to indicate that France could cover her needs by more extensive exploitation of the Normandy ironfields, the production figures for 1913 showed that the loss of Longwy–Briey would have brought French industry to a standstill for years. 81 per cent of France's total production came from Longwy–Briey. Possession of this area would have doubled Germany's reserves. In 1914 it had been calculated that Germany's reserves would last her another forty-five years, on a regular maximum production of 40 millions a year, most of this coming from Luxemburg and German Luxemburg; with Longwy–Briey Germany could have covered her needs for ninety years.[3]

What the loss of Longwy–Briey would mean to France and the gain of it to Germany is put best in the extremely thorough report by Geheimrat Dr. Schoenebeck, of the Reich Interior Office. After an elaborate analysis of reserves, production, proportion exported, German participation and concessions, he concluded that the iron industry of France would sink into insignificance if it lost French Lorraine. 'The cession of French Lorraine would be almost tantamount to the end of France's large-scale iron industry. For Germany, on the other hand, the acquisition of this area would be of incalculable importance.'

If, then, the area was not annexed – which would be 'the only satisfactory solution' – it was of absolutely fundamental importance for the further development and even the existence of Germany's

[1] 162,000 tons in 1902, 499,000 in 1910 and 619,000 in 1911. The French economist Barrès estimates that France possesses one-third of the world's whole reserves (7,000 million tons out of 22,000 millions).

[2] The total French production had risen from 2·32 million tons in 1885 to 7·4 millions in 1905, 14·61 in 1910, 16·0 in 1911, 18·84 in 1912 and 21·71 in 1913. The corresponding figures for Longwy–Briey are: 1885, 1·01; 1905, 4·68; 1910, 11·10; 1911, 12·77; 1912, 15·01; 1913, 17·58 million tons.

[3] Another memorandum writes: 'At least nine-tenths of all France's present production of ore would be taken, and although there may still be some deposits in Normandy and Britanny, they are . . . very little known or exploited.' Only 13·2 millions of France's total production of 21·7 million tons was consumed by herself. Germany, on the other hand, needed to import 11 million tons (7·5 millions, or 60 per cent from Sweden and 3 millions, or 28 per cent from France).

iron industry that it should be assured of adequate supplies of French minette ore.

In the two decades before the war German capital and German enterprise had, in spite of French legislative restrictions, gained a firm footing in both Longwy–Briey and Normandy, as they had in Luxemburg and, on a smaller scale, in Belgium. German capital had acquired control of about one-eighth of the mines and supplies, partly through direct concessions (licences to prospect), partly through participation in French concessions.[1] Counting Belgian concessions, Germany, after the occupation of Belgium, dominated one-sixth of the mining area.

As soon as war broke out, the associations of German heavy industry brought all possible pressure to bear for the acquisition of the area. Petition after petition to the governments of the Reich and Prussia asked for the annexation of Longwy–Briey, or at least, economic control over it. Bethmann Hollweg always kept this aim in view, and he was justified in protesting in November, 1916, when the Steelmakers' Association alleged that he was trying to conclude peace with France at any price, even the price of renouncing Longwy–Briey. In a personal letter to Kirdorf, the Director of the Gelsenkirchener Bergwerke, he emphasised the particular consistency of his policy in respect of France and Longwy–Briey. It was no different after his fall, under Michaelis and Hertling, and when at the end of 1917 Michaelis seemed for one moment to be wavering and to be seeking a settlement with the West, however vague, at the expense of Longwy–Briey and Belgium, the spokesmen of the industry assured him that they were prepared to carry on the war for another ten years for Longwy–Briey.[2]

The conviction that the economic world-power position of Germany was bound up with the possession of this area is reflected in an early remark by August Thyssen that 'incorporation of the Briey basin would raise the iron ore production of Greater Germany to 61·4 million tons', which would exceed America's 56 million. The production of the Belgian and French works, added to the German, would increase the lead over England and America. And he concluded: 'It would therefore be only a question of a little time before Germany caught up with and passed America; and this would ensure Germany's world domination on the iron market.'

---

[1] One-thirtieth of the minette area, as then known, was wholly German-owned, and one-thirteenth partially.

[2] The meeting took place in the train between Cologne and Aachen on August 29, 1917. The speaker was Vögler.

Belgium: a Tributary State in the West

Following up his September Programme, Bethmann Hollweg on October 18, 1914, instructed Zimmermann and Delbrück, his two closest collaborators, who had stopped behind in Berlin and taken over the key positions there, 'to find forms' which would make possible Germany's economic penetration of Belgium and secure her control of the coast, fortresses and transport system against the eventuality of further wars without 'burdening' the Reich with the political executive. Belgium was to be 'restored' in form as a 'tributary state', 'but *de facto* to be at Germany's disposal in both military and economic respects'.

Delbrück's and Zimmermann's answer, which was published in 1929,[1] saw the technical method of achieving Germany's aim in the command of the Belgian coast, the Belgian fortresses and the transport system. Further, Belgium should keep no army of her own, but 'only a local police force', but for economic reasons, since the absence of compulsory service would give Belgium an advantage over Germany in respect of labour supply, a Military Convention should be concluded between Prussia and Belgium and a Belgian army organised on the German model and '. . . trained in German garrisons'. Delbrück and Zimmermann regarded this last device as particularly well calculated to bring about 'a gradual Germanisation of the Belgian people'. They thought, however, that this military control 'absolutely necessitated imposing certain limitations on the sovereignty of Belgium'. The German garrisons must be under their own jurisdiction, Belgium 'must not be allowed to conduct any foreign policy' and should accordingly maintain no missions of her own at foreign courts and no consular representatives of her own, nor conduct her own colonial policy; she must transfer her representation abroad to the Reich. The protectorate over the Congo state should be explicitly transferred to the Reich. The Reich would have to possess a general veto over domestic legislation and administrative enactments. The 'association' was to be not only military and administrative, but also economic. The best way 'to open up new markets for German industry in this rich country, with its many potentialities', was to include Belgium in the German Customs Association (on the model of Luxemburg) and to introduce 'the current German legislation and indirect taxation'. The proposed establishment of Germany's economic preponderance could, however, be made secure only by suitable dispositions in the field of transport, and the author's last and most important recommendation was

[1] Volkmann, *Annexionsfragen*, pp. 197 ff.

therefore that Belgium's transport system should be linked with Germany's 'as completely as possible' by attaching the Belgian railway system to the German on the Prusso-Hessian model. Similarly, the Belgian inland waterways could be linked up with the German. Transport tariffs must be assimilated to the German model. Belgium could further be linked to Germany by a monetary union, must leave the Latin Currency Union, introduce the mark and conclude with Germany a uniform system of banking clearances. But the Secretaries of State strongly warned the Chancellor against 'limitations on Belgium's sovereignty' so far-reaching as to lead to a refusal to accept them and to revolts obliging the German garrisons to take action. This would result in intervention by other powers and consequently in a 'revision of Belgium's international status'.

In spite of this final warning, Bethmann Hollweg was not to be deterred from his fundamental idea of establishing military and economic control over Belgium. His policy was endorsed by the military, the heads of the Reich ministries, and also the heads of the Government-General. In March, 1915, the new Governor-General, von Bissing, circularized all offices under him with a questionnaire on economic conditions in Belgium and its relation to Germany 'in order to be able to advance the interests of Germany alone . . . with the greatest possible ruthlessness and with no unworthy lenience . . . and to lay the foundations for the future conclusion of peace'. He was primarily concerned 'to use Belgium in one way or another for the expansion of Germany's power', and to see that officials and entrepreneurs in Germany or German services in Belgium do not get the idea that this 'use is only a temporary, wartime thing. On the contrary, the population must be trained to respect order and discipline [sic] and be brought nearer to Germandom' by the strict rule of a self-administration adapted to German conditions. By these means Belgium could be made into 'a serviceable outpost for Germany's strength and power'.

In contrast to Bethmann Hollweg's idea of recognising Belgium at least as a 'tributary state', von Bissing would not allow Belgium even the remnant of sovereignty left to her by Zimmermann and Delbrück. Belgium was not to have even a shadow of sovereignty; Germany must not regard the assumption of rule over her as a burden, but as a sacred duty. He, too, however, wanted 'association', not annexation, for annexation would in the long run raise social and internal political problems in Germany. But Germany should not only be given the right to erect fortresses anywhere in Belgium, and to construct strategic railways whenever she pleased, but should also secure her rule over Belgium by strict laws on the press and the rights of association and assembly.

In the course of 1915 the policy of indirect rule gained the upper hand over that of annexation. In the middle of the year a conference in the Imperial Chancellery between Bethmann Hollweg, Delbrück, Breitenbach, Sydow, Helfferich and Heinrich the Under-Secretary of State, again sketched out the 'Belgian programme', together with the Russian frontier (Vistula–San–Dniester with Lemberg). According to Heinrich's notes, the ministers and secretaries of state agreed that it was not yet possible to lay down a definitive programme for Belgium. They agreed, however, that Belgium must be 'made harmless, and in any case, economically dependent'. Delbrück recalled the familiar aims of economic penetration. Again, it was Bethmann Hollweg who pressed for a forward policy. He judged the questions of tariff regulation and of control over the railways and waterways, as demanded by Breitenbach, entirely from the angle of a customs association. 'What do we need . . . to effect the customs association?' Helfferich, representing finance, replied: monetary union and a customs union supported by control over the railways. This was the only way of establishing 'the expansion of our economy over the territory of Belgium without assuming political authority' and of 'developing our economic bastion' – of course against Britain and France. 'Hatred of Germany,' he went on, 'is still alive in Belgium . . . so there is much resistance to amalgamation.'[1] To overcome this he suggested (he had, of course, been a private business man) 'grafting ourselves on to Belgian industry and commerce through transference of industrial shares, etc., . . . via the war indemnity'.

A central question raised by the Minister for Public Works, not for the first time, was the organisation of the port of Antwerp and its approaches. On December 6, 1914, the minister had discussed with Bethmann Hollweg the plan to link the Rhine with Antwerp by a canal. On December 12 the technical, economic and political aspects of the plan had been discussed in a conference of departmental ministers. Three lines had been considered: the Kreefeld plan, to run through the northern part of the Dutch province of Limburg, the Mönchengladbach through its southern half, and the Aachen. A connection with Antwerp by water would have given Germany an outlet to the Atlantic – and the shortest route to it at that – which would have made her independent of Dutch Rotterdam. But the idea raised the question whether Bremen and Hamburg would not suffer,

---

[1] The same phrase of an 'economic bastion' was used by Bethmann Hollweg, Delbrück and Helfferich in relation to the affiliation of Austria-Hungary, Poland and south-eastern Europe.

and also Rotterdam (Holland's consent was necessary for the construction of the canal). The numerous discussions on the construction of a Rhine–Scheldt canal and the attachment of Antwerp to the
Reich were carried farthest at a meeting on June 15. The threat to
Hamburg and Bremen was dismissed with the reply that those two
ports could in any case never handle the exports of south Germany,
for which Antwerp was the natural outlet. Breitenbach, and following him, Helfferich and Delbrück, accepted Ballin's idea of a 'German–Belgian Company' as the best solution of the problem, and this
idea of a joint administration of the port, combined with some new
arrangement for the future status of Antwerp–perhaps as a Free
City–remained a basic element in Germany's Belgian policy down
to 1918: Antwerp was to be expanded into 'the first and dominating
port of Mitteleuropa'.[1]

The central question discussed by the departmental ministries in
the middle of 1915 was the proposed customs union. Special enquiries were necessitated by the proposals to partition Belgium into
Flanders and Wallonia. In the first of these proposals Wallonia was
to be incorporated in the French customs area and Flanders in the
German. The way in which Germany's interests were secured under
this solution again shows Germany's anxiety for her own power, and
also, how closely the Belgian problem was interwoven with Mitteleuropa. The Reich Interior Office demanded that if Wallonia went
to France, France should be required to enter a customs association
with Germany and also to provide securities assuring the German
iron industry all the supplies it needed of French minette ores. The
purpose of the Franco-German customs association was partly to
give the commercial policy of the customs union more weight against
Britain and America, partly to create a more differentiated economic unit.

As on the central European customs union, so over the Belgian
question, the views of the economic experts differed widely: economic harm was balanced against advantage in the field of commercial policy. Political considerations and communications spoke in
favour of a customs union with Belgium under German control; the
ministries wrote that 'a customs union with Belgium must bring advantage to the whole of our industry through the closer connection
between the systems of communication which will necessarily come
about as result of the unification of the customs and economic area'.
It proved possible, with the help of the 'Economic Committee', to

[1] The confessed purpose was the economic annihilation of Belgium's independence by depriving her of her railway sovereignty. The postal services, customs and
banks were also to be German.

reconcile the different aims, both of the state and of private interests.

Meanwhile, the preparations for the currency union were being carried on. In the summer of 1915 the Reich Treasury, with the Reichsbank and the Prussian Ministry of Finance, assisted by the Foreign Ministry and the Reich Interior Office, completed preparations for introducing the mark into Belgium on the basis of a report prepared by von Lumm, formerly Director of the Reichsbank and now Director of the Banking Department in the General government, and Somary, an expert from that department. This report made thorough and comprehensive provision for the absorption and assimilation of the Belgian capital market, both state and private. Helfferich held the currency union to be the real key to economic penetration, and used all his influence to push it through as 'fundamentally desirable and conducive to Germany's interests'. Associated therewith were the efforts of the Reichsbank to establish itself in Belgium as the Bank of Issue, to set up branches there even during the war, and to establish control over the Belgian capital market by using them as clearing houses. As late as July, 1918, Helfferich, who was then co-ordinating the proposed peace conditions for the west, was urging most strongly the establishment of a customs and currency union between Germany and Belgium.

After these extensive preparations, it proved possible, in September, 1915, to draw up the draft of a 'Treaty on the adhesion of Belgium to the German–Luxemburg customs association'. The draft had been agreed with representatives of heavy industry, who met Geheimrat von Schoenebeck, representing the Reich Interior Office, in the Park Hotel, Düsseldorf, on August 4. The wishes and proposals of the 'North-Western Group of the German Iron and Stee Association' were considered by the ministries at a meeting on August 27, and accepted.

Other associations, the 'Association for the Maintenance of Common Economic Interests in the Rhineland and Westphalia' (the '*Langnamverein*'), the 'Association for Mining Interests in the Upper Mining District of Dortmund-Essen-Ruhr' and the Chambers of Commerce of the Lower Rhine and Westphalian industrial districts advocated the same aims in what appeared to be harder terms, but in reality went little beyond the government's own Belgian policy. A combined meeting was held, again in Düsseldorf, on November 22 to discuss proposals for attaching Belgium to Germany. On November 25 a memorandum was submitted to the Chancellor which stated: 'When the war has been won, the attachment of Belgium to Germany is an ineluctable necessity, both for the military security of our frontiers, and for the increase of our maritime weight.'

In what constitutional form the attachment was to be effected was treated as a subject for later consideration. The following conditions must, however, be fulfilled:

(i) Belgian production must be made to carry the same social charges as are borne by German production.

(ii) All communications (railways, waterways, posts, telegraphs, cables) must come into the ownership of the German Reich, or under its direct and effective control.

(iii) Belgian industry must be brought under German influence or into German ownership.

(iv) The German currency and monetary units must be introduced into Belgium.

(v) Belgian law to be adapted to German, with full allowance for the maintenance, for a period, of a state of emergency in the interests of security.

(vi) To balance the attachment, and for further security, the attachment of other foreign areas is to be considered, to serve:

(a) the supply of industrial raw materials (iron ore, colonial products) – [Meaning Longwy–Briey and the Congo.—Author];

(b) the production of a considerable surplus of foodstuffs;

(c) enlarged markets for industrial products;

(d) covering of requirements of foreign labour, which will inevitably constitute a more difficult problem in the future.

(vii) Belgium must be attached to the German customs area. There must, however, be a transitional stage, the extent and duration of which depends on a list of commodities to be drawn up in consultation with the industrial, commercial and shipping interests concerned. When this last demand is carried through, the German trade associations will act in the knowledge that the requirements of military security and of a stronger position at sea may sometimes call for sacrifices which the individual has to bear willingly.

There is a striking similarity between these demands and the aims of Bethmann Hollweg, Jagow, Helfferich, Delbrück and the Prussian departmental ministries. Point (vii) especially, reflected very briefly, but most exactly, the course which the German government had decided to take. It is obvious that Zimmermann, who had been concerned for the necessary secrecy when the conversation with industry took place in Düsseldorf in August, and Bethmann Hollweg, had no objections to the substance of this document; it was only on tactical grounds that they forbade the publication of such aims.

What had previously been plans took the form of demands put to Belgium in the secret negotiations with King Albert.

Conformably with the Chancellor's ideas of September, 1914, and May, 1915, Kühlmann proposed in April, 1916, the direct annexation of the whole line of the Meuse from Liége past Namur and Dinant to Givet in France. As minister in The Hague he had been systematically preparing the ground for a favourable reception of this very definite proposal by reports on feelings and intentions in Holland. The Dutch, he wrote, were afraid that Germany meant to annex the whole of Belgium, and would be relieved and even delighted if she confined herself to the Meuse line. Against this, Kühlmann pointed out that the military had wished to annex Liége only. Yet as late as November, 1915, Falkenhayn had confirmed his earlier demand, that Germany needed the general line Metz–Ostend to enable her to advance against France in a future war and, beyond this, the whole of Belgium as a glacis against the western powers.

The navy had put forward more precise demands for extensive annexations in Belgium in a long memorandum from Admiral von Holtzendorff to the Emperor on 'the importance of the Belgian ports for our sea-power', dated October 29, 1915. This report attached especial importance to the Ostend–Zeebrugge–Antwerp triangle of ports as a base for an invasion of England in a future war and also as submarine bases for operating in the Atlantic. On November 1 the Emperor signified his full concurrence with the ideas of the Admiralty,[1] which maintained its Belgian programme unchanged throughout the war and renounced its demand for the coast of Flanders only as late as August 31, 1918.

The hardening of opinion in favour of annexation was, however, only a passing phase; as early as February, 1916, the plans first adumbrated in September, 1915, were spelled out in a draft by the Reich Interior Office, the Treasury and the Foreign Ministry, expressly entitled 'draft binding treaty', and submitted to the Chancellor on February 9. The purpose, as the covering letter to Bethmann Hollweg said, was to ensure 'that when Belgium becomes attached to the German customs area, the predominant influence of the German Reich in the economic field shall be firmly and lastingly secured'. The familiar demands were recapitulated. This document remained the basis for the treatment of the Belgium question for the rest of the war.

It again became necessary to define the sum of Germany's demands on Belgium at the end of 1916, in connection with the German peace offer and Wilson's offer of mediation, when there was again a prospect, even an imminent probability, of negotiating a separate peace with King Albert–the German answer to Wilson expressly spoke of German conditions towards Belgium, which were

[1] The memoranda are minuted 'Agreed' and 'Very good. Wilhelm. R.I.'

to be handled in separate negotiations with King Albert. Beside demanding the annexation of Liége, Germany informed Wilson at the end of January, 1917 that she required 'military, political and economic safeguards in Belgium'. The previous history and treatment of Belgium as an object of Germany's war aims policy shows what were the aims concealed under this formula.

The consistency of Germany's intentions is also shown by the long memorandum compiled by der Lancken for the Chancellor, and presumably on his orders. This 'sketch of the peace conditions to be demanded of Belgium', which is dated December 10, 1916, distinguished a minimum and a maximum programme, according to the issue of the war. The core of the minimum programme provided for the familiar economic penetration, without politically unattainable annexations; the maximum programme, for the eventuality of a more favourable bargaining position, asked for the annexation of Liége or a permanent right of occupation of Belgium by Germany.

Lancken argued that the conditions for 'the economic conquest of Belgium' were favourable, since Belgium had already grown into a very important market for German industrial products and field of investment for German capital and was already closely linked with Germany. Like the Reich Treasury, Lancken proposed to eliminate the influence of the Entente countries in Belgium by liquidating the participation of British and French capital in Belgian enterprises. Similarly, Belgian and foreign shares in Belgian undertakings were to be transferred to the German capital market through the formation of German co-operative associations.

With the same object of capital control, Lancken further proposed to acquire an influence over the Belgian bourse and discount market and to secure a German interest in Belgium's overseas commerce through the foundation of joint German–Belgian financial institutions. Finally, he recommended forming, or expanding, industrial cartels to prevent Belgian industry from again associating itself with Germany's competitors on world markets. All this could be done without establishing any legal international link between Germany and Belgium. In addition, Lancken added the familiar demand of the Ministry for Trade and Industry that–should the Customs Union be carried through–Belgium should adopt Germany's social legislation.

For him, as for the military and the overwhelming majority of the politicians, Belgium was the corner-stone of Germany's position as a world power. The 'unalterable final aim', he said, must be 'the establishment of German supremacy over Belgium as far as the sea, in order to exploit her favourable geographical situation and natural wealth, and the productive powers of her population, for the development of Germany's World Power position.'

Germany's Flemish policy was a further instrument for drawing Belgium into the direct field of Germany's expansive force. The aim was to split Belgium administratively, politically and culturally into Wallonia and Flanders, in order on the one hand to reduce the preponderant French influence over the higher clergy, the schools and the bureaucracy in the Flemish areas and on the other to obtain in Flemish a means of putting pressure on both the king and the Belgian government in Le Havre to consent to a separate peace. If the peace did not satisfy Germany's full wishes, the Flemish would constitute a *point d'appui* for her influence in Belgium. The cultural aspect of the 'liberation of the Flemish' was thus heavily overshadowed by the power-political factor of the domination of Belgium.

In its Flemish policy the German government was able to make very substantial use of the Flemish movement as an instrument for promoting its own interests. The beginnings of this movement go back to the 1840s, when it first appeared as a reaction against the strongly French character of the unitary Belgian state established in 1830. After the introduction of a general franchise in the 1890s the Flemish had extracted from the government language laws establishing the equality of rights of the Flemish element with the Walloon–French. Since, however, this equality was never applied in practice, friction and tension were chronic. But the Flemish had strongly refused to associate themselves with the rising pan-German movement's programme of unifying all Lower-German and Germanic territories, and Germany's march through Belgium in 1914 had poisoned their hearts against Germany, holding as they did loyally to the Belgian state.

Nevertheless, as early as September 2, 1914, Bethmann Hollweg had recommended to Sandt, the head of the German civilian administration in occupied Belgium, to use the Flemish movement as an effective starting-point for acquiring political influence in Belgium, and to give it 'the most visible support possible', for this might be of use 'in view of a future understanding with Holland'. The aim of securing Holland's close friendship was a cardinal element in Bethmann Hollweg's western and central European policy. In December, 1914, he informed the newly-appointed Governor-General, von Bissing, that it was his intention 'to acquire and secure for Germany the position of natural friend and protector of a large part of the population of Belgium'. At the same time, he made detailed suggestions for putting this policy into effect: contact to be established with the intellectual and religious leaders of the Flemish movement, the Flemish language to be given the utmost encouragement (no Germanisation to be attempted), the University of Ghent to be transformed into a purely Flemish institution, and a common press for Holland and Flanders to be created. Bissing accepted these proposals and made attempts to bring together the various dissentient Flemish groups, the Activists in Antwerp (who wanted a union between Flanders and Wallonia as autonomous states), the Passivists in Amsterdam (the same aim, but without collaborating with the Germans) and the Young Flemish in Ghent (who demanded an autonomous kingdom of Flanders), on a middle line.

In the course of the next month the German occupying power put into force a number of Belgian language laws dating from before the war; in particular, it introduced the Flemish language into the elementary schools of Flanders. Bethmann Hollweg's intention of developing Ghent as a Flemish university could be realised only after the famous historian, Pirenne, who had been the heart and soul of the professors' resistance, had been arrested and deported and careful preparations made by Professor von Dyck, of the *Technische Hochschule* of Munich. The Flemish University was opened in Ghent on October 21, 1916, ten months after the issue of the order that lectures must be held there in Flemish as well as French.

The second phase of Germany's Flemish policy was again initiated by the Chancellor personally, during the negotiations for a separate peace in 1915–16. He proposed the constitution of a 'Flemish Committee' with the object of making Germany's efforts more systematic, more intense and more active. This was realised in the spring of 1917 in the form of a 'Council of Flanders'. Here again, Bethmann Hollweg's own notes (of January 1, 1916) provide the best interpretation of Germany's new move:

> As things now stand, we cannot count on doing as we please with Belgium on the conclusion of peace. The most we shall achieve – with the possible addition of the annexation of Liége – will be a defensive alliance with political, military and economic guarantees. The question is whether we shall or shall not strengthen the position achieved by us in Belgium through such a defensive alliance by energetic promotion of the Flemish movement. I should say emphatically, 'yes'.

Any connection between the German government and the proposed Flemish Committee should, however, he wrote on January 6. 1916, at first be only 'external' and chiefly cultural; only gradually should the Flemish Committee 'ripen into a political factor' and be used as a stooge in dealing with the Belgian government in Le Havre.

He warned against precipitate activities which could appeal only to a minority of the Flemish, and pointed out that hitherto he had purposely confined himself to putting into effect existing Belgian laws in favour of the Flemish, precisely in order to demonstrate the correctness and legality of what Germany was doing. He thought it still too early to set up a Flemish Committee, because the majority of the Flemish population, in any case hesitant about approaching Germany, would regard this as a revolutionary step, and their laboriously allayed mistrust would be re-awakened. The Governor-General replied that the German administration had long since combined with the 'Activists' in all important towns of Belgium to form cadres for a 'Flemish National Action Group'. This organisation was for the time being still an underground one, but its influence was far greater than that of the small radical group of the Young Flemish in Ghent or of the group of Passivists in Amsterdam.

These documents afford plain proof of the continuity of Germany's Flemish policy and of the close agreement in principle between the Chancellor and the highest representatives of the Emperor's authority in occupied Belgium. This policy was carried a step further when Germany's Flemish policy was officially announced to the Reichstag on April 5. Bethmann Hollweg said that it was one of Germany's aims 'to prevent the long-repressed Flemish people from being again submitted to Francification' (*Verwelschung*), and that Germany intended to secure cultural autonomy for the Flemish in Belgium through 'effective guarantees'. What 'effective guarantees' meant, within the framework of Germany's war aims, emerges abundantly from the documents: it meant the establishment of German supremacy over Belgium.

In October, 1916, von Bissing's relatively 'patient' policy was replaced by a less patient and more stringent one. In connection with the Hindenburg Programme of raising Germany's production of munitions, the new Hindenburg–Ludendorff Supreme Command and the Ministry of War yielded to the pleas of the industrial leaders and ordered 400,000 workers from occupied Belgium to be pumped into German industry as a short-term measure.[1] Von Bissing long resisted the compulsory deportation of Belgian workers, but the alliance of industrialists, soldiers and political groups who maintained that the war would be lost without the Belgian workers, was too strong for him.[2]

[1] Cf. on this, 'Die Zwangsüberführung belgischer Arbeiter nach Deutschland', in *Werk des Untersuchungsausschusses, Völkerrecht im Weltkrieg*, 2 Reihe, Vol. 1, pp. 187 ff.

[2] The first demand was for 20,000 workers weekly; this was later reduced to 8,000.

The deportations, taking place just when all the world was awaiting peace proposals from President Wilson, had devastating effects on opinion in Belgium, as also among the neutrals and Germany's enemies. Wilson, in particular, found that the step had excited such feeling against Germany in America as to block for a considerable period his hopes of mediating peace; the Belgian civilian population had only been existing on regular shipments of food from America.

The entry of America into the war and the revolution in Russia made it more impracticable than ever for Germany to prosecute her war aim of extending or spreading her power by simple annexation. In the spring of 1917 there began an inevitable shift towards indirect forms of control, continuance of the Flemish policy in the west and development of a new policy of granting various forms of 'autonomy' in the east.

Poland: 'Frontier Strip' and Protectorate

The 'Frontier Strip' policy[1] was still conceived as one of direct annexation. It was, however, to be limited to what was regarded as the indispensable minimum, in order to keep open the possibilities of reaching terms with Russia in separate peace negotiations. The motives for establishing the 'Frontier Strip' were partly strategic, partly—in the phrase then coming into fashion—national (*völkisch*): the 'Strip' was to be settled with nationally reliable German elements. First and foremost, the salient between east and west Prussia was to be flattened out by the acquisition of an area south of Thorn; it was also proposed to take over the crossings of the Bohr, the Russian fortresses of Ossowiec and Ostrolenka. The Suwalki district was to be east Prussia's military glacis. The colonisation policy was the direct continuation of the Prusso-German Ostmark policy, and was strongly supported by the Prussian Ministry of State and the *Ostmarkenverein* and the Association for Internal Colonisation. The governments of the Reich and of Prussia hoped to isolate the Prussian Poles and to separate them from Congress Poland by deporting the Poles and Jews from the 'Frontier Strip'. At the same time a Germanic wall against Slavdom was to be set up by settling there German colonists from all parts of east-central Europe.

It was Bethmann Hollweg himself who as early as the end of 1914 had imported this idea, including the deportations and colonisations,

---

[1] The whole question of the 'Frontier Strip' has been studied in great detail and with full documentation by Imanuel Geiss, 'Der polnische Grenzstreifen, 1914–1918, ein Beitrag zur deutschen Kriegszielpolitik im ersten Weltkrieg', in *Historische Studien*, No. 378.

into the field of active politics; his right-hand man and close collaborator was Wahnschaffe, Under-Secretary of State in the Imperial
Chancellery, himself a big landowner in the March. The Chancellor
instructed the *Regierungspräsident* of Frankfurt an der Oder, Schwerin,
and the President of the Colonisation Committee, Ganse, to prepare
detailed proposals for the solution of the problem of the 'Strip'. A
big conference of all the imperial and Prussian ministries concerned,
held in the Imperial Chancellery on July 13, 1915, resulted in the
first concrete proposals for pursuing this policy on a broad basis. On
Delbrück's proposal, the paperwork was assigned to the Prussian
Ministry of Agriculture, because all the biggest internal problems of
the 'Frontier Strip' were concerned with colonisation and population transfers; the Prussian Ministry of the Interior remained in
charge of general Polish policy. On February 1, 1916, the Prussian
Minister of the Interior, von Loebell, pressed Bethmann Hollweg to
carry through the decisions of July 13, 1915, without waiting for the
end of the war, and himself submitted proposals for the inconspicuous Germanisation of the 'Frontier Strip'. In June, 1916, he was
asking for the 'Frontier Strip' to be extended over the Bohr–Narew–
Bug line to include Modlin (a little way north-west of Warsaw), an
idea which Bethmann Hollweg was himself favouring at that time.
Loebell thought that the final measure of the cessions to be required
from Poland should depend on the degree of dependence of the future
Polish state on Prussia–Germany.

Even General von Beseler, the Governor-General, who was the
strongest supporter among all the important soldiers and politicians
of a Polish national state – in close association, of course, with Germany, which would have to determine its frontiers and the degree of
sovereignty to be enjoyed by it – and who, as Ludendorff (whose
ideas were quite different) said, 'wanted to make the Poles happy' –
even he approved both the inclusion of the new Poland in Mitteleuropa and the annexation of the 'Frontier Strip' up to the Warthe–
Narew line. In April, 1916, he submitted to the Chancellor a plan
under which the Poles were to accept the cession of the 'Frontier
Strip' and renounce that area for ever as the price, in a sense even
as a token of gratitude, for the re-establishment by Germany of a
Polish state. In a further secret report to the Emperor, dated July 23,
1916, he asked for the annexation of the area up to the Bohr–Narew–
Warthe line on the grounds that it was necessary to ensure complete
military control over the rest of Poland. When, then, the kingdom of
Poland was proclaimed in November, 1916, the determination of its
frontiers, not only with Russia and the proposed Lithuanian state
but also with Prussia–Germany, was reserved.

The objectives and claims of heavy industry constituted another factor of increasing importance in the 'Frontier Strip' question, as in the whole of Germany's war aims policy. A long series of enquiries, investigations, journeys and conferences concentrated interest on the extent and economic importance of the mining and industrial area of Polish Upper Silesia, the southernmost tip of the 'Frontier Strip'. As with Longwy–Briey, the purely economic considerations of broadening Germany's supplies of raw materials and basic industries came to determine political decisions.

Lithuania–Courland:
the 'New Germany' in the North-East

The general line of Bethmann Hollweg's September Programme for the east, the 'forcing back' of Russia, did not exclude the possible detachment of Lithuania and Courland. In fact, authoritative governmental circles in Berlin very soon drew the consequences of this, at first in the purely traditional form of annexations. Loebell for example, in his memorandum of October 28, 1914,[1] proposed advancing the Prussian frontier to the Niemen between Kovno and Grodno, i.e., prolonging the Narew line, by annexing the government of Suwalki. Suwalki was technically part of Poland, but as its population was almost entirely Lithuanian, it was always treated separately in Germany's plans. Its annexations was taken as practically automatic throughout the whole war, since it possessed considerable strategic value as the northward continuation of the Narew line. As early as December, 1914, Otto Hoetzsch submitted a memorandum extending this demand. He wanted the 'Frontier Strip' continued along the Warthe–Narew line to include not only Suwalki, but parts of the governments of Grodno and Kovno as necessary links, and finally almost the whole of Courland. Both Loebell and Hoetzsch represented an Old-Prussian Conservative point of view, and accordingly, both then and later, wanted the minimum of annexations from Russia, in marked contrast to the expansionist pan-German and Liberal schools of thought.

Schwerin, in a memorandum compiled at the Chancellor's request in the spring of 1915, went further than Loebell and Hoetzsch. He asked for the annexation and Germanisation, not only of the 'Frontier Strip', but also of the whole province of Kovno, all Courland, and – after further military advances – the province of Vilno. For the more distant future he was already counting Livonia, or at least the southern, ethnically Latvian, part of it, as a German war aim. He grouped the whole area – Suwalki, Lithuania, Courland

[1] Summary in Volkmann, op. cit., p. 187.

and parts of Livonia – together as the 'North-Eastern settlement areas'.[1]

The first representative of high authority to ask for the acquisition of Lithuania and Courland was Jagow. This was in September and October, 1915. In the former month he sent Geheimrat Max Sering, Professor of Agronomics at Berlin University, on a tour of the occupied territories of the north-east. Sering's extensive report on the results of his studies and observations thereafter formed the basis of Germany's policy in the north-eastern regions.

Sering proposed that if the successes of Germany's arms allowed it, Russia's western frontier should be pushed back to the line Lake Peipus–Drina–Rowno–R. Zbrucz – almost exactly the line laid down in 1919 and 1920 as the frontier between Russia and the new states then created. This, he pointed out, would cost Russia twenty-four million persons, one-sixth of her total population, or twenty-eight million if Finland were also detached.

Sering, too, regarded Lithuania and Courland as immediate objectives. He went further than Schwerin and asked for the immediate annexation, not only of Suwalki and Kovno, but also of Vilno which, he calculated, would make Lithuania as large as 'the three German–Russian Baltic provinces' (Courland, Livonia, Estonia). Even though not more than about 10 per cent of the population of Courland was German – landowners and the old-established bourgeoisie of the towns[2] – yet Sering thought that the Lettish peasants, workers and intelligentsia would submit to German rule. He hoped that the Letts could be Germanised through cultural influences (German secondary schools) and economic measures. At the same time, he wanted Germanisation intensified by increasing the Germanic peasant element through large-scale colonisation. The newcomers were to be settled on the Russian Crown domains, church lands and large private estates – the big German landlords had already released one-third of their total estates, about 400,000 hectares, for this purpose – and above all, Latvian peasant land. As in the Polish 'Frontier Strip', the first source of settlers to be tapped was the two million German colonists of Inner Russia, a community with the

---

[1] The areas and populations are given as follows:

	Area (sq. km.)	Population, 1897	Of these, Germans
Courland	27,286	674,000	51,000
Kovno	40,641	1,545,000	7,500
Suwalki	12,551	583,000	30,000
Total	80,478	2,802,000	88,500

[2] The census of 1897 gave 52,000 Germans, but the later colonists must be added to this figure.

highest birth-rate in Europe. But given the close connection between the country and Germany its agricultural production would rise even faster than its population – twofold and threefold: 'A determined policy would thus make Courland into a possession entirely homogeneous with the Old Country within two or three generations.' He judged the chances of Germanising Lithuania less favourable, since its ruling class was not German, but Polish or Russian, the native aristocracy and bourgeoisie having been Polonised. Lithuania was densely populated, and it would thus be difficult to colonise it, to replace the Lithuanians by 'fruitful German colonists'. Furthermore, account would have to be taken of the Polish-minded church and the Lithuanian national movement. The backbone of the latter lay in the groups of emigrants in the United States, but at the moment it was still directed against the spiritual domination of the Poles. Sering pinned his chief hopes on the economic interests of the more intelligent peasants, on the advantages offered by customs union with Germany and on the 'order' guaranteed by German rule. The local Poles should be deported into the new Polish state.

To these memoranda, and to another by the professors of Breslau which stood for the same aims as Sering and Schwerin, must, however, be added a whole chorus of publicists who from 1915 onward were quite openly clamouring for the annexation of the Baltic provinces. Prominent among these were men who had left the Baltic with the onset of Russification in the 1880s and 1890s, and particularly since the revolution of 1905–6, and who now saw their great chance.

The strongest and most influential personality in this group was Theodor Schiemann.[1] Schiemann's passionate interest in the Baltic question derived in part from his special picture of Russia, in the interpretation of which he founded a regular school, which goes by his name. Unlike Hoetzsch,[2] who regarded the Russian state as a unitary product of organic development, Schiemann held that it was no natural growth, but a conglomerate of peoples held together artificially by the iron vice of a monarchy which had degenerated into despotism, a realm which the first great shock was bound to shatter into fragments. He therefore demanded for each of its peoples the right to secede from it. His views found wide acceptance in the public

[1] On Schiemann, see Klaus Meyer, *Theodor Schiemann als Publizist* (Frankfurt and Hamburg, 1956), *Welt– und Geschichtsbild*, pp. 73 ff.; also his own numerous letters to the Emperor and members of the government and, above all, the periodical issued by him: *Die Deutschen Ostseeprovinzen Russlands*.

[2] On Hoetzsch, see Fritz T. Epstein, 'Otto Hoetzsch als aussenpolitischer Kommentator während des Ersten Weltkrieges, in *Russlandstudien, Denkschrift für O.H., Schriftenreihe Osteuropa*, No. 3 (Stuttgart, 1957).

and in military circles, and his personal relations with the Emperor enabled him to exercise a direct influence on German policy.

His supporters included Johannes Haller, Paul Rohrbach, the *Alldeutsch* leader, Class, the theologian Lezius of Königsberg and the respected Berlin constitutional lawyer, Gierke. Lezius and Gierke in particular made very extensive demands: domination of the area 'on the Roman model', 'dictatorship of the German Governors', even in time of peace. All these men, the 'Eastern experts', and also Professors Seraphim and Stumpf of the Prussian Ministry of the Interior, and likewise – although their views were more moderate – the theologians Reinhold Seeberg and Adolf von Harnack and the historians Dietrich Schäfer, Hans Delbrück and Friedrich Meinecke, agreed with Sering and Schwerin in advocating colonisation of the eastern districts with German settlers as a means of Germanising them. These groups came in the course of the war to agree with the Hoetzsch school that Russia should be left intact, peace concluded in the east and the decision sought in the west.[1]

Here, too, all these wishes were much less important than the policy actually followed by Germany. The advance in the east had brought nearly all Lithuania and Courland under German administration in September, 1915. No Government-General with a civilian administration was set up as in Belgium and Poland, but a military administration for Lithuania and Courland, to which Suwalki was attached. At the beginning of November, 1915, this administrative unit was given the designation of *Oberost*; Hindenburg and Ludendorff were in supreme charge, while the heads of the administration were von Gossler for Courland (Mitau) and Prince von Ysenburg for Lithuania (Vilno). The reasons for making the administration military were political. As early as August, 1915. Ludendorff had tried to get the newly-established Government-General of Poland put under the command of *Oberost*, but had been defeated by Falkenhayn's strong opposition. Ludendorff took this as a personal affront[2] and vented his wrath in writing to Zimmermann, who felt as he did: 'Since Poland has been taken from me, I must found myself another kingdom in Lithuania and Courland.'[3]

Oberost was 'ruled' with unremittingly active and thorough initiative, energy and harshness. A local administration which took over the Russian territorial structure regulated the daily life of the popu-

---

[1] For the leading figures in the various groups, see Lilli Lewerenz, *Die deutsche Politik im Baltikum, 1914–1918*, Hamburg dissertation (in typescript), pp. 49 ff.

[2] See also Börge Colliander, *Die Beziehungen zwischen Litauen und Deutschland während der Occupation 1915–1918*, Diss. Abo, 1935, pp. 21 f.

[3] Conze, op. cit., p. 87.

lation down to the minutest detail, with Prussian exactitude and military discipline, and reorganised the land, which had been deserted by the Russian civil servants and large parts of the population, primarily with the object of utilising it for the purposes of the war by requisitionings, the exploitation of the forests and the recruitment of labour;[1] but the political aim of Germanisation was present from the first. The language of administration and education was German, and the school system was modelled on the German.

More important still was the great colonisation work. In September, 1915, Sering, who was then working for the Foreign Ministry, expounded his ideas to Ludendorff-Hindenburg, who had already been notified of the Bethmann Hollweg–Schwerin plan for a Polish 'Frontier Strip'. Ludendorff took up the ideas, and laid the foundations of the colonisation policy in *Oberost* through an Order of April 27, 1916. He called for reports on demographic statistics, figures on the ownership of the land, on land suitable for settlement, on the possibilities of creating new smallholdings, and on war damage. After the summer of 1916 the Reich Interior Office and the Prussian Ministry of the Interior, which had been working since the spring of 1915 for the annexation of the 'Frontier Strip', took part in planning colonisation. Commissions and individual experts travelled through the country to examine its possibilities.

These activities had their precursors in efforts made by the Baltic German nobles before the war to settle locally German colonists from the interior of Russia and thus create a German peasantry as counterweight to the growing national activity of the Letts and Estonians. The leaders of this enterprise were two big landed proprietors, Silvio Broedrich-Kurmahlen and Baron Carl Manteuffel-Zoege-Katzdangen; both worked in Berlin during the war as representatives of the Baltic Germans.

The colonisation of *Oberost* which was initiated in the summer of 1916 and then taken up by the central ministries of the Reich and Prussia, was finally co-ordinated with high policy in the Reich in the summer of 1917. In February and March of that year the problems of colonisation in the east were discussed in Berlin at two great conferences of the highest authorities of the Reich and Prussia. On this occasion, again, the initiative came from the government. On February 6 Wahnschaffe had a preliminary conference in the Reich chancellery with the heads of the Prusso-German ministries. A committee, for which the Foreign Ministry provided the secretariat,

---

[1] See R. Stupperich, 'Siedlungspläne im Gebiet des Oberbefehlshabers Ost (Militärverwaltung Litauen und Kurland) während des Weltkrieges', in *Jomsburg*, 5, 1941, pp. 348 ff.

was set up, and only a week later a session of this body considered a detailed programme for questions of repatriation and settlement in the occupied eastern territories. The continuity and the authority of the committee's work is shown by the fact that it took its instructions direct from the Chancellor, and that Schwerin's proposals, among others, served as the basis of its work. The discussions, which centred round the provision of land for German settlers, assumed the early conclusion of a separate peace with Russia, the essential provisions of which would include the 'acquisition of land, repatriation and expatriation'.

The *völkisch* components of Germany's war aims policy appeared very clearly among the motives for the colonisation. The idea of re-patriating the Russian Germans and settling them in the Polish 'Frontier Strip' (in part, also in east Prussia) had come up in the Reich chancellery as early as the end of December, 1914, but it was now reinforced by the idea of bringing back to the new German east also the German minorities–'*Deutschtum's* lost outposts'–from the non-German parts of the Danube Monarchy Galicia, the Bukovina, Hungary and the Ukraine. Had these ideas been realised, the result would have been a 'protective wall' of Germans from the whole of east-central Europe.

On March 31, after the bases of the programme had been worked out, the civilian committee brought in representatives of the military for a wider discussion. The phalanx of these soldier-politicians was headed by Ludendorff, whom we shall meet again in 1917 and 1918. To support him, the Supreme Army Command (OHL) sent von Bartenwerffer, head of the Political Section of the general staff, von Schwarzkoppen, Chief of Staff of the Quartermaster-General, and Professor Ludwig Bernhard, of Ludendorff's personal staff, one of the German specialists on colonisation in the east. *Oberost* sent Baron von Gayl; the military administration of Lithuania, its chief, Prince von Ysenburg. Other participants were von Gossler, the ad-ministrative head of the military administration of Courland, and Wachs, Chief of General Staff to the Governor-General in Warsaw.

Taking as a basis the decisions of the ministerial bureaucrats' con-ference of February 13, which were taken up point by point, this second meeting determined certain further details. Von Gayl, speak-ing for *Oberost*, placed the colonisation in its proper perspective among the war aims by emphasising that it was in no way an end in itself, but entirely subordinated to the aim 'of developing the New Territory as quickly and surely as possible, but also as peaceably as possible, into a source of added economic and political strength to the Reich'.

Another and even more far-reaching plan was discussed at this great conference; that of establishing a second security belt (additional to the Polish 'Frontier Strip') to run between a reduced Lithuania and a reduced Poland from the Lomsho–Grodno line south to Brest-Litovsk. This area too was to be Germanised. This plan was accepted with no dissentients: ideas of the sort had long been familiar to the leading classes of Germany. The idea of linking up east Prussia through a southward extension with a new Ukrainian state had first been broached by Class in September, 1914, in his memorandum to Bethmann Hollweg. Bernhard made the same suggestion in the memorandum which was sent to the Chancellor in May, 1915, through von Gayl, then commanding in Münster. The idea came up again in November–December, 1915, in a memorandum submitted to the Foreign Ministry by an agent of *Oberost*, the German Lithuanian, Rittmeister Steputat, who had been negotiating as representative of the Foreign Ministry with Lithuanian exiles in Switzerland. This idea had conjured up the vision of a Jadwingia–White Ruthenia settled with Germans and turned into a Germanised province of Prussia. Steputat thought Germany's tactics should be to accentuate and exploit in her own interest the sharp differences between Poles and Lithuanians. Hindenburg made similar suggestions in April, 1916, to Loebell, who for his part entirely agreed with the field-marshal's basic idea of 'roping off the West Slavs from the East Slavs', so as to strengthen still further Germany's power-position in the east. Loebell accordingly wanted the governments of Vilno, Grodno and Minsk, if they could be detached from Russia, not to be incorporated in a future Poland but attached to the 'Baltic–Lithuanian area', which would be exposed to strong German influence. Finally, in December, 1916, the Supreme Army Command (OHL), in the opinion sent by it to the Chancellor on the official formulation of Germany's war aims, officially proposed cutting off the Poles from the Russians by a second Frontier Strip reaching to Brest-Litovsk, which was to become 'a Prussian provincial town'. Thus the decisions of March 31, 1917, led to the Kreuznach war aims programme of April 23, an important part of which – the section relating to the east – they had prepared down to the smallest detail. Only with this knowledge can we understand the deeper meaning of the simple words of the Kreuznach Programme: 'Courland and Lithuania to be won for the German Reich as far as the line traced by the OHL.'

9

GERMANY AND THE UNITED STATES

SUBMARINE WARFARE AND THE BELGIAN QUESTION

WHEN Britain upset the German statesmen's hopes of a limited war by declaring war on Germany over the invasion of Belgium, German public resentment soon concentrated on 'perfidious Albion'. The Chancellor himself was no exception; he was reputed an Anglophile, and as late as the beginning of August was still reluctant to believe that Britain would throw her whole weight into the war, and he still thought that Britain might mediate a peace after Germany had defeated France.[1] Yet in September, after Britain's intervention and the speeches of her statesmen, even he said, not without bitterness, that 'England's determination to wage war *à outrance* against Germany'[2] was forcing Germany to reply in the same terms in her conduct of the war.

This disappointment generated the idea, which was then regularly drilled into the German people, that Britain was the cornerstone of the enemy coalition. Consequently, Germany thought a separate peace possible only in the east, with Russia, or in the west, with France or Belgium; a separate peace with Britain would, in the view of her leaders, have been tantamount to initiating a general peace and would have presupposed renunciation of Germany's most cherished war aim, Belgium.

So long as Germany refused to renounce this aim, then the longer the indecisive struggle on the land went on, the louder did public opinion, supported by the Supreme Army Command and the navy, press for Britain to be 'brought to her knees' by the 'last resort' of submarine and Zeppelin warfare.

Air and Submarine Warfare against Britain

As early as the first days of August, 1914, the German military leaders had been considering plans for breaking Britain's resistance by a combined assault by sea and air. On August 23 the head of the

[1] Walter Hubatsch, *Der Admiralstab und die obersten Marinebehörden in Deutschland, 1848–1945* (Frankfurt am Main, 1958), p. 165.

[2] *Bethmann Hollwegs Kriegsreden.*

Naval Cabinet, Admiral von Müller, and von Tirpitz were discussing at General Headquarters 'preparations for air and mine warfare against England'. The new methods were to be employed the moment the German armies reached the Channel coast.[1] The nature of the ideas then current, even in diplomatic circles, on the methods and purposes of such action may be illustrated from a letter written on August 25 by the German minister in Stockholm, von Reichenau, to Zimmermann:

> I almost have the impression that the English are trying to withdraw unobtrusively from the battle-field to save their skins from being tanned. In my view, this must not under any circumstances be permitted. These wretched cowards who can only raise just enough courage to hire bravos to carry out the action which they dare not do themselves—these cowardly assassins must bleed from a thousand wounds until their vulgar huckster souls forget even how to do sums. The war must be carried into their own land in every possible way, the population kept in continuous quaking terror. For that reason I hope with all my heart that we shall occupy and keep occupied the whole northern coast of France and Belgium from Cherbourg to Ostend, that there we shall build airship hangars at a safe distance from the sea, and send airships and aircraft cruising regularly over England and dropping bombs, and that we shall make continuous attacks against the English coast with submarines and torpedo boats.
>
> If France is conquered she must give up her fleet for us to incorporate in ours, as must the Russians—and then settle with the English! England must be brought to her knees: we owe that to ourselves. She, like Belgium and France, must cede us her colonies in Central and South Africa; we must cut out of her skin new land for our surplus population. We must make France dismantle all her fortresses so that the fellows finally stop worrying us.

Important here, quite apart from the idea of forcing Britain to surrender by attack from the air, is the thought (reminiscent of Tirpitz' idea of a continental bloc) that it would be possible, after conquering in turn the two continental powers, France and Russia, to press their fleets into the service of Germany against Britain.

Germany's monopoly of the Zeppelin and her first employment of it awoke in German public opinion—as did the submarine—expectations which were at times fantastic. The more extreme the war aims entertained by the right against Britain and the west, the louder grew the clamour for England to be forced to her knees by the annihilation of London from the air. And it was by no means occasional eccentrics who tried to press the government in this sense.[2] Men of

[1] Müller, op. cit., p. 51.

[2] The most extreme among them went so far as to suspect that the Emperor or the Chancellor would prevent the employment of the decisive Zeppelin arm owing to alleged financial interests in England, or pro-British sympathies.

public weight like Erzberger and Count Zeppelin himself urged the Chancellor to stop 'hesitating' and throw all Germany's air forces into a mass assault on Britain,[1] and they went on doing so long after the losses inflicted by the defence had shown that the expectations pinned on the Zeppelin could not be fulfilled.

The Zeppelin offensive was to be accompanied by a blockade of Britain by German naval forces, operating if possible from the Belgian and French coasts. In fact, all Germany could do was to lay some mine-fields and send out raiders to bombard a few British coastal towns, whereas Britain had been able, by the end of 1914, while holding her battle-fleet in reserve, to cut Germany off from the high seas by the so-called 'distant blockade', and also to endanger her trade via the neutrals, with disastrous effects on the German economy, highly dependent as it was on imports for its food and its raw materials. Germany could not use her main High Seas fleet to enforce a decision, and in view of the extremely unfavourable ratio of forces – 1 to 1·8 – did not even attempt to do so. Von Pohl, the commander later of the High Seas fleet, who was then chief of the naval staff, therefore persuaded the Chancellor to blockade Britain, which was also highly dependent on imports, by employing the submarine arm in radical fashion against merchant shipping.

To this end the establishment of a blockade zone round Britain and Ireland was announced on February 4, 1915. In this zone German submarines – Germany possessed at that time twenty-one submarines in the North Sea, some of them still petrol driven, of which in practice only about one-third could ever be out at one time – would not only sink enemy merchant and passenger vessels without warning, but might similarly also torpedo neutral vessels. The German government regarded this as an answer to Britain's methods of naval warfare, which in its view were contrary to international law. It was hoped that the shock effects of this procedure on Britain and the neutrals would be so great as to force Britain to give way; the new Chief of Naval Staff, Bachmann, and also von Tirpitz, who at first had been against this course on account of the insufficiency of the number of vessels available, answered a query from the Emperor on

---

[1] Writing to Bethmann Hollweg on August 10, 1915, Erzberger said: 'A major attack on London would be of the highest political importance. Since I know that consent to such an attack has already been given by Headquarters, but it has not, for reasons which are obscure to me, been carried out, I would recommend Your Excellency to make representations to bring about an attack as early as possible.' Erzberger also saw in this a way of reconciling Tirpitz, who was sulking over the refusal to start unrestricted submarine warfare. Rathenau, too, in a letter written in early September, 1914, advocated 'systematically working on the nerves of the [English] towns through an overwhelming air force.' The Six Economic Associations similarly advocated systematic air warfare in September, 1916.

February 15, 1915, by assuring him that Britain would be forced to give in within six weeks.[1] This was, of course, a complete miscalculation; on the other hand Germany's procedure had, as Bethmann Hollweg had feared, provoked the greatest resentment among the neutrals, and above all very strong reactions in the United States, particularly as it was without precedent in international law.[2]

Belgium as the Key to General Peace

The idea of a general peace had first been raised in September, 1914, with President Wilson's offer of mediation, which would have hinged on an understanding between Germany and Britain on the basis of the *status quo* in western Europe. The German government had, however, replied to the first, informal soundings by demanding 'safeguards and guarantees' in east and west. The second soundings, this time official, made through the Austro-Hungarian ambassador in Washington, Dumba, in November, 1914, met with a similar fate.[3] At that time the German government, after considering the question among its own members, had laid down the principle of avoiding any general peace, and above all, any Peace Congress with neutral participation; the aim should be rather to conclude separate peaces with individual members of the enemy coalition.[4] As, however, Wilson repeated his offers, the German government – not least on grounds of domestic policy – was repeatedly faced with the question of general peace; it knew from the American ambassador in Constantinople, Henry Morgenthau, that Wilson regarded the conclusion of peace in Europe as a main aim of his policy.[5]

Contrary to the view usually taken by German historians that the German government was prepared to accept American mediation in

[1] Hubatsch, op. cit., p. 169; cf. id., *Die Ära Tirpitz*, pp. 129 f.

[2] Mgr. Marchetti wrote in September, 1915: 'Zeppelins and submarine warfare against merchant shipping are the bellows with which the otherwise faintly glimmering enthusiasm for the war is continually kindled into new life: they are thus Lord Kitchener's best allies. If Germany . . . insists on her point of view that the world must be razed to the ground before there can be any idea of peace, the Entente will – *sauf l'imprévu* – remain true to its programme of letting the Central Powers go on fighting until they have conquered themselves to death.'

[3] For this whole complex subject, see E. R. May, *The World War and American Isolation, 1914–1917* (Cambridge (Mass.), 1957); also E. H. Mamatey, *The United States and East Central Europe, A Study in Wilsonian Diplomacy and Propaganda* (Princeton, 1957).

[4] See the very thorough study by Karl B. Birnbaum, *Peace Moves and U-Boat Warfare, A Study of Imperial Germany's Policy towards the United States, April 18, 1916– January 9, 1917* (Upsala, 1958), p. 11.

[5] The first, tentative feelers towards Wilson's enterprise were made in December, 1914, in conversations between Wangenheim and the American Ambassador, Morgenthau. Pallavacini reported to Berchtold that Morgenthau was fostering this move of Wilson's in order to put pressure on England.

the spring of 1915,[1] the documents show that the Wilhelmstrasse did indeed agree to the President's request to allow his confidant, Colonel House, to make an informative tour of the European capitals, but laid down such conditions in practice that House's mission was, so far as Germany was concerned, foredoomed to failure. House had said that a meeting of the ambassadors of the Entente powers in Washington had agreed with him that the evacuation and compensation of Belgium by Germany and a plan for general disarmament would constitute a suitable basis for peace negotiations. The German government at once rejected this basis decisively. From the first, therefore, the question of Belgium was the point on which Germany refused to retract from the position achieved by her in September, 1914, and that which proved the decisive obstacle to a settlement with Britain and, later, with America.

The sinking of the *Lusitania* on May 7, 1915, and the death of a number of American citizens (118 of the 1,198 victims were Americans) a few weeks after the opening of unrestricted submarine warfare[2] produced such excitement in America that public opinion forced the White House to threaten Germany with a breach of diplomatic relations and possibly even with war. In Germany, on the other hand, Wilson's demands produced violent differences within the government on how the American note should be answered,[3] until finally, unwilling to face war with America, Germany retreated and abandoned unrestricted submarine warfare.

At that time the German ambassador in Washington, Count Bernstorff, was pressing very strongly for a settlement, and warning his government that the consequences would be incalculable if the U.S.A. entered the war on the side of the Entente.[4] When Germany's victories over Tsarist Russia in the summer of 1915 evoked a certain positive echo in American public opinion, Bernstorff asked his government to take advantage of the favourable opportunity for negotiation. This was all the more important since German propaganda in the United States had collapsed completely after the *Lusitania* incident. At the height of the crisis, on May 29, he had proposed that Germany should make far-reaching concessions in order to secure co-operation with America. He thought that this would lead to an American peace move consisting of the convocation of an international Peace Conference by the United States, at the head of

---

[1] See, for example, Rudolf Stadelmann, *Friedensversuche im ersten Jahre des Weltkrieges, Historische Zeitschrift*, 156, 1937, pp. 483 ff.

[2] Birnbaum, op. cit., pp. 27 ff. [3] Id., pp. 31 f.

[4] Graf Johann Heinrich Bernstorff, *Deutschland und Amerika, Erinnerungen aus dem fünfjährigen Kriege* (Berlin, 1920), pp. 126 ff.

the neutral powers. General peace, he suggested, would be possible on the basis of the territorial *status quo* in Europe, the freedom of the seas and an agreement between the European powers on colonial questions. Jagow rejected such a basis for a general peace categorically. His point of view, as he told Count Taube, the Swedish minister in Berlin, was that Germany was certainly not conducting a war of conquest, but that the *status quo* could not be considered after so many sacrifices and endeavours. This rejection of a general peace on the basis of the *status quo* occurred just at the moment when Germany was hoping to conclude a separate peace with Russia. On June 22, 1915, Jagow instructed Brockdorff-Rantzau – the communications with America went through Copenhagen – for his personal information, that Germany did not at that moment think it desirable to work for a general peace, but only for a separate peace with Russia. And four weeks later the Chancellor minuted on a report from the German minister in Berne on the possible participation of Switzerland in peace negotiations, 'but only in case of a general Peace Conference, which on principle we cannot desire'.

At the turn of 1915–16 the general staff and navy allied themselves with public opinion to put renewed pressure on the Chancellor to resume unrestricted submarine warfare.[1] On January 1, 1916, Tirpitz maintained that this would force Britain to surrender in two months; three days later, Holtzendorff, who had been Chief of Naval Staff since September, 1915, told the Chancellor that he gave England rather longer – four months. He did indeed now admit the risk of a breach with America, but maintained optimistically that if Germany were allowed to use submarines quite freely, she would 'finish off not only England, but also America'. The Chancellor, however, thought the number of submarines available still too limited to justify the admirals' optimism, and feared that the step would result in bringing the U.S.A. and the smaller European neutrals – Holland, Denmark, Spain – into the war, with disastrous consequences for its issue. It might mean the end of Germany. Since, however, Falkenhayn had told him that he could no longer guarantee victory, through land operations only, Bethmann Hollweg was driven into a corner. He regarded the admirals' policy as 'playing with fire', but saw no way of avoiding it.

Intensified submarine warfare (against armed merchant shipping) was resumed on February 29, 1916, on Falkenhayn's insistence, in

[1] The history of all these debates was gone into very thoroughly by the Committee of Investigation (*Untersuchungsausschuss*) of the Constituent National Assembly (of the Weimar Republic). The evidence of the witnesses may be found in the stenographic reports of the Committee, and the documents, in the appendices (*Beilagen*).

view of the Verdun offensive, and led to new tension with the United States and consequently to sharp disagreements among the German leaders. On March 6 the Emperor decided, against the votes of Falkenhayn and Tirpitz, against unrestricted submarine warfare (that is, against attacks on neutral shipping and attacks without warning) and accepted Tirpitz' resignation on March 17. The internal political struggle for power was thus decided once again in Bethmann Hollweg's favour. He had, however, only been able to maintain his position because he had not opposed unrestricted submarine warfare absolutely, but had consented, as the note of May 4 to the U.S.A. was to show, to enlist the services of diplomacy to prepare for it.

In the hope of avoiding this last resort, Bethmann Hollweg had again put out peace feelers towards Britain in the spring of 1916. Reports had reached him that Grey and Lloyd George were not entirely averse to peace, and they were confirmed by the Chancellor's conversations with Colonel House in February, 1916. House had just arrived from England, and reported that Britain was out of humour with America. Grey and Lloyd George were not at all so disinclined towards peace as he had expected. Britain's peace conditions, according to House, were the evacuation by Germany of Belgium, northern France and Poland, but no war indemnity. He said that Lloyd George had expressly assured Germany all her colonial possessions and a free hand against Russia.[1] The British offer raised what was for Germany the decisive question, the recognition of the *status quo* in the west, i.e., renunciation of Belgium. For this, however, the German government was not prepared. The Chancellor told House that the restoration of Belgium and Poland would have been possible earlier, but now Germany could not consider it. His Reichstag speech of April 5, 1916, in which for the first time he said publicly that Germany could not accept a return to the *status quo*, was inevitably taken both by the British statesmen and by House and Wilson as a further decided rejection by Germany of their proposals.

[1] See Müller, op. cit., p. 152. House seems to have regarded his mission less as an attempt to bring about an early peace in Europe, than as a move to prevent Wilson's attempted mediation from resulting in an estrangement between the two Anglo-Saxon powers. This is made clear by the Grey–House memorandum of February 22, 1916, which contains, besides a description of the bases of a possible peace, the promise that America was prepared to enter the war on the side of the Allies if Germany rejected mediation on this basis. The bases of peace given in this document are the same as those communicated by House to Berlin, except that Alsace-Lorraine is to be restored to France; House concealed this from Bethmann Hollweg. This is the more important because Wilson approved the document, including this demand to be made of Germany. In respect of the promise of armed intervention Wilson did, indeed, make the important reservation that he inserted into the memorandum the word 'probably'.

The 'Third Way': Unrestricted Submarine Warfare
Without American Entry into the War

Bethmann Hollweg's hope of preparing the way for submarine warfare through diplomacy constituted a policy which has been called 'the third way'.[1] Unrestricted submarine warfare was to be resumed against Britain, but so hedged about with diplomatic safeguards as to keep the U.S.A. out of the war. This was the objective on which Germany's policy towards America centred in 1916. Apart from this idea Bethmann Hollweg wanted to use the threat of an unrestricted submarine warfare in order to force America to urge Britain to lift the blockade. In the spring of that year, however, the preparations were still insufficient, and after the torpedoing of the *Sussex* (a result of the decision of February 29) Germany only escaped war with America by beating another retreat. The German note of May 4, however, which formally closed this crisis, did not abandon the 'third way'. It said that Germany 'reserved her freedom of decision' *in the event* of Wilson's diplomatic pressure failing to get Britain to raise her blockade against Germany.[2] The purpose of this reservation is explained in instructions sent by the Chancellor to Bernstorff via Brockdorff-Rantzau on May 5, which stated that it was the government's intention to make it impossible for Wilson to break with Germany, and to force him to take up a firm attitude against Britain. The point, however, is that the Chancellor never from the first expected Britain to give way to Wilson over the blockade. But he reckoned that Wilson, in the interest of his candidature for the Presidency, would feel bound to make up for the loss of prestige which this would involve, and could do so only by putting 'strong pressure on England to make peace' without – or so Bethmann Hollweg hoped – himself figuring as the direct mediator; the Germans did not want Wilson as mediator, because they thought that he was prejudiced against them and would prevent the realisation of their war aims.

Yet on the same May 5, 1916, Bethmann Hollweg saw that the economic position of Germany was so serious, the longing of its people for peace so widespread, that she 'must grasp at every possibility of achieving peace'. One would naturally have supposed that if the Chancellor took so realistic a view of the general situation, he would have been thankful for any mediation for peace, most of all for one coming from the greatest of the neutrals, for this would have opened up the possibilities of peace without forcing Germany to betray her urgent need for it by herself taking the initiative. Bethmann

---

[1] See on this, Birnbaum, op. cit.   [2] Bernstorff, op. cit., pp. 248 f.

Hollweg's attitude can be fully understood only when viewed against the background of the unbridled agitation of the right (in secret alliance with the navy) against his person and his policy, his alleged weakness and submissiveness, especially on the submarine question. The passionate demands for discussion of war aims made in the Reichstag on May 24–26, demands which were coupled with very sharp attacks from the right on the Chancellor, forced him to 'take refuge in publicity' in his speeches of June 5 and 6, in the hope of countering these intrigues and pacifying over-heated public opinion. He now publicly rejected mediation of peace with Britain.

Wilson had clearly indicated his willingness to undertake such mediation in his speech on May 27, 1916, to the American League for Peace;[1] but opinion in Germany would have none of it. After that speech feeling against Wilson grew so bitter in Germany that Stresemann publicly rejected his mediation; Westarp, the Conservative leader, described such an idea in the Reichstag as 'intolerable'.

Bernstroff, however, reported on May 28 that Wilson was considering calling a conference at The Hague at which the neutral powers should participate only when questions relating to the freedom of the seas were under discussion. This new threat of a general Peace Conference alarmed the German government, and on June 7 Bernstorff received a note from Jagow instructing him bluntly to nip any possibility of peace mediation by Wilson in the bud: 'As soon as Mr. Wilson's intentions of mediation threaten to assume more concrete forms and Britain shows signs of readiness to accept them, it will be Your Excellency's task to prevent President Wilson from approaching us with a positive offer of mediation.'[2]

The chief motive behind these uncompromising instructions was fear about Germany's war aims in the west, for the German government thought that American mediation would endanger these. Germany's reasoning ran as follows:

As for Mr. Wilson's intention to mediate peace, this is at the moment encountering strong opposition in England. We can only welcome it if the refusal comes from England. For it is obvious that we must be sceptical about the mediation of a statesman so strongly inclined in his whole ideas to the British standpoint and also so naïve as President Wilson, if only because the President would presumably attempt to bring about a peace essentially

[1] Id., pp. 271 ff. A despatch from Bernstorff on May 28 especially stressed the extreme importance of this speech for Germany. Bernstorff went so far as to assert that acceptance by Germany of Wilson's proposals would win her the sympathies of the American people, which was entirely behind the President's efforts for world peace.

[2] Id., pp. 273 ff.; cf. also Birnbaum, op. cit., which contains a section devoted to the instructions of June, 1916.

based on the *status quo ante*, in particular as regards Belgium. While it is not possible to say today how far we shall be in a position to bring about a solution of the Belgian question, as raised by the war, satisfactory to our interests, yet so much can be said already, that if the war continues to go well for us a peace on the basis of the absolute *status quo ante* is unacceptable to us.

This letter, with its clear instructions to block an American peace step and its notification that Germany was not prepared to return to the *status quo*, was at such gross variance with Bernstorff's own views that he telegraphed back incredulously to the Foreign Ministry on July 13 asking whether he was really 'to prevent an initiative for peace, or only a positive proposal which would bind us in respect of territorial conditions'.[1] He made it quite clear that if America's mediation broke down on Germany's refusal and Germany resumed unrestricted submarine warfare, war with America was inevitable. Even should it be the objections of the Entente on which the peace initiative broke down, war with the U.S.A. was still 'probable' if Germany reverted to submarine warfare. The government had thus been plainly warned.

Before the Foreign Ministry could answer Bernstorff's question, Germany's military position had so deteriorated on both fronts that the Wilhelmstrasse now thought it advisable after all to consider the President's proposals. Berlin still rejected an 'American peace' as unfavourable to Germany, but now thought that 'certain peace chords from a potent neutral side would perhaps not be undesirable'. On August 15 Jagow accordingly modified his instructions of June 7 as follows: 'General tendencies towards peace are rather to be encouraged, but he [Wilson] is where possible to be restrained from definite proposals, since these could only be very unfavourable to us.'[2]

In these new instructions Jagow was still holding in principle to his earlier line. He wanted a more elastic procedure, but still one which would not prevent Germany from putting through her war aims. But only three days later the further deterioration of the general situation forced the Chancellor to go a step further in his attitude towards mediation for a general peace. A general Peace Conference with the participation of the neutrals would, however, only be at best 'tolerable' after successful negotiations between the belligerents themselves.'[3]

A few days later the crisis reached its climax with the entry of Rumania into the war and the consequent appointment of the Hindenburg–Ludendorff 'OHL 3'. A prolonged conference of state

[1] Bernstorff, op. cit., pp. 276 ff.
[2] Birnbaum, op. cit., p. 124.
[3] Bernstorff, op. cit., pp. 279 f.

was held at Pless in the last days of August, 1916, and here, on Holt-zendorff's initiative, the resumption of unrestricted submarine war-fare was discussed in detail in the light of the new situation.[1] At this conference, unlike the decisive submarine conference of January 9, 1917, not only the military but also the civilians were present – the Chancellor and also Jagow and Helfferich. These last two both voted against the navy's demand, because they thought a breach with America undesirable on two grounds: American help to the Entente was not at present by any means exhausting America's full economic resources; and it was exceedingly uncertain what the effect would be on the European neutrals. Bethmann Hollweg, who accept-ed these arguments in principle, emphasised the direct military dangers, which the OHL also took seriously, and succeeded in get-ting a postponement of unrestricted submarine warfare. To prevent this last step or, if it was unavoidable, to prepare the way for it, he reverted to the possibility of peace mediation by America.

On September 2 he asked Bernstorff for his personal opinion whether mediation by Wilson would be possible and successful if Germany guaranteed the limited restoration of Belgium. If not, she must seriously consider reverting to unrestricted submarine warfare.[2]

Bethmann Hollweg was making a complex calculation. He re-alised that the resumption of unrestricted submarine warfare would bring America into the war and render the outcome of it doubtful. But if the mediation proved unsuccessful, then the resumption of submarine warfare as an answer to the 'hunger blockade' would have received sufficient diplomatic preparation; and finally, his own position, and that of the government, would be safeguarded both against the neutrals and against the rising domestic popular agita-tion for submarine warfare.

Bernstorff's answer of September 8 was calculated to confirm the fundamental correctness of Bethmann Hollweg's analysis of the political situation.[3] The ambassador drew his government's atten-tion to the U.S.A.'s central interest in the restoration of Belgium as a pre-condition for any settlement with Britain. At the same time he suggested that there was a hope of Wilson's resuming his efforts after his re-election, before the end of the year. But reference to this date warned the government that, the political situation in the U.S.A. being what it was, no move from America could be expected before the elections in early November. Bernstorff also warned the Chan-

---

[1] See the *Untersuchungsausschuss*, Vol. 2, *Beilagen*, pp. 170 ff.; debates on the resumption of ruthless submarine warfare.

[2] Bernstorff, op. cit., p. 284.

[3] Ibid.

cellor: 'Seen from this end, achievement of peace through ruthless submarine warfare appears hopeless, because that would quite certainly bring the United States into the war, whichever way the elections go, and consequently war would presumably only be prolonged.'

This warning suggested that Bethmann Hollweg's 'third way' was a dangerous illusion.

Yet although convinced that the resumption of unrestricted submarine warfare would bring America into the war, the Chancellor sent further instructions to Bernstorff on September 26 which, while they did indeed ask the President to use his influence on England to bring about a speedy opening of peace negotiations, combined this request with a notification that otherwise Germany would resume her freedom of action in conformity with her note of May 4.[1] This was, in diplomatic language, a threat to resume unrestricted submarine warfare if Wilson delayed much longer with his peace step, or should it prove unsuccessful. The threatening undertone in the message was due to the Emperor's wording, which was approved by Hindenburg.

Meanwhile, as Bernstorff wrote on September 6, Wilson had decided to put off his mediation to a later date. Bernstorff gave two reasons: Rumania's entry into the war, which had revived Germany's enemies' confidence in victory, and the approaching Presidential election, before which Wilson could not in any case work for peace with the full authority of his office. If he were re-elected and if military operations were suspended, he was ready to start his peace action immediately. 'He [the President] believes that he would then be strong enough to enforce [sic] a Peace Conference. Wilson regards it as an American interest that none of the belligerents should achieve decisive victory.'[2] What a chance for Germany to make a draw of this war, which both OHL 2 and OHL 3 had said could no longer be won on land without the *va banque* game of unrestricted submarine warfare with its grim consequences!

All through September the navy had been pressing Ludendorff and on October 1 had finally got OHL 'to consider' letting unrestricted submarine warfare be resumed on about the 15th or 18th of the month, because meanwhile the situation in the sout-east had improved and defence against a British landing in Denmark and Holland thus seemed assured. The by-passing of the political leaders on so important a question led to a dispute between Bethmann Hollweg and Hindenburg–Ludendorff, in which the Chancellor maintained

[1] Id., pp. 285 f.; Birnbaum, op. cit., pp. 135 f. and 354 f.
[2] Bernstorff, op. cit., p. 283.

his own responsibility for a decision which was not military alone, but fundamentally political, and finally forced a further postponement of the unrestricted submarine warfare by using the same arguments as on August 31:

Count Bernstorff has been instructed on the personal orders of His Majesty to induce President Wilson to issue an appeal for peace. If Wilson can be got to do this, the probable rejection of the appeal by England and her allies, while we accept it, would give us a moral justification in the eyes of the world, and in particular of the European neutrals, for withdrawing our promise to America, and would thus influence their presumable later attitude.

Germany's intentions could not have been expressed more clearly. Bethmann Hollweg saw Wilson's hopes for a peace step less as a path towards a peace without victors and vanquished, as Wilson and Bernstorff envisaged it, than as a springboard and a moral-political basis for resuming unrestricted submarine warfare against Britain.

Although Bernstorff had to write on October 6 that Wilson would in no case come forward with a peace move before his re-election, so that Germany's hopes of an immediate move were disappointed, yet in the middle of October Germany repeated her urgent request for peace mediation by the President, again combined with a notification that Germany would otherwise no longer feel herself bound by her assurances of May 4, 1916. This was conveyed in the form of an *aide mémoire* (drafted by the Emperor), which Bernstorff handed to House on October 18 and to Wilson on October 20. Although Bernstorff, as instructed, tried to pretend that this was not a threat of resumption of unrestricted submarine warfare, House and Wilson immediately recognised its true character.

In these weeks the Chancellor's freedom of movement in his struggle over submarine warfare was still further restricted from two quarters. On the one hand, representatives of the big economic associations were petitioning the Emperor and the civilian and military authorities for an early opening of unrestricted warfare, as they had petitioned in 1915 for far-reaching war aims: the famous Six Associations, for example, on September 5, and the merchants of Hamburg on September 25. Several of them went as far as to threaten that the success of the new war loan would depend on ruthless employment of Zeppelins and submarines. On the other hand, the Chancellor lost further ground against the OHL when the Zentrum's spokesman in the Central Committee of the Reichstag said that the Chancellor must 'make his decisions . . . essentially dependent on those of the OHL' on the question of the conduct of ruthless submarine warfare.[1] The Reichstag itself thus put a decision of high policy in the hands of the military.

Between Vienna and Washington

On November 7, 1916, a fortnight after the imperial *aide mémoire* had been handed in, Wilson was re-elected by a bare majority. The German government officially welcomed his plan to mediate peace, and the Chancellor again instructed Bernstorff to encourage the re-elected President in his intention. At the same time, however, the idea of a general peace took a new turn.

On October 18, at the end of the Pless Conference on the Polish question, the Austro-Hungarian Foreign Minister, Baron Burian, had proposed a joint peace offer,[2] and Bethmann Hollweg had agreed in principle. The reasons given by the Austrians were the often adduced 'difficult economic position in which the Central Powers now found themselves', and the fear that the heavy fighting expected for the next spring would not bring the end of the war. From this point onward two peace actions were proceeding on parallel lines, which frequently crossed in the course of the negotiations. The discussion on the modalities of this new peace step gave rise to a controversy between the two allied powers which directly affected Germany's war aims policy.

Austria wanted all four Central Powers to accompany the Peace Note to the enemy with the simultaneous publication of a joint, binding statement of their own peace terms. Germany, however, refused to divulge her terms simultaneously with the peace step, because they were so far-reaching in the west, especially in relation to Belgium, that the enemy would have refused to negotiate with the Central Powers at all on such a basis, whereas to the German public they would appear too modest and would jeopardise the position of the government. After a prolonged exchange of notes and a conference in Berlin on November 15–16,[3] the Germans finally consented

[1] This question thus brought together again the old War Aims Majority, from which the Zentrum had temporarily defected in the preceding March. Although Helfferich, the new Vice-Chancellor, showed skill and pertinacity in adducing all arguments against the unrestricted submarine warfare and its consequences, the plus in man-power, finance and material which the entry of America into the war would bring the Allies, and Erzberger uttered similar warnings, the Conservative forces in the Zentrum got their way when Gröber and Spahn refused to remain any longer with the Social Democrats and Progressives in a 'Bethmann coalition'. See Frieda Wacker, *Die Haltung der Zentrumspartei zur Frage der Kriegsziele im Weltkrieg 1914–1918* (Diss. Würzburg, 1937), p. 21; Willy Bongard, *Die Zentrumsresolution vom 7 Oktober, 1916* (Cologne, 1937); May, op. cit., p. 299.

[2] On the Peace Offer of December, 1916, see the very detailed work by Wolfgang Steglich, *Bündnissicherung oder Verständigungsfrieden, Untersuchungen zum Friedensangebot der Mittelmächte vom 12 Dezember, 1916* (Göttingen, Berlin, Frankfurt, 1958).

[3] For fuller details, see below, p. 315.

to bring their terms with them to the peace negotiations, if such took place. They further gave a grudging acceptance to Burian's request for a joint, binding war aims programme of all the Central Powers – a concession which on the surface appeared to carry with it the renunciation of their policy of a free hand on the war aims question. We begin, however, to doubt this when we find them henceforward postponing the joint definition of war aims by demanding that the Turks and Bulgarians should first produce their own peace conditions, after which a new date could be set for the conference. Furthermore, the despatch of the note was made conditional upon the final definition of the peace programme.[1] The Germans had thus achieved their immediate aim: they were not obliged to sit down at once with the Austrians and formulate their war aims with them. They had given their allies further proof of their will for peace, and finally the despatch of the note itself was adjourned indefinitely.

For three weeks the Wilhelmstrasse now carried on a double game which Bethmann Hollweg, for intelligible personal reasons, denied indignantly after the war before the examining committee of the National Assembly.[2]

On the evening of November 16, after the Austro-Hungarian statesmen had left the conference room, Jagow drafted instructions to Bernstorff, asking what were the prospects of early mediation by Wilson. Bernstorff answered positively in two telegrams of November 20 and 21. He emphasised that Wilson was not acting alone; all those in authoritative positions in Washington and the whole public opinion of the U.S.A. were in favour of the mediation. He had learned through House that Wilson would take the first step 'as soon as possible', probably before the New Year. Wilson made three important reservations. Firstly, before he began his action, there should be as little talk as possible in Germany, so that the Entente powers should not get the impression that Wilson was acting on the suggestion and in the interests of Germany. Secondly, all submarine incidents must be avoided, and the two recent sinkings of the *Marina* and the *Arabic* disposed of without further controversy. Finally, the German government was asked to make some concessions over the deportation of Belgian workers to Germany, which had caused a considerable public stir in America.

On December 4 Bernstorff reported that 'everything was ready for the peace action in Washington', and added expressly that Wilson's mediation might come 'overnight', especially if the German government met his wishes by an official declaration on the question of

[1] Steglich, op. cit., pp. 83 ff.
[2] *Untersuchungsausschuss*, Vol. 1, pp. 188 ff.

deportations. The American chargé d'affaires, Grew, told the Chancellor on December 6 that a peace step would be coming very shortly, and that such a step by Germany would constitute 'practical co-operation'.[1] The German government, however, not only did not accept these recommendations but on the same day energetically took up the Austro-Hungarian peace action, which had been in practice neglected for the past three weeks in favour of the American mediation.

Wilson's request for the declarations on Belgium made the Germans suspect that he would try to influence the peace conditions themselves. This brought with it the danger that Wilson might in his capacity of mediator take sides against Germany and her peace terms, in which case the Germans would be in a hopeless minority at any Peace Conference. The prospects for a peace step of Germany's own had, on the other hand, become brighter since the improvement in the military situation with the collapse of Rumania. The government thus reverted to its line of June 7, of open opposition to American mediation.

This decision was bound up with a change at the Foreign Ministry. Jagow, who saw the war from the 'racialist' angle of a struggle between Teuton and Slav and was less interested in the freedom of the seas and the defeating of Britain, and consequently attached the chief importance to the war aims in the east (counting Germany's ally, Austria-Hungary, as part of the new *Ostraum*) was, through the influence of the OHL 3, replaced by Zimmermann. Zimmermann, Ludendorff and Holtzendorff set the 'hard course' of German policy, which aimed at securing guarantees for Germany's world power position. Characteristic of all three is their east–west concept, their conviction that the peace must be a dictated one, and their further conviction that the war could be won unaided by means of the submarine arm.[2]

The Peace Offer of the Central Powers
(December 12, 1916)

The Austrians, for their part, having learnt of Wilson's intended mediation, were also pressing for the peace step proposed by them, and now even renounced the preliminary conversations between the four Central Powers on their joint peace negotiations,[3] especially in the altered and more favourable military situation on the eastern front. The capture of Bucharest on December 6 made such an offer

[1] Birnbaum, op. cit., pp. 231 f.
[2] Steglich, op. cit., p. 106; Birnbaum, op. cit., p. 233.
[3] Steglich, op. cit., pp. 123 f.

possible. 'The greater our military success,' wrote Zimmermann '. . . the deeper the impression that this would doubtless make on our enemies, who may perhaps be readier to consider *our* terms.'

It thus proved possible to 'loose off' the peace offer of the Central Powers only a week after the decision to make it had been taken. Neither the Federal states nor the Reichstag were initiated into the preparations. The Federal Council was informed of the forthcoming step only on December 11. On the same evening the Chancellor convoked the leaders of the bourgeois parliamentary parties preparatory to a general discussion between the party leaders on the next day, when the Reichstag was to meet in Berlin to hear the text of Germany's note to the belligerent powers and a declaration by the Chancellor. The whole sitting lasted only twenty minutes, and a debate on the contents and substance of the peace offer was prevented by a prior arrangement between the Chancellor and the Zentrum, the Progressives and the Majority Socialists (the later Peace Resolution Majority), which kept the spokesmen of the extreme left – Haase and Ledebour – and of the War Aims Majority – Bassermann and Westarp – from speaking. The parliamentary support from the parties of the centre enabled Bethmann Hollweg to carry on his policy of non-committal silence on Germany's war aims. The German peace offer was marked by its tone of strong confidence in victory and by the absence of any sort of concrete conditions. The Central Powers declared themselves ready to enter into immediate peace negotiations with the enemy under conditions 'calculated to assure the existence, honour and freedom of development of their peoples'.

The programme with which the German government would have come to the negotiations – it was not going to show its hand until the negotiations opened – agreed in essentials with the list of war aims which the Foreign Ministry had communicated to Vienna on November 9.[1] Berlin itself recognised that so far-reaching a programme could be put through only if the Central Powers were in a position to dictate the peace as victors. On their own evidence, however, they were far from being in that position. The Wilhelmstrasse could therefore only hope to save as many as possible of its war aims by playing off the enemy powers against one another during the negotiations. In this hope, the Germans were still trying to reach a separate understanding with Russia or France (via Spain), or with Belgium (via King Albert).

The hope of achieving a separate peace with one partner or another was the real motive behind the whole move, for hardly anyone seriously expected the peace offer to be accepted. The German

[1] See below, p. 313 f.

government assumed in advance that the Entente would reject it. But the Chancellor promised himself important psychological effects among his own people, whose confidence in the government would be strengthened if it felt that it was trying 'seriously' to bring peace about. On the other hand, a rejection of the offer must strengthen 'the determination to hold out'. Abroad, the Chancellor counted on a twofold propagandist effect in favour of Germany: On the one hand, he hoped to mobilise the longing for peace of the peoples in the enemy camp as a means of pressure against their own government, and further he expected to make 'a good impression' on the neutrals, primarily, on the United States.

The Chancellor's actions were quite obviously based on his calculation of January 10, 1916, that Germany must undertake peace soundings before she could turn to the *ultima ratio* of unrestricted submarine warfare. If peace resulted, Germany would not have to resort to submarine warfare, but if the peace move failed to produce negotiations, the offer would have played a central part in the 'diplomatic preparations' for unrestricted submarine warfare. Not the least purpose of the peace step was to provide an excuse in the eyes of the peoples of the world and of history for carrying on the war with all possible means.[1] This interpretation is justified by the last sentences of the peace offer: 'Should the struggle continue, in spite of this offer of peace . . . the four allied Powers are resolved to carry it on to a victorious end. But they solemnly repudiate any responsibility for this before humanity and history.'[2]

Six months later (on July 4) Zimmermann, the chief of this policy in the Wilhelmstrasse, in a confidential speech to the Central Committee of the Reichstag, confirmed with almost cynical frankness what motives had impelled the government to make the peace offer. In a retrospective survey of the history of the 'offer' and of Wilson's attempted mediation, he said:

It was not in our interest to let President Wilson take the affair [i.e., general peace] into his hands. As, however, we feared that he would take such a step, and we did not wish America thus to get the whole peace negotiations into her hands, in which case we should certainly have been at a disadvantage, we loosed off the peace offer of December last year. What made us hurry was the need to forestall America's intervention.

There can be no doubt that on this point Zimmermann was reproducing correctly the intentions of the government; he himself had mentioned this motive shortly after Germany's peace step in conversation with the German minister in The Hague, Friedrich Rosen.

[1] Müller, op. cit., p. 247.
[2] *Untersuchungsausschuss*, Vol. 2, *Beilagen*, pp. 99 f.

Rosen had suggested diplomatic preparation by the Missions abroad for a step of the kind. Zimmermann 'agreed with this proposal, but said that at that time it was desirable to forestall the American President's peace step'; haste would therefore be necessary.[1] Even in the summer of 1917 Zimmermann still thought this policy correct (although the failure of submarine warfare was already becoming clear); he ended his speech to the Central Committee with the words: 'It is a good thing that his [Wilson's] mediation did not come about.'

Wilson's Offer to Mediate (December 18, 1916)

Although the German peace offer could not but injure Wilson personally and seriously hamper him in his role of mediator, he did not allow Germany's action to discourage him. The essential of his note of December 18, 1916[2] was a proposal to all the belligerent powers to make public in some form—what form, he left them to choose—the conditions under which they were ready to conclude peace. Wilson thus placed himself in a position above the belligerents, whom he warned against continuing a struggle which was bringing suffering to many millions of men; but his political motive was a fear that prolongation of the war would produce an embitterment 'which might never cool off'. Then the hopes of a League of Nations would vanish, and 'civilisation would suffer harm which could never be expiated or repaired'.

Behind this apparently Utopian proposal lay a realistic train of thought: the President did not want either side to win a decisive and complete victory in Europe. His aim, as he had put it five weeks earlier in his famous speech to the American Senate of January 22, 1917, was a peace 'without victors and vanquished' which would bring with it as result a peace 'without annexations or indemnities'. Wilson, who for months had accepted uncomplainingly Britain's interpretation of the law of blockade, had now, in the autumn of 1916, become increasingly critical, even of Britain, and was approaching a truly neutral attitude. The 'knockout programme' which Lloyd George had announced in September ran entirely contrary to Wilson's views and intentions. It was the same Lloyd George—become Prime Minister a fortnight before Wilson's offer—who now opposed the chauvinistic public opinion in his own country[3] and advised re-

[1] F. Rosen, *Aus einem diplomatischen Wanderleben*, Vols. 3–4, (Wiesbaden, 1959), pp. 191 f.

[2] May, op. cit., pp. 365 ff. (also on the genesis of the note and the parts played by House and Lansing); Birnbaum, op. cit., pp. 251 ff.

[3] Page, the American Ambassador in London, reported 'a deep feeling of disappointment and . . . even of anger' in all British circles, except a small group of pacifists. May, op. cit., p. 367.

turning a conciliatory offer, with concrete conditions, as Wilson asked, in order to avoid a breach with the U.S.A. and ensure that the moral and perhaps some day the physical weight of America should not be thrown into the scales against the Entente. Although, on House's advice, Wilson had ended by modifying considerably the original draft of his offer, which had said that America would throw her weight to the side which accepted her demand, yet Germany still had a real chance of securing Wilson's goodwill by a conciliatory answer.[1]

Thus America's intervention at the end of December, 1916, offered Germany a possibility of improving her own position decisively by accepting Wilson's offer: either peace negotiations would really have resulted, in which case the United States would have worked for moderation and for a settlement between conflicting interests, or it would have been the Entente's refusal alone which had prevented the negotiations, and in that case America, with her moral, diplomatic, economic and military weight, would certainly have remained neutral. What American neutrality would have meant for the war in Europe was shown by the further course of the war.[2]

But Germany's course had been fixed by the note of December 12. The answer which she returned to Wilson's note on December 26 amounted in practice to a rejection, since the government invoked its own 'peace offer' of December 12 to exclude the participation of the President in the peace negotiations proper; it did, indeed, formally accept Wilson's proposal, but ignored the central point of his note, the request for communication of its peace terms. On December 21 Bernstorff telegraphed explaining that Wilson only wanted to serve as a 'clearing house' for further peace moves, but the Germans clearly thought this unsafe.[3] On the same day on which Zimmermann handed to Ambassador Gerard Germany's official answer to Wilson's note the Secretary of State telegraphed to Bernstorff the secret explanation of the real reasons why Germany would not have Wilson as a 'clearing house' for negotiations:

The intervention of the President, even in the form of a 'clearing house', would be detrimental to our interests, and is therefore to be prevented. We must create the basis for future conclusion of peace through direct negotiation with our enemies, unless we are to risk being cheated of what we hope to

[1] According to Bernstorff's report (Bernstorff, op. cit., pp. 305 f.), the President had initiated financial measures calculated to produce pressure in the direction of peace as early as the beginning of December, 1916, as a first warning to Britain.

[2] *Ursachen und Folgen, Vom deutschen Zusammenbruch 1918 und 1945 bis zur staatlichen Neuordnung Deutschlands in der Gegenwart* (Berlin, n.d.), Vol. 2, p. 238.

[3] Bernstorff, op. cit., pp. 318 f.

gain from the war by pressure from the neutrals. For that reason we reject also idea of conference.[1]

These words show clearly that its determination to put through definite war aims was the main reason which prevented the German government from accepting Wilson's mediation, even in the watered-down form of a 'clearing house'.

After Germany had rejected the American offer of mediation on December 26, and the Entente had refused Germany's 'peace offer' on December 30, a conference at Supreme Headquarters at Pless on January 9, 1917, decided to resume unrestricted submarine warfare, which would now 'seem to the neutrals much rather a logical conse-quence of the political situation than an act of despair'.[2] On January 12 the Emperor issued a message to the German people calling on it to work with all its strength until 'final victory' was achieved. From February 1 onwards all merchant shipping encountered in the closed zone round Britain was torpedoed.

The Entente's Rejection of the German 'Peace Offer' and its War Aims

The answers sent by the Entente powers and their allies both to the German peace offer and to Wilson's offer of mediation deserve closer analysis.[3] Where Germany's enemies differed fundamentally from Wilson was in their refusal to be put on an equal footing with the Central Powers. Their joint note to Germany repudiated Germany's assertion that the Central Powers had been the victims of aggression. It analysed the motives behind Germany's offer in terms which agreed remarkably closely with the explanation of it given by the Chancellor himself to the Federal Council on October 30–31, 1916:[4]

(i) In spite of the unlikelihood, as the balance of military forces stood, that the war would end in a military victory for Germany, the Germans in their offer had still attempted to 'force a German peace' on their enemies, i.e., to impose Germany's war aims.

(ii) To this end, the Germans had tried by their step to incite the forces of peace in the Entente countries against their own govern-ments.

(iii) A further aim of the peace offer had been to raise morale in Germany and among her allies, which had been greatly depressed by losses and economic hardship.

[1] Id., pp. 319 f.
[2] Müller, op. cit., p. 247.
[3] Text of the notes in *Ursachen*, etc., Vol. 1, pp. 80 ff., 89 ff., 68 f., 74 f., 86 ff.
[4] Müller, op. cit., p. 245.

(iv) The Germans had been trying to make a favourable impression on the neutrals through this diplomatic step.

(v) Finally, the German government had wished to justify submarine warfare, deportations, forced labour and forced recruiting of the citizens of occupied territories for service against their own countries (this was a reference to the attempts to raise a Polish army under German command).

The reactions of the Central Powers to this note were not uniform. The new Austro-Hungarian Foreign Minister, Count Czernin, thought it not unfavourable since it did not constitute an actual rejection, but only an evasion.[1] Wilhelm II, on the other hand, made it the occasion for demanding on January 2, 1917, a revision, meaning an extension, of Germany's war aims against France and Belgium.[2] The German government, however, thought it necessary to issue a special note to the neutrals on January 10, again explaining the intention behind their offer. The Entente powers' answer to Wilson was sent on January 10. Again, they refused to be placed on a moral equality with Germany and her allies, and they again refused to open peace negotiations, but unlike the Germans, they met Wilson's main request by giving an official definition of their war aims: full restoration of Belgium, Serbia and Montenegro, evacuation of the occupied parts of France and Russia, reparation for all damage. Further, they demanded:

Restitution of provinces formerly torn from the allies by force or against the wishes of their inhabitants; the liberation of the Italians, as also of the Slavs, Rumanians, Czecho-Slovaks from foreign domination; the liberation of the populations subject to the bloody tyranny of the Turk and the eviction from Europe of the Ottoman Empire.

The Allies' war aims, as made known in the demands of this one sentence, threatened the existence of Germany's two main allies, Austria-Hungary and the Ottoman Empire. The principle of nationality was used to undermine the 'fortress' of the Central Powers exactly as Germany had used it against Russia and the colonial empires of the western powers. The Entente's indirect reference to Alsace-Lorraine and to Posen–West Prussia[3] also threatened the integrity of the

---

[1] *Untersuchungsausschuss*, Vol. 2, *Beilagen*, p. 112.

[2] Id., p. 113. Grünau writes to the Chancellor on January 2, 1917: 'His Majesty told me today that after the Entente's rejection of our offer he, too, was obliged to revise our war aims, and that there could no longer be any question of conciliation towards France and Belgium. Now that King Albert had refused our offers for the third time, he could not be allowed to return to Belgium, and the coast of Flanders must be ours.'

[3] On August 16 the Grand Duke Nicholas had held out a prospect of enlarging Congress Poland by Galicia and Posen.

German Reich itself. What concrete shape these aims had already taken under mutual agreements is shown by the relevant secret treaties. The Treaty of London, concluded between the three Entente powers and Italy on April 26, 1915, had promised Italy, in return for her entry into the war, the South Tyrol, Trieste, Istria, Gorizia, parts of Dalmatia, sovereignty over Valona, the Dodecanese, territory in Asia Minor, and much more. The Straits Treaty of March 4–April 10, 1915, between Russian on the one side and France and Britain on the other, had promised Britain gains in the Ottoman Empire and Persia, while Russia was to get Constantinople. Then there was the so-called Sykes–Picot Agreement of May 16, 1916, between Britain and France on the delimitation of spheres of interest in the Arabic parts of the Ottoman Empire; and finally, a few weeks after the Entente's answer to Wilson (February 12, 1917, just before the fall of the Tsar) France and Tsarist Russia had concluded a treaty, which was kept secret from Britain and which gave Russia a free hand on her western frontier, especially in Poland, and promised France both the acquisition of Alsace-Lorraine and districts bordering on it (i.e., the Saar) and also the neutralisation of the whole left bank of the Rhine.

A discussion and appreciation of the origin, the material and political motives, and the significance of the war aims of the Entente powers would exceed the limits of this work; like Germany's war aims, they were a characteristic product of the age of imperialism. They were as incompatible as Germany's with a peace without victors or vanquished. Since, however, both great belligerent groups were deeply exhausted in the winter of 1916–17, everything depended on the future position of the U.S.A. And the mutual interaction of mediation for peace and submarine warfare decided the U.S.A. against Germany.

Wilson's Last Attempt at Mediation and the Opening of Unrestricted Submarine Warfare

In spite of Germany's refusal President Wilson continued his efforts. It says much for his persistence that on January 26, 1917, he described the Entente's war aims as exaggerated and a bluff. In his address to the Senate four days earlier he had spoken openly against them; he was still treating the Central Powers as the Entente's equals in status and importance, and throughout January he persisted in his efforts to initiate peace negotiations. In this connection he had at the turn of the year (the Entente's answer had not yet arrived, but was expected to be negative) urgently begged the German government to communicate its war aims to him personally and in confidence.[1] Bethmann Hollweg had drawn up a programme of German war aims to be sent to Wilson, but although it had been cautiously drafted, he had found it too far-reaching and had kept it back. Instead, the Wilhelmstrasse contented itself with sending instructions (drafted by Zimmermann) to Bernstorff on January 7, saying in general terms that Germany's aims 'in no respect exceeded the limits of what was reasonable'. On the Belgian question Zimmermann made only the negative declaration that Germany did not want to annex Belgium. He was completely unambiguous only over Alsace-Lorraine: Germany could not discuss this question.

For the rest, Zimmermann notified Bernstorff that Germany would find herself forced to begin unrestricted submarine warfare unless Wilson put strong pressure on the Entente, e.g., by prohibiting the export of arms and foodstuffs to Britain. He was still feeling for the 'third way', and asked the ambassador to suggest 'how unrestricted submarine warfare could be carried on without a breach with America'.

Wilson persevered with his efforts even after Germany had refused to communicate her conditions to him confidentially, and had thus put herself in a less favourable position than the Allies: their demands had been very far-reaching, but by communicating them they had done what Wilson asked. Balfour sent a covering note with the Allied answer on January 10,[2] in which he expressed the opinion, politely but unambiguously, that satisfactory conditions could not be achieved 'except through victory'. Wilson replied in his speech of January 22 with his counter-formula of 'peace without victory' and developed his views on the foundations for 'everlasting peace'. Although he insisted that the U.S.A. would not take part in the negotiation of the peace terms, several phrases in his speech could not but awaken German suspicions:

(i) The demand for Poland's independence—for the very existence of the kingdom of Poland just refounded by the Central Powers was to depend on its close attachment to Germany or Austria-Hungary.

(ii) The elastic formula of the 'just settlement of vexed questions of territory or of racial and national allegiance', which presumably covered Wilson's consent to the restoration to France of Alsace-Lorraine as already given by him in connection with the Grey–House memorandum; in any case, this wording could be made to cover the Allies' demands in connection with the liberation of national minorities.

[1] Bernstorff, op. cit., pp. 321 ff.
[2] May, op. cit., pp. 368 f.

(iii) The suggestion that the peace to be inaugurated by the Peace Conference must be worth guaranteeing 'lastingly' through a League of Nations and disarmament.

After this speech Wilson had again asked Germany for her conditions, and Bernstorff now received them on January 29 for confidential communication to the President (Austria only heard after the event of the existence and communication of this programme). They were cautiously drafted, but still could not be contained within Wilson's bases for peace. This programme, like its predecessors, refused to accept the *status quo* in the west. Like them, it insisted on the acquisition of Liége and Longwy–Briey and on guarantees in Belgium, which would have constituted severe infringements of Belgium's sovereignty.[1] But the demonstration of alleged goodwill which the conveyance of these conditions to Wilson was supposed to constitute could not be very convincing, since while communicating its conditions the Wilhelmstrasse had once again added the explicit reservation that they would have been valid if the Entente had accepted the German peace offer, but that the German government now no longer felt itself bound by them. In what sense the German government really understood its programme we see from a remark by Zimmermann, who almost at the same moment (on January 31) told the Federal Council that a particular advantage of the 'very elastic' formulation of the conditions as communicated to Wilson was 'that they leave us a completely free hand'.

The interrelation between peace efforts and submarine warfare reappeared clearly in the answer delivered by Bernstorff on January 31, for the peace conditions were accompanied by notification of the resumption of unrestricted submarine warfare, which was to begin

[1] According to the text in the *Untersuchungsausschuss*, Vol. II, pp. 74 ff., the conditions as communicated ran as follows:

'Restitution of the parts of Upper Alsace now in French occupation. A frontier against Russia for Germany and Poland which gives them strategic and economic security. Colonial restitution in the form of an understanding which assures Germany a colonial empire appropriate to her population and the importance of interests. Restoration by Germany of the French territory now in her occupation, subject to reservations of strategic and economic frontier rectifications and financial compensation. Restoration of Belgium subject to specific guarantees for the security of Germany; these to be determined in negotiations with the Belgian government. An economic and financial settlement on the basis of the exchange of territories occupied by each party, and to be restored on the conclusion of peace. Compensation for losses suffered in the war by German enterprises and individuals. Renunciation of any economic agreements and measures which would constitute an impediment to normal trade and communications after the conclusion of peace, and conclusion of appropriate commercial treaties. The freedom of the seas to be safeguarded. The peace conditions of our allies agreed with our views and were equally moderate in scale. We are further prepared to attend the international conference which President Wilson wishes to convoke at the end of the war, on the basis of his message to the Senate.'

on the following day, February 1. Discussions between the Emperor, the Chancellor, Hindenburg, Holtzendorff, Ludendorff and the three heads of cabinets on January 9 had resulted in a definitive decision in favour of this step.[1] The Chancellor informed the President that the German government had received with appreciation the President's last offer, dated January 26, to bring about a direct conference between the belligerents, but that it had unfortunately arrived a few days too late. The submarines had already put out with their new instructions and the preparations could no longer be cancelled. This appeal to technical difficulties was, however, only a pretext. Bethmann Hollweg himself confirmed in his memoirs that the naval staff had told him on January 28 that it was then still possible to recall most of the submarines.[2] But so long as he wished to abide by his previous policy, Bethmann Hollweg could not accept America's mediation, fearing as Berlin did that the President might influence the negotiations of the peace terms themselves. The Emperor had given orders that the instructions sent to Bernstorff on January 29 were to include an express and categorical rejection of Wilson as a peace mediator, and had answered all warnings that America might enter the war with the words: 'That is indifferent to me.'[3] Although the Chancellor's note did not reproduce the Emperor's drastic words, it conveyed the substance of his orders. The U.S.A. answered Bernstorff's communication by breaking off diplomatic relations with Germany. A number of further events were, however, needed to bring America into the war against Germany.

The Germans themselves threw away their last chance of delaying this event by three measures:

(i) Bernstorff had suggested at least giving neutral shipping a month's grace before opening the submarine warfare.[4] The naval

---

[1] See *Untersuchungsausschuss*, II, *Beilagen*, pp. 318 ff.; Birnbaum, op. cit., pp. 315 ff. The Chancellor had been successful on three occasions (at the end of August, in October, and again at the end of December) in getting the opening of the unrestricted submarine warfare postponed – on the last occasion, by saying that he needed to prepare the ground for it diplomatically. It seems to have been an intervention by Admiral von Scheer, the Commander of the High Seas Fleet, on January 4, that secured the decision to commence the operation on February 1. Under this pressure, Holtzendorff, who since the middle of October had been using the submarine arm in accordance with the rules of cruiser warfare, allied himself with Ludendorff, who now also pressed for unrestricted submarine warfare to begin at the earliest possible date. The two men talked the Emperor over, so that Bethmann Hollweg submitted, against his own convictions – and remained in office. See Birnbaum, op. cit., pp. 304 ff.

[2] Bethmann Hollweg, *Betrachtungen*, Vol. 2, p. 161: 'The Naval Staff assured me, indeed, positively on January 28 that they could no longer recall all the submarines which had already put out. Counter-orders would, however, not have been out of the question, although some incidents might have occurred.'

[3] Müller, op. cit., p. 251.   [4] Bernstorff, op. cit., pp. 358 f.

staff rejected this suggestion in view of what is calculated to be Britain's difficult supplies position. Britain was economically just at the most precarious stage of complete dependence on imports from overseas, and Germany must take advantage of this situation if the expected increased losses through unrestricted submarine warfare were to have their effect in breaking Britain's resistance.

(ii) Zimmermann's famous Mexico telegram broke the last threads between Germany and the U.S.A.[1] The Foreign Ministry asked the President of Mexico to conclude an alliance with Germany against the U.S.A. if the latter declared war on Germany on account of submarine warfare. As reward for her entry into the war Germany offered to restore to Mexico the states of New Mexico, Arizona and Texas, ceded to the U.S.A. in 1848. In other words, Germany threatened the U.S.A. with the loss of her south-west. At the same time the Wilhelmstrasse was speculating on a separate peace and alliance with Japan against the U.S.A. Such spacious plans to occupy the U.S.A. and to keep it from intervening in Europe by working up Mexican–American quarrels and Japanese–American tension into open warfare was typical of Zimmermann's mentality, as already observed in relation to his policy of revolution. Nothing came of it all, but the Zimmermann telegram, which the British intercepted, deciphered, and passed on to Wilson, made it easier for the President to take his weighty decision to declare war on Germany. His confidant and biographer, Baker, has described the immense effect of the Zimmermann telegram on Wilson in these words: 'No single more devastating blow was delivered against Wilson's resistance to entering the war.'[2]

(iii) Wilson still hoped to avoid bringing the U.S.A. into the war, and finally asked the German government at least to allow American shipping to pass freely to Britain without a special public declaration. The naval staff brusquely rejected this last request too, with the concurrence of the Supreme Army Command.[3] Germany's refusal to leave at least American shipping unmolested resulted in several new submarine incidents. These gave the last impetus to the U.S.A.'s declaration of war on Germany on April 6, 1917.

In retrospect it seems almost incomprehensible that Germany should have taken the risk of the U.S.A.'s entry into the war so

[1] The most recent account of this episode is that of Barbara W. Tuchman, *The Zimmermann Telegram* (New York, 1958).

[2] Tuchman, op. cit., pp. 198 f.

[3] See Holtzendorff's memorandum to the Emperor of March 18, 1917, and the Emperor's minute: 'Agreed, reject. . . . This is the end of negotiations with America, once and for all! If Wilson wants war, let him provoke it and then have it.' *Untersuchungsausschuss*, II, *Beilagen*, pp. 335 f.

lightly; even at that time the U.S.A. was no longer a *quantité négligeable*. It had more than 100 million inhabitants in one of the largest and richest continents of the globe, was already the world's strongest industrial power, and possessed a first-class fleet only a little less strong than the British. Germany's policy towards the U.S.A. shows in particularly crude colours the fundamental traits of Germany's world policy at the beginning of the twentieth century. Dazzled by confidence in their own strength, the Germans underestimated the economic and organisatory capacities of America. Nothing betrays more clearly the conventional limitations of the German soldiers' mentality than the fact that they measured America's military force by the strength of her standing army, counted up its cavalry brigades and infantry divisions and ranked it with the armies of Denmark, Holland or Switzerland.

Germany's underestimate of the U.S.A. arose from the fatal ignorance of America's power potential and American mentality which prevailed in leading circles of the Reich. Besides Bethmann Hollweg, Jagow and Helfferich, some few experts who were acquainted with American conditions did issue grave warnings during the war against underestimating the U.S.A. These included Bernstorff himself and the two bankers, Max Warburg and Bernhard Dernburg, who had been sent to the U.S.A. at the beginning of the war on a special mission. At the *Lusitania* crisis and again in 1916 these men had drawn attention to the ideological and emotional forces in the young American people. America, they said, although deeply averse to everything military and to the idea of a big war, could, if challenged and if convinced that she was fighting in a good cause, develop energies which would put into the shade anything experienced in Europe. They pointed out that private deliveries of arms and munitions from American firms to the Entente in no way represented the war potential of the American nation; in particular, America's financial power, if placed entirely at the disposal of the Entente by an American declaration of war, would definitively shift the balance of war finance to the disadvantage of the Central Powers.

Finally, Germany's American experts knew from their own experience the Americans' immense economic power and capacity for organisation. Attention had also been drawn to this factor by one of Ludendorff's most capable collaborators on the general staff, Major Wetzell, in an appreciation of the military potential of the U.S.A.[1] Wetzell recalled that the Americans had already once in their history—in the Civil War—been able to raise effective armies millions strong within a short time.

[1] *Ursachen*, II, p. 238 (extract from the memorandum of October 23, 1917).

But all these objections, political, economic, military and psychological, were brushed aside by the German military, by the bourgeois parties and by the Associations of the War Aims Movement, which manipulated public opinion. Germany's confidence that she would be able to take on the last great neutral was based exclusively on the calculation that submarine warfare would bring Britain to her knees in a very short time, before any American soldiers could arrive and before America's help as an ally could become effective. Thus Germany would have decided the war in her own favour before the U.S.A. could intervene decisively on the continent of Europe. The Germans thought that they could ignore America's small existing professional army, and that if attempts were made to bring it to Europe, even enlarged and reinforced, the transports could be destroyed in the Atlantic by the German submarines. The Americans could not come over in less than eighteen months, Admiral Capelle told the Reichstag deputies. And he promised definitely: 'And they won't come, either, because our U-boats will sink them.' Thus America's military significance was nil and nil and again nil. (In fact, only one transport was ever sunk; nearly two million men came over and they decided the war.) But the balance was finally tipped by the naval staff's firm promise that unrestricted submarine warfare would sink an average of 600,000 tons of enemy and neutral shipping monthly and would force Britain to accept terms within five months, i.e., by July 1, 1917.[1] This calculation was based partly on technical military data (the number, range and armament of the U-boats), and on the extent of the enemy and neutral tonnage, and partly on far more problematic estimates of economic factors—how far Britain herself was self-sufficient and how far she depended on her imports, how big the world harvest would be, etc. On these points, the calculations proved faulty. The submarines achieved extraordinary initial successes up to May and June, although at the cost of rising losses as new defensive weapons were developed and the convoy system organised. Nevertheless, the set term passed and Britain had still not given in. The increased figures of tonnage sunk[2] bore no relationship to the direct and indirect military and political disadvantages resulting from the introduction of unrestricted submarine warfare. And we have not even mentioned one factor which began to operate immediately after the rupture of

[1] *Untersuchungsausschuss*, II, *Beilagen*, pp. 335 ff. After the fall of Tirpitz, Holtzendorff disloyally sent the memorandum, behind the Chancellor's back, to several hundred military and political offices, and to many individuals, thus persuading German public opinion that his own prophesies had been correct.

[2] The previous figure of approximately 400,000 tons now went up by about 200,000 more.

relations between the U.S.A. and Germany, and even more when the U.S.A. entered the war: the moral effect in strengthening the confidence in victory among the Entente nations, who had also been near exhaustion, and its contrary effect on the peoples of the Central Powers, whose losses in manpower and material were becoming increasingly painful, and who saw themselves truly isolated and facing virtually the entire world.

10

WAR AIMS PROGRAMMES:

GERMANY AND HER ALLIES, NOVEMBER, 1916 to MARCH, 1917

THE hopes and suggestions of peace of the autumn of 1916 led, as we have shown, from October, 1916, to the compilation by the German government of a regular catalogue of official war aims, and to the systematic definition of them, both towards Germany's allies and among the German leaders themselves.

Austro-Hungarian War Aims, 1914–16

It is necessary to give at this point a short survey of Austria-Hungary's war aims after 1914. Although it was clear to the Austrians as early as December, 1914, that they were waging the war less to acquire territory than to assure the continued existence of the Monarchy itself, yet from the outset of the war the 'chief aim' of their policy was–as Burian put it to Conrad von Hötzendorf on December 25, 1915 – 'to get the greatest possible increase of power and security when things are re-arranged.'

The occupation of Serbia and Montenegro and parts of Albania at the end of 1915 raised the question of the future of those districts. This was discussed in the Common Ministerial Council at the great Austro-Hungarian war aims conference of January, 1916. Very soon the question arose whether it would be better to annex Serbia, in order to stamp out the focus of future pan-Serb agitation, or to reduce her to a condition of extreme dependence on the Monarchy; the latter was the course preferred by the Hungarians, who feared the internal political effects of a further reinforcement of the Slav elements in the Monarchy. Burian remarked that 'whatever solution is adopted for the Southern Slav question inside the Monarchy, it is certain that Serbia and Montenegro must be made politically, militarily and economically subject to us'. Montenegro was further to be cut off from the Adriatic; Austria proposed to annex both Mt. Lovčen (in the interests of the security of her naval base at Cattaro) and the coastal strip with Skutari, thus getting a direct connection with Albania. Albania itself, with its port of Valona, was to become an Austro-Hungarian Protectorate.

Besides these Balkan plans, another Austro-Hungarian war aim emerged soon after the outbreak of war: the attachment to the Monarchy of Congress Poland. This aim quickly involved the Monarchy in sharp differences with Germany.

The invasion of Rumania in the autumn of 1916, in which Austro-Hungarian troops took part with German and Bulgarian, suggested to Austria-Hungary her third major war aim: the *Milliardenobjekt*, as Burian put it.

These war aims were discussed in detail at the meeting of the Common Ministerial Council on January 7, 1916. In spite of the heavy reverses of the following August, they were re-stated on the old basis by Burian before he approached the Imperial Chancellor in Pless on October 18 with his proposal that the four Central Powers should make a peace move. His official list of war aims followed on November 5: a free hand in Albania, Montenegro and Serbia, 'strategic frontier rectifications' against Italy and Rumania, and (a new item) recognition of the kingdom of Poland recently created by Germany and Austria-Hungary, whose final relationship to the two Empires was, however, still unsettled.

Burian wanted the total war aims of the Central Powers fixed at the same time. He was very reserved as regards the west; Britain was not mentioned at all, France was left with her territorial integrity unaffected, Belgium was to be reinstated as a sovereign state, subject to 'safeguards for the legitimate interests of Germany', which was also to receive the Belgian Congo. Germany's war aims were to be satisfied by strategic frontier rectifications in the north-east, by which Burian meant Courland and Lithuania. His chief preoccupation was disguised behind the demand for the integrity of the Central Powers; this, in the military situation of that time, was chiefly a Turkish and an Austro-Hungarian interest, for it meant for the Monarchy that East Galicia and the Bukovina, then under Russian occupation, must be recovered.

Although the defensive element thus held first place in Burian's list, he had not forgotten his old aim of 'getting the greatest possible increase of power and security' for the Monarchy. In this respect his policy differed perceptibly from that of Count Czernin, who took his place a few days later after the death of Franz Joseph on November 21, 1916, and the accession of the Emperor Charles; although both agreed on the necessity of concluding peace as quickly as possible.

Bulgarian and Turkish War Aims

In the negotiations between Germany, Bulgaria and Turkey which opened in November, 1916, it proved particularly difficult to satisfy Bulgaria's wishes in the Dobruja. To secure Bulgaria's entry into the war on their side, Germany and Austria-Hungary had, under the secret Convention of September 6, 1915,[1] promised her the acquisition of the following territories: Macedonia up to the Morava line at the expense of Serbia;[2] if Greece should enter the war on the side of the Entente, Greek Macedonia with the Aegean port of Kavalla; and if Rumania did so, the Dobruja, the southern half of which Bulgaria had only just lost to Rumania under the Treaty of Bucharest. This was to prove of great moment. Very soon after the conclusion of the Convention Germany was trying to hedge on Bulgaria's claim to Dobruja by saying that she had only 'held out the prospect of her agreement', but had not committed herself to any kind of guarantees.[3]

The reason for this reserve was that Germany had her own ideas for the Balkans. So long as there was still a chance of Rumania remaining neutral, or being secured as an ally, it seemed necessary to keep her viable by ensuring her an outlet to the sea. This would exclude later conflicts, since Germany was tied to Rumania by strong economic interests. These considerations became even stronger after Rumania had entered the war and had been defeated in the autumn of 1916; for now Germany gave free rein to her political and economic interest in Rumania—in exploiting her resources and in developing her into a 'strong Eastern March against Russia'. Germany was especially interested in the port of Constanta and the line to it from Cernavoda, which constituted the shortest link between the lower Danube and the Black Sea. She wished to retain control over this port and railway in a Rumania dependent on herself, and therefore to return only the southern Dobruja to Bulgaria. Furthermore, Turkey was very anxious that Germany should secure a foothold in Constanta, partly because of her historic dislike of a Greater Bulgaria, partly in order to have a direct route to the Central Powers.[4] This attitude was very convenient for the Germans.

Turkey herself had at that time not put in any specific war aims. Nevertheless, the Turkish 'Foreign Minister' had told the Austro-

---

[1] The texts of all these instruments are in the archives of the Foreign Ministry. See also Carl Mühlmann, *Oberste Heeresleitung und Balkan im Weltkrieg 1914–1918*, pp. 281 f.

[2] Since February, 1916 at the latest, King Ferdinand had been expressing even more extensive aspirations towards the partition of Serbia, and even Albania. He was asking for the west bank of the Morava with the railway line from Semendria to Nish; also for the region of Prisren and Elbasan, which cut deep into Albania.

[3] Steglich, op. cit., p. 108.

[4] On the question of Constanta, see Chapter 19 (Treaty of Bucharest).

Hungarian ambassador on December 25, 1916, that Turkey would require the evacuation not only of all Turkish territory then in enemy occupation (parts of Turkish Armenia and of Iraq), but also of Egypt and Cyprus, and also rectifications of her frontier with Bulgaria.[1]

Bulgarian and Turkish wishes had not been put in binding form when the Central Powers despatched their Peace Offer on December 12, 1916. The Germans had in any case no interest in seeing common war aims formulated, and the Austrians were beginning to feel concern at increasing Bulgarian demands and consequently relaxed their pressure.

The Formulation of the German Programme

Bethmann Hollweg had at first been reluctant to put Germany's war aims in writing and to communicate them to her allies, but had ended by giving way to Austrian pressure. Between November 4 and November 14, 1916, he held various conversations with the Emperor and with the Supreme Army Command on war aims and on the text of a note to be sent to Vienna.[2] He began by sending the OHL, on November 4, a list of war aims, and asking for the soldiers' comments. His list comprised five points:

(i) Recognition of the Kingdom of Poland.

(ii) Frontier rectifications through annexations of territory in Courland and Lithuania, so that 'counting in the future Kingdom of Poland, a good strategic frontier against Russia, running from north to south, would be achieved'.

(iii) In the west, guarantees in Belgium, 'to be established, as far as possible, through negotiations with King Albert'. Should it not prove possible to secure adequate guarantees, a strip of land including Liége to be annexed.

(iv) French territory to be evacuated, except Longwy and Briey; in return, France was to restore the lost parts of Alsace, or to pay a war indemnity or compensation. Possibly also frontier rectification in favour of France in Alsace.

(v) In respect of colonies, the proposals were either the restoration of the German colonies, except Kiaochow, the Carolines and the Marianas, or 'a general colonial settlement'.

Hindenburg's reply arrived the next day. The general line of the two drafts was the same, although Hindenburg's was the more detailed and precise. Bethmann Hollweg accepted this draft, although

[1] Steglich, op. cit., p. 154.

[2] The documents quoted here are reproduced in *Untersuchungsausschuss*, II, *Beilagen*, pp. 84 ff. See also Steglich, op. cit., pp. 73 ff.

he softened it down somewhat in form when passing it on to the Emperor and to Vienna, where it was handed in on November 9.

On Point (i) the OHL has asked for frontier rectifications on the Prussian–Polish frontier, the economic attachment of Poland to Germany and 'influence over the Polish railway system' and other economic *desiderata*–all points which had for years figured, in whole or part, in the government's programme.

(ii) There was no difference in principle between the Chancellery and the OHL on the annexation of large areas of Courland and Lithuania; in particular, the Chancellor's programme had included Vilno and Grodno since the spring of 1916. Hindenburg further wanted to include Brest-Litovsk, on the east bank of the Bug, which was in any case to form the frontier between the satellite state of Poland and Russia.

(iii) The OHL's detailed list of guarantees to be required from Belgium, use of the Campine coalfields, economic attachment to Germany, control of the Belgian railways, and a right of occupation, agreed exactly with the government's Belgian programme throughout the whole war. Finally, the Chancellor had told the Committee of the Federal Council only a few days before that, besides the acquisition of Liége, the dismantling of other fortresses and the right of passage in case of war might 'perhaps' be 'obtainable'. There was only one of the soldiers' demands–a truly Utopian one–which the Chancellor rejected; they had asked for a war indemnity from Britain as compensation, in case Germany failed to obtain adequate occupation rights in Belgium.

(iv) Chancellor and Field-marshal were of one mind on the question of Longwy–Briey, only Hindenburg wanted, as Bethmann Hollweg had for two years, possible minor frontier rectifications in Alsace, not in favour of France but of Germany. In the final version Bethmann Hollweg gave way to Hindenburg on this point and also demanded war indemnities or compensation.

(v) The OHL wanted not only Germany's colonies back, but also the Congo state–the heart of Bethmann Hollweg's 'Central African' plan.

(vi) The OHL further asked for compensation for the Germans outside the Reich and the entry of Luxemburg into the German Reich: a demand accepted by the Chancellor, if in somewhat veiled form, as 'necessary in the event' of Germany's acquiring Longwy and Briey.

(vii) The November 9 version included further a 'commercial treaty with Russia', which had not appeared in either Bethmann Hollweg's or the OHL's first list, but had figured prominently whenever war aims had been discussed in connection with the soundings for a separate peace, and a detailed draft of which had been prepared as early as the spring of 1916.

This last point shows that the apparently deep divergences between the political and military leaders resolve themselves, on closer inspection, into a difference of attitudes: the politicians' attitude was elastic, deliberately impenetrable and always at pains to keep a free hand; the soldiers' was hard, open, and intent on definition. The two parties were agreed in principle on Germany's war aims; the only question between them was whether and how far it was wise to bind their hands by communicating those aims to Germany's allies, her enemies, or a mediator.

But it was precisely this question of tactics in the proposed peace move that had to be discussed again between Germany and Austria-Hungary at the Berlin Conference of November 15 and 16. Burian had contented himself with expressing regret that the Germans were still refusing to publish their peace terms simultaneously with their peace offer – they would do no more than bring their terms with them to any peace negotiations; but he insisted obstinately that a binding joint programme of the four Central Powers' war aims must be drawn up in advance of the peace negotiations, and he finally got out of the Germans a hesitant and 'academic' consent. The Germans' change of attitude when Wilson made his offer of mediation the next evening shows, however, that they wanted to avoid so binding themselves. One factor was certainly not only Burian's insistence on his own procedure, but also his criticisms of the substance of the German programme: he thought its demands in relation to France and Belgium too far-reaching and 'hardly capable of realisation', and he was convinced that the possibilities of peace stood or fell with Germany's demands in the west. Bethmann Hollweg, for his part, criticised Austria's wishes in the Balkans as too far-reaching. He urged Burian not to 'incorporate' Montenegro, except Lovčen and the coastal strip, in the Monarchy, but to let it join up with the new kingdom of Serbia which was to be established. Jagow and Zimmermann went further still; they wanted to give the kingdom an outlet to the sea at the expense of Albania. Jagow even raised the question 'whether Albania might not be partitioned between Greece and Serbia'. Serbia, thus enlarged and 'strengthened economically, as far as possible', should then be made part of the Austro-Hungarian customs and economic system.

The remarks of the German statesmen, especially Jagow, reveal the outlines of a plan for the Balkans of which Jagow had spoken a year earlier, in November, 1915, and which took definite shape at a purely German conference on Balkan problems in May, 1917: an enlarged, economically strengthened Serbia was to be attached to Austria-Hungary and thus to Mitteleuropa as a new medium state, side by side with a friendly Bulgaria and a satellite Rumania, which was at that moment on the verge of accepting defeat and already marked down as an object of German economic interests. The partition of Albania would have meant the end of Burian's pet idea of establishing an Austrian protectorate over that country; on the other hand, the Germans proposed to draw Greece thereby into the German economic system, while between New Serbia and the enlarged Greece Germany would establish an outpost for her influence on the Adriatic in Valona, the chief port of Albania, which the German Admiralty was demanding as a naval base. This intrusion by Germany into Austria's most private sphere of interest reveals what was the position assigned to Austria-Hungary in Germany's plans for the future.

The Germans not only opposed Austria's wishes in the Balkans, but also refused to meet her most important demand for a guarantee of her territorial integrity, either in the shape of a joint war aims programme worked out between the four powers or, as the Austrians desired, by way of a declaration of solidarity between Germany and Austria-Hungary. Immediately after the publication of the Peace Offer of December 12, the Austrians pressed for the conclusion of a guarantee agreement to this effect. Bethmann Hollweg could not refuse altogether, but what he finally conceded, in order to pacify the Austrians, was no more than a gesture. In an *aide mémoire* which he read out to the Austro-Hungarian ambassador on December 21 and then handed over, he assured him that in the event of peace negotiations Germany would use the 'pledges' of the occupied territories to use her influence in favour of the restoration of the Monarchy's former frontiers.[1] This assurance did not, however, give Burian what he really wanted which was that the conclusion of peace should be made conditional on the restoration of the integrity of the Dual Monarchy.

The Views of the Army, the Navy and the Colonial Office

More important than the discussions between the allies was the further definition of Germany's war aims which emerged at the end of 1916 as a result of exchanges between the military and civilian authorities. In these internal deliberations the OHL's programme of December 23,[2] produced at the Chancellor's request, opened a new

[1] Steglich, op. cit., pp. 131 f.   [2] Id., pp. 155 ff.

chapter. In the west the frontier of Alsace-Lorraine was to be recti-
fied in the Vosges and at Metz, and the Longwy–Briey basin further
secured by a glacis to the west of it. Immediately to the north, the
Belgian iron-fields of Arlon were to be annexed, if only to complete
the ring of German territory round Luxemburg (which was to be
taken into the German Reich) and to make its 'absorption' easier.
Then came the annexation of Liége with the western deployment
area beyond the Meuse, while the rest of Belgium was to be reduced
to 'the closest dependence' on Germany.

In proposing to advance the Prusso-German frontier against the
newly-proclaimed 'Kingdom of Poland', Hindenburg was doubtless
thinking of the Polish 'Frontier Strip', then running along the
Warthe–Bug–Narew–Bohr line, as a deployment area and field for
colonisation. Beside this strip a wedge of German territory was to be
thrust out south-eastward between Lithuania (to be annexed by
Germany) and the new Poland, past Bialowièza to Brest-Litovsk,
which was to become a Prussian provincial town. These proposals by
Hindenburg would have reduced the Russo-Polish frontier to only
120–150 kilometres; and it must be remembered that if, as the Germans hoped, a fully independent Ukraine were created, Poland
would be cut off from Russia altogether. This insulation of Poland
from the central Slavonic bloc would have realised the key item
in Germany's plans for a New Order in the east; it was essentially the plan set forth by Class in his memorandum of September,
1914.

The significance of this document lies less in the measure of the
various annexations which it proposed than its general admission
that its demands had been drawn up 'in the light of the present military situation'. This could mean that if things went badly in the field
some demands could be abandoned, but also, conversely, that the
demands might grow if the military situation developed even more
favourably. This was exactly what happened, at least in the east, at
the end of 1917.

On December 26, 1916, Solf, the Secretary of State at the Colonial
Office, had sent the Foreign Ministry a resumé of the war aims programme of his department with a note to say that at the moment it
expressed only his personal views, but that he had often discussed
them with the Chancellor and Jagow, who had agreed with them.
He wanted all Germany's colonies returned; further, Germany's
colonial possessions in Africa were to be 'consolidated into a German
Central African colonial Empire' through the acquisition of French,
Belgian, Portuguese and possibly also British colonies. This programme agreed broadly with Bethmann Hollweg's central African

programme of September, 1914, and Solf's own programme of the same date, but the new version was more specific. The German Mittelafrika of the future was not to be identical with his 'Central Africa', but a new conception equivalent to 'tropical Africa', and he attached most importance to the economically valuable areas. Furthermore, 'since the Congo and the Portuguese colonies would not at first bring anything in', he demanded 'the extension of this Central African Empire westward into the economically developed districts from which the coloured French are recruited'. The reasons for this demand were 'both power-political and economic'. Both the Colonial Office and the Admiralty were to frame the programme more specifically in 1917 and 1918.

The third field of German territorial demands was marked out at the same time by the Admiralty staff in two memoranda dated respectively November 26 and December 24, 1916, the former having been composed at the Chancellor's direct request. Read together, the two papers show a homogeneous vision of the foundation of Germany's 'sea-power', composed of an extensive network of bases for the German fleet. It fell into two divisions: an African–Atlantic, and a European (North Sea and Baltic).

The extension of Germany's power-position at sea in Europe was to be secured in the east by the acquisition of the Courland coast with Libau and Windau, together with the islands of Dagö, Worms, Ösel and Moon at the mouth of the Gulf of Riga (not yet conquered), and on the coast of Flanders, by 'the important maritime triangle Bruges–Ostend–Zeebrügge'. Since, however, even possession of the Belgian coast did not ensure an outlet to the Atlantic, and since Berlin was now renouncing the French Channel ports of Dunkirk, Calais and Boulogne, the Admiralty demanded in return the Faroe Islands, to be acquired from Denmark by purchase or exchange. It was hoped that it would be possible thence to outflank the British blockade and reach the open Atlantic.

The Admiralty staff assigned to the Atlantic bases two tasks, a defensive and an offensive. They were to defend Mittelafrika, when acquired, and secure the safety of Germany's overseas trade. They were also to be used in case of war to cut off Britain's and France's colonies in central and south Africa from their mother countries and damage Britain's overseas commerce. For this purpose the Admiralty staff thought that Germany must have Dakar, with Senegambia as hinterland, and the Azores–possibly the Cape Verde Islands in lieu of Dakar. Its programme culminated in the demand that the remaining Atlantic islands, the Cape Verdes, the Canaries and Madeira, should in no case be allowed to fall into the hands of another major naval power. Germany should rather acquire them herself, even if she need not develop them immediately into naval bases.

In addition to her old possessions of New Guinea, the Bismarck Archipelago and Yap, which were not to be surrendered, Germany should acquire the island of Tahiti, an effective base for destroying traffic through the Panama Canal to East Asia.

The big East African ports of the future German Mittelafrika and Madagascar were judged sufficient bases for the Indian Ocean, but in the eastern half of that ocean the Admiralty pleaded for the 'peaceful acquisition' of one of the large islands of the Dutch colonial Empire (which must in any case not be allowed to fall into enemy hands) should it not prove possible to establish a close link between Germany and Holland which placed the Dutch East Indies *de facto* at Germany's disposal.

Finally, the memorandum asked that Germany should have a base of her own in the Mediterranean; Valona would be the ideal. This town, with its immediate surroundings, should become German and should have a territorial connection with Austria-Hungary, possibly also with Bulgaria or Greece.

These three expert opinions, the army's, the navy's and the Colonial Office's, complemented and confirmed one another, par-particularly since Hindenburg explicitly adopted as his own the Admiralty's second memorandum. The Chancellor did not adopt all the proposals in every detail, but he agreed in principle with the objects, as is proved by the programme which he drew up a few days later, in January, 1917, for communication to Wilson–which in view of its destination, was intended to be a moderate one.

The Peace Conditions to be Communicated to Wilson

Before the rejection by the Entente of the Central Powers' peace offer of December 12, 1916, but in anticipation of it, Wilson had told the German government that the only possibility now remaining was to prepare the ground for a peace conference by way of confidential negotiation, and he had asked for communication of Germany's peace terms and an assurance of her readiness in principle to accept his proposed guarantees for an international rule of law in the future: limited disarmament on land and sea, machinery for the peaceful settlement of disputes and a League of Peace (League of Nations). This consent could be given without prejudice to the peace actually achieved.[1] By the time Bernstorff's message reached Berlin,

[1] Id., pp. 170 ff.

319

the Entente's refusal had already been announced. Bethmann Holl-weg drafted a reply to Wilson (which was never sent off) in his own hand.

He accepted the guarantees for the future, although with the large reservation that a Preliminary Peace must first be concluded on the basis of Germany's terms. These, as he enumerated them,[1] were:

(i) Territorial integrity of Germany and her allies.
(ii) Annexation of Liége.
(iii) Strategic frontier rectifications at Metz and acquisition of the Briey basin, just possibly frontier rectifications in favour of France in Upper Alsace in return.
(iv) Political, economic and military safeguards in Belgium, to be agreed with King Albert.
(v) Recognition of the kingdom of Poland, to be attached to the Central Powers. The frontier of Congress Poland to be advanced in the east and the line carried northward, involving the cession by Russia of Lithuania and Courland.
(vi) Colonial restitution in the form of a solid African colonial Empire, safeguarded by naval bases.
(vii) For Austria-Hungary, frontier rectifications and extensions, especially against Serbia, Montenegro and Rumania.
(viii) For Bulgaria, territorial extensions in Serbia and the Dobruja.
(ix) Regulation of trading and transport relations, no boycott.
(x) Monetary and economic compensation.
(xi) Russia to be allowed transit through the Dardanelles.

Of these eleven points, two now represented – although in fairly general terms – the interests of Austria-Hungary and Bulgaria, in conformity with the conversations and the secret Convention. The same is true of Point (i), which laid down, if in somewhat watered down form, the principle demanded by the Austrians and worded by Burian as the 'integrity of the four Allied Powers'.

The conditions relating to Germany accorded with those communicated to Vienna on November 9. Point (vi) betrayed the influence of the memoranda from the Admiralty and the Colonial Office in its more definite wording: the substance was simply that of the programme of September, 1914. The same applied also to Point (x), while Point (ix) was meant as a defence against an economic war, which the Germans feared would be the effect of the agreements reached at the Paris Economic Conference of 1916. Point (xi) repeated a concession, the necessity for which the Germans had recognised in all the discussions for a separate peace with Russia, although they had not reached any final agreement over it with their Turkish ally.

[1] Id., p. 171.

This catalogue of Bethmann Hollweg's, compiled at the beginning of January, 1917, throws more real light on Germany's war aims than the later list,[1] which was actually sent to Wilson at his renewed request at the end of the month, and reproduced Germany's purposes only in a watered down form. On close inspection the second list is seen to contain all the aims given in more concrete terms in the first – indeed, all Germany's essential demands, as they had materialised in the discussions of the preceding months. After the restoration of that part of Upper Alsace which was then in French occupation came Germany's eastern war aims in terms which disguised but by no means excluded Courland and Lithuania: 'a frontier which affords Germany and Poland strategic and economic security against Russia.' Longwy–Briey plus glacis was demanded in the wording that the restoration of the areas of France occupied by Germany could be effected only 'without prejudice to strategic and economic frontier rectifications and financial compensation'. Belgium was to be reinstated 'subject to definite guarantees for the security of Germany' to be negotiated with the Belgian government (previously it had been King Albert). Germany's colonial aims were assured by the stipulation that the measure of them must take account of the population of Germany and 'the importance of her economic interests'; given the size of Germany, compared with France and Britain, not to mention Belgium and Holland, and the stage of development, actual or prospective, of the German economy, this phrase would assure at least German Mittelafrika. The word 'understanding' appeared here, but the understanding would at best have been a very one-sided one. One must suppose the same of the 'economic and financial settlement', a phrase which concealed a demand for an indemnity, since it was to be 'based on exchange of the territories occupied by either party, and to be restored on conclusion of peace'; the German armies were standing deep in enemy territory on all fronts. The enemy might also expect very extensive demands under the heading 'compensation for losses incurred in the war by German enterprises and individuals'. America's co-operation was invited to secure the 'freedom of the seas' – a demand directed against Britain and maintained since the beginning of the war – and further to secure an assurance against an economic war after the conclusion of peace.

Quite apart from the fact that, as already noted, the Germans no longer regarded themselves as bound to the substance of this programme, it was – characteristically for Bethmann Hollweg's manner of thought and self-expression – worded in such general terms as to

[1] Id., pp. 175 f.

express Germany's war aims in a flexible and veiled form, but diminished in substance.

In the second programme the conditions in favour of Austria-Hungary were not repeated, except for the general statement that the war aims of Germany's allies were 'on a similar moderate scale'; nor was the stipulation in favour of territorial integrity. Furthermore, Vienna was not notified in advance of the communication of the German conditions to Wilson, an omission which led to further tension between the allies; for Czernin thereupon acted independently and on February 5 sent Lansing a note officially accepting the principle enunciated by Wilson in his speech to the Senate of January 22 of 'a peace without victory' and not naming any separate Austrian conditions.[1] Although the motives behind this move were largely a matter of diplomatic tactics (to keep contact with Lansing in spite of the consent which Bethmann Hollweg had given on January 31, albeit unwillingly, to the resumption of unrestricted submarine warfare) yet the main purpose of the note was to show the Americans that Austria-Hungary's attitude towards the question of peace was different from Germany's.

German Renunciations in the West?

Disappointed over the failure of the recruiting campaign in Poland, and consequently no longer interested in the creation of a Polish state, Ludendorff had at the end of 1916 demanded that the whole of Poland be taken under German rule. Bethmann Hollweg had submitted, and on January 1, 1917, the German ambassador in Vienna, Wedel, had advanced this demand strongly, to Czernin's extreme consternation. To make the loss of Poland tolerable to the Austrians, Wedel offered Czernin a bargain: if Austria left Poland to Germany, Germany would give Austria the guarantee of her territorial integrity which she had previously withheld. As further compensation, he suggested a partition of Rumania between Austria-Hungary, Russia and Bulgaria, Austria to receive the 'fat slice' of Wallachia which she could make into a 'vassal State', 'as we should do to Poland'. Czernin, however, refused this offer, as 'impossible, if only on account of Hungary and the Constitutional structure of the Monarchy'; he further rejected the proposed bargain indignantly, saying that a guarantee to this effect from her German ally was so much a matter of course that Austria should not have to pay for it.

Czernin cannot have been so surprised as he made out, for Austrian government circles had for some time past been considering the possibility of allowing Germany to compensate herself in the east for

[1] Id., p. 178.

renunciations in the west. Thus on November 5, the day of the Polish proclamation, and a few days after his own proposal of a peace offer, Burian had written to Conrad in a strictly secret letter:

> I am convinced that the key to the situation lies in the west. If Germany gives up France and Belgium, and something on top, peace is there. The Imperial Chancellor has promised me this sacrifice, in strict secrecy. I cannot put successful pressure on him here if I tell him at the same time that we shall make him all possible difficulties in the east (Poland). Only if we go into the Balkans and sell Poland to Germany can the idea of a partial cession of Alsace-Lorraine take shape.

Burian referred in the same letter to the '*Milliarden*' prize of Rumania as compensation for the loss of Poland.

This idea of balancing Poland against Rumania remained a factor in the mutual relationship of the two allies throughout 1917 – a tug-of-war for these two rich countries which the war had brought under central European domination. The key point was that the Austrians believed themselves to have detected a thorough-going change of front in Germany's war aims. Tisza put this most clearly at a Common Ministerial Council on January 12, 1917. Germany, he said, had gradually come to realise 'that the hopes she had entertained at the beginning of the war of territorial acquisitions in the west could not be fulfilled, and that she would have therefore to look for compensation in the east'. She had therefore gradually come to demand 'the political military and economic incorporation of Poland, with all her resources, in the German Reich'. Although he realised, and said, that what Germany wanted to create in Poland was not, as she said, a 'buffer State' but a 'vassal State of Germany', yet Tisza advised giving up the system of parallelism or condominium which had been in force since August, 1916. The Conference, nevertheless, decided in favour of maintaining the *status quo* in Poland for the time being. On the Emperor Charles' proposal, it drew up a maximum and a minimum programme.

Austria-Hungary's maximum programme, as conceived by Charles and Czernin, comprised the acquisition of Congress Poland (although the Conference had just considered leaving it to Germany), Montenegro and the Macsó, certain rectifications of the Transylvanian frontier, and the replacement of the Karageorgevitch dynasty in Serbia by another. The minimum programme was to confine itself to the integrity of the Monarchy, the annexation of the Lovčen, and the change of dynasty in Serbia. Czernin agreed in principle that either programme might be put forward, according to the fortunes of war, but he rather favoured the latter. He wanted at the most a few snippets off Rumania and was prepared to let Russia have Moldavia if that would make her readier for peace. In general, the idea of a new League of the Three Emperors was mooted and received with some enthusiasm, especially by the Emperor and Clam-Martinitz, the Austrian Prime Minister.

Part Two

1917

11

A HINDENBURG PEACE
OR A SCHEIDEMANN PEACE?

WAR AIMS AND INTERNAL POLICY

THE turn of the year 1916–17 marks a deep *caesura* in the history of the First World War in general and in that of Germany. The Polish Proclamation of November 5, 1916, had anticipated a peace settlement in respect of one important German war aim. Germany's peace offer of December 12, 1916, the controversy over war aims between Berlin and Vienna, the initiation of unrestricted submarine warfare and the breach with America, had shown that the rulers of Germany were resolved to prosecute the war in the west by all means at their disposal until they had achieved their war aims. All this at a moment when, the quick victory over Rumania notwithstanding, the mobilisation of all resources, the losses suffered by the nation at Verdun and on the Somme, and the privations of the third winter of war, had produced a material and physical crisis such as the nation had never before known. With the new phase of the war there set in an intensification of the home war effort embodied in the 'Hindenburg Programme'. The lifting, on November 15, 1916, of the ban on public discussion of war aims was also, primarily, a measure of psychological general mobilisation for total warfare. But the outburst of the long pent-up flood of annexationist propaganda now became a really heavy handicap on any effort to bring about a general peace, especially when the Belgian war aim (confessedly an anti-British demand) was expressly, repeatedly and publicly demanded.

The Effects of the Russian Revolution

The first effects in Germany of the outbreak of the Russian March Revolution operated in two different directions. On the one hand, the internal paralysis of Russia seemed to German public opinion to mark the first step towards the long-desired separate peace in the east; the revolution thus came as a relief, and was at first favourably received almost everywhere. On the other hand, the events and ideas of the revolution had momentous effects on the internal politics of the German Empire. Soon after their success the Russian revolutionaries had appealed to the war-weary peoples in both camps with the proclamation by the Petersburg Workers' and Soldiers' Council of the slogan of early peace 'without annexations or indemnities'. In Germany this formula found a ready hearing among the Socialist workers, whose Social Democrat leaders, though still standing by their declaration of August 4, 1914, were finding it ever harder to convince their followers of the rightness and necessity of a war which was apparently being waged very largely in order to achieve German war aims. How real was the government's fear of serious consequences for the conduct of the war is shown by a conference in the chancellery which met on March 31, 1917, specially to discuss 'the effects of the Russian revolution on internal political feeling in Germany', and came to the conclusion that the active services of the press must be enlisted to influence the public positively against revolutionary ideas.

The constitution in the spring of 1916 of the 'Social Democrat working party' (*Arbeitsgemeinschaft*), with a programme of opposition to war credits and war aims, marked a first defection of a section of the Social Democrats from the policy of the government, and an attempt to give expression to the workers' mounting discontent. Nevertheless, the influence of the left Radical groups, and in particular of the Spartacist League, was still relatively small in the spring of 1917, and its most important leaders, Rosa Luxemburg and Karl Liebknecht, had been eliminated from politics some time before by arrest.

The Social Democrat leaders soon drew the consequences of the changed situation brought about by the Russian revolution. On April 19 the party published a joint resolution by the party officers and the party committee which adopted the Russian formula of 'peace without annexations or indemnities' as the official party programme.[1] One motive behind this step was undoubtedly an honest desire for peace, but considerations of internal politics and party tactics were also unmistakably present: only two weeks earlier, at Easter, the Socialist Working Party had turned itself at Gotha into an 'Independent Socialist Party' (U.S.P.D.), and was canvassing among the workers with a definite demand for an early peace.

When the Social Democrats' resolution appeared, Zimmermann at once protested to Scheidemann, complaining that it was bound to be taken as a sign of weakness in Germany. His attitude is the more intelligible when one considers that the day of his protest – April 23 – was the very day of the great war aims conferences at General Headquarters between the statesmen and the military leaders, which laid

[1] Philipp Scheidemann, *Der Zusammenbruch* (Berlin, 1921), p. 119 (also describes the reaction of the government); see also *Ursachen*, I, pp. 387 f.

down extensive war aims for German policy. On April 28 the Conservatives issued another protest in the form of a resolution of the party officers expressing 'grave and deep concern' at the 'apparently steady growth of the influence of Social Democracy'.

The Social Democrats' resolution . . . would rob us of the possibility of a peace commensurate with the immeasurable sacrifices and the glorious feats of arms of our incomparable army and fleet, and of a nature to guarantee the prosperous development of our fatherland under a strong monarchy and to allow the healing of our war wounds through sufficient indemnities. It is only such a peace, one of victory, that we can advocate.[1]

The public discussions on war aims,[2] which from this point on raged more violently than ever under the rival slogans of 'peace of understanding' or peace of victory, 'Scheidemann peace' or 'Hindenburg peace', also reveals, ever more clearly as it proceeds, the internal political factors conditioning Germany's war aims policy. The OHL and the whole of the political right in Germany repeatedly argued the necessity of 'positive' war aims on the ground that to end the war without annexations or indemnities would endanger the monarchist order. The favourite device of the right was to conjure up the danger of revolution from the left if the workers returning from the front had to bear alone all the financial burden of the war as they would have to do under a 'peace of renunciation'. But the real threat behind this picture was one of a revolution from the right, which would be directed in the first instance against the allegedly weak regime of Bethmann Hollweg, but might possibly also endanger the Emperor and even the monarchy itself. The first draft of the 'Intellectuals' Memorandum' of the summer of 1915 had already hinted at such a possibility; now the outlines of the '*Alldeutsch* rule of the sword' which would follow Bethmann Hollweg's fall grew ever plainer. The interlocking of the war aims question and the problems of a new order at home dominated German internal politics throughout 1917, and it was this inter-connection that led eventually to Bethmann Hollweg's fall.

Leading circles in Germany were convinced that only a victorious war ending in substantial gains would enable them to maintain their political and social order; a drawn peace on the basis of the *status quo* would suffice to shatter their power position at home. It was therefore

---

[1] Westarp, op. cit., II, pp. 41 f.; *Ursachen*, l.c.

[2] Klaus Schwabe, *Die deutschen Professoren und die politischen Grundfragen des erst en Weltkrieges* (Diss. Freiburg, 1958), pp. 291 ff. For the attitude of the left see Arno J. Mayer, *Political Origins of the New Diplomacy 1917–8* (New Haven, 1959), pp. 98 ff.; also Kruck, *Alldeutscher Verband*, pp. 85 ff. and 97 ff.

necessary, in their view, vigorously to oppose the 'politicians of renunciation' but also, at the same time, to keep down the advocates of democracy and parliamentary control. If a renunciation of the aim of increasing power through war was bound to weaken the position the ruling classes in Germany, so conversely the advance of democracy and parliamentary control must endanger the attainment of the great peace by victory, since the leading advocates of political change, the Social Democrats, were also the circles which most strongly opposed a peace with annexations. The alignments on the great issues of foreign and domestic policy were almost identical, even if a few Social Democrats, or a few Liberals, were able to reconcile agitation for unrestricted submarine warfare and far-reaching war aims with demands for internal political change in the direction of more democracy and more power for parliament. These men had no intention of using parliamentary control over political power in the state to limit German acquisitiveness, still less forbid it. All they wanted was, as Naumann and Max Weber preached,[1] to use the experience of the western democracies and mobilise and activate 'the masses at the flywheel of power' to make the Reich even greater and stronger. All they would have done in the end would have been to save the pseudo-constitutionalism of Prusso-Germany from the rising wave of twentieth-century democracy, and reconcile it with the masses' demand for political rights by broadening its basis without touching its structure or its substance at any really essential point.

Bethmann Hollweg and Social Democracy

The Social Democrats had taken the Emperor's proclamation of a 'truce' in his famous speech from the throne of August 4, 1914, as a promise of what came to be called a 'new orientation'. Bethmann Hollweg, for his part, had been appointed to succeed Bülow by the Emperor in 1909 with the mission of integrating the Socialist workers into the existing political and social order,[2] and he enjoyed considerable confidence in left-wing circles; he held the positive co-operation of the Social Democrats to be vitally necessary for the state, precisely in time of war. Without the collaboration of organised labour, he was convinced, the war could not be carried on. The leaders of the right wing of the Social Democrats were prepared to go a long way to meet him, and a tacit alliance developed between them and him. As early as the end of August, 1914, one of the most prominent lead-

---

[1] Wolfgang I. Mommsen, *Max Weber und die deutsche Politik 1890–1920* (Tübingen, 1959), pp. 252 ff.

[2] See Bülow's own account in his *Denkwürdigkeiten*, II, pp. 511 ff.

ers of the revisionist wing, Eduard David, had a long discussion with Delbrück on the new attitude of the Social Democrats towards the state. David was then expecting an early victory over France, and he demanded, in the name of his section of the party, a new orientation in domestic politics, without, however, mentioning the Prussian franchise. He said that 'a big gesture from a competent quarter' was essential.[1] He wanted 'political acts', not mere words. He described his friends' goal under the term 'national democracy', but said that they could not get themselves accepted with this new programme unless the government met them with such a gesture.

Bethmann Hollweg snatched at this offer of collaboration with the right wing of the Social Democrats. He wrote to Delbrück 'that we must make every effort to seize this opportunity, which may never recur, to place Social Democracy on a national and monarchic basis'. He saw clearly that unreserved acceptance by the Social Democrats of the new line of 'national democracy' must lead to 'a new orientation of our entire internal policy'. He at once laid down one fundamental condition:

> The Social Democrat leaders must meanwhile realise that the German Reich and in particular the Prussian State can never allow any loosening of the firm ground on which they have grown up, the firm acceptance of the State (*Staatsgesinnung*) and the system which Social Democracy has been accustomed to stigmatise as 'militarism'. . . . The moment that the German Left is prepared to accept this system of the nation in arms, and to adopt the appropriate popular mentality, at that moment a re-orientation of our internal policy will be possible.

The Chancellor thus laid down that no change of political course in Germany could come unless the Social Democrats first moved away from their previous principles, and the leaders of the right wing of the Social Democrats paraphrased this new turn quite fairly when they said that they had 'made their peace' with the state and the army. The Chancellor refused, however, to make any immediate concessions, such as the lifting of the State of Emergency, because he thought that this would be a confession of internal weakness; he only held out prospects for after the war: 'If such concessions are to be made – if they can be made – this must be as reward for work done, not as a premium in advance'.

The word 'reward' recurred when the conversations between the right wing of the Social Democrats and the Reich authorities were renewed. On October 2, 1914, Solf and Delbrück arranged a

[1] The account of the interview preserved in the archives has been published by Jürgen Kuczynski, *Der Ausbruch des ersten Weltkrieges und die deutsche Sozialdemokratie, Chronik und Analyse* (Berlin (Ost), 1957), pp. 207 ff.

conversation between the Social Democrat deputy Max Cohen-Riess and Wahnschaffe, the Under-Secretary of State, on 'the transformation of the Social Democratic Party'.[1] Cohen concentrated on the question of the Prussian franchise, but contented himself with asking for a plural franchise, thereby renouncing the introduction into Prussia of the Reichstag franchise.[2] On the question of republic versus monarchy a dialogue took place between the senior Imperial official and the Social Democratic politician which Wahnschaffe summarised in his notes as follows:

> I said to Herr Cohen, that if the Social Democrats wanted to be met, they must themselves change their ways radically and accept our Monarchist Constitution. . . . Herr Cohen did not deny this, and said that he himself could see the Social Democratic Party developing along monarchist lines; the Progressives had, after all, done the same. A development of this kind could not, however, be brought about all at once. But it would come if the government took the initiative in meeting them and was not too impatient. . . .

Cohen assured Wahnschaffe that the right wing of his party, and of its deputies, was propagating his own views most vigorously. The leading revisionists were himself, Südekum, David and Scheidemann.

Bethmann Hollweg knew now that he could rely on the leaders of the right wing. While mobilising the party machine and the trade unions to steel the masses of the Socialist workers to 'stick it', even after it had become apparent that German policy had relinquished the war of defence proclaimed on August 4, 1914, these same men offered their services to the imperial government as propagandists abroad for the German cause. The government made no immediate 'big gestures', but the Social Democrat leaders made do instead with direct and indirect help from the government against the left-wing Opposition, by releasing successively party or trade union officials who took the majority line and interning or imprisoning the leaders of the left Opposition. Bethmann Hollweg's temporising policy on the whole worked well throughout 1915 and 1916: the Social Democrat and trade union leaders could chalk up the recognition of the unions under the Employment Act (*Hilfsdienstgesetz*) as a substantial success, while strikes among the workers were extremely rare. It was, at least if his own later account[3] is to be believed, consideration for

[1] Kuczynski, op. cit., pp. 209 ff.

[2] A form of plural franchise was in fact suggested in the Prussian House of Representatives in May, 1918, by the Conservatives, the Free Conservatives and the right wing of the National Liberals, as a defence against Social Democracy, after they had rejected the Franchise Bill of November, 1917, which would have introduced general suffrage.

[3] Bethmann Hollweg, *Betrachtungen*, II, p. 136.

the Social Democrats and the large section of the workers whom they represented, as much as anything, that made Bethmann Hollweg reject the thought of resigning at the beginning of January, 1917, when the decision on the submarine question went against him. He believed, and perhaps with justice, that he alone still enjoyed sufficient confidence among the workers' leaders to prevent them from swinging over to the Opposition, as would have happened inevitably if Bülow or Tirpitz had become Chancellor.

The Easter Message

When the U.S.A. broke off diplomatic relations with Germany on February 2, 1917, in protest against the resumption of unrestricted submarine warfare, Bethmann Hollweg made this the occasion for a defence of German policy in his Reichstag speech of February 27[1] which was still coloured by his disappointment over his failure to combine with America against Britain. Overshadowed as the atmosphere was by the threat of America's entry into the war, he treated the question of war aims with reserve, although in terms capable of covering all his concrete aims (Westarp, the Conservative leader, put them openly), but when he turned to internal politics he raised the question of the 'new orientation'—this being the first time that the word had been used from the government benches.[2] The poet's words 'that Germany's poorest son was also her most loyal', quoted by him, could not but sound revolutionary in the Prusso-Germany of nobles and bourgeois, officers and bureaucrats, however vague its hint of internal reforms. Since, he said, the 'national idea' 'embraced the whole people, in an entirety which transcended class or party' (thus not excluding the Social Democrats), it would be possible and even necessary when peace came to open up new paths for the nation's forces—subject to the imperative condition that 'every sober-minded champion of popular rights' accepted the existing monarchic form of state. This programme, which Naumann aptly described as 'democracy combined with Empire' (*Demokratie und Kaisertum*), was aimed expressly at the western democracies. It was an attempt to build the new elements cautiously into the existing order, so as to guarantee that Prussia–Germany could put out her full strength, in war and peace.

Strongly as these vague hints of reform insisted on the maintenance of the character of the Prussian authoritative state, they yet sufficed

[1] Thimme, op. cit., pp. 192 ff.

[2] See Ludwig Bergsträsser, *Die preussische Wahlrechtsfrage im Kriege und die Entstehung der Osterbotschaft, 1917* (Tübingen, 1929) (still the basic study of the subject). It is true that the author does not altogether appreciate the inter-connection between the Message and Germany's war aims.

to sound the alarm among the conservative elements of Prussia–Germany. Their displeasure found vent over a relatively trivial point, a proposed amendment to the Prussian law on deputies' allowances. In the debate of March 19 the conservative majority in the Herrenhaus directed bitter attacks against democracy in general and the Reichstag, as its alleged champion, in particular; von Buch, President of the College of Knights, accused the Reichstag of 'working for an unconstitutional, and in the last end, revolutionary, extension of its power'.[1] This in its turn elicited vigorous criticism of the Herrenhaus from Free Conservative, National Liberal, Centre and Progressive speakers in the Prussian House of Deputies, who repudiated passionately the undeserved accusation of revolutionary intentions. In fact, nothing was further from their minds than a wish to alter the constitutional structure of Prussia–Germany, although the National Liberals, in their annoyance, did introduce a Bill for a radical reform of the Prussian Herrenhaus. Nevertheless, this seemed the first serious threat to the inner fortress of Old Prussia, and it explains the embittered reaction of all conservative circles in Prussia against any beginning, however modest, of internal reform.

It is against this background that Bethmann Hollweg's speech of March 14, 1917–the day before Tsar Nicholas II's abdication–must be read. Only in this light is it possible to realise how greatly it provoked the Conservatives and so was bound to endanger his position as Imperial Chancellor and Prussian Prime Minister.[2] After repudiating the Herrenhaus's attacks on the Reichstag, he drew a picture of a united nation as Germany's only chance of survival after the war. 'We can carry on such a policy of strength, at home and abroad, only if the whole people, every class of it, including its broad masses, enjoys such political rights as to enable it to take an equal and willing share in the work of the State'.

In his endeavour to reach an internal settlement, Bethmann Hollweg went so far as to appeal to his listeners' reason to discard the prewar dogma of the incompatibility of the interests of the workers with those of the state and the employers, for the sake of Germany's future.

On March 28 came sharper attacks in the Herrenhaus against the Reichstag, the general franchise and the 'new orientation'. The following day the Reichstag began its debate on the new course. The debate showed for the first time that Bethmann Hollweg's 'policy of diagonals' was no longer appropriate to the internal situation in

[1] *Ursachen*, Vol. I, p. 312, n. 1.

[2] Id., pp. 312 ff. On the pre-history of the Chancellor's speech, see Bergsträsser, op. cit., pp. 117 ff.

Germany; for the right his reform proposals were too advanced, for the left they were too hesitant. The spokesmen for the National Liberals, the Zentrum, the Progressives and the Majority Socialists did indeed agree with what he had said on March 14, but they protested against putting the reform off until after the war. Stresemann was among those who pleaded most earnestly for immediate reforms, with an eye to American opinion and under the impact of the Russian revolution, which had just broken out, and Müller-Meiningen, the Progressive, begged the government 'to open a safety valve as soon as possible' in view of the growing internal unrest. The counterreaction of the Conservatives had, however, grown so strong in the meantime that the Chancellor confined himself to promising reforms after the end of the war.

It was only a few days before events outstripped his hesitances. During the first days of April the full measure of the Russian revolution and of its effects on the internal situation in Germany became clear. On April 1 Wilson advised America's declaration of war on Germany, and on April 6 Congress declared war. Wilson hailed the Russian revolution enthusiastically as a victory of democracy over autocracy. Adopting for his own (on Lansing's advice[1]) the British ideological slogan of a war of democracy against 'militarism' and autocracy, he announced that the U.S.A. would fight together with the other western democracies – not against the German *people*, but only against German autocracy. Thus the President of the classic land of democracy in the New World allied himself with the revolutionary democracy of the Old World to proclaim the war of the democracies against what they regarded as the historically outworn form of autocracy. Thereby Wilson lent to the struggle of the allies a vast, entirely new, emotional content, while at the same time hopelessly isolating the Central Powers in the eyes of the whole world.

The threat of isolation inherent in Wilson's moral appeal to the world, the increasingly difficult food situation, which brought with it the danger of demonstrations and strikes by the workers, the heightening of the internal tension with the foundation of the U.S.P.D. – all these factors made Bethmann Hollweg feel that the time had come for the 'big gesture' for which Cohen and David had asked in the autumn of 1914. He also saw clearly that it was now too late for half measures. A promise to introduce plural voting in Prussia after the war would no longer suffice to dam the wave of democracy in Germany. The situation had become so critical, the world had changed so suddenly, that the monarchy in Prusso-Germany could in his

[1] George F. Kennan, *Soviet–American Relations* (Princeton, 1956), Vol. I, p. 144.

view be saved only by a great political step: by the immediate introduction of direct, secret and equal voting in Prussia.[1]

The introduction of the Reichstag franchise in place of the Prussian three class franchise[2] was the kernel of the draft Royal Edict
which Bethmann Hollweg, in his capacity of Prussian Prime Minister,
submitted to the Ministry of State on April 5. He argued the necessity for this 'grave and serious step' in a minute analysis of Germany's
situation, caught as it was between the Russian revolution and
America's declaration of war. He openly admitted the revolutionary
character of this step for the old Prussia by saying that 'leaving aside
the enormous differences of opinion that the reform must provoke',
it would entail 'a complete shift of power-relationships in Prussia,
and was thus of decisive importance for our whole political life'. If,
however, he hoped that an appeal to political common sense would
enable him as it were to storm the fortress of the Prussian Ministry
of State at the first attempt, he found himself grievously disappointed.
A storm of protest arose among his fellow-ministers, led by von
Loebell. The Vice-President, von Breitenbach, the Minister of
Justice, Beseler, and Helfferich supported Bethmann Hollweg's
draft, but the conservative elements in the ministry forced him to
change the text to the form in which it was published on April 8 as
the king's so-called 'Easter Message'.

The Easter Message is usually extolled by German historians (or
blamed, according to their views) as the first break-through of democracy. In reality, its pre-history reveals it as little more than a
miserable remnant of what had been a grandiose attempt to place
Prusso-Germany on a new basis by an initiative from above, that of
the monarch's government. In contrast to Bethmann Hollweg's
original draft, it contained only vague promises of reforms after the
war. All it offered was reform of the Herrenhaus and the abolition
of the Prussian three class franchise, but the franchise on which the
new order was to be based was to be only 'secret' and 'direct', not
'general'.

[1] That it was not theoretical convictions that led Bethmann Hollweg to wish to
introduce franchise reform, but only his feeling (which itself does him no small
credit) that it was politically necessary, is shown by what he said to Wahnschaffe:
'With the three class franchise become impossible, and given the hopelessness of
any attempt to construct a new franchise which should in practice serve the same
anti-democratic purpose, and yet look like a victory for democracy, we should in
the end be driven into the equal franchise.' (Bergstrasse, op. cit., p. 132.) Loebell
was at heart opposed to any radical change of the existing franchise; see the various
memoranda from the Ministry of the Interior in Bergstrasse pp. 13 ff., especially
pp. 31 f.

[2] This divided the electors into three categories, on the basis of their tax returns,
leaving the broad masses, with their relatively low incomes, heavily under-
represented in proportion to their numbers.

The Internal Political Effects of the Easter Message

The Easter Message did, as Bethmann Hollweg justly claimed, bring the government an initial tactical success. Thanks to the co-operation of the loyal trade union leaders and Majority Social Democrats the dreaded protest strike of the workers took place only on a limited scale, passed off peaceably, and was called off after only a few days. The Majority Socialists had undoubtedly been able to take up this attitude only because their press and the proclamation of the General Committee of the trade unions and the committee of the Social Democrat Party on May 1 had welcomed the message and had succeeded in portraying it as a success for themselves in their struggle against the left. The first effects of the foundation of the U.S.P.D. at Easter were therefore not so far-reaching as the government and the Majority Socialists had feared.

The Majority Socialists and their allies, the official trade union leaders, had not disappointed the Chancellor; the whole right, especially the Conservatives, had. They had been intensely alarmed by Bethmann Hollweg's step, which seemed to them to confirm his rumoured democratic leanings. The threatened democratisation of their last stronghold, Prussia, could not but make them fear for their own political and social power position, since the introduction of general and equal suffrage would have revealed to the world that they constituted only a small minority.[1] After the issue of the Easter Message they took up the fight against democracy in real earnest. An official Conservative party communiqué, for example, of July 12, attacked the proposed abolition of the three-class franchise most vigorously, and declared: 'The equal franchise does not accord with the special nature and historic past of the Prussian State. It is calculated rather to shatter the solid framework of Prussia and to deliver up this State too to complete democratisation.'[2] But the left soon found the pressure of events at home and abroad too strong: they could not go on contenting themselves with the Easter Message's vague promises for after the war. In the same resolution of April 19, in which the Majority Socialists, vieing with the new U.S.P.D., had adopted as their own the Russian slogan of 'peace without annexations or indemnities', they again attacked the questions of the Prussian franchise and of democratisation, this time more vigorously than ever.[3] The resolution called for 'the immediate removal of all

[1] The Conservatives, led by Count Roon and General von Kleist, had already protested strongly against the danger of democracy in the Herrenhaus on March 28, 1917.

[2] *Ursachen*, I, 3265.

[3] As early as March 19 Scheidemann had called for the equal franchise in Prussia in an article in *Vorwärts* entitled 'The Time for Action' (*Zeit zur Tat*).

inequalities of civic rights in Reich, State and Commune, also the removal of every form of bureaucratic rule and its replacement by the decisive influence of the representatives of the people.' On May 2 this step by the Majority Socialists was accompanied and supported by a move by the Progressive People's Party in the Prussian House of Deputies.[1] It welcomed the Easter Message in principle, but called for the immediate introduction of equal franchise and for reform of the Herrenhaus. This demand went even beyond those hitherto voiced by the Majority Socialists. The Conservative majority succeeded in invoking the Standing Orders to prevent a debate on the left-wing Liberals' motion, but on the same day the parties of the left in the Reichstag, this time supported even by the National Liberals, got the establishment of a Constitutional Committee of the Reichstag voted by a big majority against only thirty-three minority votes. The importance of this success was, however, chiefly formal and psychological. The Committee was duly set up, with Scheidemann as Chairman and a Conservative as Vice-Chairman, but effective obstruction by the government prevented it from putting through any far-reaching changes.

The Counter-attack of the War Aims Movement

The establishment of the Reichstag Constitutional Committee was a prestige success for the left, but in practice it meant abandoning any prospect of early reform of the Constitution, and the right went over to an open offensive against the Chancellor. It chose for its attack a field in which it had for some time past been working with the OHL under Hindenburg and Ludendorff, the broad field of war aims. Following up their resolution of April 28 against the Easter Message, the Conservatives tabled an interpellation in the Reichstag on May 3 protesting against the Majority Socialists' resolution of April 19 and expressly calling on the Chancellor to state his position on the Socialists' demand for a peace 'without annexations or indemnities'. They naturally expected the Chancellor to reject the idea of such a peace decisively. The same day the Social Democrats tabled an interpellation asking the Chancellor to define his foreign policy in their sense and quoting the statements made in favour of a peace without annexations or indemnities by Germany's ally, Austria-Hungary, and by Russia. The Chancellor was thus caught between two fires, and as always, sought a middle way in the interests of national unity—a way whose course was determined by the interplay of forces.

Before the two interpellations came up for debate in the Reich-

[1] *Ursachen*, I, p. 320.

stag, the right had mobilised the broad front of the War Aims Movement—not merely the East Prussian Conservatives, but the innumerable associations and leagues of the middle classes and the Christian-national element among the workers—for a massive protest 'against a peace of renunciation'. The joint appeal, which appeared on May 3,[1] called in familiar phraseology for compensation for the enormous sacrifices suffered by the German people in the war to enable Germany 'to build a new future, economic, social and cultural, after concluding a victorious peace'. For this Germany needed a wider basis for her industrial raw materials and her armaments, and further, new territory for settlement and 'more sea-power'. The document culminated in the massive demand: 'Only a peace with indemnities, with increases of power and territorial acquisitions, can lastingly assure our people its national existence, its position in the world and freedom for its economic development.'

The list of the signatories to this frankly annexationist demonstration shows how widely such expectations of a victorious peace had spread among the German middle classes, and how deep they had struck their roots.

Besides specifically political associations such as the Independent Committee for a German Peace, the *Alldeutscher Verband* and the *Ostmark*, Fleet and Army Associations, it was signed by the famous six great industrial and agricultural associations whose earlier agitation for war aims and unrestricted submarine warfare has already been described, with the subsidiary vocational organisations. New recruits were the associations of the national and Christian wing of the workers, both Catholic and Protestant. The old War Aims Movement of the national associations and parties now took the field in order to use the weapon of the national slogan of a German victorious peace for the purpose of breaking up the new majority beginning to form in favour of internal reform, some of whose components (especially among the National Liberals, parts of the Zentrum and the Progressives) overlapped with the old War Aims Majority. The purpose of this great public demonstration was to commit the Chancellor to their war aims, under threat of overthrow.

Meanwhile the OHL was already at work to commit Bethmann Hollweg to its own line against any weakening on the war aims question. So far as territorial aims were concerned, this commitment had been successfully accomplished at Kreuznach on April 23, and

[1] Schulthess, *ad* May 3, 1917. The appeal was signed by twenty-two associations, political and vocational, the latter including workers' as well as employers' associations.

the success was repeated in mid-May in the war aims agreement with Austria-Hungary. Exactly a week after putting in its statement of war aims, the OHL enlarged it with a list of economic conditions which were to be imposed on Britain in the victory peace soon to be brought about by submarine warfare.

With what powerful weapons of psychological suggestion Luden-dorff operated against any idea of a 'peace of renunciation' is illus-trated by a brochure entitled *The Future of Germany Under a Good Peace, or a Bad One* which he had distributed to every unit in the army. Grotesquely distorting the data, this screed says that a 'German peace' would leave Germany 'a free people with only 5,000 millions of debt' (!) while a 'Scheidemann peace' would leave her 'a wage-slave of England's with 170,000 millions of debt'. Coloured maps of the Central Powers and the ethnically non-Russian parts of Russia show Germany's new European order, the possibilities of colonisation for the German people, the coal, iron and oilfields which were to make Germany self-sufficient in raw materials, and the continuous Central Africa which was to supplement her European basis. The War Aims Movement at this time added to its many publications the monthly *Deutschlands Erneuerung* (The Renewal of Germany),[1] which preached a populist nationalism to the educated classes and opposed most strongly both any 'peace of renunciation' and any new orientation at home.

This is the background against which we must view Bethmann Hollweg's Reichstag speech of May 15, 1917[2] In this, his last public speech as Chancellor, he remained true to himself and to his own war aims policy. As before, he refused to give way to any pressure, from left or right, or to commit himself to a definite war aims programme. On the other hand, he let it be understood that he was pursuing war aims which were entirely definite, and he expressly referred to earlier statements of principle made by him in the Reichstag on the subject. It should further be mentioned that in this same speech, made three weeks after the Kreuznach Conference, he emphasised his faith in the success of the submarine warfare and his complete agreement with the OHL on the question of war aims:

Gentlemen [he said dramatically], time is not standing still for us. We can rest fully assured that we are nearing the happy end. Then the time will have arrived when we shall be able to negotiate with our enemies on our war

[1] The editorial board consisted of the historians G. von Below and H. St. Chamberlain, Class, Geheimrat von Gruber, of Munich, who had also collaborated on the brochures, Generallandschaftsdirektor (ret.) Kapp, one of Bethmann Hollweg's strongest opponents, von Schwerin and the theologian, R. Seeberg, the initiator of the so-called 'Intellectuals' Address'.

[2] Thimme, op. cit., pp. 237 ff.

aims, in respect of which I am in complete agreement with the Supreme Army Command [tempestuous applause on the Right, from the *Deutsche Fraktion*, the Zentrum and the National Liberals, and on the Left: 'Hear! Hear!' from the Social Democrats].

He concluded his speech with a passionate appeal which, characteristically and perhaps not accidentally, contained certain verbal echoes of the appeal of the War Aims Movement:

Then we mean to achieve a peace which leaves us free to use all our forces unfettered in building up again what this war has destroyed, so that of all this blood and all these sacrifices shall be born anew a realm and a people strong, independent, unthreatened by its enemies, a garden of peace and of work [prolonged and tempestuous applause from the *Deutsche Fraktion*, the Zentrum, the National Liberals and on the Left].

Once again, as *Vorwärts* rightly said, Bethmann Hollweg's endeavour 'to pick his words so carefully as to allow the widest interpretations was triumphantly successful'.[1] The dominant note of victory naturally drowned the few words directed towards Russia on the possibilities of peace, especially as they were vague and went little beyond rhetoric. Bethmann Hollweg may well have been speaking under the influence of the War Aims Movement and of the military, he may well have felt his tactics imposed on him by considerations of both foreign and domestic policy; nevertheless he maintained the same attitude representing Germany's official policy, in the tedious discussions with the Austrians of April and May, 1917 (described below). We are concerned only with the purposes which guided the actions of the Chancellor as responsible statesman, not with the innermost promptings of his heart. Abroad, his Reichstag speech was inevitably regarded as tantamount to a renewed declaration of war, or at least an exceedingly strong expression of Germany's determination to achieve victory and power.

[1] Ibid., pp. 209 ff.

12

MAINTENANCE OF
GERMANY'S WAR AIMS PROGRAMME
PARRYING AUSTRIA'S DESIRE FOR PEACE

THE weak oppositional forces had been defeated, and the dominant economic, military and political factors joined with the imperial government in a re-affirmation of Germany's war aims and a determination to carry on the war by every means. This resolve inevitably raised to an extreme pitch the tension which for months past had existed between Germany and Austria-Hungary, which in the previous March had asked for an explicit limitation of war aims to enable the allies to take advantage of any possibility of peace which might present itself. When the full effects of the Russian revolution became apparent, Austria directed her pressure primarily towards reaching an understanding with the new Russia, but she was also extremely interested in an understanding with the west–England and France–particularly as she had no direct interests of her own in that quarter.

The German-Austrian War Aims Conferences
of March, 1917

On March 16, 1917, four days after the success of the revolution in Russia, the long promised German-Austrian conference on war aims took place in Vienna.[1] It has to be seen against the background of the Austro-French feelers, which had already been put out; not only was Count Mensdorff-Pouilly, the former Austro-Hungarian Ambassador in London, being sent to Switzerland, thence to spin threads towards France–this was all Bethmann Hollweg knew–but contact had already been made with Prince Sixtus of Parma.[2] The

[1] See (besides the archival material) Richard Fester, *Die Politik Kaiser Karls und der Wendepunkt des Krieges* (Munich, 1925), pp. 57 ff.

[2] The literature on the 'Sixtus Affair' is so vast that we must confine ourselves here to directing the reader to the latest account from the Austrian side, Reinhold Lorenz, *Kaiser Karl und der Untergang der Donaumonarchie* (Graz, Vienna, Cologne, 1959), pp. 325 ff. Poincaré had received Sixtus as early as March 5, and had given him France's terms for a separate peace with Austria (Silesia and Bavaria to go, if possible, to Austria-Hungary, Alsace-Lorraine to France). Czernin was not fully informed of the negotiations and afterwards expressly dissociated himself from the extreme French demands.

Prince and his brother, who were nephews of the Empress Zita, were serving in the Belgian army and were prepared to act as intermediaries between the Emperor Charles and Poincaré. Czernin pinned great hopes on these conversations, since he realised plainly, and also stated unambiguously at the outset of the conference, that it was 'entirely impossible' for Austria-Hungary to carry on the war longer than the coming autumn.

Czernin wanted to grasp France's 'proffered hand',[1] but Bethmann Hollweg was decidedly sceptical: France would make the cession of Alsace-Lorraine a *conditio sine qua non*, and that would mean a loss for Germany which he could not justify either to the Emperor or to the German people. Moreover, the occupied territories of France and Belgium must be kept as pledges for the return by Britain of the German colonies. The Chancellor therefore wanted the negotiator 'to be strictly receptive and not to prejudice the future in any way'. Unlike Czernin, he had hopes of the effects of the Russian revolution and of submarine warfare; that is, he still believed in the possibility of eventually concluding a separate peace on Germany's conditions.

Nevertheless Bethmann Hollweg made the motions of meeting Czernin's urgent wish that Germany's war aims should be reduced as nearly as possible to the maintenance of the *status quo* by pretending to the Austrian that Germany had now renounced far-reaching war aims against France. Czernin had proposed giving Mensdorff for his conversations a minimum and a maximum programme of the war aims of the Central Powers. The Chancellor gave him, as the maximum, the acquisition of Longwy–Briey without territorial counter-concessions by Germany, and as the minimum, 'exchange of the Briey–Longwy ore fields against parts of Lorraine or Alsace'. This was not Germany's 'last word'–although the events of the turn of the year 1916–17 and later documents show that all Bethmann Hollweg thought of ceding was a few frontier villages. The 'exchange' would have been quite illusory, especially as Belgium was excluded from the discussion.

In the east, the Chancellor simply took up the attitude of a conqueror. 'Here,' he told the Austrians, 'so long as Germany is not defeated, all that can be considered is how much we take, how much we keep; at the worst, a return to the *status quo*.' But even here, Bethmann Hollweg did not entirely disclose his cards to his closest ally; he clothed Germany's intention of dominating Congress Poland

---

[1] France herself only wanted a separate peace with Austria in order to beat Germany and take the left bank of the Rhine from her. At the beginning of 1917 she secured the support of the Tsarist government for this in return for a free hand for Russia against Germany, and in the Straits.

in the garb of Mitteleuropa. The establishment of the Kingdom of Poland would push eastward the Russian frontier in Central Europe, to the advantage of all the Central Powers. In that event Bethmann Hollweg was prepared 'not to claim any Polish territory for Germany', i.e., to renounce annexing the Polish 'Frontier Strip'; Germany would confine herself to strategically desirable acquisitions in Courland and Lithuania. The dimensions of the direct annexations – he explicitly named the governments of Grodno and Vilno – would, of course, depend on Germany's military position at the conclusion of peace. Should the Central Powers be forced to restore Congress Poland to Russia – if, that is, the general situation forced them to offer Russia a 'cheap' peace – 'then Germany would be thinking only of frontier rectifications on the Silesian and East Prussian frontiers' – that is, the Polish 'Frontier Strip', as planned two years before.

Czernin's answer reflected the dilemma of the Dual Monarchy. He put the integrity of the Monarchy – in particular the recovery of East Galicia and the Bukovina – above the acquisition of Congress Poland. He thought it, however, impossible, on grounds of prestige, to let Germany acquire large territorial prizes (in Courland, Lithuania and Poland) and Bulgaria others, while the Monarchy 'bleeding from a hundred wounds, came out empty-handed, or even diminished'. He therefore proposed that at the end of the war 'the territorial and economic gains should be brought into a certain agreement'. He was evidently thinking of putting the war gains of all the Central Powers into a sort of common pool, out of which each partner should draw his share. To safeguard Austria-Hungary's interests he proposed partitioning Rumania on the lines sketched out in January, 1917.[1]

Bethmann Hollweg and the Under-Secretary for Foreign Affairs, von Stumm, at once raised strong objections to Czernin's proposal, announcing at the same time a new turn in Germany's Rumanian policy. The Chancellor criticised the Austrian claim to Rumania as giving the Danubian Monarchy an excessive share of the spoils, and advocated instead preserving the kingdom of Rumania as far as possible within its existing frontiers. He suggested that Austria might content herself with Western Wallachia, while Russia took, not the whole of Moldavia, but only the northern tip of it. In these areas Germany was asking for 'nothing but economic advantages'. Behind this apparent modesty lay Germany's intention to secure for herself the hegemony in Rumania, an aim which she pursued tenaciously, with many changes of tactics, throughout 1917 and achieved in 1918 by the Treaty of Bucharest.

[1] See above, p. 322.

Immediately after the session of March 16 Czernin set down the proposals which he had made at the conference in even more explicit form in a memorandum to the Emperor Charles: Germany must give up Alsace-Lorraine, in whole or part, and restore Belgium; in return, she could keep Congress Poland. Austria should cede the Trentino to Italy and receive compensation in Rumania.[1]

The renunciation of Poland was the central question discussed at an Austro-Hungarian Common Ministerial Council, held on March 22 under Charles' presidency, to consider Austria's position after the conference of the 16th. Emperor and Ministers assumed that Germany was renouncing any territorial gains in the west. On this assumption, the ministers present were prepared to reserve the east for their allies as 'compensation' and 'as a logical consequence' to renounce their own aspirations in Poland. When we know that only two days earlier the Emperor had drawn up with his cousin the so-called 'first Sixtus letter' to Poincaré, promising that Charles would 'support the just claim of France to recover Alsace-Lorraine with all means at his disposal and with all the personal influence he could exert on his ally', and would call on Germany to reinstate Belgium as a sovereign state with its colonies,[2] we can realise how compulsively necessary the Austrians felt it to be to persuade their German ally to make renunciations in the west and thus somehow or other make peace. At this council the Austrians for the first time mentioned as a war aim of their own the inclusion, already suggested by Germany in November, 1916, of a diminished Serbia within the customs area of the Danubian Monarchy.

Meanwhile the effects of the Russian revolution seemed to call for another meeting between the allies. It took place in Berlin on March 26–27.[3] The exchange of Poland against the lion's share of Rumania was confirmed, although Austria stipulated that if the Entente refused to allow Rumania to be partitioned, she could not renounce Poland. Czernin, however, linked the Polish and Rumanian questions with that of Mitteleuropa, for which Germany was pressing strongly, by stipulating that both German hegemony over Congress Poland (which would also necessarily carry with it the inclusion of Poland in the German Customs Union) and the resumption of economic negotiations on the Mitteleuropa project should be conditional on Wallachia going to the Danubian Monarchy.

[1] Conze, op. cit., p. 278; see also Novak, *Sturz der Mittelmächte*, pp. 420 ff. Czernin entertained momentary thoughts of ceding Galicia to a German-dominated Poland, but dropped the idea in his memorandum.

[2] Lorenz, op. cit., pp. 329 f.

[3] See also Rudolf Neck, 'Das Wiener Dokument vom 27 März, 1917', in *Mitteilungen des oesterreichischen Staatsarchiv*, VII (Vienna, 1954), pp. 294 ff.

On principle Czernin was anxious that the Central Powers should not exclude the possibility of peace with either west or east by pitching their demands too high. Bethmann Hollweg, however, invoked German public opinion to insist most obstinately on Germany's war aims in the west, saying that to accept the *status quo* either in Belgium or in Longwy–Briey would be 'a very heavy sacrifice' for Germany. He insisted even more strongly on Germany's war aims in the east, although he said that he might make far reaching concessions, especially towards Russia, as price for a separate peace.

The results of these two conferences were committed to paper in the shape of a short resumé signed by Bethmann Hollweg and Czernin jointly on March 27. The two men agreed firstly on a minimum programme which made the evacuation of any occupied enemy territory 'primarily' dependent on recognition of the territorial *status quo* of both powers in both east and west. This programme, which was however to apply only in the case of a relatively unfavourable issue to the war, was more advantageous to Austria-Hungary, which would have recovered East Galicia and the Bukovina, whereas Germany would have got back only a few villages, since no German territory was in enemy occupation except a small corner of Alsace. More instructive for the history of Germany's war aims is the maximum programme, which was to apply if the war ended favourably. For this eventuality, for which Germany was putting out all her strength, the resumé laid down a framework which was elastic in two directions and amounted to another success for the German standpoint: if the Austrians had talked in Vienna of 'a certain agreement' and even of 'an automatic equalisation' in the division of the spoils of war, they now had to accept the German *fiat* that 'the territorial acquisitions of the two Powers must be made proportionate to the achievements of each'. Acceptance of military efficiency as the criterion for the division of the spoils at the end of the war could only work in Germany's favour, since the German troops were undoubtedly bearing the brunt of the war effort of the Central Powers, in the east as well as the west; German forces had played by far the greater part, even in the conquests of Serbia and Rumania. Finally, the resumé also indirectly left Germany a free hand in the west. While Austria's territorial gains were to be 'primarily in Rumania', Germany was to get acquisitions 'chiefly in the east'–thus partly also in the west.

The Kreuznach War Aims Programme of April 23, 1917

The Chancellor obviously cannot have informed the OHL of the Vienna agreements, and the Foreign Ministry and Bethmann Hollweg's own successor afterwards showed themselves unaware of the existence of the document.[1] Consequently, when the Austrian Emperor and Empress, with Count Czernin, came to Bad Homburg on April 3, the OHL pressed for an Austro-German conference to define the war aims of both states. The military thought it necessary for the German military and political authorities to meet beforehand to discuss Germany's war aims between themselves.[2] Bethmann Hollweg again opposed a fixed programme of war aims, because he thought it would hamper possible negotiations for a separate peace with either France or Russia. On April 16 he again said that the unaltered aim of his policy was to break the enemy coalition, if possible, even to draw one of the former enemies over to Germany's side.

Pressed by Hindenburg to define Germany's war aims, the Chancellor replied that he was informed of the wishes of the OHL and the naval staff from their memoranda of the previous December, and meant 'to achieve the very utmost possible of those demands which are directed towards increasing our military security'. The Chancellor further declared himself ready to subordinate general political and economic considerations to military ones, thus giving the military priority over the civilian in the matter of war aims. From this point onwards he found it very difficult to oppose even the exaggerated annexationist demands of the OHL. Nor was this all. He lost even such limited freedom of action as had been left him in the discussion of war aims when Hindenburg and Holtzendorff, mistrusting him, went to the Emperor at General Headquarters and got him to order the Chancellor on April 20 to draw up a specific war aims programme, with maximum and minimum demands, in view of the possibility of peace with Russia and of the approaching negotiations with Austria-Hungary. The Emperor also prejudged an important issue in the sense desired by the OHL by laying down, in respect of Lithuania, that for strategic reasons Vilno, Kovno and Grodno were in no case to be allowed to go to Poland.

On April 20 the Emperor told Bethmann Hollweg to come to Kreuznach on the 23rd for the big debate on war aims. The necessity of producing a war aims programme agreed between the government and the OHL could no longer be evaded. On the 21st Bethmann Hollweg held a strictly secret conference with the inner ring of the Prussian Ministry of State, preparatory to the meeting. At this

[1] So Hertling, Kühlmann and Helfferich told Czernin on February 5, 1918; see Volkmann, op. cit., pp. 217 f.

[2] See also A. J. Mayer, op. cit., p. 116. Hindenburg had proposed 'immediate consultations on a high level' to determine Germany's minimum demands, 'since it is to be anticipated that the war will be decided . . . this year . . . and that peace negotiations will take place before very long.'

meeting Helfferich, in agreement with the Chancellor, produced the new formula of 'autonomy', which was to be applied in the areas which Germany had hitherto proposed to 'annex', viz., Lithuania, Courland, Livonia and now Estonia also.

The Kreuznach Conference was attended by the Imperial Chancellor, Zimmermann, Hindenburg, Ludendorff and the head of the Political Section of the Government-General in Brussels, von der Lancken. The minutes of this meeting were published shortly after the war, but have hitherto been taken too much in isolation and regarded as a specific expression of the German military's annexationist ambitions. It is true that the formulation of war aims reached at this conference was primarily dictated by the wishes of the OHL, but a survey of the development of Germany's war aims from Bethmann Hollweg's programme of September, 1914, to the visible unfolding and realisation of Germany's wishes in the east at Brest-Litovsk reveals not only continuity of intention but also general agreement in principle between the military and civilian authorities.

The OHL's memorandum of December 23, 1916,[1] was taken as basis for the discussions. The main conclusions reached were the following:

In the East

(i) Besides the acquisition of Courland and Lithuania up to the line designated by the OHL on December 23, the further acquisition of parts of Livonia and Estonia, including the islands at the mouth of the Gulf of Riga, was also desirable. If the anticipated disintegration of Russia did not provide an opportunity to seize the last-named districts, they would have to be conquered by arms (as was in fact done in the case of Riga and the islands in September, 1917, and Livonia and Estonia in February, 1918).

(ii) On the question of Poland, the OHL and the civilians confirmed Germany's old intention of establishing complete military, political and economic domination over Congress Poland. If this could be achieved, the OHL would be ready to renounce part of the 'Frontier Strip' and to content itself with the Narew line and its prolongation through Ostrolenka–Mlawa and a few other trivial annexations. In theory the new Polish state was allowed the possibility of expanding eastward, but since Courland and Lithuania were reserved for Germany and the ethnically Polish district of Bialystock was also earmarked for annexation, it is not easy to see where the Polish state's new territories were to be found.

(iii) At this point of the discussions the war aims of Germany's allies, as they had emerged at the recent discussions with the Aus-

[1] See above, pp. 316–17.

trians in Vienna and Berlin, were considered. The remarkable proposal was made that Austria-Hungary should pay Russia for Germany's acquisition of Courland and Lithuania by the cession of East Galicia, which she allegedly no longer wanted to recover, compensating herself for this loss in Serbia, Montenegro and Albania which were to be attached to Austria-Hungary in the form of a Southern Slav state. Austria-Hungary was to receive further compensation in western Wallachia. The German leaders wished in their own interest to keep conquered Rumania 'as large as possible' and to safeguard Germany's oil interests. Bulgaria was not to get the Cernavoda–Constanta line, which was to be left 'Rumanian', i.e., under German control, on account of Germany's interests in Turkey.

In the West

(i) As in all programmes after September, 1914, Belgium was to be a German vassal state, and was also to cede to Germany the coast of Flanders with Bruges, and Liége with an extensive approach up to Tongeren. These cessions were described as conditions 'indispensable for peace with England'.

(ii) The OHL demanded the annexation of Arlon 'for reasons of war economy', 'on the assumption that it contains deposits of iron ore'. Luxemburg was to become a German federal state.

(iii) The annexation of Longwy–Briey figured in this, as in all previous programmes; there were also to be certain 'frontier rectifications' in Germany's favour in Alsace-Lorraine.

(iv) The cessions to France, of which Bethmann Hollweg had spoken to the Austrians in March as proof of Germany's good will, would consist 'at the very most, of certain frontier salients and a narrow strip south-west of Mülhausen'. Astonishingly, this was conceded 'to prevent peace with France breaking down on this point'.

(v) In general the conference expressly laid down that any armistice could apply only to the war on land, while the war at sea, i.e., unrestricted submarine warfare, was to be carried on, even after an armistice by land, as a means of pressure against Britain.

The above list of war aims in eastern and western Europe did not, however, exhaust the sum of Germany's wishes: 'further questions relating to the Balkans and Asia Minor' and those of the overseas bases demanded by the naval staff and of the colonies were referred to the departments for discussion in detail.

The sum of these demands leaves on the reader who surveys them in retrospect the same impression as they made at the time on Admiral von Müller, the Chief of the Naval Staff: 'My impression: completely immoderate, in east and west alike.'[1] These war aims could, of course, only be realised if Germany was in a position to dictate the peace as victor. Bethmann Hollweg expressly pointed this out immediately after the conference in a minute which did not go outside the Foreign Ministry; he declared himself not obliged to continue the war, under all circumstances, until these aims should have been achieved. In this minute the Chancellor took exactly the same line as in his letter to Hindenburg of April 16, in which he had admitted the primacy of the military war aims, as he did at the conference, but refused to commit himself finally. The special significance and meaning of this reservation related to the feelers which were being put out by Erzberger at the same time for a separate peace with Russia.

The criterion for the appreciation of Germany's war aims policy is the intention to realise as much of these aims as the military situation and any unavoidable consideration for her allies allowed, not how much tactical freedom the Chancellor enjoyed in his pursuit of them.

The primacy of Germany's own war aims over those of her allies was confirmed immediately after Kreuznach by Zimmermann, when he opposed categorically a suggestion that a conference of all four Central Powers should be convoked to define their war aims. 'Such joint conferences,' he wrote,[2] 'jeopardise the realisation of our own war aims, and it is of those that we must think first.' He therefore said that the first step – which would be hard enough – should be to reach an understanding with Austria-Hungary alone, through normal diplomatic channels; only afterwards should discussions be opened with Bulgaria and Turkey.

When, then, the Kreuznach Conference is viewed in its historic

[1] Müller, op. cit., pp. 278 f.: 'One could read what the Chancellor and Zimmermann were thinking in their eyes: "it does no harm if we lay down maximum demands; it will work out differently, anyhow".' A different view is taken by Hans Herzfeld, "Kontinuität oder Permanente Krise" in *Historische Zeitschrift* 191/1, July, 1960, pp. 67 ff.; but see my reply (*Kontinuität des Irrtums*), ibid., pp. 83 ff. In a marginal note on a memorandum from Grünau, dated April 24, 1917, Bethmann Hollweg wrote that he had consented to the peace conditions laid down at the conference only on the assumption 'if we are able to dictate the peace'.

[2] See also the letter written by Bethmann Hollweg on January 26, 1918, after his fall, to Hertling, reproduced in Schwertfeger, *Politische und militärische Verantwortlichkeiten*, pp. 142 ff. Bethmann Hollweg writes of the Kreuznach programme: 'The peace demands here were not drawn up by me as my war aims programme, but by the OHL as a military necessity, and when the negotiations opened they were far more extensive, in both west and east, than as finally agreed.' In other words, the 'immoderate' Kreuznach programme had already been modified, compared with the original demands of the military. Czernin thought that the meeting 'again proved that Germany does not want peace with Russia on a basis of mutual renunciation of annexations and reparations. . . . I ask myself again and again in astonishment whether these gentlemen are really still blind to the gravity of the situation; whether they would dare let a separate peace break down on the rock of their wishes for annexations.'

context, it becomes plain that what Hans Herzfeld calls its 'terrifying list' of proposed annexations is no isolated testimony to the greed of the German military. Its programme fits smoothly into the list of war aims discussions and programmes which preceded and followed it.

Czernin's Memorandum of April 12, 1917

A new phase in the struggle between Germany's war aims policy and Austria-Hungary's need for peace was opened by the famous memorandum[1] addressed by Czernin on April 12 to the Emperor Charles, and immediately forwarded by him to Wilhelm II. It opens with a drum-roll: Czernin announced, quite soberly, that the military strength of the Danubian Monarchy was approaching its end. In view of the complete exhaustion of reserves of material and manpower, the chronic starvation and dull despair of the masses and the effects of the Russian Revolution on the Slavs of the Monarchy, revolution among the workers and revolts of the nationalities were to be expected shortly. There would be revolutionary upheavals within the Monarchy (and also in Germany) if it were asked to carry on the war through another winter. Such upheavals seemed to Czernin, as a defender of the principle of monarchy (he wrote, with an eye on his two imperial readers) far worse than 'a bad peace concluded by the Monarchs', which would at least leave the old political and social order in being. His warning culminated in the prophecy: 'If *the monarchs* of the Central Powers are unable to conclude peace *within the next months,* then the peoples will make it over their heads, and then the waves of revolution will sweep away everything for which our brothers and sons are still fighting and dying today.'

Finally, Czernin queried the effectiveness of unrestricted submarine warfare, the immediate successes of which had been more than outweighed by America's entry into the war. So anxious was he for early peace that to achieve it he was willing for the Monarchy to make heavy territorial sacrifices.

Charles strongly endorsed his minister's warnings in a personal letter to Wilhelm II, whom he begged 'most earnestly' 'not to shut his ears against [Czernin's] considerations'. And he ended with the pathetic appeal:

We are fighting against a new enemy, which is more dangerous than the Entente: against international revolution, which finds its strongest ally in general famine. I implore you not to overlook this most momentous aspect of the question, and to consider that a speedy end of the war – possibly at the

[1] The text of the memorandum has been published in *Deutsche Allgemeine Zeitung,* July 26, 1917, and in Ludendorff, *Urkunden,* pp. 375 ff.

cost of heavy sacrifices—will offer us the possibility of meeting successfully the revolutionary movements which are now gathering.

The leaders of Germany took Czernin's memorandum for a piece of nervous pessimism,[1] a view which reveals how diametrically opposed were both the analyses of the situation and the policy aims of the Wilhelmstrasse and the Ballhausplatz.

Germany's 'No' to Austria

Germany's official standpoint was set out at length in a letter drafted by Bethmann Hollweg for Wilhelm II to send back to his imperial cousin, and in an official exposé which he himself, as Chancellor, sent to Charles at the same time.[2] Both documents were based on a speech on the submarine question made by Helfferich in the Central Committee of the Reichstag on April 28, and on appreciations of the military situation submitted by the OHL and the naval staff.[3] The German leaders had clearly recovered from the shock of America's declaration of war and of the strike threat of mid-April. The depressed atmosphere of the beginning of April had given place to one of pronounced optimism within a month.

It is remarkable how the German leaders, while holding tenaciously to their fundamental aims, always adapted their strategies to their changing views of their own prospects in the war. This was true of Bethmann Hollweg in May, 1917. In his answer to Vienna he adopted Helfferich's and Ludendorff's optimistic views of the situation, and went so far as to write: 'Time has become our latest ally.' This bold assertion was based on the view that Britain and France were exhausting their strength in the current offensive, that Russia was crippled and on the verge of collapse, that the United States would not be able to intervene in Europe within an appreciable time and that submarine warfare would produce a crisis in Britain, the approach of which the Chancellor claimed to see in the introduction there of food rationing. He therefore answered Czernin's gloomy picture with a more sanguine view of the general situation. While the Austrian saw risings among the Slavs and revolution among the workers as the consequences of continuing the war, the German on the contrary thought that a 'cheap peace' would be extremely dangerous to the Monarchy. In May, 1913, the German statesmen still thought an upheaval in Germany similar to the Russian completely out of the question. His confidence in the internal solidarity of the Prusso-German political system led the Chancellor to the opinion

---

[1] See Fester, op. cit., pp. 85 ff.
[2] The text is in Ludendorff, *Urkunden*, pp. 379 ff.
[3] Ibid.; see also K. Helfferich, *Der Weltkrieg* (Berlin, 1919), p. 419.

that 'the conclusion of peace at any price, simply for the sake of ending the war, would be absolutely fatal'. What he wanted was not the end of the war as such, but a peace which enabled Germany to achieve at least a part of her war aims. He even wanted the possibility of a separate peace with Russia treated without 'ostentatious enthusiasm'. The Emperor, in these days, was taking up in advance a strongly negative attitude towards the peace feelers from Britain, which were expected to be forced from her by submarine warfare.[1] Exactly the same stiffness which the Emperor wanted to manifest against Britain was shown towards Austria-Hungary's further pleas for peace. Through her answer, Germany not only forced Austria to continue the war, but committed her indirectly to Germany's own war aims. That is the significance of the Kreuznach programme of May 18, 1917.

The Emperor's War Aims Programme and the German–Austrian War Aims Conference of May 17–18, 1917

What the Emperor and his military advisers meant to come out of the negotiations with the Austrians appears from Wilhelm II's own personal war aims programme, which he had sent to Zimmermann in the Foreign Ministry on May 13.[2] Broadly, it agreed with his earlier programme of April 17, but in certain nuances it was even more extreme.

As his grandiose demands show, Wilhelm saw himself victorious over Russia, France and even over America. Of France, as before, he demanded Longwy–Briey, with the threat that the 'prolongation of the war raises claims'. His requirement of Britain was freedom of the seas with 'guarantees', by which he obviously meant the cession of Britain's Mediterranean possessions with Malta going to Germany and Gibraltar to Spain. Cyprus, Egypt and Mesopotamia were to fall to Turkey, the Azores, Madeira and the Cape Verde Islands to Germany (together with the French and Belgian Congos); Germany's colonies were to be restored. Belgium was to be divided into Wallonia and Flanders and put under German rule. In the east Wilhelm wanted the direct or indirect annexation of Poland, Courland and

[1] We ought to pitch our demands against England very high, and carry on the submarine warfare with the same intensity, and go on at her until she gives way.' On another memorandum submitted to him by Bethmann Hollweg on May 14 he wrote: 'The English scoundrels must come to us, not to the Austrians! Till they do, we'll flail on and shoot on and submarine on. The fellows are to swallow our conditions, not the Austrians theirs!'

[2] A.A. rok. Gr. Hg. Friedensanknüpfungen, Vol. 1. See also Klaus Epstein, 'The Development of German–Austrian War Aims in the Spring of 1917', in *Journal of Central European Affairs*, Vol. XVIII, April, 1957, p. 42.

Lithuania. The Imperial 'minimum demands', as Wilhelm entitled his programme, culminated in demands for massive war indemnities. As in his earlier draft he hoped, in the event of a German victory, to extract from Britain, the U.S.A., France and Italy (Russia was not mentioned in this connection) the fantastic indemnities of 30,000 million dollars from each of the first two, 40,000 million francs from France and 10,000 million lire from Italy; and in addition 12,000 million marks each from China, Japan, Brazil, Bolivia, Cuba and Portugal, at first not indeed in cash, but in kind: wheat and oil from Russia, cotton, copper and nickel from America, wool and iron from Britain and Australia. France was to transfer her interest in the big Russian loan to Germany and to deliver iron ore and edible oils. The chief value of this document lies in its revelation of how the world, and also the objectives and potentialities of Germany, appeared to the Emperor's imagination.

Czernin had come to Kreuznach expecting to be able to reach agreement with the Germans on the basis of an early peace with Russia. The Chancellor's Reichstag speech of May 15,[1] with which the Austrians were, as it were, received on their arrival, acted like a cold shower on Czernin. The cup of his disappointment was filled when the Germans never even listened to his peace proposals, so that there were no negotiations on the point at all. What the conversations brought instead was recognition by Austria-Hungary of Germany's claims in the east.[2] The Germans were able to book Courland and Lithuania for themselves uncontradicted, and Austria conceded to Germany exclusive influence in Poland. Germany's return for Austria's *désintéressement* in Poland consisted in her allowing Rumania to go, as before, to Austria-Hungary, subject however to numerous reservations; in a complete guarantee of the integrity of the Monarchy; and in accepting Austria's programme for the settlement of the southern Slav question. While the Austrians wanted only the creation of three small states – New Serbia without an outlet to the Adriatic, Montenegro and Albania – all to be kept militarily, politically and economically dependent on the Monarchy, the Germans wanted to combine the small Balkan states into an enlarged New Serbia, consisting of West Serbia, Montenegro (which would give it an outlet to the sea) and Northern Albania, and closely attached to Austria. Southern Albania was to be attached to Greece.

The first of Germany's special wishes in the Balkans was the expulsion of the Italians from Valona, which the German naval staff had

[1] See above, pp. 340–41.
[2] The texts of the agreements were first published in Ludendorff, *Urkunden*, pp. 388 ff.

marked down as a Mediterranean naval base for Germany. They wanted Austria to give them a free hand to conclude an agreement with Bulgaria on the exploitation of the natural resources of 'New Bulgaria', i.e., Macedonia. They made this an absolute condition of any agreement with Austria. Since Germany's aspirations in Bulgaria included control over the Macedonian railways, the claim to Salonica, as the terminal point of those railways and a free port, reveals with great clearness what German policy hoped to achieve when peace was concluded. Nor, finally, should we overlook the economic advantages which Germany, if closely linked with Austria-Hungary in a customs union, could expect to derive from the wealth accruing to the Danubian Monarchy by the resources of the New Serbia.

More important still is the proposed reorganisation of the south-eastern Balkans. In return for yielding on Poland, the Germans were prepared to allow their allies to attach Rumania to the Monarchy as a separate state. In fact, however, the Germans had secured for themselves all that was really valuable in the *'Milliarden'* prize of Rumania: the exploitation of the Rumanian oilfields, the use of the Danube and the Rumanian railways. In addition Constanta was to become Germany's gateway to the east. Just as in Poland at one stage, the Germans were prepared now to leave their allies the political responsibility in Rumania, while keeping the real economic advantage for themselves.

This solution seems, moreover, to have been suggested chiefly as a tactical move and not to have been regarded by the Germans as final, for later they evicted Austria again from the position they now granted her in Rumania. It was none other than Bethmann Hollweg who–following and modifying in his own way a suggestion from Fieldmarshal von Mackensen, commanding in Rumania–had written to Hindenburg as early as February, 1917, pressing very strongly the idea that Germany's policy must be to collaborate with the conservative elements in Rumania in order to draw it back into its old relationship with Germany and build it up as a 'strong Eastern March' against Russia. He was against the plan, which the military circles were clearly entertaining, of turning Rumania into a German military colony on the grounds that it would impose too heavy a strain on Germany's strength after the war; he also opposed partitioning Rumania between her neighbours, but he strongly advocated reorganising the country entirely, with a new constitution, a new dynasty and a reformed administration, and orienting its economic and cultural life towards Germany.

The use of Valona, Salonica and Constanta would have provided the foundations for a German economic imperium in the Balkans, especially since German policy at Kreuznach combined German penetration of the Balkans with a resumption of the Mitteleuropa plans, which had been in cold storage for some time. These plans seemed to provide the best way of assuring Germany's economic interests in the Balkans, and definite outlines now appeared of a German-dominated economic *Raum* from Antwerp to Brest-Litovsk (or Rostov) and from Riga, if not Reval, to Salonica and Constanta, and on to Baghdad and Suez.

German Economic Expansion in the Balkans

The agreements on the Balkans outlined above were based on the conclusions of a conference held in the Foreign Ministry on May 12, in preparation for the conversations with the Austrians and attended by officials of the Foreign Ministry, headed by von dem Bussche, the Under-Secretary, a delegation from the Reich Interior Office, and two representatives of the OHL, one of them the very influential head of the Political Section of the general staff, Colonel von Barten-werffer. It was characteristic of Germany's attitude towards her closest ally, Austria-Hungary, that the participants differentiated carefully between the points on which something could be told to Czernin and those which were to be concealed from him. The aims worked out at this conference accorded closely with those of certain private financial and economic interests; one example is the demand that French and Belgian interests in 'Serbian Macedonia' should be liquidated and taken over. Here the Disconto-Gesellschaft, the Dresdner Bank, the Deutsche Bank and the Deutsche Erdölgesell-schaft were particularly engaged, being chiefly interested in copper, coal, gold and shale oil. When the German Reich demanded a general option on the exploitation, after discovery, of the still un-known natural resources of Serbian Macedonia, it was advanced in the interest of these financial and economic groups. As in Poland and Belgium, great importance was attached to the control of the rail-ways, and it was therefore proposed to set up a German–Bulgarian railway company with a capital of 310 million marks. German domi-nation over the Danube was to be assured by expelling Britain, France and Italy from the International Danube Commission. Whether or no Rumania were left an 'independent' state, the meet-ing demanded for Germany the entire mining royalties on Rumanian oil, i.e., an unlimited right to all deposits of oil whether opened or not yet exploited. Rumania was to guarantee carriage of the oil out of the country by rail, waterway or pipe-line. Here, too, the Germans justified their claim to a controlling interest over the Rumanian

1. Wilhelm II, Alfred von Tirpitz and Henning von Holtzendorf

2. Theobald von Bethmann Hollweg, Gottlieb von Jagow and Karl Helfferich

3. Walther Rathenau

4. Arthur von Gwinner

Arnold von Wahnschaffe

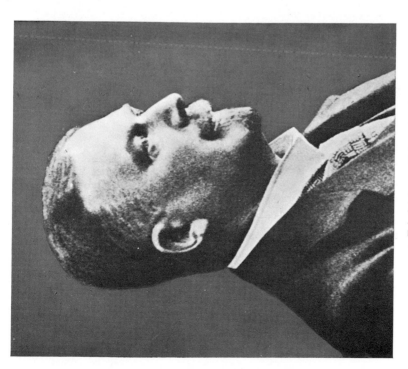

5. Friedrich von Schwerin

6. Arthur Zimmermann

Alexander Parvus Helphand

7. Baron Hans von Wangenheim

8. Count Ulrich von Brockdorff-Rantzau

Hans Delbrück

9. Max Sering

10. Gustav Stresemann

11. Clemens von Delbrück

Hugo Stinnes

12. August Thyssen

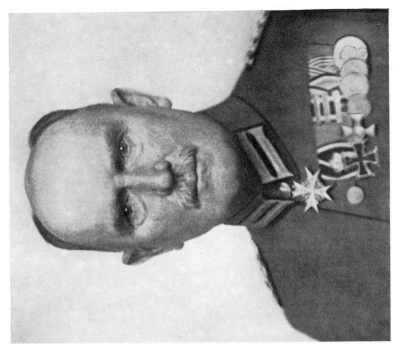

Hans Hartwig von Beseler

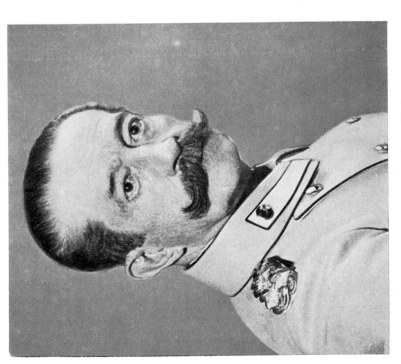

13. Moritz Ferdinand von Bissing

Paul von Breitenbach

14. Friedrich Wilhelm von Loebell

15. Erich Ludendorff

16. Matthias Erzberger

17. Richard von Kühlmann

18. Negotiations at Brest-Litovsk: Hoffmann, Czernin, Talaat Pasha and Kühlmann

19. Baron Hans Karl von Stein zu Nord- und Ostheim

20. Paul von Hindenburg, Pavel Skoropadsky and Erich Ludendorff.

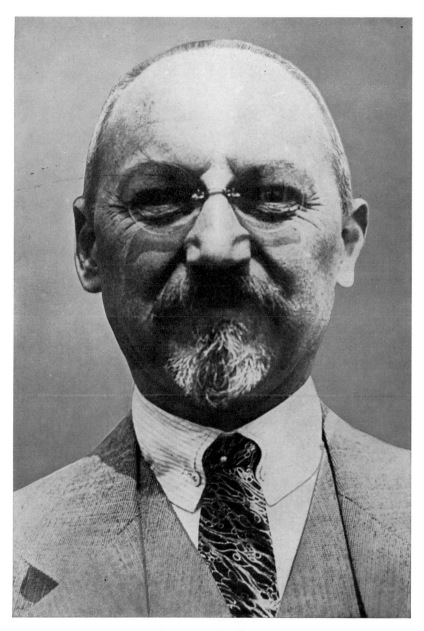

21. Otto Wiedfeldt

Hilmar von dem Bussche-Haddenhausen

22. Wilhelm von Stumm

23. Paul von Hintze

24. The *Deutsche Gesellschaft* in 1914: Gutmann, Rizoff, Solf, Helfferich, Wahnschaffe, Salomonssohn and Johann Albrecht von Mecklenburg.

railways by 'the preponderant share taken by the German troops in the conquest of the country'.

But the core of Germany's war aims in Rumania was possession of or control over Constanta. This was incompatible with Bulgaria's receiving the whole of the Dobruja, and the Foreign Office was therefore at pains to pursue the policy (which Germany had hitherto adopted towards her ally) of holding out to her certain hopes that she might receive the whole area, but avoiding a precise commitment. If, however, the Bulgarians proved obstinate and appealed to the Emperor's promise of December, 1916, so that the cession of the whole Dobruja could not after all be refused, then the Germans hoped at least to have Constanta and the Cernavoda–Constanta line internationalised – in other words, put under German influence, like Salonica.

Since Germany would still need Bulgaria in the future as a link with Turkey and a market for German exports, King Ferdinand's 'land greed' had to be handled very delicately. On the other hand Germany too could bring pressure to bear since the economies of the two countries had been extensively interlocked through officially supported enterprises such as the 'German–Bulgarian Company', of which Prince Ernst Günther of Schleswig-Holstein was President, and through Bulgaria's extensive exports to Germany.[1]

The OHL's Economic Peace Conditions:
Bases and a Colonial Empire

The definition of economic war aims and the questions of colonies and bases had been left aside at the Kreuznach Conference, since the authorities principally involved had not yet reached agreement on them. The OHL took the occasion to re-state the economic peace aims already put forward at the beginning of April; and similarly the Chief of the Naval Staff and the Secretary of State in the Reich Colonial Office again re-stated their programmes, the latter in a public address which differed from the others in its general outlook.

The OHL's memorandum, which was dated May 11, was signed by Hindenburg but drafted by Ludendorff. It began by assuming the

---

[1] Hohenlohe wrote to Czernin on April 18, 1917, that between 1889 and 1911 Germany's exports to Bulgaria rose by 2,000 per cent and her imports from Bulgaria by 2,200 per cent; the rate of growth of Germany's trading figures was far higher than that of Austria's. Germany would 'work consistently after the war for the domination of the Bulgarian market'; Bulgaria was 'necessary and indispensable' as a transit area 'if Germany wished to realise her grandiose plans in the east', which was where she saw 'her real and chief objectives'. See also K. H. Müller, 'Die Unterwerfung Bulgariens unter den deutchen Imperialismus am Vorabend des I. Weltkriges', *Jahrbuch für die Geschichte der USSR und der volksdemokratischen Länder Europas* (Berlin, 1960), pp. 265 ff.

probability of another war in the near future. Germany must anticipate that her enemies, Britain above all, 'will, even after the conclusion of peace, aim at attacking us again, before we have recovered our
strength'. Germany must therefore 'regain her military and economic
power of resistance' as fast as possible, while preventing the recovery
of her enemies. The conditions of peace must be framed so as to
render ineffectual the economic war already launched by Britain
through the blockade and the decisions of the Paris Economic Conference. In anticipation of a second war, the 'fortress of Germany'
must be supplied with foodstuffs and raw materials to last 'at least as
long as the present world war', at least three years, in order to prevent the Reich from again running short of foodstuffs and raw
materials, as in the present war. The importance of fodder, phosphates, cattle, horses and machinery must be absolutely assured in
order to ensure the speedy reconstruction of Germany's industry and
the reorganisation of its agriculture (on which special stress was laid),
both in the old Reich and the 'new German Lands'. Sufficient stocks
of certain raw materials 'not found domestically' were to be accumu-
lated to make Germany independent of imports for three years. The
tonnage of Germany's fleet was declared insufficient for this programme, even if the greatest energy were devoted to enlarging it.
The Peace Treaties must therefore secure new tonnage; the 'occupation' of a substantial part of the enemy's merchant shipping would
alone guarantee that Germany could acquire her supplies quickly,
and would at the same time slow down the enemy's economic recovery. By making the enemy nations dependent for their supplies
exclusively on German or 'German-occupied' bottoms, Germany
could prevent them from sabotaging the reinforcement of 'Fortress
of Germany'. 'Only such an occupation of the enemy tonnage would
enable us to enforce the execution of the Peace Treaties *vis-à-vis* England and America, a security which we already possess *vis-à-vis* our
other enemies in the form of occupied territories.'

In order to achieve these peace conditions, which the OHL described as 'absolutely indispensable' – 'apart from the regulation of
commercial relations through commercial treaties and of the costs of
war through reparations' – Germany must fight on until Britain's
resistance had been broken by the submarine warfare.

The generals produced their programme in time for Bethmann
Hollweg's last Reichstag speech, in which the Chancellor – although
he envisaged post-war developments rather differently – publicly announced his full agreement with the OHL in the matter of war aims.

The good behaviour of Germany's enemies after the war was further to be guaranteed by the system of bases, which was again worked

out by Holtzendorff in May, 1917, on the Emperor's express orders, and submitted to him. Holtzendorff had discussed his proposals with the Secretary of State of the Reich Colonial Office, and was able to tell his master that 'by and large, there was general agreement on principles on the question of bases'. As in his exposés of November and December, 1916, he asked, in the Atlantic, for the Azores or part of them, and Dakar with a sufficient hinterland – the acquisition of Dakar and Senegambia being also necessary as a way of enabling military pressure to be exerted on the spot to prevent France from recruiting black troops from her central African possessions. In the Mediterranean he repeated his demand for Valona; if that was impossible, Germany's allies must be induced to allow her to keep permanent garrisons in Cattaro and Alexandretta. A new demand was for a wireless station in the East Indian Ocean, perhaps in the Portuguese part of Timor (if Germany gave up her East African ports, she must try to obtain a second base there, perhaps Réunion). New Guinea and the Bismarck Archipelago were to be retained, and the Colonial Office recommended acquiring New Caledonia with its deposits of nickel and cobalt. It would be unnecessary to have any military bases in China if the Peace Treaties assured Germany further concessions on the pattern of the existing trading colonies, Tientsin and Hankow; sites suggested were Tsingtao, Wuhu on the Yangtse-Kiang and 'a place in South China, the choice to be dictated by purely commercial considerations'.

While the Kreuznach Programme outlined Germany's demands in Europe, including the coasts of Flanders and Courland, the naval staff's exposé presented a grandiose picture of Germany as a maritime world power. It is true that Bethmann Hollweg, unlike the Emperor, thought it 'premature to go more deeply into the question just now', but he had no objections of principle whatever to such a programme. And these ideas were further pursued after his fall, throughout 1917 and 1918.

A month later Solf expounded Germany's colonial aims in a lecture to the German Colonial Society in Leipzig. What is important here is not the extent of his demands but the fact – which the Austrian diplomats at once realised – that he here 'for the first time presented to the wider public a clearly defined war aim, consisting of the creation of a geographically continuous colonial empire'. The facts that his speech was public, and that it constituted an answer to certain English utterances, explains the relative modesty of his aims compared with the programmes of August, 1914, and December, 1916. Invoking the agreement on the Portuguese colonies initialled by Germany and Britain in June, 1914, he demanded Angola and a part of the Congo (meaning Katanga with its mineral resources) which, he said, Portugal had already once offered to sell. These territories, with German East Africa and Mozambique, would constitute a 'strong Central African colonial empire'. Solf even said that he would be ready, 'provided the plan as a whole succeeds', to cede German South West Africa to the Union of South Africa, because when its diamond fields were exhausted it would be of no further economic use. Germany would also, at a pinch, give up her South Sea colonies.

The key to this speech lies in Solf's view that a general peace of understanding was possible only on the basis of a settlement of the colonial question. This was an attempt – which could certainly not have been made without the Chancellor's consent – to divert part of Germany's attention to Africa, away from the demands for annexations in Europe, especially France and Belgium, and at the same time represented a cautious peace feeler towards Britain. Contrary to Ludendorff's opinion, and also to views repeatedly expressed in public by Bethmann Hollweg, Solf held 'that England had not wanted this war and that a peaceful settlement was possible'. This view of Solf finds no parallel in the general discussion of Germany's war aims. The Chancellor and the Foreign Ministry, and even more the OHL and the War Aims Majority, the great trade associations and public opinion – all demanded European 'safeguards' in east and west and colonial gains as well: in other words, not one or the other, but both. This had just been made clear by the maintenance of Germany's war aims at the conferences of April and May.

Austria-Hungary's Last Remonstration and the Compromise

On June 7 the Emperor Charles sent another urgent letter to Wilhelm II begging strongly that Germany should make an unambiguous declaration that she was ready to accept peace on the basis of the *status quo*. He had received various reports from the Russian front which had satisfied him that Russia would be prepared to cease hostilities on this basis. He reproached his imperial cousin with having provoked a violent reaction in Russia and rekindled her readiness to fight on by the German government's demand for 'substantial territorial extensions in Russia'. He again appealed to the increasingly difficult internal situation of the Monarchy, and said openly:

that the non-Germanic majority . . . in my Monarchy, in particular, is beginning to find it incomprehensible why we do not end the war. So long as the people believed that it was beyond their power to end the war, they accepted that fate; but now they are beginning to see that there is a glimmer of possibility of finishing with Russia, and that it is Germany's demands that have made the elimination of Russia impossible.

He demanded a separate peace with Russia 'at any price', because this would guarantee definitive victory. A separate peace with Russia on the basis of the *status quo* would also bring Italy out of the war, and the Austrian eastern front would be so effectively relieved that German troops could be sent to the west. 'Peace with Russia is the key to the situation. It will bring the war to a speedy and favourable end.' On this sentence Wilhelm II made the revealing marginal minute: 'If we give way!'

It is an open question whether the Russian provisional government, which was at the time under strong political and financial pressure from France, Britain and America, would have considered an unconditional offer of this sort from Germany and Austria, but in any case Germany went only a very little way to meet her ally's request. A few days later she took the occasion of President Wilson's message to the Russian provisional government to make an official declaration, in the form of an inspired article in the *Norddeutsche Allgemeine Zeitung*, to the effect that Germany was ready to make peace with Russia on the basis of renunciation of annexations and indemnities. By this move Germany hoped to clear herself of the reproach that her attitude was making peace with Russia impossible. But Zimmermann instructed the Foreign Ministry explicitly that this 'by no means implied that we renounce our wishes in Courland and Lithuania'.

The announcement was meant at once to pacify Austria and to blunt the edge of Wilson's invective. In anticipation of his answer to the Pope's peace note and of his own Fourteen Points, Wilson had indicted Germany of autocracy and of working by force and intrigue for world domination; and he had sought to avert the danger of Germany and Russia concluding a separate peace by describing Germany's wishes for peace as incompatible with Russian democracy and by contrasting them with his own aims of peace and freedom. Zimmermann counter-attacked: he demanded publication of the secret treaties, which would have proved the crass irreconcilability of the Entente's war aims with Wilson's ideals. The German government was aware that, shortly before, Briand had been forced to admit in a secret session of the French Chamber that France and Britain had promised Russia Constantinople, and that Russia had in return promised France not only Alsace-Lorraine but also the left bank of the Rhine. It further knew that the Entente had drafted a complete

plan for the partition of Asia Minor which had only not been definitively agreed because Italy wanted more territorial booty than Britain and France were prepared to give her. Zimmermann further
declared himself astounded at the change in Wilson, who only a few
months earlier had been prepared to negotiate peace with this same
'autocratic' Germany; he forgot how deeply the German government had disappointed Wilson by proclaiming unrestricted submarine warfare at the very moment when Wilson had undertaken
for the second time an attempt to mediate peace.

If the *Norddeutsche Allgemeine Zeitung* article represented an attempt
to convince world public opinion of Germany's honest desire for
peace, Austria-Hungary now took her ally at her word. On June 18,
a month after the German–Austro-Hungarian Conference, Czernin
very belatedly sent the German government a note setting out his
definitive attitude towards the decisions of the conference, to which
he had previously given only provisional assent subject to the agreement of the Austrian and Hungarian Prime Ministers. He asked for
the economic agreements to be referred to specialist discussion; he
agreed to the political points, subject to two conditions. He obviously
thought that the *N.A.Z.* article, which had been communicated to
him officially, meant that Germany might not be annexing Courland
and Lithuania. If that were so, he said that Austria-Hungary would
be prepared to renounce attaching Rumania fully to the Monarchy,
and would content herself with claiming in Rumania 'that position
and those prerogatives which would accrue to Germany in Poland'.
He further declared specifically that Austria would only be able to
maintain her promised renunciation of a condominium in Poland
and her political and military *désintéressement* in that kingdom if this
concession were kept strictly secret until the end of the war; otherwise she would regard the whole agreement as null and void.

This communication by Czernin was the last attempt of Austrian
diplomacy to persuade Bethmann Hollweg's government to reduce
its claims in the east. It also constituted an attempt to evict Germany
from her position of economic predominance in Rumania, where
Austria-Hungary, while renouncing the direct constitutional link,
hoped to secure for herself all the essential key positions, political and
economic.

Since, however, Germany stood by her war aims, in particular
Courland and Lithuania, the bargain was doomed in advance to
futility. How obstinately Germany stuck to Rumania, as to Poland,
the later plans for exchange were to show.

Thus the possibility of a peace on the basis of the *status quo* remained
as distant as ever. In spite of the Austrians' insistence, Germany was

not prepared to give up her eastern war aims and to reduce her western. Instead the inter-allied negotiations had only led to Germany's confirming her aims in the west and re-formulating them in the east, under the catchword of autonomy, while extending them still further by the proposed detachment of Livonia and Estonia from Russia and the advancement of German economic interests in the Balkans under the protection of the Reich.

13

GERMANY AND THE NEW RUSSIA

THE PROMOTION OF REVOLUTION
AND ATTEMPTS TO MAKE A SEPARATE PEACE

THE news of the outbreak of the Russian revolution reached Berlin in the middle of March. The belief at once obtained that the Russian state had been shaken to its foundations, and the most far-reaching hopes were entertained. A few weeks later (April 19) Ludendorff thought that Russia had been so weakened that he need no longer fear an offensive on that front and could readjust the balance of forces on the western front in Germany's favour by sending troops to it from the east.[1] In contrast to his views at the turn of the year, he now 'regarded the future with the utmost confidence'. This inevitably increased his faith and steeled his will to impose the desired separate peace on Germany's terms. Bethmann Hollweg, for his part, saw in the confusion prevailing in Russia primarily the political possibility of achieving the same end by promoting social and national revolution.

At first these hopes were disappointed. On May 18 the new Lvov–Milyukov government (in which Lvov was only a figurehead, Milyukov, the Foreign Minister, being the driving force) announced that it was carrying on the war at the side of the allies in conformity with the treaty obligations of the Tsarist government, and rejected the idea of a separate peace. This attitude earned the speedy recognition of the Entente Powers, which was even anticipated by the U.S.A.; on March 22 Wilson gave the new Russian democracy a solemn and enthusiastic welcome.[2] The Russian government's attitude, however, did not accord with the feelings of the war-weary Russian people, to whom the war had brought heavy suffering and enormous losses. From the first day of the revolution the Liberal government had on its flanks the Socialist Soviets, who, speaking for the workers and soldiers – most of the latter being peasants – voiced a general longing for peace. The reaction to Milyukov's 'militarist and imperialist foreign policy' was the famous proclamation to the peoples of the

[1] See Werner Hahlweg, *Lenin's Rückkehr nach Russland, 1917* (Leiden, 1957), p. 11.
[2] Kennan, op. cit., pp. 25 ff.

world, issued on March 27 by the Petersburg Soviet, which called (with echoes of Wilson's Senate speech of January 22) for a peace 'without annexations or indemnities' on the basis of the self-determination of the peoples. The effect of this proclamation was so great that the provisional government was forced, on April 4, to declare its agreement with its principles, though the phraseology was admittedly vague and the move was a tactical one to take the wind out of the Soviet's sails.

There were from the first two elements in the Russian revolution – on the one hand, the Liberals and Democrats, who represented chiefly the interests of the propertied middle classes and were therefore satisfied with the introduction of a parliamentary system of government, wished as far as possible to prevent land reform, and wanted to carry on the war with the support of the allies; on the other, the Socialist-Proletarians, who wanted to go further than bourgeois democracy, to combine social with political revolutions, and to bring about a general peace. This division gave the rulers of Germany a welcome chance to step up their programme, both of revolution and of separate peace.

The Despatch of Lenin

In this situation the Germans had two courses open to them. Brockdorff-Rantzau analysed the possibilities acutely. If Germany was not in a position 'to carry on the war to the end of this year with a prospect of success, she must . . . attempt to approach the moderate parties now in power in Russia'. Milyukov and Gutchkov must be convinced 'that if they insist on carrying on the war, they will only be doing England's work for her, smoothing the path for the reaction and thus endangering even what has been gained for liberty'; it should, indeed, be suggested to them that it was quite possible that England might reach an understanding with Germany 'in view of the uncertain situation in Russia'. This course would have meant a radical scaling down of German war aims, for only on that condition, if at all, were peace negotiations with the provisional government conceivable – not to speak of the growing uncertainty whether the moderates would be able to stabilise conditions in Russia without themselves being overthrown. This course should therefore be followed only if Germany was extremely weak. If, however, she was in a position, as the OHL had expressly and repeatedly declared in April, 'militarily and economically, to carry on the war successfully until the autumn', Brockdorff-Rantzau strongly advised the Wilhelmstrasse 'to create the greatest possible chaos in Russia', and especially to support the extremist elements, in Germany's own interest, 'because this would do the work more thoroughly and bring the conclusion sooner'.

To this end, any outwardly discernible intervention in the course of the Russian revolution should be avoided. On the other hand, we should in my view do everything we can secretly to intensify the differences between the moderate and extremist parties, for it is very greatly in our interest that the latter should gain the upper hand, because the upheaval (*Umwälzung*) will then be inevitable and will assume shapes which must shatter the existence of the Russian Empire. . . . We should in all probability be able to count on disintegration proceeding far enough in about three months' time to guarantee that military intervention by us will bring about the collapse of Russian power.

Brockdorff-Rantzau accordingly advised letting Russia's power of resistance disintegrate through the advance of the revolution, without outside intervention; above all, there should be no premature offensive by Germany, for that 'would serve to bring together all the centrifugal forces and perhaps also unite the army in the struggle against Germany'.

Such being his ideas, it was only logical that Brockdorff-Rantzau should send his confidant and revolutionary expert, Parvus Helphand, to Berlin to propose personally to the Chancellor that Lenin should be helped to return to Russia from Switzerland. In Berlin, Helphand was supported by Erzberger and Baron Ago von Maltzan, of the Foreign Ministry.[1] Although Helphand himself belonged to the right wing of the Social Democrats and disagreed with Lenin on questions of revolutionary principle, he believed that the Bolshevik leader, being a much 'wilder fellow' than the two Socialists in the Lvov government, Cheidse and Kerensky, would 'push the latter aside and be ready for peace without delay'.[2]

On April 5 Brockdorff-Rantzau gave Helphand an introduction to Zimmermann, whom he asked 'to receive him kindly', writing: 'because the latest aggravation of the situation in Russia seems to me so important for the final decision on the development of our whole future, as I am convinced, radical decisions have to be taken to ensure us victory at the twelfth hour.'

The idea of sending the Russian revolutionaries home from Switzerland was not, however, Brockdorff-Rantzau's alone, nor did it derive exclusively from Helphand's interview with the Chancellor.

---

[1] Epstein, *Mathias Erzberger*, pp. 168 f.

[2] Hahlweg, op. cit., p. 14, following Scheidemann, *Memoiren eines Sozialdemokraten*, Vol. 1, 1928, pp. 427 f. Hahlweg's work contains full details of Lenin's journey and the negotiations connected with it.

As early as March 23 Romberg, in Berne, had reported that 'outstanding' Russian revolutionaries had been pressing to return to Russia since the outbreak of the February revolution and wanted to travel across Germany, and Zimmermann had consented in principle, subject to the agreement of the OHL which arrived two days later. Zimmermann's words prove that he realised that the main purpose was to send back the left Radicals; he thought they should be allowed passage across Germany 'because it is in our interest that the radical wing should gain the upper hand in Russia'. It is impossible to suppose that the Secretary of State should have taken so momentous a decision without the Chancellor's consent in principle. In fact Bethmann Hollweg, in a report to the Emperor on April 11, claimed as his own work that 'immediately after the outbreak of the Russian revolution' he had set on foot the return of the left-wing groups to Russia. This report throws a revealing light on the position of the Emperor. Perhaps because he was expected – as it turned out, quite wrongly – to object, he was left to learn from the newspapers of the possibilities open to German policy, and was only informed of what was really going on after the first transport of emigrants had already passed through Germany. The despatch of Lenin is to be regarded only as one move, if the most successful one, in Germany's policy of revolution, an integral part of her efforts to achieve her war aims through a separate peace.

How strongly Germany was interested in Lenin's journey is shown by the fact that the German government at once accepted his conditions, with one unimportant exception; it also agreed that he should be accompanied by a party of pro-Entente Mensheviks, even larger than the Bolshevik group, so that the Bolsheviks should not be compromised as German agents.

Lenin was anxious to demonstrate his independence, and he therefore concluded a regular treaty with the German authorities, the main condition which he 'demanded' of them being that the permission for the group to cross Germany should not be made conditional on 'their attitude on the question of war and peace'. The help given by the German authorities to him and his group in connection with their journey and the financial support subsequently given by imperial Germany to the Bolsheviks, before and after the October Revolution, inevitably brought Lenin under suspicion of being a paid agent of Germany.

The co-operation between the German government and Lenin has been regarded as a German–Bolshevik plot.[1] This is a political rather than a historical judgment, and one which reflects the standpoint of

[1] S. T. Possony, *Jahrhundert des Aufruhrs* (Munich, 1956), pp. 449 f.

that 'democracy' which had been made an ideological objective of the enemies of the Central Powers by Wilson's welcome to the Russian revolution and his declaration of war on Germany. It was a policy of interests on both sides that brought monarchist Germany and the leaders of the Russian revolution into their short-lived cooperation. The German government was aiming, not simply at achieving any kind of peace, but at realising its definite and far-reaching objectives in the east. For this purpose the Germans needed Lenin, who had declared the question of peace to be central to his political plans and actions. But Lenin, on his side, used the interest of imperial Germany in him and his party to turn the Russian revolution, which was in danger of being frustrated by a Liberal–Social-Democrat coalition, into a victory for the Bolshevik revolution as the first stage of a world revolution. He made use of the peace slogan to get into power,[1] and he needed peace to bring about and consolidate the revolutionary transformation in Russia. Even in Switzerland he had opposed the provisional government, the Mensheviks and even his own adherents in so far as they supported the continuance of the war. After reaching Petersburg on April 16, where he was welcomed enthusiastically by the workers, he at once intervened in the revolution and pressed for conclusion of peace with the Central Powers. His success was delayed by a consolidation of those forces in Russia which wanted the war to be carried on with the moral and financial help of the Entente powers. Bolshevik *putsches* (attempted by Lenin's adherents against his own will) in May, in June, during the First All-Russian Council of Soviets, and finally on July 4 after the failure of the Kerensky offensive, were unsuccessful; their authors failed to turn street demonstrations into a popular upheaval, or to drive the Executive Committee of the Soviets into action against the provisional government. Lenin had to flee. Only after months of agitation did he succeed in gaining a majority in the Soviet of the capital and organising an armed upheaval. In spite of their reverses the Bolsheviks, like the separatist nationalities, enjoyed continuous support from Germany. Thus Zimmermann's successor, Kühlmann, was able to write on December 3, looking back on the successful October Revolution:

It was only the resources which the Bolsheviks received regularly from our side, through various channels and on various pretexts, that enabled them to develop their chief organ *Pravda*, to carry on a lively agitation, and greatly to expand the originally narrow basis of their party.

[1] Cf. Georg von Rauch, *Die Grundlegung des Sowjetsystems* (Göttingen, 1957), pp. 50 ff.; also Erwin Hölzle, *Lenin 1917, Die Geburt der Revolution aus dem Kriege* (Munich, 1957), pp. 10 ff.

This deliberate support of the radical revolutionaries shows how determined Germany was to persist in her war aims, however they had to be modified. Monarchist Germany's share in the October Revolution reveals the secular explosive force of Germany's will to power, which not only sought radically to transform the previous form of the Russian state, but did not even shrink from pulling down the existing social order at one point in the enemy world.

The revolution had also re-activated the national question in Russia, and Germany at once reinforced her agitation in this field. Zimmermann, for example, asked the Finnish delegation in Stockholm as early as March 15 'to make the present situation in Russia the occasion of *immediate* energetic action'. 'The moment for the proclamation of Finnish independence seemed to have arrived.' The Stockholm Finns, however, who were wavering between looking to Sweden or to Germany for support, preferred to wait and see how the Russian revolution developed, so as not to 'compromise themselves'. Zimmermann criticised their hesitations sharply. Finland, he said, 'had every interest in heightening the current confusion in Russia by energetic action'.[1]

Towards a Separate Peace with Russia

In the spring of 1917 Germany still felt herself strong enough to reject obstinately both Wilson's attempt to mediate a peace 'without victory' and also Russia's proposal for peace 'without annexations or indemnities', and to pursue instead a separate peace embodying exclusively Germany's own terms. Even if the bourgeois forces in Russia, and perhaps Kerensky personally, rejected a general peace on such a basis as incompatible with their own war aims, and a separate peace with Germany as contrary to their pro-Entente orientation, yet on the left there were, besides the Bolsheviks, other big groups which might be considered as possible peace partners. Considerable fractions of the Social Revolutionaries and the Mensheviks, who rejected Lenin's internal political programme and whose foreign political leanings were towards the west, were entirely ready to take action in favour of a general peace and to put pressure on the western powers, perhaps to the extent of threatening a separate peace. They were not ready for peace at any price, for the pre-condition for any peace approach laid down by the Russian non-Bolshevik left was a categorical declaration from Germany renouncing all annexations and indemnities.

[1] On this, besides the archival material, see C. Jay Smith, Jr., *Finland and the Russian Revolution 1917–1922* (Athens (Georgia), 1958), pp. 11 ff. Germany's promise, given in June and July, to supply arms to the Finnish underground army (Skyddskar) was honoured in October.

The Germans were well informed of this attitude. Before the second transport, comprising some 250 émigrés, left Switzerland to cross Germany in the middle of May, representatives of the groups concerned discussed the situation with the utmost frankness with German and Austro-Hungarian diplomats in Switzerland. Even if, as Bethmann Hollweg pleaded in his memoirs,[1] 'the practical value' of such a declaration by the German government 'would have been extremely dubious . . . in view of the general tendencies of the Russian government and its complete dependence on the West', yet an official renunciation of annexations and indemnities, made by Germany to these groups, would have created the first real possibility of achieving peace – quite apart from the fact that it was the only way to lend plausibility to Germany's thesis that her war was one of 'self-defence'. The indispensable condition for such a declaration would, however, have been the abandonment of Germany's war aims and, as at the turn of 1916–17, official Germany was by no means ready for such a decision.

The disputes within Germany over a Hindenburg or a Scheidemann peace and the rejection of Austria's appeal for peace – both of which took place under the impact of the Russian revolution – show what powerful forces were marshalled in Germany against any far-reaching revision of Germany's war aims, and how successful they had been, in the struggle between Vienna and Berlin over a separate peace with Russia on the basis of the *status quo*, in forcing the Chancellor – if indeed force was needed – to follow their line. While the German government was letting Lenin and his associates travel through Germany to Russia, and while it was defeating Czernin's and the Emperor Charles' desperate endeavours to make a separate peace with Russia on the basis of the *status quo*, it was trying at the same time to start conversations on a separate peace alike with the provisional government, the Russian armies or representatives of the Petersburg Soviet – always on Germany's own terms. In all the contacts attempted between March and June, 1917, the continuity of Germany's war aims appears with crushing monotony.

Thus the question of annexations figured centrally in the first, tentative conversations which took place a fortnight after the outbreak of the revolution. The Russian Councillor of State, Joseph von Kolyshko, who was married to a German wife and had been living in Stockholm since the beginning of the war and writing for the Liberal press, had asked Erzberger for a meeting at the beginning of March, before the outbreak of the revolution. Meanwhile the provi-

[1] *Betrachtungen*, p. 61.

sional government had invited him to return at once and had offered him a post in the government as Secretary of State. Before leaving he again invited Erzberger to meet him in Stockholm. Erzberger, who had just been visiting General Hoffmann at *Oberost* and receiving from him an unvarnished picture of the military situation,[1] accepted the invitation with Bethmann Hollweg's consent. He had prolonged conversations with Kolyshko on March 26, 27 and 28, in the Stockholm flat of a Polish industrialist named Gurewicz. He reported on the 27th to the Chancellor, who was preparing a speech to the Reichstag on the latest events for the 29th. It had seemed to Erzberger, after his talks with Kolyshko, that this speech would offer Bethmann Hollweg his great chance to do something for peace. As Bismarck in 1866 had imposed political moderation against the will of the king and the army, thereby—and thereby alone—making possible the foundation of the Empire in 1871 and the alliance with Austria in 1879, so Bethmann Hollweg now had the choice between two courses: he could offer moderate conditions for an honourable peace, thus initiating good relations with the new Russia, or he could put forward exaggerated demands which would make her a deadly enemy. There was no third course, for any talk of destroying Russia as a political and military great power was simply Utopian.[2]

Kolyshko wanted peace with Germany because he regarded the question of peace as decisive for the internal political development of Russia. If there was no peace, he warned Erzberger, the left would overthrow the Liberal government, and that meant chaos. He therefore tried to bid up the value of a peace with the Liberal government by saying that it was by no means certain whether a Socialist government would get itself accepted everywhere in Russia. More likely, the war would 'peter out' in general anarchy, leaving the Germans with no partner at all with whom to conclude peace. With what was certainly an excess of optimism, he maintained that the Liberal government was ready to conclude peace, and that Germany had it in her sole power to bring peace about. He insisted strongly that the peace movement already existing in Russia could be strengthened if the Chancellor were to address himself as soon as possible to the Russian people. He named three concrete assurances which would strengthen the will for peace. Erzberger passed these on and they actually appeared in Bethmann Hollweg's speech of the 29th. They were:

(i) Germany was not interfering in Russia's internal affairs, i.e.,

[1] Epstein, op. cit., pp. 164 f.
[2] Id., p. 116.

as Bethmann Hollweg put it in plain words, Germany would make no attempt to restore the Tsarist regime.

(ii) Germany was not waging war against the Russian people as such.

(iii) Germany was not asking Russia to accept a dishonourable peace (Kolyshko had expressly described this assurance as essential for any approach to the Russian army).

Bethmann Hollweg included these points in his speech, but in the single sentence in which he touched on conditions of peace he spoke ambiguously of a peace 'on a basis honourable for all parties'. 'Honourable' was a very elastic term, and how the Germans understood it at once became clear when Erzberger and Kolyshko began discussing concrete terms. The Russian said that his most important condition was 'no big annexations'; only 'frontier rectifications' could be accepted. Erzberger reported that Kolyshko viewed such frontier rectifications 'by Russian standards' which in current German terms could still, as Erzberger said himself, comprise 'considerable areas'. Kolyshko objected to the cession of Vilna or the *whole* of Lithuania, the *whole* of Courland, or the *whole* of Poland. The annexation of parts of these areas seemed therefore not to be excluded. The two men arranged to meet again in Stockholm on April 20, after Kolyshko's return from Petersburg.[1]

On April 9, meanwhile, the provisional government had, mainly for reasons of internal policy, published a declaration in which some of the slogans from the Proclamation of the Workers' and Soldiers' Soviets of March 27 were drowned by affirmations of firm determination to restore and maintain the nation's will to resist. Nevertheless, when the Germans read it on April 12, they thought that they could read into it an encouraging answer to the Chancellor's speech of March 29. The busy Erzberger at once went into action.[2] The very same day he conferred successively with Bethmann Hollweg, Helfferich, Zimmermann and Stumm on the question whether and in what form the German government should reply to the Russian declaration without showing too much eagerness. Erzberger wanted an open letter from the Emperor to the Chancellor, which would strengthen the position of both men in the public eye. The letter should welcome Russia's wish for peace and empower the Chancellor to open negotiations. In this connection the Chancellor had proposed to the Emperor an open telegram to King Ferdinand of Bulgaria and

---

[1] Kolyshko refused to negotiate with other Germans, especially not with Stinnes, who had repeatedly visited him and had offered him 15 millions to found Russian newspapers.

[2] Epstein, op. cit., pp. 167 f.

a public statement to be issued by the Emperor himself. The reasons given by Wilhelm II personally for rejecting this suggestion are most characteristic for the problem of war and peace aims:

> If we answer the last manifesto of the Russian government with so solemn a declaration, we are committing ourselves and running the risk of Russia's replying that she, too, is ready for peace, but on condition that we renounce any acquisition of territory. Then we should have to reject the Russian offer, which would put us in a very much more difficult position, abroad and at home, than if we do not for the present react officially at all to Russia's tones of peace.

The Emperor gave orders that, instead, the threads were to be spun further, unofficially and through the press. Ludendorff supported the view of his imperial master. The Emperor's order to the man responsible for the policy of the Reich, in no case to allow Germany to abandon her war aims by committing herself to the principle of a peace without annexations, shows most exactly the connection between Germany's war aims policy and the question of peace, and again confirms the primacy of war aims in the German mind. At the same time, the monarch's intervention shows that in spite of his notorious aversion (of which Admiral Müller's diaries provide shattering evidence) from hard work and responsibility, he was entirely capable of taking important decisions in moments of crisis.

With the full agreement of Bethmann Hollweg and Zimmermann, Erzberger met Kolyshko again, as arranged, on April 19 and 20, having in the meantime helped Helphand to send Lenin to Russia. These further negotiations in Stockholm were marked by the unrealistic optimism of both parties regarding their own importance and the feasibility of their own wishes. Furthermore, Kolyshko took the Chancellor's speech and what he called the 'world-historical' declaration in the *Norddeutsche Allgemeine Zeitung* of April 15 at its face value. Nevertheless, he remarked to Erzberger on the strong discrepancy between the official utterances of the government and the meagre support given them by the German public. On the other hand he had to admit that 'feeling was still undecided' in the struggle going on in Russia between the war and peace parties, chiefly owing to the massive counter-influences of Britain, the Entente Socialists and Plekhanov. To counter these, he recommended buying the Petersburg Workers' and Soldiers' Council with cash. He welcomed Lenin's arrival in Russia.

At Erzberger's request, Kolyshko agreed to go back to Petersburg in a few days, but thought it unlikely that his peace efforts would have any success unless he could take back something more definite on Germany's conditions than the very general declaration in the

373

N.A.Z. The first condition, he said, was an armistice on the whole eastern front. Erzberger's instructions were to let the Russian do the talking. Doubtless in the hope of advancing the conclusion of peace substantially, he seized the opportunity and at once worked out, with Kolyshko, the draft text of an armistice and the bases of 'a lasting peace, honourable for both parties'. Both men promised to try to persuade their governments to accept peace on this basis.

The first paragraph, which is basic, formally recognised the principle of peace without annexations: 'Russia's frontier of August 1, 1914, is restored; the possibility of frontier rectifications is, however, expressly reserved.' German war aims figure under the familiar designation of 'frontier rectifications'. Even if one failed to recognise the war aims policy pursued by Germany since 1914 under the headings 'frontier strip', 'frontier rectifications', etc., Erzberger's commentary on this paragraph would suffice to show what were the bases of Germany's policy towards Russia in 1917:

> On 'frontier rectifications', the early conversations of March have already shown that this term is to be interpreted by Russian standards. The word 'annexation' is not to be mentioned, even if a frontier rectification amounts to an annexation. Given good negotiations, Germany's wishes can be satisfied in the most far-reaching measure. J. v. K. asked for a statement that Russia, too, would receive frontier rectification. I explained to him that it was not necessary to put that in writing, since the text spoke of frontier rectifications, in the plural.

Point (ii) assumed as a fact the new Polish state, whose frontiers were to be fixed by Russia, Germany and Austria-Hungary jointly. A plebiscite, to be held not later than June, 1917, was to determine 'whether Poland should be constituted under Russian sovereignty or as a free republic or a hereditary monarchy'; Erzberger, the Catholic, explained in his notes that he was sure that, with the help of the Polish clergy, 'a result favourable to Germany was absolutely certain'.

One remnant of Russia's aspiration survived in Point (iii): 'Russia agrees to the abolition of the Capitulations in Turkey, while Germany, on her side, promises her good offices over the regulation of the question of the Dardanelles and of Armenia.'

Points (iv) to (ix) dealt with private legal relationships, a commercial treaty and provisions, reminiscent of Wilson's principles for international arbitration. Point (vi), which spoke of the mutual renunciation of indemnification for war costs, is important. Russia's road to a separate peace was smoothed by a declaration (Point (x)) that Germany was prepared at any moment desired by Russia to conclude an armistice with the other belligerent powers preparatory to the conclusion of a general peace. Instruments of ratification were to be exchanged within four weeks, by May 18 at the latest.

Erzberger returned to Berlin in high spirits on the morning of April 21 and was at once received in the Foreign Ministry by Bergen and Zimmermann. Both were delighted with the results of his journey to Stockholm, for they were still under the shattering effects of Czernin's memorandum and therefore interested in an early peace. How deeply they were disquieted by Czernin's picture of the situation is shown by the fact that they gave his memorandum to Erzberger to read that same day.

Again on the same day, Erzberger talked to the Chancellor, who also signified his approval of the Erzberger-Kolyshko agreement but wanted closer definition of the 'frontier rectifications'.[1]

The Genesis of the 'Autonomy' Policy

Wishing to save as much as possible of Germany's aims, but forced to pay consideration to the Russians' national susceptibilities, Bethmann Hollweg reshaped the agreement between Erzberger and Kolyshko in his own fashion, trying to find a way round both the partial annexations as devised by Erzberger (which were too small for the OHL) and total annexation (which seemed unacceptable to Russia). Both his own policy of annexation in Lithuania and Courland, followed by him at least since the autumn of 1915 and expressed most recently and most specifically at the two conferences of February 13 and March 31, 1917, and also the massive demands of the OHL for the 'acquisition, come what may' of the whole of Courland and Lithuania, forced him to seek a middle road going beyond Erzberger's proposals and acceptable to the military.

He worked out his proposed solution at a secret meeting with the innermost ring of the Prussian Ministry of State on that very same evening of April 21. This meeting took place, after the routine meeting of the Ministry of State, under Bethmann Hollweg's chairmanship, and the only other persons present were the Vice-Chancellor, Helfferich, the Ministers of State Breitenbach (Public Works), Schorlemer (Agriculture, State Lands and Forestry), and Loebell (Interior), Under-Secretary of State Heinrichs, and Wahnschaffe to take the minutes. Surveying the general situation, the Chancellor said that Germany must, if possible, conclude peace with Russia, for in spite of the successes of submarine warfare general victory was not 'in the bag'. The Russian revolution had, however, created an

[1] Id., p. 172. Erzberger made notes of this interview on the day it took place. His statement that the Foreign Ministry received his proposals favourably cannot therefore be coloured retrospectively by his disavowal by the Emperor and the OHL.

entirely new situation; above all, it had made the old-style annexationist policy impossible. Even should 'frontier rectifications measured by Russian standards' prove possible, they would still turn out smaller than the OHL imagined. Schorlemer proposed giving Lithuania and Courland a form of autonomy compatible with the new formulae of the Russian revolution which would make them economically profitable to Germany, and Loebell supported the idea of autonomy, pointing out the necessity of securing land for settlement. Helfferich too took up the idea, saying that he was in favour of a 'middle road' and advocating autonomy for Poland, Lithuania, and – here he went further than Schorlemer – all the Baltic provinces, Courland, Livonia and Estonia. These autonomous areas should be free of Russian troops, associated economically with Germany, provided with guarantees for their native German populations and opened for settlement to the Germans of Inner Russia. Bethmann Hollweg agreed with Helfferich's programme; he thought it would be possible to proclaim autonomy the moment chaos broke out in Russia. He summed up his 'middle way' in the formula: 'annexation only of what is militarily necessary, and beyond this a non-military autonomous belt.'

This new idea of limited direct annexation and 'autonomy' under German influence for a wider area farther east meant applying to the north-east the policy already initiated towards Poland. Thus Lithuania and Courland too were to be divided into a relatively narrow frontier strip and two areas under indirect control. The idea of a policy of border states, already mooted in 1914, thus assumed concrete form. The idea of autonomy for Poland (beyond the 'Frontier Strip') had been current since the beginning of the war, since the whole of Poland had been thought 'more than Germany could digest', but the leaders of Germany had at first thought it possible to assimilate the whole or almost the whole of Lithuania and Courland, and had only been forced by the Russian revolution to renounce the policy of annexation for the greater part of these territories and to adapt themselves to the new conditions.

With this new idea in mind Bethmann Hollweg went two days later to the Kreuznach conference, but apparently did not yet submit it to discussion with the generals. Although Bethmann doubted the wisdom of a rigidly annexationist programme his own 'autonomy' plan was merely more flexible and expedient. The traditional picture of a difference of principle between Bethmann Hollweg and Ludendorff, between political and military thinking, between moderate, non-annexationist war aims and unlimited, annexationist ones, is reduced in the end to divergences over the forms by which Ger-

many's domination should be exercised. Hindenburg and Ludendorff, in wanting the annexation of the coveted areas in Courland and
Lithuania, and perhaps also in the other Baltic provinces, represented
the unbroken continuity of the purely annexationist line which had
undoubtedly held the field in German official planning up to the
spring of 1917. Bethmann Hollweg, however, also represented a
continuity of German war aims since the autumn of 1914; all he
could do now was to make concessions of form to the forces in world
politics which had been emanating from America and the new Russia
since the spring of 1917 by disguising a part of the previous annexation
policy under the mask of 'autonomy'. Such considerations also
accorded completely with Bethmann Hollweg's own ideas and with
the policy actually followed by him in Belgium and Poland, where
he had first developed the combination of limited direct annexations
with indirect control through 'guarantees' with internal 'autonomy'.
In conformity with the programme of April 21, he issued on May 7 his
'touching-up order' to German negotiators engaged in any conversations for a separate peace with Russian plenipotentiaries; the triad
of military, economic and political links with Germany, familiar
from the cases of Poland, Belgium and Mitteleuropa, reappeared in
the plans for Courland and Lithuania.[1] The military only took over
his autonomy programme later.

The differences between the political and military leaders at the
Kreuznach conference were only of degree. Incomparably more violent were the disputes on the form which the association was to take.
Hindenburg demanded on April 20 that Russia should 'be told at
once what we want'; i.e., Germany should demand unquivocally the
annexation of the whole of Courland and Lithuania, Russia being
possibly allowed parts of East Galicia and the Bukovina as compensation. This suggestion was based on a report from Ludendorff that,
in the course of conversations at the front, the Russians had mentioned among other conditions that 'if Germany demands Courland,
Russia will ask for the Bukovina and East Galicia'.[2] The military
thus believed that they could impose their programme quite openly,
while the more diplomatic Bethmann Hollweg feared devastating
reactions abroad, especially in Russia and in Austria, which had
already refused to pay the price for her German ally's gains in the
east.

After the political leaders and the OHL had again agreed at

[1] See below, pp. 457 ff.

[2] The other conditions were: (1) Russia desires no territorial acquisitions;
(2) Poland to be independent; (3) Serbia and Belgium to be restored; (4) Russia
retains North Moldavia and otherwise leaves Rumania alone. Austria can be
compensated in Serbia and Wallachia.

Kreuznach to reject the *status quo*, the military could not but feel that they had been badly duped when they learned the next day through Admiral Müller and Grünau of the draft agreements worked out by Erzberger and Kolyshko. The recognition in principle of the *status quo* for Russia expressed in these documents reawakened and seemed to confirm all their suspicions of Bethmann Hollweg's 'weakness'. The consequent mood at General Headquarters was therefore one of 'heavy thunderclouds along the whole line, with periodical discharges of lightning', as Grünau described it picturesquely to the Foreign Ministry. In their indignation they concealed from the Emperor – *mala fide*, Grünau thought – Erzberger's commentary on the paragraphs relating to frontiers, and gave him the impression that these really related only to frontier rectifications in the usual sense of the term, and not to disguise annexations. The Emperor was furious; Grünau had the greatest difficulty in explaining to him at table 'what was meant by "frontier rectifications by Russian standards"' and in getting him to understand that this was not a regular draft treaty at all, but only a written note of what Kolyshko thought might constitute a possible basis for getting his friends to initiate a peace move.[1] Wilhelm's and his generals' excitement did not die down, although meanwhile Zimmermann had disavowed Erzberger by saying that he had been authorised only to listen to what the Russian said and not to make proposals. Erzberger had been sent to Stockholm only in the hope of learning from Kolyshko, 'who claims to have close contacts with Kerensky ... something about Kerensky's wishes, without committing ourselves, and to prevent him ... from using the German Socialists as middlemen'. He could not regard the conversation between Kolyshko and Erzberger 'as constituting a serious approach or offer from the enemy'.

In spite of the Foreign Ministry's repudiation of Erzberger, Bethmann Hollweg had to submit to a burst of unbridled rage from the Emperor on account of this enterprise. Wilhelm was particularly enraged by Hindenburg's report that Erzberger had 'without authorisation' communicated his report to the armies, together with the conditions – which Wilhelm described as 'impossible and hairraising, both from the military and the political point of view'. He told the Foreign Ministry that in future its agents must be furnished with 'absolutely binding instructions' approved by himself. His greatest anxiety, now as two weeks earlier, was that the Russians might accept some such unauthorised proposals, and that he, the Emperor, would be forced to disavow his agents. The same rules

[1] Müller, op. cit., p. 280 (completely borne out by the archives).

must apply to peace feelers by the Foreign Ministry as to the propaganda in the trenches. Any German offer, he wrote, signing himself 'Wilhelm, R.I.', 'must follow the lines laid down here under My Presidency' at the Kreuznach conference of April 23.

Peace Feelers at the Front

The Emperor's rude telegram to the Imperial Chancellor had referred to the peace propaganda in the trenches. In fact, from the first days of the Russian revolution, the OHL had been distributing leaflets, approved by the Foreign Ministry, calling on the enemy to cease hostilities. These leaflets told the Russian soldiers that they were being misused as tools of the English warmongers. When various more or less self-appointed Russian negotiators appeared at the front, the Foreign Ministry issued on April 9 instructions, signed by Zimmermann, laying down the basic line to be followed in propaganda and negotiations on the fronts. The German soldiers were to hammer into the Russians' heads that the entire blame for the war and for the failure of all peace negotiations lay with the old Russian regime. Germany had no idea whatever of restoring the Tsarist system and 'was prepared at any time to give Russia an honourable peace'. With this formula the OHL and the Foreign Ministry adopted the basis for peace suggested by Kolyshko and Erzberger, and by him to the Chancellor. If, however, the Russian negotiators at the front wanted to leave the official peace negotiations to their government in Petersburg, the latter was to be branded as a 'tool of England' and there-fore not acceptable to the Germans as a negotiating party. On the other hand, Germany was prepared at any moment to negotiate for peace with representatives of the Russian army.

Zimmermann's intention in these manoeuvres was, as he himself said, 'to enhance the general confusion in Russia', i.e., as far as possible to embroil the army with the Petersburg government. If they were thus brought into conflict, Germany would have eliminated both army and government as power-factors and would have facilitated the passage of her own plans. Here, again, accents of peace were serving war aims.

The necessity of having concrete conditions to give to the Russian negotiators at the front led to the production, on April 29, 1917, of a Five Point Order by Ludendorff, which again was completely approved by Zimmermann. It was meant to be handed to the Russians at the front. Besides (1) demanding an armistice of three to four weeks and (2) repeating the promise of non-intervention in Russian internal affairs and (3) the offer of good offices over the Dardanelles and extra-European questions 'if Russia renounced the conquest of

Constantinople', it contained two further points, which stated Germany's territorial demands in very innocent language:

4. Financial assistance in the reconstruction of Russia and active economic participation; no war indemnity, but frontier rectifications, so far as Germany is concerned consisting of Lithuania and Courland.
5. Poland to become a state.

It is noteworthy that the words 'frontier rectification', which Erzberger had just been scolded for using, were here adopted as a mask behind which to hide Germany's intentions on Courland and Lithuania. Zimmermann had been just as indefinite and cautious on the previous day in talking to the Majority Socialist, David, who had again asked the government to consent to a peace 'without war indemnities or reparations'. Zimmermann had taken shelter behind the old formula of 'a fair, good and honourable peace' and had said that he was expecting 'a fair offer from the Russian side'.

On the 29th Ludendorff again came out strongly, as he had ten days earlier, in favour of the idea of inducing Russia to cede Courland and Lithuania by leaving her part of East Galicia, which was then occupied by her troops.[1] On May 6 he demanded categorically that the Chancellor's forthcoming Reichstag speech should contain nothing incompatible with this line. The Secretary of State hastened to assure the general that the civilian authorities were completely of one mind with him. 'The Chancellor entirely shares the opinion of General Ludendorff, as I do myself'; the Chancellor would appear personally at General Headquarters and agree with Ludendorff on the substance of his Reichstag declaration.

Before the Chancellor made his declaration on May 15 for all the world to hear, one more tangible possibility of peace seemed to present itself to Germany. In the course of conversations at the front, which had been going on for weeks, two Russian spokesmen suggested on May 7 that while Cheidse, the Chairman of the Petersburg Soviet of Workers and Soldiers, who had Menshevik sympathies, could not be spared, his first deputy, Stecklov, might be available for peace talks. They therefore asked that the German participants in any further talks should likewise include a 'party comrade'. At the same time, however, it was made entirely plain to the Germans that any possibility of peace depended on the honouring of the published renunciation of annexations.

When asked how our propaganda principles (of April 29) had been received, deputies answered that they could not accept annexations by Ger-

---

[1] In Rumania, Ludendorff wanted the dynasty replaced and the country 'chained to Austria-Hungary and Germany by an alliance'.

many. If Germans accepted this condition, Russians would not feel bound to consider the Entente, but would conclude a separate peace.

Even express references by the German Intelligence Officer conducting the conversations to the large amount of Russian territory under German occupation, and the large number of Russian prisoners of war, the surplus of which (over German prisoners in Russia) the Russians had offered to ransom for cash, could not induce the Russian negotiators 'to abandon the standpoint, expressed by them at the outset, of no annexations by us'. When the question of 'a general Peace Conference' came up, the Germans said that 'that would be for the Russians to arrange'. The Germans wanted to make the question of war guilt a central one, but the Russians were quite uninterested in this: 'the one, burning question for the whole country was the speedy conclusion of peace'.

Ludendorff at once took up the Russians' offer in spite of their fundamental reservation, and asked the Foreign Ministry to send two parliamentarians, one 'reliable' Social Democrat and one representative of the 'national' parties. To head the negotiations, which were to begin by arranging an armistice, he proposed Colonel von Winterfeld, formerly Military Attaché in Paris and now Quartermaster General in Mitau, to whom he suggested that the Foreign Ministry should attach a junior diplomat. Bethmann Hollweg had proposed 'to consider attaching Lithuania and Courland [to Germany] under a Prince of their own'; he wanted to discuss this first with *Oberost*, and agreed 'to replace the term "annexation" by "frontier rectification"'.[1]

The government found this message so exciting and promising that it answered the same day in a telegram drafted personally by Zimmermann and checked by Bethmann Hollweg. The Chancellor saw a possibility of official negotiations and had the minister, Friedrich von Rosen, attached to Colonel von Winterfeld. For the 'reliable' Social Democrat he nominated David, 'who is reasonable on the question of frontier rectifications against Russia'. He wanted a clause on trade relationships added to the programme previously arranged, perhaps in the form of a provision that the existing German–Russian commercial treaty (which was greatly disliked by the Russians) should remain in force, not subject to denunciation, until the conclusion of a new one. But the most important passage in the telegram was that in which the Chancellor dealt with the Russians' insistence on the renunciation of annexations, as a pre-condition to any peace negotiations. To get round this difficulty, Bethmann

[1] Only a fortnight earlier the Emperor and the Generals had objected indignantly to the use of the word 'attachment' (*Angliederung*).

Hollweg gave instructions which were not indeed to be realised until Brest-Litovsk:

> To avoid using the word 'annexations' or 'frontier rectifications', which they also dislike, I think it worth considering the idea already put forward by me, in order to make the renunciation of Courland and Lithuania palatable to the Russians, of dressing them up as independent states, leaving them their own, autonomous internal administration but attaching them to us militarily, politically and economically.

This sentence contains the whole programme for 1917 for policy in the north-east. Ludendorff agreed the same day to the proposed formula for disguising Germany's demands for annexations, but asked the Chancellor, 'at *Oberost*'s request, not to send the gentlemen to Mitau, but to let them come first to H.Q. *Oberost* in Brest-Litovsk to talk things over', meaning presumably, to be given Ludendorff's ideas on what to say at the negotiations.

The Austrians were told in quite general terms that a delegation would be going to the Commander-in-Chief on the Eastern Front 'to discuss there how an armistice with the Russians could be arranged'. Germany's ally was told nothing of her terms. These terms for the anticipated negotiations had been re-formulated by Ludendorff on May 12 on the basis of his and Zimmermann's 'Principles' of April 29 and sent to Zimmermann for approval. The Foreign Ministry agreed almost completely with Ludendorff's suggestions, as we see if we compare Ludendorff's text with Zimmermann's version when he transmitted these conditions for peace with Russia to the ambassador in Constantinople.

Both versions promised non-intervention in Russia's internal affairs. Both promised good offices over the settlement of the Straits and other extra-European questions, 'if Russia renounces the conquest of Constantinople'. Both stated that the Central Powers were prepared to negotiate with Russia's allies 'if Russia undertakes the role of mediator'. The Foreign Ministry further stressed 'close economic and financial relations'. Both asked for 'no war indemnity, but monetary compensation for the keep of prisoners of war', which would have meant a financial settlement favourable to Germany. The only difference was the way in which the territorial claims were put. Ludendorff's wording was:

> Attachment of Lithuania and Courland to Germany. It is our intention to show far-reaching respect for the national (*völkisch*) claims of the Lithuanians and Courlanders in the way in which their association is effected.

> Independence of Poland. Determination of the frontier between Lithuania and Poland in accordance with military requirements. It is assumed that England will not set foot in Oesel, Dagoe or Livonia.

Zimmermann put it:

> Attachment of areas of Lithuania and Courland to Germany in form of frontier rectifications, with allowance for their national claims.
>
> Independence of Poland. England not to establish herself in Livonia or the islands off her coast.

The seemingly more modest, but in reality only more elastic, formula chosen by the Foreign Ministry – 'attachment of areas . . .' – becomes less important when one remembers that Bethmann Hollweg had been talking to Ludendorff at the same time of 'renunciation' (unqualified) by the Russians of Courland and Lithuania, and of the 'attachment' of those countries. The Foreign Ministry's omission of the sentence on the 'determination of the frontier between Lithuania and Poland . . .' was only made in order to keep a free hand in the dispute going on inside Germany on the allocation of the districts disputed between Poland and Lithuania.[1]

The hoped-for armistice and peace negotiations did not materialise, because Stecklov, on whose personality and position the Foreign Ministry had just succeeded in informing itself, did not appear at the rendezvous. The preparations made for these negotiations are, however, of importance for the appreciation of Germany's eastern war aims in May, 1917.

What was going on at that time in Russia, what were the potentialities, is still not clear and perhaps never will be. It is, however, plain that the question of peace, and with it the question of Germany's annexationist demands, was in the foreground of the internal Russian disputes.

The impact of the despatch of Lenin and of the money spent by Germany to oppose the policy of the provisional government is perceptible.[2] Propaganda directed by Germany was helping to 'inflame the anti-English feelings of the masses' and to strengthen the longing for peace. So much is shown by a report to the Foreign Ministry from Petersburg dated May 10:

> Agitation for separate peace gaining the upper hand. . . . The propaganda has been carried into the streets. . . . On Sunday vast masses gathered there [sc., in the Petrogradskaja-Storona quarter]. The war is the sole topic of discussion. As means to agitate against war agitators talk against England.

---

[1] A little later, when the peace feelers towards Russia were under discussion, Ludendorff, in the presence of Lucius, insisted that 'on grounds of military necessity' the frontiers must coincide exactly with those submitted by the OHL to the Chancellor on December 23, 1916 (above, p. 316 ff.) and shortly before reconfirmed at the Kreuznach Conference (above, pp. 348–9).

[2] The Chancellor received proposals to spend 300–400 million marks on getting a separate peace with Russia.

England is represented as our real enemy. . . . Calls for treason.[1] . . . Defenders of England isolated individuals, whereas accusers of England are an organised society working on a definite plan. Whether German agitators are among them it is hard to say. In any case, the character of this agitation is pro-German.

About the same time the Foreign Ministry instructed Lucius in Stockholm and Romberg in Berne 'to agitate' through middle-men, especially among the émigrés returning to Russia, for the publication of the military and political agreements concluded by the Tsarist regime with France and Britain before and during the war. Publication in fact took place, although only after the October Revolution, when Trotsky arranged for it. Other reports still further encouraged German expectations of chaos in Russia, so that concessions were not thought necessary; Jansson, for example, a member of the General Committee of the German Trade Unions, who had made a vain attempt to get a word with Lenin during his journey across Germany, reported from Stockholm that Russia was in chaos and that communications, administration and supplies had broken down. 'The general position is as favourable for us as we could wish. . . . The process of disintegration has gone so far that the curve is bound to change.' He therefore advised waiting for the peak point, in any case allowing the Soviet peace offensive to work itself out, and, if possible, postponing the Chancellor's speech for a few days, 'for as things stand'—meaning, given the attitude of the OHL and of the forces behind it—'what he said could hardly finally paralyse the agitation of the Ententists'. This could have been achieved only by a German renunciation of annexations in the east which the Chancellor was either not willing or not able to pronounce.

In these days the Chancellor was pressed from the most various quarters to make a declaration which would paralyse the agitation of the Entente. For example, the Social Democrat, Adolf Müller, who was also working for the German government, sent him a message from Berne through Romberg that 'the whole world is awaiting Your Excellency's declaration on May 15; the decision of the war will depend on it'. Conscientious enquiries had led him to the bitter conclusion

that peace with Russia could only be got by clear renunciation of annexations and war indemnity. Unless this condition were fulfilled separation of Russia from her allies was out of the question. But if it were fulfilled an early separate peace with Russia could almost be guaranteed.

Bundesrat Hoffman, the head of the Swiss Foreign Ministry, expressly confirmed to Romberg the next day that Müller's view was

[1] I.e., demands that Russia betray her allies.

also his own, and added that after Britain and France had rejected the peace offer – as it could be assumed with complete certainty that they would do – the Russians would regard themselves free to negotiate a separate peace.[1]

The Georgian, Prince Machabelli, who was also in Germany's service and was taking a leading part in the agitation among the 'foreign peoples' in Russia and was at that time in Stockholm, also asked for a clear official statement by Germany on the future of the Russian territories conquered by her. Only a renunciation of annexations and indemnity, and a solemn assurance that the occupied areas would be evacuated immediately on the conclusion of peace, would make it possible to dislodge the Russian war party. Machabelli thought it desirable that this declaration should be accompanied by a promise that 'the fate of these territories should be determined by the representatives of the indigenous nationalities themselves'. A contribution along these lines to the Polish, Lithuanian, etc., questions would gain Germany the sympathies of the nationalities and of the neutral powers. Even if the declaration did not lead to immediate peace with Russia, it would bring about a further split in the Russian people and army, so that the country would be further paralysed and could be compelled by force of arms to accept a separate peace.

In spite of these warnings and this advice, Bethmann Hollweg made no unambiguous declaration in his speech of May 15. The successes in the submarine war and hopes of disintegration in Russia had brought him round to the OHL's view that the situation need not be judged so deadly dangerous that he need renounce Germany's war aims in the east – in spite of the change in the world situation brought about by America's entry into the war. Just at this time – on May 6 – Ludendorff had reached the conclusion that 'with Russia crippled and America unable to help within an appreciable period, time has become our latest ally'; and Bethmann Hollweg made this view his own.

The Failure of the Grimm-Hoffmann Mission

In the middle of April a leading Swiss Socialist, Nationalrat Robert Grimm, asked the Foreign Office for a transit visa to Sweden. The application was supported by both Hoffmann and Romberg, to whom Grimm had applied direct on April 14, two days after Lenin's

[1] Brockdorff-Rantzau took, in substance, the same line, and asked the Chancellor to show even stronger inclination towards peace in his forthcoming Reichstag speech, in order to encourage the Council of Workers' delegates, who were wanting to convoke an international conference.

departure.[1] The ostensible reason for Grimm's journey was that he wanted to persuade the provisional government to exchange the Russian émigrés still in Switzerland against German civilian internees. His real hope, however, was to promote the possibilities of peace, in which he was interested as a pacifist and a member of the Zimmerwald movement. Although he had attacked Germany publicly, and although 'our Governmental Socialists' were dead against him, as Romberg reported,[2] the Foreign Ministry sanctioned his journey in the hope of using him for its own ends.

Grimm's purpose in Petersburg was to attack the 'anti-peace activities' of the Swedish Socialist, Branting, and to sound out the possibilities of peace; he hoped that the situation might lead to a separate peace with Russia, out of which a general peace might develop. He thought, indeed, that he could hope for success only if Germany strengthened the peace party by an official declaration renouncing annexations and indemnities – a hope which was not fulfilled. He reached Petersburg four weeks late, because the Milyukov government, so long as it was in office, refused him permission to enter Russia. Meanwhile, the Petersburg Workers' and Soldiers' Council, working in parallel with the Scandinavians, had decided to convoke an international conference in Stockholm. Grimm got in touch with this movement and telegraphed to Hoffmann that there was a general desire for peace, which was 'imperatively necessary, on political, economic and military grounds alike'; 'authoritative quarters' recognised this; the only difficulties were coming from Britain and France, who were trying to keep Russia in the war through the Socialists in their governments. In the hope of exploiting the possibilities in Russia, Grimm asked Hoffmann for information on the war aims of the governments (in the plural) 'as known to him'. Hoffmann, however, sent him only a slightly modified edition of Germany's aims, as communicated to him by Romberg.

The enterprise failed because the two telegrams were intercepted and thus became known both to Russia and to the world. Grimm was regarded as a German agent and expelled. He had compromised the Socialist members of the provisional government who wanted a general peace. Hoffmann was forced, largely owing to representations from Britain, to resign on the ground that he had committed a breach of neutrality. It is hard to say what the chances of such a

[1] See R. Fester, *Die politischen Kämpfe um den Frieden und das Deutschtum (1916–1918)* (Munich and Berlin, 1938); also Olga Hess Gankin and H. H. Fisher, *The Bolsheviks and the World War* (Stamford, London and Oxford, 1940).

[2] In fact, Scheidemann and Ebert advised against giving Grimm the transit visa, on the grounds that he was pronouncedly favourable towards the Entente (Hahlweg, op. cit., p. 56, n. 67).

peace move might have been, given the political situation in Petersburg during those weeks; but the obvious importance of the episode
lay in the fact that Germany's annexationist aims were revealed to
the public – even if in veiled form and perhaps not completely – and
thus not only was any chance of peace made more difficult, but the
German 'Governmental Socialists', who were just at that moment
engaged in making the preliminary arrangements for the international Socialist conference in Stockholm, were saddled in advance
with the odium of annexationism, if they attempted to follow the
government's line.

Germany's peace conditions, as transmitted to Hoffmann through
Romberg, agreed in essentials with the 'Principles' laid down on
April 29 for peace conversations at the front, and with the conditions
drafted on May 12 for the anticipated negotiations with Stecklov.
The earlier assurance that Germany was prepared to negotiate with
Russia's allies on the mediation of Russia was, however, completely
altered by the addition of the words 'at their wish' – at the wish, that
is, of the allies, without Russian mediation. After the exchange of
prisoners of war and civilian internees and the restoration of normal
legal conditions for the subjects of both contracting parties came a
sentence which is important for Germany's colonisation policy:
'Free return for Russian expellees of German ethnic origin.' But here
again the heart of the programme lay in its undiminished territorial
demands, which, however, Hoffmann passed on to Grimm in a somewhat modified form:

3. Amicable understanding on Poland, Lithuania, Courland, which shall
   have regard to the national characteristics, language, culture and religion
   of their inhabitants. . . .
4. England not to establish herself in Oesel, Dagoe, Livonia or other places
   in Russia.

The whole list was headed by an inviting Point 1, which spoke of 'a
peace honourable for both parties as the basis of a lasting friendly
relationship between Germany and her eastern neighbour'; further,
of 'financial support of Russia in her reconstruction: close economic
and commercial relations'. What form these 'relations' were to take
we know from earlier preparations for peace in the east. The professed
aim of a 'lasting friendly relationship' between Germany and Russia
looked beyond the separate peace to a new power-constellation which
envisaged, not indeed a formal alliance between Germany and Russia
– this had been considered and rejected – but semi-dependence of a
Russia without other allies on Germany. This apparent readiness of
Germany to meet Russia was strictly limited on what was perhaps the

most important point for Russia, for while the first draft had taken over from the programmes of April 29 and May 12 the offer of 'good offices over the regulation of the question of the Straits, the sovereignty of the Porte to be respected', Zimmermann had cut this out.

These plans, envisaging as they did a Russia under German tutelage from the Dardanelles to the Gulf of Bothnia, and with a frontier pushed back to a straight line running from Riga to Tarnogrod, foreshadowed the Peace of Brest-Litovsk—the more so when one remembers that since the spring of 1917 Germany had resumed with renewed vigour her efforts to promote the secession of Finland and the separation of the Ukraine.

The Stockholm Conference

The idea of an international Socialist peace conference had first been suggested by the Secretary General of the Second International, the Belgian Camille Huysmans, then in London, and had been taken up by Dutch and Scandinavian groups. When the plans took firmer shape, the government of the Reich had to consider whether it should forbid the German Socialists to attend. The OHL wanted to do this, because it feared that propaganda for a general peace might weaken the war spirit. The Foreign Office, however, although regarding it as objectionable 'that a political party should put itself forward officially as a peace mediator', refused to impose the ban. In explaining his reasons to the OHL, Zimmermann gave a most characteristic estimate of the 'Governmental Socialist' leaders and of the part played by them in German politics.[1] He doubted whether the Social Democrat leaders themselves expected the Stockholm conference to have any immediate effect in bringing about peace. He supposed that the chief advantage they expected to gain from attending the conference was a propagandist one: they would be able 'to go on posing before their electors, as per the party programme, as active champions of the idea of peace, and thus retain their control over the masses'. This was undoubtedly what the national interest required, especially since the difficulties with which the workers' leaders had to contend were very appreciable. He thought that the conference was certain to be a fiasco, and that it would make the national role of the Majority Socialists easier, because it would cure their followers of their pacifist ideas. If the delegates came back from Stockholm with a failure to report, this would 'consolidate and strengthen the whole party in the German national sense'; the arguments over the questions of annexations and indemnities would

---

[1] On the Stockholm Conference, see J. Meenzen, *Aussenpolitik und Weltfriedensordnung der deutschen Sozialdemokratie 1914–1919* (Diss. Hamburg, 1951), pp. 59 ff.

die away as soon as it became clear how the military operations were going to end:

> With victory immediately in sight, German Social Democracy itself will no longer be feeling favourable towards renunciations. If the further developments of the military situation are favourable, then the worse the experiences it has had meanwhile with its fellow Socialists abroad, the more safely can we count on getting its support for all demands necessary for the welfare of the Fatherland.

To prevent the Majority Socialists appearing as 'agents of the Wilhelmstrasse', the Foreign Ministry also issued passports to a few Independent Socialists, afterwards described by Hertling, when speaking of the episode, as 'an unimportant little clique of political eccentrics'.

The German delegation, which included Ebert, Scheidemann and Legien of the Majority Socialists, and Bernstein, Haase, Kautsky and Ledebour of the U.S.D.P., arrived in Stockholm on June 2, 1917, the day on which Robert Grimm sent his telegram to Hoffmann from Petersburg. Although there were no Socialists present from the Entente states, whose governments had refused them passports, the Germans were from the first driven on to the defensive; the Dutch van Kol and the Swede Branting attacked them in the opening session of June 4. At Ebert's request, David answered these attacks in a big speech which, taken in conjunction with a memorandum which the party leaders had composed,[1] gave a comprehensive picture of the Social Democrats' policy since the outbreak of the war. The memorandum rejected all 'forcible' annexations and demanded that, if any frontier rectifications were made on the basis of mutual agreement, the populations affected must be given legal and material safeguards if they wished to emigrate. Restoration of Germany's colonies was assumed as axiomatic; war indemnities were rejected. Turning to the 'right of self-determination' which had begun to figure so prominently in German policy, the memorandum demanded its application in three cases: (i) states which had lost their independence during the war (Belgium, Serbia); (ii) states which had recovered their former independence through the present war (Poland, Finland); such states not to be denied the right to self-determination; other districts inhabited by national minorities to be granted at least autonomy; (iii) peoples which had once been independent and had fallen victims to imperialist conquest at an earlier date, but whose national status had experienced no change during the war (Ireland, Egypt, India, Tibet, Korea, Tripoli and Morocco).

[1] Meenzen, op. cit., pp. 61 ff.

In this application of the right of self-determination the Social Democrats were following exactly the line of government policy. Point (ii) permitted the realisation of Germany's aspirations in the east as conceived by Bethmann Hollweg in April; Point (i) called for 'restoration' for Belgium and Serbia but did not define the term and left the way open for any form of satellite status.

The question of Alsace-Lorraine brought another clash.[1] The neutrals demanded self-determination for Alsace-Lorraine and for the Polish and Danish inhabited parts of Germany. This the Germans refused, while agreeing to cultural autonomy for the minorities and for the French-speaking parts of Lorraine. Their case was that only 11·4 per cent of the population of Alsace-Lorraine was French-speaking, and that the area was ethnically and historically German, had been forcibly torn away from Germany by Louis XIV, and had recovered its original affiliation in 1871. To meet the strong criticisms raised against Alsace-Lorraine's position within Germany (as a 'Reichsland') they supported its promotion to the status of an independent federal state. They maintained, in this connection, that the principle of 'peace without annexations' did not exclude frontier rectifications by mutual consent, thereby obviously keeping the door open for the acquisition of Longwy-Briey. The one demand made by them which differed from the government's policy—the promotion of Alsace-Lorraine to be a federal state—remained irrelevant, since the annexations which Prussia proposed to make in the west and the north-east had brought the imperial government to accept the necessity of partitioning Alsace-Lorraine as compensation for the non-Prussian dynasties.

The Socialists from the Entente states had, as we have said, failed to appear, and Albert Thomas, the French Socialist Minister of Munitions, returning from Petersburg via Stockholm, announced: 'The war will go on; we can do nothing about it.' David and Scheidemann returned to Germany on June 19, leaving only Hermann Müller behind to wait vainly for the opening of a real peace conference.

[1] Id., pp. 63 f.

14

WAR AIMS
IN THE JULY CRISIS OF 1917
CHANGE AND CONTINUITY

THE Brusilov offensive of the end of June, 1917, destroyed the German public's last hope of getting speedy relief for Germany through a separate peace with Russia. At the same moment the first doubts of the effectiveness of the submarine war were beginning to appear, in spite of the apparently impressive successes. Fear of a fourth winter of war and the renewal of the tension in the military situation at last really produced that internal crisis in Germany which had so often been prevented from erupting by delaying half-measures. The fall of Bethmann and the Peace Resolution seemed to cast doubts on the internal political development of Germany and at times also on her war aims policy.

Depression and a Peace of Understanding

The internal crisis was ushered in by an attempt by the German military to transfer the responsibility for Germany's unhappy situation from their own shoulders on to those of the political leaders. As recently as April 5 the Chief of the General Staff, Hindenburg, had supported his demand for a fixed programme of war aims with the argument that the war would 'presumably be decided this year' and that there was 'a prospect of peace negotiations in the near future';[1] and up to the middle of May the OHL, basing its view on statements by the naval staff in an 'open' private letter to Hindenburg's wife, had put the end of the war at August and had persistently fostered an optimistic belief in victory, its confidence being responsible also for the optimism in the German answer to Czernin and the Emperor Charles, and in Bethmann Hollweg's Reichstag speech. But in June the generals were abandoning this attitude. Only three weeks after the Chancellor's 'strong' speech in the Reichstag, their views on the military situation had changed radically. Up to this point the OHL had encouraged the Chancellor to use a firm tone in the Reichstag; now they complained of the 'absolutely irresponsible optimism' of the

---

[1] See above (n. 9 to c. 12). On Hindenburg's letter to his wife, see Mathias Erzberger, *Erlebnisse im Weltkriege* (Stuttgart, 1920), p. 251.

political leaders, which was spreading the illusion that the war would be over in a few months.

On June 10 the representative of the OHL in Berlin, Colonel Bauer, had a conversation with Erzberger, to whose great astonishment the colonel revealed for the first time that the military command was now reckoning on a fourth winter campaign.[1] On top of this, Bauer spoke frankly of the crushing material superiority of the enemy on the western front, and said that this superiority would increase as time went on. At that moment the enemy's superiority in munitions was four to one; by the spring of 1918 it would have risen to at least six to one. It may have been Bauer's report on this conversation with Erzberger and his impressions in Berlin which now caused the OHL to inform the Chancellor officially that it was not possible to count on Britain's early collapse as a consequence of the submarine war and that a fourth winter of war was to be expected. Writing on June 19, Ludendorff placed the responsibility for the outcome of the war on the home front.[2] By stating that 'time is working for us if only the will to hold out remains alive at home', Ludendorff laid the foundations for that shift which, after Germany's military collapse, gave birth to the legend of the stab in the back; other factors were made responsible for military failures of judgment.

The military's proposal to make up for Germany's shortage of material resources in this threatening situation by a massive psychological propaganda campaign at home coincided with a similar proposal by Erzberger.[3] In his interview with Bauer that experienced politician drew the conclusion that the critical military situation called for the establishment of a central organisation for propaganda, 'a sort of spiritual war food office', as he called it rather cynically, for the conduct of which he, the busy chief of the 'foreign information service', seemed to be predestined. About the same time Wilhelm II instructed his Chancellor to hammer into the German people faith in the submarine arm and consequently in final victory. Psychology was thus to replace guns as means of dispelling the disappointment over Britain's failure to collapse.[4] Bethmann Hollweg promised the Emperor immediate action.

The Chancellor's answer to the OHL dated June 25, 1917,[5] showed him disillusioned as never before. Under the influence of the pessimistic view of the situation taken by the military, he did indeed

[1] Id., p. 252.
[2] See also Ludendorff, *Urkunden*, pp. 395 ff.
[3] Cf. Epstein, *Erzberger*, pp. 186 f.
[4] Ludendorff, op. cit., p. 400.
[5] Id., p. 397.

declare himself ready to start the desired propaganda campaign at home, but he made a number of strong reservations against the course proposed by the OHL. In direct contradiction to the military, he thought that the continuation of the 'new orientation', as promised by the Easter Message,[1] was necessary for the maintenance of internal unity. He also said that, the prospects of a peace dictated by Germany being now so small, it would be unwise to throw away the last possibilities of a compromise with Britain, especially by pitching colonial aims too high. Solf's 'war aims' speech of June 17[2] could serve as a first 'invitation' to Britain, since in that speech Solf had not touched on Europe at all and had only asked for some moderate additions to Germany's colonial empire at the expense of Portugal and France, and not of Britain. It is true that Bethmann Hollweg pressed for energetic prosecution of the submarine war in order to weaken Britain as far as possible, but at the same time he showed himself clearly opposed to any strong public rejection of a peace of understanding and against a renewal of the public discussion on war aims. He further called attention to the extraordinary embitterment occasioned by the last German bombing attacks on London: 'No English government which tried to negotiate with Germany after this sort of thing would be able to maintain itself for a single day in face of the popular fury.'

Hesitant as were these first beginnings of a realistic attitude on the Chancellor's part towards both domestic and foreign political questions, they were yet enough to put the military up in arms again at once. In their answer of July 7 they rejected with the utmost decision any idea of a peace of understanding or of a new course in internal politics in the sense of the Easter Message. They thought–and here they were in complete agreement with an opinion voiced by Bethmann Hollweg on July 2 at a session of the Prussian Ministry of State–that if Britain made an offer for a peace of understanding this would be a sure sign of her approaching death agony, and that it would therefore be unnecessary for Germany to accept such a peace:

. . . in my opinion it would be a disaster for our political and economic future if we accepted such a 'peace of understanding' with England, unless the defection of Austria-Hungary and equally critical conditions at home forced us to conclude immediate peace.[3]

---

[1] See above, p. 336.

[2] See above, pp. 359–60.

[3] Ludendorff, op. cit., p. 401. Bethmann Hollweg said here that the submarine warfare had been initiated in order to make the enemy ready for peace. The best thing would, of course, be if they capitulated, but he did not think this would happen, for when Britain felt 'the catastrophe approaching' she would presumably

In July, 1917, however, the OHL still regarded such an 'unfavourable coincidence'—the defection of Austria-Hungary and the simultaneous exhaustion of Germany—to be 'extremely improbable'.

The bombing attacks on London were continued and the conflict between Britain and Germany sharpened into real hatred between the peoples. Bethmann Hollweg had grown 'flabby' again, as he had at the time of the decision in favour of unrestricted submarine warfare. The OHL openly reproached the Chancellor with the same lack of decision in his internal policy:[1] he had not succeeded in maintaining solidarity and enthusiasm for the war in the nation—the pre-conditions for a victorious end to the war. What was depressing the home front was not 'the disappointed hopes of a speedy end to the war' but the weak attitude of the political leader who had allowed 'private, party and particular interests' (by this the generals meant the advocates of franchise reform) to take precedence over the 'general good of the state'.

Internal crisis, peace and franchise reform

On June 27, with the internal situation deteriorating rapidly, the Majority Social Democrats David and Scheidemann again visited the Chancellor.[2] Their attitude bore unmistakable testimony to the growing pressure of the U.S.P.D., which itself was only the articulate expression of growing war-weariness and the increasing desire of the masses for equality of status. The Chancellor asked the two men to put their wishes in writing, and the Majority Socialists accordingly produced their demands the very next day: the government must unequivocally dissociate itself from the war aims of the *Alldeutschen*, accept the formula of peace without annexations, and carry through without delay a measure of internal political 'reorientation' by introducing the equal franchise in Prussia. The memorandum repeated the threat already made by its authors in the Reichstag at the beginning of July to vote against the next war credits. At this juncture the Emperor was not even ready to accept Bethmann Hollweg's modest suggestion of taking Spahn, the Zentrum leader and spokesman of the War Aims Majority, into the government as First Parliamentary Minister.[3] On the day that he rejected this 'reform',

'come round' (*einlenken*) one way or another. . . . He therefore thought that it would be wrong to announce that Germany was ready to make peace if the enemy came round; 'our task can now only be to show that we can and will carry on the war longer than our enemies'.

[1] Müller in his *Kriegstagebuch*, pp. 277 f., is very revealing on the inner connections between war aims, internal politics, and the fall of Bethmann Hollweg.

[2] Scheidemann, *Zusammenbruch*, pp. 160 f. (with full text of the memorandum).

[3] Müller, op. cit., p. 298; entry of June 29, 1917.

he also gave the Papal Nuncio, Pacelli, who had appeared at General Headquarters with a first, cautious suggestion of mediation by the Vatican, plainly to understand that he was not interested in peace.[1]

Bethmann Hollweg's meeting with the party leaders on July 2 opened a new chapter in the development of the crisis.[2] The government had arranged the meeting (at which, besides the Chancellor himself, Helfferich, Roedern, the Secretary of State for the Treasury, and Capelle, Secretary of State for the Naval Office appeared to represent the government) to prepare for the next war credits vote. It hoped to arrange at the same time that the debate in the Central Committee of the Reichstag should be confined exclusively to the granting of the credits, and above all to exclude in advance any general political debate, either on war aims or on internal reforms. Since Bethmann Hollweg was unwilling to appear in the Central Committee—which would inevitably have provoked the unwanted political debate—he now resorted to the device, frequently used with success during the war, of a meeting of party leaders, whose little circle could be reassured, encouraged and further bound morally to the government by the confidence shown to them. In the conference itself both the Chancellor and Capelle, in agreement with the OHL's letter of June 19, still maintained the optimistic view that it would be possible to achieve victory through the submarine arm, if not within the term of five months originally given. But a fourth war winter had obviously become unavoidable. The debate on a peace of understanding took place under the chilling influence of these remarks. Only Scheidemann came forward with his programme of a peace without annexations or reparations; he alone called on the Chancellor to accept the Russian formula 'without shilly-shallying'. Yet, lest the representatives of the bourgeois parties and the government should regard him as 'nationally unreliable', Scheidemann stated expressly that he had only decided to adopt this principle when he had been forced to recognise that Germany was beyond doubt 'the weaker party'. He found no seconder for his appeal. If Bethmann Hollweg failed to secure full conviction with his argument that a 'weak peace' would bring Germany a 'helot existence', yet his attitude remained the same as in every crisis: to wait and let the enemy make the move. On this point he received strong support, especially from Westarp, who spoke vigorously against a peace without annexations. Thus the government apparently succeeded in banishing for the moment the 'danger' of a peace of understanding.

[1] Ibid.; cf. also Bethmann Hollweg, *Betrachtungen*, II, pp. 214 ff.

[2] Besides all the main parties, the Poles and Alsace-Lorraine were represented at this meeting.

On the other hand Scheidemann's demand for internal reform met with much support. Both Payer and Stresemann spoke unequivocally in favour of the immediate introduction of the equal franchise in Prussia.

The first, immediate effects of the new and soberer feeling were perceptible when the Central Committee of the Reichstag met the next day. Ebert, who had meanwhile become the chief spokesman of the Majority Social Democrats, initiated a massive attack against Bethmann Hollweg's government. He sharply criticised the 'conscienceless agitation' which had exaggerated beyond measure the prospects of submarine warfare; he warned the Reichstag equally sharply against underestimating the United States, as Germany had previously misjudged England. He concluded gloomily that 'confidence in the government has been completely destroyed by the failure of food supplies and submarine warfare.' Like Scheidemann the day before, he called on the government clearly to define its attitude on the question of war aims, on the basis of the Russian formula. He ended with a categorical demand for the introduction—at once, before the end of the war—of the general franchise in Prussia as a pre-condition for the solidarity of the domestic front.

Before the Chancellor could act came Erzberger's famous move of July 6 in the Central Committee, which set the ball of the war aims question rolling.[1] On July 3 Erzberger had criticised the government severely, but his second attack, on July 6, was much more decisive, for in it he proposed bringing in the Reichstag in order to get a speedy 'compromise' peace—a peace which 'took account of the power-relationships as they had taken shape during the war, a peace which brings no enforced repression of peoples and frontier areas'. Erzberger's arguments were based on the sober calculation that continuation of the war, as things stood, could only make Germany's position worse, so that the 'power-relationships as they had taken shape during the war' were bound to develop more unfavourably for Germany. Under closer inspection, however, his negative description of a basis for general peace was so elastic that the government's most uncompromising aims could have been realised under it. The impression made by Erzberger's speech was extraordinary; the idea that the Reichstag should take an independent initiative was revolutionary. The suspicion that Erzberger, who had acted often enough during the war as an agent for the government, was playing into the government's hands was obvious: thus the shock to the Reichstag

[1] The literature on this subject is immense; the latest comprehensive account is that of Epstein, op. cit., pp. 182 ff.

was all the greater.[1] Yet according to the evidence of all concerned,[2] there had been no previous conversation between Erzberger and the government, nor do the documents give grounds for supposing anything of the kind. On the contrary, Bethmann Hollweg could not but regard Erzberger's move as a breach of the gentleman's agreement reached with the party leaders on July 2. He had now got into great difficulties, both over the franchise reform and over the question of war aims. The next day Capelle tried to allay the Committee's fears by emphasising the rising tally of tonnage sunk by submarines. Scheidemann contradicted Capelle's official optimism most decidedly and said that he doubted whether Germany could reckon at all with a military decision in her favour. He went further than Erzberger and asked not only for the adoption of his 'defensive formula for Germany' (a peace without annexations), but also for a precise declaration to this effect from the Reichstag, in order to allow peace to be concluded as quickly as possible. In face of these strong attacks, the government abandoned its original purpose, which had been to reserve its fire, and immediately after Erzberger's speech, von Stein, the Prussian Minister of War, called Hindenburg and Ludendorff to Berlin from General Headquarters. On July 7 Bethmann Hollweg appeared personally in the Central Committee in the hope of saving the situation for the government.

Answering Erzberger, who had called on the government to return to its defensive standpoint of August 4, 1914, the Chancellor declared that his policy had never departed from this line during the war. Characteristically, however, he still allowed the idea of 'defence' to include 'safeguards for Germany's future' which previously had had no defensive meaning at all. He promised that Germany would not wage war a day longer simply to make 'further' conquests. We may certainly credit him with not wanting, in July, 1917, to prolong the war exclusively for the sake of 'further' conquests. Germany had already occupied so much territory in east and west that her leaders might hope to achieve a peace without being forced back to the *status quo*. Bethmann Hollweg therefore rejected decisively the suggestion that the Reichstag should make a public declaration on the subject of peace. It was only through strong military pressure, especially through the submarine arm, that Germany could make her enemies ripe for peace; not through a Peace Resolution, which must rouse the impression that the German Reich was near collapse.

Bethmann Hollweg did not touch on the franchise question, which

[1] On this and the next paragraphs, see Epstein, op. cit., pp. 190 f.
[2] Bethmann Hollweg, op. cit., p. 224.

the Majority Socialists always linked with that of war aims, although petitions from quarters ranging from the Majority Socialists to the National Liberals had convinced him how urgent it now was and how strong the demand for it had become among the overwhelming majority of the Reichstag, except the Conservatives. In spite of the Reform Majority's move of May 6 and of his own readiness in principle to carry through extensive internal political reforms, the Chancellor could not venture on July 7 to express approval of the equal franchise. For this he needed first to get the consent of the monarch and of the Prussian Ministry of State.

On July 9 the Emperor, at Bethmann Hollweg's request, held a Crown Council to consider the question of the equal franchise in Prussia.[1] All present, even those Secretaries of State who were not also Prussian ministers, were allowed to express their opinions for or against the equal franchise, with their reasons in detail. The strongest supporter was Bethmann Hollweg himself, in his capacity as President of the Ministry of State, and he emphasised with almost exaggerated sharpness the key position of the Majority Socialists and the trade unions for the winning of the war. The most decided speaker for the opposition was the Prussian Minister of the Interior, von Loebell, who drew an equally strong picture of a Prussia dominated by Social Democrats and Poles, and suggested the introduction of plural voting as an expedient to check the advance of Social Democracy. The Emperor, however, was still unable to make up his mind, in spite of Bethmann Hollweg's urgent warnings. He saw quite clearly what were the two positions between which he had to decide:

In the one side's view the introduction of the equal franchise would mean the decline of Prussia, in the view of the other, failure to introduce it would probably mean the loss of the war and thus the decline of both Germany and Prussia.[2]

The Emperor thought that before 'imposing' the equal franchise on 'his Prussians' he ought to consult, not only the Crown Prince, but

[1] See Helfferich, *Der Weltkrieg*, pp. 445 f. The minutes of the Crown Council are reproduced by Leo Stern, op. cit., p. 588. Bethmann Hollweg's concluding words were: '. . . So far it had proved possible to keep the Social Democrats quiet (*an der Stange halten*), and especially the Social Democratic Trade Unions had . . . rendered excellent service. The longer the war lasted, the worse the distress became, the more would the power of the radical wing grow. The Trade Unions were complaining that they no longer had their members under control, that they were being egged on by the Radicals, who were telling them that the Imperial Social Democrats were doing nothing for them. It was absolutely necessary to make the right wing of the Social Democrats stronger again. For what would happen if the government was no longer able to use the help of the Trade Unions in combating the strike movement?'

[2] *Untersuchungsausschuss*, 4th series, Vol. II, p. 152.

also the parliamentary parties in the Upper House. Bethmann Hollweg protested vainly that this had made his position untenable and he then offered his resignation. The Emperor refused to release him, saying that any government would have to find a solution to the franchise question. He was supported by the Crown Prince, who on the 11th expressed himself in favour both of keeping Bethmann Hollweg as Chancellor and of conceding the equal franchise. Bethmann Hollweg seemed on the verge of victory; the Ministry of State met again that afternoon at 4 o'clock and the Chancellor informed it of the king's decision and laid before it the draft of an 'All Highest Order regarding equal franchise'. Wilhelm II signed it the same evening, for publication on the following morning. Equal franchise for Prussia had been accepted in principle, although not yet enshrined in legal form. But this was a Pyrrhic victory for Bethmann Hollweg; the very next day he was overthrown by a combined move by the Crown Prince and General Ludendorff.

The fall of Bethmann Hollweg and the antecedents of the Peace Resolution

One reason for Bethmann Hollweg's fall was the franchise question; another was the question of peace, which had become dominant since Erzberger's move. Not only were the two questions exactly synchronised, but they were solved by the same persons. The Crown Prince and the OHL, assisted by the Reichstag, determined Bethmann Hollweg's fall.

After July 6 a committee had come into being with a membership which extended from the Majority Socialists via the Zentrum and the Progressives to the National Liberals, for the purpose of considering the urgent questions: internal reform and, above all, what the Reichstag should say on the peace question.[1] The National Liberals had withdrawn after a few days, saying that the preparation of a peace resolution was 'inexpedient', but the other three parties, which now took the joint designation of 'parties of the majority', went on to work out a joint resolution. On July 10 Bethmann Hollweg had agreed to a first draft, which had even been accepted by the Emperor, except for the words 'peace of understanding', which he rejected as 'unclear'; but on July 12 the Emperor was in a 'brusque and unfriendly mood', could not recall anything, and took shelter behind the attitude of the OHL. The generals abruptly rejected the resolution, as put before them, as too weak; they objected above all to a 'peace of understanding' which excluded as

[1] On the history of this committee see the numerous documents in *Quellen zur Geschichte des Parlamentarismus*, Vols. I/I and II.

'incompatible' with it 'territorial acquisitions imposed by force and political, economic and financial violence'. Their sight of the draft and the announcement that the equal franchise was to be introduced were enough to bring them hot-foot to Berlin, where they tendered their resignations in writing, if Bethmann Hollweg remained Chancellor any longer. The OHL was going *va banque*.[1]

Meanwhile the Crown Prince, who had 'swallowed' the equal franchise and the retention of Bethmann Hollweg only with the utmost reluctance, had not been inactive in Berlin. On July 11 and 12 he had got in touch with the party leaders, with the result that on the 12th only one party – the Progressives – was left supporting the Chancellor's policy unreservedly. The Majority Socialists supported him only on the condition that he did not oppose peace as they conceived it. Erzberger of the Zentrum, Stresemann of the National Liberals, not to speak of the Conservatives, Free Conservatives and the 'German fraction', openly declared themselves opposed to Bethmann Hollweg remaining in office.

This transient co-operation between the Crown Prince and the parliamentary leaders, which took place in an atmosphere of real conspiracy, deprived Bethmann Hollweg of the last parliamentary support which he had enjoyed for his new policy. The Emperor had called for his resignation before Ludendorff and Hindenburg had reached Berlin.[2] The Crown Prince, however, hoped in this way not only to get rid of Bethmann Hollweg, but also of the Peace Resolution. He proposed adjourning the Reichstag until a new Imperial Chancellor had been appointed and thus 'preventing a parliamentary debate on the Peace Resolution'; the parliamentarians had done their duty when Bethmann Hollweg fell.

The idea that Bethmann Hollweg, who in any case was no fighter by nature, could have carried the equal franchise and the Peace Resolution with the support of the Progressives and Social Democrats against the OHL and the Crown was, given the whole structure of Prussia–Germany, unimaginable. Moreover, the two parties together still constituted a minority in the Reichstag. Even if Bethmann Hollweg had been able to enlist the Zentrum and secure a parliamentary majority, no Chancellor of imperial Germany could have maintained himself for a single day against the Conservatives and their allies in the army, the bureaucracy and the business world.

With Bethmann Hollweg's fall under the attacks from right and left, the confusion in high places reached its apogee. Bethmann

[1] See also Bernhard Schwertfeger, op. cit., in *Werk des Untersuchungsausschusses*, Series IV, Vol. II, pp. 154 ff.

[2] Müller, op. cit., pp. 304 ff., entry of July 16, 1917.

Hollweg had suggested Count Hertling to the Emperor as his successor. Hertling, however, had at once refused the appointment on the grounds of his advanced age (he was 74) and his disagreement with the OHL's views on the question of war aims. After considerable consultation between the Heads of Cabinets, the candidature of Michaelis emerged. Michaelis, Under-Secretary of State in the Prussian Ministry of Finance and Commissioner for Food Supplies, was an unknown figure, both to the public and to the Emperor; he said of himself that until appointed Imperial Chancellor he had 'run by the side of the carriage of politics as a disinterested contemporary'.[1] Hindenburg at once agreed with the suggestion. Michaelis had been to General Headquarters several times and certain drastic turns of speech had made a favourable impression on general staff officers with whom he had talked. He could be taken as entirely the OHL's man. The day after his appointment he told representatives of the Majority Parties that he proposed to act in constant agreement with the OHL.[2] (He obviously thought that the OHL and the Majority Parties had already reached agreement over the Peace Resolution.) All the conflicts of the coming weeks were foreshadowed in this declaration.

A Peace of Understanding and War Aims: The Peace Resolution

Things did not fall out as the Crown Prince had meant when the Chancellors changed. Even under the new Chancellor the government had to give all its attention to the Reichstag's Peace Resolution.

In the spring of 1917 Erzberger had begun to move away from his annexationist line, mainly under the impression of Czernin's memorandum of April 12 and of his own observations in Vienna. At the beginning of July, when it had become clear that submarine warfare would not break Britain's resistance with in the term announced (if at all), and the United States entered the war and the bourgeois-liberal revolution in Russia converted the war of the Allied and associated powers into an ideological struggle of democracy against autocracy–then Erzberger, the propagandist and parliamentary leader, saw how a public declaration in favour of peace could be used as a political weapon to justify, and above all to retain, what had been achieved. It furthermore seemed opportune to present parliamentary institutions to the outside world more prominently than hitherto. These were the considerations which prompted the

---

[1] Erzberger, *Erlebnisse*, p. 265. On the 'intervention' of Michaelis, see Magnus Frh. von Braun, *Von Ostpreussen bis Texas* (Hollkamm, 1955), pp. 113 ff.

[2] Braun, loc. cit.

Reichstag's appeal to the enemy peoples. On Erzberger's initiative, and after previous discussion with the government and the OHL,[1] the Peace Resolution was accepted on July 19, 1917 by the three parties of the majority – the Zentrum, the Progressive People's Party and the Majority Socialists – against the votes of the Independent Socialists, the National Liberals and the Conservatives.

It was no coincidence that these were the parties which had voted in 1916 for acceptance without debate of Bethmann Hollweg's peace offer. The spirit of the resolution was the same as the spirit of the offer. Once again the Reichstag majority, reverting to Wilhelm II's declaration of August 4, 1914, proclaimed the old thesis that Germany was waging war solely in order to retain 'the integrity of her own territory'. The Reichstag would therefore never aim at any other end than 'a peace of understanding'. Like the offer, this resolution closed on a note of decision and confidence. The majority parties announced that should the enemy reject Germany's offer, she would 'hold out and struggle until her right and the right of her allies to life and development is assured'. Between the slogans of 'peace of understanding' and 'holding out' came, very inconspicuously, the politically decisive central sentence '*territorial acquisitions imposed by force*[2] and political, economic or financial violence are incompatible with such a peace'.

The Peace Resolution is generally taken as proof of the readiness of a broad inter-party front in Germany to conclude a peace of understanding, it being tacitly assumed that the basis of such a peace would be approximately that of the *status quo*. The nationalist opposition of the day, and of later, interpreted the resolution as the first open sign of Erzberger's treachery to Germany; the journalists and historical interpreters of a liberal-democrat brand in Germany hailed with delight the co-operation between the majority parties and saw in the resolution the beginnings of the defeat of the Prusso-German authoritarian state by the forces of democracy. But neither view does justice to the historical situation. Erzberger, in particular, the key figure behind the resolution, was neither a traitor to Germany nor an angel of peace; he was only pursuing his old, nationally conscious course. The resolution marked no fundamental abandonment by him of his earlier political convictions, but only a new tactical turn, the consistent continuation of what had been his policy since the beginning of 1917 – to achieve by diplomatic methods as much as

[1] For an exhaustive discussion of Erzberger's motives for his action in July, 1917, see Epstein, op. cit., pp. 185 ff. The conversation had taken place on the afternoon of July 14, after the appointment of Michaelis.

[2] Author's italics.

possible of Germany's war aims in a general peace. And in this he was in full agreement with the official policy of the German Reich. This interpretation is justified by his later attitude towards Brest-Litovsk, and confirmed even more fully by his own explanations to the government at the moment when the resolution was accepted.

On the day of the vote in the full house of the Reichstag, Erzberger explained to the new Chancellor, Michaelis, his real intentions in promoting the resolution.[1] As regards the west, he contented himself with the obscure remark 'that the regulation of the Belgian question today no longer presents any obstacle', while he wanted Alsace-Lorraine promoted to the full status of a Grand Duchy, thus anticipating 'France's wishes'. His glosses on Eastern war aims betrayed clearly the disguised annexationist purpose of what the resolution called 'a peace of understanding without territorial acquisitions imposed by force'. He did not find it necessary to waste any words on the Polish question. He regarded the attachment of Lithuania to Germany in the form of an 'independent Duchy' with the German Emperor as Duke as an expression of Germany's conciliatory spirit. Lithuania would not become a member state of the German Reich, but it would be attached closely to Germany by a 'customs union' and a series of other agreements as well as by the dynastic link. He thought that Russia would be unable to protest against this arrangement and he went on:

Then we have assured our frontier in the east through understanding. But what we are doing here is not 'imposing territorial acquisitions by force', but securing the optimum protection for our eastern provinces. The faster the organisation of the state proceeds, the sooner we shall get peace, for another important obstacle will have been surmounted and our wishes fulfilled.

The Peace Resolution thus meant no renunciation of Germany's war aims. The Zentrum politician was as far from accepting the *status quo* as the end of Germany's war policy as the Emperor Wilhelm II, who at about the same time had rejected, with the marginal minutes 'quite impossible' and 'can't be done', Austria's request that Germany should declare 'that she would not prolong the war for the sake of conquests and indemnities should the enemy ask for a peace on the basis of the *status quo ante bellum*'. The new Chancellor took the same line. In his first Reichstag speech, made on July 19, he devalued the government's acceptance and the Peace Resolution itself—so far

[1] After the event (in January, 1918), Solf gave an unintentionally exact description of the Peace Resolution: there was nothing objectionable in its substance, because it did not mean any 'renunciation by Germany of a satisfactory peace', and did not affect 'concrete war aims'. 'The best instincts of the German people would, indeed, today call for repudiation of the resolution.'

as it had been accepted at home and abroad at its face value—by his famous gloss 'as I understand them', and publicly testified to the continuity of Germany's war aims policy by repeating Bethmann Hollweg's formula of 'safeguards and guarantees for Germany'. The world immediately recognised the true character of the peace resolution, and Michaelis himself was the best crown witness for the justness of this view when he wrote to the Crown Prince on July 25 on the acceptance of 'the notorious resolution': '*I have deprived it of its most dangerous features by my interpretation of it* (italics in the original). 'One can make any peace one likes with this resolution'.

The rulers of Germany had thus assured themselves a completely free hand, even after accepting the resolution. It betrayed a certain cynicism—which also revealed the weakness of the parliamentary forces—when the Chancellor continued with satisfaction, in the same context: 'Thereupon the credits (15,000 million) were accepted, against the votes of the Independent Social Democrats. After this achievement, which disposed of the conflict, the Reichstag was closed.'

15

MICHAELIS AND KÜHLMANN

RENUNCIATION IN THE WEST?

MOTIVES of both foreign and internal politics lay behind the fall of Bethmann Hollweg and the Peace Resolution. One factor was the attempt by the Conservatives and *Alldeutschen* to pin the Chancellor down to extensive war aims, and also their opposition to the equal franchise in Prussia and their fear that the Chancellor might give way on the question of making parliament a force in the Reich; another was the desire of the so-called majority parties to keep the Social Democrats in the war by an apparent scaling down of war aims, and to make an impression alike on Germany's allies, the neutrals and the enemy. The task of the new Chancellor and the new men in authority under him was to restore internal solidarity without basic changes in the monarchic-constitutional system.

Renewed rejection of the Austro-Hungarian desire for peace

Michaelis had no experience of foreign affairs, but the Vatican's peace move at once brought him face to face with the problem of possible peace conditions – in other words, he had to occupy himself with the formulation of Germany's war aims as soon as he took office. It was therefore natural for him to use his first official visit to Vienna, on August 1, for a conversation with Germany's ally on the situation in general and on possible peace conditions in particular.

The detailed minutes of this conference surprise the reader by the frank and serious tone in which the new Chancellor spoke of the general situation of the Central Powers. Michaelis began by saying that he 'could not say with absolute certainty' whether Germany would be able to hold out through a fourth year of war. On this point he was thus clearly no more optimistic than his predecessor had been immediately before his fall, but Michaelis, like Bethmann Hollweg, drew no positive deductions from his correct appreciation of the facts. In theory he approved the Austrians' urgent desire to get peace before a fourth winter of war, and thought that it would be wrong to reject any possibility of peace 'on account of questions of extensions of power'. In practice, however, he wanted to treat his conversation with the Austrian statesmen as provisional only, saying that he could not reach complete clarity on the situation until he had spoken to 'the other competent authorities', i.e., the OHL. The mentality of the military being what it was, it could, however, be taken for granted that they would oppose any renunciation of 'extensions of power' simply for the sake of peace.

At this meeting there recurred the three great complexes of questions which had been debated between Vienna and Berlin in the meetings of March to May, 1917: the possibilities of a separate peace with France, the Polish problem (in particular the question of the Polish Legions), and Balkan questions. It was especially significant that von Stumm of the Foreign Ministry thought an understanding with France quite possible. Thereupon Czernin, who did not believe a general peace possible at that moment, proposed officially that Germany should induce the French to make peace by meeting them over Alsace-Lorraine. To compensate Germany for her territorial sacrifices in the west, Czernin offered complete *désintéressement* in Poland and the cession of Galicia to the new Poland. Since the Germans, no less than Czernin, referred to the great difficulties which they were having in Poland, the idea of giving Poland her independence momentarily broke surface, but even so Michaelis expressly insisted that Poland would have to take her place in a belt of buffer states against Russia. In practice Czernin very soon gave up the idea of an independent Poland, because his offer had been designed only as a tactical means of prising France out of the Entente. With a Polish settlement achieved through a separate understanding with France, Czernin thought that the Central Powers would have won the war and would have a free hand in Poland even if nominally independent. Czernin's views certainly accorded exactly with Germany's Polish policy, which was far from intending to allow the Poles to dispose freely of their national destinies.

The monolithic continuity of Germany's Eastern policy after August, 1914 was again clearly revealed in Vienna in this context. Stumm, whose relations with the Secretary of State, Zimmermann, were very similar to those of Zimmermann with Jagow, stated with special emphasis that a solution of the Polish question was only one part of what Germany was working for, which was 'the disintegration of the Russian Empire'. The detachment of the Ukraine from Russia, vaguely considered in 1914, was now beginning to take definite shape in Germany's plans. Stumm told the conference that the Foreign Ministry was in touch with the Ukrainians; but to win them over it was necessary to satisfy their claims on Chelm and East Galicia. This, he said, was possible only if the Danubian Monarchy would cede East Galicia to Poland, from which, he added, not without Machiavellianism, it could then at once be taken away again and given to the Ukraine. Czernin, like his predecessors, treated Germany's Ukrainian plans with reserve. His attitude was obviously governed by the fatal dilemma into which polyglot Austria-Hungary had been plunged by the development of the new historical forces which were becoming so potent since both America and the new Russia had officially sponsored the 'right of national self-determination'. Czernin expressly emphasised how impossible it was 'to propound and recognise the right of national self-determination within the framework of the Monarchy'. The restoration of Galicia to a re-born independent Poland could have been justified in conservative political thought as deference to the historic principle, but the detachment of the Ukraine from the Russian Empire, with the inevitable and immediate effects on the Ruthenes of East Galicia, would have been a further step towards the recognition of the right to self-determination.

On closer examination the Balkan question too was found to be closely bound up with the possibilities of peace with France. Czernin maintained quite consistently the attitude which he had adopted since the previous March, that if Austria lost Galicia, with its bread, grains and oil, she must receive compensation in Rumania. He accordingly insisted on the division of spheres of influence agreed at Kreuznach in May—Poland for Germany, Rumania for Austria-Hungary—and asked for support for the movement in Rumania which favoured its attachment to the Central Powers, or rather to Austria-Hungary. The Germans agreed but went a step further when Stumm demanded 'that united Poland' (i.e., Congress Poland and Galicia) 'and Rumania should be attached to the bloc of the Central Powers'. This demand revealed Germany's grandiose aim of creating a vast *Raum* dominated by Germany's economic and military power – the aim which Bethmann Hollweg had had in mind in his Mitteleuropa programme of September, 1914, and which reappeared in the 'Principles' which Kühlmann extracted from Czernin on October 22, 1917.[1]

Czernin at once saw the implications of the German demand. He tried to maintain Austria-Hungary's equal status in the alliance and her complete independence against Germany's ill-disguised claim for domination. Germany's proposal, he said, could be realised only if the Monarchy and Germany concluded a new Treaty of Alliance – 'in which case, if each of the two contracting parties attached its allotted country to itself militarily and politically, those lands would *eo ipso* be participants in our Treaty of Alliance'. The negotiations in

[1] See below, p. 437 ff.

Vienna ended at this stage of the discussions, which in appearance left everything open, but in reality made the final order in Mitteleuropa after the hoped-for victory dependent exclusively on how much vitality and political determination each of the two partners could show in dealing with the other.

The Austrians and Germans were to meet again in Berlin on August 14 to continue and expand their discussions. Before this happened, the Chancellor met Hindenburg and Ludendorff on August 9 – as he had told the Austrians – for the second purely German Kreuznach conference. Although the results of this conference have long been known, the student of the continuity of Germany's war aims policy will find a closer analysis of them profitable, since nearly all those war aims which Germany had set herself since August, 1914 re-emerged at this point.[1]

Germany's Eastern war aims had previously been confined to Courland, Lithuania and Poland. In Kreuznach, however, they were quite formally extended in two directions: to the Ukraine in the south-east and to Livonia, Estonia and Finland in the north-east. German policy had included the detachment of the Ukraine from Russia as one of its aims as early as August, 1914, and in May, 1917 the Emperor again described the Ukraine as a German war aim; both Stumm and Michaelis had taken up the same plans in Vienna on August 1. Now, on August 9, the political leaders and the OHL expressly agreed to exploit the separatist movement in the Ukraine 'for tacit, friendly adherence to ourselves'. A secret conference of Prussian ministers, held in Berlin on April 21, 1917, had described Estonia and Livonia as districts to be detached from Russia and settled with German colonists – another old established claim. Now the political leaders and the OHL agreed in Kreuznach to co-ordinate their propaganda activities, which had hitherto been conducted separately, among the Baltic peoples. The same decision was reached for Finland. The Chancellor and the OHL agreed 'that the Duchy of Finland and the Grand Principality of Lithuania must be attached closely to Germany'; they only left the 'form of the association' undefined for the present.

The conference occupied itself in detail with Alsace-Lorraine: the Chancellor and the OHL alike felt that any division of the Reichsland was militarily disadvantageous. The OHL thought that the 'best solution' would be to attach it to Prussia. If, however, it was made a German federal state, as suggested by the Reichstag Majority parties, the OHL could accept this solution, given the early enactment of far-reaching political and economic measures calculated

[1] The 'results' ap. Volkmann, op. cit., p. 204.

to ensure its integration in the Reich; in particular, the railways must be attached to the Prusso-Hessian railway system. All these measures, like those in Poland, Lithuania, Courland and Belgium, were meant to serve the single purpose of 'assuring intact the military supremacy of the king of Prussia' and putting an end to previous particularist institutions. Alsace-Lorraine was thus treated as an object of war aims policy.

In respect of Belgium the OHL repeated the demands already presented to Bethmann Hollweg on April 23: Belgium must remain in German hands as a 'special state'. Should, however, Germany be unable to insist on this or to 'chain' Belgium to Germany in this way, 'then, for the sake of the industrial area of Aachen, we must at least have Liége with a glacis north of it'.

The incorporation of Luxemburg as a German federal state was to be achieved as 'inconspicuously' as possible by attaching the Luxemburg railway system to the Prusso-Hessian. Longwy–Briey – for the sake of which the leaders of Germany's heavy industry were ready, as Michaelis was told on August 29 in a special audience, to carry on the war 'another ten years' – was described as economically 'indispensable' to Germany. The OHL did, however, adapt itself to the new and more elastic philosophy of the day by agreeing to a provisional arrangement which could be based on private legal commitments without the express incorporation of the area in Germany.

On the Polish question the Chancellor and the generals agreed that the Austrians must at last be openly ejected from Poland before the end of the war. Vienna must evacuate the Austrian zone of occupation and accept the appointment of a German Regent (Duke Albrecht of Württemberg). Should the Poles oppose attachment to Germany, the Germans were willing to have a fourth partition of Poland, as Michaelis had already hinted in Vienna. In this case – if, that is, Germany's military, political and economic control over Poland were not assured – the Germans proposed to cut off a considerably larger Polish Frontier Strip, viz., 'the whole Narew line' reaching almost to Warsaw, and to regard the cession of Rumania to Austria-Hungary as null and void.

The structure of the second Kreuznach war aims programme was crowned by a survey over an extended Mitteleuropa: the continuance of the Quadruple Alliance – Germany, Austria-Hungary, Bulgaria and Turkey – after the war was to be assured by economic and military agreements and, if possible, a great Central European economic alliance stretching from the North Sea and the Baltic to the Red Sea.

Of decisive importance for Germany's negative attitude on the question of peace was the inconspicuous sentence: 'We are not at the moment interested in Austria renouncing (all of) Galicia.' Czernin's offer to this effect had been meant as a counterpart to a concession by Germany in Alsace-Lorraine – 'a piece of Alsace-Lorraine'. If German policy no longer attached any value to Austria's sacrifice in Galicia, it relieved itself of the necessity of meeting its ally's wishes by renouncing parts of Alsace-Lorraine in order to make possible an agreement with France, such as even the Foreign Ministry had envisaged. The second Kreuznach conference was thus entirely consistent in refusing the cession of any considerable areas to France.

The natural sequel to the refusal of any concession in Alsace-Lorraine was the failure of the Austro-German conference in Berlin of August 14, 1917. The OHL had again expressly communicated to the participants at this conference the principles agreed with the Chancellor. These participants, besides Michaelis and Czernin, were Hohenlohe, Helfferich and some others, including, for the first time, the new Secretary of State, Kühlmann, formerly minister in The Hague and ambassador in Constantinople.

Immediately on his appointment Kühlmann had set out his foreign political ideas 'shortly but precisely' in a memorandum to Michaelis.[1] The central idea was that, Germany's military, naval and internal situation being what it was, Kühlmann's immediate task must be to obtain peace as early as possible. He agreed with the widespread opinion that Germany's most important enemy, England, would realise that peace talks would be profitable for herself 'before the beginning of winter'. But, unlike the OHL and the naval staff, he thought it quite out of the question that Britain, or the Allies as a whole (including America), could be 'forced to their knees' by military or naval operations. He did, however, think a settlement possible if Germany would meet Britain's real aims, as distinct from propagandist catchwords. He thought these to be:

(i) Maintenance of France as an effective ally and independent Great Power.
(ii) Maintenance of Belgium as an independent state.
(iii) Preventing Germany from establishing herself on the Belgian coast.

He thought that the key position occupied by Belgium in British political thought went back to historic-political traditions which held it to be axiomatic that no great power should be allowed to establish itself on the continental coast opposite England. The seizure by

[1] Cf. Kühlmann's evidence before the Parliamentary Committee of Enquiry, Series 7, Vol. II, p. 60.

Germany of the Belgian coast, or the inclusion in Germany's peace conditions of effective restrictions on the freedom of action of the Belgian state, would make a compromise peace with England impossible. Kühlmann's philosophy was thus decidedly one of withdrawal in the west and security in the east and overseas, something on the lines advocated by Friedrich Meinecke and Hans Delbrück. He thought it possible to obtain the Congo state and therewith a continuous German African colonial empire, which Britain had declared to be compatible with her interests before the outbreak of war. Strong pressure should be applied to obtain what was militarily necessary in Belgium, such as the acquisition of Liége. He wanted to open the peace negotiations by making very far-reaching claims in respect of Belgium and then buy Britain's goodwill by retreating.

In the interests of a settlement with France, he rejected any partition of Alsace-Lorraine for the benefit of the federal states and demanded the continuation of the policy of autonomy initiated by Bethmann Hollweg in the 1912 constitution. He recognised the importance of the Briey deposits for Germany's industry and armaments, but thought annexation impossible if Germany wanted peace before the autumn. The inclusion of Luxemburg in the Reich was 'imaginable'. In the east he would not go beyond the Frontier Strip and its continuation in Courland, with perhaps some enlargement of Upper Silesia. He would not even insist strongly on the kingdom of Poland, as proclaimed, but rather sound the ground for an arrangement between Germany and Russia on which a new relationship between the two states could be built up.

The new Secretary of State had thus expressed himself on all the chief questions of foreign policy, largely indeed in a sense which contradicted Germany's policy since 1914. But whether his ideas could be put into effect depended primarily on the internal power position, on whether Kühlmann could overcome the resistance of the Emperor, the OHL and the navy, his own Foreign Ministry, industry, and the parties of the right; he also had to hold his ground against the Prussian departmental ministers and the military and civilian heads of the occupied territories and, above all, against the Chancellor himself, who had already laid down his own foreign political line in agreement with the OHL.

Kühlmann's appointment was made on August 7, and a week later, on August 14, war aims and questions of peace were discussed with the Austrians at the second Kreuznach conference in Berlin.

Czernin hoped that the conference would bring agreement on the deal proposed by him on August 1, whereby separate peace with France and victory for the Central Powers were to be achieved by

Austria renouncing Galicia, and Germany, Alsace-Lorraine. Kühlmann insisted that it would depend on the internal situation whether
such a step proved necessary. Helfferich emphasised that the situation in Germany was not as bad as in Austria. The hardening of the
German attitude can be explained by the more optimistic view of the
military situation which the German statesmen were now taking.
Helfferich prophesied that the effects of submarine warfare would
soon 'force the British statesmen to accept a peace of the sort that
we want'.

Helfferich, Bethmann Hollweg's chief adviser after Jagow and
Zimmermann, who was not a bureaucrat but the representative of
economic thought and planning among the leaders of the Reich and
occupied a variety of leading positions, personified in interesting
fashion the continuity of Germany's war aims policy. Now, as in the
previous May, he allied himself with the sailors and was largely
successful in nipping Kühlmann's diplomatic plans in the bud.
Michaelis, a product of the higher ministerial bureaucracy, agreed
with Helfferich's general view of the situation in Germany: her
internal conditions were not yet so bad as to force her to accept a
'premature' peace. There was no objective justification whatever for
ceding Alsace-Lorraine. The discussion therefore centred on Rumania and Poland. The cession of Galicia to Poland and the attachment of Poland to Germany would be 'no equivalent for renunciation by the Reich of Alsace-Lorraine'. If Germany gave up Rumania,
she would have to be paid for it by the immediate cession to herself
of the Government-General of Lublin, which the German generals
had so long demanded.

The conversation then reached an unprecedently dramatic tenseness. Czernin had defended his hint that Austria might conclude a
separate peace by maintaining excitedly that Austria had not been
the sole author of the war.[1] Thereupon Kühlmann rejected any
possibility whatever of peace with France on the basis of territorial
concessions in Alsace-Lorraine. Instead he brought Britain back into
the foreground as the 'centre of the coalition'. When Czernin replied
by asking, 'What are your conditions?' the Chancellor only repeated
the latest Kreuznach agreements with the OHL – a proof of the importance and official character of the Kreuznach results. When
Michaelis made the reservation – as Bethmann Hollweg had done in
April, and even the OHL only five days earlier – that the Belgian
war aim could only be achieved after Britain had been defeated,
Czernin was provoked to the sharp retort: 'You are playing *va banque*,

[1] Because Germany had insisted on a strong ultimatum to Serbia. See above
pp. 91–2.

you are waiting for the submarine warfare.' Hohenlohe sprang to his help, saying: 'We cannot carry on war *à outrance*.' The Germans evaded this unexpected attack with Helfferich protesting, no less unexpectedly, that Germany wanted the *status quo*.

Helfferich's sudden retreat on the *status quo*, which the Germans had rejected again and again for three long years, was, however, only a tactical manoeuvre. The only point which was seriously meant was that the Germans were not prepared to grant any cessions worth mentioning, except perhaps a few frontier villages in Alsace-Lorraine. Czernin, however, at once took the Germans at their word and told them plainly that Austria would immediately grasp any possibility of peace on the basis of the *status quo*. The dramatic character of the clash, in which the Germans again, as in May, most strongly resisted their ally's pressure for peace on this basis, is enhanced by the summarised version of the verbal exchanges in the official minutes:

Czernin:	We are talking at cross purposes; in a few months Austria is done for.
Von Kühlmann:	Concessions in Alsace-Lorraine excluded. Then war alone.
Czernin:	Suppose: Entente makes peace offer on the *status quo ante*; you say fight on. We say end. Then *casus foederis* drops.

Before this ultimate threat from their ally, the Germans beat another retreat. Kühlmann now suddenly announced that the conversation of August 9 with the OHL, which the Chancellor had just described officially as containing Germany's official peace terms, had only been 'maxims of the Supreme Command' – a tactical attempt to depreciate the importance of the Kreuznach agreements. Helfferich immediately sprang to his help, enlarging for a second time on the *status quo*. Czernin at once responded gratefully and tried to pin the Germans down to this basis for peace. Unfortunately Michaelis, inexperienced as he was in diplomacy, had no ear for the tactical refinements of the resourceful Helfferich and the experienced diplomat Kühlmann. He contradicted Helfferich quite openly and stated plainly that Germany could not accept the restoration of the *status quo*, although he did hint that the OHL's war aims in the west were unattainable. Helfferich, however, did not let the Chancellor's objections discourage him, and coined a new formula for disguising Germany's war aims: the *status quo* as a 'general basis'. When Czernin insisted on the absolute *status quo*, the Germans gave some indications of how they understood Helfferich's 'general basis'. Michaelis thought that Germany could accept it only 'if Courland and Lithuania adhered voluntarily'. Helfferich backed a similar suggestion about Belgium with a reference to the Flemish movement, so that even Czernin allowed Germany the 'attachment' (sc. of Belgium), 'which appeared to be voluntary'. The German statesmen's ideas on war aims and peace, so vividly reproduced in the minutes, were, although veiled in diplomatic language, identical with those of the Emperor and the OHL. The Crown Prince, however, whom Czernin visited after the meeting, shared the Austrians' serious view of the situation of the Danubian Monarchy and thought it impossible to deny the necessity of an early peace.[1] The Emperor on the other hand, in an answer personally drafted for him by Ludendorff, justified his own and his government's policy by painting a more optimistic picture of the general situation, both in Austria-Hungary and in Germany. He was particularly sanguine on the question of 'man-power and horses' which the Crown Prince had thought to be critical, saying that this justified 'complete confidence in the prospective further development of the situation'. 'Should our enemies . . . pro-pose to resume the struggle next spring with American help, we shall be equal even to this.' None the less, he wrote, his own earnest wish was always for peace – though only a peace such as 'would ensure the position of the Reich in the world'. What Germany must do was to hold out 'ten minutes longer' than the enemy; otherwise she could not count on an 'honourable' peace.

Two days later, in an effort to smooth down the tension which had arisen so violently in Berlin, Michaelis, while yet maintaining Germany's war aims, handed Czernin a written *aide-mémoire* describing Germany's policy, as it then stood.[2] He said that Germany could not come forward with another peace offer of her own, and reverted to the idea of separate peace treaties with Russia or France. In view of this possibility, he defined what the Germans meant by Helfferich's phrase 'the *status quo* as a general basis'. He did protest (referring to his Reichstag speech of July 19) that Germany 'was not aiming at any violent shift of power-relationships after the war'. This, however, would not exclude the possibility 'of bringing about by negotiation close economic and military connections between Germany and economic areas previously in enemy possession, even without the alteration of the present frontiers of the Reich; this would mean

[1] The Crown Prince's letter to the Emperor was dated August 18, 1917. The Emperor replied on August 25: 'Given a monthly requirement of about 160,000 men (for wastage and new formations) we shall still have about 190,000 men on hand at the end of 1917; this figure, it is true, includes the 1899 class . . . but the position is improving every week, especially as the wastage of the field army in July was considerably below the monthly average. For replacements after January, 1918 we have, first, former casualties reporting back (about 90,000 a month) and persons combed out from rejects, of whom there were on July 15 1,026,387 in all. . . . The position in respect of horses is, however, serious.'

[2] Printed ap. Georg Michaelis, *Für Staat und Volk* (Berlin, 1922), p. 333.

Courland, Lithuania and Poland'. Michaelis wanted to apply this system, which basically was simply the masked extension of Germany's power in east and west, even to Belgium and Longwy–Briey. From this vaguely formulated welter of aspirations there emerges very clearly what was perhaps Germany's most concrete war aim, the Polish Frontier Strip. Michaelis openly threatened to fall back on this if Austria-Hungary continued to refuse to vacate her military government in Lublin and hand it over to the German occupational authorities without waiting for the end of hostilities. He further threatened, if Austria continued obstinate, to hand back Congress Poland to Russia. Germany would then annex the Polish frontier districts necessary for her strategic security, while Austria-Hungary came away empty handed in Poland.

This letter has long been known, but the real significance of its apparent modification of Germany's war aims only becomes clear when it is read in connection with the earlier negotiations in Bingen on July 31, in Vienna on August 1, in Kreuznach on August 9, and in Berlin on August 14 and 15. The new wording, adopted out of tactical necessity, towards an ally which was now not willing to fight for more than the *status quo*, nominally altered Germany's old war aims from direct annexation to indirect domination of spheres of influence through economic and military treaties, but in substance yielded nothing essential.

The hint of negotiations between Vienna and Paris constituted only a part of the wrangle which went on between Germany and Austria-Hungary over the question of peace. In spite of the failure of the Sixtus mission in May, 1917, the line between Vienna and Paris was working again so well by the end of August that Painlevé, the French Minister of War who had become Prime Minister on September 12, said that he was ready to meet Czernin in Switzerland. Czernin wanted to meet him, but Kühlmann prevented the meeting, allegedly because the negotiating parties might not be of equal status, but in reality because he thought it 'might gravely endanger Germany's most vital interests . . . if we left the mediation of peace to Austria . . . our interest is so great that polite and moderate, but . . . unambiguous language is called for, even should this provoke annoyance'. Kühlmann was willing to accept Austria's mediation (if at all) only if it was limited to bringing together negotiators from the two camps, including Germans, on neutral ground. Germany's real motive for refusing mediation even by her own ally was concern for her war aims, for the Foreign Ministry feared that the Austrians might be too yielding, especially 'over the purely German sphere of interests, Belgium, North France and

Alsace-Lorraine'. Although Czernin had rejected what Painlevé put forward as a basis of negotiation as a 'bad joke', he nevertheless announced his readiness to enter into conversations. His counter-proposals tried to safeguard the interest of his own state, but attempted also loyally to represent those of Germany.

The Foreign Ministry had been notified on August 13 of Czernin's intention of making contact with Painlevé in Switzerland, and only two days later Kühlmann had hurried to Vienna to insist on Germany's reservations. At this interview Czernin begged Kühlmann, as Austria had so often begged Germany, at least to give France an 'outline' of what Germany was demanding on the most important point, Belgium. Kühlmann, however, refused to define more closely the German government's views 'as already made known' on August 1 and 14; he would not go beyond acceptance of 'the *status quo* as a general basis'. Nevertheless he was successful, for nothing more came at this time of a meeting between Czernin and Painlevé, or someone else of equal standing. On the other hand, when Czernin returned the visit in Berlin on September 6, he obviously succeeded in getting the German statesmen to adopt something of his proposals about Belgium, as may be inferred from the negotiations on Belgium which now opened in connection with the Vatican's peace move.[1]

German war aims and the Pope's peace moves

The tug-of-war between Vienna and Berlin, whether over a separate peace in east or west, or over a general peace, was hidden from the public eye, since the negotiations were carried on in strict secrecy. We can thus understand the agitation of the German public, already excited over Bethmann Hollweg's fall and the Peace Resolution, when it learnt of another peace move, especially as in this case political power-questions and controversies were complicated by a deep-rooted religious mistrust. We refer to Pope Benedict XV's peace move in August and September, 1917. Although the origin and course of this move have been cleared up in extraordinary detail by historians, the decisive role of Germany's war aims in the rebuff to Austria-Hungary, the last Catholic great power and author of the suggestion, has not been clearly recognised and evaluated.

The preliminaries to the Pope's action, combined with the possibility of separate negotiations with Belgium in 1916, and also the negotiations with Wilson, had shown the German government

---

[1] Here, again, the literature is immense. The following works may be mentioned: Kühlmann, *Erinnerungen* (Heidelberg, 1948), pp. 475 ff.; Michaelis, op. cit., pp. 337 ff.; F. Meinecke, *Kühlmann und die päpstliche Friedensaktion, SB. der Pr. Ak. der Wiss., Phil. Hist. Klasse,* 1928, pp. 3 ff.; Epstein, *Erzberger*; Mayer, *New Diplomacy.* Further material in the *Quellen zur Geschichte des Parlamentarismus.*

clearly the central position of Belgium in international politics. Pacelli, the Papal Nuncio in Munich, had had a preliminary meeting with the Emperor on June 29, followed by visits to Bethmann Hollweg and then Michaelis, and the conversations opened in earnest in the middle of August. The Belgian question remained the starting-point for any move towards general peace. On August 1 Benedict XV had issued an earnest appeal for peace in an Encyclical addressed to the heads of the belligerent states. It was handed to them on August 15, the second day of the German–Austro-Hungarian conference in Berlin. Like Wilson and the Stockholm Socialists, the Pope called for a negotiated reduction of national armaments and an international court of arbitration. Proposals of immediate bearing on a possible ending of the war were that all parties should renounce reparations and should evacuate occupied territories, including colonies. The Pope made express mention of the Balkan, Armenian and above all the Polish questions, which he said should be treated in a spirit of equity and justice; he was plainly advocating the restoration of Poland. This was already calculated to cause displeasure in German circles, which could not but harden when the Pope described cessions by Austria to Italy and Alsace-Lorraine as 'disputable questions' on which he asked for 'conciliatory mutual concessions'. Nevertheless Czernin and Michaelis agreed in Berlin on the 15th to accept his offer of mediation.

On the same day the Cardinal Secretary of State, Gasparri, conveyed the wish of the Holy Father that Germany should return a 'simple answer' in the sense that the government of the Reich was prepared to accept the Vatican's proposal 'as a basis for further discussions'. Stronger pressure still came in a letter sent by Pacelli in August to von Bergen in the Foreign Ministry, which painted in very strong colours the danger which Germany would incur if she publicly rejected the Pope's initiative, while conversely the Central Powers would necessarily gain in moral prestige if the Entente rejected it; and he asked for the text of Germany's reply to be communicated to him in confidence, to enable the Vatican to suggest amendments if it thought fit.

On August 19 the German government conveyed to Vienna the outlines of its answer, which could also serve as a basis for a peace conference. This draft, which the Austrians approved on August 22, indicates Germany's war aims under Michaelis. They differ little from those of Bethmann Hollweg. With respect to the Pope's proposals, the note asked for the 'freedom of the seas', to be realised 'by the establishment of real guarantees'; it agreed to a limitation of armaments 'subject to consideration of the special situation of each state' and to a court of arbitration. For herself, Germany asked for the restoration of her colonies and in addition, 'a colonial empire commensurate with the importance of her economic interests'; further, a 'territorial compromise' (meaning Longwy–Briey) was to be reached in the west by way of separate negotiations between Germany and France. Germany applied to Belgium the same principle of treating each question separately, admitting 'the restoration of the Belgian state, subject to safeguards for the security of Germany', but stipulating that the attendant economic questions should be clarified in separate negotiations between the German and Belgian governments. Belgium could not be evacuated until England had 'withdrawn from the Continent'. The paragraph on 'economic peace' concealed the lurking shape of Mitteleuropa. In the east Germany declared herself ready to recognise the newly created state of Poland, and to champion the rights of the other national units, naming the Ukraine, Finland, the Baltic provinces, the Flemish Netherlands, Ireland, Egypt and Persia (cf. the instructions given to the German Majority Socialists for Stockholm). Further, Germany agreed that, 'provided the interests of her allies are safeguarded', the future of Serbia, Rumania and Montenegro should be decided in a way conducive to European peace.

Austria-Hungary raised no objections to these general principles. Only for Belgium did Czernin ask for an express assurance that no change in the existing frontiers was intended, in order to disclaim clearly any suspicion of annexations – a proposal which Germany, however, did not accept. Czernin's further wish that the German government, like the Austrian, should confine itself to describing the Pope's suggestions as 'a suitable basis for the initiation of peace negotiations' had already been adopted by Michaelis as the German government's standpoint when he spoke to the Federal Council's Foreign Affairs Committee on August 20. He said that the German government would reply to the note in terms of 'general sympathy', but without entering more closely into the allies' war aims. He emphasised that on this point he was in complete agreement with the OHL. The government accordingly took the Pope's move as offering 'a basis for an understanding' and on August 24 returned both to Pacelli's letter and to the note answers which were, as the Pope had wished, 'simple' and avoided detail, stating that 'the basis of a peace honourable for all parties' should be 'guarantees of the real freedom and general use of the seas and limitation of armaments through definite rules and subject to certain safeguards', and accepting the principle of arbitration. Without reverting to the problem of Belgium (which Bergen had mentioned in his first draft) the government said

that it saw in the Pope's train of thought 'a suitable basis for the preparation of an approach to future peace'.

Only after this had been done was the Reichstag, in the form of the
constitutional innovation of the 'Committee of Seven', formally
consulted on the answer – a step thought to be necessary in view of the
internal political situation after the Peace Resolution. The meeting,
which took place on August 28,[1] was attended by six members of the
Federal Council in addition to the seven parliamentary deputies.
Kühlmann, Helfferich and Wallraf, Under-Secretary of State in the
Reich Interior Office, represented the government. While Ebert and
Erzberger thought some mention of Belgium necessary, Westarp and
Stresemann opposed it sharply, and the diplomats of the Federal
Council supported them unreservedly; The meeting ended by adopt-
ing Scheidemann's and Fehrenbach's proposal and cast its remarks
in idealistic and general terms.

On August 21, meanwhile, the British government had informed
the Cardinal Secretary of State, through its representative at the
Vatican, that it thought 'any attempt to produce agreement between
the belligerents useless' in the absence of 'a definite declaration by the
Central Powers on their war aims, in particular on their intention
to restore the full independence of Belgium and to make good the
damage done to her'. Pacelli passed this answer to Michaelis on
August 30 in a personal letter and asked Germany in the name of the
Cardinal Secretary of State: (i) to issue a definite declaration on the
intentions of the imperial government in respect of the 'full independence of Belgium' and reparation for war damage, and (ii) 'also to
state definitely what were the guarantees required by Germany for
political, economic and military independence'. Thus the Holy See's
public peace move was now accompanied by other, confidential
soundings of the German government.

The government recognised that Britain might be putting out
serious peace feelers, but did not feel certain that, if the desired
declaration were given, Britain would open (separate) peace negotiations on a basis acceptable to Germany in other respects. Kühlmann
therefore suggested, and Michaelis agreed, that the British government should first be sounded through a neutral diplomat. In order
to secure for itself the necessary freedom of action and to establish
general principles for answering both to the Pope's public peace
move and the secret Pacelli note, the government thought it necessary to get a decision from the Emperor in a Crown Council. This
should be attended by the OHL and the navy, who could then not
raise later objections. After this course had been decided, Kühlmann

[1] See *Ursachen des deutschen Zusammenbruches*, IV ser., Vol. II, p. 380.

succeeded at the second and last session of the Committee of Seven, on September 10, in persuading Ebert and Scheidemann to drop their demand for a declaration on Belgium and to agree to include in the answer to the Pope – as they had themselves proposed – a reference to the Peace Resolution (which Michaelis had reserved the right to interpret himself) and to collaboration between the government and parliament in drafting the note. Erzberger had already been converted to the government's tactics. Incidentally, Kühlmann gave the deputies only a very vague intimation of Pacelli's request for a definite declaration on Belgium; he even left Scheidemann (to whom he had personally given a hint of his intention of sounding the British government through a neutral) under the belief that the Holy See had agreed and did not expect Germany's reply to mention Belgium. This was the exact contrary of the truth, although we may credit Kühlmann with the subjectively honest wish to prevent his diplomatic game, for which he was working with the 'pledges theory' (i.e., the use of an occupied country as a bargaining counter), from being spoilt by a public declaration of renunciation over Belgium.

Much has been written by historians on the episode, but in fact the significance of the government's victory, won over a hesitant opposition reduced at the last to a single party, and obscured into the bargain by the emphasis on the tactical elements in the situation, was only secondary; for the substance of its answer had been decided before the first meeting of the Committee of Seven, not to mention the second. The Reichstag had no influence on the shaping of the government's decisions.

A separate peace with Britain:
the Bellevue Crown Council of September 11, 1917

The political leaders of Germany regarded the British communication to the Pope, as transmitted to Pacelli – of which, however, only Kühlmann, the Chancellor and the Emperor were informed – as a serious peace feeler, but they wished to answer it, not through the Pope but in their own way. The efforts to bring about political agreement between the leaders of the Reich were therefore directed rather towards planning the projected diplomatic step than towards answering the Pope (this answer, though bound up with the Belgian question, now retreated into the background). Before the Crown Council Michaelis visited the western front, where he found full agreement on concessions on the Belgian question in various quarters, including both the Prussian and the Bavarian Crown Princes.

Further, Michaelis called together his Secretaries of State on September 8 to explain to them in detail that he was willing to work for 'an honourable peace' and did not propose to prolong the war for the sake of individual and not absolutely essential aims, such as possession of the coast of Flanders as hitherto demanded by the navy. Recognising that peace with Britain would depend on the Belgian question, he strongly emphasised his approval of 'the restoration of the territorial integrity of Belgium with far-reaching respect for its sovereignty'. A promise to this effect, however – and this he said equally clearly and decidedly – could not be given unconditionally, but must depend on 'partly military, partly economic guarantees' which would have to be achieved through private German–Belgian negotiations; for he was, he said, convinced that the Belgians themselves 'would see the best guarantee of a bright future in a close relationship with Germany'. All present agreed except the Secretary of State for the Navy, von Capelle.

Kühlmann had already composed two memoranda, dated respectively August 21 and September 3, setting out his belief that peace with Britain could be achieved if Germany was conciliatory on the Belgian question. Information received from The Hague, even before Pacelli's communication, had led Kühlmann to believe that Lloyd George wanted to end the war at any price. Even demands for Alsace-Lorraine would not prevent Britain from concluding peace. There must, however, be soundings, which need in no way bind German policy, to make certain whether a German declaration on Belgium would lead to the immediate initiation of peace negotiations. He rejected only the far-reaching war aims of the navy, which amounted in practice to the annexation and military subjection of the whole of Belgium. We learn from his memoranda that the navy was asking, not only for a semi-circular zone 45 kilometres deep behind the towns of Ostend, Zeebrügge and Bruges, which were to be German bases (i.e., all West Flanders and much of East Flanders), but also a corridor running diagonally through Belgium and including Brussels as well as Liége. Kühlmann rejected this corridor, which would have been 180 kilometres long and would have cut Belgium in two and would have been quite indefensible, and he likewise rejected the demand for strong German garrisons in all important Belgian towns. Like Michaelis, he thought Germany's interests would be sufficiently safeguarded by establishing close economic links with Belgium.

In preparation for the meeting of Secretaries of State and for the Crown Council to be held in advance of the anticipated private negotiations with Belgium Helfferich had already obtained certain detailed proposals from von der Lancken, the Head of the Political Section of the Government-General in Brussels. These were elaborated by the Reich Interior Office into 'Notes for a Peace Treaty with Belgium' and then personally re-written by Helfferich himself as his proposed basis for the Belgian discussions. Helfferich, too, now renounced annexations, in whole or in part; Belgium was to retain her sovereignty, but only on condition that Germany's interests, military, economic and international, were safeguarded; for otherwise Belgium would infallibly 'drift into complete dependence on our enemies'. Belgium was to be divided into two autonomous states, in a personal union under one king; she might conclude treaties only if she first submitted them to all signatory powers. The economic guarantees were very precise. The economic relationship between Flanders-Wallonia and Germany was to be so close as to make Belgium regard her own interests, pragmatically, as identical with those of Germany. This relationship was to be effected primarily by including Belgium in the German Customs Association for twenty to twenty-five years; Belgium was also to adopt Germany's tariff legislation, certain German taxes, Germany's legislation on monopolies, and her social and workers' protective legislation. If possible she was to be attached to the German–Austrian Economic Alliance. There was also to be a currency union and Belgium was to renounce the Latin Currency Convention. Agreements were to be concluded on the railways and waterways under which Belgium would cede her rights to a mixed economic company in which German influence would predominate. Similar arrangements were to be made for the port of Antwerp, and for the protection of all German undertakings existing in Belgium before the war or founded during it. Helfferich thought that the question of a war indemnity could be solved by the cession of the rich coal supplies of the Campine, the exploitation of which, in conjunction with the minette ores of Longwy–Briey, was of the greatest importance for the economic development of Germany. They were, however, to constitute only a part of the war indemnity, which was to made up out of contributions from the Belgian state and Belgian private companies.

These 'safeguards' and 'guarantees' again followed Bethmann Hollweg's middle line between annexation and freedom, but they were strongly influenced by the Reich and Prussian departmental ministries and by the civilian administration of the Government-General. These 'guarantees' figured three times in the subsequent answer to Pacelli, and were not 'relics of annexationism' but the expression of political intentions which were believed to be practicable.

The OHL set out their demands in memoranda which gave a minimum and maximum programme. The minimum demand was the annexation of Liége and the Meuse line, to protect the Rhineland-Westphalian coal basin. The OHL agreed with Helfferich in seeing Germany's interest best secured by close economic links between the two countries and by an administrative partition. On military grounds, however, they added further demands: control of Belgium's war industry, dismantling of the fortresses, and occupation of the country until the military, economic and transport terms of the peace had been fulfilled. There should be a customs union, joint management of the public transport system, joint administration of the ports, a currency union and identical trade, industrial and social legislation. These demands comprised the OHL's minimum demands for a 'release of Belgium'. The maximum demands envisaged a permanent annexation of the coast of Flanders in order to constitute a permanent threat to Britain and to strengthen Germany's power position.

On this point the OHL was most strongly supported by the sailors, led by the naval staff. Holtzendorff, in this respect a faithful disciple of Grand Admiral Tirpitz, declared it to be a *conditio sine qua non* of peace with England, the very pre-condition of Germany's existence even as an economic world power.

The different parties concerned had now defined their positions. It remained to get from the Emperor a decision binding on them all. The Emperor's feelings and views were nearer to those of the navy and the military, but on September 9 Michaelis, by representing to him the prospect of an early conclusion of peace with Britain – which was expected to follow in three or four weeks – persuaded him to renounce the coast of Flanders and to agree to a conciliatory step designed to ensure the success of Helfferich's programme.[1] It is true that Wilhelm afterwards relapsed, probably under the influence of the navy, and demanded at least an equivalent, in the form of overseas bases, for the renunciation of the coast. Nevertheless, in the Crown Council he left Michaelis 'a free hand'.

At the Crown Council[2] the Chancellor began by assuming that serious peace feelers would be coming from England, elicited, as Kühlmann put it, by the fear of America becoming too powerful in the future; this appreciation had confirmed Kühlmann in his conviction that the 'key to the political situation' and thus to peace lay not with France – of which he had said as lately as September 3 that

[1] Michaelis, op. cit., pp. 344 ff.
[2] The official minutes have not been preserved. See Michaelis, op. cit., pp. 349 ff.; Helfferich, *Weltkrieg*, p. 485; and Kühlmann, op. cit., pp. 481 ff.

'a sea of hatred separates us from France' – but with Britain; for Britain was not fighting for Alsace-Lorraine but for her own war aims which were the freedom of the coast of Flanders and the liberation of Belgium. Such being the situation as they saw it, Michaelis, supported by Kühlmann, asked for authorisation to announce *le cas chéant* that Germany was prepared to consent 'to the restoration of the territorial integrity and sovereignty of Belgium', and further 'to discover through discreet reliable channels what were the Western Powers' minimum demands in respect of Belgium . . . and whether a declaration on the future development of affairs in Belgium, to be given, at first, discreetly by government to government, but in binding form, would lead to the opening of peace negotiations'.

The complete renunciation of annexations was opposed by Ludendorff, speaking also for Hindenburg. He insisted on the annexation, both in east and in west, of a 'glacis' for the protection of the industrial areas near the frontiers; as regards Belgium, this meant the annexation of Liége. He too hoped that very close economic association would lead to political union. Although he thought that complete security could be achieved only through the military domination of the whole of Belgium – his maximum programme – nevertheless for the sake of peace, if it was certain and of nature to prove lasting, he was willing to abandon it and to renounce the coast of Flanders. He was, however, all the more obstinate in insisting on his minimum programme. As Capelle accepted the OHL's view, Holtzendorff was left isolated in a vain defence of Germany's permanent occupation of the coast of Flanders.

To the Emperor, who had to take the decision, Britain's feelers seemed to confirm his policy; he saw in them the effect of submarine warfare. 'Now England was coming'; she 'was throwing in her hand'. Even more decidedly than Kühlmann, he discerned the effects of Russia's collapse and fear of American supremacy. He regarded Britain's peace move as the 'great success', precisely because Britain might act as 'a wedge to split the other Powers'. He too, he said, turning to the soldiers, had, like Falkenhayn, thought of annexing the whole of Belgium,[1] and he had never been blind to the strategic importance of the Flanders coast; but the coast could not be held without annexing the whole. For these reasons, and in view of the possibilities of peace, he said in brief 'that Belgium could be restored, and King Albert might return to the Belgian throne'. The restoration of Belgium must not, however, be unconditional; it must be

[1] Müller, op. cit., p. 137. On a visit to Flanders on October 20, 1915, the Emperor said, in a conversation with Valentini: 'I shan't give this up again, I swear to you.'

made conditional on 'definite economic and military safeguards' to be worked out in bilateral negotiation. Finally Emperor, statesmen and (although only reluctantly) the OHL agreed that the Chancellor should be empowered to act in the sense of his two proposals. If, however, peace on this basis had not been reached with the western powers by the end of the year, the Emperor reserved his right to reconsider the Belgian question.

Kühlmann's freedom of action was thus doubly restricted: on the one hand, he could not make any declaration on Belgium without having received Britain's previous consent to immediate peace negotiations; on the other, the declaration could not be unconditional, but must contain hidden reservations. Kühlmann had won an apparent victory, but the particular interests had got their way.

No minutes had been taken of the Council, and the next day the Chancellor tried, for safety's sake, to pin down the Emperor, the OHL and the naval staff. First he drew up an account of the meeting and got the Emperor to initial his own words; then he sent letters of thanks to Holtzendorff and Hindenburg. In his letter to the OHL Michaelis made another attempt to get round their demand for the annexation of Liége: if the Belgians fulfilled all Germany's demands for close economic association, then military safeguards, including the annexation of Liége, could presumably be given up. Hindenburg, however, objected immediately and most decidedly, saying that the close economic association could not be forced through without pressure, viz., without permanent possession of Liége. Ludendorff made his reluctant renunciation of the Flanders coast the occasion to put in world-embracing demands for compensation, which looked very grandiose but were entirely in the tradition of Germany's official war aims: Russia and South America must be secured as markets, a colonial empire acquired in Africa, and naval bases for its defence. If it was no longer possible to use Flanders as a means of pressure on Britain, Holland must be brought in for this purpose 'especially since its colonial territories will be guaranteed by an alliance between us and Japan'.

That Michaelis himself entertained absolutely positive war aims appears most clearly from his letter to Hindenburg,[1] in which he implored Hindenburg (as he implored Holtzendorff in respect of 'your officers and the influential men who are your associates or supporters') to support him against the pan-German annexationists.

They must be told . . . what we are getting: in the west, intact frontiers and an assured prospect of exploitation of the raw materials in the occupied areas, favourable economic and technical conditions on the railways and

[1] Meinecke, op. cit., p. 10.

waterways, privileged positions in the Port of Antwerp, influence over the pro-German Flemish population, our neighbours made to pay for the heavy damage inflicted by them on us, elimination of British influence on the coast of Flanders and north France, and the demand for the restoration of our colonies, perhaps as part of an exchange. On top of this comes any increase in power and influence, in political, economic and military respects gained by us in the east.

In the east Michaelis envisaged not only the cession of the Polish Frontier Strip, to which he, as a Prussian, attached particular value, but also Courland, Lithuania, Poland and now Rumania also, and as the Vienna conference of August 1 had shown, he already had an eye on Finland and the Ukraine when Russia should collapse.

After the Crown Council the feelers for immediate conversations with Britain and the negotiations with the Vatican on the public answer to the Pope's peace move went on in parallel. As instructed by the Crown Council, Kühlmann immediately pursued officially the secret soundings which had been initiated by the Spanish minister in Brussels, the Marquis de Villalobar, a personal friend of his from earlier days when both had been stationed in London and a man who had been highly respected both by the British government and the Court. Villalobar, however, sent Kühlmann's message – a modified version of the decisions of the Crown Council – to the Spanish minister at The Hague by wireless. The message was intercepted by both the Germans and the French, who at once took counter-measures, so that this line was cut. Another attempt was made through the Spanish Foreign Minister, who was in touch with the British ambassador in Madrid. This attempt failed to produce the assurance required by Germany that Britain was ready to open immediate negotiations, but it did elicit a message that the British government was prepared to receive any communication from the German government relating to peace, 'which they would then discuss with their allies'. This, however, was an offer of which Kühlmann was prevented from taking advantage, both by the conditions laid down by the Crown Council and by his own maxim of not giving up the 'pledge' of Belgium without return.

For the sake of this slender thread, and on the basis moreover of a false assessment of Britain's position and attitude – whether attributed to submarine warfare, to Russia or to America does not matter – Kühlmann thought himself in a position to reject the Pope's offer, and he gave it no more than a vague answer which ran quite contrary to the Holy See's intentions.[1] The Holy See had emphasised

[1] See Kühlmann's evidence before the Committee of Enquiry, *Untersuchungsausschuss*, 4th series, Vol. VII, p. 97.

strongly the moral effect which a public declaration on the unrestricted restoration of Belgium would have on world public opinion, including America and those circles in Britain which were anxious for peace (Labour, Liberals, the circle round Lansdowne, even Lloyd George himself). But Kühlmann thought he could do without this. How far the preference for the more diplomatic and secret course over the revolutionary and public one was due to indecision on the part of Michaelis and his Secretary of State, how far the insistence on the Belgian war aim was determined by renewed pressure from the OHL and the navy, or the *vis momenti* of Germany's own policy since September, 1914, how far super-diplomatic refinement defeated its own object in spite of an honest desire to achieve peace through a renunciation of Belgium – all this is hard to judge definitely. One factor, however, was undoubtedly the limitation of Kühlmann's own personality. A jurist and diplomat of the old school, he was not capable of carrying on revolutionary diplomacy appropriate to the age of Wilson and Lenin, and he could not bring himself to toss the catchword of 'unconditional restoration of Belgium' to the masses of the Entente peoples and so provoke a popular crusade for peace. But the personal factor was only subsidiary. The objective factors were decisive. Kühlmann was indeed formally bound by the decision of the Crown Council forbidding him to renounce Belgium without counter-services, but the resolution itself expressed the essence of the power relationships of Germany; it marked the extreme limit of the possibilities of an understanding, for a public renunciation of Belgium would certainly have resulted in the fall of the Secretary of State, if not of the Chancellor.

Kühlmann accordingly retained the general wording of the first answer to the Pope, which omitted mention of Belgium, and in spite of urgent warnings from the Cardinal Secretary of State, who had, as agreed, been given the test of the note and now sent two telegrams (of September 18 and 20) warning him that the attempted mediation would fail unless the wording of the note was altered, and urging postponement of the communication and publication of it, he insisted on handing over the note unaltered on September 20 and publishing it without delay on September 27. Two days later came the definite answer to Pacelli's letter of August 31. It said that Germany 'was not yet in the position to make a definite statement on the intentions of the imperial government in respect to Belgium and the guarantees required by us'. The guarantees described as 'inescapable' (the word figured three times in the document) again conveyed unmistakably those German war aims which made a public declaration on Belgium such as the Vatican had wanted impossible. All that the German government offered was that a declaration on Belgium might be given 'at a not very distant date' and 'after certain pre-conditions had been cleared up', meaning, after Britain had promised to open peace negotiations in reply to Villalobar's soundings. This, however, never happened, since the soundings via Spain broke down on October 6. Therewith the partial renunciation of Belgium, laboriously extracted at the Crown Council, became null and void again and the men and forces of the harder line regained the upper hand.

Confidence in Germany's military leaders and faith in her power and in the invincibility of her armies, provided only the unity of the home front could be preserved, remained the dominant feeling at least in public opinion, outweighing the wish for a peace of understanding. This feeling was expressed and at the same time fostered by the manifesto (which Michaelis said 'touched him pleasurably') issued by Hindenburg on his 70th birthday in tones of Germanic–Christian sentiment, with the two warnings: 'Think not on the Prussian franchise! doubt not in the realisation of the war aims!'

'With God's help our German strength has withstood the tremendous attack of our enemies, because we were one, because each gave his all gladly. So it must stay to the end. "Now thank we all our God" on the bloody battle-field! Take no thought for what is to be after the war! This only brings despondency into our ranks and strengthens the hopes of the enemy. Trust that Germany will achieve what she needs to stand there safe for all time, trust that the German oak will be given air and light for its free growth! Muscles tensed, nerves steeled, eyes front! We see before us the aim: Germany honoured, free and great! God will be with us to the end!'

16

THE RE-SHAPING OF WAR AIMS POLICY

MAINTENANCE OF EASTERN AIMS

THE Bellevue Crown Council took place under pressure from a new War Aims Majority, which was then forming. In the course of the next few months this body, in co-operation with the OHL and civilian leaders, succeeded in emasculating the offers of the Peace Resolution, which had been taken abroad as evidence of Germany's readiness to reach an understanding.

Against a peace of renunciation and democratisation: the reconstitution of the War Aims Majority

The national committee of the Zentrum party met in Frankfurt-am-Main on July 23–4, 1917, only a few days after the acceptance by the Reichstag of the Peace Resolution. The party opposition protested most vigorously against the parliamentary party's change of front on war aims, and it was only with difficulty that Erzberger succeeded in repelling the attacks by reading out Czernin's secret reports on the economic collapse of Austria-Hungary. The committee finally agreed to a resolution which accepted 'a peace of understanding and compromise', but only on condition that it 'safeguarded the political security and further economic development of Germany.'[1] The idea of a peace of understanding had thus been largely modified in its most important respect. The Zentrum party was not behind its parliamentary representatives.

After the Peace Resolution had accomplished two of its three real purposes – enabling the Majority Socialists to continue to justify to their followers their consent to the war credits, and preventing Austria-Hungary from leaving the war – the Zentrum deputies quickly returned to their old line, partly under the influence of the improved military situation, partly under pressure from the right wing of their own party. The Bavarian-Christian Peasant Union, for example, at its twelfth war session on September 12, adopted a resolution pledging it to fight 'against attempts at democratisation which are a danger to the federal structure of the Reich, and against a

[1] On the negotiations, see Epstein, *Erzberger*, pp. 206 ff., and Karl Bachem, *Vorgeschichte, Geschichte und Politik der deutschen Zentrumspartei*, Vol. 9 (Cologne, 1932), pp. 437 ff.

peace which submits us like slaves to the yoke of King Dollar of America', and to reject most decisively any kind of peace of renunciation. Erzberger, addressing a meeting in Ulm on September 23 on his party's aims, said: 'We are renouncing nothing whatever that is necessary to Germany's greatness, Germany's development, Germany's freedom in the world.'[1] The Zentrum rejected co-operation with the Fatherland party (*Vaterlandspartei*) and the idea of a 'peace of victory', but dissociated itself no less decidedly from Social Democracy's 'peace of renunciation'. When, finally, a member of the right wing of the party – Count Hertling – came to occupy the highest position in the state, Erzberger's influence declined still further. In January, 1918 a large proportion of the party wanted to repudiate the July Resolution altogether.[2] The path had been smoothed for the acceptance by the Zentrum of the Eastern Peace Treaties, and it was symptomatic that Gröber, not Erzberger, was picked to speak for the party on that occasion.

Similar voices were heard among the second of the three Majority parties, the Progressive People's Party.[3]

There were also violent dissensions among the National Liberals, some of whose parliamentary representatives had originally intended to vote for the Peace Resolution. A section of the party, especially the 'Old National Liberals', thought that the counter-declaration produced by their parliamentary representatives had not dissociated them sharply enough from the Peace Resolution. In view of this dissatisfaction, the Central Committee of the party met on September 23, 1917. Stresemann tried to forestall attacks by adopting a strong, confident tone, very different from his despondent one of the summer. Speaking of the Pope's note, he said explicitly that besides her official answer to the Vatican, Germany was carrying on separate negotiations through the neutral powers, and that in these negotiations the question of war aims was being discussed in detail; and he declared: 'Unless all appearances deceive, the foundations of Germany's position in the world are being laid at this moment.' With Austria's re-occupation of Galicia and the Bukovina in the latest offensive, Russia's offers of a separate peace to Austria had lost their attractiveness, and Austria was again standing firmly by Germany's side; Germany, too, was in occupation of wide areas of enemy territory, 'so that,' said Stresemann, 'with these great pledges in our hand we shall be able, when peace negotiations begin, to extract whatever is to be extracted by virtue of the brilliant situation in which we are'.

[1] Wacker, *Haltung der Zentrumspartei*, p. 38.
[2] Westarp, op. cit., II, p. 566.
[3] Volkmann, *Annexionsfragen*, pp. 137 f.

Stresemann was critical of all political moves which did not show a strong determination to secure Germany's aims 'in view of the brilliant situation'. Speaking of Germany's Polish policy, he feared that the proclamation of Poland's independence might lead to the real loss of that country. On Belgium, he was strongly against Germany declaring herself disinterested without absolute guarantees of her interests. He warmly advocated 'a quite close political association' between Germany and Courland and the occupied parts of Livonia, 'because these old nurseries of German greatness and German genius . . . would be driven straight into the arms of the Russian hangman, were we to surrender them again'.

This speech, with its complete return to the old arrogance of 1915, was nevertheless followed by a long and acrimonious discussion, which ended in the committee repudiating the declaration of July 19 by 100 votes to 8. The committee regarded the Peace Declaration as

seriously endangering the future development of Germany. . . . Germany's future security cannot rest only on treaties between peoples; it must be based on German power and strength. Unless we extend our power in east and west and assure our world-political positions overseas, and unless we get adequate war reparations, we should have no security against future threats to our existence and should be set back for decades, politically and economically. The military situation gives us the assurance that Germany's frontiers will receive the necessary improved protection and that the political and economic future of Germany will be secured.

The committee also found fault with the line adopted by its parliamentary representatives on internal policy; it had thus repudiated their policy completely.

Stresemann was nevertheless able to secure his own re-election, by acclamation, to the Deputy Presidency of the party. Under his leadership the party's parliamentary representatives now backed far-reaching demands, to derive from a peace of victory, as vigorously as in the first years of the war.

But the most important internal political reaction produced by the Peace Resolution and the attempt to moderate Germany's war aims was the foundation of the Fatherland Party[1] as a focus for all advocates of extreme war aims. This party had originally been conceived by Tirpitz and Dietrich Schäfer as a 'movement' standing above the parties, and had at once been joined by a number of politicians from all parties of the right. It had quickly expanded into an ultra-nationalist mass organisation with a membership which in July, 1918 topped 1,250,000 – considerably more than the 1,000,000 which was

[1] Karl Wortmann, *Die Kriegsziele der Vaterlandspartei* (Halle/Saale, 1926) contains valuable material.

the highest figure reached by the Social Democrats (in 1914). Besides its prize, the party enjoyed especial weight through the high positions occupied by its leading members in Germany's political, economic and social life, and was thus the most powerful organisation representing the political bourgeoisie of Germany during the First World War. The leaders of Germany's material and intellectual life were clearly more firmly convinced than ever that only a victorious and profitable conclusion of the war could secure their political and social order against pressure from below: even a 'drawn' peace on the basis of the *status quo* would shatter their internal position.

The Fatherland Party embodied the mass protest of the German bourgeoisie against any yielding over war aims, especially to the west, and against any invasion by Western democracy of the traditional structure of the Prusso-German form of state; for democracy threatened the greatness of Germany. The Peace Resolution, and even more fear that the German government and liberal circles were prepared to accept a 'peace of renunciation' with Britain, had sounded the alarm throughout all nationalist circles in Germany. But the special feature of this party's policy was its attempt to raise Germany's economic and military claims on to the plane of a fundamental opposition of world philosophies which must – and was intended to – make a peace of understanding between Britain and Germany impossible. Tirpitz announced this categorically at the party's founding meeting on September 2, 1917:

> The war has developed into a life and death struggle between two world philosophies: the German and the Anglo-American. The question today is whether we can hold our own against Anglo-Americanism or whether we must sink down and become mere manure for others [*Völkerdünger*]. . . . The colossal struggle which Germany is now waging is therefore not one for Germany alone; what is really at issue is the liberty of the continent of Europe and its peoples against the all-devouring tyranny of Anglo-Americanism. Germany is fighting for a great deal, and therefore I would cry out to every corner of our Fatherland: 'Germany, awake! Thine hour of destiny has arrived.'[1]

The slogan of an irreconcilable conflict of world philosophies was taken up by the Emperor in the summer of 1918. Tirpitz was the man who, with Wilhelm II and the admiral's intellectual mouthpiece, Dietrich Schäfer, had since the turn of the century introduced the new style of mass agitation for the promotion of Germany's power, conducted by influencing the press, founding associations and collecting funds. In the autumn of 1917 he was able, with Ludendorff's

[1] Hans Resch, *Grossadmiral Alfred von Tirpitz* (Stuttgart, n.d.), p. 82.

surreptitious support, to draw on the rich experience of his agitation for a navy before the war and for unrestricted submarine warfare during it and, unhampered by the restrictions of public office, to make himself a national figure as never before. By combining the aims of the right with the techniques of mass propaganda which had hitherto been thought the prerogative of the left, Tirpitz and the Fatherland Party went beyond the old monarchic-constitutional Prusso-Germany; their professedly supra-party 'movement' was a step towards the anti-parliamentary, dictatorial, one-party state.

Since the stronghold of the Fatherland Party was in the Prusso-Conservative Protestantism of north Germany, it is understandable that the Pope's move, occurring when it did, helped to inflame nationalist feeling still further. As early as 1912 Hans Delbrück, in a polemic against the equal franchise, had maintained that the threatened majority of Socialists and Catholics both in the Reich and Prussia would inevitably destroy the Prussian–Protestant character of the German state.[1] The same feelings now led large numbers of Conservative-minded German Protestants to attack sharply the alliance between the Zentrum and the Social Democrats which they regarded as already a political reality. The quartercentenary celebrations of the Reformation in October, 1917[2] provided a welcome occasion for mobilising the immemorial resentments and deep-rooted anti-Catholic emotions of the German Protestant bourgeoisie against the Pope's peace move and against the key position in Germany's internal politics held by the Zentrum under Erzberger. In these months preachers and teachers went further than ever before in their invocation of Martin Luther, as symbol of Germany against Western democracy in the cause of monarchist Prussia–Germany with its buttresses in the army and the bureaucracy. The Emperor himself felt that he had a mission to support the Protestant imperial crown against rivals at home and abroad, not least against the House of Habsburg–Parma. He saw this own special plans of extending the power of Prussia north-eastward endangered by conspiracy between Rome and Habsburg–Parma in Catholic Poland and Lithuania. Thus in the course of the controversy over the dynastic question in Lithuania, he wrote after a visit by Erzberger to that country in the summer of 1918:

The ultra-bigoted House of Parma, in league with its fanatical father-confessors, hates the Protestant House of Hohenzollern; its standpoint is one

[1] Annelise Thimme, *Hans Delbrück als Kritiker der Wilhelminischen Epoche* (Düsseldorf, 1955), p. 38.

[2] See Gottfried Mehnert, *Evangelische Kirche und Politik, 1917–1919* (Düsseldorf, 1959), pp. 43 ff. and 48 ff.

of mediaeval obscurantism. It is working for a confessional encirclement of Germany under the hated House of Hohenzollern. Under the leadership of Vienna, and *allied* with it, Italy—won by the restoration of Trentino and the Tirol—France, Poland, Lithuania *to the sea* are to be united! Hence Poland's *independence*, and the resumption of the *Austro-Polish* solution which had been dropped in Homburg. Hence an *independent* Lithuania under *Cathol.* Prince; hence the resistance to our incorporation of the *Baltic Provinces* inc. Liv. and Estonia, which are to be attached to Lithuania and Catholicised, to cut us off from the sea. The deputy *Erzberger* has *criminally* [elsewhere he calls him a 'traitor and scoundrel', even a 'poisoner of wells'] personally *assisted* these plans, against the interests of Germany and the German Emperor; hence his journey of agitation to Lithuania. He has been *consciously* serving Rome, Parma and Habsburg against *Hohenzollern*; a scoundrelly traitor, who must be rendered harmless. The whole unsavoury Parma–Rome–Habsburg campaign of agitation is represented, inspired and directed by the *Jesuit General Count Ledochowski* and Prelate *Strydmont* in Rome. Erzberger is now the *personal enemy of My House.* Anyone who *uses him or associates with him is just such another!* And will be treated as such!

With all this going on, the Catholics ask us to repeal the Jesuit Law!!!! The House of Parma, under the aegis of Rome, makes anything of the sort impossible.

W.

Rumania, Poland and Mitteleuropa in the autumn of 1917

While Germany's will to conquer and annex was thus being fanned to new vigour by the Fatherland Party in the autumn of 1917, the war aims policy of her leaders was also becoming more active again. This turn was the result of very heavy pressure from the OHL under Ludendorff, who obviously hoped to make up for the temporary and conditional withdrawal in the west by a thrust forward in the east. At this stage Poland and Rumania joined Lithuania and the Baltic provinces as central objectives of Germany's war aims policy.

In September Germany's intention of drawing Rumania more closely under her own authority was published to the world by a journey undertaken by the Emperor through the conquered country. The sight of the rich country, its leagues of wheat and maize fields and the great officials with their refineries, inflamed Wilhelm's excitable imagination. In an extensive report on his impressions he expressed a strong wish to maintain Germany's dominating position in Rumania by exchanging it against Poland. With Rumania organised by her, Germany, he thought, would have unrestricted access to the Black Sea and also a powerful means of exerting pressure if tension should ever arise between her and Austria-Hungary.

However, the very thought of abandoning the treasured prize of Poland to Germany's ally immediately evoked the strongest opposition from the OHL, which was supported in this instance by German public opinion. A great Conference of State was called in Kreuznach for October 7, and here an attempt was to be made to resolve the differences between the OHL and the government occasioned by the Emperor's suggestion.

Kühlmann began with a survey of German–Russian relations in the past, and like his predecessors, Jagow and Zimmermann, said that he anticipated in future an 'aggressive Russia', the more so since Poland, Lithuania and Courland would produce new points of friction. It was 'not practicable today' to restore Poland to Russia. Its incorporation in Germany would, however, be difficult, in view of the Poles' reluctance, and he therefore made a plea for the Austro-Polish solution, the dangers of which he thought would be neutralised by Germany's 'penetration of Austria' – a phrase behind which lurked the great plan for a Mitteleuropa which he had inherited from Bethmann Hollweg. The moment was propitious for exacting a high price for the Austro-Polish solution: Austria's consent to a military convention (which would have political repercussions) and to a customs union. If Rumania were taken in exchange, Germany would get primarily economic gains, 'Austria disinteresting herself completely'. Ludendorff opposed both the Russian and the Austro-Polish solution. Kühlmann's proposal would make Poland an equal partner in a trialist monarchy, a development which would render both the military convention and the customs union valueless. Hindenburg supported him and, with his specifically Prussian prejudice against Austria, went even further than Ludendorff in his mistrust of Austria. 'There was a danger of the Hohenzollerns becoming vassals of the Habsburgs.' Like Falkenhayn before him, he reckoned with the possibility of a war against a reinforced Austria. He also agreed that further wars with Russia were probable. 'Racial hatred is the reason for the antagonism between Russia and ourselves.' He therefore judged the Polish question exclusively from the angle of Germany's need for a 'deployment area' in the east; political considerations did not bother him. He rejected even Kühlmann's idea of a customs union with Austria, maintaining that German capital could be better employed in Belgium, Bulgaria and Rumania. On the other hand Count Roedern, Secretary of State in the Reich Treasury Office, supported Kühlmann; he thought that the dangerous features of the Austro-Polish solution would be eliminated by the creation of 'a great commercial-political bloc in Central Europe'.

Thus the OHL clung to the Prusso-military solution, while the diplomats were thinking in terms of a future central European economic bloc. Michaelis tried to bridge the difference by saying that the aim of German policy was 'the closest relationship with Austria', for 'the power in Central Europe must be ours', 'combined if possible with friendship with Russia'. He wanted the military convention imposed on Austria, while Ludendorff wanted both that instrument and the customs union to be given her 'as an act of grace' after Austria had pledged herself 'to stick to us to her last breath' – when exhaustion would finally force her to beg for it, thus making it unnecessary to give her Poland now. Should, however, the Austro-Polish solution be unavoidable – if the politicians thought that Poland must be given to Austria in return for getting Rumania – then Germany should still make whatever conditions were required by the OHL on military grounds.

The Chancellor asked the OHL to define these conditions. They fell into two groups. The first related to the safeguarding of German interests, territorial, economic, transport and military, in Poland itself. If these had been fulfilled, the Austrians would have been left with only a shadow of authority in a Congress Poland substantially diminished by the Frontier Strip. The second group comprised concessions and obligations to be undertaken by Austria-Hungary in the interest of the further extension of Germany's power-position outside Poland. The most drastic of these was undoubtedly the demand for the cession of Austrian Silesia, in order to give Germany direct communication by rail with Hungary (and via Hungary, with Rumania) this transfer would also have cut off Galicia from the other lands of Cis-Leithania. Rumania herself was to be nominally 'independent', but politically and economically at Germany's disposal. The OHL further demanded the enlargement of Rumania by three districts of Bessarabia, and Vienna's complete support for Germany over the Dobruja. Germany must have an Adriatic base at Valona or Cattaro. Austria should renounce any claim to compensation for the control acquired by Germany over the Serbian and Bulgarian railways and the Orient line. Austria was to support Germany's claims in the colonial field, Lithuania and Courland, and 'leave Germany the sole voice in the settlement of all Western questions [Belgium]'. The list of guarantees and obligations reached its climax in point 20, which pledged Austria-Hungary to continue the war. The struggle between Berlin and Vienna for an early peace now entered on a new phase, in which Germany absolutely forced Austria to remain in the war 'until Germany's war aims have been achieved'.

The discussions lasted many hours. The next day Michaelis reported to the Emperor. At the conference he had tried to mediate,

but now he took the generals' line completely. He told the Emperor
that their guarantees 'should be demanded of Austria most vigorously and to their full extent, and Austria made to accept them', and
he submitted the list of twenty-four points only slightly modified. He
warned the Emperor not to offer Charles the Austro-Polish solution
before he was assured of the 'return services', adopting undiminished
even the strongest demand – 'recognition of our interest in Belgium
and the colonies and holding out to the end at our side' – which committed Austria also to Germany's war aims in the west.

As Germany's will to power reached its culminating point on the
eve of the Russian October revolution, a divergence of method again
became apparent between Kühlmann on the one side and Ludendorff and Hindenburg on the other. The generals continued to stand
for the traditional hard power-policy of the most extensive annexations possible as the way to assure Germany's domination in Europe.
They were thinking in terms of the next war and, like Falkenhayn,
saw not only the enemies of the day, but also Austria-Hungary as a
potential enemy of the future.[1] Kühlmann, on the other hand, was
thinking in terms of Bethmann Hollweg's Mitteleuropa. His ideas
were in every respect larger than those of his military counterparts –
larger in terms both of space and time – but he was also more liberal,
or at least more adaptable, in his methods. He did not want his wider
vision of German power in Europe, as assured through 'Mitteleuropa', to be spoiled by insistence on the last inch of direct annexations, as demanded so obstinately by the soldiers. He hoped to over-
bid the OHL with a 'grand ready-made programme', which would
do as much for Germany as theirs, and he got the Austrians' consent
in advance after weeks of conversations with Hohenlohe, who advised Czernin to accept on the grounds that the plan provided the
only possibility of regenerating Austria and enabling her later to resume an independent policy.

While the OHL's intentions had been made unmistakably apparent by their twenty-four points of October 7, Kühlmann's
method of procedure emerged clearly from certain so-called 'non-
binding principles' agreed between him and Czernin on October 22
in pursuance of the Emperor's instructions of the preceding month.
These 'principles' constituted the first step towards what is known as
the 'reversal' of the Kreuznach agreement. Germany now agreed to
the purely formal association of Poland with Austria-Hungary

---

[1] The view expressed by Ludendorff was: 'We do not want to make Austria
strong, Poland will bring war with Austria'; and by Hindenburg, on the same
occasion: 'The alliance with Austria must remain, but the conflict with Austria is
bound to come.'

through a personal union, but exacted numerous concessions in return: dominion over Rumania to be transferred to Germany (subject to safeguards, to be negotiated later, in favour of Austro-Hungarian interests), Poland to be linked to Germany through close economic and military ties, and the Austro-Hungarian Monarchy as a whole to be bound to the German Reich by a twenty years' offensive and defensive alliance and by treaties establishing close military and economic links between the two states. To banish any doubts that Poland was to be attached firmly, if only indirectly, to the German Reich, point 3 stated expressly: 'The Kingdom of Poland is to be attached to the German Reich in military and financial and economic respects, as is Austria-Hungary.' To this was added 'autonomy' for Courland and Lithuania, which were also to be 'closely attached to the German Reich'.

Beyond the purely formal cession of Poland to Austria-Hungary, Kühlmann made only the single concession that, as agreed at the Crown Council of September 11, he would meet the Austrians over Belgium. Since, however, he phrased even this concession only in a negative form which bound Germany only to a solution 'which constituted no impediment to peace', German diplomacy still retained a free hand, even in the west, the more so since Germany continued to reserve to herself the right to conduct direct separate negotiations with King Albert, and the Emperor never made the reassuring pronouncement on Belgium which Kühlmann had promised.

These 'principles' amounted to capitulation by Austria before Germany's claim to domination, disguised under the mask of Mitteleuropa, and we may therefore ask what induced Czernin to sign them, 'non-binding' as they were. His strongest motive was assuredly the hope of achieving peace before the end of the year by getting Germany to renounce Belgium in one form or another. The Austrians clung to this hope up to the middle of December and were appalled when a violent attack by Tirpitz against the surrender of Belgium met with practically no disapproval from German public opinion. The prestige which would result from the Austro-Polish solution must also have counted heavily with Czernin, who expected from it a diminution of the internal tensions within the Danubian Monarchy. The decisive consideration for him seems, however, to have been another. The war had greatly weakened the Monarchy, and he hoped that the economic unification of Mitteleuropa would be of much help to her in her economic reconstruction after the war. He was fully aware that Germany's economic and financial help would have to be paid for by closer association with the stronger party. But like Hohenlohe in Berlin, he hoped that after the Monarchy had recovered economically, with Germany's help, she would be able to re-cover equality of status with her ally; for, as he argued in February, 1918, Germany would be 'the best-hated state in the world' after the war, and would thus be forced to look to Austria as her only ally. In other words he meant to use the Central European alliance to enable Austria to recover, to become once more an independent great power and so perhaps be able to cut loose again from Germany. He accepted the risk that the Germans might try, as Count Tisza in particular feared, to use Austria as a stepping-stone towards their objectives in the east, which had in fact been exactly the intention of the Foreign Ministry under Jagow and remained so under Zimmermann and Kühlmann.

The war aims conferences
on the eve of the October revolution

After the Czernin–Kühlmann conversations of October 22 Czernin had announced his intention of coming to Berlin on November 5 to settle finally the procedure for putting the Austro-Polish solution into effect. Michaelis had consequently arranged for conferences on war aims to be held on October 29–30. Owing to the crisis over the Chancellorship these meetings had to be postponed to November 2–3, when they were followed by a Crown Council on November 5, immediately before the meeting with the Austrians.

When the conferences opened, a new man had been Chancellor since November 1. The fall of Michaelis was due to considerations of internal policy, and chiefly to his reactionary attitude towards franchise reform in Prussia.[1] This attitude had brought down on him the wrath of the Majority parties, who had always been reserved towards him, and on October 24 the three parties and the National Liberals had made joint representations against him to the Emperor.[2] Wilhelm II had hoped – following a suggestion from Michaelis himself – that it might be possible to appoint the Bavarian Prime Minister and ex-President of the Zentrum, Count Hertling, to be Chancellor of the Reich, to separate that office from that of Prussian Prime Minister, and to retain Michaelis in the latter capacity; but he had had to drop this plan because Hertling, prompted by Erzberger, refused to take the one office without the other.

The activity of the parliamentarians in these days was astounding, their search for a suitable man for Chancellor almost tortured.

---

[1] Michaelis, op. cit., pp. 365 ff.

[2] The letter to the Emperor was drafted in the inter-Party Committee; see *Parlamentarischer Untersuchungsausschuss*, I, pp. 253 ff.; also Michaelis, op. cit., p. 368; Helfferich, op. cit., pp. 505 f.

Bülow, Kühlmann, Rantzau and Solf were suggested in turn. In the end the Emperor made his own choice, but by raising the slogan of more authority for parliament the politicians managed to force Hertling to hold consultations with them on his programme and on his choice of new assistants, in respect of which he had constitutionally a free hand. Finally they secured the appointment of two parliamentary politicians as deputies: Friedberg, the leader of the National Liberals, as Vice-President of the Prussian Ministry of State, specially in charge of the question of franchise reform, and Payer, the South German Progressive, as Vice-Chancellor, replacing Helfferich. Payer's office was no longer tied to that of Secretary of State in the Reich Interior Office, and his position was essentially that of liaison officer with the Reichstag. Friedberg too, unlike his predecessor, was not given a department.

The appointment of Hertling and his two 'adjutants' was hailed – and reprobated – as the first step towards 'parliamentarising' the government of Germany, and the main object of appointing parliamentary politicians was in fact to lend the government a certain 'tinge of democracy' to impress opinion in Europe and America;[1] it did not affect in any way the determination of policy in the Reich. And if this was true even of internal policy, where the Conservatives' opposition prevented a solution of the franchise problem in Prussia until the collapse of the Empire in November, 1918, it was even more true of foreign policy. Germany's war aims underwent no important change: they survived undiminished, even heightened by the collapse of Russia. Furthermore, the 'democratic' element was balanced by the creation of counter-weights which were far more effective than they: the Reich Supply Office was taken over on November 20 by a collaborator of Helfferich, Baron von Stein, previously head of the Department of War Economy in the Reich Interior Office and a sympathiser of Ludendorff; and on November 9, when Helfferich ceased to be Vice-Chancellor, he was made head of a special office in charge of preparations for the peace negotiations, which played a very large part in the safeguarding of Germany's economic interests in the Eastern Treaties.

Hertling put Helfferich, who remained Vice-Chancellor for another fortnight during the change of Chancellors, in charge both of the internal German and of the German–Austro-Hungarian conferences. These discussions therefore marked no change in the continuity of German policy, especially since Kühlmann remained Secretary of State in the Foreign Ministry, and – to the great annoyance of the parliamentary politicians – Hindenburg and Ludendorff at-

[1] See also Kühlmann, *Erinnerungen*, pp. 511 ff.

tended both the conferences of November 2–3 and the Crown Council in Berlin. The agenda comprised every aspect of war aims: first colonies and then bases, freedom of trade, evacuation by Britain of such occupied territory as Calais, Egypt and Mesopotamia, Germany's war aims against France, and the war aims in the east from Persia through Rumania and Poland to Lithuania and Courland.

The two most delicate problems were, as before, Belgium and Poland. Accepting the conditional renunciation of Belgium to which the Crown Council of September 11 had agreed, these meetings also discussed what safeguards could be obtained which would leave Belgium safely in Germany's hands without formal infringement of her sovereignty or direct annexations. On the Polish question the Chancellor and his assistants took over the OHL's Twenty-Four Point Programme of October 7 complete as a basis of discussion. The aim of both the civilians and the OHL was to retain for Germany as much influence as possible over Poland even after formally accepting the Austro-Polish solution, and they agreed that Poland's connection with Austria must be 'as loose as possible, preferably in the form of a simple personal union, without constitutional links'. As regards the western frontiers of the new state, they agreed to insist on the Frontier Strip, whatever Poland's international orientation. The only differences between them were over the dimensions of the frontier changes to be effected, and over the question of deporting the Polish and Jewish populations from the areas to be annexed. On the Polish-Lithuanian frontier, the OHL adhered to its old proposal of December 23, 1916 of extending Lithuania, which was to be autonomous but dependent on Germany, southward as far as Brest-Litovsk inclusive, so as to include in it two districts of Vilno and Grodno. The civilians also adopted completely the other points of the programme of October 7, including the clause binding Austria to remain in the war. In this respect the wording of October was now made more precise: 'Austria-Hungary must pledge herself to carry on the war until Germany's war aims have been attained.'

The most important difference between civilians and soldiers was, once again, the plan to establish a Mitteleuropa including Austria-Hungary enlarged by Poland. Ludendorff again rejected this plan and it was the problem round which most argument centred when the German–Austrian discussions opened.

November 5 was devoted chiefly to discussion of questions of economic policy raised by a Central European union. On November 6 came the military problems, especially the 'safeguards' for Germany's eastern frontier. The central question was the Frontier Strip, or more accurately, its dimensions. The Germans asked for nearly one-third of Congress Poland under the heading of 'frontier rectifications'; Czernin and his advisers objected that this would amount to a fourth partition of Poland, which would be so resented by the Poles of the Monarchy and of Congress Poland itself as to make it quite unacceptable. Czernin's own wish was to see Galicia united with Congress Poland under Vienna – if only to get the Poles out of the Austrian half of the Monarchy; he therefore told the Germans that either a German–Polish solution, or the big territorial cessions which they were demanding, would fatally obstruct both the conclusion of an alliance with Germany and the realisation of the Mitteleuropa plan. The Galician Poles' wish for unification with their fellow-countrymen in Poland would be a permanent apple of discord between Germany and Austria. This move brought Ludendorff on to the stage with a vigorous defence of Prusso-German interests. He in his turn feared that if the Austro-Polish solution were adopted, the Poles would develop aspirations towards Danzig, Posen and Vilno, inevitably bringing the Polish crown into sharp conflict with Prusso-Germany. Far-away Rumania, he went on, was no equivalent to the increase of power which the incorporation of Poland would bring to the Danubian Monarchy. The price which the Germans finally demanded of their allies for the Austro-Polish solution consisted of the twenty years' offensive and defensive alliance, the complete customs union, the military convention (in other words, the Mitteleuropa plan), Rumania, a free hand on the Baltic, the Frontier Strip in Poland, and thirteen points which comprised all the essentials of the OHL's twenty-four points. Kühlmann's policy thus joined hands with that of Ludendorff and Michaelis, in the hope that the wider framework would compensate for the harshness of the territorial and economic provisions; the formal grant of the Austro-Polish solution had to be bought by this long list of 'guarantees', and the prospect of a Mitteleuropa (the details of which still remained to be settled) could make it little more tolerable for the Austrians.

No real agreement could be reached. The question of the partition of Poland stood between the allies; and as Czernin gave notice on November 26, this meant that no decisions could be taken on Rumania, on the plans for Mitteleuropa, or even on the great joint economic conference which it had been proposed to hold at the end of the year.

These were the days immediately preceding the outbreak of the October revolution in Russia, and the historian must note at this very juncture the birth in Germany of a great new wave of self-confidence and self-assertiveness, directed towards the conquest of a wider sphere of domination in east and west. 'Mitteleuropa' was still the basis on which Germany's claims to domination in Europe were to rest. With the inclusion of Bulgaria and Turkey, Mitteleuropa with its adjuncts under German or Austro-Hungarian domination would have stretched from Antwerp via Hamburg, Vienna, Sofia and Constantinople to Baghdad; if it also proved possible to detach Finland from Russia, a German Mitteleuropa would extend from the North Cape to the Persian Gulf.

17

THE OBJECTS OF WAR AIMS POLICY, II

BETWEEN ANNEXATION AND SELF-DETERMINATION

WITH the Russian revolution and America's entry into the war, and with the idea of national self-determination invading the world from east and west, Germany's war aims policy, if it was to retain its old plans, had to find new forms of domination different from those of annexation or economic exploitation carried out without regard to national claims. It is within this world-historical framework that we must view the change-over from a pure policy of annexation in Belgium, Poland, Lithuania and Courland to the more elastic methods of 'association' through which Germany tried to turn the new principle of self-determination into a channel for the indirect exercise of her domination without renouncing her old aims.

Belgium: Flemish policy and the Council of Flanders

In January, 1917 Warburg, concerned over the future of Germany and the consequences of the United States' entry into the war, had written to Zimmermann, urging once more, most earnestly, that Germany should make an unambiguous declaration on Belgian independence, as the only possible chance left of avoiding a breach with America if unrestricted submarine warfare were initiated. Instead, Bethmann Hollweg had tried to re-activate his Flemish policy.[1] When the decision in favour of unrestricted submarine warfare had been taken and the breach with America seemed imminent, he thought the time had come to play the Flemish card openly, obviously in the hope of impressing President Wilson as Warburg had suggested. Fortunately for him, the 'activist' Flemish leaders, the 'cadre' in the towns, were ready for action, since they wished to present themselves as an organised movement at the peace negotiations which were expected to follow the German peace offer of December 12, 1916. The Governor-General thought the move premature, but accepted Bethmann Hollweg's decision.

On February 4, 1917 some 200 Flemish leaders met in Brussels

[1] On Germany's Flemish policy, see (besides the archives) J. Pirenne and M. Vautier, *La législation et l'administration allemandes en Belgique* (Paris, New Haven, 1925).

under the patronage of the Governor-General and formed the so-called Council of Flanders,[1] which issued its first manifesto on the same day. This document declared the aims of the movement to be administrative partition and cultural autonomy for the Flemish and Walloon parts of the Belgian state. The Council was composed of representatives of all three Flemish groups: 29 from the Young Flanders group, 13 from the Catholic Free Flamands and 8 Autonomists. The more radical element was thus in the majority; the two first-named groups determined the 'official' aims of the Flemish movement in a measure quite disproportionate to their real influence in the country or to the numbers of their followers. Furthermore, the 'Council' was under the permanent supervision of the German occupying authorities. An official of the German civilian administration sat in at its weekly meetings. It had very little administrative experience, and all proposals coming from it were first considered by a so-called Inner Committee, composed of plenipotentiaries of the Council and twice as many representatives of the civilian administration and the Political Department of the Government-General.[2] The Council of Flanders was thus a typical product of Bethmann Hollweg's policy: not to dominate Belgium by force, but to work through the native pro-German elements, leaving the reins slack but seeing to it that while the right of self-determination was exercised in appearance, German authority in fact remained unimpaired.

Only four days later, Bethmann Hollweg asked the Emperor to receive a delegation of the Flemish. He said that Germany's policy had met with considerable success.

A substantial strengthening of the Flemish national spirit, which Governor-General Freiherr von Bissing has been working systematically for more than two years to bring about, seems to me to constitute, politically, the best real guarantee for the future development of our relationship with Belgium.

The Emperor was delighted and asked for '*most extensive*' support for the Flemish independence movement, although care must be taken that 'the development of their national forces . . . proceed in close economic and spiritual association with ourselves'. He at once appreciated the propagandist value of such a demonstration of 'the Flemish people', and wanted the reception by the Chancellor to take place 'in good time, before the coming spring offensive'. Germany should 'point to the development: Polish university and Polish state; Flemish university and Flemish independence' and thus reduce *ad*

[1] See also Rüdiger (A. Wullus), *Flamenpolitik, Suprême espoir allemand de domination en Belgique*, 2cd. ed. (Brussels, 1921), pp. 17 ff.

[2] On the Inner Committee, see *Les Archives du Conseil de Flandre, publiées par la Ligue Nationale pour l'Unité Belge*, n.d., p. xxix.

absurdum the Allies' phrase of 'the liberation of the small peoples'. The Emperor thought that the reception could be made more important still: 'Flemish propaganda' must prove a counter to Allied propaganda, especially in the Allied countries, and it would invest policy with the nimbus of a cultural mission. He was so enthusiastic that he at once sketched out a summary programme for the Flemish – including, of course, firm military and political obligations – which he hoped that they would accept:

Military:
1. Flanders independent, convention relating to military.
2. Flanders coast (lease or servitudes).
3. Antwerp (Port company, lease).
4. Inducement for Flemish to stop fighting in Belgian army; possibly Flemish Legion under German command, as in Poland, for frontier defence.

Political:
1. Flemish separated from Walloons.
2. Flemish associated with Dutch, thus embroiling latter with Belgians,
3. Walloons nipped between Flemish and us.

Wilhelm even believed that if this programme, which was only a variant on Bethmann Hollweg's and Bissing's, was carried out, one reason for Britain's carrying on the war would cease to be operative, and that 'we should thereby be meeting Wilson's wishes on the principle of nationality', i.e., that with Germany figuring as the new champion of that principle, the United States would no longer need to enter the war against her.

The deputation's address at the audience showed that the radicals of the Young Flanders group, although less numerous in the country than the Autonomists, were predominant in the delegation. They not only asked that all measures taken by the occupying power during the occupation should be recognised and guaranteed when peace was concluded; they also said that the only right way of giving Flanders independence was 'to grant Flanders self-administration and self-government' – not the Autonomists' programme of autonomy for Flanders and Wallonia and union of the two areas under one crown. They went further still: independence should be conferred as quickly as possible, before the end of the occupation, for only with German help could 'the domination of Latin [*welsch*] capital and Latin culture be broken', the 'administrative separation', which should begin with partition of the Ministry of Arts and Sciences, must be carried through as quickly as possible, 'completely, by making all official bodies bi-partite and delimiting all administrative units to correspond with the linguistic frontier'. The ethnic motif was strongly emphasised throughout, especially in the eloquent concluding sentences:

Only ... Germany's intervention can save the existence and national future of the Flemish people. At the same time Germany will thereby be safeguarding her own most intimate and supreme interests and fulfilling her supreme world-historical mission by saving from destruction this advanced outpost of Germanism represented by the Flemish of the Western March.

Bethmann Hollweg promised to meet the request for administrative separation, but ignored the demand for self-government. He told the speakers: 'The German Reich will do everything, at the peace negotiations and after them, calculated to further and assure the free development of the Flemish people.'

Although this answer was deliberately framed in very general terms, and was accordingly received with disappointment by the delegation, yet it did contain a 'moral obligation'[1] and Germany was now publicly committed. All the further developments proceeded according to the programme as fixed: on March 21 the administrative separation between Flanders and Wallonia was carried out—von Bissing's last important act as Governor-General, for he died a few weeks later (on April 18).

Four days after receiving the deputation, Bethmann Hollweg made an attempt—not least with the object of breaking down von Bissing's opposition—to enlist Hindenburg's agreement and support for his new policy.[2] He gave his reasons for the forthcoming administrative division, which was intended to give Flanders more independence, and emphasised the importance of Germany's interests in Belgium. He was indeed well aware that the fate of Belgium must depend in the last instance on the fortunes of Germany's arms; but whatever the result achieved, he argued:

A Belgium whose internal organisation is divided, one in which the Flemish majority is emancipated from the domination of the pro-French Walloon minority, will be a much more convenient instrument of Germany's interests than a Belgian state as at present constituted.

Hindenburg replied that he would, of course, loyally support the Chancellor in the policy which the Emperor had approved; yet on the insistence of Ludendorff, the imperial Treasury and the Ministry of War, he pressed for a big contribution from Belgium to the costs of the war. He wrote that after the promises which had been made to the Flemish it was no longer possible to maintain his earlier objective

[1] Volkmann, op. cit., p. 105.

[2] This letter, and Hindenburg's reply, are published in *Les Archives*, pp. xxiv, 469 ff., 478.

of making Belgium more anxious for peace by so exploiting her that the government in Le Havre would be forced to sue for peace. Nevertheless Belgium must still be weakened economically more than the war was weakening Germany, for only so could she be kept dependent on Germany.

As soon as Bissing's successor, Baron von Falkenhausen, took over, Bethmann Hollweg confronted him with a long memorandum by von der Lancken, the head of the Political Department in the Government-General, on 'Considerations relating to policy in Belgium'. Dated only one day after the Kreuznach war aims conference, it read like a sort of commentary on Kreuznach. Although Lancken recommended (besides the continuance of the existing policy on the church and Flemish questions) a certain relaxation of 'economic exploitation' and of the exercise of martial law in the interests of German political objectives, none the less the political purpose behind his remarks was uncompromisingly directed towards the *'furtherance of Germany's world power position'*.[1]

The eventual establishment of German domination over Belgium, up to the sea, to ... exploit its favourable geographical situation and natural wealth and the industry of its inhabitants would [he wrote] edge out England and France and now America too, who will make the Belgian question the corner-stone of their policies.

Although Lancken's proposed solution masked its real aim, the policy which he advocated was exactly Bethmann Hollweg's own.

To this end, he went on, a solution must be found which enables the Entente Powers, especially England, which allegedly entered the war because of Belgium, to make peace, and which appears tolerable to the Belgian people itself, which sets especial store by the outward appearance [sic] of independence.

Bethmann Hollweg's address to the deputation had given enormous fresh encouragement to the annexationists, especially to Dietrich Schäfer's 'Independent Committee'. In the same month two associations were founded, which combined in September, 1917 in a 'German–Flemish Association', exactly parallel to the German–Ukrainian, German–Georgian, German–Lithuanian and other similar propagandist associations. Its chairman was von Reichenau, sometime minister in Stockholm, the strongly pan-German President of the 'Association for Germans Abroad' (*Verein für das Deutschtum im Ausland*), whom readers will remember as a fiery Anglophobe in August, 1914. Other members of the Association included Falken-

[1] Author's italics.

448

hausen, Tirpitz, Kapp, Count zu Reventlow and Schäfer–the moving spirits of the later Fatherland Party–and the Conservatives Wangenheim and Westarp.

The October revolution also had its effects on the Flemish movement, although it had there no social revolutionary accompaniments. Uneasy lest the Flemish might ask for too much real political power and that the politicians give it them (a quite unfounded fear), Ludendorff sent a bellicose letter to Kühlmann as early as November 29, 1917 protesting against the allegedly over-conciliatory attitude of the Government-General in Brussels towards the Flemish. This latter must not be given more than 'an advisory voice' in public affairs; this was the first principle of Germany's 'policy of autonomy'. Finally, the Flemish should be told 'honestly, that we are following German aims, that we do not want to incorporate them, but do want to protect them. Then they will accept our leadership trustfully'. The civilians' answer was again composed by Lancken. He admitted that there were signs of too wide-spread activism and too vigorous recruiting among the Flemish and that, unlike the Poles, the Flemish were beginning to build their own administration from the bottom upwards, but he too was consistently against giving them more than 'an advisory voice in national affairs', and had consequently regularly rejected the 'Young Flamands'' attempts to achieve independence. This national conflict in Belgium 'was being pressed into the service of German aims, also in connection with the natural economic aims'; Flemish nationalism, reinforced by the economic dependence of Antwerp in particular on the Rhine, guaranteed success for the 'officially approved' policy of von Bissing and Falkenhausen. Their main object was to use the conflict between Flemish and Walloons and between the Flemish movement and the Belgian state to extricate Belgium from the influence of the western powers, 'and in the last instance to destroy the central authority of the state altogether'. He assured Ludendorff that:

The Flemish with whom we Germans have entered into at all close touch have never been left in doubt that the Flemish policy of the German government is primarily governed by *Germany's*[1] interests, and that their aspirations can therefore only be considered in so far as they do not conflict with legitimate German interests.

This policy was, however, meeting with great difficulties, because 'Germanic racial feeling among the masses had been considerably weakened by political and religious influences.' Furthermore, the Flemish, 'with their pronouncedly democratic mentality', were

[1] Author's italics.

449

ill-adapted to becoming 'simply objects in the hand . . . of a policy serving exclusively foreign objectives'.

On December 22, only ten days after these words had been written, the Council of Flanders proclaimed the independence of Flanders and, confidently expecting early negotiations for a general peace, dissolved itself in order to secure confirmation of its mandate through new elections. The German government was greatly taken aback by this step, and only allowed the Council's proclamation to be issued after the weaker word 'autonomy' had been substituted for 'independence'. On January 20, 1918 the Flemish then really proclaimed their 'autonomy', but at once got into renewed difficulties with the German occupying power, because the Six Point Programme of the new Council of Flanders[1] asked not only for its own legislature, executive and judiciary, but also for its own diplomatic representation abroad. The Government-General vetoed the publication of the proclamation; Germany proposed to keep the future of Belgium in her own hands.

Before their spring offensive opened, the Germans approached King Albert once again, half-threatening, half-imploring, with a last offer of a separate agreement with Germany on Germany's terms. Their revived interest in making a deal with the king was due partly to the political relief which a separate peace with Belgium would have brought them, and partly, beyond doubt, to economic considerations. For experience had shown meanwhile that the partition of Belgium was not such a simple matter, and that it was a two-edged sword which was bound in the last resort to injure certain German economic interests very severely. Consequently in the spring of 1918 the German government was still working for 'administrative separation', but was also aiming at keeping the economic unity of Flanders and Wallonia intact. It is noteworthy that its plans envisaged giving Flanders and Wallonia not only a common monarch, but also a common Ministry of Economics. The problem of Belgium's final shape was thus still entirely open in the summer of 1918.

Poland: an eastern outpost: Regency Council, Military Convention and economic Raum

As early as the summer of 1916 the German government had, under the direction of Helfferich who had just been appointed Secretary of State for the Interior, addressed itself to the question of a constitution for Poland to be framed by Germany, and by the middle

---

[1] See the notes on the sessions of the Council on December 24, 1917 and January 12, 1918, in *Les Archives*, pp. 31 ff.; also the account in A. W. Willemsen, *Het Ulaams Nationalisme, 1914–1940* (Groningen, 1958, pp. 29 ff.).

of August very detailed discussions were going on in Warsaw on drafts of a military convention, a customs treaty and agreements on railways and inland waterways, and on posts and telegraphs. In the course of these preparations von Kries, head of the administration in the Government-General, worked out a 'draft fundamental law for the kingdom of Poland'. On November 15, ten days after the proclamation of the kingdom by the two Empires on November 5, and six days after the issue (against Austria's wish) of the appeal for recruits for a Polish volunteer army, Bethmann Hollweg sent Kries's draft to the ministries for their comments. Kries had assumed that the constitution would be enacted 'as a gift from the Central Powers, who had liberated the country from Russian domination, but without any decisive collaboration from the Polish people'. As he explained in his foreword, his draft

avoids as far as possible emphasising too strongly in the constitution . . . the *de facto* relationship of dependence in which the new state will stand towards the German Reich in the exercise of certain essential prerogatives of sovereignty.

He preferred to reserve these provisions '*for the inter-state treaties with the German Reich which will form part of the constitution*'. The conception and shape of 'independent' Poland's future dependence were thus entirely parallel with the similar objects and procedure followed in Lithuania and the Baltic provinces.

Kries wished to secure Germany's influence through a constitutional structure which left the leadership firmly in the hands of conservative elements. It is true that he advised against introducing the Prussian franchise for the Lower Houses (*Landbotenkammer*); he thought that a House of Deputies elected on the democratic 'Reichstag franchise' would be sufficiently balanced by a 'senate' on the model of the Prussian Herrenhaus, containing hereditary representatives of twenty families of Polish magnates and a strong contingent of the *sklachta* or lesser nobility; and he also hoped that the peasants, once 'dissociated from the subversive influence of Russia', would vote Conservative, especially as they would have learnt collaboration with the landed proprietors in the local *Kreis* councils.

Besides this constitutional structure, which was designed to orient Poland towards Prussia–Germany, Kries envisaged Poland and Germany bound together by 'the economic unity which we desire, and must establish'.

In shaping the future economic relationship between the kingdom of Poland and the German Reich we must be clear that a close economic tie is the only sure chain by which this people, whose nature, race and sympathies are alien to the German people, can be *permanently* attached to Germany.

The structural adaptation of the Polish economy which would necessarily follow the establishment of a customs union between Poland and Germany would bring ruin to the 'hot-house growth' of Russo-Polish industry; on the other hand, it would bring unprecedented prosperity to Polish agriculture, thus creating 'a far greater measure of unity between Germany and Poland'. Consequently, not even the smallest internal tariffs could be allowed to exist between Germany and Poland, because then the new Polish state would 'take energetic measures to develop and protect its industry'. Poland would, without any obviously dictatorial measures, be turned into a producer of raw materials for the German industry of the future, and her political destinies would become inseparably linked with those of Germany. At the same time a customs union raised, in Poland as in Belgium, Austria-Hungary and the north-east, difficult questions of organisation, for the Poles would have to be assured in advance of an equal footing in the tariff parliament. Even if there are only 12·5 million Poles,[1] Kries thought that a system like that introduced between Germany and Luxemburg impossible; his solution was to let 'Polish tariff deputies' attend the Reichstag and the Federal Council when questions of 'Polish tariffs' were to be discussed; this provision would have the further great advantage that every Pole wishing to play a part in public life would have to learn German.

Helfferich approved Kries's suggestions, but wished that they had included drafts of the inter-state treaties. Suggestions for meeting this demand comprised the bulk of the ministries' commentaries, the most important of which were those of von Loebell, whose ministry was responsible for Polish policy. Von Loebell was flatly opposed to giving the Poles any representation, even if only as 'tariff deputies'; partly to avoid strengthening the Poles as a party, and partly to deprive the Reichstag or the Prussian Landtag of any chance to meddle in Polish policy. He strongly stressed Germany's claim to have Poland permanently attached to the Reich, rejected any connection between it and Austria-Hungary, and demanded the creation of a German-minded administration and uninterrupted prosecution of Prussia's Polish policy. He thought that the safeguards for Germany's influence in Poland should consist partly in obligations to be laid down in the 'foundation charter' (which should also delimit the frontiers and was to be 'imposed on the Poles unilaterally and bind-

[1] According to Kries, the future Poland would have about 12½ million inhabitants, of whom roughly 10 million would be Poles, 2 million Jews, and 600,000 Germans. These figures include the populations of Byalistok and its surroundings (government of Grodno) and Chelm, both of which districts Kries expects to be included in Poland. Suwalki is to be detached from Poland and included in Lithuania.

ingly for all time') and partly in obligations to be settled by international treaty for limited periods. Germany must have the right to occupy the key places in Poland, and a right of inspection in time of peace and of supreme command in war. If possible, she should conclude with Poland a 'customs union' 'for all time', but only on condition that there were no 'tariff deputies' in the Reichstag or the Prussian parliament. If this last provision could not be avoided, Germany's interests should be secured through a thirty years' commercial and tariff treaty. Contractual provision must be made for the free entry of seasonal workers (280,000 Poles came to Germany in 1913).

The association would be sufficiently safeguarded by making Poland a hereditary monarchy with an order of succession determined by Germany (only a German or an Austrian prince could occupy the throne), for Poland was not to be denationalised – as Bethmann Hollweg said, the Poles were to be allowed 'to enjoy their national life to the full'.

Besides these long memoranda there were others from various departments, which differed only in nuances; thus the Reichsbank asked for a currency union and the establishment of branches of its own in Poland. In general, there was broad agreement on what amounted to a confirmation of Germany's Polish policy, the Austro-Polish solution notwithstanding. This was the more essential as it was becoming plain that the hopes of recruiting a volunteer army had been entirely misplaced; neither the clergy nor the pro-German aristocrats supported the plan, and the Poles were insisting ever more strongly on their own independent national institutions.

The German government could not go on for ever resisting these wishes. It hoped that the Poles would be satisfied with the appointment of a Provisional Polish Council of State, a kind of advisory body which was to have only very limited powers, while its composition was manipulated to consist of conservative and pro-German elements; and Ludendorff anticipated that this institution would also help to provide the soldiers which his own appeal had failed to produce.[1]

The outbreak of the February revolution in Russia and the issue by the Russians of a manifesto promising the Poles an independent state including West Galicia and the Polish parts of Prussia – it was to be required to conclude a military union with Russia – put the Polish Council in a difficult position. Eventually, on April 13, it announced that it accepted the Proclamation of November 5 and refused to fight against the Central Powers. On Beseler's advice the administration of education and justice was handed over to the Council on the

[1] Conze, op. cit., pp. 239 ff. and 249 ff.

453

same day.[1] But its powers were too limited to satisfy it, and the next stage was—largely owing to the rivalry between Germany and Austria-Hungary—slow in following, while the Russian revolution stirred up further excitement. On May 1, two days before Poland's national day, the Council of State called for the appointment of a government and a regent (the Archduke Karl Stefan was suggested) who should appoint a cabinet and then convoke a Polish parliament; only if these conditions were fulfilled would the Council be able to work with the Central Powers. Its demands were not accepted, and it accordingly suspended all activities on May 15, thus making clear to the whole world the fiasco of the Central Powers' Polish policy. A wave of anti-German feeling swept over the country; the Warsaw students struck at the beginning of May with the consequence that the university was closed on June 22. Although the winds of democracy and socialism blowing from Russia were forcing the church and the conservative aristocracy to declare for co-operation with monarchist, aristocratic Germany, German policy had not succeeded in getting broad popular support.

Meanwhile the Kreuznach agreement of May 17–18 had assigned Poland to Germany in exchange for the surrender of Rumania to Austria.[2] Four weeks later the secret so-called 'Monarchs' Agreement' revealed the hard core of Germany's aims. While the administrative partition between Warsaw and Lublin was retained, Austria-Hungary conceded to Germany control over the entire future army of Poland, which was to come under German leadership for organissation and training and to continue under German command after the end of the war, irrespective of how Poland's international status was settled. The compromise formula of the 'Beseler–Kuk oath'[3] was accepted as the oath of loyalty to be administered to the Polish army.

It was the army policy that produced the great débâcle at the beginning of July. Pilsudski and the representatives of the left had protested and resigned from the Provisional Council of State, but the rest of the Council had, on July 3, accepted the Beseler–Kuk oath; but nearly two-thirds of the Polish troops raised in the meantime refused to take it. At the same session the Council adopted two drafts of a provisional constitution, and these were discussed between German and Austrian representatives in Warsaw on July 28–30. It was decided to set up a Council of Regency, which should exercise the

[1] Id., pp. 279 f.   [2] See above, pp. 353 ff.

[3] The oath of the Polish troops was to be taken to 'the future king of Poland', the two Emperors not being named. Kuk was the military Governor-General of Lublin, the centre of the Austro-Hungarian zone of Poland.

functions of the Head of State of the future Monarchy 'without prejudice to the international position of the Occupying Powers'; under
this council there was to be a new Council of State, which should not
be purely advisory but should exercise certain legislative and executive functions and thus constitute a sort of government.

This 'further step towards the creation of a Polish state' was announced on September 12 in a proclamation by the two Emperors;
'a Polish King, wearer of the venerable and glorious Crown of the
Piasts and Jagellons' was to work together with 'a popular representation built up on democratic principles'. The rights of the new Polish
government were strictly limited. The legislative functions exercised
by the Council of Regency—a triumvirate which was not appointed
until October 27—with the assistance of the Council of State were to
extend at first only to those matters which had already been transferred to the Provisional Council of State, and the Governors-Gener-
al retained a veto. The occupying powers had the deciding voice in
the choice both of the members of the Council of Regency and of
the Prime Minister and Council of State.

Meanwhile the Reich Interior Office and the Prussian Ministries
had been pursuing their plans for taking over the Polish railways
without regard to these high-level constitutional dispositions. The
OHL's Twenty-Four Point Programme of October 7 included this
railway plan together with a demand that German capital should be
given a preponderant share in the expansion of heavy industry in the
Kreise of Sosnowice, Kielce and Radom, the first of which lay in
Polish Upper Silesia and the two others in Congress Poland. The
Programme also repeated the supply of seasonal labour, the potash
monopoly, and shipping on the Vistula. Breitenbach suggested the
formation of a great railway joint-stock company with predominantly German capital and with the Reich owning such a holding and
occupying such a position as would enable Germany to exercise permanent and effective control over the Polish transport system and
thus over the whole Polish economy, without any formal transfer of
the ownership of the railways to Prussia or the Reich.[1]

At the end of 1917 and the beginning of 1918 all the ministries and
the civilian administration of the Government-General were further
engaged in setting out Poland's obligations in the form of a state
treaty with an Austro-Poland, should it emerge. Much attention was
again devoted to the Frontier Strip and the deportation from it of its

---

[1] Breitenbach calculated that the German Reich would be able to acquire for
itself about 70 per cent of the share capital of the company. The plan of incorporating the railways in the Prusso–Hessian system 'could unfortunately not be realised,
since the mistake had been made of promising the Poles independence without laying down conditions in advance'.

Poles. The inter-German discussions on the conditions to be laid down by Germany in the event of the Austro-Polish solution showed plainly that the departmental ministries, the Reichsbank and also Beseler were opposed to that solution, and were trying to work against it by proposing extremely far-reaching 'safeguards'; only Kühlmann, Helfferich, and the Emperor sincerely approved of the exchange of Poland for Rumania.

The struggle over the dimensions of the Frontier Strip and the safeguards for German interests in Poland reached a climax in Berlin in January, 1918. There were heated debates, and the Government-General sent in a series of memoranda, recapitulating its aims and demands: Poland must 'look towards both Central Powers', as envisaged in the Proclamation of November 5, but Germany, as the economically stronger partner, must hold the dominant position. Since the establishment of the currency union was no longer guaranteed, it was essential that German trade and German industry in Poland be promoted by favourable customs and railway tariffs, by most favoured nation treatment, by complete freedom to practise trades and acquire real property, by protection for German patents and designs, by the introduction of the metric system of weights and measures and, as in Belgium, of German social legislation. All claims and concessions for exploiting or prospecting for mines acquired under the occupation must be registered in the 'objective public law' of the new state. Even without customs association or customs union, Poland, even if attached politically to Austria-Hungary, was Germany's economic hinterland and indirectly dependent on the Reich; moreover, 'the most important deposits in Poland, as so far known . . . are situated almost exclusively in the Frontier Strip, and the Strip will exist in the event either of an Austro-Polish or a Polish-Polish solution'.

These memoranda demanded securities not only for the export of raw materials but also for 'the export of workers from Poland' for German agriculture and industry. Finally, the Government-General, like Loebell, opposed the idea of minority protection and advocated colonising the Frontier Strip with Germans 'as completely as possible'. We need not therefore be surprised that the Emperor Charles told the Emperor Wilhelm in February, 1918 that 'under certain circumstances' he thought Poland hardly worth having.

The foundations of the new 'autonomy' policy in the North-East

In the first half of the war the north-east – Lithuania and the Baltic provinces – had been the field *par excellence* of Germany's annexationist dreams. Since then, however, the Russian revolution and the proclamation of the right of national self-determination, America's entry into the war and the ideals proclaimed by President Wilson, had introduced into world politics a new element which the rulers of Germany had to take into account.

It was difficult enough in any case to reconcile two such mutually exclusive principles as peace without annexations and national self-determination on the one hand, and annexations on the other. The problem was made twice as difficult by the world's obvious mistrust of Germany's agressive intentions. The German government therefore tried to mask Germany's eastern war aims by developing more elastic methods. This was done by using the new catch-word of 'autonomy' which was now applied to the north-eastern territories.[1]

But little would be left of any 'autonomy' for Courland and Lithuania when it was combined with economic dependence on Germany and large-scale settlement of German colonists from the interior of Russia.[2] It was in this sense that the Chancellor expounded his new programme of 'autonomy' for these two areas on May 3, 1917, in an address to the leaders of the parties of the centre from the National Liberals to the Progressives (thus excluding the Conservatives and the Social Democrats). Four days later, on May 7, he issued his famous 'touching-up' instructions for German representatives taking part in any negotiations for a separate peace with democratic Russia, which envisaged allowing Courland and Lithuania internal administrative autonomy, combined with military, political and economic association with Germany. Major-General Hoffmann, Chief of Staff, *Oberost*, outlined his ideas – which he was later to realise at Brest-Litovsk in collaboration with Kühlmann – on May 31; they agreed exactly with Bethmann Hollweg's 'touching-up' policy:

> One can, he wrote, imagine a formula whereby Germany renounces annexations, while Russia defers to the principle of the liberty of small nations by releasing the lands now occupied by us from her body politic, for Germany to regulate their future political form.

Gossler, the head of the civilian administration of Courland under *Oberost*, only accepted the Chancellor's policy of autonomy under strong protest. On July 10 – four days before Bethmann Hollweg's fall – he sent him a memorandum on a future constitution for Courland, saying that he ought to have 'announced clearly in advance that Germany regarded Courland and Lithuania as permanent acquisitions'. Then (before the February revolution) even the Social

[1] See above, p. 348.
[2] See above, p. 375.

457

Democrats would have raised no objections. Now, however, Germany would have to make do with the 'makeshift solution' of a loose association, 'consented to by the peoples concerned'. The best course would have been to annex Courland and Lithuania as Prussian provinces; they could then have been Germanised later–although he thought that it would be harder to Germanise the Lithuanians than the Letts of Courland. The two lands should therefore be kept separate even after the establishment of the personal union with Prussia, and be administered by two local governors with the widest possible legislative and executive powers. For Courland he suggested a Diet on the Estates basis–thus consisting almost entirely of Baltic Germans–to meet every two years with the right of considering and approving legislation and confirming the appointment (which was to be made by the Emperor) of the head of the administration. These suggestions were a particularly plain embodiment of the policy of annexation masked under the formula of autonomy.

Meanwhile, as decided on April 21, a further conference had been arranged in Bingen to regulate in detail future procedure in Lithuania and Courland. Ludendorff had had a detailed preparatory programme for this meeting drawn up on July 21, and Zimmermann had accepted it in principle on July 25. The ideas of the Secretary of State differed from those of the general only marginally: whereas Ludendorff wanted Germany to proclaim publicly and immediately the personal union of Lithuania with Prussia, Zimmermann thought that it would be better for a native Council to ask for Lithuania to be taken under the protection of the Reich.

The ground having thus been cleared, the Bingen Conference, which met a fortnight after the fall of Bethmann Hollweg and the Peace Resolution, achieved agreement between the civilians and the OHL on 'procedure' in Lithuania and Courland. Its decisions were fully in line with Bethmann Hollweg's whole policy. The two administrative chiefs, Gossler in Courland and Prince zu Ysenburg in Lithuania, should have 'Trustee Councils' (*Vertrauensräte*) convoked, the Lithuanian to be 'purely Lithuanian', but that in Courland to have a German majority. No further details were settled in respect of Lithuania where, according to Ysenburg, it would be very difficult to arrange for such a Council, but the composition of the Courland Council was laid down exactly. The 'Trustee Councils' were to be turned into 'Provincial Councils', again by the military administration. As a return for this concession the new representatives were immediately to beg for 'the protection and shelter of His Majesty and the mighty German Empire'; the Lithuanians and the Letts of Courland would thus have recognised Germany's proposed dispositions.

The military and the diplomats agreed even on the wording of the addresses to be made by the administrative chiefs to the 'Trustee Councils' and of the replies which the latter were to make to the representatives of the occupying powers, so that no hitch should occur in the ceremonial of the 'Inauguration of the States'. There was, of course, no suggestion of modern constitutionalism, still less of parliamentary life of the Western democratic type, for the Councillors (how they were to be chosen was, incidentally, left entirely open) were only to enjoy the right of commenting on legislation; even taxation they might not approve. German was to be the language of command in the army, and also, in Courland, of the administration.

The policy of Bingen reappeared on the eve of the Russian armistice. On November 4 a conference on Courland and Lithuania met under the chairmanship of Helfferich, then still Vice-Chancellor; present were Kühlmann, the heads of the departmental ministries, representatives of the OHL and *Oberost*, and the Governor-General of Warsaw. All present agreed that it would be possible to Germanise Courland by settling Germans in it, introducing German as official language, and integrating it with the Reich, while Lithuania could be 'led to *Deutschtum*' by meeting the Lithuanians' wishes over the frontier (i.e., giving Vilno to Lithuania rather than Poland) and settling German colonists in thinly populated districts. Hoffmann and Ludendorff, however, were against conciliation: 'if we threaten the Lithuanians that they will be partitioned unless they are attached to Germany', they would opt for Germany soon enough. Hoffmann thought that a friendly settlement between Poles and Lithuanians, as advocated by Beseler, would be a misfortune for Germany: 'the Lithuanians must be our allies in the struggle against the Poles'; and Hindenburg concurred with the laconic and unambiguous remark: 'the policy of *divide et impera* is the one for these dubious elements'.

This meeting actually laid down the exact forms under which the two countries were to be attached to the Reich: they were to be duchies, linked with the Reich by a personal union, not a part of Germany in international law, 'but linked with the German Reich by international treaties' [especially foreign affairs, army, navy, customs union as with Luxemburg] guaranteed under imposed constitutions 'which reproduce the essential parts of the treaties'. Helfferich emphasised that it was necessary to have these treaties ready before any possible conclusion of peace, so as to create a '*fait accompli*'.

It would be pointless, said a memorandum of November 29 (the day on which the Chancellor announced his acceptance of the right of self-determination as the basis of the peace negotiations) to set up

Courland and Lithuania 'as buffer states between Germany and Russia with autonomy for the Letts, Estonians and Lithuanians', because they would not be strong enough 'to constitute a secure future barrier against Russian expansive ambitions'. Courland and Lithuania, 'and if possible, Livonia and Estonia', were only valuable if 'brought and permanently kept in a relationship of complete dependence on the Reich, militarily, politically and economically'.

Courland, Livonia, Estonia: the contribution of the Baltic Germans

The Bingen decisions could only be realised if Germany had at her disposal in the countries in question persons on whom she could depend as reliable instruments. This condition was fulfilled in Courland by the Baltic German landowning aristocracy and 'educated' bourgeoisie, which since the occupation of the country by German troops and, in particular since the outbreak of the Russian revolution, had themselves followed a policy consonant with the interests of the German Reich. Although the Baltic Germans numbered only about 7 per cent of the populations of the Baltic provinces, the great majority being Letts or Estonians, the 'capitulations' concluded by their ancestors when the countries passed under Russian rule two centuries earlier had enabled them to retain their own class privileges and to rule the provinces with little interference from the Russians almost up to the outbreak of the First World War.

The German government was egged on by the Baltic émigrés in Germany, who had succeeded in the course of the war in acquiring a direct influence over German policy.[1] There was also much pressure from public opinion. In March, 1917 the historian, Friedrich Meinecke, the National Liberal, Eugen Schiffer, and the industrialist, Friedrich von Siemens, collected 20,000 signatures for a mass petition, which said: 'The lands belong to us. The soul of the people revolts against abandoning the Germans of the Baltic Provinces.'

The Chancellor, who was again occupied with ideas of a separate peace, said that the petition must not be published and that the moment was unpropitious for a move on Livonia and Estonia, but he expressed clear agreement in principle with the aims of the petition. The demands should for the present be confined to Courland; 'but that is very essential, and my decided wish is for the detachment of Courland. . . .' The Baltic Germans' own organisation was reinforced in May, 1917 by the 'German–Baltic Society', an association

[1] See Lewerenz, *Baltikum*, pp. 167 ff. The 'Ostland Company, Ltd.' had the task of preparing the way for the incorporation of the Baltic coast by collecting statistical and other material. Its founder and moving spirit was Adalbert Volck, an advocate from Dortmund.

brought into being chiefly on German initiative. The prime mover was von Schwerin, who was in close touch with the 'Baltic Council'. The presidency was assumed by Duke John Albert of Mecklenburg who was also President of the German Colonial Association, and from September 2, 1917 onwards Honorary Chairman of the Fatherland Party.

In March, 1917 the Knights' Estate of Courland sent an address to the German government declaring themselves ready to undertake any sacrifice in the war, and their efforts were recognised officially in August when Baron Manteuffel-Zoege was appointed their representative. In the following autumn, after the Bingen conference, they formed a representative body (which was intended to be merely provisional). On September 18 the old Diet, the 'Knights and Landsmen of Courland' which constitutionally had ceased to exist in the previous spring, met for a single session and resolved, again in accordance with the Bingen decisions, to form an enlarged representative body of eighty deputies, among whom Germans would form the majority. Three days later this body met in the throne room of the ducal castle at Mitau, Gossler also being present.[1] It accepted *verbatim*, unanimously and by acclamation, the address prepared for it in Bingen.

'As the representatives delegated by the population of Courland,' they announced, 'we beg for the protection and shelter of His Majesty and the mighty German Reich. We entrust our destinies confidently to the hands of His Majesty and the German military administration appointed by him.' The meeting further asked that a National Council composed of representatives of all vocational and national classes should be allowed to collaborate in the preparation of the future constitution.

This motion was accepted on September 22, and elections were thereupon held for a National Council which was 'to consider, under the guidance of the head of the military administration, the fundamental rights of the future state and the principles of its future administrative and economic institutions in the light of the historical development of Courland'. The Council was composed of twenty members, again elected unanimously and by acclamation by the enlarged Provincial Assembly. This, again, was obviously a well-thought-out political manoeuvre, the fruit of collaboration between the German military administration and the local Baltic Germans, concerned on the one hand with keeping up the appearance of

---

[1] This body was composed of 27 representatives of the large landed proprietors, 4 of the Knights, 5 of the clergy, 17 of the towns and 27 of the peasants. It also drafted a Bill for the cession of one-third of the large estates.

popular representation and on the other with limiting the influence of the Latvian element and satisfying the most important provision laid down at Bingen – that the majority of the Advisory Council must consist of Germans.

Conditions were different in Livonia and Estonia in that these areas were at first still under Russian rule; Riga was not occupied by German troops until the beginning of September, 1917,[1] the islands until the middle of October, and the rest of the country until the end of February, 1918. The Russian provisional government, soon after taking over power, had met the desire of the Lettish and Estonian nationalists for autonomy by replacing the Russian governor by native commissioners.[2] On April 22 it had divided the district on national lines: instead of Estonia and Livonia and the islands of Oesel there were now the districts of Estonia and Latvia, each with a Government Council to be elected on a general franchise – which would, of course, have deprived the German section of the population of all its political influence. On June 22, 1917 the Knights' Estates were deprived of their political rights, and the local administration was transferred to the Government Councils.[3]

To counter their loss of political influence, and presumably also in the hope that military developments would be favourable to them, the Germans in Estonia and Livonia had formed their Trustee Councils in March, 1917 for the protection of their interests. The Livonian Council wanted Livonia to be incorporated in the Reich as a province of Prussia. The Letts and Estonians were to be completely Germanised. The Council wanted neither sovereignty nor its own army; instead it wanted a customs, currency, postal and railway union with Germany.

A slightly different line was taken in Estonia, where a similar Trustee Council took the view that Courland, Livonia and Estonia constituted a single unit and asked for an autonomous association with the German Reich.

Besides the local councils on the spot, individual persons from these districts had been working in Berlin since 1916 for adhesion to the Reich.[4] This unofficial but very influential agitation reached its

[1] When this occurred, the Emperor wrote: 'With God's help, Riga is ours! To Him be the praise and the glory! A splendid proof of the efficiency and the steel-hard will to victory of our splendid troops! Forward with God!'

[2] See Reinhard Wittram, *Geschichte der Ostseelande Livland, Estland, Kurland, 1180–1918* (Munich and Berlin, 1945), pp. 212 f.

[3] Lewerenz, op. cit., p. 179.

[4] A. v. Tobien, *Die livlandische Ritterschaft in ihrem Verhältnis zum Zarismus und russischen Nationalismus*, Vol. I (Riga, 1925), pp. 224 f. This contains many details of the activities of the Livland deputy, Heinrich von Stryk and the plenipotentiary of the Livonian Knights, Alfred, Baron Schilling.

climax after the October revolution of 1917 and in the spring of 1918. On November 6, 1917 a deputation from the Knights in the occupied parts of Livonia waited on Hindenburg and Ludendorff with a petition[1] asking for Livonia and Estonia to be taken under the protection of the Prussian crown or under the military administration of an imperial viceroy. This development was accelerated by the Bolshevisation of the two lands. On November 24 all Estates were abolished, the whole nobility expropriated and Soviet committees put in place of the Estonian and Latvian administrative offices. Excesses by the revolutionary troops added to the distress among the Baltic Germans, so that on December 4 the Knights of Livonia again begged the OHL to send German troops into the country. Even before the first conversation with the OHL on November 6 Ludendorff[2] had reported that they wanted to extend the protected zone as far as the Narva, but Germany had to respect the principle of 'the right of self-determination'; the decision to secede from Russia must therefore proceed from an expression of the wishes of wide circles of the population. This advice sounds like an echo of the Bingen decisions. It was followed: the Baltic Germans collected signatures among the non-German populations for the decisive resolutions of the Livonian Nobles' Assemblage of November 30 and the Estonian Committee of Knights on December 14. On December 24 the Municipal Council of Riga asked for the protection of the German Reich, and many similar petitions came from cultural and communal German organisations in Riga and the occupied parts of Livonia.[3] On December 30 an Extraordinary Diet of Livonia resolved to secede from Russia.[4]

The events in Livonia and Estonia produced intensified agitation among the Baltic Germans in the Reich. On February 5 the Knights of Livonia and Estonia addressed an urgent appeal[5] to the German Emperor, Hindenburg and the king of Saxony, begging for the help of the Reich. While the German–Soviet arguments were going on in Brest-Litovsk, the Crown Council of Homburg[6] decided on February 13 to arrange for regular calls for help from Livonia and Estonia, so that German troops could be sent in. This was done on February 18 and by February 25 the occupation was complete.

[1] Lewerenz, op. cit., p. 187.
[2] Tobien, op. cit., pp. 226 f.
[3] See M. Martna, *Estland, die Esten und die estnische Frage* (Olten, 1919), pp. 109 ff.
[4] Von Stryk handed the declaration of independence to the Soviet Chargé d'Affaires in Stockholm on January 27.
[5] Tobien, op. cit., pp. 321 f.
[6] See below, pp. 501 ff.

Lithuania: the Taryba's
contest with the German authorities[1]

The problem of reconciling Germany's war aims in Lithuania and Courland with the principle of national self-determination was made more difficult by the treatment which the Lithuanians and Letts had received from the German military regime since 1915. They had not been at all hostile to the German troops when the latter first entered their homes, but the ruthless exploitation of the country in the interests of German operations, the harsh treatment of the population by both civilian and military occupying authorities, and the measures of Germanisation introduced in connection with the annexation programme, inevitably produced increasing embitterment and hostility among the Lithuanian and Lettish populations.

This hostility was fed by the agitation of the Russians and of the émigré Lithuanian committees in the west (Sweden, Switzerland and the U.S.A.), which made the Germans' task in Lithuania ever more difficult. As early as November, 1915 the Foreign Ministry, at the suggestion of Romberg in Bern, had therefore successfully approached a certain Gabrys (Garlava), editor of the Lausanne *Pro Lithuania* and one of the most influential Lithuanian publicists in Switzerland, and with the help of a German–Lithuanian captain named Steputat, had taken him and his paper into the service of Germany under a formal contract. In the course of their propaganda for liberation from Tsarism they had also secured Lithuanian signatures for an appeal from the 'League of non-Russian Peoples' organised by them in April, 1916 – although Ludendorff demurred out of fear of prejudicing the policy of straight annexation. On May 2, 1917 Ludendorff had accordingly issued political principles for the north-eastern territories, to the effect that everything possible should be done to win over the Lithuanians to Germany, while the White Russians were to be reconciled with them. The Lithuanians were therefore not to be Germanised. Meanwhile, however, world developments had outstripped these attempts to clear the path for the annexation of Lithuania by administrative manipulations in a patriarchal spirit. The Russian provisional government, in which the Lithuanians were represented by an Under-Secretary of State in the person of their former deputy in the Duma, Ytchas, had held out the prospect of autonomy within the framework of a federalised

---

[1] An authoritative account, with many documents, of Germany's policy towards Lithuania, is given by Paul Klimas, *Der Werdegang des litauischen Staates von 1915 bis zur Bildung der provisorischen Regierung in November, 1918* (Berlin, 1919). See also B. Colliander, *Die Beziehungen zwischen Litauen und Deutschland während der Okkupation von 1915 bis 1918* (Abo, 1935, diss.).

Russia, and the American Lithuanians, who had sent a deputation to Petersburg, had approved these proposals.

For months Bethmann Hollweg had believed it possible to allay the disappointment and mistrust in Lithuania by temporising pronouncements. This, however, was only one side of his policy of 'touching up'. In May, 1917, when it became clear that straight annexation of Lithuania was no longer practicable under the altered world conditions, he found himself compelled to announce the appointment—vaguely promised many times before—of an 'adviser' (*Beirat*) for Lithuania, attached to *Oberost*. Contrary, however, to his instructions, *Oberost*, when making the appointment the next day (May 31), gave its holder only the title of 'consultant'(*Vertrauensrat*).

The Germans looked for support for their policy to the conservative country clergy[1] and the small peasants who followed their lead, to the exclusion of the urban intelligentsia and the workers, who leant pronouncedly towards democratic Russia. The government was, however, well aware that a referendum would show an overwhelming majority against attachment to Germany. This they could not risk. Yet Lithuania was essential to them, as the territorial bridge to Courland, Livonia and Estonia. Other ways of winning it over had therefore to be devised. This was the purpose of the Bingen decisions of July 31, 1917.

Pursuing those principles, the representatives of Germany in Lithuania opened negotiations with the leaders of the Lithuanian-Clerical National Party, with whom they had held many non-committal conversations on the future of Lithuania since August, 1916. they were, however, forced to realise that even this Conservative group, which was the one most likely to agree to co-operate with Germany, refused association with her, fearing 'that connection with Germany would mean that in place of the Russifiers and Polonisers we should get the German colonisers and Germanisers, who would be even worse'.

At the end of July, 1917 the Lithuanians of Vilna managed to secure permission from the occupying authorities to set up a committee to organise the convocation of a Lithuanian conference. J. Staugaitis, A. Smetona and J. Schaulys were elected officers of this body.[2] Since the military authorities had forbidden all elections,

---

[1] One object for which the Germans worked hard was to get a Lithuanian bishop appointed to the See of Vilno. The Foreign Ministry pressed the Vatican to transfer the then occupant of the see, Bishop von dem Ropp, to another diocese. The Administrator, Michalkiewicz, was not available for the see, as he was earmarked for that of Minsk. The new see was to be enlarged to take in the diocese of Sejny and the archdiocese of Warsaw. The discussions dragged on throughthe whole of 1918.

[2] Klimas, op. cit., doc. No. XIII.

the meeting resolved 'to settle on the candidates by private conversations, or larger meetings'.

Even before the committee met, the Lithuanians had been told by the military authorities 'that independent Lithuania must get in touch with Germany on the basis of a *military convention*, a *customs union*, and *co-ownership of the strategic railways*'.[1] The Germans invited the Lithuanians to choose: either they might opt for Germany, with close association with the Reich, in which case Germany would support the unification of Lithuania as far as the chain of lakes east of Vilno, independent of Russia, or, if they refused, the country would be partitioned between Germany and Russia, the area west of the line named being simply annexed. This was the policy which Germany afterwards tried to put into effect.

The Lithuanians did not reject Germany's conditions *a priori*, but they asked for much larger political powers for the projected National Council and the replacement of Ysenburg whom they detested as the embodiment of the harsh German occupying regime. *Oberost* feared that when the Lithuanians got a representative body of their own, they would proclaim their complete independence instead of the association with Germany, and proposed that the position should be consolidated before the National Council was constituted. The government disagreed. Its aims was the same as that of *Oberost*: 'to chain Lithuania to us so closely that whether the end of the war finds it an independent state or an annexe of Germany, it must itself seek rapprochement with or incorporation in us'; but it hoped that this result could be achieved by replacing Ysenburg, introducing a 'milder' regime and giving the Lithuanians economic and cultural support. The conference organised by the preparatory committee met in Vilno from September 18 to 22 and elected a Lithuanian Taryba (National Council).[2] Twenty Lithuanians were nominated at the session, and provision was made for co-opting representatives of the minorities. The Lithuanians asked for sanction for this 'national representative body, drawn from all classes of the population', and on September 23 a proclamation issued by Ysenburg in the name of Field-Marshal Prince Leopold of Bavaria, General Officer Commanding in the East (*Oberost*), convoked a 'National Council for Lithuania' under the control of the military administration.[3] The candidates put forward by the conference were nominated members. The Taryba was recognised by the émigré Lithuanians in Stockholm in October and by those in Switzerland in November as

[1] Ibid.
[2] Id., p. xiv and doc. XIV.
[3] Id., XVII and XVIII.

the supreme organ of state of the Lithuanian nation,[1] but their interpretation of its status was different from that of the Germans, who regarded the National Council as a mere consultative body, neither a repository of sovereignty nor a government.

The formation of the National Council concluded a chapter in the political negotiations with the Lithuanians. Thereafter Germany exercised her influence chiefly through the administration. The Germans tried to divert the national aspirations of the Lithuanians, and particularly the activities of the National Council, to the non-political fields of school, language, church, welfare institutions and communal activities. The Foreign Ministry's new representative on the administration, von Maltzan, promised on October 3 'to oppose benevolently but firmly' all attempts to engage in wider political activities. The Lithuanians proved, however, much more stubborn in the defence of their national interests than the Germans had expected. At the end of October the Taryba and the occupying authorities came into open conflict over the language question.[2] The Lithuanians objected to the introduction of German as the language of proceedings in the Taryba and to the appointment of a German official as its President, and sent a protest to the Majority parties of the Reichstag against the stubborn attitude of the German authorities on the question of obligatory instruction in German in the primary schools.[3] The OHL made a paper concession. A new head of the administration was appointed in the person of Under-Secretary of State von Falkenhausen, who was, incidentally, a Prussian of the strictest type;[4] but under him was a purely military administration, which by agreement between the government and the OHL 'was to remain for years under G.O.C. Ost'. Falkenhausen was not even allowed to correspond directly with the Chancellor on current administrative questions: all correspondence had to go through *Oberost*.

The parliamentarians, led by Erzberger, nevertheless succeeded in helping the Lithuanians to get the detested Ysenburg removed. On November 29 Ludendorff had met Smetona, Kairys and Schaulys in Berlin, and had again threatened them with the partition of Lithuania, although this time he gave somewhat different reasons: in view of the forthcoming negotiations with the Russians the Germans must have the Lithuanians' declaration of adhesion to Germany in

[1] Id., XXI.

[2] Id., XIX.

[3] The Central Committee for the civilian administration in Lithuania and Courland began work on October 28, 1917.

[4] Lewerenz, op. cit., pp. 206 ff.

their hands, or they would not be able to defend Lithuania's interests at Brest-Litovsk, and might possibly even find themselves forced to agree with the Russians over their heads. Smetona and Schaulys gave in for the moment and promised to accept the OHL's draft of this declaration, with the substance of which they 'agreed in principle'. On the same day, however, the new Chancellor, in his opening speech to the Reichstag, announced that he accepted the right of self-determination for the countries formerly subject to the Tsar, and said that he expected 'that they would express themselves in whatever form corresponds to their conditions and the direction of their cultures'. This declaration had certainly been forced out of Hertling by pressure from the Reichstag majority. The Lithuanians at once sent him a telegram of thanks with a request for an audience.

The Chancellor received them in the Foreign Ministry on December 1 in the presence of the Under-Secretaries of State Radowitz and von dem Bussche and of Nadolny.[1] The Lithuanians then promised to ask the Taryba to proclaim an independent Lithuanian state in perpetual 'close alliance' with Germany in the form of a *military, customs, currency and transport union.* It is true – and this was to prove decisive later – that the Lithuanians reversed the order of the steps to be taken when constituting the independent Lithuanian state. The Germans had asked for the declaration first, after which they would concede formal independence; the Lithuanians insisted that they must first proclaim their independence and receive an assurance from Germany that she would recognise the new state not later than the conclusion of peace. The OHL, however, wanted to avoid any declaration on Lithuania, and Hindenburg consequently objected to it on the old grounds; particularly he objected to a military convention, 'since the Lithuanians will be doing their service in German regiments for many years'.

On December 6 and 7 a big Conference of State between the civilians and the OHL decided to make the Lithuanians accept retrospectively a much shorter version of the Protocol of December 1, which entirely disregarded their wishes and complaints. At the same time it was agreed to embark on an immediate confidential exchange of views with the Federal governments 'on the personal union between Lithuania and Courland and the Prussian Crown'. In view of the difficult political situation and of the imminence of the Brest-Litovsk negotiations, the Lithuanians had to do as the Germans

---

[1] On this occasion the Lithuanians again presented a list of grievances and suggested that unless they were remedied. it would be impossible to get the Taryba to accept the Declaration.

wished or risk seeing their country partitioned. On December 11 the Taryba accordingly produced a declaration[1] proclaiming

(i) an independent Lithuanian state with Vilno as its capital
(ii) an alliance between this state and the German Reich, to be realised chiefly by a military, transport, customs and currency union.

The German leaders had attained their object of an 'independent' and 'free' Lithuania in close association with Germany, and at Brest-Litovsk they in fact invoked these dictated 'declarations of independence' by their Lithuanian and Courland nominees as justification for detaching those countries from Russia and reserving their future disposition to themselves.

When, on the resumption of the Brest-Litovsk negotiations, the Russians asked for a second notification of Lithuania's Declaration of Independence, the Taryba resolved on January 8, 1918 to repeat the first half of the declaration of December 11 without essential alteration,[2] but said that it could not repeat the second part on Lithuania's relations with Germany, without the consent of a democratically elected constituent assembly. The Germans very naturally objected, and the next day the Taryba agreed to send the Russian government a notification of the first half of their declaration only, but it made this offer conditional on receiving a number of binding assurances:

(i) The national administration to be transferred to the Taryba within a reasonable period.
(ii) The German occupying forces to be withdrawn and a Lithuanian militia formed.
(iii) Recognition by the German Reich of the independent Lithuanian state.[3]

The German representatives insisted that the Lithuanians should be forced to notify Russia of their declaration; their message made no reference to the Lithuanian conditions. The only concession finally made by the Germans – to convoke a constituent assembly – was of little value; it was only a tactical move to facilitate the negotiations with the Russians, and the Germans were determined in advance that it should be no more.

On February 16, however, the Taryba adopted a new declaration[4] disavowing the contractual relationship with Germany. This led to a conflict with the military authorities. The censorship vetoed publication of the declaration.[5]

[1] Klimas, op. cit., No. XXIX and p. xviii. The declaration had no perceptible effect (see Colliander, op. cit., p. 150).

[2] Klimas, No. XXXII, p. xix; Colliander, pp. 159 f.

[3] Klimas, No. XXXIII, p. xxi.   [4] Id., xxi f., XXXVIII.

[5] Only a few papers were able to print the Declaration (Klimas, XXI; Colliander, p. 165).

A Conference of State met in Berlin on February 20, two days after the resumption of the German advance, under the presidency of Vice-Chancellor Payer to consider the altered situation in Lithuania. There was much indignation at the behaviour of the Lithuanians; Payer talked of 'Lithuanian boorishness'. The civilians and the military were agreed that the declaration would have to be revoked. All speakers agreed in principle with Radowitz's definition of Germany's aims in the east as keeping 'on our frontiers countries which are bound to us and offer good security'.

Certain differences, which were however of minor importance compared with the basic agreement, arose over the forms which the monarchs were to take. Two alternative solutions were discussed; a real and personal union of Lithuania and Courland with Prussia, or the establishment of two duchies under dynasties of their own from German princely houses. General von Bartenwerffer, who was representing the OHL, von Radowitz of the Imperial Chancellery, and the heads of the military administration in both Lithuania and Courland were strongly for the Prussian solution, but others argued that the Federal states might object. Payer disliked the idea of the personal union as bearing too close a resemblance to annexation. The Reichstag had been allowed to send 'representatives' of the 'democratic' parties to the meeting, and they signified the agreement of the Reichstag majority with the government's policy on the ground that 'they, too' (sc., the parties) wanted no republics in Lithuania and Courland. Those sections of the Reichstag which were 'against conquests' had, however, some objections to too obvious an association. Payer thought the essential was 'to establish the link'. Von dem Bussche agreed; he thought it better to leave the question open and said laconically: 'We can chain these countries to ourselves, even without a personal union.'

Once the Treaty of Brest-Litovsk had been signed on March 3, the velvet glove was no longer necessary. The changed atmosphere can be whiffed in a minute sent by Nadolny to the Chancellor on March 8. 'We shall,' he argued, 'still be there even after we have recognised their independence and we shall be able to decide policy far more freely than in Germany itself, because there will be no constitutional deadweights.'[1]

The majority of the Taryba being anti-German, Nadolny thought it unusable for the present as an instrument of German policy, but it should still be required to pronounce the revocation of the declara-

[1] As a counter to the danger of Polonisation, Nadolny proposes solution of the problem of the see of Vilno in the Lithuanian sense, and immediate initiation of an anti-Polish land policy by buying up Polish-owned estates, on the model of the Prussian Ostmark policy in the Polish provinces of Prussia.

tion of February 16 and to re-affirm that of December 11, on which earlier basis the independence of Lithuania could then be recognised. Then the Taryba would have to dissolve itself. There would follow a transitional period of indefinite length, without popular representation, and Nadolny suggested the following principles to govern Germany's policy in Lithuania during this stage:

Meanwhile, a Lithuanian government of about seven departments should be set up, to carry through the organisation of the country with German help and under German guidance. It will be possible to find seven reasonable [!] Lithuanians to form a government.

As the last touch to his policy of the 'slack rein', Nadolny proposed replacing the military regime at an early date by a civilian administration unconnected with the OHL. His reasons were purely political:

Until we change the present system, which the Lithuanian independents regard as simply a façade for the benefit of foreign countries and left-wing deputies in the Reichstag, and which exploits the country as booty of war at the conqueror's will, we cannot achieve any of the results which we want; we shall only make the country, which at first welcomed us with great sympathy, increasingly antagonistic to us.

The one important result of Nadolny's recommendations for a relaxation of the German occupying regime was the appointment of Count Keyserlingk[1]–who had called for the annexation and Germanisation of Lithuania and Courland in October, 1914, when *Regierungspräsident* of Königsberg–to the post of 'commissioner for the handling of Lithuanian, Courlandish and other Eastern questions, with the exception of Poland', *directly* responsible to the Chancellor. But constitutional objections by the ministries against this new post and strong opposition from the OHL drove Keyserlingk to resign it only six weeks later.

Nadolny's notes were taken as the basis for a further discussion between the civilian authorities and the OHL on March 10 and 11 on 'the political situation in Lithuania and the Baltic provinces'. The basis of German policy was again defined in the following two sentences:

Germany must retain the real power in these areas by bringing them under her sovereignty. The degree of limitation of the sovereignty of the Eastern States will be determined by the treaties of alliance to be concluded in due course, the initiative for which must come from the individual states.

[1] The civilian government of Germany tried to use the Commissioner's office to put through its policy against that of the OHL. After Keyserlingk's resignation the office was placed under the Reich Interior Office, and on October 7 Baron von Falkenhausen was appointed Commissioner, while retaining his previous post of head of the civilian administration of Oberost.

The political situation being so unfavourable for them, the Lithuanians were forced to make further concessions. It was only on condition that the Taryba should unambiguously endorse the declaration of December 11 that the Chancellor consented to receive a deputation conveying its Declaration of Independence. At first the Taryba refused to go back on its declaration of February,[1] but the imminence of the ratification of the Treaty of Brest-Litovsk forced it to take a quick decision. As the Entente was uninterested in the Lithuanian question, regarding Lithuania as a part of Russia,[2] the Taryba had no choice but to accept the Germans' demands if it wanted a Lithuanian state to be created by the end of the war. On March 20 it empowered Staugaitis, Dr. Jurgis Schaulys and Dr. Jonas Vileischis to notify Berlin of the Declaration of Independence as resolved on February 16 and to ask Berlin to recognise the Lithuanian state; at the same time, however, it adhered to the declaration of December 11 in respect of the definition of Lithuania's relationship with the German Reich.[3] On this basis the Emperor signed a 'Charter of Recognition of the Independence of Lithuania', but with an important amendment. The conditions of December 11 were included in the Charter as conditions for Germany's recognition of the Lithuanian state—i.e., no treaties with Germany, no Lithuania.[4]

The recognition made no change in conditions in Lithuania. In spite of busy and obstinate endeavours the Taryba was given no opportunity to negotiate on a real Lithuanian government. The military administration continued to use the country for Germany's purposes and retained sole disposition over the country of Lithuania, whose own inhabitants had in practice no voice in their own destinies.

[1] Klimas, No. XXXVIII and pp. xxii f.
[2] Colliander, p. 175.
[3] Klimas, No. XXXIX.
[4] The left and the Zentrum supported the Lithuanians in their endeavours to obtain recognition, thinking that this would be an antidote to ill-effects of Brest-Litovsk on world opinion of Germany's world policy. When the Treaty of Brest was given its second reading in the Reichstag on March 22, 1917 (the third reading was taken on the same day), the Majority parties submitted a resolution to the Reichstag, expressing the hope that when the Treaty was through, 'the agreement with the German Reich desired by the present popular representatives (of Poland, Lithuania and Courland) be concluded as speedily as possible'.

Part Three

1918

18

THE PEACE OF BREST-LITOVSK

THE FIRST REALISATION OF GERMAN WAR AIMS

LENIN's victory over Kerensky on November 6 and 7, 1917 could not but seem to the German government to be the crown of their military and political campaign against Russia since the autumn of 1914. At last the Russian colossus had collapsed under the pincer movement of military pressure and the social revolution fostered by Germany through the Bolsheviks and the revolt of the nationalities. The Bolsheviks, who had come to power in Russia with the slogan of 'Peace and Bread', promptly fulfilled Germany's expectations of a speedy peace. The very day after seizing power in Petersburg they issued the famous 'Message to All', the appeal of the Congress of Soviets to peoples and governments to conclude a general peace without annexations or reparations and with full respect for the peoples' right of self-determination.[1]

From a general peace to a separate peace

The German government was the first to react to this invitation to initiate negotiations for a general peace. It did so because messages from Stockholm had made Kühlmann doubt whether the new government would be able to maintain itself longer than a few weeks.[2] This situation induced the German government to continue its previous policy of supporting the Bolshevik regime, especially with financial means,[3] in order to find a partner with which to conclude peace in the east, since according to reports from German 'informants'[4] Lenin 'needed Germany's support to carry out his programme'. Reports, said these informants, that Germany intended to choose this moment to detach Poland and Lithuania from Russia 'had weakened confidence in the policy of the German government'. It was therefore necessary for the German government to identify itself publicly

---

[1] General works on this question include von Rauch, *Geschichte des bolschewistischen Russland*, pp. 104 ff.; William Henry Chamberlin, *The Russian Revolution, 1917–1921* (New York, 1954), Vol. I, pp. 389 ff.; John W. Wheeler-Bennett, *Brest-Litovsk, The Forgotten Peace* (London, 1938).

[2] Zeman, *Germany and the Russian Revolution*, p. 73.

[3] Id., p. 75.

[4] Id., pp. 79 f.

with the war aims of the majority parties. The Foreign Ministry at once replied that 'the Imperial Government took its stand, as before, on the Reichstag resolution in respect of war aims'[1] – thus, given the nature of the resolution and the interpretation given it by Michaelis, renouncing no war aims.

The same basic idea was contained in a memorandum which Czernin had addressed to Hertling even before hearing the 'Message to All'.[2] Czernin assumed that Lenin would start by asking for a general peace without annexations or reparations, as a move towards the conclusion of a separate peace with the Central Powers if, as he expected, the Western Powers refused to make peace on this basis but the Central Powers agreed. The Central Powers should therefore accept this formula as the only way of entering into conversation with the Russians. The Bolsheviks' acceptance of the right of self-determination for the non-Russian peoples in Russia would make it possible to decide the future of Courland, Livonia and Finland at the peace negotiations. Hertling expressly approved these considerations.

Kerensky's attempt to recover power and the revolt of the Kadets delayed the consolidation of the Soviets' authority. It was therefore not until November 20 that the declaration of November 8 was handed to the ambassadors of the powers allied with Russia. When, however, the Allied powers refused to recognise the Soviet government or to follow up the peace move, Trotsky, as People's Commissar for Foreign Affairs, wirelessed direct to the German Supreme Command proposing the conclusion of an armistice for the purpose of reaching 'a democratic peace without annexations or reparations'. Hoffmann brought the message to Ludendorff,[3] who decided to accept it, and on November 27 it was agreed to open official armistice negotiations on December 2. These led first to a suspension of hostilities, and on December 15 to the conclusion of an armistice, at first running only till January 14, 1918. An armistice had meanwhile been concluded on the Rumanian front on December 8. On November 30 Trotsky had informed the Allied ambassadors of the impending armistices but again they had not answered.

The opening of these negotiations, as a step towards a separate peace with Bolshevik Russia, was the first success for German tactics.

The Bolsheviks were understandably nervous at the prospect of

---

[1] Id., pp. 75 ff.

[2] Von Rauch, op. cit., p. 104.

[3] See Max Hoffmann, *Die Aufzeichnungen des Generalmajors M.H.*, ed. Friedrich Nowak (Berlin, 1929), Vol. I, pp. 184 f.; id., *Der Krieg der versäumten Gelegenheiten* (Munich, 1924), p. 189.

having to face the Central Powers alone, and receive from them conditions which might well be so humiliating as to endanger their political position, which was still very precarious. Immediately on seizing power they had sent a message to the Germans via Stockholm that if Germany's conditions were too severe they would be overthrown by a bourgeois reaction which would try to restore the front against Germany with Japanese help. The new rulers in Petersburg were in a dilemma: on the one hand, they had come to power with the slogan of peace, and they therefore needed an immediate end to hostilities, if only for reasons of internal policy. On the other hand, they could not accept peace at any price, for fear of strengthening the right-wing Social Revolutionaries and the Mensheviks, or creating a threat of bourgeois-monarchist reaction. Moreover, they lacked authority within their own frontiers, for the soldiers were flooding back in ever-increasing numbers from the front, in order to be at home when the promised division of the land took place. The Soviets' policy at Brest-Litovsk is therefore to be understood primarily as an attempt to steer between the Scylla of extreme and humiliating German conditions and the Charybdis of a split in their own party and a counter-revolution.

The German government saw the Bolsheviks' dilemma and decided to exploit it ruthlessly, in order not only to secure the comprehensive solution in the east for which it had so long been working, but also, by concluding a separate peace with Russia, to decide the issue in the west and thus achieve the whole of their war aims. When Ludendorff gave his consent to an armistice on November 27, he had just decided,[1] under the impact of the news of the Russian revolution, to seek a military decision in the west by a great offensive in the coming March, into which he would be able to throw all the forces released from the east. The Emperor had agreed. Hence Ludendorff was pressing for the speedy conclusion of peace in the east, although he was not prepared to renounce Germany's war aims there.

Hertling too recognised the unique chance of peace in the east. Conformably with the considerations submitted to him by Czernin and Kühlmann on November 10 and 13, and with his promise to the German 'informants', he had told the Reichstag on November 29 – his first speech to that body – that he hoped for peace and was accepting the Russian offer, and he expressed the hope 'that we shall return to a good-neighbourly relationship especially in the economic field. . . . As for the lands previously subjected to the Tsarist sceptre, Poland, Courland, Lithuania, we respect the right of their peoples to

[1] See on this *Der Weltkrieg*, from the Reich Archives, Vol. 13, pp. 331 f. and 342; id., *Bundesarchiv* (*1956*), Vol. 14, pp. 53 ff.

self-determination.' This declaration, which Kühlmann himself described[1] as the sub-structure for the *whole* negotiations, was the bridge
to the peace without annexations or reparations demanded by the
Russians and also a tactical method of nevertheless detaching the
border states to Germany's advantage.

The Emperor was aiming higher still. On the same November 29
he proposed to Kühlmann that, should peace negotiations with
Russia come within a reasonable time, he should try to 'enter into a
sort of relationship of alliance or friendship with Russia'. Kühlmann
was unwilling to go so far, for Germany, he said, was strong enough
to wait. Von Bergen, who was the organiser of the Foreign Ministry's
policy of revolution and Kühlmann's closest adviser (greatly es-
teemed by him as 'the most gifted man, politically, here' and consulted over all important political decisions), drafted the answer to
the Emperor. It expressed in most striking form the continuity of
German policy since the autumn of 1914.

The splitting of the Entente and the formation thereafter of new political
combinations agreeable to us is the most important diplomatic war aim.
Russia seemed the weakest link in the enemy chain; the task was therefore
gradually to loosen and, if possible, detach her. This was the purpose of the
destructive work carried on by us behind the front in Russia, primarily
encouragement of separatist tendencies and support of the Bolsheviks.

These are the same considerations as were adduced by Bethmann
Hollweg in November, 1914 and August, 1915 to explain Germany's
attempts to conclude a separate peace and to promote revolution in
Russia. Only the chances in favour of a peace in the east were much
greater now: the Bolsheviks, Kühlmann thought, 'need peace to establish their own position'. And in close agreement with Czernin's
reasoning, he went on: 'we have every interest in using their term of
office, which perhaps will only be short, to reach an armistice, and
then, if possible, a peace also'.

By December 3 the Germans had at least a prospect of a separate
armistice. The task of Germany's and Austria-Hungary's diplomats
was now to evolve out of it the separate peace which was their sole
objective. The Germans were well aware – Kühlmann himself said so
later[2] – that it would be very difficult, even for a revolutionary
government which had repudiated all tradition, to break an alliance
under the eyes of the whole world and its own people, and immediately to conclude a separate peace. It was therefore advisable to meet
this government half-way by the détour of a general peace – taking
precautions that such a peace did not ensue.

[1] Addressing the representatives of the parties in the Reichstag, January 1, 1918.
[2] Ibid.

Internal preparations: the definition of political aims, economic interests, peace with the Ukraine

The shape which Germany wanted the peace to take was decided in detail in a series of preparatory conferences between the Germans themselves. The principal problem governing the German–Russian conversations in Brest-Litovsk was whether Germany would be able to achieve and justify her old war aims in Lithuania, Courland and Poland, in spite of its public acceptance of a peace without annexations and of the right to self-determination. The German government was now able to reap the fruits of the policy of 'autonomy' initiated in Berlin and Bingen on April 21 and July 31, 1917. Kühlmann, as he admitted in his recollections as late as 1948,[1] was determined from the first 'to use the right of national self-determination to undermine the point of peace without annexations'. He went on:

My plan was to entangle Trotsky in a purely academic discussion on the right of national self-determination and the possibility of applying it in practice, and to get for ourselves through the right of national self-determination whatever territorial concessions we absolutely needed.

When the negotiations opened in Brest-Litovsk on December 22, the tactical basis for the German delegation was afforded by the declarations produced in the course of the preceding weeks, under more or less strong German pressure, by the newly constituted National Councils in Courland, Lithuania and Poland, and parts of Estonia and Livonia (Riga and the Islands). Kühlmann had defended these declarations as 'genuine expressions of popular opinion' against attacks by the Social Democrats and the U.S.P.D.[2] The Russians, although they did not know that the declarations had been arranged in Bingen on July 31, refused to recognise the composition of the National Councils as representative of the will of the peoples, and insisted that new elections be held on a general franchise – a demand which the Germans were bound to refuse, knowing as they did that the overwhelming majority of the populations would have declared for complete independence and for a democratic republican form of state.

Kühlmann himself was thus well aware that the basis of his arguments was a purely tactical device for detaching these countries from Russia without mobilising the public opinion of the whole world against Germany and destroying her internal unity. He was less concerned with repelling Bolshevism as such, than with preventing the

[1] Kühlmann, *Erinnerungen*, pp. 523 f.
[2] At a session of the Inter-Party Committee.

creation of a pro-Western belt in east-central Europe (the system which in fact came into being later, although then in the form of a *cordon sanitaire* against Bolshevism). Looking on things as he did from a Prusso-German angle, Kühlmann also saw the possibility that Austria might defect to the West, and needed to keep her under control no less firmly than the nascent border states from Finland to the Ukraine.

The first internal conference between civilians and OHL to prepare for Brest-Litovsk was held on December 6–7, 1917. Some time was spent on the situations in Lithuania and the Ukraine, but the principal subject discussed was the instructions to be given to General Hoffmann, who was to be in charge of the armistice negotiations. He was given two main orders. First, he was 'to put a strong demand to Russia to evacuate Livonia and Estonia', without, however, letting the negotiations break down on that point; the same was to apply to Finland. Secondly, should the Entente contrary to expectation, offer a general armistice, thereby endangering the separate peace, the offer was to be accepted only subject to the condition that submarine warfare was to go on.

Finally, Brest-Litovsk was designated as the *venue* for the negotiations.

After the conference Ludendorff gave Hoffmann his detailed instructions, which agreed with his own 'principles' of the previous April and May, and were in reality purely annexationist, although clothed in other forms to make them appear compatible with the principle of peace without annexations which the German government had accepted as the basis for negotiations out of consideration for Austria-Hungary, the internal position in Germany itself, and world opinion. Their substance was:

   (i) Non-interference in Russian affairs.
  (ii) No war indemnity in cash. Attachment of Lithuania and Courland, including Riga and the islands, to Germany, 'since we need more land to support our people'.
 (iii) Far-reaching 'respect for the national claims' of the Lithuanians.
 (iv) Independence of Poland, in close connection with the Central Powers.
  (v) Respect for the principle of national self-determination: Russia to evacuate Finland, Livonia, Estonia, Moldavia, East Galicia and Armenia.
 (vi) Economic help in the reconstruction of Russia and the closest economic relations between Russia and Germany; after this perhaps an alliance with Russia (as proposed by the Emperor at the end of November).

The OHL brought these instructions to the Crown Council which was held at Kreuznach on December 18[1] to settle finally what Ger-

[1] Volkmann, op. cit., pp. 215 ff.; Wheeler-Bennett, op. cit., pp. 107 ff.

many was to demand at Brest-Litovsk. The most remarkable feature of this conference was the way in which confidence in coming victory again, as in the Kreuznach programmes of the preceding April–May and August, welded Germany's western and eastern war aims into a complete unity. Thus the conditional renunciation of Belgium resolved at the Crown Council of September 11 was modified on the Emperor's insistence, on the ground that its pre-condition – 'peace before winter' – had not been fulfilled. And this background of western war aims must always be kept in mind when we consider Germany's pursuit of her eastern aims during the following months.

These constituted, of course, the main point on the agenda on December 18. For Lithuania and Courland the Emperor thought personal union with Prussia–Germany the only possibility. He agreed with the OHL that the military administration should be maintained for a period after the war and only gradually replaced by a civilian one. The non-German peoples must be ruled 'with a slack rein'. Again in agreement with Ludendorff, he wanted the antagonism between Lithuania and Poland intensified and he therefore suggested getting the Vatican to appoint Lithuanians to the Lithuanian diocese, and re-delimiting them, as soon as possible. In respect of Poland, for which the Austro-Polish solution was still officially in force, the Emperor thought Austria's proposals for the frontiers unacceptable and demanded that Germany insist on 'complete security for our frontiers' (even against an Austrian Poland).

After Germany's claims on Lithuania and Courland and in Poland, the main point discussed that day was how to extend Germany's 'sphere of influence' to Livonia and Estonia, a point strongly pressed by the OHL, as its instructions to Hoffmann for the armistice negotiations will have shown. Hertling and Kühlmann, on the other hand, had political qualms in view of Germany's future relations with Russia. Hindenburg produced military arguments in favour of the demand – he wanted room to manoeuvre his left wing in a future war – and favoured attaching Estonia and Livonia with Riga and the islands to Prussia–Germany by means of a personal union. The Emperor advised diverting Russia's ambition to reach the open sea to the Persian Gulf. He recommended – and this decision, which went part of the way to meet the OHL, was accepted –'waiting for the Estonians and Livonians to come to us', but agreed with Ludendorff that they must be given the possibility to express their own wishes.

The next day Kühlmann reported on the state of preparations to the Central Committee of the Reichstag. The day after that, December 20, immediately before leaving for the negotiations in

Brest-Litovsk which were to start on the 22nd, he explained Germany's programme to the party leaders of the Reichstag in terms which showed that he envisaged the disintegration of the old Russia into more or less autonomous formations, of which the three lying within Germany's sphere of rule had already been recognised as independent by Germany, while the others (among which Finland had already declared its independence in July, while the Ukraine had become autonomous in July and was about to declare itself independent) would be recognised as soon as Russia set the example.

Germany's peace conditions were: 1. Free right of self-determination for *Poland, Lithuania and Courland.* The Russian Government already knew that the representatives of the peoples in those countries had seceded from Russia. Germany would recognise the secession of *Finland, the Ukraine, the Caucasus and Siberia,* only if the Russian Government did so also. 2. Resumption of regular trading relations, the old Commercial Treaty to be prolonged initially for three years. 3. Repeal of all war legislation. 4. Mutual exchange of prisoners of war. 5. Mutual renunciation of war indemnities.[1]

Once again we see that ideological motives played no part in German reasoning, or only a very secondary one. For the attainment of her 'security programme' Germany cared little whether she had to deal with the Tsar or with Kerensky, with Lenin or with a counter-revolutionary government; the essential was that whoever was in power in Russia at the time should accept peace on Germany's terms. This 'security programme' could, however (as Kühlmann explained in his report to the Central Committee of the Reichstag and again in his big speech to the same audience in January), only be helpful to Germany's policy of destruction and revolution in Russia if that Russia crumbled into a multiplicity of weak little states needing German protection and a weakened Rump Russia.

The Prussian Ministry of State agreed to this programme on December 21, the day before the negotiations in Brest-Litovsk opened.

When it became clear that a separate peace in the east was possible, the question of a central office for preparing the peace – which had been discussed before – became urgent. Helfferich, who had offered his resignation as Vice-Chancellor on November 9 – he had already handed over his duties as Secretary of State in the Reich Interior Office to Wallraf on October 13 – now gave way to the pressure of the Chancellor and the Emperor and accepted the post of head of a special office, directly subordinated to the Chancellor in a fashion not exactly defined by the constitution,[2] and with the task of

---

[1] Author's italics.
[2] See also Helfferich, op. cit., pp. 533 ff.

collaborating with the Prussian ministries and Reich offices concerned in co-ordinating the wishes advanced by business circles as a basis for the negotiations with Russia. The military authorities, the army and navy, immediately elbowed their way in, and the OHL succeeded in getting a regular representative of their own appointed to Helfferich's office to look after 'war-economic necessities'.

The immediate object of the military was, as Ludendorff wrote to Helfferich, to safeguard 'the interests of the operations against the Western Powers' – in other words, Germany's supply of armaments. They did this by pressing for rubber, cotton, asbestos, copper, nickel, tin, ores of every kind, and particularly for sufficient supplies of petrol. But besides this legitimate interest, they were always alert to create for Germany a strong power position for the future. For example, since Galicia if attached to Poland, might drop out as a source of oil, and since the production of petrol from lignite at home was still in its first stages, the navy demanded safeguards for the importation of Rumanian and Russian petrol by sea from Poti and Batum across the Black Sea to Constanta and up the Danube to Germany. Consequently Germany must try to secure a firm hold on Constanta. Again, the Secretary of State of the Reich Naval Office explained that it was 'necessary' for Germany to receive a substantial war indemnity because she could not otherwise finance her naval construction programme for the next war. Both Capelle and Ludendorff wanted Russian prisoners of war to be employed in armaments factories during the war, and Ludendorff went still further and wanted Germany to have a permanent right to recruit voluntary labour in Russia.

But the strongest pressure came from German industry itself. The *Verein Deutscher Eisen-und Stahlindustrieller* set out what the iron industry wanted from a peace with Russia in a letter to Hindenburg, of which, characteristically, they sent Helfferich only a copy. Heavy industry's chief interest was to secure the import of high-grade Ukrainian iron ores and of Caucasian and Ukrainian manganese ores which it needed for steel production. Very large quantities were involved – up to 1914 50 per cent of the world production of manganese had come from Russia, which had supplied three-quarters of Germany's total requirements of this ore. As the rest of the manganese ores imported by the German steel industry came from Brazil and India, and as these countries would, as the letter said, 'be subject to the raw materials control of our Anglo-Saxon enemies in the future world economic struggle' – in consequence of the Paris economic conferences – the German iron and steel industry was particularly interested in securing its imports from the nearer source of

Russia. Every precaution should be taken to see that the export of iron and manganese ores was not impeded by transport or customs barriers, and Germany must receive preferential treatment in every respect for all imports and exports from Russia. Germans must be guaranteed complete freedom to establish and carry on economic activities in Russia; in particular they must be allowed entire freedom to acquire and work mines formerly owned by the Russian state. The two heavy industrial associations of west and east Germany demanded quite nakedly measures to hinder the economic exploitation of Russia by other foreign countries, so that Russia should be converted into a supplier of raw materials, dependent on Germany. A very strong demand was made for the cancellation of all American and Anglo-French separate agreements with Russia; another demand was for free immigration of labour from the Russian industrial districts.

The *Deutscher Handelstag* declared that Poland, Finland and the Baltic provinces should first be annexed, and that thereafter Rump Russia be 'made an object of exploitation by the imposition of appropriate economic agreements'.

The Thyssen concern, which had long been engaged in the production of manganese as part-owner of the Chiaturi manganese mines in the Caucasus, expressed the same wishes to Helfferich on December 14 in even greater detail. Thyssen mentioned especially the high-grade ores of Krivoi Rog, whose iron content of 68 per cent made them particularly suitable for the production of steel. The import of ores from Russia was the more important because the Swedish export had been limited by the Swedish government and that of Spain was on the decline. Similar considerations applied to the Caucasus: here the chief demand was for the opening of the port of Poti, the grant of concessions, and facilities to expand and modernise that port. As always, special interest was shown in the railways and their tariffs on the lines leading to the ports of Nicolaev, Cherson and Poti. It was these concrete economic interests which inspired Germany's efforts in 1918 to dominate the Ukraine and Georgia.

The railway problem was considered separately at a conference of all ministries and the OHL which met on December 22 in the Reich Interior Office under the presidency of Helfferich (who had previously brought the Reich Economic Office and the Reich Treasury into agreement). The conference considered what provisions should be introduced into the separate peace with Russia for taking over the railways in the border states to be ceded by her. Among other points, it was decided to introduce the German gauge on these lines, a proposal followed shortly afterwards by the new independent

Ukraine. It was further decided to claim for Germany all state properties in Courland, Lithuania and Poland, including the forest of Bialowièza.

Innumerable representations from heavy and light industry and from commerce produced a demand from Helfferich to the Secretary of State for Foreign Affairs, dated January 2, 1918, that the peace treaty with Russia should contain provisions which not only ensured to Germany Russia's sources of raw materials, but also completely eliminated Anglo-American competition and left the Russian market open without restriction to German capital.

Brest-Litovsk also offered an opportunity to realise an objective for which German policy had been preparing since the spring of 1916: to impose Germany's economic interests by renewing her commercial treaty with Russia, an instrument which the Russians had regarded as most disadvantageous in its 1894 form and still more so in the even less favourable version of 1904.

The efforts to re-negotiate the Russian commercial treaty, which could not under the most favourable conditions have fulfilled such far-reaching demands as were being made by German heavy industry, explain Germany's Ukrainian policy. Renewal of the 1904 treaty, which was based on the most favoured nation principle, would have ensured for Germany the chief Russian market of Rump Russia; but the demands of the heavy industry in particular would hardly have been satisfied by that treaty, but only by separate agreements with the Ukraine. When the Bolsheviks resisted Germany's demands more stubbornly than had been expected this became one of the leading threads in Germany's eastern policy. The different national groups which were breaking away from the Russian Empire were to be isolated from one another, each was to be linked directly with Germany, and the whole 'Ostraum', its political and economic unity smashed beyond repair, was to be made into a 'Hinterland' for Germany.

After the spring of 1917, when the movement for autonomy set in in Russia, the agitation which Germany had been carrying on among the Ukrainians since 1914 became more vigorous. Still more did Germany exploit the confusion of the Russian revolution to press with vigour her own interests in the Ukraine. When the Lvov government fell and Kerensky took over on July 12, 1917, the Ukraine claimed the right of self-determination, and after long argument this was conceded on July 16 by the Foreign Minister Tereschenko and the Minister of the Interior Tseretelli.[1] This concession cleared the

[1] See John S. Reschetar, Jr., *The Ukrainian Revolution, 1917–1920* (Princeton, 1952), p. 65.

field for German policy. The first 'Universal' had still pronounced decidely against separation from Great Russia, but its successor proclaimed the autonomy of the Ukraine and thereafter its Rada (Council) was the supreme authority of the democratic Republic of the Ukraine.

The separate peace signed with the Ukraine in Brest-Litovsk on February 9, 1918 can no longer be considered solely or chiefly as a 'bread peace', important as that factor was for Austria-Hungary. For Germany the decisive considerations were expounded to the Chancellor by General von Bartenwerffer[1] as early as October 25, 1917, a fortnight before the October revolution. Bartenwerffer, who was then Head of the Political Department of the OHL, drew the Chancellor's attention to the central importance of the Ukraine for the economy of Russia. From it, he explained, came one-third of Russia's agricultural production and 70 per cent of her coal and ores. The loss of this area, with its rich supplies, would thus be a decisive blow to Russia. Bartenwerffer, however, was not satisfied with proposing that the Ukraine should be detached from Russia and dominated by Germany. The domination of the Ukraine was for him by no means only a worthwhile object in itself; it was also an important piece of German world policy. He set out in precise form the innermost motives of a Ukrainian policy which was afterwards followed by Kühlmann after discussions with Hertling and the Emperor: to curb the Poles by exploiting the antagonism between them and the Ukrainians; to thrust Russia back from the Black Sea and the Straits, and finally to separate Russia from the Balkan peoples and so secure Germany's road from Berlin to Baghdad.

What Bartenwerffer was recommending had been widely discussed in Germany for years past.[2] As early as August, 1914 Bethmann Hollweg had put down the detachment of the Ukraine from Russia as a German war aim, and in August, 1917 von Stumm had reported from Vienna that the German government was in close and constant touch with the Ukrainians.[3] This continuity in Germany's civilian policy explains how the OHL came to insist so strongly on direct separate negotiations with the Ukraine. It is therefore no accident that a separate peace with the Ukraine was being considered very seriously only a few days after heavy industry announced its demands in southern Russia to the OHL and the government, i.e.,

[1] See the author's article, *Deutsche Kriegsziele, Revolutionierung und Separatfrieden im Osten, 1914–1918, Historische Zeitschrift*, No. 188/2, p. 287 and n. 1.

[2] See Hans Beyer, *Die Mittelmächte und die Ukraine, 1918, Jahrbücher für Geschichte Osteuropas*, 1956, Beiheft 2, pp. 20 ff., especially p. 23 with n. 29.

[3] Cf. Czernin, *Im Weltkriege*, p. 327.

in the first days of the Brest negotiations. The German plans were greatly facilitated by Austria's wish to get peace with Russia at almost any price. Czernin himself suggested a separate peace with the Ukraine as a tactical method of putting pressure on the Russians. The Ukraine had created the pre-conditions when on Christmas Eve its Rada had produced a note 'to All' of its own in favour of the principle of peace without annexations – its purpose, of course, being to emphasise its own independence in view of the armistice concluded between the Central Powers and Russia on December 15, and to carry on an absolutely independent policy pending the formation of an all-Russian Federal State.[1] The Central Powers immediately – on December 26 – invited the Ukrainian government to take part in the peace negotiations at Brest-Litovsk. The Ukrainian delegation arrived on January 1, 1918. As early as December 27 Ludendorff had been pressing that, when the delegation arrived, the negotiations with it should be carried to a conclusion with all speed; and he wanted the bilingual district of Chelm to be assigned to the new Ukrainian state[2] without regard to the wishes either of the Poles or the Austrians (Czernin was in favour of peace with the Ukraine but had at first assumed that Chelm would go to Poland). Ludendorff's motives, like Bartenwerffer's, seem to have been partly to secure the road to the east, partly to gain a source of raw materials, to weaken Russia and to 'bottle up' Poland by extending the Ukraine to the north-west and a German-dominated Lithuania to the south-east; the idea of a bridge between the German-dominated Baltic and a Ukraine allied with Germany is obviously the same as that put forward by Class in his memorandum of December, 1914.

The great misunderstanding: the first phase of negotiation

Elaborately prepared and attended by high hopes, the peace negotiations began in Brest-Litovsk on December 27. The choice of *venue* itself was not without symbolic importance. The negotiations reached their first climax with the submission by the Russians of a six point programme and the joint answer of the delegates of the Four Powers returned on December 25 by Czernin.[3] The six points which, were read out by Joffe, the leader of the Russian delegation, followed

[1] Reschetar, op. cit., p. 103.

[2] The province of Chelm had been established only in 1912–13, when it was detached from Congress Poland. The Orthodox Bishopric of Lublin had been established in 1905, being a suffragan of Warsaw until 1912. See Fr. Heyer, *Die orthodoxe Kirche in der Ukraine 1917 bis 1945* (Cologne, 1953), p. 12.

[3] Wheeler-Bennett, op. cit., pp. 177 ff. On the reply of the Central Powers, *Ursachen*, II, p. 125.

the Soviet peace declaration of November 8. They may be summarised as follows:

(i) No annexations by force. Speedy withdrawal of troops from occupied territories.
(ii) Complete restoration of their political independence to the peoples which had lost it during the war.
(iii) National groups inside existing states to be allowed to decide freely by referendum whether to attach themselves to another nation or to form independent states.
(iv) Assurance of the rights of national minorities.
(v) No war indemnities.
(vi) Application of points (i)–(iv) to colonies.

Czernin's answer, which had been drafted by the German delegation, went through the motions of agreeing completely in principle, but suggested such modifications to each of the six points as completely to alter their sense.

(i) Evacuation of occupied territories to be left to be regulated at the peace settlement.
(ii) Point 2 said only that it was not the intention of the Allied Powers to deprive hitherto independent peoples of their independence.
(iii) The status of national groups within a state was a matter for metropolitan, not international, regulation (this reservation nullified the principle and was made in view of the multi-ethnic character of Austria-Hungary and Prussian Poland).
(iv) Minority protection was recognised only in so far as it seemed practically enforceable.
(v) The regulation of the costs of war was made conditional on the Allies' participation in the negotiations.
(vi) The restoration of Germany's colonies was demanded.

These modifications permitted the attainment of all Germany's war aims. With the consent of her allies Germany could on these terms have concluded what Kühlmann, speaking to the Inter-Party Committee, had called 'a completely honourable peace and one completely satisfactory to our vital interests'. But this was not all: by their general reservation the Germans, while appearing to pave the way towards a general peace, had left themselves a free hand by making the basis (renunciation of annexations and reparations) conditional on the consent of all belligerents, 'without exception and without any reservation', within a definite period which was fixed at ten days, that is, by January 4. While making certain of their own aims through the formula of self-determination the Germans dropped the same formula like a bomb into the empires and colonial possessions of their enemies. The reference to the countries often named in this connection, Ireland, Egypt, India, Morocco, etc., was meant to make it impossible in advance for the Entente powers to join in the negotiations.

At the Russians' request, the negotiations were carried on in public; the world was thus able to follow speech and counter-speech through the press. The Russian declaration and Czernin's reply, which was taken as an acceptance of it, produced a shock in German public opinion. In the course of years of discussion and agitation the German War Aims Movement had laid down concrete, firmly defined aims. The majority of the people expected German diplomacy to use the victories in the east to bring home the fruits of Germany's victory swiftly and amply. But these negotiations seemed to be sacrificing the realisation of Germany's war aims in the east now, and her war aims in the west in the future. A press review of the Ministry of War reported that only the Independent Socialists were satisfied; a storm of indignation was sweeping through almost all the other papers and parties. So it was too in the OHL. Ludendorff called on Hoffmann to explain how this was possible; Hindenburg saw in what was being done betrayal of the Kreuznach agreements of December 18.

The deep consternation of German public opinion and the German military was matched in the Russian delegation by optimistic illusions that the Central Powers had renounced the principle of annexations; Joffe had telegraphed in this sense immediately to Petersburg. The day after Czernin's declaration, that is, on December 26, Hoffmann, in agreement with Kühlmann, explained to the Russians that they were deceiving themselves, for they were obviously giving the words 'renunciation of annexations imposed by force' a different interpretation from that given them by the Central Powers, who understood them as allowing the voluntary secession of certain areas from Russia, to wit, Poland, Lithuania and Courland (and from that point onwards, also Livonia and Estonia). Hoffmann reported that Joffe was absolutely stunned by this revelation, and burst into protests, while Kamenev raged and Pokrovsky asked in tears: 'How can you talk of a peace of understanding when you are tearing away nearly 18 districts from Russia?'[1] The thin veil of appearances had been wrenched brutally aside. After this unofficial 'explanation' by the general, Kühlmann stated his bases for the preliminary peace when the commission met the next day, December 27. Here the tactics and aims of Germany's procedure were shown in a nutshell. The Russians were required to accept as expressions of the popular will the

---

[1] Hoffmann, *Versäumte Gelegenheiten*, pp. 201 f.

artificial demonstrations from Poland, Lithuania, Courland, and parts of Estonia and Livonia. When the Russians asked for confirmation of these 'declarations of secession' Kühlmann referred their request to a special committee, thereby rejecting *de facto* any general and free referendum. Germany's political and military representatives were in full agreement; the harmony was not troubled for one instant (as Kühlmann himself said on January 1 when reporting back to the parliamentary leaders). The Russian delegation left Brest-Litovsk to obtain further instructions and was to be away for ten days. As Helfferich put it, from that moment onward Joffe was a political corpse.

Nevertheless the Germans, and also the Western Powers, took Joffe's threat to break off negotiations so seriously that they reckoned with the possibility that the Russians might not return to Brest-Litovsk after the ten days' interval. Germany's insistence on war aims so far-reaching that even a regime as weak as that of Lenin and Trotsky refused them would have necessitated the resumption of the war in the east. But Czernin's instructions, and the critical condition of the Monarchy, made it absolutely essential to avoid the resumption of war, and he therefore threatened the German delegation that he would conclude a separate peace with Russia. It is characteristic of General Hoffmann's extreme anti-Austrian bias that he answered this threat with the laconic remark that he found the idea 'brilliant' since it would allow him to withdraw twenty-five divisions from the Austrian front and throw them against Russia.[1] Kühlmann took Czernin's move no less coolly, but was glad to use the threat as a lever against the OHL and its extreme pressure – it was especially furious at the ten days' delay – and secure for himself the support of the Chancellor and the favour of the Emperor.

Both parties used the pause in the negotiations to clarify their positions. Kühlmann addressed the representatives of the political parties on New Year's Day, and it was all he could do to defend himself against the criticisms of the right and the no less vigorous attacks from the left, who saw a regrettable discrepancy between the declarations of the 25th and the 27th. He hoped to be able to get over the difficulties with the Russians by concluding separate treaties 'with more or less autonomous bodies' (of the old Russia) especially with 'by far the largest and most important of them, the Ukraine'. By mentioning the Ukraine as 'a lever' Kühlmann revealed to the parliamentary leaders the latest device by which Czernin was trying to force through peace in the face of the policy of the German Foreign Ministry and the OHL. When Stresemann reproached him with

[1] Id., p. 202.

laxity in the defence of Germany's economic interests, he retorted by appealing to the larger aim of Mitteleurope:

We must leave ourselves the possibility of according special treatment, including special economic treatment, to those states which are territorially contiguous with us and closely bound to us by historic and other links. We must leave ourselves the possibility of reaching a special relationship with Austria now, when we are dealing with Russia.

The same day a conference of the economic ministries, under the chairmanship of von Stumm of the Foreign Ministry, submitted the results to date of the economic negotiations in Brest-Litovsk to unsparing criticism. Kühlmann had not found it too difficult to talk the parliamentarians over, as the sessions of the Reichstag on January 3 and 4 were to show; but Johannes, who was leading the German commercial delegation, was sharply attacked by Helfferich, Baron von Stein and their collaborators, who described the Russians' consent to the 'negative most favoured nation principle' (which the trade delegation had extracted and which Johannes had thought a good achievement) as a 'last refuge', something to which Germany should have consented only as a last resort. Stein wanted the Russian customs frontier pushed back and Rump Russia (called Great Russia) isolated. Johannes, driven into a corner, had to promise

to obtain a formula which allowed the inclusion of Belgium, Lithuania, etc. among the countries to be given preferential treatment. When the Russians talked of 'seceding states' they had been thinking chiefly of Finland; in the cases of Poland, Lithuania, etc., the principal point in his view was that we should dominate these states economically. In this case it had been made impossible for them to enter into a close economic relationship with Russia . . . all representatives of all Departments invited supported this wish.

The OHL, for its part, had made its position clear in a speech by Ludendorff of the same date to the Committee of the Federal Council, which raised no objections of principle. Starting with the military position, which he said was better than ever, Ludendorff announced that Germany had now no longer any military need of Austria-Hungary, while Bulgaria's help was unimportant and Turkey was a burden. As in Kreuznach on December 18, he linked Germany's war aims in west and east: secure frontiers, colonies and naval bases, annexations of Liége, partition of Belgium between Flemish and Walloons for the protection of German industry in the west. He saw the east as a deployment area against Russia; in the kindred Polish question he stood uncompromisingly for the German-Polish solution.

The Crown Council of January 2[1] has attracted more attention than its due owing to a *faux pas* by the Emperor. The central point under discussion was the question of the Polish Frontier Strip which, if the Austro-Polish solution was retained, had to be settled, not between Germany and Russia, but between Germany and Austria. Asked to choose between the OHL's far-reaching line, which would have included between two and three million Poles in Prussia, and a more modest line put forward by Hoffmann, which confined itself to direct strategic needs, the Emperor, against Kühlmann's advice, chose a line between the two.[2] Hindenburg and Ludendorff regarded this independent decision by the monarch as an insult to their persons and positions and expressed their displeasure openly, challenging the imperial prerogative. Although the Emperor promised to reconsider the question and asked for their views, they made the incident the occasion to threaten to resign.

In the exchange of letters which followed between the OHL, the Emperor and the Chancellor,[3] the point of decisive importance on the war aims was Hertling's communication to Hindenburg that the ten days' grace had expired without the Western Powers joining the peace negotiations. Germany was thus 'now entirely free in respect of the Western Powers and in no way bound any more (equally not to the Russians) by those proposals'. Hindenburg again referred to the Crown Council of December 18, stating most decidedly that Germany's aim was 'to beat the Western Powers ... and thus ensure ourselves that political and economic position in the world which we need'. He prayed that the diplomats would not again throw away the fruits of victory after the heavy offensive in the west ordered for the coming March.

But that Kühlmann's ideas, at least as regards the east, were no less 'imperialist' – perhaps, indeed, even more spacious – is shown by his notes on eastern policy sent to Hindenburg with Hertling's letter:

For the rest, high as I rate the military value of the acquisition of certain protective frontier strips, I can in no way agree that the whole of German policy ought to be thrown out of course for the sake of a small plus or minus to these strips. Our relationship with Austria-Hungary is the pivot of Germany's whole policy. As regards Russia, we have to solve the extraordinarily

---

[1] Wheeler-Bennett, op. cit., pp. 130 f.; for Ludendorff's statement in the Federal Council, *Ursachen*, II, pp. 130 f.

[2] Description and map in Geiss, *Grenzstreifen*, pp. 131 f.

[3] *Ursachen*, II, pp. 131 ff.; cf. also Kühlmann, op. cit., pp. 527 ff. and 534 ff. 'The chief thing,' said Hertling, 'is that the ten days' grace has expired, and no answer to the Russian invitation has come from the Western Powers.'

difficult task of establishing a good economic and political relationship with the new Russia, in order to keep our rear militarily completely free, while at the same time detaching huge areas from the present Russia and building up those districts into effective bulwarks on our frontier.[1]

Such an aim, he admitted, could doubtless be achieved through annexations, on the basis of victory. But in view of Germany's internal conditions and of her intention of return to a friendly relationship with the new Russia, open annexation appeared impracticable. 'We were therefore faced with the task of reaching our aim without annexing these areas.' Kühlmann pursued this policy, with the support of Chancellor and Emperor, tenaciously and ingeniously throughout the negotiations of the following weeks, hoping that the weakness of Bolshevik Russia would enable him to achieve his aim.

In Russia itself the short period of confident expectation had been followed by the cold shower of December 25. Lenin replaced Joffe as head of the delegation by the People's Commissar for Foreign Affairs, Trotsky, who thereafter fought with extreme tenacity to gain time and put off the final decision in the hope of help from world revolution and from the Allies, especially America. The world has become familiar with Trotsky's efforts to establish contact with the Allies and America through unofficial agents, the Briton Bruce-Lockhart and the American Robins of the Red Cross Mission in Petersburg, after the ambassadors of the Western Powers still left there had failed to help.[2] Although the governments felt strong repugnance towards the Soviet regime, which they were refusing to recognise, so that true cooperation was impossible, yet Trotsky's expectations helped to encourage him in his delaying tactics. Furthermore, these efforts inspired Wilson with the idea, suggested among others by Mr. Sisson (then representing Creel, the Head of the American War Propaganda in Petersburg), of competing with Lenin's peace declaration by a public announcement of America's war aims. He hoped that this would have an effect on the liberals of the west who had begun to doubt the idealism of those aims after the Russians had published the secret treaties with the Allies, on the Russians themselves (above all), whose will to resist he hoped to strengthen, and finally on the Germans whom he hoped to split and whose war will he hoped to weaken. The result was the famous Fourteen Points, announced on January 8, while Wilson was still under the impression that the

[1] Kühlmann, op. cit., pp. 540 f.

[2] Kennan, op. cit., especially cc. 2 and 5; also the author's article, *Das Verhältnis der U.S.A. zu Russland, Historische Zeitschrift*, No. 185/2, pp. 300 ff., especially 309 ff.

Russians were not going to return to Brest-Litovsk. They included an *amende honorable* to the Bolshevik leaders (although Wilson refused to recognise them as a government) and to the democracy-thirsty Russian people – which he viewed through the spectacles of an American Professor of Politics rather than as they really were – but above all they called for the immediate evacuation by the Germans of the occupied areas of Russia. Wilson's speech, copies of which Sisson had distributed by the hundred thousand in Russia and on the German eastern front, made little impression on the Germans at the time. It was only when their backs were to the wall in October that they seized on it for salvation against the war aims of the Entente.

The continuity of Eastern war aims policy: the second and third phases of negotiation

On January 8 the Russians returned to Brest-Litovsk, to the relief of the Germans and the consternation of the Allies. Trotsky, who now led the delegation, put up stiffer resistance to Germany's conditions. The Russians refused to accept Germany's demands. Although the Bolsheviks were, as the Germans very well knew, anxious to conclude an early peace, if only for reasons of internal policy, they were still not yet prepared to accept a dictated peace which threatened Russia with losses so heavy as to endanger their political existence no less than would the resumption of the war. In this dilemma the Russians used the publicity of the negotiations to appeal to the world. Trotsky tried to heighten popular longing for peace by propaganda over the heads of governments and to bring about the hoped-for world revolution, which would enable him to conclude peace with proletarian governments. Had the right of self-determination been honoured, as the Russians demanded, Germany would undoubtedly have lost Lithuania and the Baltic provinces. As this right was interpreted differently by the Russians and the Germans, Germany being less interested in the peoples than in securing her aims by a purely nominal appeal to that right, the negotiations could make no progress. Kühlmann ended by saying that the votes in Lithuania and Courland might be taken again provided the troops remained in the country, but the Russians rejected his offer on the grounds that a second vote of the kind would, if conducted under German conditions, have produced the same result as the first.

The negotiations had thus reached deadlock. The Russians did not give up their resistance to the German conditions; on the contrary, they made the strongest efforts to carry their revolutionary propaganda into the ranks of the army of the east. The Germans, from similar internal, foreign and military considerations, insisted on their demands as victors. In order to end the talking match, General Hoffmann, in agreement with Kühlmann, produced the legendary and symbolic 'Thump of the Fist' of January 18.[1] He laid a map before the Russians. On it was drawn the line marking the territory which they had to evacuate if they were not prepared to risk resuming hostilities with Germany. This line offered nothing new in substance, for all the territories marked were those which Germany had required the Russians to evacuate as early as December 28, 1917 – although the future of Livonia and Estonia in Germany's war aims had become much more definite in the meantime, for whereas on December 28 this evacuation had only been hinted at, Hoffmann now openly demanded it of Trotsky. Trotsky, like Joffe before him, said that he must first return with his delegation to consult with his party. Germany's war aims had again interrupted the Brest-Litovsk negotiations.

The crisis at Brest-Litovsk was followed by crises both in Russia and in the Central Powers. The crucial hour of the Soviets' political existence had come:[2] the choice between maintaining the revolution in mutilated Rump Russia or defending Greater Russia was no longer to be postponed. Lenin had realised that the hour of world revolution was not yet particularly near and that the hopes reposed in the proletariat of Central Europe would not be fulfilled. His path was clear to him: to save the revolution by all possible means, even if this meant accepting a dictated peace. On the other hand Trotsky, and above all Bukharin, and with them the overwhelming majority of the Central Committee, thought that acceptance of such a peace would cause the collapse of the revolution, and they wanted resistance. The voting took place on January 21. Only Sverdlov, Sokolnikov, Smilga, Stalin and not more than ten others voted for Lenin, whereas forty-eight voted for Trotsky and Bukharin. It was only with the greatest difficulty that Lenin succeeded in persuading the meeting to accept his view of the need for a 'breathing space' to consolidate the Soviet Republic. The next day the Central Committee agreed on Trotsky's middle line of 'neither war nor peace'. Both Bukharin's proposal to resume the war at any cost, and Lenin's to accept the peace, were rejected. The real decision was postponed, but the crisis was surmounted in appearance; hopes were again reposed in world revolution. Trotsky went back to Brest-Litovsk.

Meanwhile Kühlmann and Czernin had been in Berlin and Vienna respectively. The Secretary of State had again been heavily attacked from the right and the left. On January 23 he again addressed

[1] Wheeler-Bennett, op. cit., p. 173; Hoffmann, II, p. 209.
[2] Wheeler-Bennett, op. cit., pp. 183 ff.

the party leaders in the Chancellor's palace in an attempt to explain the position, soothe excited feelings, and emphasise his agreement with the OHL. Again he defended the tactics of the 'right of self-determination'. 'When,' he said, 'we met the Russians at Brest-Litovsk, the only point on the agenda was the conclusion of a general peace . . . but what we needed was to find a bridge which the Russians were willing to cross, which would lead us to a separate peace.' Self-determination, no less than the Polish proclamation, he went on, 'was one of the planks of the platform which the Chancellor had announced as principles of his policy'.

The Secretary of State's speech was much more than a mere report. It was a profession of faith in the traditions and continuity of Germany's war aims policy, 'the principles of which had been established very long since'. He said that the idea of not asking any gains from Russia

was not possible without a fundamental transformation and scaling down of Germany's whole Eastern policy as followed since the beginning of this war by the responsible authorities in the German Reich; such a scaling down does not fall within the bounds of what is politically possible. The idea of attaching Poland, Courland and Lithuania closely to Germany, in accordance with their own wishes, was not his invention or creation. The fundamental determination of the policy which I now . . . have the honour to represent . . . goes back at least to the spring of 1917, when Herr von Bethmann Hollweg was Chancellor.

This detailed answer had been elicited by the sharpness of the attacks. War Aims had become a 'mirror' whose political implications were meeting as at a focal point. Our previous investigations have traced the course of German policy through the war. The political leaders of Germany had steadfastly followed the line laid down in September, 1914 without great deviations or abrupt changes, although they were of course influenced by the internal situation and by conditions abroad and had adapted their line on points of detail to the current situation. Undeterred by crises and failures, they had pursued the aim of expanding Germany's power and hegemony in Europe by all means at their disposal.

Inside the Central Powers the internal political effects of the renewed impasse in the negotiations were considerable. In Austria-Hungary a general strike took place at once, with its centre in Vienna, and helped to produce a similar series of strikes in Germany. Although the great strike of January 28–February 1, 1918 was triggered off by the difficulties in the supply situation and the internal political situation (the delay in dealing with the Prussian franchise), its real political motives stemmed from Germany's attitude at Brest-Litovsk. Although these strikes had no effect on the policy of the German government, they had big effects in Austria, whose economic and moral forces seemed to be at their end and which was now pressing vehemently for any possible peace.

Here we must take a brief backward glance. The differences between Germany and Austria had appeared during the first phase of the negotiations. The first crisis, and one which put a heavy strain on the alliance, was occasioned by Austria's threat to conclude a separate peace with Russia and to regard herself as released from the conditions of November, 1917. At the end of the year the imperial court and the government in Vienna were being subjected to constantly increasing pressure from the nationalities. In Hungary and among the workers in the big towns of Cis–Leithania, all of whom attributed the difficulties and threatened failure at Brest-Litovsk to Germany's hard conditions, resentment manifested itself in January, 1918 in mass strikes and major demonstrations, sometimes of an openly anti-German character. In Budapest, for example, the German consulate was assaulted on January 8. The German ambassador in Vienna, Count Wedel, reported again 'that public opinion in Austria and Hungary refuses to go on with the war for the sake of German conquests'.

In view of this tension the German government thought it necessary to send the German military representative at the Austro-Hungarian Army General Headquarters, General von Cramon, on January 5 with a personal message from Wilhelm II to the Emperor Charles, in the hope of countering the Austrians' growing desire for peace. The Emperor Charles, however, told Cramon that after so many protestations of desire for peace, he found it difficult to get his peoples to understand 'that they might perhaps have to go on fighting simply in order that Germany should receive Lithuania and Courland as prizes of victory'. Cramon offered the Austrians Montenegro, Serbia and Albania as compensation for Germany's gain in Courland and Lithuania, but the Emperor expressly rejected the offer, saying that he 'only' wanted a settlement of the Polish question in the Austrian sense.

But here too things had taken an unfortunate turn for Austria in connection with the peace with the Ukraine. The report on the course of the negotiations and the crisis in Brest-Litovsk made by Czernin to a Crown Council in Vienna on January 22 referred to this turn. The Ukraine, he said, was, with German encouragement, demanding the inclusion of Chelm and East Galicia in its new state, or at least the creation of an independent Austrian province of Galicia and Bukovina, which involved the partition of Galicia.[1] Czernin supported the partition, and the Crown Council agreed to it, for the sake of a separate peace and in spite of the gravest fears of its consequences for the future of the Monarchy. But the supply situation in Austria was catastrophic. There were only reserves of bread grains for two more months, and there was no other way of getting at the stocks in the Ukraine with which it was hoped to surmount the crisis. This concession to the Ukraine, as the Ministers agreed, would embitter all Poles against the Monarchy and make the Austro-Polish solution no longer worth having.

Czernin's closest adviser, Gratz, of the section for commercial policy in the Austrian Foreign Ministry, had already come to the conclusion that the Austro-Polish solution was no longer feasible even apart from the Ukrainian question, since Germany would dominate Poland as her own hinterland by throttling Polish industry and making herself co-owner of the Polish railways and state properties, not to speak of the enormous territories which she was slicing off Congress Poland. The Emperor, however, still left the decision on the Polish question open, in spite of the twofold difficulties from the Ukraine and Germany.

Armed with these instructions, Czernin returned to Brest-Litovsk on January 28, determined to get peace with the Ukraine as fast as possible. Meanwhile, Trotsky had brought to Brest-Litovsk the representatives of the Kharkhov district of the Bolshevik Ukraine, and furthermore Kiev had been taken by the Red army on January 29 and the Rada had been put to flight, so that Trotsky was no longer prepared to accept the Rada's delegates as representing their country. All that Kühlmann and Czernin, both of whom had (although for different reasons) received instructions to play the Ukrainian card, could do was to confront the two delegations with one another, embroil them irreconcilably, and get the Rada to conclude peace quickly. This was the outcome of the transitional phase of January 28–February 7.

On January 5 a long-announced conference was held in the hope of reconciling the differences between Germany and Austria. This showed once more that Germany's war aims were the real bone of contention between the two allies. The kernel of the discussions, which took place under the shadow of the recent mass strikes, was Czernin's demand for a plain definition of the Dual Monarchy's obligations under the treaty of 1879. Czernin invoked the so-called

[1] Czernin wrote in his diary on January 21, 1918: 'It looks as though the Germans had long since made up their minds on this wretched business' (the cession of Cholm and East Galicia) (op. cit., pp. 327 f.).

'Vienna Document' of March 27, 1917, in which he and Bethmann Hollweg had outlined a minimum and a maximum programme, to maintain that Austria was not bound 'to go on fighting for Germany's lust of conquest' beyond the *status quo*. As in August, 1917, he raised the question whether Austria-Hungary was bound to go on fighting if the Entente offered the Central Powers peace on the basis of the *status quo*, and Germany rejected it. On this occasion, as previously, Helfferich evaded this precise question and contented himself with a vague reference to Germany's need to secure her future – above all, to have a certain supply of raw materials for an economy of sixty million persons. Ludendorff, on the other hand, said openly that Germany had always followed both economic and territorial war aims, and announced frankly:

A peace which only assured the territorial *status quo* would mean that we had lost the war. Such a peace in the east has never been considered. In the west things are not yet clear. If, however, we keep the old frontiers there, we shall be worse situated militarily after the war than before it.

Neither Hertling nor Kühlmann nor Helfferich dissociated himself from Ludendorff, and when Hohenlohe expressed 'surprise' that Alsace-Lorraine was now not 'the only obstacle to peace', but that German annexationist ambitions had suddenly emerged as obstacles to peace, Kühlmann thought it a sufficient answer to refer to the London Protocol on the Entente's war aims, recently published by the Bolshevik government, as justifying Germany's own 'active war aims'. He thought that the way to keep Austria in the war would be 'to give Austria-Hungary too positive war aims and thus make it possible for her to agree to active German war aims' beyond the obligations of 1879. Nevertheless, Hertling relegated Austria-Hungary's one 'positive' war aim, the Austro-Polish solution, to the distant future by laying down Germany's conditions for such a solution in words which justified Gratz's suspicions. Austria-Hungary had just consented to the partition of Galicia, and Czernin had conceded Chelm to the Ukrainians without further reference back to the Crown Council;[1] yet now Germany confronted the Austrians with territorial and economic conditions which made Poland, like Rumania before it, seem to the Austrians no more than 'a squeezed lemon'. The breach between the allies widened.

Czernin warned the Germans flatly that they were ruining the Mitteleuropa plan with their insistence on Poland, and he threatened

[1] Id., p. 326. 'I shall take responsibility for the question of Chelm. I cannot and will not watch hundreds of thousands of human beings starve, while there is still a possibility of help, in order to retain the Poles' sympathies for us.'

to dissolve the alliance between Germany and Austria-Hungary after the war.

The only point on which the allies agreed was the tactical one: to utilise the conflict which had emerged between Petersburg and Kiev to make a separate peace with the Ukraine as fast as possible, with the twofold aim of securing their own supplies and putting pressure on the Bolsheviks.

The discussions between the delegations were resumed on February 6. In spite of the Bolsheviks' opposition, the chief point was the speedy conclusion of a separate peace with the Ukraine, regardless of the impotence of the Rada, which had proclaimed the complete independence of the Ukraine on January 22. A treaty of peace between the four Central Powers and the Ukraine was in fact signed on February 9.[1] Its peculiarity lies in the fact that it was quite consciously concluded with a government which at the moment of signature was unable to exercise any authority over its country, its rule, as Trotsky said sarcastically, not extending beyond its own rooms in Brest-Litovsk. The result for the Germans was that the numerous advantages which they had secured on paper could be realised only if they conquered the country and reinstated in Kiev the government with which they had signed the treaty. The treaty was thus a sort of distraint order issued by the Germans for their own benefit, and they did not hesitate to take immediate steps to secure their interests.

The line of Germany's Eastern policy described and defended before the party leaders on January 23 had thus reached its logical conclusion. As Wedel, writing from Vienna on February 10, recommended, Germany was staking all on the disintegration of Russia.

As regards Russia, he wrote, there are, after all, only two possibilities. Either an Imperialist Russia will come back, or Russia will disintegrate. In the former case Russia will be our enemy, for she will want to recover the ice-free ports of Courland, and quite apart from this, an Imperialist Russia will always be pushing forward again towards the Balkans and . . . Austria-Hungary. An Imperialist Russia could perhaps make friends with Germany, if we do not rob her of her coast, but never with Mitteleuropa. In my opinion, we must therefore stake everything on the other card, the disintegration of Russia, which would be helped by thrusting her back from the Baltic. If the Ukraine, the Baltic provinces, Finland, etc. really fall away from Russia permanently, which seems to me still very uncertain, especially as regards the Ukraine, then what is left of Russia is simply a Great Siberia. If Russia is reborn, our descendants will probably have to fight a second Punic War against another Anglo-Russian Coalition; then the further eastward our power extends, the better for us.

[1] For the text of the treaty, see G. F. de Martens, *Nouveau Recueil Général de Traités*, Ser. III, Vol. X, pp. 752 f. and 762 f.

On February 9 the Russians found Hoffmann demanding of them both their Black Sea coast and their Baltic coast (they were asked to evacuate Livonia and Estonia). Since resistance was impossible, Trotsky, to avoid submitting to these dictated terms, issued next day his famous declaration, 'No war, no peace!', and left Brest-Litovsk with his delegation. The negotiations had been broken off for the fourth time on account of Germany's demands.

The German negotiators were at first taken completely aback by Trotsky's unexpected change of front, but very soon they saw how greatly he had played into their hands. The armistice on the eastern front expired on February 17 and could not be renewed if the Russians were not in Brest-Litovsk. The Germans seized the chance to carry on the war and to put the blame for it on the Russians. The resumption of hostilities would allow them to occupy the Ukraine, Livonia and Estonia, so that the Russians' bargaining position would have grown much worse before peace was finally concluded. As early as February 5, at the Austro-German negotiations in Berlin, Ludendorff had announced that he was taking military action against the Bolsheviks if they remained recalcitrant over the German conditions; the Emperor minuted the record with the characteristic addition: 'Have already given the order in advance!'[1] In preparation the eighth army corps, which was stationed in the Baltic provinces, had received instructions on February 3 to hold itself ready to advance on Reval. The military, who were long since tired of the negotiations in Brest-Litovsk and of Bolshevik obstinacy, were now solely concerned to find the best political excuse for resuming the campaign, especially as there were signs of a strong democratic movement in Estonia and Latvia which was clearly hoping to achieve independence, and in particular independence of Germany, and eliminate the German Baltic element. Germany's intentions in the north-east would then no longer have been realisable. A quick way had to be found of making these provinces seek association with Germany. This was the purpose of the Homburg Crown Council of February 13.

The Homburg Crown Council of February 13, 1918, and the resumption of the advance in the east

This Council was held under the presidency of the Emperor, who was, however, absent most of the day, The others present were Hertling, Payer and Kühlmann from the political side and Hindenburg,

---

[1] The Emperor's marginalia on Hertling's report to him on the conference of February 5 ran: 'I have already ordered him to do this.' Then: 'Estonia and Finland must be *occupied*. The Bolsheviki and British must get out, quick! The line Narwa–Pleskau–Dünaburg must be occupied!'

Ludendorff and Holtzendorff from the military. Both groups assumed that Russia had already fallen into three parts, that Germany was at peace with the Ukraine and Finland,[1] but still at war with Great Russia. The military, headed by Ludendorff, called for immediate action and an advance on Petersburg, whereupon the Bolsheviks would be overthrown and a new Russian government set up to conclude peace on Germany's terms. They also wanted the immediate occupation of the Ukraine, Estonia and Livonia.

The civilians did not object on principle to military action; their hesitations were purely political and practical. Kühlmann doubted whether even the capture of Petersburg would suffice to bring about the fall of the Bolsheviks. On the contrary, he feared that the entry of the German army into Petersburg would only awaken Russian nationalism and strengthen the revolution. He further maintained the doubts expressed by him in the previous December on the advisability of taking over Livonia and Estonia, which would, he thought, greatly endanger future relations between Germany and Russia; the Russians he thought, would never endure a 'German bolt' shutting them off from the Baltic. Von Payer said that the resumption of the war in the east would produce 'paralysing horror' among the German people, and that the Reichstag too would make difficulties. This warning, however, only had the effect of rousing all the Emperor's resentment against parliament. He indulged in violent abuse of the Reichstag and threatened that if it interfered in the conduct of the war it would 'suffer for it'; the German Reichstag was no Convention. Like the soldiers, he wanted the Bolsheviks overthrown as fast as possible; he saw Germany as having a sort of police duty to perform in the east, especially since otherwise the British and Americans would gain in influence there, and a Russia organised by the Anglo-Saxons would constitute a permanent and great danger for Germany.

The cardinal question had, however, still not been settled: what political reason could be given for the advance? The Emperor himself found the way out. His formula was: 'Not a new war, assistance.' His calculation ran as follows: to stimulate the bourgeoisie of Petersburg into counter-revolution against the Bolsheviks, German troops must occupy Livonia and Estonia. This move, however, must be justified by appeals to Germany from those countries, which must ask for 'help against bandits'. The same applied to Finland and the Ukraine. Germany's military intervention would then acquire the character of a 'police operation' in the interest of humanity against the Bolshevik danger, and not the character of a war.

[1] Germany had recognised that Svinhufvud government on January 6, 1918.

The Chancellor, who was reluctant on political grounds to take on himself the 'odium' of an 'annexationist procedure', welcomed the Emperor's suggestion: 'We must have appeals for help, then things can be discussed'–whereupon Wilhelm interrupted: 'We must find some window-dressing.' Hindenburg fixed the date: 'Appeal must be here by the 18th.' Ludendorff then read out a ready-made telegram from Riga, and asked: 'Is that enough?'. It was not enough for the Chancellor; he wanted more 'appeals' from Finland and the Ukraine to cover himself better against the Reichstag. The Crown Council agreed to regard the armistice as expiring on February 17, according to timetable, to start the military advance on the 18th, and to order 'appeals for help' from the areas to be occupied so that the military operation could be explained as one of liberation.

These measures were carried out exactly up to February 18, so that the occupation of the Ukraine, Livonia and Estonia was able to begin. Contemporary German propaganda, and German historians, have seen in the resumed advance an anti-Bolshevik campaign of liberation, undertaken largely to protect the Baltic Germans. It is true that Baltic German nobles in unoccupied Livonia and Estonia were in difficulties, and their appeals for help were certainly not artificial. The general social revolution in Russia was threatening their positions no less than those of the Russian nobles, for now, as in 1905, the Estonian and Latvian peasants thought the moment a good one to get rid of the German ruling class. Besides, the Livonian and Estonian Knights and Estates had already, on December 30, 1917 and January 27, 1918 respectively, declared their separation from Russia under pressure from the Reich and particularly from the German army.[1]

There was fairly widespread sympathy in Germany, due partly to the influence of the many Baltic Germans in the Reich, with the difficulties of this class[2]–the feeling of *völkisch* solidarity with the Germans outside the Reich was one of the products of this first World War. Emotional factors did not, however, weigh very heavily in determining the resumption of the German advance on February 18. Greatly as the German press of those days dramatised the difficulties of the Baltic Germans by publishing their 'appeals for help', for the leaders of Germany anything that happened in the Baltic provinces was only an excuse for finally achieving their aims in the east by resuming the military advance. Their real train of thought is vividly summed up in a note by Ludendorff for the Homburg meeting:[3]

[1] The text of the declaration is reproduced by Tobien, op. cit., II, pp. 321 f.
[2] See Lewerenz, *Baltikum*, pp. 243 ff.
[3] Ludendorff, *Urkunden*, p. 472.

If we act, we strengthen our position against the Entente, confirm peace with the Ukraine, achieve peace with Rumania, confirm our position in Lithuania and Courland, improve our military situation by the occupation of Dünaburg and parts of the Baltic, perhaps deal a death blow to the Bolsheviks, thereby improve our position at home and our relations with the better classes in Russia, and can liberate strong forces in the east and throw our whole military and moral force into the great blow which His Majesty has now ordered in the west.

The advance began on the 18th. As the Russians put up practically no resistance, it became, as General Hoffmann described it,[1] a military excursion by rail and car, and went off according to plan. After only one day the Russian government announced its readiness to sign peace on the basis of Germany's terms of February 9 (i.e., recognition of Ukrainian independence, cession of Courland, Estonia and Lithuania).[2] If the rulers of Germany had really only wanted to put military pressure on the recalcitrant Russians to force them into peace, they could now have broken off the advance again. This, however, was not what was done. In the north-east the German troops continued their advance until they had occupied the whole of Livonia and Estonia up to the Dünaburg–Narva–Lake Peipus line in order to ensure a 'free' vote under the protection of German 'forces of order'.[3]

The position in the Ukraine was rather more complicated. Here it was hoped to reinstate the government which had been expelled by the Bolsheviks. The German advance, in which the Austrians joined under extremely heavy pressure from Germany, encountered local resistance from Red Guards and the Czech Legion, and thus led to the immobilisation of strong German forces, amounting finally to some thirty divisions.

Germany did not, however, content herself with detaching the Ukraine from Russia, but made the Ukrainians pay further for her 'help' (the military operations). On February 19 the representative of the Foreign Ministry, who had remained behind in Brest-Litovsk, recommended that Germany should insist on further economic privileges in return for her help and suggested the rich ore-fields of the Ukraine, for which German heavy industry had put in demands two months earlier. He further drew attention to the possibility of dominating the future Ukrainian grain trade by the construction of silos and control of the shipping on the Ukrainian inland water-

---

[1] Hoffmann, *Aufzeichnungen*, p. 187 (entry of February 22, 1918).

[2] Wheeler-Bennett, op. cit., p. 138.

[3] See Hoffmann's notes, op. cit., pp. 186 f.: 'In any case every day's delay [in answering Trotsky's offer] is something gained for us. He [Trotsky] seems to be in the devil of a hurry; we aren't.'

ways. The farms of the German colonists in the Ukraine must be protected.

The Prussian Minister of War, von Stein, duly asked for all this as the price for Germany's 'military help' to the Ukraine, and beyond this, 'German participation in the Ukrainian railways, to give Germany a decisive influence over economic conditions in the Ukraine and ensure that the products of the country be made fully available for the economy of Germany'. Additions to this effect should be made to the existing treaties. A conference held on March 5 under the presidency of Helfferich and attended by the Secretary of State in the Reich Economic Office, Baron von Stein, settled the detailed financial and economic demands to be made of the Ukraine. Helfferich himself summarised them as 'Germany's programme for the Ukraine'. Their execution was left partly to the German occupation forces in the Ukraine, partly to the mixed economic committees to be set up under the peace treaty. The result of the advance of February 18 was thus not only to bring the Russians back to the negotiating table, but also to reveal still further German aims reaching beyond 'Russia'.

The Peace Treaty and its ratification

The expectations which the Germans had reposed in their 'railway advance' were fulfilled as regards Russia. The Central Committee of the Party and the Central Executive Committee of the Soviet Congress held their decisive debate on the German ultimatum of February 21 on the night of February 23–24. There was the greatest excitement and bitterness, and everyone expected the Germans to advance on Petersburg. Lenin argued that it was necessary to accept the harsh dictated peace for the sake of the world revolution and its chief–and at the time only–base, the Soviet Republic. He won acceptance of his view, although by the narrow majority of 116 votes against 85 with 26 abstentions. The German Reichstag was told of the stiffened terms of the ultimatum only on February 26, when Hertling communicated them and said that he entirely agreed with the use of military force as a decisive weapon to bring about peace. A day later Erzberger welcomed the peace and described its conditions as conformable with the Peace Resolution, while Stresemann, for the National Liberals, said that what had secured peace had been not Trotsky, not the Peace Resolution, not the answer to the Pope, but Germany's unbroken military prowess.

Both sides were represented at the signing of the treaty on March 3 by minor figures only, the Germans and Austrians because Kühlmann and Czernin had already left for Bucharest for the negotiations with Rumania, the Russians because Trotsky opposed signing up to the last minute. The Russians declared that the terms were 'dictated to them' and signed under protest. They ratified them, as provided, on March 18–again only after difficult internal arguments–at a general Soviet Congress which had been called to Moscow for the purpose. Lenin got the ratification through by his argument of a breathing space, while Trotsky hoped up to the last moment for help from America.[1]

In Germany the Reichstag debates on the Brest-Litovsk treaty were less violent, the points raised being in general ones of procedure and not of substance. The debate on ratification took place on March 22. The Conservatives and National Liberals approved the treaty in principle, but criticised it as not going far enough, but the decision lay with the centre parties, i.e., the Peace Resolution majority. The Zentrum and Progressives succeeded in reconciling the self-determination clause in the treaty with the principles of the Peace Resolution, since it only forbade 'annexations imposed by force'. Apart from minor reservations, both parties accepted the treaty completely.

The spokesmen of the Majority Socialists began with a purely formal criticism of the way in which the treaty had been concluded, especially of the fact that the Reichstag had not been given a voice in it. They then expressed disagreement with large parts of its substance, especially with Germany's action in securing the immediate separation of Poland, Lithuania and Courland, without first guaranteeing an honest exercise of the right of self-determination on a broad democratic basis. They also criticised the 'annexationist mentality' prevailing at Brest-Litovsk as having thrown away the chance of securing for Germany an economic hinterland reaching to Vladivostok. In spite, however, of all these objections, the Social Democrats did not vote against the treaty, but abstained on the grounds that it had after all brought peace in the east.

Only the Independent Socialists voted against both treaties, on the grounds that both constituted breaches of the solemn assurance of August 4 that the war was a defensive one, and would presumably have deep effects on how world opinion judged Germany. Their leader, Hugo Haase, further called attention to the remarkable contradiction between Germany's advance into Livonia, Estonia and the Ukraine, in order to liberate those countries from Bolshevik 'bandits', and the German government's simultaneous conclusion of an important treaty with the same Bolshevik government, which had been allowed to accredit a diplomatic representative to the German government.

[1] Kennan, op. cit., ch. 1.

The contents of the treaties are familiar, and could in any case be deduced from our account of Germany's policy and of the negotiations. The economic clauses did not constitute a formal renewal of the commercial treaty of 1904, but in effect went beyond it. Otherwise, the central point was the cession by Russia of Poland, Lithuania and Courland. Even more galling for the Russians perhaps was their forced consent to the separate peace with the Ukraine, which in practice amounted to ceding the Ukraine. Livonia and Estonia still remained parts of Russia on paper, but were to be occupied by German 'police forces . . . until security should be guaranteed and order restored there through those countries' own organisations' – in other words, until those countries also should have been drawn into Germany's power sphere with the help of the Baltic Germans. The final separation from Russia was effected at the end of August, 1918 under supplementary treaties, at a time when Russia's position had been made even weaker by the internal and foreign difficulties of the Bolshevik regime.

The Peace of Brest-Litovsk is undoubtedly one of the most important political events in which Germany herself took a direct and active part between the outbreak and the end of the war. Judgments on the 'forgotten peace' range between condemnation of it as a peace of force, as foreign critics saw it at the time, and the ebullient praise given to it by Wilhelm II as one of the 'greatest successes of world history, whose significance only our grandchildren will truly appreciate'. The broadest circles of German public opinion agreed with the Emperor, and German Protestantism, or at least one of its leading organs, saw in the triumph of Germany's sword over Russia a sort of divine judgment in favour of Germany's cause in general Here is what the *Allgemeine Evangelisch-Lutherische Kirchenzeitung* wrote:

Peace without annexations or indemnities! So men resolve. The slogan was coined by Germany's enemies when Germany's sword grew too heavy for them. The wolves wanted to escape unpunished for having ranged abroad, spilt German blood, ravaged German prosperity and inflicted wounds which will be long in healing. What was to remain was to be an impoverished, diminished Reich on which anyone thereafter could wreak his will . . . but here, too, God willed otherwise. He made Russia's masters drink of the cup of madness, so that they fell like robbers on their own peoples, until the latter at last called for German help. And out of the same cup drank the Russian negotiators, who fooled all the world and at last thought up the master stroke of breaking off the negotiations. That was God's hour. Germany's armies pressed on, took city after city, land after land, everywhere greeted as liberators. And Russia, who wanted to give no indemnities, was forced at the last minute to yield up uncountable booty: 800

locomotives, 8,000 railway trucks with every kind of treasure and supply; God knew that we needed it. And we also needed guns and munitions for the last blow against the enemy in the west. God knew that too. So He freely gave us, since God is rich, 2,600 guns, 5,000 machine guns, two million shells for the artillery, rifles, aircraft, lorries, and innumerable other things. . . . England and France had paid for it and made it, Germany received it. Only when Russia had given all that up, was she allowed and indeed compelled to make peace. Thus it was decided by God, a true Peace of God, contrary to everything that men had planned and wanted. Whatever may happen to the liberated border states, Russia will never get them back, and the protection and support which they seek they will find in Germany.[1]

A later generation may look on such a paragraph as a piece of hysteria and an abuse of religion. It cannot, however, be denied that it reflects what was in the spring of 1918 the feeling of a great majority of the politically dominant classes of Germany – and it is only they who matter when we consider Germany's policy in the war.

After 1919 the Allies often retorted to German criticisms of the Treaty of Versailles by pointing to the ruthless severity of the Peace of Brest-Litovsk. By that time German public opinion had come to regard the treaty more soberly. In view of Germany's political situation new judgments were almost always apologias, and they have coloured German historiography up to the present day. One of the most important participants on the German side, General Hoffmann, has, for example, replied to all critics of the treaty in his memoirs, which appeared in 1929, by pointing out that the Allies technically annulled the German–Russian Treaty at Versailles, but used the situation created by Germany as the basis for their re-organisation of eastern Europe when they set up the ring of states nicknamed the *cordon sanitaire*.[2]

It is also often pointed out that the Brest-Litovsk Treaty did not take away a single square yard of ethnically Russian territory, so that they cannot be held up as examples of German annexationism. Kühlmann used this argument as early as January 23, 1918, when pleading the case for the treaty before the Central Committee of the Reichstag, and we still hear it today. In each case the argument is seductive because it is, technically, absolutely correct. If, however, we are to reach a correct and just appreciation of the whole problem of Brest-Litovsk, we need to relate later events as they emerged after the collapse of Germany in November, 1918 with Germany's actual aims. Then what we have said, and what innumerable documents in the German archives confirm, can leave no doubt that Germany's

[1] Gottfried Mehnert, *Evangelische Kirche und Politik*, pp. 64 f.
[2] Hoffman, *Versäumte Gelegenheiten*, p. 216.

aim was not to confer independence and national liberty on Poland, Lithuania, Courland, Livonia, Estonia and the Ukraine, but on the contrary to fetter them closely to the German Reich and to Mitteleuropa by treaties which were only nominally international and by personal unions, economic and customs unions, and military conventions. 'Germany as the power of order in East-Central Europe' regarded the separation from Russia of all these countries, and also of Finland and later of Georgia, only as a means of thrusting Russia back and extending Germany's sphere of power far eastward.

Furthermore, German policy towards Russia did not even stay within the limits marked out at Brest-Litovsk. In the summer of 1918 it reached out far beyond these limits, as far as the Caucasus. In a message to the Hetman of the Don Cossacks Wilhelm II elaborated a regular plan of dividing Russia, after Poland, the Baltic provinces and the Caucasus had been detached from her, into four independent states: the Ukraine, the South-Eastern League (the anti-Bolshevik district between the Ukraine and the Caspian), Central Russia, and Siberia.[1]

The Treaty of Brest-Litovsk brought no real peace in the east. Strong German forces had to be left in the east to maintain the situation created at Brest-Litovsk and afterwards, and these could not be used for the decisive battles in the west. But politically the most serious consequence of Brest-Litovsk was its effect on the western allies, and in particular on the attitude and feelings of President Wilson.[2] He had already been disappointed by Hertling's rejection of his Fourteen Points, and he saw in the Peace of Brest-Litovsk proof that there was in Germany no opposition to a policy based purely on power and self-interest. What disappointed him most was the attitude of the German Majority Socialists, for he had thought to see in them a liberal oppositional party and the kernel of a democratic Germany. Now they had, as he saw it, submitted to the policy of 'autocracy' by abstaining on the vote.[3] It was only after this episode that he dropped all hesitation and mobilised every resource to help the Allies defeat monarchic-military Germany.

[1] Wheeler-Bennett, op. cit., pp. 326 f.

[2] Id., pp. 366, 368.

[3] See John L. Snell, 'Wilson's Peace Program and German Socialism January–March 1918', *Mississippi Valley Historical Review*, Vol. 38, 1951, No. 2, pp. 187–214.

19

THE ELABORATION OF MITTELEUROPA

THE PEACE TREATIES WITH FINLAND
AND RUMANIA—POLAND AND MITTELEUROPA

WHILE the Brest-Litovsk negotiations were going on, Germany was also working to extend her sphere of interest still further eastward by other peace settlements. Finland was brought into line in the north-east, and Rumania in the south-east. This outward thrust brought Germany into conflict with her allies, especially in the Balkans. Although Kühlmann managed to reconcile Germany's interests with those of her allies in the Peace of Bucharest, the eastern peace treaties again brought up the Polish question in an acute form and produced an open conflict between Germany and Austria-Hungary. Germany's great Eastern Idea, which went far beyond Brest-Litovsk, prevented the completion of Mitteleuropa which, in the last phase, was dropped by Germany in favour of absolute domination of the *Ostraum* – a goal as old as the Mitteleuropa idea itself.

Finland as the corner-stone of the north:
the Treaty of Berlin and intervention

The situation of Finland had been changed by the outbreak of the Russian February revolution, but although urged to do so by the Foreign Ministry, Finland was not yet prepared to break with Russia openly and proclaim herself a fully sovereign state. The developments which followed the July crisis in Russia were no better calculated to encourage Germany's hopes of an independent Finland leaning on Germany.[1] Only when Svinhufvud was made President[2] did a man arrive whose programme was complete independence for Finland. On December 6 the Diet proclaimed Finland an independent republic, and it was recognised on January 4 by Soviet Russia after personal negotiations between Svinhufvud and Lenin, and after strong pressure had been applied by Germany. Sweden, France and Germany followed suit.

[1] A useful general work on the history of Finland under Russian rule is M. G. Schybergson, 'Politische Geschichte Finlands, 1909–1919' (Gotha-Stuttgart, 1925), in *Geschichte der europäischen Staaten*, I. Abt., No. 41, pp. 410 ff.

[2] E. Räikkonen, *Svinhufvud baut Finland, Abenteuer einer Staatsgründung* (Munich, 1933), pp. 40 ff.

The position in Finland itself was exceedingly uncertain, for the Russian troops, although formally recalled by the Soviets[1] and in many cases half disbanded, had not left Finland. The semi-independent Red Russian units worked together with the Socialists after the October elections, which the latter refused to recognise. At the same time the Socialists began raising Workers' Guards, and tried after the middle of November to organise a general strike. The peasants and bourgeoisie of the more agrarian northern provinces replied by forming their own defence formations. The conflict between Whites and Reds reached the dimensions of civil war in January and February.

At the end of January, 1918 Helsinki fell into the hands of the Reds.[2] Four ministers of the bourgeois government retired to Vaasa, where they set up a rump government and organised a self-defence corps, and Svinhufvud appointed von Mannerheim, a former Russian cavalry general, to command the White troops. Although the final aims of the two men were identical, they differed sharply on methods; Mannerheim was very insistent that Finland must secure her unification with her own forces, without foreign intervention, to save her from falling later into dependence on another country, in particular Germany. He did, however, agree to buy arms, which were solely needed, from Germany, and to ask for the repatriation of the 'Prussian' Finnish chasseur battalion, which had been incorporated into the German army in 1916 and sent to the Courland front.

After Sweden had refused to intervene actively in favour of the bourgeois government, Svinhufvud appealed to the Germans. In August, 1917 there had been conversations in Stockholm – continuations of contacts established in 1914 – between bourgeois Finland and the Political Department of the German general staff, and the Germans had promised to send arms. The Finnish partner to these negotiations, Edvard Hjelt, Vice-Chancellor of the Finnish University and a Councillor of State, became the organiser-in-chief and moving spirit behind the co-operation between Germany and Finland. On November 26, 1917 he told Ludendorff in Kreuznach that the aim of the bourgeois Finns was to create an independent state, closely associated with Germany: 'Finland would form the northernmost link in the chain of states forming a wall in Europe against the east.'[3] Ludendorff still hesitated to intervene, on tactical grounds,

[1] During the Brest-Litovsk negotiations Germany had forced Russia, not only to recognise the independence of Finland, but also to order the withdrawal of all Russian troops stationed there.

[2] Schybergson, op. cit., p. 423; also C. Jay Smith, op. cit., pp. 55 ff.

[3] Schybergson, op. cit., pp. 456 ff.

owing to the armistice and the hopes of peace with Russia. On January 30, 1918 the Foreign Ministry gave its final consent,[1] and the Finnish battalion was released from the German army and transferred to the Finnish bourgeois, where it played an important role in Mannerheim's army. Hjelt was made Finland's official representative in Berlin and was given special instructions to arrange for German military 'assistance'. It was, however, only when the Brest negotiations were broken off on February 10 and 11 by Trotsky's formula of 'no war, no peace', that the OHL decided to occupy Finland, as well as Livonia-Estonia, as a means of applying pressure. The Homburg Crown Council of February 13 decided to order 'appeals for help', and on the next day Hjelt appeared in person in Bad Kreuznach with an official memorandum asking very urgently for armed intervention by Germany in the Finnish civil war. On February 21 Ludendorff told him that Germany had finally decided to intervene. As in the Ukraine, the German government had thus pledged itself to a government which was master of only a small part of its own country. As in the Ukraine, it demanded the conclusion of a peace treaty and a commercial treaty before undertaking any military operations.

The three treaties (for a secret treaty was added to their number)[2] were signed on March 7 and approved on March 10 by Svinhufvud, who had come to Berlin. The provisions of these instruments formed, as in the cases of Rumania, the Ukraine and Russia, the basis for the absorption of Finland into Germany's political and economic sphere of influence. These treaties were accepted in Germany (where they were ratified on June 3) without opposition, except for a little criticism in the Reichstag. The political treaty covered the conclusion of peace, the recognition of Finland's independence, renunciation of costs of the war, and the regulation of questions of private legal relationships and finance. Its other chief provision was an undertaking by Finland to cede no territory to a third power and to conclude no alliance with a foreign power without Germany's permission. Even more important for the future relationship between Germany and Finland were the provisions of the commercial and secret treaties. The former provided that each party conceded national treatment in respect of trade and economic enterprise to persons and trading corporations of the other, a provision which, in view of the

---

[1] See Joose Olavi Hannula, *Finland's War of Independence* (London, 1939), pp. 169 ff.; Carl Gustav von Mannerheim, *The Memoirs of Marshal Mannerheim* (New York, 1954), pp. 159 ff.; Rüdiger von der Goltz, *Als politischer General im Osten 1918 und 1919* (Leipzig, 1936), pp. 27 f.; Jay Smith, op. cit., p. 61.

[2] On the treaty see Jay Smith, op. cit., pp. 61 ff.; Schybergson, op. cit., pp. 461 ff.

great difference between the commercial and economic potentials of Germany and Finland, would have left the latter an open field to German enterprise and capital. Furthermore, this treaty, like that with Rumania which was being negotiated at the same time, provided for commercial advantages which were not equal but unfavourable to the country which would be producing chiefly raw materials. Finland bound herself to admit all German goods dutyfree, while Germany reserved herself the right to tax Finnish imports on entry. This arrangement would undoubtedly have turned Finland into a market for Germany's industries, exactly like Poland.

To the economic protective belt was added a military one, for under the secret supplementary treaty Finland pledged herself not to allow any foreign power to establish bases on her territory during or after the war, but to allow Germany the right to establish naval bases (opposite a German-dominated Reval) and a telegraph station at Torneo (Tornio). She further promised to pay for all deliveries of material of war during the civil war by offering her exports only to Germany or to states approved by Germany.

The northern corner-stone had been laid on March 7, at least contractually. As in the Ukraine, however, the plans had to be made into reality by military help, and that not only within the framework of the frontiers of the old Grand Duchy of Finland, but–if only in view of the military necessity of a Murmansk front–within Greater Finland, inclusive of Karelia, in order to cut Russia off completely from the ice-free North Sea and thrust her frontiers back to the line before Peter the Great's conquests.

When the Central Powers won their great successes on the eastern front in the summer of 1915, the Finnish revolutionaries in Berlin had thought the moment ripe to ask for independence for a Greater Finland, including eastern Karelia, to form a link in the 'chain of states' allied with Germany from the White Sea across Lake Onega to the Black Sea. They repeated this request in May, 1916. Germany, however, at this time still refused to commit herself, although Jalmari Castrén, who had been in touch with Bethmann Hollweg as early as 1914 and was to become a senator in the Svinhufvud government in 1917, wrote to Hindenburg and the government proposing that Germany should take Petersburg by troops sent through Finland, thereby striking Great Russia in a vital spot. To dispel German hesitations, he suggested at the same time offering the throne of Finland to a Prussian prince and concluding an alliance between Finland and Prussia. These men, who were among those governing the destinies of the young state in 1917, conceived of Finland, including Russian Karelia, as the 'northern bridge' to the Arctic Ocean, as constituting at once a 'link' with the northern waters and an economic partner and corner-stone of the monarchic-constitutional Mitteleuropa. In Karelia itself the pre-conditions for its attachment to Finland had been created years before by the awakening, with the help of church and school, of a national movement appealing to the right of self-determination. These feelings were voiced in *Sovnarkom* (the Karelian assemblage) on December 31, 1917.

In spite, however, of Ludendorff's consent, and in spite of the signature of the commercial and economic treaty, the German government still thought the political situation not yet ripe for military intervention. After many previous discussions, another meeting of the military and political leaders of the Reich–only Kühlmann was absent, in Bucharest–was held on March 12, the Emperor being present, to consider 'the proposed enterprise in Finland', with all its complications. Hertling, in particular, wanted the move postponed, if possible, a little longer–at least until March 17–so as not to endanger the ratification by the Soviets of the freshly concluded Peace of Brest-Litovsk. He was also uneasy about the possible effects inside Germany of an indefinite extension of the theatre of war in the north on top of the advance in the Ukraine, and thought the juncture psychologically very unfavourable for intervention in Finland, since the people would see in it another resumption of the war. The strongest argument advanced was that the ratification of the Peace of Brest-Litovsk by the Soviets would impose on them a legal obligation to evacuate Finland, 'and if they do not do that, we are free', especially since action against 'bands of marauders' did not mean resumption of hostilities against Russia. Holtzendorff thought that the campaign in Finland did not amount to a military expedition, but an operation similar to that which had been followed in Livonia and Estonia. The Emperor summed up:

> Position is this: Finns have been robbed by Bolshevik government. Government twice overthrown. Finns asking for help. Sweden refuses. Therefore ask me. I have consented (Bolsheviks must be beaten, because revolutionary). Military reasons: threat from Russia. Mannerheim has said he is ready also to go to Petersburg and take Ingermanland.

The Emperor thought it was Germany's duty 'to play the policeman in the Ukraine, Livonia, Estonia, Lithuania and Finland'. He was certainly influenced by dynastic considerations–by the hope that the feeling in favour of a monarchy which, as he emphasised, had arisen spontaneously in Finland, would develop and might there (and nowhere else) really form a 'dam against Bolshevism'.

The despatch of the expedition was delayed, not only by internal and international complications, but also by ice in the Gulf of Bothnia. A force of about 15,000 men under von der Goltz crossed the gulf at the end of March and the beginning of April and at once opened an attack from the south in support of Mannerheim's offensive, which achieved its biggest success when it took Tampere on April 25. By the middle of May the Finnish White army and the Germans, who were acting under Mannerheim's command, had defeated the Red forces, taking about 80,000 prisoners and eliminating the Socialists as a political factor. Finland had now to consider the future form of her state, the choice lying between a bourgeois-democratic republic which would have been tantamount to an orientation towards the democratic West, or a monarchy of strongly conservative character which menta close relations with the constitutional monarchy of Prusso-Germany. By choosing a 'regent', Finland indicated her preference for Germany. A strong party in the country came out in favour of a monarchy, and the leaders of the Reich began haggling over candidates. Both the Emperor and the OHL wanted one of Wilhelm's sons, perhaps Prince Oscar; but in view of the question of compensation within Germany for the Federal princes and of world public opinion, a German Protestant prince was finally proposed: the German Emperor's 'brother-in-law', Prince Friedrich Karl of Hessen, who had already been suggested for the throne of Rumania. The Finnish Diet elected him king on October 9, 1918, but the issue of the war led him to renounce the throne.

No less important than the dynastic connection and the economic link was a plan to organise a Finnish army on the German model, with the help of the German troops left in Finland, and to conclude a military convention with Finland (as with Estonia–Livonia–Courland, Lithuania, Poland, Rumania and Bulgaria) as a northern bulwark against Russia. Ludendorff was thus able to talk of 'the infinite importance to us of the Ukraine and Finland, the corner-stone of the East, with their incalculable wealth' – a view completely endorsed by Kühlmann.

The Treaty of Bucharest: the Balkan balance and economic colonialism

An armistice had been concluded with Rumania on December 9, 1917, following that with Russia, and since then German policy had been directed towards consolidating through a peace treaty the dominating position in Rumania conceded to Germany under the revised Kreuznach agreements. First, however, the Germans had to find a government ready to negotiate with them, and neither King

Ferdinand nor the existing Prime Minister, Bratianu, who were the two men responsible for Rumania's entry into the war, answered their purposes. The Central Powers eventually succeeded in coming to terms with the leaders of the pro-German Conservative Party who had remained in Bucharest, the octogenarian Carp, Marghiloman, Arion and Stere, who hoped to save the integrity of the country by replacing the dynasty by a German prince, Friedrich Karl of Hesse or Prince Oscar, who was to conclude peace after a brief regency. But Carp's hopes were dashed the moment he stated his terms: he asked for a guarantee that the northern Dobruja with Constanta should remain with Rumania if the armies at the front issued a declaration deposing King Ferdinand and his government. Germany was not prepared to give such a promise. On the one hand, she was bound by obligations towards her ally, Bulgaria, and on the other, she was following the Emperor's instructions not to let the disposal of the Dobruja and Constanta pass out of her own hands prematurely or definitively before the Balkan question, with its problems of Bulgaro-Turkish, Turkish–Transcaucasian and Bulgaro-Rumanian relations, had been settled. Although left isolated by the Ukrainian peace, the Rumanians resisted the severe territorial and, as it soon appeared, no less heavy economic demands of Germany and her allies most obstinately, and it was not until three months later that they 'bowed to force' and agreed to sign a preliminary peace. After even longer delays, a government was formed under Marghiloman, and it again fought hard until peace was at last signed at the beginning of May.

Since the Emperor's journey to Rumania, German interest, encouraged by the relevant business groups and by the General Officer Commanding, Mackensen, had begun to turn away from Poland towards the oilfields and granaries of Rumania. Wilhelm II was prepared to meet Austria over Poland if she made a generous announcement of disinterest in Rumania, and at the Crown Council of January 2 he had accordingly proposed asking for a less extensive Frontier Strip. The OHL, which still inclined towards a Great Bulgarian solution, opposed this concentration on Rumania by continuing to insist on a wide Frontier Strip in Poland, while at the same time demanding for Germany Rumanian oil and wheat and territorial possession of Constanta and the railway line from Cernavoda.

The Emperor poured out his wrath against the generals in a flood of violent marginal comments. With great determination he demanded a Rumanian solution in which the country was to figure as a sort of crown colony or dominion under a German prince. The issue was decided by the Chancellor and the Foreign Ministry. The civilians' policy was still that of Bethmann Hollweg; the Rumanian problem was a function of Mitteleuropa. Austria-Hungary and Bulgaria must be satisfied without imposing crippling territorial cessions on Rumania, while Germany, as mistress of Constanta and the real power in Rumania, must be in a position to hold the balance between the Balkan states—not only Rumania and Bulgaria, but also Greece and Turkey—and to ensure her own preponderant influence, if necessary (since it seemed even harder here than at Brest-Litovsk to reconcile all interests) by playing off her other allies against each other.

Bulgaria was asking for the whole Dobruja. The southern or 'Bulgarian' part of it had been promised her in the treaty of 1915, but she also clung very stubbornly to her demand for the northern part, thereby holding up the conclusion of peace, especially since she refused to restore to Turkey, as compensation for her own gain, the Maritsa Bend received by her in 1915. Turkey tried to link the Dobruja question with the recovery of West Thracian areas along the Maritsa and with gains in the Caucasus—Georgia, Armenia and Azerbaijan, thereby at once pressing her allies to go beyond the terms of Brest-Litovsk and impinging immediately on Germany's proposed sphere of influence in the Caucasus. The conflict was made more acute by Turkey's claim to influence over the other Islamic areas of Russia. The Turks were thus asking for much more, in Europe and in the Caucasus, than their agreements with Germany had promised them. The German government had the greatest difficulty in getting Turkey to consent in the Peace of Bucharest to the Dobruja solution, even to the condominium.

Another difficulty was caused by the claim of Austria-Hungary to Wallachia, or at least to frontier rectifications which would have carried her frontier south of the Transylvanian passes. Given so much disunity between the Central Powers on what form the future of Rumania was to take, it is not surprising that the negotiations ran into a dead end on January 31, 1918. Although Kühlmann believed that Bulgaria's strategic position as key to the east and her economic potentialities predestined her to be the leading Balkan power after the war and the most desirable ally for Germany, without whose alliance Germany's eastern policy 'would lack any firm basis', yet the government was reluctant to 'sacrifice' Rumania to Bulgaria; its solution was to give the northern Dobruja to the one and the southern to the other, and to keep the port and railway for Germany herself. Germany and Austria had settled the question of Rumania in the preceding October by allowing Germany the ruling voice in Rumania in return for her consent to the Austro-Polish solution. From mid-February, 1918 onwards, however, Germany began again to call in question the Austro-Polish solution, though without giving up Rumania in return.[1] Now, the Rumanian question, like the Polish, was treated as a preliminary to Mitteleurope. Only thus could the territorial gains which Austria would get at the expense of Rumania – on top of Poland – be balanced out. 'This natural differentiation,' thought Hertling, 'can only be partially balanced out if Austria disinterests herself contractually in a Rumania attached to us politically, militarily and economically.'

But beyond this, Rumania, like Poland was to be directly linked with the German Reich by economic and military treaties.

The substance of Germany's dominating position – and here Emperor, Chancellor, Secretary of State, Minister of War, OHL, Mackensen's General Headquarters, the economic departments and the economic interests behind them were completely at one – was to be secured through German participation in the economy of Rumania so extensive that even Austria-Hungary was to be allowed only a few advantages in the shape of a share in Rumanian exports. Since Rumania's geographical situation made it impossible to extend German rule over her directly – as with the Ukraine and later with the new states carved out of south-eastern Russia – a modern form of vassaldom was devised which, by concentrating almost exclusively on economic connections (however differently viewed by different groups of interests), was something quite new in politics, distinct both from traditional annexationism and from the policies pursued in Poland and Belgium. The overriding principle of German policy was, as Kühlmann put it when conducting the negotiations in Bucharest, 'not to let Rumania wither away as a colony of the Central Powers' but to make it permanently 'efficient'.

The moulding of Germany's economic-political plans took place at a series of internal German conferences between the beginning of February and the beginning of April. At these conferences Germany's economic aims in Rumania were settled on the basis of joint memoranda submitted by the Foreign Ministry and the OHL. The principle underlying these decisions was that Germany must 'enjoy the leadership and the preponderant influence in the economic field', assure herself of 'Rumania's surplus products', and make Rumania

[1] This latest turn can already be sensed in Wilhelm II's comments on a telegram sent to him on February 16 by the Emperor Charles, advising less severity in the conditions to be imposed on Rumania. On this Wilhelm notes: 'If H.M. wants good-neighbourly relations with Rumania, let him renounce his own frontier rectifications in the Carpathians at her expense! Rumania long ago privately offered, or rather, promised us the oil. H.M.'s request is simply monstrous. I refuse to fulfil it. . . . He is frightened of the Poles, chucks away the Austro-Polish solution, and decides to put us out of Rumania.'

financially dependent on her. The original drafts prepared for the first great conferences of state on February 15 and 16, which still envisaged protecting German interests by more traditional methods, provided for the transfer of Rumanian state lands – above all, those containing oil deposits – to a 'Central European Oil Company', controlled by German capital, to which were to be transferred also the mining royalties formerly enjoyed by the Rumanian state and its unlimited right of expropriation. All sales, exploitation and deliveries were to be in the hands of a trading monopoly, the capital of which was again to be mainly German, to ensure that Germany's requirements should, as far as possible, be covered from Rumanian oil. The OHL and the naval staff also wanted Constanta made into an extra-territorial German base on the Black Sea, a canal (which would have cost 95 million marks) constructed between Cernavoda and Constanta to shorten the passage to the Black Sea, and ownership of the Rumanian railways. These last demands were regarded by the civilians chiefly as a means of putting pressure on Austria-Hungary; retreat from a maximum programme would make it easier for them to get their demands in Poland, especially control over the railways; but as regards the economic demands in Rumania, the old aims were in substance consistently retained.

The Emperor Charles wrote a personal letter to Wilhelm II protesting against these exaggerated economic demands as likely to prove fatal to the much desired peace with Rumania, since no state could be expected to renounce 'its most important economic assets ... on which the possibilities of its economic development depend' without resorting to a desperate appeal to arms. Wilhelm II said that 'His Majesty's request was absolutely unprecedented', refused it, and said that if the peace negotiations did break down, it would be as much on account of Austria-Hungary's territorial claims in the Carpathians as of Germany's demands. The delegation left Berlin without having much modified its programme or its aims.

The conferences of February 18 and 20, over which Helfferich presided, were held to check over once more 'the principles laid down by the Chief of the General Staff ... on the basis of the proposals of the military administration in Rumania and of the drafts of the Foreign Office' in order 'to secure to ourselves as far as possible the maximum political and economic profit from Rumania'. Helfferich expressly laid down that there could be no departure from the substance of the aims previously laid down; only different forms could be chosen. The 'different form' suggested by Helfferich was, first, that new conditions should be substituted for the transfer of ownership and the unlimited appropriation of the royalties, namely:

(i) the long-term leases of state lands as already introduced by the military administration, and (ii) the enemy oil companies liquidated by it should be transferred to the 'Central European Oil Company', and (iii) all agreements concluded during the war between America, England and France, conceding them rights to oilfields, should be cancelled. Second, and still more important, a trading monopoly was to be established which would prevent the sale of oil to a third party. As Germany would both control and own most of the capital both of this monopoly and of the producing company, she would be able to supervise all sales of Rumanian oil, and also to control sales and deliveries of crude oil or its products, including refinement and distribution by pipe-line, rail or sea. The Rumanian state was to have a 20 per cent share in the crude oil company, while the remaining 80 per cent was to be left to Germany and Austria-Hungary in the proportions of 70 :30. This last provision was criticised very strongly in Germany as not sufficiently safeguarding Germany's interests, although it would in fact, while leaving Rumania a figment of sovereignty, have given Germany control over Rumania's economy and the lion's share of her oil production. Germany's real domination was disguised as 'return for our help in reconstructing Rumania's economy', as Count Roedern, Secretary of State in the Reich Treasury, put it. The machinery was modelled on that of the German oil company in Rumania before the war, the Steaua Romana (owned by the Deutsche Bank).

The hold which Germany sought to establish on Rumania's agricultural production was very similar. The so-called 'economic agreement', which was worked out in the course of the same discussions, laid down that the whole surplus of the harvest of 1918 and 1919 and of the following seven years, was to go to Germany and Austria-Hungary. Rumania was to be required to issue a prohibition on exports, which was not to be lifted unless Germany's and Austria-Hungary's needs had been completely satisfied. The final aim was to include Rumania in the Central European Customs Union. Meanwhile, Germany demanded the conclusion of a direct military convention with herself, which would make Rumania a part of the defensive belt against Russia.

The Rumanian government in Jassy accepted both the economic and the military conditions as bases for peace negotiations, and even consented to the cession of the southern Dobruja and to Austria-Hungary's frontier demands, but it refused to agree to Bulgaria's larger demand (which Germany, although reluctantly, and Austria-Hungary were now endorsing) for the whole of the Dobruja. This delayed considerably the conclusion of the negotiations; on the other hand, the Dobruja question was the real lever by which Kühlmann and the German government could put pressure on Bulgaria.

As early as February 28 – even before the Jassy government had accepted the German ultimatum – the OHL had laid down the terms which Germany was to ask from Bulgaria in return for conceding her claim to the northern Dobruja. The list included the regular demands for Constanta, the Constanta–Cernavoda line and control of the Danube, with the right to construct the canal from Constanta to Cernavoda, and various additional conditions relating to Bulgaria alone. Bulgaria promised to conclude a military convention immediately; she renounced any share in 'booty of war' from Rumania or in any possible economic profit from her; and she promised to meet her war debt by borrowing on the German market. Other conditions echoed Germany's Polish policy. The enemy-owned mines, most of which lay in the newly acquired territories of Serbian Macedonia, were to be expropriated; in particular, the Bor mines and the railways of this area (which ran down to Salonika) were to be transferred to German ownership. In the Dobruja Germany retained 'for the transition period' the rights hitherto exercised by her authorities along the lines of communication, particularly in respect of raw materials, exploitation of mines, industrial and agricultural enterprises, fisheries, and the use of local railways. Germany had thus secured a considerable influence over Greater Bulgaria to add to what she enjoyed in Poland, the Ukraine, Rumania and Austria-Hungary.

When the negotiations with Rumania reached another deadlock over the Dobruja question, Kühlmann tried to break it by putting his demands in the form of an ultimatum. Presented on February 27, it was repeated on March 1. It led to another crisis between the allies, since the Emperor Charles said that he would not reopen hostilities against Rumania for the sake of the demands contained in the ultimatum. The crisis, however, passed, for the Rumanians, whose military situation had been rendered exceedingly precarious by the opening of the German advance into the Ukraine and the big 'withdrawals' of Russian troops, submitted on March 2 and signed the preliminary peace of Buftea on March 5. The wranglings of the Germans with each other and with their allies went on the whole of March; there was moreover no one in Bucharest officially entitled to negotiate. It was only on March 21 that the new Prime Minister, Marghiloman, at last appeared and the peace negotiations proper could be opened in Bucharest. The peace was initialled on the 26th, subject to the reservation that the final form of the economic conditions was still to be established. The treaty was signed in Bucharest on May 7. The important provisions are, however, not those of the main treaty, but those contained in its five annexes on oil, economics, shipping, finance and law respectively. The Secretary of State in the Reich Economic Office, Baron von Stein, said afterwards that the central purpose 'of ensuring Germany's influence over the production and export of oil' had been completely achieved, as also had been the substance of all her other aims – not, however, the territorial possession of Constanta but a free port with control of the railways and the Danube, and not the mining royalties but the trade monopoly.

Private interests, however, were less well satisfied with the treaty. They regarded the commercial monopoly as a threat to the realisation of their own plans, which they had expounded in numerous memoranda purporting to satisfy both the state and private enterprise. These objections were supported by Helfferich, who in all the preliminary negotiations had pressed very strongly for a solution based on private enterprise, and by some of the ministries.

The way in which the economic negotiations with Rumania are being carried on is evoking very strong criticism here from Helfferich and the Ministries, and also from the big private interests. The Deutsche Bank is grumbling, Stinnes raging, Ballin up in arms. All these are people who get listened to. . . .

On the same day on which this warning was sent to Kühlmann, Ludendorff followed it up by saying that it was impossible to conclude a political treaty without first securing the economic demands in respect of oil, wheat and finance; it was precisely in the interest of those demands that he had left his troops in the country, so that they could apply the necessary pressure.

Led by Ludendorff, the extremist wing of the War Aims Majority began to criticise the diplomats, especially Kühlmann, sharply for weakness, saying that the power position attained by Germany in Bucharest was far too modest in view of Germany's victories and by comparison with what she could have achieved. The treaty, like that of Brest-Litovsk before it, contributed largely to Kühlmann's fall. The Emperor, under the influence of Ludendorff and private interests, already wanted to drop him, and he was again only saved by Hertling in the interest of the wider objective of Mitteleuropa. Hertling sent the Emperor a letter (drafted personally by his Under-Secretary, von Radowitz), defending the policy of his Secretary of State against the numerous and envenomed attacks upon him. He denied strongly that Germany had failed to achieve anything 'which was in her economic or political interest' and insisted that the real aim of his policy was not to concentrate on a single objective, but to hold together, now and after the war, the coalition of the Central Powers, the corner-stone of which was Germany's relations with Austria-Hungary.

If these relations were clouded, the value of our alliance with Bulgaria and Turkey and all advantages achieved in Rumania would become illusory. The strengthening and firm establishment of the alliance on the basis of common interests would, on the other hand, create a *Central European bloc* of a strength *never yet witnessed in the history of the world*.[1]

'The only protection for Germany, east or west, in the new war which must follow the Central Powers' present victory could, he went on, come from 'the new bloc now coming into being', to which Holland and the Scandinavian states would probably first attach themselves, in their own economic interests. Russia could be eliminated as an enemy in the immediate future, but only if a *modus vivendi* with her present rulers could be found; this depended on 'practical handling' of the problem of the border states.

Hertling said that Kühlmann's special merit was to have come back both from Brest and from Bucharest with Germany's relationship with her allies untroubled–and that was the essential condition for the larger Central European solution. His dismissal would mean the collapse of the present system, which had succeeded so far in holding together the people and its representatives. Even in the Reichstag there was an unmistakable swing 'away from the resolution (sc. of July, 1917) on no annexations or indemnities'; in this way the government had been able 'with the help of parliament, to keep alive in the people faith in its intention of reaching a peace honourable to Germany'.

The Reichstag later accepted the Peace of Bucharest without serious objections.

Austria-Hungary, Poland and Mitteleuropa

Immediately the Treaty of Bucharest was signed, Ludendorff revoked the consent given by him at the end of 1917 to the Austro-Polish solution on the grounds that the treaty had not given Germany the position in Rumania promised her in October, and that she was therefore no longer bound. The old German demands, which would have made Poland a satellite of Germany irrespective of her political status, reappeared undiminished, supported by the OHL, the Prussian ministries, and private interests. As Germany also wanted to make Austria-Hungary as a whole dependent on herself, Poland was not only a war aim, but also the key to Germany's hegemony in Europe.

[1] Author's italics.

But the two most important political factors in Germany, the OHL and the civilian government, had different ideas on how to achieve that hegemony. Thus in spite of the decision of the Crown Council of January 2, 1918, the OHL opposed a military convention with Austria-Hungary on emotional anti-Habsburg grounds; while the civilians advocated it as the way to chain Austria-Hungary to Germany. The OHL insisted strongly on its demand for a big Frontier Strip, and thereby so prejudiced the Austro-Polish solution that Austria-Hungary was prepared to give up both Poland and Mitteleuropa. That, however, Kühlmann and Hertling wanted by all means to prevent.

The military and political plans for the east now came into head-on collision. Czernin complained to Kühlmann that 'his persistent efforts to create closer unity between Germany and Austria' were being thwarted by the German military's obstinacy, and Kühlmann implored the Chancellor to get the generals to yield.

If we succeed in bringing about the economic and military attachment to Austria which, given at all skilful leadership, must also greatly increase our influence over the foreign policy of the Habsburg Monarchy, I see in this an enormous and permanent gain for the cause of *Deutschtum* in the world.

The success of this policy, which Kühlmann called 'an absolute necessity' in Germany's interest, must not be thwarted by the military-technical narrow-mindedness of the Prussian generals with their excessive demands in the Frontier Strip.

Kühlmann also accused the generals of having no programme of their own. Nevertheless, they were not prepared to give up their aims for the sake of the political Mitteleuropa idea. Their aim was, by securing the centres of raw materials and industry near Germany's frontiers, to bring not only Poland and Austria-Hungary, but also France and Belgium into dependence on Germany and keep them weak, under German domination, but without Mitteleuropa. As regards the east, this idea emerged clearly in conversations between the AOK and the OHL on where the German–Polish frontier was to run in Upper Silesia. The Germans demanded the whole coalfield of Dombrowa under the pretext of ensuring supplies for the Silesian industrial districts. The Chief of the Austro-Hungarian General Staff, Baron Arz, at once saw what was Germany's real purpose: 'What Germany is trying to do is, by getting possession of the coalfields of Dombrowa, to accentuate our dependence on her and make Poland, which will then have no coal mines at all, dependent also.'

The first clash between Germany and Austria-Hungary was

followed on February 5 by another and still grimmer one, when Czernin's hope that by yielding over Chelm he would get Poland undiminished by a Frontier Strip was not fulfilled; on the contrary, the Prussian policy represented by the Ministry of State and the departmental ministries, in alliance with the OHL, began to prevail over Hertling–Kühlmann line. On top of this, the Ukrainian peace had drawn down on Czernin, who was the chief Austrian supporter of the Mitteleuropa idea, the implacable hatred of all Poles inside and outside the Monarchy. On February 28 the Poles vented their wrath in the Austrian Herrenhaus, 'raging' over the loss of Chelm and saying that Czernin had betrayed Austria-Hungary to 'German imperialism' and sacrificed Austria in order that Germany 'should make herself mistress of the lands from Riga to Constantinople'.[1] Czernin's position was shaken; the support which he enjoyed from the extremists of the right, the champions of 'Austria's place in the world', was barely enough to defend him against the Poles. The situation in Austria-Hungary after the treaty with the Ukraine was thus deeply divided; the 'Bread Peace' produced only a meagre return. The Emperor's longing for peace was diametrically opposed to his Foreign Minister's hopes of victory, and Austria's annexationists were by no means pleased with the peace treaties.

Under the impact of unbridled Polish reactions and of the internal difficulties of the Monarchy, the Emperor Charles visited the German Emperor in Homburg on February 22 to express *désintéressement* in the Austro-Polish solution and – at least if Wilhelm II understood him aright – to consent to the so-called 'candidates' solution' which, given the latest change of feeling among the Poles, would certainly have resulted in the election of the German candidate. He asked only for certain safeguards for Austria-Hungary's interests. Wilhelm II, however, set forth Germany's conditions for any solution of the Polish question in their full magnitude: he must conclude a military convention with the king of Poland and reserve to himself the right to inspect the country's military installations and a certain measure of influence over the organisation and training of the Polish army. He attached no less weight to the economic safeguards, in the form of a guaranteed German influence over the Polish railways, roads and waterways. Wilhelm felt himself already victor in the east, and wholly confident of victory in the west, and when Charles pressed for a 'quick' peace, he replied that he was firmly resolved to achieve a 'good' peace, for which Germany could carry on the war for another two or three years. When Charles agreed

[1] The Poles in the Reichsrat had talked of 'German imperialism, Germany's attempts to build a bridge to the East.'

to the 'candidates' solution', Wilhelm II in his turn dropped the Austro-Polish solution, to which he had hitherto been faithful, and his Chancellor followed him. Only Kühlmann continued to advocate it as the only way, as he saw it, of realising the Mitteleuropa plan with Austria-Hungary.

The Polish question was discussed again in Kühlmann's absence (he was in Bucharest) at a Crown Council on March 13, and a middle line was found which diverged only a little from the Emperor's wishes and included in essentials all demands evolved since 1915. Beseler, who had hurried in from Warsaw, gave a reappraisal of the Polish situation after the Brest peace. Militarily Poland 'jutted out like a wedge' into the belt of German-dominated Russian border states from Finland to the Ukraine, and must therefore be kept dependent on Germany. Politically Poland was of key importance for Germany from every point of view, not only the military, and to prune its frontiers too severely would produce lasting discontent and turn it into 'the focal point of all intrigues of enemy Powers against Germany'. Although, therefore, the two parties could not 'negotiate as equals', the 'state treaty' must 'be up to a point voluntary'. This was relatively easy, because the Poles, whose leading class consisted of landed magnates, were frightened of Bolshevism and had themselves recently approached Germany, and had offered her a military convention and a commercial treaty. Germany, said Beseler, should use the might of her army to 'establish the Polish state on firm foundations' and give it the frontiers, already fixed by the Brest treaties, which 'encircle it south and north'.

The Russian danger has been banished for a long time to come. We have decades before us in which to build in the ex-Russian border states an advanced frontier bastion for the defence of our country. Behind this must lie a second defensive sector. That I see on the Vistula.

Beseler (who was strongly criticised as too pro-Polish, not only by the OHL but also by the Prussian ministries) thought that this meant 'that we must have the Bobr–Narew line, up to about Ostrolenka'. He did indeed plead that the iron and coal mines on the Upper Silesian frontier, which the OHL wanted to include in the Frontier Strip, should be left to Poland, since German industry was in any case guaranteed the use of them. The *conditio sine qua non* of his proposals was, however, that Germany must be complete master of Poland's army and communications; this was the only condition on which she could renounce large annexations. Not one word was said on this occasion in favour of Kühlmann's Austro-Polish solution; the meeting agreed in principle to Beseler's Prussion–Little Poland proposals, and left the Secretary of State completely isolated. The idea of a Mitteleuropa via the Austro-Polish solution was dead. Germany tried to separate the two aims and to achieve the former without herself making concessions. On top of this, Czernin resigned on April 14, leaving Kühlmann without a partner in the other camp on either Poland or Mitteleuropa. Czernin's fall had only been a question of time since the Ukrainian treaty and the Poles' reaction to it, but it was precipitated and made inevitable by his unfortunate intervention in the Sixtus affair and his speech against the Czechs. Further, his resignation and the publication of the Sixtus letter,[1] with its reference to France's 'just claims' on Alsace-Lorraine, compromised the Emperor Charles' position towards Germany no less severely.

Germany's reaction was immediate. Kühlmann now accepted the view of the OHL and the Prussian Ministry of State that the moment had arrived to impose Mitteleuropa and clear up the Polish question in accordance with Germany's wishes and without considering Austria. 'According to the historic course of events, a long-term alliance, economic association and military agreement would represent Austria's returns for German counter-concessions on the Polish question.'

The publication of the Sixtus letter had, however, altered the situation considerably to Germany's advantage, and it would thus now be possible to secure the threefold alliance even without counter-concessions in Poland. Kühlmann indeed thought that Austria would be forced 'to link her further destinies demonstratively with those of the German Reich' through these agreements, in order to dispel the doubts raised by the letter about her loyalty to the German alliance.

Most careful advance arrangements were made for Charles' 'pilgrimage to Canossa' (he was expected in Spa on May 12). Hertling, Payer, Roedern, the two Steins, Stumm, Bussche and Radowitz held a number of conferences, Kühlmann, Bergen, Wedel, Ludendorff and Hindenburg being called in in the later stages, which defined in what could now be called definitive form Germany's aims towards Austria-Hungary and Poland. The 'hard line' won: Austria-Hungary, Poland and Mitteleuropa were to be treated separately, and each objective reached separately on its own merits. Austria-Hungary – still more Poland – was to be bound by threefold treaties, the object being 'to dominate Austria-Hungary economically, like Poland and Russia'. The Emperor, like Kühlmann, called for 'an alliance which shall be as long-term as possible, and conspicuous to

[1] See Lorenz, *Kaiser Karl*, p. 153.

the world'. Baron von Stein, however, who was the stiffest representative of Germany's economic interests, regarded a long-term alliance as only one aim of German policy; he (and with him the OHL) thought it even more important that Austria-Hungary should leave Germany an entirely free hand, economically, in Poland and allow her to conclude a customs union with Poland, leaving open the question of the possible adherence to it of Austria-Hungary. Thus the Kühlmann-Czernin agreement was dropped in favour of a central Europe as conceived by Ludendorff, von Stein, Helfferich and Roedern. There were differences of nuance, according to the more or less strictly Prussian mentality of each, but all agreed in rejecting the Austro-Polish solution in favour of one which on the one hand showed Germany to be the complete master, and on the other made Poland into a German hinterland in which Austria-Hungary had nothing to say. The results of the first conference formed the basis of the discussions at all the others; the general line of policy thus laid down was not thereafter substantially modified.

The conference of May 10 put the economic alliance first among the obligations to be imposed on Austria-Hungary; that of the 11th, at which the OHL participated, dealt chiefly with the political side. 'All competent organs' again agreed on the necessity of a political alliance, a military treaty and a customs union. Hertling, it is true, now thought that it would be a tactical error to ask Charles, who was ready to accept the three treaties, at the same time to renounce Poland, Austria's single war aim.

This was how things stood on May 12 (five days after the Peace of Bucharest), when Charles arrived in Spa, accompanied by Czernin's successor, Burian. The discussions lasted many days, and Burian, whose appointment had not been welcomed in Germany, succeeded in forcing the Germans to agree reluctantly to make the validity of the Mitteleuropa treaties dependent on a prior settlement of the Polish question. The agreements concluded between Germany and Austria-Hungary were thus only provisional. The Germans, however, paid little attention to this qualification; as early as May 16 they were describing the Austro-Polish solution as 'done with', and exploiting the signature of 'Mitteleuropa' as 'a step of world-historical importance'. Germany's Austro-Hungarian policy was 'settled' by (i) a long-term, close political alliance, (ii) a military treaty, (iii) a customs and economic alliance, with the ultimate purpose of bringing about completely duty-free traffic between the contracting powers. Economic details were to be considered further in special committees, and it was hoped that the Polish question would be solved easily at the beginning of June, when Burian came back.

When Burian did come back, on June 12, Germany's western offensive seemed on the verge of bringing her victory, and her self-assurance was even greater than in May. This increased confidence found expression when the Polish question was debated again on May 30 at a conference in the Imperial Chancellery. As in the previous conferences of that month, eastern and western aims were treated exactly alike; the eastern march was to be matched by a western, both screening Germany's industry, both serving as deployment areas in another war, both colonised with Germans. Poland and Belgium figured equally as satellites of Germany. Belgium was to be restored as an independent state, tied economically to Germany and partitioned administratively between Flemish and Walloons – as Poland, by means of the 'candidates' solution', was to be 'closely attached to the Central Powers, Germany enjoying preference'.

While Kühlmann for reasons of policy still wanted Austria-Hungary treated *pro forma* as a partner and thought it necessary to get her consent to the transference of the Polish railways to Germany, Roedern brushed this aside almost contemptuously, arguing: 'Without Prussia-Germany the railway question is entirely insoluble. Poland is starving. . . . Coal, railways our best weapon. . . . We are creating something permanent there, so that we can use that too as a lever to squeeze Austria.' Roedern's was no isolated voice; Stein supported him most vigorously: 'We need Poland, we must be the masters there.' The commercial policy of the Foreign Ministry was 'impossible'; 'it contents itself with preferential duties, while we need customs union or commercial treaty'. The Chancellor agreed with Roedern and Stein. He looked beyond Poland, even beyond Rumania, and found full assurance that Germany would be able to hold out in the anticipated economic war with the Western Powers only with the economic domination of Russia. 'Russia must become our economic domain'; it is 'an ineluctable necessity that we should dominate the Russian market'. Therefore no internal tariffs with Poland!

Germany's aims emerged even more nakedly in the discussion over what was to be done with Poland during the transitional period which all departments agreed must intervene before Mitteleuropa was fully established. Roedern, Wallraf and the Chancellor agreed that the regulation of the Polish question during this period must be one favourable to Germany. If it took 20–25 years to bring the customs union with Austria-Hungary into effect, Poland must not slip out of German hands during this interval; so 'Austria-Hungary must get out of Poland'. Kühlmann's arguments on the other side failed to convince; he wanted to create a relationship between Germany and Austria-Hungary like that of Britain and her dominions, but Hertling, Roedern, Wallraf, Stein and their supporters were entirely unconvinced. His objection that the Russian market could not be dominated by German industry without massive state help was practically disregarded. His argument that the way to prevent both Austria-Hungary and Poland from shutting themselves off from Germany by tariff barriers was to establish close connections with the two countries together met with opposition which he was unable to overcome even by pointing to the secret agreement with Rumania, under which that country had pledged itself to enter the customs union. Stein produced economic arguments to counter the political: the economic structures of Germany and Austria-Hungary were so different that to link them together without first making sure of Poland would be an 'economic fetter on Germany'. He proposed to try to get a provisional customs union with Austria-Hungary in which Austria and Germany would be on the same footing *vis-à-vis* Poland. This was generally approved, because the gainer by this situation could only be the economically stronger party, Germany.

During Burian's two-day visit he quickly agreed with Hertling and Kühlmann on the outlines of a new treaty of alliance. The Polish question, however, was in no way solved. Burian surprised the Germans by the obstinacy with which he clung to the Austro-Polish solution, and that with a territorially unmutilated Congress Poland. The alliance again threatened to founder on war aims. Burian said that unless Germany agreed to the Austro-Polish solution, not only could he not discuss Mitteleuropa any further, except purely academically, but Austria must in that case also keep her hands free for the future (i.e., to change allies). In spite of this threat, Hertling and Kühlmann flatly rejected Austria's proposals, declaring themselves bound by the Emperor's instructions. The negotiations were broken off, leaving the two positions irreconcilably opposed. This was apparent from the instructions prepared by the Reich Economic Office in preparation for the negotiations with Austria on the customs union which were to take place in Salzburg. Stein's basic thesis was that Germany, Austria-Hungary and Poland were 'to constitute a unitary economic territory' with complete customs unification, unification of financial, currency and banking legislation and mutual assimilation of their transport systems, in which Germany was to control the Polish railways and the possibility of a German–Polish currency union was left open, while a Polish–Austro-Hungarian union was expressly ruled out. Domination of Poland, which Stein regarded entirely in the light of a transit area leading to Great Russia, the

Ukraine and the Caucasus, was a more vital aim than Mitteleuropa. Radowitz, it is true, rejected these instructions as unacceptable from the point of foreign policy, but nevertheless Germany's policy remained basically that of Stein up to the middle of 1918.

Another great war aims conference, at the beginning of July, 1918, showed this plainly. Here, once again, Germany's war aims were discussed, under the presidency of the Emperor, in a spirit of full self-assurance. Again the leaders of Germany confirmed their decisions of May and June, this time without a dissenting voice, since Kühlmann's place as Secretary of State for Foreign Affairs had since been taken by Hintze:

(i) The personal union between Poland and Austria was rejected;
(ii) The Poles were to be allowed to nominate a (German) candidate;
(iii) Poland, being the most important transit area to the east, must be economically dominated by Germany; therefore Germany must:
(iv) possess a dominating influence over its railways.
(v) Military conventions;
(vi) Cession of Frontier Strips to be determined by purely military considerations.

With these six demands, which Hertling proposed should be presented to Austria-Hungary 'in almost the form of an ultimatum', the Chancellor hoped to eliminate the differences between Germany and the Dual Monarchy. His proposal was agreed by all. Ludendorff, however, thought it necessary to sketch once again the standpoint of the OHL – no concessions to Austria-Hungary, no retreat over the Frontier Strip, a Poland economically dependent on Germany, a Poland saddled with part of the war bill; then (Poland) 'is so dependent on us that it must seek to attach itself to us' and will ask for a military convention.

The result of this basic agreement on the German–Polish solution and on its economic-political conditions was that the only question left for the Germans to discuss between themselves was the delimitation of the Frontier Strip.

In the voluminous memorandum on this question, submitted on July 5, the OHL went far beyond their demands of February 18, 1918. In particular, they now demanded the inclusion of the towns of Karlish and Konin, in order to secure a new connection by rail, and also by canal, via Mlava and Augustovo, which would facilitate the deployment of troops in a future war and also provide a close connection between the Silesian industries and coalfields and the 'German North-East' of East Prussia and Lithuania. The proposed frontier followed in general the old Bobr–Narev–Warthe line, taking in the Polish-Upper Silesian coalfield. The OHL also again reverted to the idea of expelling the Polish and Jewish populations, expressly recalling the plans bruited by Bethmann Hollweg, Wahnschaffe, Schwerin and Ganse at the conference of July 13, 1915.[1] During these weeks the OHL had arranged for a new flood of memoranda from east German civil servants, communal authorities and business circles, all opposing any renunciation, and could now claim that its demands accorded with those of 'the authoritative quarters and the best experts on our East', that the 'battle for the soil' against the Poles made the deportations necessary, if Germany's eastern provinces were not 'to perish in the Slav masses'. This ethnic argument could not be disregarded, for Beseler's policy of 'enlightened despotism' (which had also been supported at the last by Kühlmann) was recognised, very realistically, to be fruitless.

The Polish question, especially the population transfers which the political leaders now no longer favoured, was discussed at several inter-ministerial conferences in the middle of July and the beginning of August. In view of the insolubility of the Polish question the decision was taken on August 9 (the morrow of the black day on the western front) to go back to the old line of a military convention and a political and economic alliance.

Meanwhile, the 'ultimatum' framed on July 2 had been presented in Vienna, and Burian had accepted the conditions as a basis for discussion, but with so many reservations as to make it clear that he was not prepared to accept Germany's demands but was only playing for time.[2] The situation having changed in the west, the Emperor Charles reappeared in Spa in the hope of initiating a peace move by the Central Powers and at the same time solving the Polish question, but the Germans had blocked any possibility of reviving the Austro-Polish solution. On August 13, the day before Charles' arrival, Hintze had told two Polish spokesmen, Count Ronikier and Prince Janusz Radziwill, that they could choose between two alternatives: adhesion to Germany and a small Frontier Strip, or adhesion to Austria and big Frontier Strips.[3] And on August 27 he repeated, now officially, the threat that if Poland chose Austria-Hungary she would lose the Hindenburg Strip, including the Sosnowice coalfields. Thus the military crisis had in no way bridged the gulf between Germany and Austria; on the contrary, Germany was now pressing forcibly for a *fait accompli* in Poland before the military situation forced her to ask for a general armistice and peace. At the end of August the

[1] Cf. the Bernhard–Wegener plan (above, p. 172).
[2] Conze, op. cit., pp. 371 f.
[3] Id., p. 372.

situation became so critical that even Ludendorff pressed for a final settlement of the Polish question. On August 31 he submitted to Hintze – at the latter's request – his 'programme for an understanding with Poland':[1] an alliance, with military, railway and economic conventions, duty-free transit for German goods, Poland to take over part of Germany's war debts, and the bridgeheads of Lomsha, Ostrolenka and Ossowiec.

Germany's aims in Poland were formulated once more, by Hintze to Burian, on September 5, 1918, only three weeks before the collapse:

(i) Frontier rectifications – parts of Polish Upper Silesia in the *Kreis* of Bendzin, and in front of Thorn, Lomsha and Ossowiec, in return for which Poland should get compensation in Chelm and White Ruthenia [which Count Ronikier had asked of Hintze on August 28].

(ii) A military convention on the model of the Prusso-Bavarian military alliance of 1870.

(iii) Poland to come into the Central European customs union, and

(iv) Foundation of a railway company under predominantly German influence.

Once again, at the end of September, the mutually irreconcilable intentions of the allies clashed, when Burian produced another plan for an Austro-Polish solution, worked out down to the last detail.[2] Never before had Austria defined her demands so exactly; it was probably only the hope of holding together the centrifugal elements of the Dual Monarchy by offering them a major war aim, that led him now to take this step. Germany refused sharply, but by this stage no real 'solution' of the Polish problem was any longer possible.

This brought with it the collapse of the Mitteleuropa plan which had been so closely knit up with the Polish question. It had really become a secondary issue, for on the one hand Burian believed that the only way of saving the existence of the Monarchy was through the Austro-Polish solution (with an intact Congress Poland), while on the other Germany needed Poland not so much as a corner-stone of Mittleuropa but rather as a necessary bridge and link with Russia, the Ukraine and the south-east, areas on the complete domination of which Germany's will had been fully concentrated in the months after Brest-Litovsk. The resignation of Czernin, and still more that of Kühlmann, mark the end of Mittleuropa both for Austria-Hungary and for the German Reich. Thereafter both states tried to follow an 'autarky policy' of their own – the one out of consciousness of weakness, the other in an illusion of strength.

[1] Id., p. 374; Geiss, *Grenzstreifen*, p. 146.
[2] Conze, op. cit., p. 377.

20

THE ELABORATION OF THE *OSTRAUM*

THE UKRAINE, THE CRIMEA,
THE DON TRANSCAUCASIA

THE Ukraine had first figured as a German war aim within the framework of Germany's policy of promoting revolution, a policy resumed with vigour in August, 1917.[1] On February 8, 1918 peace had been concluded in Brest-Litovsk with a government which neither enjoyed any authority in the Ukraine nor possessed the means, force or popular support to recover it. Only two days after the Homburg Crown Council of February 13 had decided to solve the impasse reached at Brest-Litovsk by 'appeals for help' to Germany, one such appeal reached Berlin from the fallen Rada government.[2] The 'rescue expedition' set out on February 18. Kiev was occupied on March 1. For the sake of appearances the OHL allowed the Ukrainian units which had been raised in Germany from among Russian prisoners of war of Ukrainian origin to take part in this operation.

The military foundation of the German power position in the Ukraine

But the capture of Kiev and the return of the Rada by no means meant the end of the campaign. A Bolshevik–Ukrainian counter-government was still in Kharkhov, and enjoyed much sympathy among the workers and small peasants. The Rada could not possibly extend its control over the Ukraine east of Kiev without German support. On March 15 further 'appeals for help' (announced by Hoffmann as early as February 26) came in, begging Germany for further help in liberating the districts of Kharkov, Ekaterinoslav, Tauris, Poltava and Cherson.[3] These brought Germany–so far unaided by her allies–to the Black Sea coast and the Donetz basin.

Austria hesitated long before joining in the 'police operations' in the Ukraine. It was only after the Rada had made concessions to

---

[1] See above, pp. 136 ff.

[2] See above, p. 500.

[3] Ludendorff, *Kriegserinnerungen*, p. 453.

Poland over the frontiers of Chelm that she sent some small forces, which however she did not, as the German Emperor asked, place under German command. The Austrians' chief goal was Odessa. As Austria's aspirations revealed themselves, they were followed by the Germans with extreme mistrust, and it was only reluctantly that Germany allowed Austria, whose supply situation was worse than her own, to take what steps she could to squeeze all possible supplies of bread grains and other commodities out of the areas occupied by her troops. These activities were very damaging to Germany's policy which was quite the opposite. Germany regarded the Ukraine, like Belgium, as a valuable source of raw materials, and also as a political counter to be used against Russia and the Balkans; she therefore wanted to follow a long-term policy. The result was quarrels and tension which was only slightly relieved in June by concessions by Generals Arz and Krauss, the Austrian Commander-in-Chief and the General Commanding Austria's Eastern Army.

Thus military-tactical and political purposes led Germany to answering the second appeal by continuing her advance beyond Kiev and Kharkov—in the north to the railway junction of Byelgorod, half-way to Kursk in the district of that name (which no longer belonged to the Ukraine), and in the east through the iron and coal fields on the Donetz, which were occupied, and across the Ukrainian frontier almost to the main southern railway line joining Moscow with Voronezh and Rostov.[1] The capture of Rostov, after hard fighting with Russian Bolshevik forces, cut the chief line of communications between Great Russia and the Caucasus, and furthermore brought the chief port on the Don under German control. Austrian troops had by now occupied Odessa, and German units now entered the Crimea, thus thwarting attempts by the Ukrainian Rada to attach to itself this area which, like Rostov and the Donetz basin, belonged technically to Great Russia. The occupation of Sebastopol not only established Germany in another Black Sea port, but brought Moscow's second great southward line of communications, through Kursk to Sebastopol, under German control as far as its terminal point. And the extension of the German zone of occupation also meant the expansion of the now re-established Ukraine, by the inclusion in it of areas regarded by Germany as a necessary military glacis. Great Russia was thus cut off from the Black Sea and from

[1] See also Groener, *Lebenserinnerungen* (Göttingen, 1957), p. 395. Groener praises the Austrians' policy as 'practical' . . . 'whereas we went on doing the egg-dance round the "government". . . . One must admit that if we wanted to make a long-term policy in the Ukraine, the German method was the right one.' On the differences between Germany and Austria-Hungary, see *Die deutsche Okkupation in der Ukraine, Geheimdokumente* (Strassburg, 1957), pp. 173–191.

the valuable corn lands of the Kuban area and from the Caucasus.[1] Disregarding repeated protests from the Moscow government, which looked on the occupation of Cherson, the Crimea, etc. as a violation of the treaty of Brest-Litovsk, the Foreign Ministry and the satellite government of the Rada settled the frontiers of the Ukraine. The Ukraine, the Foreign Ministry informed Moscow, consisted of the nine districts of Volhynia, Podolia, Cherson, Tauris (excluding the Crimea, for the occupation of which another pretext had to be found in the shape of the right of self-determination), Kiev, Poltava, Chernigov, Ekaterinoslav and Kharkov. The OHL went further still; it wanted these frontiers regarded as only 'provisional', and in particular it pressed forward at Taganrog beyond Rostov into the Don and Kuban areas, in order to secure and consolidate a bridge to the Caucasus, a region in which German policy was at the same time pursuing further objectives.

Iron, coal and wheat:
German policy to the fall of the Socialists

Germany's plans, however, encountered unexpected difficulties. The more she pressed for concrete profits out of the Peace Treaty, the less suitable an instrument did the Rada government prove for her purposes. It failed to raise an army deserving the name;[2] it failed to organise an administration which commanded respect and authority in the country;[3] it could not produce the promised supplies, nor keep prices from rising. Conditions were chaotic. Withal, while possessing no real power, the Ukraine government was highly recalcitrant and unsubmissive towards the Germans.

The present Ukrainian government, wrote Colin Ross, an officer sent down by the British Foreign Office to report on the situation, is nothing else than a club of speculative political adventurers who are engaged in doing wonderful business with the support of 'German bayonets'.

Feeling in the country was still pro-German, the hope of 'procuring goods in unlimited quantities' still alive, and realisation that the country had now been linked with 'Central European shortages' had not yet dawned. But when the disappointments arrived, feeling would change. For the moment, the 'club' would continue to accept Germany's orders, if reluctantly; but if permanent collaboration

[1] The provisional eastern and northern frontier, as proposed by the Ukrainian Minister of War, ran from Taganrog south of the government of Voronezh to Bobrov (50 miles south-east of Voronezh), thence Kursk–Rylsk–northern boundary of the government of Chernigov–Shlobin–Lake Vygonovskoye.

[2] The total force consisted of 2,000 men, in 'theatrical costumes', with no military value. Their commander was Petlura.

[3] Groener, op. cit., pp. 391 f.

with the Ukraine was to be achieved, 'peaceful penetration by German forces' of the government, the army and the whole country was essential.

Germany had already initiated this 'peaceful penetration' by sending Field-Marshal von Eichhorn and Lieutenant-General Groener,[1] the former to command the Kiev Army Group with the latter, who had previously been employed to organise the Office of War Economy and to head the railways in the field, as his Chief of Staff. With the two soldiers came an 'ambassador', Mumm von Schwarzenstein, the son of a family of industrialists and a man with much experience of the east. Besides these official representatives of Germany's interests there were others, including a very active group of long-term planners from the Reich Economic Office under a director of Krupps, Wiedfeldt, released for the purpose. This 'economic office', which was specially established to organise the economic penetration of the Ukraine, became very active. With the backing of the German occupation force of eighteen divisions (over 300,000 men with the Austrians) Wiedfeldt and his equally alert collaborator, Melchior, of the Max Warburg bank in Hamburg, succeeded in preparing the ground for a supplementary treaty which would have laid the Ukrainian market completely open to Germany.

As the troops advanced in the south-east, the economic plans in the Ukraine began to take concrete shape in the course of countless conversations. The new possibilities were discussed as early as February 19, and agreement was reached in principle that the situation would offer 'ample possibilities . . . for agreements which might be of extreme value for our domestic industry and for the national food supply'.

South Russia, wrote Helfferich in a survey of future prospects, will be a much more important market for German industry than the north, which has been economically much weakened by the loss of its grain producing areas, and should in future be relatively unimportant, compared with the Ukraine, as a consumer.

It was, however, necessary to seal the Ukraine off from the north and reorientate it to the west partly, according to Helfferich, through control of its railways (which were to be linked with the central European network and have their tariffs adjusted) and partly by indirect control of the mines through German-dominated iron and coal monopolies. These plans were strongly supported by von Stein, the Prussian Minister of War, who further wanted a treaty ensuring

[1] Id., p. 395.

for Germany the Ukraine's whole export surplus of cereals 'for a number of years'. After the railways the Foreign Ministry began to interest itself chiefly in the problem of the indirect domination of the Ukraine's raw materials. Thyssen (of the *Deutscher Kaiser* works) and Kirdorf (of the *Gelsenkirchener Bergwerkgesellschaft*) had been interested in Krivoi Rog before the war. Forms of organisation previously worked out in Belgium and Poland were taken over and amalgamated with the Rada's own plans for a state monopoly of mineral deposits, concessions for coastal and river shipping (the latter on the Dnieper), and licences to construct new railways and to construct and operate grain elevators on the American system.

On March 5 there were further conversations between the departments and Helfferich, and the interests and wishes thitherto disclosed were co-ordinated. The financial claims for the 'expedition' in the Ukraine were distinguished sharply from the economic demands, which were to be put into a supplement to the peace treaty with the Ukraine and, in Helfferich's words, worked out 'in free collaboration' with the Ukraine. Germany now adopted as the aim of her economic policy what before had been only the demand of an occasional individual: in spite of the difficulties of the supply situation in Germany, the Ukraine was to be sealed off from Great Russia, and also from any third power, and its economic system was to be geared to that of Germany and its exports directed to her. All concerned – Helfferich, von Stein, their colleagues in other ministries, also the OHL – agreed that the first way of ensuring 'the unimpeded export, not only of bread grains but iron ore . . . and manganese ore' was to alter the gauge of the railways to the west European and to assimilate tariffs. For safety, Germany should ask for the port of Nikolaev, on the Don, so that the export of the mineral ores would be possible under any conditions.[1]

The foundations of a new Ukrainian policy had thus been laid – barely two days after the signature of the Peace of Brest-Litovsk.

A fortnight later von Stein sent Kühlmann a memorandum containing even more ambitious plans: capital connections with Germany were to be used to prevent a customs union between the Ukraine and Rump Russia. The main point, for him, was to seal off the Ukraine; if this were not done, 'that part of the old Russia which is economically most considerable and most important for Germany's supply of raw materials is lost, treaties or no treaties'. The peace

---

[1] Ludendorff's proposals to Hertling are characteristic: since Germany would be obliged to employ 'methods not consonant with the dignity of the highest representative of the German Reich' in getting in the bread grains and raw materials, the economic work should be left to an 'independent' commission, which should be under the orders of the G.O.C. the German troops in the Ukraine.

treaty between the Ukraine and Russia must therefore be concluded as early as possible, and under German supervision. In the draft the 'Ukraine' was laying territorial claim to 'not only a considerable part of the Black Earth Belt but also the important ironfield of Krivoi Rog, the industrial district of Kharkov, the coalfield of the Donetz basin and the tobacco plantations of the Kuban'.

She was asking also for one-third of the annual production of all Russia's most important raw materials: gold, silver, platinum, copper and naphtha; of these products, Stein proposed, Germany must keep a quota for herself, including up to 90 per cent of the platinum. Similarly, the trade in timber, cotton and manufactured goods which would normally be carried on with Russia must be stopped by customs barriers.

Collaboration between the Germans and the 'kiddies' in their 'Ministerial baby-carriages', as Groener put it,[1] grew more and more difficult as the new treaties neared completion. While the Foreign Ministry wanted to go on working with the Rada, as did Ludendorff, out of anti-Polish sentiment, the German delegation in the Ukraine came increasingly to favour collaboration with the big landlords (who had been expropriated under the Rada's agrarian legislation) and rich peasants, and the installation of a government resting on these elements. Berlin, however, thought it impossible to establish an open military dictatorship within the framework of a German Government-General of the Ukraine, for it thought it essential to preserve the fiction of an independent government, particularly since Germany had concluded with the Ukraine a peace treaty which was the legal basis of its separation from Russia. When the supplementary treaty of April 25, with its twenty annexes regulating the collection of the harvest through a state monopoly assisted by a German purchasing company, had been initialled and signed, the system and personnel of the Rada lost their value for Germany. It had to be overthrown and the country reorganised.[2]

At the end of April, after a considerable search, Groener found the right man in the person of General Skoropadsky, a former Tsarist Guards officer of an old family of Ukrainian nobility; the part of chorus in the 'revolution' he assigned to a group of landlords, most of them of only local importance.

On April 23 Ludendorff himself made the decisive move.[3] He hoped, as he told Groener, that 'powerful pressure' would succeed in overcoming the stoppage of deliveries and the obstinacy of the Rada.

[1] Groener, op. cit., p. 399.
[2] Beyer, op. cit., p. 35.
[3] Groener, op. cit., p. 398.

The issue was forced when the Rada objected strongly to an order by Eichorn introducing compulsory labour in the fields – the first open infringement of the government's sovereignty – and by the abduction of a bank director named Dobry, who had been working with the German Economic Commission.[1] Wilhelm II personally laid down conditions required of a new government:

> Recognition of the Peace of Brest, dissolution of the Rada, new elections only when order had been completely restored, formation of a Ukrainian army by agreement with the German Command, recognition of the German–Austrian courts martial for military offences, local committees, etc. to be dissolved and a regular administration put in, adoption of the Central Powers' legislation on compulsory deliveries, abolition of all limitations on free trade with Germany, the agrarian question to be solved by restoring the right of property, land distribution with compensation . . . retention of the large agricultural enterprises . . . conclusion of a military convention and a long-term economic agreement . . . which places surpluses of foodstuffs and raw materials at our disposal.

Skoropadsky accepted these conditions with a few reservations.[2]

On April 28 the Rada was surrounded and summoned to yield. The members of the government were arrested and the legislature dissolved. The next day an assemblage of great landlords, meeting in a circus, again under military 'protection', proclaimed Skoropadsky Hetman of the Ukraine. Two days later again, Skoropadsky produced a list of ministers which had been agreed with the Germans.

Thus, under the transparent disguise of an internal Ukrainian counter-revolution, Germany had set aside the parliamentary socialist regime in the Ukraine and put in a government which had even less roots in the people than the Rada, but being, unlike the other, quasi-monarchic, was better fitted to cover the fact that Germany had now entered on a second phase of her Ukrainian policy, in which her purpose was to make the Ukraine a relatively stable state, orderly and peaceful in its internal conditions and completely dependent on Germany. The complaints voiced in the Reichstag against the crude behaviour of the military and the violation of a parliament's immunity did not alter by a hair's breadth the policy actually followed by Germany.

[1] Dobry was Director of the Russian Bank for Foreign Trade and financial specialist of the Ukraine, who was working with the German members of the Economic Commission on the preparation of the economic treaty. He appears to have been trying to get the industrialists and 'banking circles' to combine, in order to form a new ministry. The German delegates seem to have had no objections to this.

[2] Groener, op. cit., p. 399.

The Skoropadsky era:
the achievement of aims in the Ukraine

The change of government effected, the economic penetration of the Ukraine set in apace. In the few months allowed them by fate Wiedfeldt and Melchior, who were the two chief brains of the German delegation in the Ukraine, and Freiherr von Stein laid the foundations for the economic domination of the country. Wiedfeldt in particular opposed most strongly any participation by the military. He wanted the relationship of the Ukraine to Germany to be modelled on that of the British dominions with the mother country – absolute primacy of the civil arm with dependent natives filling honorific positions. The military was to remain in the background as far as possible and to confine itself exclusively to police duties.

The activities of the Reich were deployed especially in three major fields: agrarian reform, railways and banks, and iron ores and coal.

As early as April Germany's attitude towards the Rada's policy of nationalisation had undergone a change. The delegation had demanded compensation for expropriated landlords. The Rada, whose position in the country was based solely on land distribution without compensation, refused. The Germans contacted the so-called All-Ukrainian Farmers' Congress and achieved their object on April 29.[1] The Congress not only demanded the liquidation of the Socialist Land Committee and the revision of all distribution, but after the fall of the Rada (which it welcomed) called for the election of a new legislature on a class franchise modelled directly on the Prussian. Germany, however, wished to prevent the restoration of over-large estates by creating 'a conservative class of prosperous peasants'. A State Agricultural Bank was to afford financial support to this new class, and a number of further laws was issued to round off what was called 'the re-enactment of Stolypin's land reform'. On July 15 agrarian committees were set up with the further purpose of creating a class interested in defending the independence of the Ukraine against Russia and against the small peasants and the landless elements in the population. At the same time Ludendorff's maxim that 'the Russian must still be made to feel the knout' was honoured by the enactment of laws on compulsory work on the land and forced labour in other fields, with the severest penalties against strikes and sabotage.[2] Therewith Germany achieved her immediate aim of changing the socialist structure of Ukrainian agriculture into one designed to deliver to Germany the harvests of the Black Earth Belt.

As early as April 18 Wiedfeldt proposed the formation of a

[1] Reschetar, op. cit., pp. 147 f.   [2] Id., pp. 175 f.

German–Ukrainian iron ore company on the Belgian model, to which Germany, with her foundries, would contribute most of the finished and half-finished products and the Ukraine, with its mines, more of the raw materials. The production of manganese was to be controlled through an analogous company. Here again the still small voice of German heavy industry was heard, as in Belgium. Carl Duisburg, Director-General of I.G.-Farben, Germany's biggest chemical concern, suggested forming an 'industrial and land company' to exploit the potentialities of Ukrainian industry through the channels of private enterprise; this was meant as a way of circumventing the state monopolies which the Reich Economic Office was devising for the east as well as the west. The participants in the company were to be the biggest and financially strongest representatives of Germany's heavy and electrical industries, the men who had headed Germany's industrial expansion before the war: heavy industry was represented by the Deutsch-Luxemburgische Bergwerks- und Hüttenaktiengesellschaft, the Fried. Krupp A.G., the Gelsenkirchener Bergwerks-A.G., the Gutehoffnungshütte of Oberhausen and the Phoenix A.G., the electrical industry by the two biggest firms in it, the A.E.G. and Siemens; the mining industry by the Harpener Bergbau A.G. and the Zeche Rheinpreussen; the chemical industry by I.G.-Farben; and the circle was completed by the Hapag and the Internationale Bohrgesellschaft in Erkelenz.

The fears of the private industrialists were not without foundation for the Reich Economic Office and the Economic Office for the Ukraine were already thinking that the best way of utilising the economic potential of the Ukraine would be through the foundation of an iron ore syndicate under the joint control of the Ukrainian state and the Reich. Stein, Wiedfeldt, Melchior, Mumm and Groener were for liquidating the industrial and mining companies which had previously been entirely or mainly owned by Entente capital and transferring state monopolies and mining rights to this new, German-controlled monopoly. As, however, in the agrarian question, Germany's efforts laboured under great difficulties, including internal insecurity often approximating to civil war, strikes and sabotage; Germany's own shortage of capital; opposition from the Austrians; and widespread mistrust among the population, enhanced by Germany's open support of reactionary elements.

In the long run everything would depend on whether Germany could solve the problem of the railways. On May 2 – the date of the switch in Germany's Ukrainian policy – Wiedfeldt asked Berlin what were the government's fundamental intentions. If it meant to make the Ukraine a German 'colony', complete control over the railways was essential. The policy afterwards followed by Wiedfeldt shows what the government's aims were. He and Melchior regulated the question of the railways, and the closely linked question of the banks, in a way calculated to make the Ukraine Germany's most valuable source of materials and trading partner. The gauge was to be altered and new lines built westward and southward to give the Ukraine a transport system with its centre inside the country itself. Millions were voted for these purposes. Here, too, the form was to be that of a private company, in which the German Reich was the biggest shareholder. The crucial question was finance. On May 11 Melchior asked the Reich Treasury for 'a single, comprehensive railway loan for the Ukraine', arguing that it would give Germany, once and for all, a 'powerful economic strategic position' which would 'assure her a lasting influence over the railway network of the Ukraine'.

The Treasury was unenthusiastic, Roedern thinking conditions in the Ukraine too uncertain. On the other hand von dem Bussche-Haddenhausen, the head of the Foreign Ministry's section on commercial policy, supported Melchior in a long memorandum which put his objectives in the general pattern of Germany's Eastern policy. The railway question was for him the real political means of securing Germany's influence far beyond the border states, not only in the European parts of the disintegrating Tsarist Empire—Finland, the Ukraine, the Caucasus and Rump Russia—but also in its Asiatic parts, Siberia and central Asia. This policy required not only loans, but also help in construction, delivery of materials and administrative and technical control; and Bussche proposed that the contractual and practical foundations for all this should be laid by creating suitable organisations and staffing them with the necessary personnel. While the railways had not been mentioned in the Brest negotiations, the question must be included in the new treaties to be concluded with the Ukraine and the Caucasian states in such fashion that in all these states, and everywhere in the east, 'whatever form the German participation took, it must be made clear to the world, the state in question being only a figurehead'. He realised that the German economy was at that moment strained to the limit by the war effort, so that it would be difficult to raise the required capital, material, managerial personnel and labour, but the question was one of 'productive investment', an enterprise 'of quite outstanding economic, political and strategic importance', so that 'every effort must be made to supply the means of achieving it'.

Germany's aims in the east were set forth even more specifically and crudely in another memorandum by Bussche, dated June 14,[1]

[1] *Ursachen*, II, pp. 202 f.

which also contained the political instructions for Mumm. Bussche wrote that the fundamental principle of Germany's Ukrainian policy was 'to press all pro-Russian, federalist tendencies', the perpetuation of the dismemberment of the Russian empire being the only means of preventing its recovery as a great power and of keeping both the Bolsheviks and Skoropadsky under control. For Germany's further aims: 'Russia's transport system, industry and entire economy must come into our hands. We must succeed in exploiting the east for ourselves. There is where we draw the interest on our war loans.'

Private interests made their voices heard in the railway question, as over the mines. The Disconto-Gesellschaft planned to secure a long-term influence over the Ukrainian transport system through a German–Ukrainian railway syndicate, in which its pre-war interests were revived. Salomonssohn, uncle of the Solmssen who represented the Disconto-Gesellschaft's oil interests in Rumania, succeeded in getting the support of other big banks for this plan and interesting the government in it. On May 28 Melchior and Wiedfeldt jointly advised that the railway interests should be financed, or at least the necessary loans arranged, through private channels. This could be done either through the old Russlandsyndikat – Mendelssohn, Bleichröder, Berliner Handelsgesellschaft and Disconto-Gesellschaft – or through a new group of underwriters, which should include the Deutsche Banks and Dresdner Bank, besides Max Warburg and the Disconto-Gesellschaft. A German–Ukrainian study group was set up, which produced plans for new lines from the Donetz via Krivoi Rog to Poland and Germany, and from Kiev to Odessa, thus giving further shape to the policy of the Foreign Ministry and the Economic Office of dissociating the Ukrainian network from that of Rump Russia. More and more of these private and state plans emerged during the summer, and even in October and November, in close connection with the still more extensive planning being carried out at the same time for the economic penetration of Russia.

The Germans took a similar interest in the Black Sea ports along Russia's southern coast. As early as March 28, 1918, when she had not yet occupied nearly all Russia's Black Sea ports, Germany had made an agreement with Austria-Hungary partitioning their spheres of interest; Austria was to get Mariopol, and Germany Nikolaev on the Bug, the nearby Cherson on the Dnieper (which were indispensable for the export of the Krivoi Rog iron), Sebastopol, Taganrog on the Azov, Rostov on the Don and Novorossisk on the south coast of the Kuban district – these last being well outside 'Ukrainian' territory. The reason given by the OHL for occupying Novorossisk, which they did only six months later, was that they had to seize two

Russian ships of war which had taken refuge there, but the move shows most clearly that the Ukraine itself had become only a bridge, a bridge to the northern Caucasus; the occupation of Rostov only makes this the plainer, for it cut Russia off both from the sea and from the Caucasus.

The Economic Office in Kiev was the headquarters for Germany's economic domination of the Ukraine. Created by Wiedfeldt to act as a sort of corporative commercial attaché for all economic planning, it was something quite new in German economic policy. It guaranteed Germany a permanent influence over the whole economic system, over the Ukraine's customs, tariffs, loans, foreign trading–in short, over its entire economic policy–and enabled her not only to observe, but also to intervene actively, for example, in the foundation of banks and the establishment of economic centres, information services and port installations. The threads from the Foreign Ministry, the Reich Economic Office and Treasury, the Ministry of War, the Department of War Materials, the Prussian Ministry of Public Works (railways, roads, inland waterways) and the Reichsbank all converged at this centre. Divided into fourteen departments, it was in a position to control the entire economic potential of the Ukraine, both directly and indirectly.

Skoropadsky had by now signed a new supplementary treaty, the counterpart of those planned for Poland, Lithuania and Courland, under which the Ukraine had agreed to Germany's military and economic demands, which were linked together by a political covering agreement. Thus in spite of the political uncertainty, the Ukraine seemed securely established as the 'corner-stone' of the south. But even this acquisition depended on the decision in the west.

Crimea, Don and Kuban: a colony for German settlers? A bridge to central Asia and India

In the Crimea a Tatar Republic had been proclaimed in the winter of 1917–18 but had been overthrown by Bolshevik forces in the early spring of 1918. When the German troops entered the Ukraine and advanced to the Black Sea coast, the intervention of the Russian fleet in the fighting round Cherson provided Germany with an excuse to occupy the Crimea, and in particular Sebastopol–Ludendorff called it 'smoking out the pirates' nest in Sebastopol'–and securing for herself the supplies and outlets of the Crimea. This operation involved Germany in fresh disputes, partly with Russia which rightly regarded this attack on a non-Ukrainian area as a a breach of Brest-Litovsk, and partly with Turkey who herself aspired to found a Turkish colony in the Crimea. Although Germany would have preferred (in view of Russia's case) to leave the occupation of the Crimea to non-German troops, she could not let either Ukrainians or Turks share in the operation, as either country would have used the excuse to 'claim' the Crimea for itself. At the end of March, moreover, the Crim Tatars had appealed to Turkey for help, and Enver Pasha had promised to send a division, or at least a regiment and officers to the Crimea. Germany opposed this move: she was not even prepared to allow Moslem troops who were ex-Russian subjects – a force of Volga Tatars from Kazan whom the former Russian General Sulkiewicz had collected on the Rumanian frontier – to take part in the Crimean opertions. As Bussche put it, she must see to it that after the Ukraine had been created, 'a branch of the Russian Soviet government did not set itself up on our southern frontier, and the Crimea remain Great Russian'. Kühlmann expressed himself with equal reserve to Turkey: even should she take part in the military operations 'she was not to use this as a pretext for political demands – against us'. After Germany had occupied the Crimea, a decision on its political future became still more urgent. The Tatar parliament had reconstituted itself and applied directly to Germany with demonstrations and petitions. As, however, only 13·5 per cent of the 1,500,000 inhabitants of the Crimea were Mohammedans, it was clear that a Tatar republic could not maintain itself there except as a Turkish satellite. This the German government did not wish, and it tried to enlarge the basis of the regime in the Crimea by including in it Ukrainians and Germans. Germany meant first to secure her own economic interests and those of the local Germans; later, the Crimea might perhaps be given to the Ukraine, but only, as Kühlmann put it (in a letter to Hertling), 'as reward for good behavior and fulfilment of their obligations'.

On May 30 the Tatar parliament dissolved itself. A coalition government was formed, in which there were now only two Tatars: Sulkiewicz, who later became its head, and Djafer Seidamet, the Foreign Minister, who was now the only man to keep up the contact with Turkey, mistrustfully watched by the Germans. The Foreign Ministry had thus attained its immediate aim here also, although consideration for the Soviets and the treaty prevented it from formally recognising the government which was in practice dependent on the German army. There were already many eastern delegations in Berlin: Georgians, Armenians, Prince Tundutoff from the Kalmuks of south-eastern Russia, and Osman Tokumbet,[1] Vice-President of the Military Council of Russian Mohammedans. These were joined in August by a delegation from the Crimean government in

[1] Groener, op. cit., p. 402.

THE "NEW ORDER" IN THE EAST

The Central Powers

Territories of direct German influence: Kurland;
Lithuania (planned for annexation); Poland

Territories of economic and administrative
dependency

Territories of closest economic involvement
with Germany

Projected Tartaric Republic (area of German settlements)

Territories of political and economic connection
with Germany

Project of a Transcaucasian Republic,
closely connected with the Central Powers

Spheres of influence and raw material bases
demanded by Germany

Direction of further German expansion

Front Line, March 1918

Main transit routes

Mineral deposits

Industries

SWEDEN

WHITE SEA

Finland

Petrozavodsk

BALTIC
SEA

Helsinki

Reval

Norwa

Estonia

St. Petersburg

Dorpat

Livonia

Courland

Mitau

Riga

Lithuania

Dünaburg

GERMANY

Wilno

Polotsk

Vitebsk

Volga

Moscow

Warsaw

Poland

Lake Vygonovskoye

Shlobin

Prużany

Tula

Brest Litovsk

Tarnogrod

Volhynia

Orel

Lemberg (Lwow)

Chernigov

Rylsk

Kursk

AUSTRIA
HUNGARY

Podolia

Kiev

Byelgorod

Bobrov

Ukraine

Kharkov

Voronezh

Bessarabia

Poltava

Krivoi-rog

Ekaterinoslav

Province of
the Don Cossaks

Tsaritsyn (Stalingrad)

Odessa

Nikolaev

Cherson

Mariupol

Taganrog

Tauris

Navocherkassk

Rostov

Astrakhan

RUMANIA

Bucharest

Crimea

Kuban

Sebastopol

Novorossisk

Danube

BULGARIA

BLACK SEA

CASPIAN

Vladikavkaz

Constanța

Constantinople

Poti

Batum

Chiatura

Georgia

Tiflis

SEA

Baku

Ardahan

Alexandropol

Kars

Armenia

TURKISH EMPIRE

Aras

Julfa

PERSIA

Konya

Mosul

Alexandretta

Cyprus

Bagdad

MEDITERRANEAN SEA

Miles

0   100   200   300   400

which the leading role was taken by a Russian landed magnate, Count Tadistchev.

The Crimean problem was complicated by the private policy followed by Ludendorff, who first wanted the Crimea made into a German colony and then, when even he thought a German colony would be too isolated, wanted a German-dominated state of Crimea-Tauris to be attached to the Ukraine in a relationship similar to that of Bavaria to Prussia. In this state all the colonists of German stock were to be assembled from the whole of Russia – Volhynia, the Volga, the Caucasus, Siberia, etc. – and it might possibly be enlarged to include the three Bessarabian circles of Bender, Akkermann and Ismael, unless their German colonists were moved too. The colonisation specialists von Lindequist (a retired Secretary of State of the Reich Colonial Office) and Winkler (a Protestant clergyman and spokesman for the Black Sea Germans) propagated these ideas among the German colonists, with the support of the OHL and with such success as to produce among them an excited belief that the areas inhabited by them in the Ukraine and the Crimea were going to be 'attached to the German Reich' with colonial status. This development disquieted Mumm, who wrote to Kühlmann and Hertling warning them that 'with all understanding for the ethnic point of view', the idea of a Crimean colony was 'incompatible with our policy of an independent Ukraine in southern Russia, detached from Great Russia and friendly to ourselves'. The Ukraine was already deeply disquieted by what was going on, and if the colony was established, it would inevitably 'be driven back into the arms of Great Russia'.

Hertling and Kühlmann agreed with Mumm. Ludendorff modified his plans after a meeting with Lindequist, but still insisted on the essentials: if there could be no colony, then at least he hoped 'so to strengthen the German element in southern Russia' by collecting the colonists in one area as to make possible the establishment of a 'polity' of Crim-Tauris, attached to the Ukraine, yet 'under predominantly German influence'. The movement into the Ukraine and the repatriation into the Reich and its '*newly acquired* territories' – 'Lorraine, the Polish Frontier Strip, Lithuania, the Baltic' – should be organised and supervised by the state. Besides the Russian Germans – in so far as these were not concentrated in the state of Crim-Tauris – he wanted the overseas Germans brought back to Germany. One of Ludendorff's motives was to get colonists for the new areas which Germany was to acquire, but he was still more interested in securing replacements for the manpower of his army. He wanted recognition of German citizenship for the colonists, and the admission of some 80,000 Mennonites, made conditional on 'service with the armed forces'.

Against these plans Bussche maintained the Foreign Ministry's policy of first keeping a free hand and later 'trying to get the Crimea gradually passed to the Ukraine'. The Foreign Ministry's policy was, however, no less far-reaching in substance than Ludendorff's, as Kühlmann himself made clear. 'What must guide us,' he said, 'must not be sentiment, but Germany's interests'; and those interests would be endangered by the establishment of a German colony in Crim-Tauris. Whether the Ukraine survived or not made no difference; neither independent Ukraine nor Russia could tolerate such a state. It would also be intolerable to Turkey, to whom Germany had just refused permission to found a Turkish colony in the Crimea. Germany could protect the colonists only through such influence as she could exercise in Russia and her successor states, and the German colonists could serve Germany's interests best 'if they can remain scattered over all Russia working everywhere as political and economic factors in our favour'. As to the 'preservation of their national character' and 'maintenance of their Germandom', Germany must create guarantees in the different parts of the old Russia and be strong enough to see them observed.

Even more important than the Crimea, which in spite of the supplementary treaties remained *de facto* in Germany's hands, were undoubtedly the districts of the Ukraine, the Don and the Kuban.[1] Germany had cut Russia off from her Black Sea ports and from the Caucasus, partly by direct occupation of certain areas and partly by establishing relations with the Don Cossack Republic, under a certain Hetman Krassnov. The Don Cossacks, who were concentrated in the area of Novocherkassk, east of Rostov, were supplied by the OHL with arms and considerable sums of money.[2] The Foreign Ministry was not formally informed of this activity and was thus able to deny to the Soviet ambassador that it had recognised *de facto* and was supporting a pronouncedly anti-Soviet state. Germany thought it necessary to give this support, not least in order to prevent the Entente from gaining influence over these anti-Soviet groups, as it had over Siberian, and setting up a new front against Germany with the 'Czechoslovaks'. The OHL, however, for a time had great hopes of forging these 'states' into a 'Federation of the South-East',

[1] The frontier proposed by Ludendorff ran from Bataisk (south of Rostov)–Don–Donetz–Kalitva (on the Upper Don), Valuiki (railway junction on the lines from Kharkov to Voronezh and Saratov).

[2] Ludendorff sent 15 million roubles and arms to the Don Cossacks under the Ataman Krassnov, with whom General Alexeyev was staying. Mumm described Ludendorff as 'chasing after the phantom of an anti-Slav bloc in the south-east'.

extending from the Crimea and the Ukraine to the Caucasus. The Reich Economic Office and the departmental ministries had even more extensive plans for exploiting the Don and Kuban areas economically as German satellites, and for reaching beyond them to Transcaucasia.

The Austrians saw very clearly what the Germans were aiming at. Arz wrote in June, 1918:

> The Germans pursued a definite economic aim in the Ukraine. They want . . . to keep permanently in their own hands the surest road to Mesopotamia and Arabia, to Baku and Persia, which the advance into the Ukraine has played into their hands. To this end the Germans . . . mean to keep the Crimea under one form or another . . . as a protectorate, a colony, or in some other form.

To make full use of this road the Germans needed also ownership or control of the main railway crossing it, and – since it was impossible to supply that railway with coal from Germany – possession of the chief mines of the Don basin. They would incidentally use the Ukraine as their granary, selling their manufactured products to the Ukraine in return. Arz actually wrote – and he said expressly that he was quoting Groener – that 'so long as England cuts Germany off from the west, Germany's chief interests must lead her to India via the Ukraine and the Crimea'.

These observations are confirmed by a report by the Reich Interior Office which discussed the possibilities of air traffic in the south-east and suggested Odessa as a nodal point for Germany's future traffic to the Caucasus and to the Balkans, Egypt and Constantinople either via the Danubian Monarchy or via Poland and the Ukraine.

South Russia was thus becoming the bridge to Georgia, central Asia and India.

Germany and Turkey:
the struggle for control of the Caucasus

Transcaucasia had been an object of Germany's policy of promoting revolution since the beginning of the war.[1] Germany had found a suitable instrument for her policy in the Georgian Committee, founded by émigrés in Berlin. Prince Machabelli, Tseretelli and the brothers Leo and George Kereselidce were lavishly subsidised. Nevertheless, in spite of supplies of money and arms, the revolution and proclamation of solidarity with the Central Powers did not materialise, because, contrary to the hopes of the émigrés, what the mass of the population, both nationalists and Menshevik Social-

[1] See above, pp. 134 ff.

ists, hoped for from the fall of the Tsarist regime was nothing more than federal status for Transcaucasia within a Russian republic.

When the March revolution came, the administration of the country was taken over by a 'Special Transcaucasian Committee' composed of the Caucasian members of the Duma, which however did not break off connections with Petersburg, especially since the Russian front remained intact in the Caucasus up to October. Chenkelli, the leading personality among the Georgian Mensheviks, succeeded in introducing the Menshevik programme in Georgia; in Armenia and Mohammedan Azerbaijan, on the other hand, the landlords, clergy and bureaucracy were able to maintain their old positions in the state. The first attempts to bring into being a unified and uniform Transcaucasia had thus broken down at the outset. Even the October revolution failed to bring about a radical breach with Russia. The connection became less intimate, but only the small Bolshevik Party of Georgia recognised the Lenin–Trotsky government; a new 'Transcaucasian Commissariat' was established and took over the administration, but 'only pending the convocation of the All-Russian Constituent Assembly'. It was only when the Caucasus front collapsed and the constituent assembly was dissolved on January 19, 1918 that Chenkelli, who had refused to send a peace delegation to Brest-Litovsk, found himself driven into an independent policy, which he hoped to conduct in co-operation with the Ukraine and the 'League of the South-East' of the Don.

Meanwhile, however, all Transcaucasia had become an object of both Turkish and German war aims. What Turkey wanted was to isolate Transcaucasia through a separate peace treaty, if necessary imposed by force of arms, whereas Germany's aim was to prevent the establishment of a Turkish sphere of influence, so as 'not to allow access to Central Asia and Persia to lie exclusively in Turkish hands'. Pan-Turanian ideas and Enver's plans clashed with Germany's political and economic purposes. The situation was complicated by internal differences between civilians and military in Germany; the OHL supported Turkey's ambitions with the intention of building up a front in Persia, while the Foreign Ministry was strongly opposed to any Turkish expansion, both on account of the complications with Russia and in view of Germany's interests in the Caucasus.

When Chenkelli showed no signs of agreeing to Germany's wishes, Germany took advantage of the presence at Brest-Litovsk of the Turkish Minister of War, Talaat Pasha, to arange a meeting between him and Machabelli in Warsaw. Machabelli, whose programme was really that of the Germans, asked Turkey to respect the integrity of Georgia, and Talaat Pasha agreed, promising not to occupy either

Batum or Adzhara and not to intervene in Transcaucasia's internal affairs. This promise, however, was only an empty one, as became apparent when Talaat on the one hand refused to initial the minutes of the Warsaw meeting, and on the other Germany began to give Machabelli active support and openly to disavow Turkey's aims. On February 12 the Turks broke the armistice and began an advance to 'liberate' and 'protect the Mohammedan populations of the frontier districts'. The differences between Germany and Turkey became acute. Rather than let the negotiations in Bucharest break down over the Dobruja and Maritsa questions, Germany was prepared to allow the three provinces of Kars, Ardahan and Batum (its southern half, not including the harbour) to be 'placed at Turkey's disposal', but rejected uncompromisingly all Turkey's further proposals, to advance north-eastward from Trebizond and Erzerum and eventually annex Achalzich and Achalkali (on the main Baku–Batum line not far from Tiflis) north of the '1878' frontier.

> Before the war, wrote the Foreign Ministry in a memorandum on German policy towards Turkey and in the Caucasus, we went to great pains, against Russia's resistance, to clear ourselves a path to Persia across Transcaucasia, and we have spent millions on creating a pro-German Caucasian state to give us a bridge to Central Asia.

All this work would be labour lost if the Turks took Transcaucasia; the immediate aim must therefore be to create a Georgia dependent on Germany and an independent Transcaucasia. Should, however, political considerations make it unavoidable to allow Turkey some degree of influence over Transcaucasia, this concession must be subject to conditions, of which the first was unlimited access for Germany to the economic systems of the Caucasian states. There must be an independent Georgian state to include the port of Batum; a free port for Germany in Batum, German law in all trading centres, German administration of all railways, especially the main lines between Batum and Baku and between Tiflis and Djulfa, a monopoly of railway construction, a regulation of the oil question similar to that in Rumania, and duty-free transit. This programme would have left the districts falling to Turkey as completely in the hands of German interests as those becoming nominally independent.

When the Turks began their advance, the Georgians, who hoped to succeed in retaining Kars, Ardahan and Batum, asked for another armistice and opened peace negotiations, which took place in Trebizond.[1] While these were proceeding, the Turks succeeded in

---

[1] See on this Joseph Pomiankowski, *Der Zusammenbruch des ottomanischen Reiches* (Zürich, Leipzig, Vienna, 1928), pp. 362 ff.

winning Azerbaijan to their side, thus isolating the Georgians and Armenians. The Georgians, who had previously rejected Macha-belli's policy, now accepted it, and appealed publicly to Germany to mediate and guarantee a settlement between Turkey and Caucasia. On March 25 the Sejm in Tiflis confirmed this turn of policy and invested Chenkelli with extraordinary plenipotentiary powers to conduct the peace negotiations. Turkey insisted on recognition of the Brest-Litovsk peace; Chenkelli submitted but the Sejm did not. In a short campaign (March 25–April 15) Turkey occupied the stra-tegic key-points south of the Caucasus. Chenkelli, who had been anxious to avoid war and was now working with another 'friend of Germany', Ramishvilli, was given dictatorial powers. He formed a new government on April 22; on the same day the formation of the democratic-federal Transcaucasian Republic of Georgia, Armenia and Azerbaijan was proclaimed.

Meanwhile, however, the Turks' new advance had alarmed the Germans; it was plain that the Protocol of Warsaw provided no de-fence against Turkey's ambitions. On April 18 Helfferich asked Kühlmann for a definitive statement of Germany's attitude in the Caucasus. He drew attention to Germany's great interests in the manganese deposits of Chiaturi and to the possibility of further finds of copper and oil, and polemicised on strategic grounds against the policy of the OHL and its representative on the Turkish general staff, Seckt, of leaving Caucasia to Turkey. This policy, he said, would de-prive Germany of any possibility of influencing the economic de-velopment of Caucasia. The possession of the Batum–Baku line, which Seckt seemed prepared to cede to the Turks, was decisive for the fate of Transcaucasia. Its ores, oil, cotton, wool – all raw ma-terials needed by the German factories – would simply fall into Tur-key's lap. This memorandum was reinforced by another, long report by a doctor called Dieckmann who had been a prisoner of war in Russia. Dieckmann wrote that the Georgians were strongly pro-German. There were 60,000 Germans near Tiflis, on whom a Ger-man policy could be built up. The cutting of Caucasia's life-line from Baku to Batum was the surest way, not only to 'block the road to rich cotton-lands like Turkmenia and northern Persia', but also to damage the export of oil and mineral ores. Helfferich asked Kühl-mann to convoke a big inter-departmental conference to discuss the whole problem of Transcaucasia, and this was arranged for April 22; but before it met, the Foreign Ministry sent instructions to the Ger-man ambassador in Constantinople to call attention to Germany's interest in Batum as an export port for oil and mineral ores. 'There are,' it wrote, 'political and economic reasons for not wishing the

Turks to establish themselves permanently in Batum and on the routes leading to the Transcaucasian oil and mineral fields, and to Central Asia and Persia.'

The conference was held on April 22, the day of the proclamation of independence of the Federated Transcaucasian Republic. All ministries were represented, and it was agreed that the Foreign Ministry should use every means to secure the speedy recognition of the Transcaucasian Republic, not only by the Central Powers, but also by Rump Russia. The conference also accepted Helfferich's economic policy. The interrupted Trebizond negotiations were being re-opened in Batum, and the conference decided that a representative of the OHL should be sent there as an observer, who was to try to get Batum, the line thence to Baku, and with it Georgia, Armenia and Azerbaijan drawn into the German sphere of influence, without offending the Turks. Contact was to be made with the new Georgian government through representatives of the Georgian delegation in Berlin; it was hoped to secure a dominating influence over the railway by accepting it as security for a loan, for which the Georgians had asked.

On April 26 von dem Bussche drew up a long memorandum for the Emperor, outlining the principles of German policy in the Caucasus. Once again the continuity of Germany's war aims since 1914 is striking. Germany, wrote von dem Bussche, had since the beginning of the war done everything in her power to bring into being in the area between Russia, Persia and Turkey – the gate to central Asia – a state favourable to herself, comprising the Georgians, the Tatars and the mountain peoples of the northern Caucasus; the leading role in this state was to go to the Georgians, who were in the closest touch with Germany. A tripartite federal state of Georgia, Armenia and Azerbaijan had now in fact been formed, while the mountaineers of the north had formed their own state in Vladikavkaz and would attach themselves to the federation which had come into being between the Caucasus and the Don. Von dem Bussche sharply criticised the attempt made by the Turks in Trebizond to extend their own authority to the whole Caucasus, or at least the southern half of it up to Baku. In any case, he said, Batum, whose population was Georgian and Christian and which was the port of Georgia, must be kept out of Turkish hands. Friendly relations must be established with the Transcaucasian state, 'which must be brought as far as possible under our economic and political influence'. The cause of Georgia was the cause of Germany. 'And what applies to Batum, applies to the whole hinterland of Transcaucasia.'

On April 29 the Bavarian von Lossow, of the general staff, was empowered to conclude the preliminaries of a peace between the German Reich and the government of Transcaucasia. This meant that the OHL, too, had dropped its earlier standpoint, for von Lossow's views were the exact opposite of Seckt's. He was an uncompromising advocate of German supremacy in the Caucasus and was prepared to oppose Turkey's plans flatly.

When the peace negotiations re-opened in Batum on May 11, Germany's position was difficult. Turkey was now asking for the 1828 frontier, while Chenkelli stood for the integrity of Transcaucasia. The Germans had hoped[1] that if they made the concession of not concluding a treaty of alliance with the Transcaucasian Republic, Turkey would consent to a compromise peace which allowed her annexations on the Brest basis and left Germany the economic domination over Transcaucasia, Batum being internationalised. They asked Turkey to consent to the transfer of the ownership of the railway and port of Batum to a private German–Turkish–Transcaucasian company. The exploitation of Transcaucasia's sub-surface resources was to go to a state monopoly in which Germany and Transcaucasia would share equally. Mining companies owned by Entente capital were, as in the Ukraine, to be liquidated. Turkey did not accept these proposals; she was deeply offended by Germany's intervention in the Caucasus and was not to be pacified by Germany's offer to let her occupy the Alexandropol–Djulfa line.

It was necessary to reach a decision quickly. The Turks refused to let themselves be diverted towards Baghdad and Teheran – as Ludendorff had hoped, when the subject was discussed at Spa on May 11 – but resumed their advance on the 15th and occupied the Alexandropol–Djulfa line, thus establishing themselves in 'the heart of Armenia'. Chenkelli was now entirely dependent on Germany's help. On the 15th von Lossow intervened in the negotiations, threatening to leave Batum if the German government accepted Turkey's demands in disregard of all his warnings; for this, he said, would be tantamount to 'totally abandoning the Caucasus and handing it over to the Turks lock, stock and barrel'. Ludendorff supported him entirely. A peace on the Brest basis had now become impossible. Turkey's and Germany's aims were mutually exclusive, and as Turkey's pan-Islamic propaganda had succeeded in drawing Azerbaijan largely into her camp, nothing remained for Germany but to give up the larger aim and at least keep a local foothold in

[1] G. Jäschke, 'Der Turanismus der Jungtürken', in *Die Welt des Islams*, Vol. 23, No. 1/2, p. 311.

Georgia. This she secured when Chenkelli told Lossow on May 15 that

under certain circumstances Georgia would apply to the German government for incorporation in the German Reich, either as a federal state under a German prince, or in a relationship like that of a British dominion under a German viceroy.

If, however, Germany was more interested in the continuance of the federation, she must intervene with Turkey immediately and emphatically. He assumed that Armenia would follow the example of Georgia, and that even the Tatars 'would try to achieve union with Germany'. Thus the wider solution could still be salvaged, even if the Federal Transcaucasian Republic had disintegrated. Lossow was for trying this possibility, as was the Emperor (very strongly); Kühlmann agreed on the undesirability of letting Turkey have Transcaucasia and thought that the best solution might be to conclude peace and an alliance quickly, and then to recognise Georgia. Germany could then negotiate separately with Georgia and would thus not lose her *point d'appui* in the Caucasus.

Meanwhile, Lossow had already, as instructed, opened separate negotiations with Haidar Bammatoff, president of the North Caucasian delegation. Although both the German government and the German embassy in Constantinople had qualms about the legality of the proposal, Lossow recommended recognising North Caucasia as an independent state and thus creating a *fait accompli* before anybody had had a chance to protest. He argued that if Germany wanted to secure North Caucasia's enormous wealth of oil, minerals and cereals, she must take advantage of the elemental urge of the pent-up forces in the area. Under no circumstances must North Caucasia be allowed to re-unite with Russia, in spite of the open frontier to the north and in spite of the loss to Rump Russia which would be far heavier for Russia than the loss of Transcaucasia. In spite of the mountain frontier, the two slopes of the Caucasus were, economically, mutually dependent.

As political means of securing this end, Lossow proposed that a 'politically skilful general', and, if possible, two divisions, should be sent to Novorossisk and Tuapse. The one way of ensuring the continued existence of the North Caucasian state was, he said – and Bammatoff expressly agreed with him – to attach it closely to the German state, not by an ordinary alliance, but by a close union: 'unity of government on the highest level, of foreign policy, of currency, customs area, army and navy'.

We could attach to ourselves a rich economic area with great resources of oil, minerals and raw materials which otherwise can be obtained only from overseas countries. All this with secure communications with Germany across the Black Sea. It is clear that attachment of the Caucasian state to the German Reich, in one form or another, would provide a complete solution for all the difficulties which have arisen during the war over Turkey's, Austria's and Bulgaria's participation. Here is a great, rich land for the taking, an opportunity which might not recur for hundreds of years. The question is vast, the time for decision short.

Lossow's private policy shows most vividly how Germany's power claims were expanding.

Georgia a German protectorate: understanding with Turkey and Russia

Under the impact of the Turkish advance, the Tatar and Armenian provinces proclaimed their secession from the federation on May 22. The next day Georgia proclaimed its independence and asked Germany to take the country under its protection. Armenia had appealed to Lossow on the 20th for help 'in its desperate situation'. When on the 23rd Turkey resumed her northward advance, without issuing an ultimatum, the Armenians repeated their 'promise' 'to remain eternally true to Germany' and begged the Emperor to extend them defence and formal protection.

The northern Caucasus, threatened by a Bolshevik offensive, also asked to join Germany. Lossow begged for at least a weak division and some men-of-war to protect Germany's interests and Germany's prestige. There were, however, no military forces available, so that Germany had no other resource than that of political intervention. Hertling protested against Turkey's advance in very strong and sharp language; Ludendorff agreeing, he informed Turkey that he disapproved of her military procedure, announced that Germany had recognised Georgia *de facto* and said that she was keeping a completely free hand with respect to all further developments in the Caucasus. Ludendorff further demanded that the operations be brought to a halt.

The Batum negotiations had, however, broken down. Lossow decided to go to Berlin and force a decision on the future of the Caucasian states. He left for Poti, taking with him Chenkelli, as the plenipotentiary representative of Georgia, an Armenian similarly accredited, and Prince Tundutoff, representing the Kalmuks. Before reaching Constanta he wirelessed that he had concluded a series of treaties with the Georgian government on the basis of the Brest treaty; these 'would bring Georgia's railways and ports, her natural resources and her raw materials and her shipping entirely under

German influence and introduce the German currency as the official medium of exchange'. Germany's special envoy to Tiflis, von Wesendonck, who was returning to Berlin by the same boat, agreed with Lossow's estimate of the situation. He too thought that Berlin's instructions for Batum had been calculated to eliminate Turkey and give Germany a firm foothold in the east, and would have enabled her to develop political activities in Persia, central Asia and the Russian lands between the Ukraine and the Urals. Domination of the Caucasus should have been the keystone of Germany's Asiatic policy. With Baku had been lost 'the second largest naphtha field in the world', with the Mugan steppe 'limitless cotton plantations, capable of great development', and finally, the numerous German colonists settled in the Tatar steppes had also been lost. He ended his report:

> What Germany has lost in Caucasia in the last few weeks . . . can be built up again from the base of Georgia (which has been saved from the 'wreck') and Germany's predominance in these politically and economically important districts can yet be re-established in spite of all difficulties.

During this period Berlin's mounting difficulties with Turkey and the grave warnings which she was receiving from Bernstorff, her new ambassador in Constantinople, had been leading her to treat the question of Georgia and Transylvania increasingly from the angle of Germany's relations with Turkey and Russia, and to link Georgia's aims with the questions of Livonia and Estonia, and of the Dobruja, much more closely than her representatives in Batum had done. This attitude changed when Lossow and Wesendonck arrived in Berlin on June 3. A conference was immediately convoked in the Imperial Chancellery, and Lossow was again able to paint a convincing picture of the enormous economic value of the Caucasus and to stigmatise Turkey's policy as 'imperialism' directed against Germany and the settlement with her as 'second-rate'. Kühlmann, without discussing Lossow's preliminary treaties in detail, accepted his main thesis and defined Germany's new political tactics. She must steer between 'the Scylla of a breach with Russia and the Charybdis of a breach with Turkey', and her first task must be to secure Great Russia's consent to the secession of Georgia. Lossow himself suggested the basis for a compromise with Turkey: the Mohammedan and Tatar lands should be left to Turkey 'at least in political and religious respects', while Georgia and Armenia, as Christian countries, must come under German protection, 'but we must insist everywhere on economic participation'.

The next day, June 4, there was an even larger conference in the

Foreign Ministry, at which the OHL was represented by Barten-werffer, the Reich Economic Office by Stein, Flach and others, the Foreign Ministry by Kühlmann, Rosenberg, Göppert and Wesendonck; also present was Colonel Kress von Kressenstein, who was to go to Georgia. Tactics having been unanimously agreed the day before, the discussions were chiefly concerned with the preliminary agreements concluded at Poti between Lossow, Chenkelli and Ramishvilli. Referring to the treaty of Brest-Litovsk, Kühlmann repeated Hertling's sharp disapproval of Turkey for having concluded a separate peace with Caucasia. He said that Germany no longer regarded herself as bound unconditionally by her promise to Turkey. Any further advance by the Turks towards Baku must be prevented in the interests of Germany's relations with Russia. He recommended using a velvet glove in dealing with Turkey but trying to induce Russia to give up Georgia; the other political formations in the Caucasus were still so nebulous that it was unnecessary to give them *de facto* recognition. The recognition of Georgia was not, however, dependent on Russia's consent. 'We have expressly refrained from accepting the thesis that the consent of the metropolitan country is necessary for the secession of a border state.' The recognition would be granted 'when the situation allows it, even should Russia protest'. Kühlmann thereby identified himself with Germany's pan-Caucasian aspirations, on the assumption of course that a favourable decision would be reached in the east and that Germany would then no longer need to take into account the still precarious nature of her relationships with Russia and Turkey.

How essentially Germany regarded the limitation of her field of interest to Georgia as merely temporary is again shown by a long memorandum which Bussche thought it wise to draw up in view of reports from Bernstorff on plans for a confederation for a so-called North Caucasian Republic.

Now that the Transcaucasian Federation has broken up, wrote Bussche, the idea of partitioning Transcaucasia into a Georgian–Armenian and a Tatar half is certainly our only hope of saving at least something. It is, however, only really valuable for us to establish ourselves in Georgia and Armenia if we still keep in view the plan of re-uniting *all* Transcaucasia in the future and, if possible, attaching the mountain peoples to it.

Only 'in a federal Transcaucasian state under *German* influence [italics in the original] would it be possible to acquire complete influence over the economic resources of the country: manganese and iron ore, oil, cotton plantations, wool and agricultural products of every kind – paper agreements do not guarantee vital interests'.

This document indicated clearly the position of the Foreign Ministry. Germany was not giving up her Eastern policy; on the contrary, the Reich Economic Office strongly criticised the preliminary treaty for only making sure of 50 per cent of the prospecting for manganese, although 75 per cent of the licenses were already in private German hands – a view which Ludendorff endorsed on June 28. As an *ad hoc* measure it was decided to send out Kress von Kressenstein.

The Emperor himself, who received Lossow's report in the royal train, was 'quite carried away' by his plans and agreed emphatically with his proposals that Georgia 'should be attached to the Reich in one form or another' and an army raised there. His Majesty recommended treating the Caucasian question in such fashion as 'to leave all possibilities open' and emphasised at the same time 'how important it would be, politically and economically, if we succeeded in getting Transcaucasia under our influence . . . as a bridge to Central Asia and a threat to England's position in India.'

On June 8 the OHL announced its agreement with the aims settled at the conferences. It ordered Turkey, in the name of the Supreme War Command, to withdraw her troops from the Caucasus (except the three provinces given to Turkey under the Brest treaty) and to concentrate her forces on the Mesopotamian front. The OHL's sudden activity went further still; without waiting for Kress's reports. Ludendorff pressed for recognition of Georgia and the speedy conclusion of a peace treaty in Berlin. As in Finland, so in Georgia he wanted to supplement Germany's own weak forces by raising a local army and then take the Georgian state under Germany's official protection, thereby 'making sure of the raw materials of the Caucasian areas'. The OHL had already begun delimiting the recruiting areas in the Caucasus, sent a detachment of its air force to Poti, and pressed for exact delimitation of the areas occupied by Turkey.

In further negotiations, which were meant to result in the recognition and reorganisation of the Georgian state and the establishment of its relations with Germany, the policy of the Foreign Ministry emerged ever more plainly as representing the kernel of Germany's policy towards the future of the Caucasus: Georgia, as a state, was to be kept as nearly intact as possible and attached to Germany through a military convention and economic alliances. The economic treaty was to be reinforced by three other agreements. A group of interested enterprises headed by the Disconto-Gesellschaft would create a Georgian currency and at the same time raise the necessary loan, while a manganese export company would assure Germany's ore supplies and finally a railway company would guarantee the extra transport and shipment in Poti. The financial agreement would itself be buttressed by securities giving Germany preferential rights of participation in Georgia's railways, telegraphs, telephones and wireless stations, so bringing the country's entire communications under German control.

Even the set-back on the western front in July, 1918 hardly weakened Germany's determination to expand, for the shortage of oil had made possession of the Baku oilfields 'an ever more vital question', as Ludendorff said. The struggle for the occupation of Baku again caused a diversion of councils. The Foreign Ministry's view was governed, not only by consideration of the effects in Russia, but above all by the situation in the northern Caucasus. But if Turkey continued her advance towards Daghestan, there was a danger that she might establish herself there and oust Germany from the position which she was trying so hard to establish. In view of such possibilities, Bernstorff warned Berlin not to overdo its Georgian and Armenian policy; in his view, Lossow had already gone too far in Batum. He advised Bussche to confine his demands exclusively to economic safeguards and to refrain from any political activity such as would offend Turkey. 'This,' he wrote, 'is really a typical case of what Bismarck called playing Pericles outside the political sphere which God had assigned to us!' Germany should confine herself to mediating between Turkey and Russia and secure her economic interests by impartial action. But these words were drowned in the chorus, now increasingly reinforced by private interested sections of German industry, which was clamouring for complete domination of the Caucasus zone.

Baku was taken not by the Turks, but by the British. Germany needed the oil imperatively. Ludendorff therefore demanded on August 18 that Russia should be asked to agree to the expulsion of the British by German and Turkish troops, and to the occupation of Baku. 'During' the occupation Germany would have to be in control, and also in charge of the oil-wells and transport. The ownership would remain Russian, and Russia would get a share of the oil. On September 10, after the conclusion of the supplementary treaties with Russia, Ludendorff issued orders for the attack on Baku, to be carried out if possible with German troops only. Baku was in fact occupied with the help of some Russian units and a cavalry brigade newly brought up from the Ukraine. On September 23 Ludendorff asked for specialists to be sent at once to get production going again. But the end was already at hand. On September 30 Bulgaria concluded an armistice. Germany was no longer able to use the Baku oil.

Before this, however, the idea of a Bulgaro-Turkish deal over the

Dobruja and the Caucasus had come up once more. Bulgaria was in haste to create a *fait accompli* and told Germany[1] that, if the Turks would renounce their rights in the Dobruja and all claims in Thrace, she would put her signature to any agreement concluded by Germany with Turkey over the Caucasus question. Germany had this card in her hand when Talaat Pasha arrived in Berlin at the end of September.

When the negotiations began, Turkey at first expressed strong displeasure at Germany's supplementary treaty with Russia, because it recognised the independence of Germany's protectorate without mentioning Armenia and Azerbaijan. After difficult negotiations a secret treaty was concluded with Talaat Pasha. Turkey declared that she recognised the three republics of Azerbaijan, Armenia and Georgia. Germany recognised only Georgia but would establish *de facto* relations with the other two by sending consular representatives to them. Should Turkey's recognition of the three states result in complications between her and Russia, Germany would do everything in her power to avert a conflict and would even try to bring about an understanding between Russia and Turkey. Turkey promised to withdraw her troops from Armenia and Azerbaijan forthwith.

Thus after her reverses in the west at the end of the war Germany was trying to reach agreement with both Russia (Bernstorff, for example, thought that this would help her to secure a good peace) and Turkey by moderating her own aims and granting advantages to the other party. In both cases, however, she held fast to the core of her position: Georgia, whose legal status was now assured, and Estonia and Livonia, in the supplementary treaty with Russia concluded at the same time. The Don country and the Caucasus outside Georgia were abandoned, but not the essential war aims.

---

[1] Koluchev, the Bulgarian minister in Constantinople, came to Berlin to deliver this message.

21

GERMANY BETWEEN WHITES AND REDS

POLICY TOWARDS RUMP RUSSIA

In Brest-Litovsk Germany had succeeded in implementing her great border states programme of August, 1914, and thereafter she had carried on her policy of 'crumbling' the Russian Empire in Karelia, the Ukraine, the Crimea, the Don, the Kuban, and the Caucasus, causing it to disintegrate from Finland to the Black Sea, from Lapland to Baku. Her remaining problem in the east–and it became more urgent with the development of her South-eastern policy–was what was to happen to what was left of Russia.

The great plan for the economic penetration of Russia

So dynamic was Germany's aims policy in the east, that after the early summer of 1918, she was both pushing forward beyond the Ukraine to Transcaucasia and at the same time trying to draw what was left of Russia, now generally called 'Great Russia', into her power sphere. Preventing the formation of a new second front in Russia against the Central Powers was only a surface consideration. Germany's deeper intention was to hold Rump Russia, whether it was red or white, under her own lasting control. The aims of political domination and economic penetration are so closely interwoven in Germany's Russian policy that it is difficult to say definitely which really came first.

The treaty of Brest-Litovsk provided for supplementary agreements under which the economic and financial relations between Germany and Russia were to be regulated in greater detail. After diplomatic relations had been re-established, the negotiations on these supplementary treaties began in Berlin in the middle of May, with Kühlmann presiding.[1] They dragged on for more than three months and the treaties were only signed at the end of August by Kühlmann's successor, Admiral von Hintze.

When the discussion on these agreements was beginning the leaders of Germany's heavy industry met in the Stahlhof at Düsseldorf at the invitation of the Director of Krupps, Dr. Bruhn, 'to

[1] For the negotiations on the supplementary treaties, see the documentation published by H. W. Gatzke in *Vierteljahreshefte für Zeitgeschichte*, 1955, No. 1, pp. 67 ff.

consider how the business with Russia, the Ukraine, the Balkans and the so-called border peoples should be handled'. Although Germany's economic interests had been given very full consideration in the treaties of Brest-Litovsk and Bucharest, Germany's heavy industry had been criticising these treaties as early as April and May as insufficient to guarantee it lasting protection. The wishes expressed in December, 1917 for a peace treaty with Russia were now heard again, with increased urgency and insistence. The fifteen gentlemen present represented Germany's twelve most important iron and steel companies. They were: Thyssen (Thyssen & Co. and Gewerkschaft Deutscher Kaiser), Stinnes (Deutsch-Luxemburgische Bergwerks-A.G.), Kirdorf (Gelsenkirchener Bergwerks-A.G.), Hugenberg and Bruhn (Krupp), Reusch (Gutehoffnungshütte A.G.), Klockner (Lothringer Hüttenverein Aumetz-Friede), Röchling (Röchlingsche Eisen- und Stahlwerke), Fahrenhorst and Poensgen (Phönix A.G.), Nothmann (Oberschlesische Eisenbahn-Bedarfs-A.G.), Ohly (Vereinigte Königs- und Laufrahütte A.G.), Gerwin (Stahlwerksverband) and Hasslacher (Rheinische Stahlwerke).

There were two aspects of the general development which disquieted these gentlemen. They were afraid that after the war Germany would be squeezed right out of the world market. They hoped to make good the loss of overseas markets by 'conquest of the continental market', meaning in particular Russia, the ex-Russian territories and the Balkans, where local industries were little developed so that there was a big demand for industrial imports. But they had received alarming reports from Russia and were afraid that the Western Powers might even squeeze them out of that country, which they regarded as Germany's natural future market.

On May 16 they recommended two counter-measures to forestall Anglo-American competition: that Germany's exports to Russia should be financed by large-scale credits in which all the big private banks and the Reich should participate; and that an attempt should be made to bring the chief transport undertakings in the east – i.e., the railways and inland waterways of the whole former Russian Empire and the Balkans – under German control. They thought that this would require the sum of 2,000 million marks, which however would be beyond the capacity of industry and the banks. They therefore appealed to the state for help, asking it to mobilise the widest popular support for a public loan to raise the necessary sum for the 'economic opening up of the eastern regions.' Apart from getting the loan issued on good terms, heavy industry was concerned 'to anchor Germany's influence securely in the management of the state or private transport enterprises in question'; only thus would it be possible 'to secure the interest and amortisation of the loans and to ensure that the big contracts were placed in Germany'. It would, however, not be possible, in spite of all economic guarantees, to invest such large sums of capital without 'assuring Germany's lasting predominance in the east'.

They therefore demanded 'that the political position of the German Reich in the eastern territories should be anchored in the most effective manner, in any case far more extensively than the peace treaties appeared to date to provide'. They were not, however, satisfied with laying down these general principles; they also put forward detailed demands: 'permanent military occupation by Germany and her allies of European routes to the north of Russia', viz., the Murmansk coast, the islands off the Gulf of Riga, and the Aaland and Finnish islands; and they also drew attention to 'the enormous importance for Germany's iron and steel industry of the Swedish ore-fields'–here, too, Germany must get ahead of Britain.

On May 25, 1918 Bruhn, who was acting as spokesman for German heavy industry, suggested intimate consultations between a few representatives of heavy industry, the big banks, the departmental ministries concerned and the OHL. On June 1 he submitted a proposal for the creation, with official help, of a syndicate for the economic penetration of Russia and the Ukraine. On June 4 the conference was held in the Reich Economic Office under the presidency of Freiherr von Stein. Representatives of the Diskontogesellschaft and of the Max Warburg Haus appeared for the banks, and of Krupp, the Phoenix Iron Works and the Stinnes concern for industry. The conference duly resolved on 'the early foundation of a sort of syndicate'. This was to be a purely private enterprise, and industry and the banks were prepared to contribute 50 million marks each to its initial capital. The remaining 1,900 millions were to be raised either by public subscription or by direct subsidy out of Reich funds, the Reichstag being consulted as little as possible.

The syndicate was to be provided with two separate daughter companies, one each for the Ukraine and for Great Russia, which were to control the transport systems of both countries, to afford financial 'support' to industries in each, and to co-ordinate supplies of raw material, production and sales. The conference agreed to approach wider circles in the worlds of banking, shipping and industry, so that the syndicate should have as broad a basis as possible.

Besides this state-guaranteed private initiative, von Stein produced a plan for attaching an 'economic staff' to the German mission in Moscow with the purpose of co-ordinating Germany's economic activity in Russia and providing her economic policy with a secure and influential basis. This 'staff' was to be organised on exactly the same lines as the 'Economic Office' in the Ukraine.

It was this collaboration–after certain inter-departmental difficulties had been smoothed out–between the Foreign Ministry the Reich Economic Office, the Imperial Treasury and the Ministry of War that created the real pre-conditions for the conclusion of the supplementary treaties. Only by means of this 'staff' would Germany be able to keep Russia to the fulfilment of the treaty. The man appointed as its head, List, had worked for years in Russia and had long occupied a leading position in the bank of Schröder & Co.; he was thus familiar with the Russian capital market. Characteristically, the expansion and status of this commission formed the chief theme of the current diplomatic negotiations between Germany and the Russian embassy.

Germany's haste to establish this economic staff was due to the imminence of the conclusion of the supplementary treaty and the promise of big contracts and bigger concessions. The syndicate was very quickly founded, partly with the object of putting in the claims of private enterprise as quickly as possible, partly to put through the Prusso-Bavarian claim for a monopoly. Von Rieppel, Director of the M.A.N. and an Imperial Councillor of the Bavarian crown, was put in charge of it. It never produced any effective results, since the military collapse of Germany came only a few weeks after its establishment.

German policy in Russia between Revolution and Restoration

The success of all plans for the economic penetration and domination of Russia depended, however, on the restoration of more or less stable relations between the German Reich and Russia. Theoretically the German government could bring this about in either of two ways: either it might achieve such an absolute domination in the east as to reduce Rump Russia to the status of a German satellite, or their internal and foreign difficulties might bring the two states together approximately on the equal footing accepted by Germany in the summer of 1918. The negotiations in Berlin preceding the conclusion of the supplementary treaties to the Peace of Brest-Litovsk are to be understood in the light of this situation.

The Peace of Brest-Litovsk had shaken the position of the Soviet government in three ways: it had turned the differences between Lenin and Trotsky within the Bolshevik Party into an open crisis; it had led the Left Social Democrats to leave the government coalition; and it had evoked increased activity among all opposition groups, old and new, in collaboration with the Entente. Since the dissolution of the Constituent Assembly in January, 1918, Monarchists, Liberals, Mensheviks and Right Social Revolutionaries had seen no possibility of overthrowing the Bolsheviks except by civil war. As all these groups passionately rejected the Peace of Brest-Litovsk and were prepared if necessary to resume hostilities against Germany, their interests agreed with those of the Entente, which wanted to bring Russia back into the war. For this reason, if none other, the Allies were intervening in the political chaos in Russia in a variety of ways: by military intervention in Murmansk and Archangel, and later in Baku and Vladivostok (where they were helped by the Japanese and later the Americans), by financial support to all anti-Bolshevik forces in Russia, and finally through agents such as Lockhart, Sadoul and Sisson.[1] But their most active allies in Russia in the summer of 1918 were the Left Social Revolutionaries who, after their breach with the Bolsheviks, began an open campaign of terror in two directions: attempts on the lives of Bolshevik leaders (Lenin and others) and of leading representatives of Germany in Russia, with the idea of provoking the Germans to sharp reprisals against the Bolsheviks and so destroying the political association between Lenin and Germany. The assassinations of the German ambassador in Moscow, Count Mirbach, on July 6 and of Field-Marshal von Eichorn in Kiev on July 29 very nearly brought success to these plans. The assassination of Mirbach caused the German government for the first time to reconsider its whole policy towards Russia. It was well informed of the exceedingly precarious situation of the Bolshevik regime, and in the summer of 1918 was expecting its fall almost daily. In this situation some members of the government regarded collaboration with the Bolsheviks with very mixed feelings, as a policy to be justified only by military necessity. The leaders of this line of thought were the Emperor, Prince Henry, Ludendorff and Helfferich. They thought that the moment had arrived to overthrow the Bolsheviks in Russia and replace them by a monarchist-bourgeois government, with which they hoped to bring about an understanding between Germany and Russia by modifying the terms of Brest-Litovsk.[2]

The Emperor was naturally personally averse from the tacit alliance with a world revolutionary such as Lenin, and he was also subject to psychological pressure from White Russian émigrés, Baltic barons and emissaries of the Cossack republics, all of whom pressed him to dissociate himself from the Bolsheviks in order to clear Germany

[1] On Lockhart and Sisson, see Kennan, op. cit.
[2] See Helfferich, *Der Weltkrieg*, pp. 650 ff.

of the suspicion that she was making common cause with the murderers of the Tsar. Similar pressure came from the bourgeoisie, who found further collaborations with the Bolsheviks objectionable on grounds of internal politics, not least on account of its effects on the German workers and the morale of the army. They wanted Germany to act as the advance guard of Europe and the West against Bolshevism, a 'power of order' in the East, and in virtue thereof to force the Western Powers to admit her claim to a position of supremacy in the East. Some such ideas had been voiced as early as the Bad Homburg conference of February 13, 1918,[1] when the decision had been taken in favour of the military advance in the east. But they also accorded with the proposals of Colonel von Haeften who, in January and again in July, 1918, proposed, with Ludendorff's full approval, that Germany should undertake a propagandist offensive for the political preparation of her military offensive in the west.

The strongest representatives of the anti-Bolshevik school among the German leaders were Ludendorff himself, who was in close contact with leading industrialists and with the head of the Catholic clergy in Germany, the Cardinal-Archbishop of Cologne, von Hartmann, and Helfferich. Helfferich had been appointed ambassador in Moscow in July, 1918 to succeed the 'Bolshevised' (as the Emperor called him)[2] Count Mirbach. He was perhaps the most vigorous and consistent advocate among leading Germans of an immediate revision of German policy towards the Bolshevik regime. He therefore spent his few days in Moscow largely in a permanent wrangle with the new Secretary of State of the Foreign Ministry, Admiral von Hintze, to influence German policy in the direction which he wished it to take. As early as August 1 he urged taking advantage of the Bolsheviks' inner weakness to overthrow them at once, for in his view it needed only a touch to do this. He summarised his considerations and recommendations as follows:

It is impossible for us to go on waiting any more. All we should gain would be that we should be involved in the Bolsheviks' fall, and that the new Russian regime . . . and public opinion would be most heavily prejudiced against us as the Bolsheviks' friends and protectors.[3]

The immediate occasion of Helfferich's proposal for action was an appeal for help addressed by Chicherin to the German embassy on August 1. Chicherin proposed that German and Russian troops

[1] See above, p. 501 ff.

[2] In a marginal note on a report from Mirbach to the Chancellor.

[3] The Emperor's marginal comment ran: 'Of course! I told Kühlmann so a month ago.'

should advance in 'twofold co-operation' on the Murmansk railway and the Don district, which would have brought extraordinary relief to the Bolshevik regime, both at home and abroad. Chicherin, it is true, wanted the co-operation to be disguised (a plan considered at times by Ludendorff), probably mainly in view of the internal political situation in Russia.

Helfferich forwarded the proposal to Berlin but recommended that only a show should be made of accepting it; troops should be assembled, but then used not to support the Bolshevik regime, but to overthrow it. Then Germany should 'hasten to rid herself of that connection with the Bolsheviks which is discrediting us in the eyes of all elements which will count in the future Russia' and build a bridge to the anti-Bolshevik forces. To this end, Germany should collaborate with all opponents of the Bolsheviks, including the Latvian regiments, which should be turned against Lenin. This plan, he thought, could be realised in three steps. First, Germany should dissociate herself demonstratively from the Bolsheviks by moving the German legation from Moscow to some point near the German front line. Secondly, he recommended a 'modification of the Peace of Brest', beginning with the minimum demand made by all Russian groups for revision of Germany's Ukrainian policy, i.e., restoration of the Ukraine to Russia. Thirdly, he advocated 'effective military support' by Germany for the counter-revolutionary forces; this would 'substantially improve our position *vis-à-vis* the new regime and ensure the success of a blow against the Bolsheviks'.

Ludendorff's attitude towards Chicherin's request and Helfferich's recommendations was not clear cut. On August 4 he said that a German army could not accept 'a military alliance and close partnership in arms with the Bolsheviks', but thought that an operation might be carried out against the British in East Karelia on condition that the Finns co-operated and that the Germans were able to use the Murmansk railway from Petersburg. He even wrote that 'the occupation of Petersburg is politically of supreme importance', but admitted the practical difficulties, since it would then be necessary to feed the entire population of that great city. As regards the Don, he was prepared to order *Oberost* to concentrate as large a force as possible at Rostov against the White Russian general Alexeyev, and also along the line from Rostov to Voronezh, although the use of this line must be completely denied to the Red troops. If the Bolsheviks wanted to advance against Alexeyev, their best route was from the south-east, via Tsaritzin (now Volgagrad) and Astrakhan. He did not want to attack the 'Whites' himself, but to let them be put under pressure from the Reds. And he saw it, the Russians, White and Red, should be allowed to weaken one another, so that whichever won should be the more dependent on Germany.

If Ludendorff's first remarks were still somewhat impenetrable, two days later he revealed with absolute clarity the political intentions behind his planned military advance. Telegraphing to Hintze on August 6, he described the six or seven divisions which he was in a position to supply for military operations in the north, with several more in the south, as the power with which Germany could install a new government in Russia 'which had the people behind it'. The Emperor expressed himself in similar terms about the same time.

Against these tactical deviations born of ideological scruples, Hintze in August, 1918 was advocating with all his power an Eastern policy true to the line pursued since 1914. For him, as he put it to the party leaders on August 21, the immediate aim, until peace were concluded, must be 'to prevent or at least delay the re-constitution of a front in the east'. He held no less firmly to what had been the great ultimate object since 1914, the weakening of Russia as a precondition for Germany's supremacy in the east. For him the basis was there in the Peace of Brest-Litovsk. To all political objections to this treaty he replied coolly by stating its great advantage. 'It is there.' Nothing would therefore induce him to abandon this basis, and in his view the fall of the Bolsheviks would have been the first step towards it. On these grounds he rejected categorically any idea that Germany should overthrow the Bolshevik regime; he preferred to retain it as an instrument of his policy of disintegrating and exploiting Russia.

Unlike Helfferich and Ludendorff, Hintze did not think the position of the Bolshevik regime particularly critical, since so far neither the Russian villages nor the Red guards had risen against it. For this reason he did not share Ludendorff's belief that the Bolshevik government could be overthrown and an anti-Bolshevik government set up with the help of a few German divisions. This would only be possible – and Ludendorff himself had made the reservation quite correctly – if the new regime 'had the people behind it'. Hintze put his finger on the weak spot in Ludendorff's argument by retorting that a government which had the people behind it would not need military support from Germany. But if it had no broad popular basis, a German intervention in favour of the Whites would need far more divisions than were actually available in the east. There was in Russia only one single group which wanted German intervention for its own sake – some of the monarchists, who wanted the Russian autocracy restored. They could not maintain themselves against the people without the help of German bayonets. Hintze was not on principle opposed to such a policy, but felt himself bound to reject it in practice, for the simple reason given by himself: 'We have not got the necessary bayonets.' This applied even more to an attack on Alexeyev, who was in the pay of the Entente, so that a victory by him over the Bolsheviks would be tantamount in practice to re-establishing the eastern front.

If, however, this eventuality was to be avoided, Hintze thought that Germany must not commit herself to a war of indefinite duration against the Bolsheviks, which was the logical conclusion of what Ludendorff and Helfferich were asking. She must also try, so far as she could, to make it impossible for the Whites to seize power in Russia. 'Social Revolutionaries, Kadets, Octobrists, Monarchists, Cossacks, gendarmes, officials and Tsarist hangers-on' – all had inscribed on their banners: 'War against Germany, overthrow of the Brest-Litovsk Peace.' Hintze went so far as to treat the Whites as enemies even where, as in Alexeyev's Cossack republic – they had already established themselves as power factors. His reasoning was simple: 'Alexeyev is a pillar of the Entente. If we make war on him, we are making war on the Entente. I am not worried if the Bolsheviks are fighting against him too, although I should like to avoid having our troops march together with Bolshevik troops.'

Hintze himself was far from 'hanging round the Bolsheviks' neck' as Helfferich insinuated; he was not even fundamentally well disposed towards them. He was the Emperor's Secretary of State, and his only criterion for the Bolshevik regime was how far it could be used to strengthen and uphold Germany's power position in the East. He was never blind to the possibility of its fall, and always wanted Germany's policy to be ready for this eventuality. He put his political calculations clearly in the following passage:

> It is policy to use the Bolsheviks so long as there is still something to be got out of them. If they fall we can quietly watch the chaos which will probably ensue, until we think resistance has been so far weakened that we could create order without great sacrifices. If chaos does not ensue, but another party comes to power, at once we must intervene under the slogan of no war with Russia or with the Russian people, no conquests, but order and protection of the weak against the treatment by our enemies.

It would thus only be if the fall of the Bolsheviks was followed, not by renewed chaos, but by a new stable order, which would of course be directed against Germany, that German troops would again have to intervene openly in the internal politics of Russia, this time claiming to represent a factor of order against the Western Powers. Unless and until the Bolsheviks fell, the Germans should remain neutral, which would in the last instance mean that they were giving the Bolshevik system decisive support in its crisis. The primacy of Germany's war aims in Hintze's philosophy, which was free of any ideological trimmings, was put by him in such forceful and convincing terms that it is best to quote him *in extenso*. After sketching the principles to be followed by German policy if and when the Bolshevik regime fell, he went on:

Meanwhile, we have no reason to wish or to bring about a quick end of Bolshevism. The Bolsheviks are very evil and antipathetic people; that did not prevent us from imposing the peace of Brest-Litovsk on them and, after that, taking away from them successive slices of land and their inhabitants. We have got out of them what we could, and our drive for victory demands that we should go on doing so, so long as they are in power.

Whether we like working with them or not is irrelevant, so long as it is useful. History proves that to introduce feelings into politics is an expensive luxury. In our position it would be irresponsible to allow ourselves such a luxury. A man who works with the Bolsheviks as the men *de facto* in power and then sighs over the nastiness of the company, is harmless; but to refuse to benefit from working with the Bolsheviks out of reluctance to incur the odium of having to do with Bolsheviks–that is dangerous. Politics have always been utilitarian, and will be so for a long time to come. . . . What, then, do we want in the East? The military paralysis of Russia. The Bolsheviks are producing this better and more thoroughly than any other Russian party could do, without our giving a man or a mark for it. We cannot ask them or any other Russians to love us for squeezing their country dry. Let us therefore content ourselves with Russia's impotence.

The next paragraph shows that Berlin's mind was concentrated on using the Peace of Brest as an instrument for realising Germany's war aims in the east, over and above this general weakening of Russia.

The Bolsheviks are the only Russian party which has got into conflict with the Entente. This became clearer every day. Our duty is to foster this conflict, and recently we have had the opportunity. The Bolsheviks are the only champions in Russia of the Brest peace. His Excellency Helfferich admits that co-operation with other parties is possible *only on condition* that the Brest peace is modified; above all, the Ukraine would have to be restored to Great Russia. Now we are told of much more far-reaching demands: the restoration of Russia within the frontiers *quo ante bellum*. Are we, then, to give up the fruits of four years' battles and triumphs merely to rid ourselves belatedly of the odium of having exploited the Bolsheviks? For that is what we are doing: we are not working with them, we are exploiting them. That is good politics, and policy.

Hintze concluded his reflections, which Germany's later official policy embodied, with a provocative rhetorical question to Ludendorff the general–whose victories in the east had laid the foundations of Germany's power position – and to Ludendorff the politician of *Deutschtum* and *Raum* – who wanted to preserve and extend the fruits of those victories:

> Is the Supreme Army Command prepared, and does it think it would be profitable and practicable, to begin now on a revision of the Brest Treaty which would end in our giving up the Baltic, Lithuania and the Ukraine? Not to speak of the Crimea, Tauris and the Donetz basin, which of course would be asked for back at once? [Poland is not even mentioned.]

The Secretary of State answered his own question by invoking the pragmatic and the legal arguments for his view that the basis of Brest-Litovsk must under all circumstances be preserved. 'The Brest Treaty,' he said, 'bears the signature of our most gracious sovereign, it has been concluded by us and our allies together, it separates Austria from Russia by creating the Ukraine [sic]; it has been submitted to the Reichstag.

This retort by Hintze to Ludendorff's and Helfferich's new policy is a key document for the understanding of Germany's Eastern policy in 1918. It is as historically important for Germany's war aims policy in 1918 as Bethmann Hollweg's September programme of 1914. The memorandum represented at once the highwater mark and crown of German policy in its efforts to realise its far-flung war aims in the east, a purpose for which the revolutionisation of Russia and the support of the revolutionary system proved indispensable. The policy of revolutionising and decomposing Russia, as initiated by Bethmann Hollweg in August, 1914, had in the course of the war developed its own *vis momenti*, which became increasingly operative. For all the deviations a continuous line runs from Bethmann Hollweg and Zimmermann via Kühlmann to Hintze, reaching its highest point, if only in the radicalism of the words used, in the middle of 1918.

Almost all the men who for four years had kept steadily in view the aim of expanding Germany's power through war were, it seems, so impressed by Hintze's logic that they shelved their ideological scruples and returned to the old line. Ludendorff, who had already begun to waver, signified his agreement with the Secretary of State and ordered German troops to advance outside Petersburg, now with the unambiguous purpose of supporting the Bolsheviks. He was prepared to allow troops to be sent against the British on the Murmansk coast without overthrowing the Soviet regime. He too thought revision of the Treaty of Brest out of the question.

The Emperor had backed Helfferich completely in the first days of August, probably in part under the shattering impression of the murder of the Tsar's family. Now, after Hintze's decided intervention, he again agreed that Germany should put her money on Lenin, at least for the time. Helfferich was not convinced by Hintze, but he resigned himself. He left Moscow and returned to Germany in the hope of renewing there the struggle for a change of policy.[1]

The supplementary treaties of August 28, 1918: compromise without renunciation of control

Hintze's victory in the struggle over Germany's future relationship with the young Soviet state had far-reaching consequences. Once Berlin had decided not to overthrow the Bolshevik government, the German government was necessarily interested in binding the Soviet government to Germany still more closely and inescapably than ever. The way was now clear for the conclusion of the supplementary treaties for which the Treaty of Brest-Litovsk had provided. As will be remembered, the negotiations had been begun in Berlin at the end of May under Kühlmann.[2] The initiative for resuming them had come from Russia.[3] The difficult position of the regime, surrounded by enemies within and without, the catastrophic supply position in the big towns, and also the wish to revive foreign trade, had made the Russians anxious for agreements which would make it possible for them to obtain at least a part of the Ukrainian harvest, put a stop to the Germans' advance, and turn against the Whites. But the Germans, too, were not unwilling to negotiate. Germany saw herself threatened by the Entente's landing on the Murmansk coast. Furthermore, neither in May nor in June had a decision been achieved on the western front.

The negotiations, however, dragged on, and were interrupted by Kühlmann's fall. At that time different forces and views in Germany were still struggling for mastery, and in June and July the influence of the OHL, the Emperor and Helfferich, all of whom wanted the Bolsheviks overthrown, was still uppermost. At the great war aims conference at Spa on July 2, 1918,[4] Ludendorff was still full of confidence in Germany's power and in the approach of victory, and produced his programme of German expansion as the surest basis for establishing Germany's influence—without regard to White or Red—in Russia and its successor states. The task of German policy, he said, must be to support the Don and Kuban Cossacks and to extend the frontier of Estonia and Livonia and incorporate them in Germany, thus getting additional land for settlement. Reval should be made,

[1] Helfferich, op. cit., pp. 665 ff.
[2] Gatzke, op. cit., pp. 71 f.
[3] Id., p. 70.
[4] Id., pp. 84 ff.; also *Ursachen*, II, pp. 206 ff.

not indeed into a naval base like Kiel and Wilhelmshaven – Libau was that – but into a submarine base. Ludendorff's attitude on the Ukraine was ambivalent: he saw that the Ukrainian government was dependent on Germany's military power and he envisaged the possibility of its return to Great Russia, but in reply to Hertling, who wanted the Bolsheviks supported in order to keep Brest-Litovsk intact, he maintained his own view, saying that any Russian government could be forced to accept the treaty by the baits of the Ukraine and Crimea – leaving open the question whether Russia could not be reorganised from the south. He hoped for especially good 'soldier material' from Georgia; 'our western front needs men'.

The Emperor agreed with Ludendorff and endorsed his warning against concluding the treaties with the Russians at the expense of the Kuban Cossacks. He again spoke up for the Ataman of the Don Cossacks, who had sent the duke of Leuchtenberg to Berlin to conclude an agreement. The Emperor wanted to make Tiflis, the capital of Georgia, the centre of anti-Soviet agitation. This July Council took no decision between White and Red.

Fearing further secessions from Rump Russia and a counter-revolution supported by Germany, the Russians not only offered an economic agreement – they would be able to get more cereals out of the Ukraine than the Germans had yet succeeded in doing – but also hinted that they would regard these agreements only as the first step towards a more intimate relationship between Soviet Russia and Germany, perhaps even an alliance.[1] The fate of the supplementary treaties was decided by the fact that Stresemann, who was taking part in the German–Russian negotiations,[2] changed his line early and became an advocate of agreement.

Up to the end of June, he had still been completely in favour of what he called 'a long-term, lasting policy of alliance with monarchic forces', a policy (just like Helfferich's) of 'restoring an Old Russian, federally organised constitutional monarchy in alliance with ourselves', and he had submitted his views to the Chancellor in a long memorandum on the day before the preliminary conference of Spa. But he had changed these views, which had probably been influenced by his conversations with Milyukov in Kiev, after talking to Joffe and Krassin, who succeeded in persuading him that the position of the Soviets was not so hopeless, that their radical socialism was only a practical socialism analogous to Germany's war economy, and that if they got 'some measure' of peace and security, they would be able to deliver arms, would recognise Brest-Litovsk and

[1] Gatzke, op. cit., pp. 77 ff.

[2] Id., pp. 79 ff.

would – perforce – work for an alliance with Germany as no other
Russian party would do. In any case, after July 7 Stresemann was of
all the German negotiators the most eloquent supporter of agreement with the Soviet. He supported Hintze against Ludendorff and
Helfferich and threw his whole weight into the scale in favour of a
settlement with Great Russia, which should also secure Germany's
economic interests.

The minutes of July 7 show very clearly both the precarious situation of the Soviets and the aims of German policy.[1] Joffe and Krassin were again offering economic inducements in the hope of finding
the basis for a common policy. At the same time they assured the
Germans that, unfavourable as the Treaty of Brest-Litovsk was for
them, they meant, and indeed would be obliged, to abide by it, for it
had meanwhile become a sort of protection for them and they were
fighting to preserve it since Germany and Turkey were threatening
increasingly to cut Russia off from her 'life lines' by their 'policy of
expansion'. Their chief point, however, was that Germany must give
up the Don and Kuban districts, for then Russia would be able to
deliver cereals, oil, manganese, iron and cotton. The demarcation
lines in the south of Russia had been repeatedly altered, 'so that no
one really knew what would be left of Russia'; however much Herr
von Kühlmann denied that the Reich had recognised the Republic
of the Don as an independent state, the German troops entering it
would yet 'recognise a Russian there as ruler' (i.e., recognise Krassnov as Ataman). The purpose was obviously to cut Russia off from
the cereals of the Ukraine, the coal of the Don and the ores of the
Caucasus. 'These continuous losses of territory and the prohibition of
trade between those countries and Russia' had evoked 'immeasurable embitterment' among the Russian people against Germany, far
greater than the Tsarist government had ever succeeded in rousing
with its propaganda. 'Russia . . . had to look on while one piece of
land after the other was torn from her, now by Germany, now by
Turkey, like rags being torn off a body. . . .' Meanwhile, although
Germany had big forces tied down there, she had not been able to
produce order and secure the hoped for imports.

Stresemann recognised in the Soviet overtures a possibility of
achieving a treaty based on Brest which would 'place Russia's economic resources at our disposal so amply as to render us impregnable'.
He had numerous conversations with the Chancellor and the soldiers, in which he represented these factors as the central political
argument for German consent to negotiating the supplementary
treaties with the Soviets: peace in the east at the expense of the Don

[1] Ibid.

576

and Kuban, and perhaps also the Ukraine, concentration in the west—and, as a result, imports of cereals and raw materials safeguarded.

In the middle of July—when German forces in east and west were strained to the utmost pitch—the commercial specialist of the German committee, Litwin, replied to a Russian draft of an economic supplementary treaty with demands which showed a certain readiness to make allowances for Russia's difficulties, but in no way renounced Germany's economic aims.[1] Henceforward Russia was to be treated like Rumania and Georgia.[2] Litwin met some of Russia's wishes by agreeing to secure Russia's supplies of cereals, coal, iron and oil, and promising that Germany should not advance further. Most important of all, the line of communication between northern Russia and the Kuban and Caucasus should be restored by the return of the railway line through Byelgorod and Rostov to Vladikavkas (the terminal point of the Georgian army road which commanded the main crossing of the Caucasus) and Baku. In return, Russia should pledge herself to deliver a percentage, to be fixed, of the cereals and raw materials derived from the Caucasus and Kuban. Litwin wanted to reserve 50 per cent of production for Germany and also to have the practical execution of the obligations contracted on the spot by a mixed commission. The same commission was also to decide what Germany was to deliver in return for the raw materials, a device which would have enabled the Germans to secure the complementary raw materials which they needed for their own economy and at the same time make certain of a market for their industrial products without troubling themselves further over the problematic Cossack republics of the Don and Kuban. They would thus in practice have largely shifted the economic orientation of this area towards themselves and away from Great (northern) Russia without putting up a customs barrier on its northern frontier. The formula proposed by Litwin—that Russia *must* give Germany the first offer of 'all its surplus raw materials and cereals' – shows even more plainly that Russia, like Rumania, was to be forced into the position of a supplier of raw materials for Germany.

Heavy as these conditions were, the Russians accepted them as a basis for negotiation in the belief that the restoration of the Don and of the railway line would bring about a change of feeling in Russia which, as they gave the Germans to understand, would enable them to conclude an alliance with Germany. Krassin went even further in his promises, the propagandist nature of which became obvious when

[1] Id., pp. 83 ff.; also *Ursachen*, II, pp. 215 f.
[2] Cf. Stern, op. cit., Vol. IV/3, p. 1387.

he undertook to offer armed resistance to any anti-German enterprise on Russian territory. These extensive promises were, however, made with the intention of altering Ludendorff's mood and persuading him to evacuate Rostov, without which Russia would be cut off from the Donetz as completely as from the Kuban and the northern Caucasus.

In spite of the reversal in the west which began with the Allied and American counter-offensive at Villers–Cotterêts on July 18, and in spite of the results of the negotiations with the Soviets, the OHL still stood its ground and insisted that the treaty should at least compel Germany to evacuate Rostov *only if* the military situation permitted. On August 8 Stresemann, acting through Colonel Bauer, tried to persuade the OHL to yield in view of events in Livonia and Estonia, but in vain, nor did his plea for 'an understanding with Russia' meet with any better success. He wrote that:

> If our enemies see that we are collaborating with Russia, they will give up the hope of conquering us economically, as they must long since have despaired of conquering us in the field [this was written on August 8, the Black Day on the Western Front] and we shall be strong enough to resist any assault.[1]

While, however, the arguments of Stresemann and Hintze, of the lawyers in the Foreign Ministry and the business men in Berlin, failed to move the OHL, the developments on the western front after the middle of August at last forced them to give way. These developments created the necessary conditions for the conclusion of the supplementary treaties, and they were signed in Berlin on August 27.

Germany ratified them at once, without submitting them to the consideration of the full Reichstag. The reason given by Payer for this step is most characteristic: 'If we delayed acceptance of the treaties, there would be a danger of the present Russian government falling.' For that reason, this democrat was even against convoking the Central Committee of the Reichstag; he himself agreed without reservation to the 'favourable' treaties. So did Gröber for the Zentrum: 'We will accept the new treaties as we accepted the Treaty of Brest.' Westarp for the Conservatives and Stresemann for the National Liberals expressed themselves in the same sense. Only Ebert raised objections on the part of the Majority Socialists, who had originally asked for the treaties to be submitted to the plenary Reichstag; he pointed out that on the one hand the treaties represented the 'continuation of a false policy', and on the other, that the 6,000 million roubles being asked of the Russians were nothing but an 'indem-

[1] Gatzke, op. cit., pp. 192 ff.; also *Ursachen*, II, p. 216.

nity'. Germany was thus not making the promised 'peace without annexations and indemnities'. The voice of the Majority Socialists did not, however, affect the decision – still less did the opposition of the U.S.P.D.

The supplementary treaties consisted of a political and an economic part, supplemented by a secret exchange of notes. Livonia and Estonia, which had been occupied by German police forces ever since Brest-Litovsk, now ceased altogether to be Russian. Russia recognised the independence of Georgia and agreed to pay 6,000 million roubles in fine gold, currency and kind. She also promised to deliver one-third of the Baku oil in return for its surrender by the Turks.

Germany's counter-concessions were laid down in article 4, described by Joffe as the only acceptable article in the whole treaty. In it Germany promised not to advance beyond the frontiers laid down in Brest-Litovsk and in the supplementary treaty, i.e., in no way further to assist the abstraction of more states from Rump Russia. She further promised to evacuate the territory occupied by her beyond the new demarcation line (essentially, that is, White Russia and the Black Sea districts).

The secret exchange of notes confirmed the Soviet obligation to drive out the Entente troops, if necessary with the help of Finnish and German troops. The economic treaty set out the obligations defined in the preliminary treaty, with Litwin's additions. Germany had assured her influence. The Russians had come to the negotiations hoping that the treaty would lead them out of their isolation and that they would find a certain support in Germany, even though they thought a regular treaty still impossible in view of the strong anti-German feelings of the Russian people. For the sake of this greater end Joffe was prepared to make extensive concessions: complete renunciation of Livonia and Estonia, and delivery of big quotas of iron and managanese ore, oil and cereals. All the greater was the Russians' disappointment over the results and over Germany's policy during the negotiations. They felt the treaty to be 'the most humiliating' yet required of Russia, far worse than 'the peace of humiliation of Brest-Litovsk'. Germany, so Joffe and Krassin complained, 'had cut the body of Russia into two parts and now wanted it to function like a normal body'. The provisions of the economic treaty were tantamount to 'the complete paralysis of Russia's economic life', and the demand for 6,000 millions was 'absolutely monstrous'. Their bitterness vented itself in a warning that Germany 'would certainly raise the whole Russian people against her', and that their own government would probably reject it. Should, however, the Bolsheviks fall,

all three Russian representatives prophesied 'that a solid and unitary Great Russia, which would again include the Ukraine, would at once be there, confronting Germany'.

This severe judgment by the Russian negotiators in August, 1918 agreed exactly with the analysis of Germany's Russian policy made by leading Germans, both critics and defenders of it. Lucius, who was one of the critics, had warned his government strongly at the beginning of May, 1918 not to cross the Brest-Litovsk frontiers, in particular not to allow Finland to extend beyond its historic frontiers by expanding into Karelia. He gave economic considerations for this advice, pointing to 'the enormous Russian market on which our industries are already waiting greedily'. He therefore thought good relations with an economically effective Russia important. His idea was what he called 'real peace with Russia'. The Emperor retorted (in a marginal note) with his racialist axiom that peace 'is completely impossible between Slavs and Germans' but:

The gentleman is mad! That is a policy of fear! My view is absolutely different. Peace with Russia can only be maintained by fear of us. The Slavs will always hate us and remain our enemies! They are only frightened of a man and they only respect him if he hits them hard! S. [see] Japan! So it will be with us, too! The Entente, if it wants, and if my diplomacy is too stupid, can always do what it likes in Russia – it has driven it into war; but our preponderance in the German area is necessary to keep Russia away from our eastern frontier once and for all; no peace with Russia, however favourable, will give us that!

When the discussions on the eastern orientation were going on, Kühlmann had already put into words Germany's interests in keeping Russia from consolidating herself:

The territorial losses which Russia is suffering, especially in being cut off from the Baltic and the Black Sea, would force any future, better consolidated, regime to carry on an imperialist policy and to call for war for the recovery of the lost territories.

Count Wedel had expressed the same view even before the conclusion of the Treaty of Brest: 'Either an imperialist Russia will come back, or Russia will disintegrate.' At that time he had expressed his preference for the collapse in extraordinarily sharp and radical terms: 'the further our power is pushed eastward, the better for us'. Hintze, too, had just defended this policy of 'chaos': 'If chaos does not come about . . . we must march in. . . .' When meeting the party leaders on August 21 to discuss the supplementary treaties, Hintze again represented the continuity of that border states policy which Ebert had ventured to criticise as 'the continuation of a false policy'.

Any other party in Russia would reject Brest and the supplementary treaties; 'it is therefore not our intention and duty ... to appear in Russia as schoolmasters', but to wait: if the Bolsheviks fall, 'then there will be chaos in Russia ... then we shall have a free hand indeed ... to put through a border states policy in our own interest'. The political head of the Foreign Ministry took exactly the same view as Ludendorff of the role of the border states in a second war – another instance of the continuity of Germany's war aims: 'We want to strengthen the power of resistance of the border peoples as much as we can, for the war with the resurrected Russian colossus which may, after all, come one day sooner or later.' At the same time he turned on Helfferich, who even after his return from Moscow was preaching his policy of counter-revolution in Russia and a peace of understanding.[1] Helfferich's objects were, indeed, identical with those of the German government; he too wanted 'the establishment one day of a good political and economic relationship with Russia, which is of quite special importance for us in view of the probability that antagonism between Germany and the Anglo-Saxons will last beyond the conclusion of peace'. He only took a different view from Hintze, Stresemann, Kriege and their followers, of what were the decisive forces in Russia. 'People have talked to me,' retorted Hintze scornfully, 'of the Monarchists as possible vehicles of a counter-revolution'; 'they are officers without an army, the Kadets do not go out into the street. . . .' 'Some people have also proposed presenting Russia with the Ukraine' (Helfferich had even thought of Livonia and Estonia, but the secession of those territories was the one condition on which the Emperor and the OHL had given up their policy towards the Cossacks, the Monarchists, restoration and expansion). 'Why?' asked Hintze. 'We can get good relations without making a present like that!' His justification of Germany's claim to domination was all of a piece with this 'psychological warfare'; four weeks before Germany's military capitulation he announced to the representatives of the major parties in the Reichstag:

In the view of the OHL the military situation gives no cause for depression. There is no reason to doubt in victory. Only if we doubt whether we shall conquer, are we conquered. In the OHL's view we can justifiably hope for a military position which will allow us to attain a peace agreeable to us.

Gröber, speaking for the Zentrum, warned against a premature peace – now, after the reverses in the west – and was again reassured

[1] *Ursachen*, II, pp. 226 ff.

by Hintze that by 'peace' 'he naturally meant only a peace agreeable and satisfactory to us'. He entirely disregarded Ebert's objections. 'We are told,' he dared to go on, 'that more and more Americans are coming over and people believe that the military strength of the enemy is thus constantly increasing and our own diminishing.' These warnings and the military situation did not prevent the party leaders from again endorsing the border states policy. The ring was closed. Bethmann Hollweg's plans of August, 1914 had found their consistent fulfilment in Brest-Litovsk and its supplementary treaties.

The position reached in the east in the summer of 1918 seemed to the Germans both then and later to be so favourable as to enable them either to keep what remained of Russia in anarchy and lasting impotence, or, as Ludendorff hoped, to reorganise it in Germany's interest. But the *Pax Germanica* proved no lasting order of peace, not only because the Germans were not able to achieve a military decision in their favour in the west, but also because Germany's new order in eastern Europe mutilated Rump Russia too drastically and negated the historic reality of the Russian Empire. Germany could not allow the peoples of the east to recover in any respect, for they would then try again to overthrow in a second war the intolerable hegemony which Germany had established at Brest-Litovsk, Bucharest and Berlin.

22

THE VISION OF WORLD POWER

OBJECTIVES OF WAR AIMS POLICY, III

THE concentration of Germany's political interest on the domination of the east – Finland, the Baltic, Lithuania, Poland, Rump Russia, the Ukraine, the Caucasus and the Balkans – since the spring of 1917, and in particular since the collapse of Russia, provided certain fears that she was going to renounce her aims in the west, overseas and in the Far East. As the documents show most amply, these fears were entirely without foundation. The victory and the peace treaties in the east were, as the Emperor himself saw, the pre-conditions for a victorious peace in the west. Further, the colonial programme, both in regard to central Africa and to bases, had remained unchanged.[1]

Germany's pre-war Asiatic policy remained equally unchanged throughout the war. Since Turkey was meant to be the terminal point of the Berlin–Baghdad line in the future Mitteleuropa system and the bridge to the Persian Gulf, Afghanistan and India, and was at the same time to be economically and militarily allied with Germany and Austria-Hungary, the German government needed to turn the war time alliance into an equally assured peace-time one.

Turkey: outpost against Britain.
Oil and soldiers

Germany's aims in Turkey were fixed for the first time during the war in the summer of 1915, when she was expecting a separate peace in the east after her successful eastern offensive.[2]

Her object being on the one hand to keep the Turks in the war against Britain and France even after Russia had dropped out of the Entente front, and on the other, to secure and if possible extend, even before the conclusion of peace, 'the economic political position in the area of the Baghdad railway'. Germany concentrated her efforts on three objectives: the Mesopotamian oilfields, shipping

---

[1] See above, pp. 357 ff.

[2] A memorandum by Lohmann, forwarded to the Chancellor in February, 1914, had asserted: 'If peace, justice, order and security are established under European control, the purchasing power of this country will so rise that it will become the best market for German trade and German industry.'

concessions on the Euphrates and Tigris, and concessions in the copper mines of Arghana. These objects were at that time in the hands of Entente capital, and Turkey, uncertain what her capital position would be after the war, had refrained from liquidating them. The concessions were to be transferred to the Baghdad Railway Company (which was controlled by the Deutsche Bank), Turkey being allowed a certain participation, in order to facilitate the liquidation and smooth the way for further concessions.

The financial burden of the war had exhausted Turkey, and she was only able to carry it with the help of big German loans; by 1917 she had borrowed no less than 3,000 million marks. She was thus heavily in debt to Germany, and the German politicians were determined to take advantage of this situation to achieve their aims, which would have guaranteed an alliance with Turkey of indefinite duration. The Turks hoped that their debt would be carried over or reduced, if not entirely remitted, but for this the Germans demanded securities – 'real compensation'.[1]

Kühlmann, who at that time was still ambassador in Constantinople,[2] pressed the Foreign Ministry to appoint a study group to value British and French assets in Turkey. He argued that the only way to secure Germany's loans, and simultaneously to establish her in an unchallenged position in Turkey and prevent the Turks from entering into trading and financial relations after the war with all the European great powers, was to insist strongly on the Turkish government liquidating these assets. 'The existence,' he wrote, 'of a big German financial claim on Turkey is an arm which (used cautiously but firmly) can prove very useful in the reshaping of our later relationship.' Berlin agreed with this policy. The armament of Turkey, in which Germany herself was very strongly interested, would, as the Foreign Ministry saw it, 'if placed on a sound commercial basis', offer new opportunities for German industry, and the loans themselves, if Turkey offered 'reliable securities' for their interest and amortisation, would open up prospects for increasing Germany's influence. Zimmermann thought that these 'securities' could be found in 'the systematic grant of concessions for the development of communications, trade, agriculture and industry. German capital, German machinery and German engineers could be brought in everywhere.' Turkish companies should, however figure on paper as the concessionaires.

[1] This difference between the interests of the two partners existed long before the war; it was particularly apparent in Germany's policy on the Baghdad Railway; see above, pp. 21 and 46–7.

[2] He occupied this post from September, 1916 to August, 1917.

Von Stumm, the Under-Secretary of State, emphasised that no time must be lost if the objects were to be acquired and the political hold on Turkey made secure before the conclusion of peace.

Germany's aims in Turkey were defined a little more exactly at a conference held on April 7, 1917 between representatives of the Foreign Ministry, the Imperial Treasury, the Imperial Office of the Interior, the Ministry of War, and the Prussian Ministry for Trade and Industry. The meeting resolved unanimously 'that measures should be taken immediately to secure for Germany the economic exploitation of Turkey in peacetime'. The first step should be the appointment of a 'study group' in which all war enterprises concerned, and also the Deutsche Bank (which had particularly long experience of Turkish conditions), should be represented. The objects with which this 'study group' was to be concerned were the following:

(i) The hard coal deposits of Heraklea,[1] which should be secured by liquidating the French company and transferring the concession to Germany;
(ii) The Turkish copper mines of Arghana Maden, which were owned by the Turkish state, should be transferred to Germany;
(iii) The iron and zinc deposits of Berlia and Bulgar to be brought under German control partly by liquidating the French company, partly by transferring Turkish rights to Germany;
(iv) The Baghdad railway's claims on the oil of Upper Mesopotamia and Mosul must be realised under all circumstances, as must the safeguarding of transport to the Persian Gulf by the acquisition of the majority of shares in the shipping companies of the Euphrates, the Tigris and the Shatt-el-Arab;
(v) The phosphate deposits on the Hejjas line and at Es-salt must also be transferred to Germany, as must the asphalt deposits in the Yamuk Valley and at Ladikiye;
(vi) Complete possession of Turkey's ore supplies to be achieved by the liquidation of the Borax Company, which would give Germany the borazite deposits at Panderma and the transfers of the Turkish concessions for the manganese ore deposits in the Vilayet of Bursa would give Germany the means of refining the steel.

In 1917, however, political and military aims were added to the economic. Besides her economic alliance, Turkey was also to be bound to Germany by a military convention which should make her, as the Chancellor himself put it, 'a strong pillar of our policy'. Germany, he said, needed a virile Turkey, 'so long as we maintain our present policy in the Orient'. For that reason he asked colleagues

[1] The coal deposits of Heraklea had been discovered by Professor Frech, of Breslau, who in 1914 had asked, with the support of the Foreign Ministry, for concessions for the exploitation of them.

585

how the Ottoman Empire was to be revitalised into a 'great' and 'strong state' – 'if we do not do this, the Entente will erect a barrier against our eastward path on its [Turkey's] ruins'. When Germany was at the height of her self-confidence in 1918, and Turkey asked her for another war loan, the conditions formulated by Ludendorff were: expropriation of enemy property; mining concessions, especially for chromium ore; concessions in the Mesopotamian oilfields, preferential deliveries of Turkish wool, vegetable oils, hides and skins; in the case of railway construction preference to be given to German firms in all contracts, concessions, etc.

The reverses in the west, even the Black Day of August 8, brought no break in Germany's Turkish policy. The aims remained the same: economic penetration, military and political links with Germany. Another conference was held on August 9 between representatives of the Foreign Ministry, the Reich Economic Office, the Constantinople embassy, the Reich Naval Office, the Ministry of War and the Ministry for Trade and Industry, and these resolved unanimously that 'the Mesopotamian oil-wells must in any event come within Germany's sphere of influence' – because the Rumanian oil secured by the treaty of Bucharest ('the acquisition of which is foreseen in the Bucharest peace') would not suffice for Germany's needs.

Germany as a Colonial Power: Mittelafrika and bases

Both in the spring of 1917 after the opening of unrestricted submarine warfare and its first successes, and in the spring of 1918 after the conclusion of the eastern peace treaties and the first successes of the offensive in the west, it looked as though the war would soon end in victory and the realisation of Germany's war aims. Her colonial war aims,[1] in particular, were re-formulated both in 1917 and 1918. The business interests, the OHL and above all the civilian authorities – in this case the Reich Colonial Office – alike hoped to be able to realise all their ambitions, at the expense of both Britain and France, and expressed them accordingly.

On December 23, in the middle of the preparations for Brest-Litovsk and simultaneously with those for the western offensive, Ludendorff sent the government the OHL's colonial programme: 'A great African colonial empire running through Africa from coast to coast, with naval bases on the coasts of the Atlantic and Indians oceans.'

Solf wrote to the Foreign Ministry on January 30, 1918 that he

---

[1] For the colonial aims of 1914, see above, pp. 102 ff and 109 ff.

was 'pleased' that the Chief of the General Staff of the army in the field 'recognised the need for an African colonial empire with naval bases on the coasts of the Indian and Atlantic oceans', adding: 'I have long been advocating the creation of this colonial empire.' Solf had been in charge of Germany's colonial programme during the war and like Ludendorff he thought it necessary to concentrate Germany's aims on Africa in order to ensure the supply of tropical agricultural products – 'fruit, coffee, etc., oilseeds, rubber, hides, skins, wool, hardwoods' and the exploitation of the Katanga district with its rich deposits of copper and other metals. He did not, however, support Ludendorff's suggestion that Germany should renounce her possessions in the South Seas (the OHL would have kept only Samoa, for its phosphates), because he feared that this would involve 'a severe blow to Germany's prestige in an important part of the globe'. He was therefore emphatic that both the South Seas and Africa should be taken as vital war aims of Germany's.

The German Colonial Association also approached Solf again in the spring of 1918 through Johann Albrecht; since, it said, the decisive victory in the west now seemed to be imminent, it wanted to set down anew 'what seems to be necessary for the rational expansion of our future Central African colonial empire'. Solf received this document too with agreement and 'great satisfaction', and said that his most important tasks would be 'to influence public opinion in a sense favourable to our colonial plans and to keep alive and strong in all circles the idea of a mighty German colonial empire'. '*Since the beginning of the war* [author's italics] I have been advocating strongly that we should acquire colonial possessions of economic, political and military value on the greatest possible scale.' What were these acquisitions demanded by Johann Albrecht and described by Solf as having been 'in every case' 'carefully discussed' in the Reich Colonial Office and there 'assigned their appropriate urgency value'? In the west the Colonial Association asked for 'the productive lands of the Senegal and Niger basins, and thence southward to the sea', territories which had long been under cultivation and whose surpluses 'would make it possible to cover the expensive long-term operations of opening up the Congo basin and Angola without subsidies from the Reich'. Then Germany was to take over the Cape Verde Islands, Principé and São Thomé with Senegambia, the acquisition of whose 'industrious peoples' Solf announced publicly as an aim. In the east German East Africa was to be enlarged by British Northern Rhodesia and Portuguese Northern Mozambique, to link it up with South-West Africa and Angola; in the north Uganda and Kenya were to be attached to German East Africa, 'so as to provide a common frontier with Egypt'. The Comoro Islands and Madagascar were to provide bases for German trade; similarly Djibuti at the mouth of the Red Sea, 'as a counter-weight to Aden'. Germany would thus acquire a Central African colonial empire comprising the Congo, Angola, Northern Rhodesia, Nyasaland, Northern Mozambique, German East Africa (Tanganyika), Kenya, Uganda, and German South-West.

How little these ambitions of 1918 differed from earlier ones will appear from a glance at Johann Albrecht's first programme, put forward in September, 1914 and received with approval by Solf and also by Zimmermann; in that version the northern frontier of German Central Africa was to run south of latitude 20° – but north of the Niger and Senegal and of Lake Chad to the Sudanese frontier, thence to Kismayo on the Indian Ocean, leaving the whole of Uganda and Kenya with Germany. The proposed southern frontier was to run south of the Orange River and south of the Zambezi to Beira. In 1918 the southern frontier was retracted to the line of those rivers; in West Africa territory was sought only in the big river bends ('the business of satisfying the Saharan nomads' was left to France); the northern frontier of Central Africa was extended to latitude 5° – to include the Ubangi, but the Central African core and its heart, Katanga, were not given up. Both the Colonial Association and the Colonial Office proposed to safeguard the main eastern line of communications, the Suez Canal, by taking over the Anglo-French majority holding of its shares.

The following letter, written to Solf by an industrialist on March 27, 1918, was by no means untypical:

In all human expectation our troops will be occupying the French channel ports in the next few weeks and will, it is to be hoped, stay there for ever. Therewith the final hour of England's world power and England's world empire will have struck. In the course of centuries North America and Australia were Anglicised, South America Latinised. The time is at hand when Germany will be granted the power to Germanise virgin Africa.

Although cultural considerations influenced the idealists and the need of tropical products played a part in the Central African picture, yet for Germany, as an industrial power, the real aim of the new German Central African colonial empire was to secure the raw materials of Katanga. On January 12, 1917 – three days after the decision to begin unrestricted submarine warfare – the Imperial Commissioner for the banks in Belgium, Lumm (formerly a director of the Reichsbank), proposed that Germany should safeguard her claim to the ore-fields of the Congo by acquiring a controlling interest in the *Union Minière du Haut-Katanga*, preferably by invoking the 'reprisals legislation' enacted by Germany as occupying power to take over a majority of the shares in the company. This would create a *fait accompli* which would ensure Germany at least a share, with Belgium and Britain, in the exploitation of the ore-fields, in spite of any counter-moves by the *Union Minière* (the property and ownership of the capital were not under German control). This suggestion was considered departmentally in 1917, and in the spring of 1918 – characteristically – both the Foreign Ministry and the Reich Economic Office gave their consent to the liquidation of the *Union Minière*. On May 10 the Secretary of State of the Reich Colonial Office concurred.

Private initiative also worked hand in hand with state policy in taking over the Katanga mines – the Otavi Mining Company had registered a claim to the copper mines even before the war. On June 19, 1918 representatives of the Reich and of a group of entrepreneurs agreed on the aims and procedure to be followed towards the *Union Minière*. It was agreed in principle that the *Union* should be liquidated and the British and Belgian shares transferred into German hands, but the liquidation itself was to be postponed long enough to prevent counter-moves by Britain and Belgium, though executed soon enough 'to create a *fait accompli* before the opening of the peace negotiations'. Finally, the banks, especially the Disconto-Bank, insisted that the Reich must guarantee the enterprise, and that the *Union* must continue to enjoy the privilege of exemption from stamp duty. The state was also to guarantee the North Rhodesian and Benguele Railways, and would thus be standing surety for production and profit. The guarantee of the Benguele Railway, the use of which Solf had wanted to see assured to Germany as early as 1916, shows that the inclusion of Katanga among Germany's war aims dated from that year and not only from 1917–18.

Central Africa was to be equipped with a system of naval bases, trading and coaling stations. On Solf's proposal the ministries busied themselves in the spring and summer of 1918 with deciding where these should lie. On July 4, 1918 the Chief of the Naval Staff sent the following minute to the Secretaries of State in the Foreign Ministry and the Reich Naval Office and to the OHL:

> The main war aim of our naval warfare seems to me to be that we should be able in the future so to threaten England's sea approaches in the Atlantic and the Mediterranean that she shall be forced to keep the peace. This is possible only through the acquisition of island bases and the command of the West African coast, if possible from Cape Blanco (north of latitude 20° on the southern frontier of the Spanish Sahara) to German South-West Africa.

Admiral (retired) von Crapow and the big shipping companies collaborated in a most detailed study of the climatic, naval, military and economic qualifications of possible bases on the West Coast. From the military point of view Dakar was the first choice; it was highly developed, ready for immediate use, and its port had workshops and docks; it would however, be indefensible without a sufficient hinterland. The next best port for both military and trading purposes was Bathurst in British Gambia; it was Solf's own first choice. About on a par with Bathurst came Bissao on the Rio Grande in Portuguese Guinea, a little further south, and then Bolama, also in Portuguese Guinea. Both were protected by a defensive screen of islands, but Bissao was capable of more economic expansion and was preferable from the technical naval point or view. Conakry, the capital of Guinea, was carefully considered but rejected on technical military grounds, as was the mouth of the Congo; here the only place considered was Gabun (Libreville) in the Gulf of Guinea, with an excellent harbour, not far from the mouth of the Congo, which it could command. The two favourites to emerge in the middle of the summer were Dakar for its technical equipment and installations, and Bathurst for its natural advantages; the strategic situation of both was excellent. This concentration on the Atlantic coast and islands (the Cape Verde Islands were considered as bases) did not, however, mean that Germany was not also thinking of places further afield in the Indian ocean (Réunion) and even the Pacific. Northern Borneo, for example, was considered, partly for its iron; private interests, in the shape of the New Guinea Plantation Company, also made strong representations in favour of keeping the colony.

Even had the government been prepared, for reasons of high policy, to renounce Kiaochow as the price for a *rapprochement* with Japan, it was by no means ready to give up 'the huge economic area of China with nearly 400 million inhabitants of advanced purchasing power' for the sake of a 'little developed' Central Africa, however large; it asked for the continuance of the international status of Shanghai and Canton and the transfer to itself of the Belgian and French concessions in Tientsin and Hankow.

Although neither the bases programme nor the Central Africa programme was achieved by the war, they illustrate the global aspects of Germany's claim to become and maintain herself as a world power.

It is true that the colonial questions did not figure largely in the discussions on Germany's war aims; it was generally assumed that if Germany won the war they would practically realise themselves. The foreground of these discussions was occupied by European questions which were regarded as the foundation for any overseas policy. This order of importance was clearly expressed in a marginal note by an official in the Reich Interior Office to one of the numerous 'insatiable' representations received by it: 'Far more important than any colonial policy is a determined and extensive Germanisation of the new glacis to be acquired in east and west. Any money and manpower not needed there may be employed in colonies.'

The European glacis were Longwy–Briey in the west and the Polish frontier strips, Lithuania and the Baltic in the east.

Longwy–Briey: the Reich's mineral chamber

The minette field of Longwy–Briey in French Lorraine continued to constitute Germany's most important war aim in the west, and that to which government, OHL and private interests adhered most obstinately. In December, 1917, and January, 1918, Longwy–Briey was again the subject of memoranda submitted by the *Verein deutscher Eisen- und Stahlindustrieller* and the *Verein deutscher Eisenhüttenleute*. As in 1915, the representatives of German heavy industry called for 'the incorporation of the ore-fields of French Lorraine in the territory of the German Reich'. The minette of Longwy–Briey was ranked with the 'Bessemer red ores of Krivoi Rog' (so essential for Upper Silesia), the manganese ore of Chiaturi and the magnetic iron ore of Nicopol. The acquisition of Longwy–Briey was demanded as 'an absolutely vital necessity for the future development of the German iron and steel industry in Germany'.

In the spring of 1918, when they were expecting early victory in the west, the Imperial and Prussian Ministries themselves again took a particularly active interest in the question of Longwy–Briey. Baron von Stein, Secretary of State of the Reich Economic Office, told Ludendorff and Sydow, the Prussian Minister for Trade and Industry, that it was 'vital for Germany to secure a sufficient part of these ores'. Even favourable long-term contracts would not, in his view, suffice to assure Germany's 'part' and influence. 'Even the best-devised agreement is still only paper.' Stein wanted a company organised before the peace negotiations opened to take over the mines, six-sevenths of which were French-owned. Both Ludendorff and Sydow agreed that the ownership of the mines must be assured; the only way of doing this permanently was to incorporate the area in the Reich. Sydow thought that if this was done, it would be particularly necessary to make certain that the expropriation applied also to the land, buildings, furnaces, rolling mills, etc. connected with the mines. To make sure that no French proprietor was left with a share in the mines taken over, inventories must be compiled of all objects with data of their value and owners. Sydow said still more forcefully that there were two possible ways of taking over ownership: compulsory liquidation before the conclusion of peace, or transfer to the Reich under the peace treaty. He was strongly in favour of the former course, partly in order to create a *fait accompli* before peace negotiations and partly in order to enable Prussia—not the Reich and not private enterprise—to take over the administration of the mines. Stein agreed with Sydow's proposals, especially with 'the expropriation of all foreign titles to the mines and concessions'; he also agreed that Longwy–Briey should be put under state administration as 'national property', and not be given to private persons. 'The decision, however, whether the administration shall be Prussian or Imperial depends on whether the Briey basin becomes Prussian or Reichsland.' In any case, no more foundries were to be built in the basin; in the future only mining must be carried on there. On August 12 Stein asked Ludendorff to set foot on the necessary preparations for the expropriations.

Although agreeing in principle, the Foreign Ministry thought that liquidation could be effected only in conjunction with the incorporation of the area. It thought immediate liquidation, as advocated by Sydow, Stein and Ludendorff, dangerous on grounds both of foreign and domestic policy, since it would be regarded as a sign of impending annexation. It therefore asked for further consideration in committee. On August 17 Ludendorff invited the departments to meet on September 17, clearly hoping that by that time the military situation would have improved, but on September 15 he found himself forced to postpone the conference again. Not until October 15 did Stein announce that any further preparations for the incorporation of Longwy–Briey and the expropriation of the mines and foundries 'had been rendered otiose by recent developments in the political situation'.

Longwy–Briey was, however, also the key-stone of the proposed commercial treaty with France. If the basin was to be ceded, Germany was according nothing more than most favoured nation treatment, but if it was left with France, conditions were to be imposed which guaranteed to Germany at least one-third of her supplies of ore from France. Stein further wanted a preferential treaty allowing Germany to 'lay hands on' France's Thomas meal and slag, silk, vegetable oils, wool, bauxite, phosphates, chromium and nickel. France's industry would then have stagnated and the country would have sunk into the position of a supplier of raw materials to Germany.

Belgium: the vassal in the west

In 1918 the customs union was still the most important war aim in Belgium. It was defined ever more closely in innumerable inter-departmental conferences and memoranda. Through it and other economic agreements (currency, tariff and transport unions) the German political leaders hoped to enlarge Germany 'by a land blessed agriculturally and industrially' and to 'increase her weight in commercial negotiations'. Economic penetration was to be the basis for 'drawing Belgium into the German power sphere'. When Belgium had signed a military convention and customs union, linked her tariffs and transport systems with Germany's, had adopted the Reich's legislation on monopolies, social legislation and indirect taxation, had left the Latin currency union and adopted the mark, she would have become a tributary state, Germany's vassal in the west, without Germany having to proceed to direct annexation. Up to July and August, 1918 preparations were being carried on for a peace treaty on the basis of 'two separate states, Flanders and Wallonia', each with its own parliament, linked by one crown and *one* Ministry of Economics. It was only in October, and then only reluctantly, that the departments retreated from their more extreme demands, but even then they still demanded a preferential economic position in Belgium.

As in Poland and the Ukraine, the most important objective in this connection was the integration of Belgium's communications – 'the life-lines of the Belgian economy' – with those of Germany. The leading and most active mover in this policy was von Breitenbach. In the summer of 1918 Breitenbach was pressing for a number of agreements 'based on our experience in the east': the establishment of a joint Belgian–German railway board, a tariff agreement and the linking of Belgium's inland waterways with those of Germany, with the twin objects of influencing Belgium's economic potential and getting the lines to the port of Antwerp completely under German control. Breitenbach's plans were supported by the Governor-General, by von Stein and Helfferich, and also by the governments of the south German states, Bavaria, Baden, Württemberg and Hesse, the Chambers of Commerce of Frankfurt, Mannheim, etc. and the Hanseatic towns of Hamburg and Bremen.

As early as January, 1918 the Department for Trade and Industry in the Government-General worked out 'principles for handling the question of the port of Antwerp'. These principles were communicated to the federal governments, the Imperial and Prussian Ministries and business organisations. They contained the usual demands, and also asked for complete equality of treatment for German and Belgian subjects in all questions of trade, industry and shipping as a basis for a German–Belgian economic treaty – a demand which Stein adopted in June in his draft of a definitive treaty, and advised Helfferich to accept. But the nub of the 'principles' was a complete blueprint of a Port Authority for Antwerp. This authority was to have an initial capital of two million francs. The German government was to be allotted 60 per cent of the shares at par and an option on a similar proportion in any future increases of capital. Forty per cent of the shares would go to the city of Antwerp. Three-fifths of the Directors and Commissioners (inspectors) must by statute be German nationals. The German government was also empowered to nominate a Special Commission and a Vice-Commissioner. The authority was exclusively responsible for the administration of the port, in which the Belgian state had no voice.

The federal states agreed to the proposals; Hesse went even further and wanted the port annexed to the Reich (as the German government itself had proposed in 1914, 1915 and 1916). At the Governor-General's wish, a great conference was convoked for late July or early August, to be attended by representatives of the Reich and the Prussian Ministries, interested Chambers of Commerce (particularly those of south-west Germany) and the industrial associations of Brussels and Antwerp. Only the deterioration in the military situation led Breitenbach to limit the inspection of the port installations to a smaller number of visitors – a big assemblage of notables would have betrayed the intentions of the German Reich too clearly.

On August 3 a preliminary conference of all Reich and Prussian authorities interested was held in the Reich Interior Office. The meeting again strongly endorsed the idea of the Port Authority, the detailed statutes of which were already before it, and discussed and adopted an agreement for taking over the port.

Military plans, too, were being discussed up to the very end of the war. The OHL, although forced to retreat from its more advanced positions, still clung to the possibility of local annexations, including at least Liége. Similarly, the navy was still asking for the annexation of the Flanders coast in the early summer of 1918.[1] The OHL was also much concerned with the questions of raising a new army for Belgium, and of the duration of the occupation. On May 25[2] representatives of the OHL and the Government-General (the Foreign Ministry and the Imperial Chancellery were not invited) decided

[1] Rüdiger, op. cit., pp. 143 ff. (the demand was made by Scheer's successor, Holtzendorff).

[2] Id., p. 168.

that the occupying force must comprise at least eight divisions, and the occupation last ten years. Belgium herself was not to be allowed an army, but only a police force. Later, a Belgian army should be trained in German garrisons under German supervision; it was to be employed exclusively on the frontier against France. These precautions were meant to consolidate the proposed administrative partition of Belgium into Flanders and Wallonia, and also Germany's economic objectives.

The Flemish policy too was prosecuted with energy, if in the face of mounting difficulties. On December 22, 1917 the Council of Flanders had resolved to proclaim the autonomy of Flanders.[1] Internal differences at once broke out between the Young Flamands, who wanted an 'independent' Flemish state, and the Unionists, who were still asking for two autonomous but united states of Flanders and Wallonia. The Young Flamands were in the majority in the Council, but the German Government was reluctant to endorse a proclamation embodying the wishes of the radical group, which did not accord with Germany's own ideas. It was only under pressure from Ludendorff, who thought that publication of the declaration would split the Belgian army, that the government agreed to publication on January 19 without, however, recognising the autonomy of an independent Flanders.

In March a second Council of Flanders was constituted on the basis of 'elections' held in January and February, a step on which Wallraf in particular had insisted in order to give the Flemish movement an appearance of legality.[2] The elections were, however, no free expression of opinion; this second Council was 'elected by acclamation' by a series of mass meetings, at which 50,000 signatures were collected. It pressed for independence and political autonomy, including its own legislature, administration and judicature, but the German government ignored these demands as completely as it had ignored the appeal of the first Council to the German people to abolish the 'artificial creation' of Belgium.[3]

The decisions of the war aims conference in Spa[4] make it abundantly clear that Germany's Flemish policy was only a political device to establish Germany's economic, political and military domination over Belgium.

Belgium, it was said, must remain under German influence, to prevent it from ever coming under Franco-English influence and being used by our enemies as a deployment area. To this end the separation of Flanders and

[1] See above, p. 450.
[2] *Archives du Conseil de Flandre*, pp. 50 ff.
[3] Rüdiger, op. cit., pp. 6 f.   [4] Volkmann, op. cit., pp. 223 f.

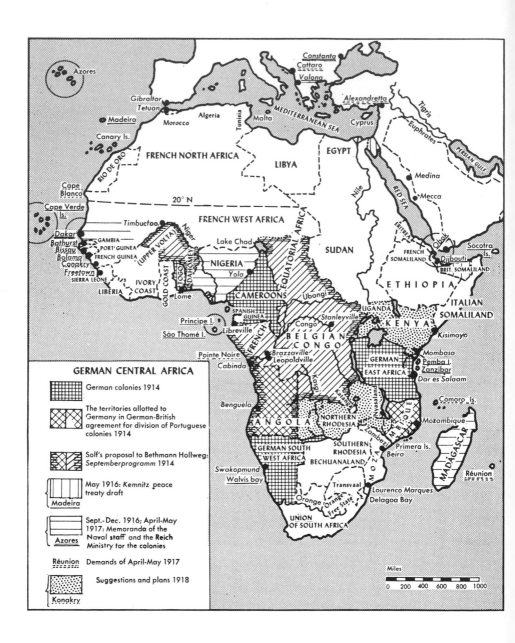

GERMAN CENTRAL AFRICA

German colonies 1914

The territories allotted to Germany in German-British agreement for division of Portuguese colonies 1914

Solf's proposal to Bethmann Hollweg: *Septemberprogramm* 1914

May 1916: *Kemnitz* peace treaty draft

Madeira

Sept.-Dec. 1916; April-May 1917: Memoranda of the Naval staff and the Reich Ministry for the colonies

Azores

Réunion   Demands of April-May 1917

Suggestions and plans 1918

Konakry

596

Wallonia into two separate states, united only by a personal union and economic agreements, is to be encouraged. Belgium will be brought into a very close relationship with Germany through a customs union, joint railway system, etc. For the present, there must be no Belgian army.

Germany ensures herself a long occupation, gradually reduced, so that the last areas to be evacuated are the Flemish coast and Liége. Complete evacuation depends on Belgium's attaching herself to us very closely. In particular, there must be completely reliable guarantees of the defence of the coast through Flanders.

These decisions formed the basis of Hertling's famous declaration on Belgium to the Central Committee of the Reichstag on July 11 when, like Bethmann Hollweg and Michaelis, he gave a solemn assurance that Germany did not intend 'to take permanent possession of Belgium', but only to keep it as a 'pledge' for future peace negotiations, i.e., Belgium would be restored only after Germany's 'guarantees' had been assured. Hertling was also pursuing the old political tactics of seeking a separate peace between Germany and Belgium; he repeated that 'close relations with Belgium in the economic field' would be in Belgium's own interest, for which reason Germany was trying to reach a direct understanding with her on the political issues. This speech, which left all questions relating to Belgium open, was applauded by the Zentrum, the Progressives, the Conservatives and the National Liberals, so that the government's hands remained completely free.

The Flemish activist groups and the Council of Flanders were disappointed by this speech. The Flemish movement and Germany's policy were not mentioned at all; indeed Hertling had talked of 're-instating Belgium'. Tension between the Council of Flanders and the German government became so acute that on July 25 the Governor-General forbade the Council to meet until further notice. The Chancellor, however, had been carrying on detailed negotiations both with the Young Flamands and the Unionists.[1] At the end of July Hertling told the president of the second Council of Flanders, Professor Devreese, and the leader of the unionists, Oboussier, that although he had not expressly said so to the Reichstag, his attitude towards the Flemish was exactly the same as Bethmann Hollweg's. A few days later, on August 3, Hertling again defined his attitude to the president of the first Council of Flanders, Tack, and De Decker, entirely accepting the unionist programme of two states under one sovereignty. The Flemish put forward far-reaching requests for the appointment of a constitutional committee and a provisional government and the transfer of the administration of the towns to the

[1] Archives, pp. LV ff.

Young Flamands, but Hertling evaded them by his promise to create two states. He had further conversations with the Unionist leaders, when the question of changing the communal councils into Flemish bodies – but without new elections – was again discussed, but the turn in the military situation soon made these discussions purely academic.

The Baltic and Lithuania:
Conventions and Personal Union with Prussia or Germany

The original annexationist purposes of German policy survived in purest form in the attempts to 'attach' Lithuania, Courland, Livonia and Estonia. On March 8, 1918, five days after the signature of the Treaty of Brest-Litovsk, the Courland 'National Council', in which the Baltic Germans possessed an absolute majority, met under the presidency of Baron Rahden-Mayhoff and resolved to beg the German Emperor and king of Prussia to accept the dual crown of Courland for himself and his heirs. It further expressed the wish that the three Baltic provinces, of which Livonia and Estonia still belonged technically to Russia, might be united in a single state with a common constitution and administration and be attached permanently to the German Reich. Thirdly, it suggested the conclusion of a military convention and conventions on customs, weights and measures, and the transport systems.

On March 15 a delegation from the Council carried this resolution to Hertling, who announced Germany's recognition of the independence of Courland in the name of the Emperor. He left the question of a personal union with Prussia open. He treated the question of the unification of the three provinces with reserve, on foreign political grounds.

The official recognition of the independence of Courland was pronounced by the Emperor on March 29.[1] At the same time he said that the German Reich was ready 'to conclude with Courland such treaties as would ensure a close economic and military connection between the two countries'.

Events followed a different course in Estonia and Livonia, which had been occupied by German 'police units' since the Peace of Brest-Litovsk. The Chancellor, the OHL and the Reichstag all held held different views on the futures of these two countries. Ludendorff took his own line, contrary to Kühlmann's wishes and warnings. In obedience to his initiative, and following exact instructions laid down by him, an Estonian National Assembly met in Reval on April 9 and a Livonian in Riga on April 10. Both announced their secession from

[1] See Lewerenz, *Baltikum*, p. 179.

Russia and then met in Riga on April 12 to constitute the 'United National Council of Livonia, Estonia, Riga and Oesel.' The new bodies were so composed as to ensure the Baltic Germans the absolute majority, exactly as had been arranged at Bingen on July 31, 1917.[1] On April 12 the 'United Council' duly resolved to beg the Emperor 'to keep Livonia and Estonia permanently under German military protection'; it furthermore endorsed the wish already expressed by Courland that the whole Baltic coast should be formed into 'a unitary and undivided monarchist, constitutional state with a unitary constitution and administration, and be attached to the German Reich through a personal union under the king of Prussia.'

Finally, it asked for the conclusion of 'conventions' between this new state and the German Reich.

Ludendorff now pressed the Chancellor to receive at the earliest possible date the deputation for which he had arranged from the United National Council. There was disagreement among the civilian leaders whether Germany should inform the delegation that she recognised the independence of Livonia and Estonia unasked and immediately, as she had done with Courland. The Chancellor thought that this step would be politically correct, but possibly not opportune, and he was therefore rather inclined only to promise the delegation support for their requests, in particular for military protection. Payer had warned him that the Reichstag felt that consideration for both German and world opinion, and also the need to preserve good-neighbourly relations with Russia, forbade recognition of the independence of these countries on such a basis. For recent moves had revived the mistrust of the left about official policy in the north-east. Two Estonians, Karl Menning and Martna, representing the democratically elected government which had been forcibly ousted by the Germans on their entry into Reval on February 24, had entered protests against the conduct of the German military administration and against the United Council convoked by them and its resolutions. They denied the Council any competence to speak for the country and protested both against the disbandment of the Estonian troops and the liquidation by the Germans of the organs of self-government.

The majority parties were not, however, opposed on principle to the policy of the OHL (which Hertling had himself adopted). The point was to gain time; as Payer told the Chancellor, characteristi-

---

[1] Marna, op. cit., pp. 103 f. Of the 58 members of the Council, 34 were Baltic Germans, 13 Estonians, and 11 Letts. The non-Germans had been carefully hand picked.

cally, if the government moved slowly Gröber's party 'would not utter a squeak'.

After consulting the departments and talking to representatives of the parties, the Chancellor told the OHL on April 20 that, 'to avoid the difficulties which might be expected to result from *immediate* recognition of Estonia and Livonia', he proposed in his answer to adhere strictly to the text of the United Council's address. When therefore he received the deputation on April 21, he spoke of independence for the whole Baltic as prospective and repeated once again that the German Reich was prepared to afford it military protection.[1]

While the question of recognition was thus for a time postponed, the question of the form under which the Baltic and Lithuania were later to be attached to the Reich now became the subject of lively argument between the different German authorities.

On May 14, after Germany's second successful offensive in the west, a meeting of commissioners was held in the Reich Interior Office to consider 'the future constitutional relationships between the German Reich on the one hand and Courland and Lithuania on the other'. The conference had before it the so-called *Oberost* draft, which had been composed by Professor Bredt, an authority on political science. It began by remarking that a simple contractual obligation was insufficient, since it could be denounced; the association must take the form of a real or personal union. How far the German Reich could take into consideration the wishes of the various nationalities must remain an open question. The contractual guarantees (the so-called conventions) should not, however, be so far-reaching as to take from the countries their 'independent character'; they should retain their internal self-administration, while in respect of foreign policy the predominance of the German Reich, which must represent the border states at both the diplomatic and the consular levels, must be absolute.

The most important economic provision of the draft was that the German Reich should form 'a single customs area' with the Duchy of Courland and the Grand Principality of Lithuania, whose financial and transport systems should be closely attached to the German.[2] The Prussian Minister of the Interior wanted the administration also to be transferred to Prussia, but this was not accepted, chiefly owing to the objections of Gossler, the head of the Courland administra-

[1] Von Stryck and von Bevern tried to get Joffe to recognise the secession of Livonia and Estonia, but Joffe refused to do so before the conclusion of the supplementary treaties.

[2] The two countries were also to be required to pay 7 million marks towards the cost of the war, but as this sum would have exceeded their capacities, the state domains and forests were to be pledged to the Reich.

tion, that nothing at all would have been left of Bethmann Hollweg's promised 'autonomy' if the countries became simply Prussian provinces.

Elucidatory provisions attached to the draft by General Hoffmann were too tame for Ludendorff,[1] who produced annexes which dealt with the economic and transport systems of the countries entirely from the angle of a possible new war. He wanted the treaty of alliance extended immediately to Estonia and Livonia.

In transmitting the decisions of the conference to the Chancellor, the Secretary of State for the Interior advised 'consideration of the further possibility of attaching Livonia and Estonia to the Reich'. In order to elucidate the problems raised by the association, first of Courland, then of the whole Baltic area, with the Reich, and to get round as far as possible the competence of the Federal Council as representative of the federal states, the Chancellor had two Opinions drawn up in the summer of 1918 which examined in detail the question of the relationship between Courland and Prussia. The first of these stressed the necessity of consulting the Reichsrat and the Federal Council, while the second approached the problem from the political rather than the legal angle and pointed out that the Emperor-King must be covered by the consent of his responsible advisers, viz., the Imperial Chancellor and the Prussian Ministry of State.

The second document formed the basis for further consultations in the Prussian Ministry of State on July 12. The Minister of the Interior said that the first step must be to consult the Prussian Diet; the next must be to set up a central constitutional authority in Courland itself, with which a treaty could be concluded. The existing 'National Council' could be regarded as representing the people, but not constituting a sovereign body; sovereignty must therefore be assumed by the king himself by a proclamation. The king, *qua* duke of Courland, would then have to conclude the treaties with the Reich, i.e., with himself *qua* Emperor. Similarly, he would have to impose a constitution, which would then have to be confirmed by the national body. Similar views were expressed by Spahn, the Prussian Minister of Justice. Both Spahn and the Minister of Finance, Hergt, wanted the whole Baltic area attached to Prussia, but under a real and not a personal union, in order that the area might later be turned into a Prussian province.

Thus Prussia remained true to herself to the last hour: the new state was not to rest on the basis of popular sovereignty, but on an

---

[1] The annexes included 'measures to be taken to prevent emigration of the Jews'.

authority created from above by the hereditary monarchy, only slightly restricted, within bounds chosen by itself, by a constitution imposed at its discretion.

A similar authoritarian solution was under consideration for Lithuania, but the deliberations were overtaken by events. Lithuania's relationship to Prussia–Germany was still completely unclarified, since neither the constitutional question nor the question of the conventions had been brought any nearer to solution, although on March 23 the Emperor had officially notified the Taryba of his recognition of Lithuania's independence.[1] Erzberger, who had been working on a 'solution' of the Lithuanian question since the beginning of April, 1918, now intervened.[2] Thanks to his endeavours the Taryba, on June 4, secretly elected to the throne the duke of Urach of the Catholic Württemberg line (under the name of Mindaugas II) – and secured his consent. At the same time Erzberger spoke in the Reichstag advocating that Lithuania should have its own government. This suggestion was officially rejected by Falkenhausen. On July 11, after Kühlmann had resigned and when there were consequent fears of a military dictatorship, the Taryba constituted itself a 'Council of State', viz., a governing body on the Polish model, proclaimed Lithuania a constitutional Monarchy and, offered the crown to the duke of Urach. This was a move designed to exclude any possibility of a personal union with Prussia or Saxony. The news had a shattering effect in Germany. The Chancellor rejected the election and had a declaration printed in the *N.A.Z.* on July 21 to the effect that the recognition of Lithuania's independence had been conditional upon the prior conclusion of the conventions necessary to safeguard Germany's interests. 'As things stood', however, this condition had not been fulfilled.[3] Almost the entire German press condemned the Lithuanians' move.

The controversies which followed led on August 1 to the division of the former military administration of *Oberost*. Courland, with Riga, the Islands of Oesel, Moon and Dagoe, the rest of Livonia, and Estonia, were grouped in a 'Military Administration of the Baltic Lands', under the Eighth Army. Lithuania, including Augustovo, Suwalki and the military forestry administration of Bialowièza, Byalistok and Grodno, was converted into a 'Military Government of Lithuania' with headquarters in Vilno. The central administra-

---

[1] See above, p. 472.

[2] Colliander, op. cit., pp. 192 f.

[3] Klimas, op. cit., p. 152. For the Taryba's Declaration and the Council of State's letter to Hertling, ibid., pp. 144–7. On the reaction of the press, see Colliander, pp. 197 f.

tion of *Oberost* was liquidated and Under-Secretary of State von Falkenhausen, who had previously been attached to it, was taken into the Reich Ministry of the Interior as 'Reich Commissioner for the Baltic Areas and Lithuania'. The result of this reshuffle was that Prusso-German policy concentrated on the Baltic, while Lithuania was given a special position; interest in that country gradually came to be confined to its position as an anti-Polish factor in the belt of border states.

Further discussions between the Prussian ministries produced a long report by the Ministry of State – one more testimony to Prussia's obstinate determination to expand – 'On the attachment of Courland, Livonia, Estonia and Lithuania.' The sequence of technical independence followed by alliance could not be followed in all four countries. The report recommended recognising the independence of Estonia and Livonia, and strongly advised 'announcing a simultaneous and identical settlement of the political future of all three Baltic countries'. If this result were to be delayed until the conclusion of general peace, at least an irrevocable *fait accompli* must be created in Courland and Riga. The Emperor annotated the word 'delayed' in the margin: 'Must not be! This must be settled first. This is no business whatever of the Americans.'

The Ministry of State was against attaching the countries to the Reich and strongly advocated a personal union with Prussia, which would better secure the 'indispensable economic unity' between the border states and the Reich'. The Emperor too was flatly against personal union with the Reich. 'No! That would be a second Alsace-Lorraine.' Nor should the Reichstag intervene in what was a part of the royal prerogative.

His Majesty deigned to remark that He did not want to object further to the Reichstag being officially consulted on personal union between Prussia and the new Baltic state, but expected that when this was done, the fact that it was not constitutionally competent should be strongly stressed. His Majesty did not want to curtail in any way the rights of the Reichstag, but was particularly insistent that the rights of the Crown must be equally respected.

These were the views of Wilhelm II *qua* king of Prussia, and of the Prussian Ministry of State, but they were strongly opposed by von Hintze, now representing the Reich as Kühlmann's successor, and also by Falkenhausen.

1. The German Reich, wrote Hintze on September 18, has in its proclamations rejected annexations, but the proposed solution amounts to that. 2. Viceroys in these countries would cause difficulties. 3. The differences

between natural, economic and social conditions in Prussia and the border states make it impossible to rule them on the same principles. 4. Like the Ministry of State, he dislikes the idea of a Saxon dynasty for Lithuania, because of the Poles. 5. Personal union with Prussia would lead to big parliamentary difficulties.

Hintze accordingly begged the Emperor to reconsider the question of a personal union.

The last discussion of Baltic problems was held in Hertling's Chancellery on September 20. Hertling too rejected the 'Prussian' treaties. The Foreign Ministry produced new drafts for the alliance with Courland, including the financial and legal appendices. Under these, Courland was to retain its formal independence, but decisions on war and peace were to rest with the Reich, and German interests must be considered when important foreign treaties were concluded and in economic relations with foreign countries. Von dem Bussche thought that 'in practice, German influence is secured everywhere'.

The interest of German public opinion in the 'German Baltic' reached another peak before the war ended – on the glorious occasion, hailed in Germany with extreme enthusiasm, of the re-opening of the University of Dorpat on September 15, 1918.[1] This idea of re-founding a German university on old German colonial territory as an eastern outpost of German culture was a result of a systematic cultural policy which was put into effect step by step as the German troops advanced along the Baltic.

As early as 1913 a large number of idealistic and patriotic German savants from the Reich had met in a so-called summer university in Riga with the intention of promoting a 'movement of world philosophy' which should 'save from cultural isolation this part of the German people which politically is separated from us'. The participants included such men as Adolf von Harnack, Ernst Troetsch and L. von Schroeder from Vienna.

When Riga was taken in September, 1917 lecture courses by German professors were instituted 'as desired and resolved by the High Command of the Army' (the suggestion had come from Max Sering, the author of the memoranda on which the colonisation policy was based). In the spring of 1918 they were extended to Dorpat and Reval. The leading figures of academic Germany took part: Max Sering (on 'The Meaning of the World War'), Reinhold Seeberg (on 'The German spirit and the cultural significance of Protestantism'), Dietrich Schäfer ('The historical role of the Baltic countries'), Erich Marcks ('Goethe and Bismarck, intellectual and political

[1] Roderich von Engelhardt, *Die Deutsche Universität Dorpat in ihrer geistesgeschichtlichen Bedeutung* (Munich, 1933), pp. 535 ff. and 524 ff.

Germany'), Georg Kerschensteiner, Hans Driesch, Eduard Meyer, Alois Riehl, Ulrich von Wilamowitz-Moellendorff, and many others.

At the end of March, 1918 Professor Karl Dehio was instructed by General von Estorff, then commanding the Eighth Army, to produce a memorandum on Dorpat University. He submitted it on April 2. The Prussian Minister of Education, Schmidt-Ott, provided the funds. A teaching staff of sixty-three was collected, partly by releasing serving soldiers. Dehio was chosen to be the first rector. As curator Wilhelm II personally appointed Theodor Schiemann, the man who, with Johannes Haller, had worked most closely to bring about the attachment of Livonia and Estonia to Prussia.

All lectures were to be in German, although the students of the old university, of whom there had been about a thousand in 1915, had consisted of Germans, Estonians and Letts in about equal numbers. This was a political move of the first importance, for it showed once again that at the end of the war and in conditions entirely different from those of 1914 the same policy of Germanisation was being followed. The consequent protests, from both enemy and neutral countries, were so sharp that Wilhelm II himself could not disregard them. German, and especially academic, public opinion, had welcomed the decision as an expression of the nation's confidence in itself and its mission. The rector of the university of Frankfurt-am-Main, for example, Professor A. Bethe, sent a message to the teachers and students in Dorpat: 'The teaching shall be German again, the language shall be and remain German, for the weal of the land, the weal of the Reich.'

Although the Germans were pinning high hopes on the Baltic as late as September, in Lithuania their cause continued to stagnate. After the Taryba's resolutions of July 11 had yielded no fruit, the Lithuanian 'Council of State' continued to press for recognition of its new position as representing Lithuania. On September 14 Hertling repeated that recognition of the Council of State still depended on the conclusion of the conventions with Germany; in the absence of these the Taryba had no competence beyond what was assigned to it in the autumn of 1917. The Council of State was at last recognised on October 20 by the new Chancellor, Prince Max of Baden, who said that he was leaving it to the Taryba to form a government, and that Germany would not intervene either in the matter of the constitution or in that of the frontiers. These last words were a veiled threat that Germany would leave Vilno to the mercy of the Poles.[1]

[1] For instance: Polish self-defence organisations had been organised in Vilno, with the agreement of the German authorities.

The Council of State adopted a provisional constitution on October 28, and on November 2 it revoked the election of the duke of Urach, thereby – contentious as this candidature had been – breaking a link with Germany. On November 5 Voldemaras, who had been elected Prime Minister, formed his cabinet, the new independent state was constituted, and the war aim so long pursued by Germany fell from her grasp.

Germany did not give up her ambitions so quickly in the Baltic provinces, especially Courland. On October 6 Ludendorff agreed with the Secretary of State for the Interior and the Minister of War that all communications on important questions of principle between those two offices and the military administrations of the Baltic lands and Lithuania should pass through the OHL – so tenaciously did the military regime oppose any attempt by the 'civilian' government to assert itself.

Not until October 15 did Payer open negotiations to replace the military administration by a civilian one. The military administration set up in the autumn of 1915 was terminated on November 3 by a cabinet decree signed by the Emperor 'on the appointment of civilian administrations on the Baltic and in Lithuania'.

But Germany had by no means given up her Baltic plans. The Emperor had recognised the independence of Estonia and Livonia on September 22, but on November 7, two days before the revolution, a Council of Regency for Courland, Livonia and Estonia, elected by the National Councils,[1] was established to bring into being a unitary state comprising all these lands, and on November 11 this Council established a Baltic militia.

Meanwhile, however, revolution had broken out in Berlin and, encouraged by it, a provisional Estonian government had been formed, to which the German occupying authorities handed over their functions on the 12th. As this government was sympathetic to the Bolsheviks, Germany could exercise no influence over it. The prospects seemed different in the republic of Latvia, which had been proclaimed within its ethnographic frontiers on November 28, with the peasant leader K. Ulmanis as Prime Minister. Here the German Right-wing Social Democrat August Winnig,[2] who had been appointed Plenipotentiary General for the Baltic four days before and had been given over seven million gold marks in cash with which to operate, was still in a position to do something to promote one of Germany's oldest war aims, her colonisation plans – though now only

[1] Reinhard Wittram, 'Zur Geschichte des Winters 1918-19', in *Baltische Lande*, ed. A. Brackman and others (Leipzig, 1939), Vol. IV, No. I, p. 20.

[2] August Winnig, *Am Ausgang der deutschen Ostpolitik* (Berlin, 1921), pp. 36 ff.

in collaboration with the Latvian democracy, which itself was being threatened by Bolshevik forces. On November 29 Winnig concluded a treaty with the Ulmanis government[1] under which the latter promised to grant Latvian citizenship to any German soldier who did four weeks' military service for the country. Winnig described this treaty as his crowning achievement for Germany; later he invoked it to claim that all the German soldiers were entitled to colonise land in Latvia.

Thus the plans evolved between 1915 and 1918 by Schwerin, Sering, Ludendorff and Gossler survived even after Germany's defeat in the west and helped to project the idea of a German colonists' land in the north-east into the Weimar period, which inherited an anti-Bolshevik, anti-democratic nationalism, untainted by any feeling of defeat, from the German 'Free Corps', the men of the *Balticum* who had set themselves up on the Baltic and were recalled thence to Germany under pressure from the Entente.

Imperium Germanicum

A survey of Germany's aims at the beginning and in the middle of 1918, when German self-confidence was at its peak in the expectation of early victory, discloses a picture of an *imperium* of grandiose dimensions. In the west: Belgium, Luxemburg, Longwy–Briey linked with Germany on such terms as to make possible the adherence of France and Holland and to isolate Britain and force her to recognise Germany's position; in the east: Courland, Livonia, Estonia and Lithuania, from Reval to Riga and Vilno, the Polish Frontier Strip and Rump Poland all closely fettered to Germany; in the south-east: Austria-Hungary clamped into Germany as a cornerstone, then Rumania and Bulgaria, and beyond them the Ottoman Empire as an object of Germany's Asiatic policy. Command of the eastern Mediterranean was to compel the adherence of Greece and secure the route through Suez, while the domination of the Black Sea guaranteed the economic mastery of the Ukraine, the Crimea and Georgia, and the command of the Baltic compelled Sweden and Finland, with their riches, to take the German side. On top of all this was the position of at least economic hegemony in Rump Russia.

The counterpart overseas of this European extended basis – Mitteleuropa surrounded by a ring of vassal states – was to be the central African colonial empire safeguarded by naval bases and linked with the Near East through the Sudan and Suez. With this economic and political power in Africa, reinforced by the command of the strategic and technical key-points on the route to South America to expand

[1] Id., pp. 83 f.

and consolidate the strong economic interests already established there before the war, Germany was to make herself a colonial and economic power of world status. Yet concentration on the African empire implied no withdrawal from the eastern hemisphere. Germany was maintaining her interests in Samoa and New Guinea and trying to initiate in China a more elastic policy, confined purely to the safeguarding of her economic interests. Above all, she hoped that by ceding Kiaochow to Japan she would be able to renew her old connections with that country against both Russia and the Anglo-Saxon powers.

Germany's political and economic *imperium* would have represented a concentration of force far surpassing Bismarck's empire in resources and human material. The old industrial areas of the Ruhr and Luxemburg, the Saar, German Lorraine, Saxony and Upper Silesia were to be reinforced by French Lorraine, Belgium, Poland and Bohemia. For her supply of ore, besides her own production and the assured imports from Sweden, she could have drawn on the ores of Austria, Poland, Longwy–Briey, the Ukraine, the Caucasus, Turkey and Katanga. To the oil of Galicia was added that of Rumania, the Caucasus and Mesopotamia, to her own agricultural production that of the Balkans and the north-east, to her previous imports from her old colonies in Africa, the abundant produce of central Africa; markets previously contested would be replaced by near-monopoly in Georgia, Turkey, Russia, the Ukraine, the Balkans, the north-east, the north and the west. The weight of the German Reich in matters of commercial policy would unquestionably have put Germany in an impregnable position of world-economic power. The economic agreements were, moreover, to be safeguarded by military treaties.

Military conventions with Finland, the Baltic states, Lithuania, Poland, the Ukraine, Georgia, Turkey, Bulgaria, Rumania and Austria-Hungary, and in a negative sense also with Belgium, had been planned, and most of them at least initialled. Through these economic, political and military links Germany would have created a European bloc which would have put her on a level with the three world powers of America, Britain and – if she could still be counted – Russia, and have given her a rank far above that of any European power of the old days.

The realisation of this world-wide aim depended on victory in the west, where the fresh and unexhausted power of America had come to the assistance of the British, French and Belgian armies.

23

IN EXPECTATION OF FINAL VICTORY

CLIMAX OF POWER AND REVERSE,
AND THE CONTINUITY OF WAR AIMS

IN the spring of 1918 Germany had in appearance reached the
zenith of her power. The political changes from Finland to the Black
Sea revealed the outlines of the German New Order in Eastern
Europe. They were at once an end in themselves and a means to
bring the war in the west to a favourable conclusion by eliminating
the Allies' second front on the Arctic coast and by the economic
mobilisation of the eastern territories now dominated by Germany.

The decision in favour of a western offensive
and psychological warfare

At the beginning of 1918 the Germans had two possible ways of
assuring the mighty German imperium in the east: either 'retreat
eastward' and defence in the west, or an offensive in the west. In the
former case, the east would have become Germany's real war aim
and she would have had to seek an accommodation with the Western
Powers. Such an accommodation could not, however, have been
achieved without an explicit renunciation of Belgium, for which
Germany was not ready at the beginning of 1918. She therefore embarked on the second road of realising her war aims in the west also
by a military decision; and in view of the imminent intervention of
the Americans this victory could not be achieved through the defensive, but only by an offensive.

The decisions to attack in the west had been taken at the end of
1917. First, in October, 1917,[1] Lieutenant-Colonel Wetzell, Chief of
the Operational Department of the general staff, had drawn up a
report, on the basis of which Hindenburg, the Chiefs of Staffs of the
two army groups, the German Crown Prince, Crown Prince Rupprecht of Bavaria, and Generals Count Schulenberg and von Kuhl,
meeting at Mons on November 11, 1917, only three weeks after
Lenin's victory in Petersburg, had decided to force a decision in the
west in the following spring by a major offensive in France.[2] After

[1] *Ursachen*, II, p. 238. See also *Der Weltkrieg*, Vol. XIII, pp. 330 ff.
[2] *Der Weltkrieg*, Vol. XIV, pp. 53 ff.

this military decision, the political decision in favour of the offensive was taken at the Crown Council of December 18, three days after the entry into force of the armistice in the east, when the leaders of the Reich concurred with the demands of industry in again promoting Germany's hegemony in Belgium to the status of official Reich policy and revoked the conditional renunciation of Belgium pronounced on September 11, 1917.[1]

At the Crown Council of Bellevue on January 2, 1918, when the ten days' grace of Brest-Litovsk had yet to expire, Ludendorff referred to the 'blow in the west' for which peace in the east was a necessity,[2] and in the course of the famous correspondence between the Emperor, the OHL, and the Imperial Chancellor, Hertling[3] wrote to Hindenburg on January 7 expressing his pleasure at the coming offensive:

> If, then, with God's gracious help, the proposed new offensive should, thanks to Your Excellency's tried leadership and the heroism and determination of our soldiers, lead to the decisive success for which we hope, we shall be in a position to lay down such conditions for peace with the Western Powers *as are required by the security of our frontiers, our economic interests, and our international position after the war.*

After the war in the east had ended in victory for the Central Powers, confidence in victory in leading circles in Germany naturally again ran very high. Von Grünau, the representative of the Foreign Ministry at General Headquarters., wrote that they were counting there on 'shattering the enemy'. At about the same time the Emperor[4] who, according to Admiral von Müller's diary, was 'on top of the world', laid down the lines for the political aims of the coming western offensive in one of his famous marginal notes:

> The victory of the Germans over Russia was the pre-condition for the revolution, which was the pre-condition for Lenin, who was the pre-condition for Brest! The same applies in the west! First victory in the west and collapse of the Entente, then we shall make conditions which they have to accept! And they will be framed purely in accordance with our interests.

Here Wilhelm II summarised with almost classic brevity the succesive stages of Germany's war aims policy and their mutual interdependence. Moreover, the general political ideas prevailing at the beginning of 1918 were entirely in the tradition of Germany's war aims policy. Bethmann Hollweg's idea of a separate peace in the east

[1] See above, pp. 424–5.
[2] Ludendorff, *Erinnerungen*, p. 438.
[3] Schwertfeger, op. cit., pp. 128 f. (author's italics).
[4] Müller, op. cit., p. 342.

had included the intention, after concluding peace with Russia, of 'so beating France to her knees by force of arms that she must accept any peace we desire'. Then Germany would be able to go on and impose her will similarly on Britain. Even if Germany's continental aims in the west had become more limited and somewhat more moderate in form, the great aim of destroying Britain's world power position was in essentials intact. On January 7, 1918, another imperial minute in which, as in May, 1917, Wilhelm wanted Britain to surrender Gibraltar, Malta and Egypt, shows how German policy remained shot through with anglophobia. The idea of detaching Egypt revived the old plan of August, 1914 of dealing the British world empire mortal blows in Egypt and in France. The war aims outlined in earlier programmes seemed to have come within Germany's grasp subject only to a victorious offensive in the west.

But Germany's reserves of power had become so exhausted after nearly four years of war that before the great attack opened Hindenburg himself admitted frankly to intimates that he could not guarantee that the spring offensive would bring final victory over the Western Powers in France.[1] It was therefore natural to think in terms of giving the military offensive some psychological preparation and support by means of a political offensive, a 'peace offensive'.

Two initiatives, one an intervention by the Liberals Naumann, Jäckh and Bosch with Ludendorff, the other a memorandum by Colonel von Haeften, both strongly advocated preparing the way for the military operations by a politico-psychological offensive.[2] The Liberals, speaking for numerous men of their mind, strongly urged an unambiguous peace move by the German government, combined with a declaration of renunciation of Belgium; for in that case, they said,

> Mitteleuropa would have been created and welded together—we should have attained a position of economic, military and political equality among the World Powers and therewith a war aim which we can put to our credit independently of any changes of frontiers in east or west.

They also thought that such an offer would isolate the Allies, thereby revealing its tactical aspect: if the war went on, Germany would place the full guilt on the Allies (who would then only be fighting for Alsace-Lorraine) and Germany would then be able to bear the terrible sacrifice of a fourth year of war, and especially of an

---

[1] See Hindenburg, *Aus meinem Leben* (Leipzig, 1920), pp. 298 f.; also *Der Weltkrieg*, XIV, p. 67.

[2] *Ursachen*, II, pp. 245 ff.; Ludendorff's answer, ibid., p. 250.

offensive in the west. Germany's own position would also be greatly strengthened among the foreign neutrals, as would the peace parties in the Entente countries, and this would be a powerful support for the military offensive if that operation proved unavoidable.

Ludendorff snubbed his Liberal visitors sharply, principally, one must suppose, because they had said that a limitation of Germany's war aims in the west was indispensable to the success of the political offensive. He had no objection to their idea of preparing the offensive in the west psychologically by assertions of Germany's willingness for peace, for at the same time he had given complete approval to Haeften's long memorandum of January, 1918, which promised the same effects from the psychological campaign, without however touching Germany's aims. Haeften was a soldier. He regarded the offensive as a thing settled, and it did not occur to him to moderate, still less give up, Germany's war aims in the west in favour of a compromise peace, as the Liberals were now proposing, in order to avoid the *ultima ratio* of the bloody western offensive. His aim was 'to defeat England in the field and at the same time to let the effects of this defeat develop into a collapse of the English war machine at home'.

He did indeed calculate that after a few more months of expensive war the peace party in Britain would in any case 'automatically' get its way against Lloyd George, but by that time the victory of the British peace party would no longer be of interest to Germany. 'Then it [the peace party] will only help us to get peace. We, however, need a policy which first helps us to win the war.'

In other words Haeften was not interested in a 'common' (*ordinar*) peace – to adapt a well-known saying of Moltke's – but only in a peace on Germany's terms. Britain's early collapse was the pre-condition for the realisation of Germany's war aims, and to bring it about Haeften proposed suggesting to the people of Britain, through public declarations by German statesmen and suitable influencing of the press, that the blame for the continuance of the war lay exclusively with the Allies and their 'imperialist' war aims. By contrast the German people's readiness for peace was to be emphasised, in order to turn the mass of waverers in Britain and the pro-peace opposition against Lloyd George's government. The discontent of the British people, combined with the blows of Germany's offensive, must lead to a 'psychological catastrophe'; Lloyd George would fall, peace be imposed; the full fruits of Germany's military offensive could then be harvested in a peace framed as Germany wished it.

Ludendorff passed on these proposals to the Chancellor. Hertling's two speeches of January 24 and February 25, 1918 may therefore be regarded in the light of Haeften's 'political offensive'; indeed they must be so regarded, for both accorded absolutely with his ideas, sometimes even *verbatim*.

Wilson's Fourteen Points, Lloyd George's speech and the German reply

On January 8, 1918, the day on which Hertling had agreed 'with joy' to the Emperor's order to prepare for the offensive in the west. President Wilson announced his famous Fourteen Points. This was the third important utterance made at this time by the West on the question of peace. First the French Foreign Minister, Pichon, had publicly rejected the Brest-Litovsk summons. Then Lloyd George had dwelt in detail on the question of peace in a public speech on the Entente's war aims. Wilson, like Lloyd George, assumed that the Central Powers' negotiations with the Russians at Brest-Litovsk had broken down and that the Russians would consequently re-enter the war. This being so, Wilson's address, while also containing general and ideological aspects which conjured up the vision of a final peaceful order after the war, had a direct tactical purpose – as also had Lloyd George's speech, seeking as it did in its practical phraseology to use the right of self-determination to establish a lasting peaceful order in Europe without depriving Germany of her great power status or dismembering Austria-Hungary, and above all without allowing America to intervene in Europe and depose Britain from her old role of preserver of the European balance of power.

The general principles in the Fourteen Points, such as the freedom of the seas, elimination of all trade barriers, general limitation of armaments and adjustment of all colonial claims, would have worked out not unfavourably for Germany and would probably have hit Britain and France harder. Their decisive importance for German policy (and particularly for the war aims hitherto pursued by her) lay in Wilson's territorial conditions, to which Germany would have had to submit if she accepted the Fourteen Points. Points 6 to 8 called for the evacuation by Germany of all occupied territory in Russia, Belgium and France. Further, 'the wrong done to France by Prussia in 1871 in respect of Alsace-Lorraine must be made good'. Finally, there was to be an independent Poland, including 'all districts inhabited by indisputably Polish populations', which would have forced Germany to renounce at least the province of Posen and Austrian Galicia. Wilson's pronouncements on the political future of Poland and Alsace-Lorraine were even clearer than those of Lloyd George, who had only gone through the motions of identifying himself with France's claim and had asked only for a 'reconsideration of the great injustice of 1871'.

Had Germany accepted the Fourteen Points as the basis for a future peace, the effects would have been twofold. On the one hand, Germany would have been obliged to renounce all her war aims and therewith her aspirations to hegemony in Europe and to world power rank; she might also have had to accept territorial losses in both east and west. Secondly, her position as a European great power would have been assured her by the retention of her indisputably German territories, since the Fourteen Points excluded all the more extensive British and French aspirations of an economic or territorial nature. Finally, Germany would have had a chance to recover her colonies in whole or part.

Thus the German statesmen were again faced with a decision of principle, like that which had confronted them in the autumn of 1916 during the controversy over unrestricted submarine warfare. At that time Germany's last military trump had lain in the unrestricted employment of her submarines; now, at the beginning of 1918, her last card was the gamble of a final offensive in the west, on which, however, was staked at the same time the existence of the Reich itself. The general military situation, as compared with the autumn of 1916, had improved in one respect by the Russian withdrawal from the war, but had deteriorated with the American entry into it. Germany's terms for a negotiated peace had meanwhile risen since the earlier date. In view, however, of the balance of forces in Germany, of the powerful agricultural and industrial associations organised in the Fatherland Party, the extensive public propaganda by the *Alldeutschen* for the western war aims, and the excitement over the allegedly 'weakly' handling of the negotiations in Brest-Litovsk, any government which accepted the Fourteen Points and abandoned Germany's previous aims in east and west – not to speak of Alsace-Lorraine and Posen – without previous military defeat would at once have been overthrown. Renunciation of Germany's aims and acceptance of Wilson's programme would have been possible only after a radical reshaping of power relationships within Germany, i.e., after the overthrow of the Monarchy and of the existing social order. But the forces of resistance in Germany were still too strong and the forces of revolutionary change too weak, as the outcome of the major strike at the end of January, 1918 had proved most convincingly.

There is therefore nothing surprising in the answer which Hertling gave to Wilson and Lloyd George on January 24 in the Central Committee of the Reichstag.[1] That answer was a categorical refusal, only

[1] Id., II, pp. 145 ff.

slightly tempered by acceptance of those of Wilson's general points which contained something favourable for Germany, although Hertling admitted that in their last speeches the Anglo-Saxon statesmen had abstained from polemics against 'Prussian militarism' and 'Hohenzollern autocracy'. But even while accepting the general principles, Hertling contrived to turn them against Britain. He made 'freedom of the seas' depend on Britain renouncing Gibraltar, Malta, Aden, Hong Kong, the Falkland Islands and other bases.

Hertling rejected decidedly any intervention by Wilson in the question of the future of the territories occupied by Germany. In respect to the east, he appealed to the ten days' grace period of Brest-Litovsk, which the Allies had allowed to pass unutilised. 'Consequently,' he said, 'we are dealing here [in the east] with questions which concern only Russia and the four allied Powers.' True to Germany's autonomy policy, he operated with the formula of the 'self-determination' of the border peoples of Russia, saying that Germany hoped thereby 'to achieve good relations both with these peoples and with the rest of Russia'—the familiar paraphrase for Germany's war aims in the east: 'the restoration of orderly conditions which guarantee the peace and prosperity of the country'.

When he turned to the west—to Point 7—Hertling again confined himself to insisting in the familiar words, 'that at no time during the war has the forcible annexation of Belgium constituted a point in Germany's political programme', and he said the same of French territory. He flatly rejected any cession of German territory in east or west, while saying that the governments in Vienna and Constantinople would answer any questions of frontiers or autonomy concerning Austria-Hungary and Turkey. He gave, however, a formal guarantee to the Ottoman Empire, because by raising the question of the Straits and through other utterances which threatened the territorial integrity of Turkey, Lloyd George had touched on 'what were also important vital interests of the German Reich'.

The exchanges between the enemy statesmen on a possible peace went on during February. On the 11th of that month Wilson developed his 'Four Principles' for peace in a speech to the Senate—again after a period of stagnation in the Brest-Litovsk negotiations and coming immediately after Trotsky's declaration of 'No war, no peace'. The Four Principles repeated the Fourteen Points in even more general form. The Chancellor answered in the Reichstag on February 25.[1] He again described the President's message as 'a small step towards a mutual rapprochement'; but while accepting Wilson's

[1] Id., pp. 376 ff.; Hertling's answer, ibid., p. 170. On March 8, 1918 Hertling again insisted that he accepted Wilson's Points.

general principles in theory, he returned in his concrete proposals to the old line of German policy. He accepted the new Poland, saying that it had the Central Powers to thank for its re-birth, but at the same time he made the first public revelation of the German government's intention to ask Poland for territorial cessions, although he added reassuringly 'that . . . in regulating the frontier question Germany . . . would only ask for what was indispensable on military grounds' – the long established current formula used among Germans to describe the Polish Frontier Strip. He gave slight, but unmistakable, hints, in a much sharper tone than he had used on January 24, of Germany's intention to make Poland, the border states and Russia herself, indirectly dependent on Germany in the economic field. There was even a hint at the purpose of Germany's Ukrainian policy, the 'sealing off' of Poland.

In respect of Belgium, the Chancellor again chose a negative way of describing Germany's war aims. It had never been Germany's intention 'to make the Belgian state a part of the German Reich'. Germany must, however, ensure, as she had already said in her answer to the Papal peace note, that Belgium did not become 'the object or field of deployment of hostile intrigues'. An international guarantee of Belgium's independence was not enough for Germany. Hertling asked the Belgian government in Le Havre to make proposals for the future of its country of a nature to meet Germany's wishes for a guarantee – again recognisably the old policy of a separate peace.

For the rest, the Chancellor's speech had been born chiefly of the need to justify the resumption of the war in the east before the Reichstag and world public opinion. Hertling thought to prove the defensive character of Germany's military operations 'even when she advances aggressively' by appealing to the 'calls for help' from the Ukraine, Livonia and Estonia, which had imposed on Germany a moral obligation to intervene. The operations in the east were 'rescue operations undertaken in the name of humanity'.

In thus stressing the defensive theme, the Chancellor proceeded to the psychological preparation for the western offensive, now imminent. To this end he threw back in the Entente's teeth their reproach of 'imperialism'. He accused them of having followed 'aims of conquest' since the beginning of the war: that they had been fighting for Alsace-Lorraine, the South Tyrol and Istria, and for the German colonies, and to detach Palestine, Syria and Arabia from Turkey. The Chancellor's speech was delivered eloquently and was impressive, because he showed that he understood the historic importance of the hour.

The world, he said, is now facing its supreme and most fateful decision. Either the enemy will decide to make peace–it knows the conditions on which we would be prepared to enter on negotiations–or it thinks fit to carry on the criminal lunacy of a war of conquest. In that case our splendid troops will fight on under their brilliant leaders.

Hertling's answer returned the initiative to the Allies, without departing from the basis of Germany's war aims policy or making any such concrete and reasonable offer on Belgium as the Allies had been hoping for for months. Although he said that Germany's conditions were known to the enemy, it is not clear to what he was referring. The context suggests that he may have been speaking of Germany's peace offer of December 12, 1916, but that 'offer' had been framed in such vague and general terms that it held out nothing which could be taken up by the other side. Germany's declaration to the neutrals of January 10, 1917, after the Entente had rejected her peace offer, had similarly described her aims only in negative terms and without clear-cut conditions; and the same was true of all her official statements on her war aims, either in connection with the Pope's peace move or the negotiations for separate peace. Nor could what Hertling said in his speech of February 25–or in that of January 24–be interpreted as reasonable peace conditions. Although, as always, his demands were framed negatively, they still comprised safeguards against Britain for Germany's position in Belgium (i.e., something more than Belgian neutrality); German domination over Poland and the annexation of the Polish Frontier Strip; recognition of the Treaty of Brest-Litovsk with the consequent recognition of German domination over the Ukraine as far as the Donetz and Rostov, the Caucasus and Finland, and of the dependent status of Rump Russia; the attachment of Lithuania and Courland–and also of Livonia and Estonia, although this was not explicitly stated–to the Reich under the pretext of national self-determination, manipulated in one way or another; German domination over Rumania, which Hertling said Germany wanted to gain as a 'friend' after concluding peace. Hertling's silence on the future of the areas of France under German occupation was still more significant, and was the more calculated to awaken the mistrust of the Entente because the German press was repeatedly calling for the annexation of French territory, at least Longwy–Briey. And at this time the German government was clinging to this aim with especial and extreme tenacity.[1] Germany's demand that the classic balance of power between the European great powers should be replaced by a world power

---

[1] See above, pp. 591 ff.

system composed of herself, Britain, America and Russia was irreconcilable with the aims of the Allies, not to speak of the position of Austria-Hungary and Turkey whose territorial integrity Germany wished to see maintained.

Western offensive, peace through victory, the War Aims Majority and the fall of Kühlmann

On March 21 sixty-two divisions launched the long-awaited great offensive in the west. The initial successes gained by Germany's shock troops seemed once again to open up brilliant prospects for Germany's future power position in the world and for the German system at home and abroad. Admiral von Müller has a vivid entry in his diary[1] on the reactions produced at Imperial Headquarters by the first reports from the front. As usual when real or alleged German victories were reported, spirits bubbled up and no one contradicted the Emperor when he said: 'If a British parliamentarian comes to sue for peace, he must first kneel before the imperial standard, for this is a victory of monarchy over democracy.'

Wilhelm II was reverting to the much quoted 'ideas of 1914' on the fundamental contrast between Germany's political philosophy and that of the West, which he developed to an ever higher pitch during the last year of the war. Speaking on June 15, 1918 – the juncture when the extension of Germany's power in the east and her claim to power in general reached their all-time high – at a banquet given at General Headquarters to celebrate the thirty years' jubilee of his reign, he said that 'this war is a struggle between two world philosophies'. As reported by the Austrian ambassador, Prince Hohenlohe, he described the alleged alternatives before the world as follows:

Either the Prusso-German-Teutonic world philosophy – justice, freedom, honour, morals – persists in honour, or the Anglo-Saxon – which means succumbing to the worship of the golden calf. In this struggle one or the other philosophy must go under. We are fighting for the victory of the German philosophy.

But behind the imperial wish to dictate peace in the west stood the very realistic interests of influential groups which were again raising their voices loudly now that final victory seemed in sight, and bombarding the government and the OHL with innumerable memoranda. It is no coincidence that Wilhelm II chose this very moment to adopt as his own, in greatly exaggerated form, the Fatherland Party's

[1] Müller, op. cit., p. 366 (entry dated March 26, 1918).

old thesis of the struggle between world philosophies, for that party's agitation in favour of annexations now reached what was perhaps its peak.[1] At the same time the rejection of franchise reform in the Prussian Lower House – its opponents increased during the year – was an impressive affirmation of the German system. The 'bourgeois' parties in the Diet took their cue from Ludendorff, who 'attached no value whatever to equal franchise in Prussia'. Colonel Bauer of Ludendorff's staff told Röchling – the confidence is symptomatic of the relationship between the OHL and heavy industry – that it was 'a stinking lie' to say that the generals had wanted the franchise reform accelerated. 'The Social Democrats would not stop fighting until everything was democratised', so that the idea that the introduction of the reform would appease and consolidate the home front was as fallacious as the hope of Drews, the Prussian Minister of the Interior, that the Social Democrats would in return give the government a free hand over war aims. Strikes – as the last one had shown – would neither unsettle the front nor seriously delay the movement of supplies, and the field censorship reported that the demand for equal franchise was not strong at the front.

The government's policy was generally accepted, both in the Prussian Chamber of Deputies and in the Reichstag, except by the Social Democrats. The appointment to the Vice-Chancellorship of the 'representative' of the parties, Payer, who began by appealing 'to all forces in the Reich to rally together', was acclaimed by Trimborn, amid applause, as a new token of the advent of a parliamentarianism adapted to 'the German genius'. But this uniform acceptance of Germany's political system was not the only conspicuous endorsement of Wilhelm II's thesis; the registered demands of the *Alldeutschen*, the National Liberals and the leading representatives of west German industry show the elemental energy with which forces in Germany were pressing in the spring of 1918 for the expansion of German power. Once again Thyssen, Vögler, Stinnes, the *Verein Deutscher Eisen- und Stahlindustrieller*, the *Metallarbeiterverband* of the Christian trade unions, the *Wehrverein* and numerous other individuals and organisations[2] demanded to be heard, and called for the annexation of Longwy–Briey and for political, military and economic 'safeguards' in Belgium.

There was yet another way in which Germany's determination to expand and assure her power position in the west manifested itself in these weeks. At the Chancellor's big conference of May 30, 1918 von

[1] See on this, Kruck, *Alldeutscher Verband*, pp. 118 f.; Gatzke, *Drive to the West*, p. 263.

[2] Gatzke, op. cit., p. 264.

Stein, the Secretary of State of the Reich Economic Office, addressed himself to the 'Westmark Association' (*Landgesellschaft Westmark*), 'which was following in the west a policy of colonisation like that in the *Ostmark*'. This association, which had Schwerin for its president and was supported by the 'old colonising men', Kapp, Hugenberg and 'Bernhard of Poland', had, at the request of the Foreign Ministry, been working with heavy industry, especially Krupp, on the expropriation of French property in Alsace-Lorraine as land for 'military colonies'. All the preliminary work had been carried out by the Reich, especially by Stein's predecessor, Schwander, and now Stein too supported the association's work with the agreement of the Chancellor, Payer, Wallraf, Roedern and Kühlmann, although the chief figures in it were *Alldeutschen*. As Stein said, 'it would be pointless to disguise the fact that we prefer reliable Germans to Frenchmen'.

At the end of July Kühlmann, who had been hated by the whole war aims movement since Brest-Litovsk for the alleged weakness of his conduct of the negotiations there, was forced to beat a retreat before the new tide of annexationism which had been rising throughout the spring and summer. After the disappointing outcome of the western offensive, he told the Reichstag that he accepted Haeften's 'propaganda campaign'.

The house was debating the vote for the Foreign Ministry, and he treated it to 'a broad survey of the government's whole policy'. He again described the purpose of the eastern treaties, in the usual veiled terms; then, turning to the possibilities of peace, he referred to the Pope's note and described Germany's positive aim in the words: '*mutatis mutandis* . . . we want to live in the world . . . secure, free, strong and independent within the frontiers drawn for us by history, we want to own overseas possessions . . . commensurate with our position'. He made, however, the famous admission that the war would no longer be won for Germany by *purely* military decisions. The OHL and with it the whole war aims movement took this statement as open defeatism. Kühlmann's 'cautious' preparation of German public opinion 'for the possibility of our having to content ourselves with a so-called peace of understanding' was incompatible with the political line and the aims of the classes who held power in Germany.

To cushion the shock effect of his words on the German people, Kühlmann answered the spokesmen of the bourgeois parties in the Reichstag immediately and very sharply. The moment that he had 'spoken very openly of the question of peace', with an openness which, as the Berlin press reported, 'we are not accustomed to get from the government', the old War Aims Majority of the 1914–17 Reichstag which, after the intermezzo of the Peace Resolution, had begun to re-form under the influence of Brest-Litovsk, recovered its complete unity. Gröber, for the Zentrum, answered Kühlmann's realistic acceptance of facts with an affirmation of faith in Germany's victory: 'Since our peace offers have met only with scorn . . . the German sword will have to enforce peace in the west also.' Westarp, for the Conservatives, sharply rejected Kühlmann's thoughts of a compromise: 'Germany must find security, and security requires that the coast of Belgium and Flanders must be brought under German influence. . . . Negotiations must be enforced by our victory, and that victory will be won.' Stresemann, in the name of the National Liberals, also repudiated Kühlmann's ideas categorically: 'The effect of the speech has been absolutely shattering. . . . Never had we less cause than now to doubt in Germany's victory. When victory has been achieved, we must use it to secure the real safeguards which we need.'

This spontaneous repudiation of Kühlmann by the old War Aims Majority was the Imperial Reichstag's last great expression of its political will, before the admission of military defeat at the beginning of October, 1918 changed the internal political situation.

The next day Kühlmann was also disavowed by the OHL and his fall became inevitable.[1] The soldiers resorted to the unusual device of a press conference, at which they attacked the Secretary of State for Foreign Affairs sharply and before all the world. On June 25 an organised campaign began against him on a wide front. It was not checked by a feeble attempt by Hertling to defend him in the Reichstag, nor did his own attempt, also made in the Reichstag, to weaken the effect of his earlier word allay the excitement, since it did not strike the expected note of robust confidence in victory. From that moment on Kühlmann was, as Helfferich put it,[2] 'only a political corpse'.

The great Spa Conference, July 2–3, 1918

Two important conferences took place in the 'pause' between the fourth German offensive in the west, which was broken off on June 14, and the last, which was to open on July 15 and enforce the final decision in favour of Germany by carrying her arms over the Marne. On July 1 the OHL and the Ministry of War discussed with the Chancellor how to introduce a total war-production economy and

[1] See Kühlmann's *Erinnerungen*, pp. 572 ff. and Müller, op. cit., pp. 388 f. For the Spa conversations between the OHL and the Chancellor, *Ursachen*, II, pp. 272 f. and Müller, op. cit., pp. 387 ff.

[2] Helfferich, *Der Weltkrieg*, p. 631.

enlist all possible forces by 'bringing in more women', 'tieing workers to their jobs', limiting consumption, etc. Germany's war aims were once more discussed exhaustively at Spa on July 2 and 3.[1] When the conference took place, there was an interregnum at the Foreign Ministry. Kühlmann was already out of things, for the OHL and the Chancellor had taken a joint decision on his 'case' the day before, and although his successor had not yet been appointed, he did not attend this last great conference of the leaders of Germany on her war aims.[2]

In the east, Germany's programme seemed fulfilled at last. Her eastern frontier was 'satisfied', 'the Austro-Polish solution dead', the border states allied with Germany, Russia isolated and economically 'opened up'. As in the east, so also in the west aims had remained fundamentally unaltered. Although direct annexations had been reduced to Longwy–Briey and Luxemburg, Germany had kept to her aim of establishing her supremacy in Belgium through a customs union, amalgamation of the railway systems, Flemish policy, etc. If Belgium was closely enough linked with Germany, the German leaders thought that they could entrust her with the defence of the Flanders coast against Britain, although even so the country was to be occupied by German troops for many years; when the occupation was gradually reduced, the military would possibly not insist on additional 'small annexations up to Liége' to make a bridge to Flanders. If the programme of veiled domination over Belgium could not be achieved in the peace, both the Emperor and Ludendorff wanted to fall back on direct annexations. The military justified their unbending attitude over Belgium by the need to afford absolute protection to the Rhineland–Westphalian industrial district against attack from Britain. The statement of these alternatives also answered Hertling's question whether Germany was prepared to prolong the war for the sake of dominating Belgium, if Britain refused to conclude a general peace on such terms. As before, so on July 3, 1918, the supreme leaders of Germany were prepared to carry on the war to enforce Germany's aims in the west.

The importance of the Spa conference with its consistent re-statement of Germany's aims is enhanced by the rank of its participants. The Emperor presided. He had brought with him his three Heads of Cabinet and his Adjutant-General, Colonel-General von Plessen.

[1] See above, pp. 532 ff.

[2] Müller, op. cit., p. 393 (entry dated July 15, 1918); also Kühlmann, op. cit., p. 572. Kühlmann, indeed, writes that only Hertling had been initiated into the secret. Both he and Müller say that the speech had been shown in advance to the Emperor and the Chancellor. If this is so, these two men had gone back on to the old line of war aims policy.

The others present were the Chancellor, the man who alone was formally responsible for Reich policy, with his Under-Secretary in the Imperial Chancellery, von Radowitz, and Minister von Rosenberg to represent the Foreign Ministry; the Foreign Ministry's and the Chancellery's liaison officers with the OHL, Freiherr von Lersner and Count Limburg-Stirum; the Prussian Minister of War, von Stein; the Secretary of State of the Reich Naval Office, von Capelle, and Vice-Admiral Hebbinghaus; and a strong delegation from the OHL, including Bartenwerffer, Oldershausen and Winterfeldt, besides Ludendorff and Hindenburg themselves.

The conference met in a mood of full confidence in victory – the one man who had dared to depart ever so little from the general line had just been got rid of. Without any doubt Spa expressed far-reaching agreement between Emperor, civilians and military in respect of the aims of expanding Germany's power. Moreover, the ideas and aims of the leaders reflected exactly the ambitions and political philosophy of the overwhelming majority of the German people. It was not Bethmann Hollweg or Kühlmann, with their ideas of possible compromise, who represented the will of the German people, but the forces which forced them to go.

Kühlmann's resignation, which was accepted by the Emperor in spite of objections from Hertling and Payer 'that there might be grave internal consequences', removed the last man with a voice in the formation of German policy who hesitated to impose the approved war aims by force. This lends additional importance to the fact that his successor, whose appointment was announced on July 8, was Rear-Admiral von Hintze, for Hintze was regarded, both in political circles in Berlin and abroad, as speaking with the voice of the *Alldeutschen*. He was certainly cast for the role of carrying out the Spa programme after the anticipated victory in the west and 'stamping sure victory with the seal of a victor's peace'. The Reichstag had worked with the OHL to compass the fall of Kühlmann, and there could be no question of objections to the appointment of Hintze from the War Aims Majority. Hertling took Hintze, who had been military attaché in Petersburg before the war and minister in Christiania during it, with him to Berlin in order to assure the Reichstag that there would be no change in the direction of foreign policy. On July 13 he was able to report to the Emperor that 'the Kühlmann crisis was peacefully over in Berlin'.[1] The same day the Reichstag confirmed its approval of the political and military leadership of the Reich – or its own political impotence – by approving war credits to the tune of

[1] Schwertfeger, op. cit., p. 207; note on the Chancellor's report to the Emperor, ibid., p. 347.

13,000 million marks. Only the Independent Socialists voted against this, the twelfth, appropriation which brought the total of war credits to 139,000 million marks. Elbert explained his party's vote by saying: 'As the enemy refuses a peace honourable to all parties, we will once again approve the means to achieve peace.' This declaration was received with great applause, contrasting with the booing which greeted Geyer, the spokesman of the Independent Socialists, when he said: 'This time again we shall vote against the war credits. The war has never been one of defence . . . in the west too Germany is seeking a peace of conquest and violence.'

After voting the credits the Reichstag went into recess until the end of October and excercised no perceptible influence over the further development of the political situation in Germany.

Two days before the re-opening of the long prepared German offensive on the Marne was surely the most unpromising moment imaginable for new peace feelers. This is the only possible explanation for the Emperor's repeated rejection, on July 14, 1918, of a last opportunity for undefeated Germany to enter into peace negotiations. Since the spring Kühlmann had been working pertinaciously to make contact with America through Daniel McCormick, the tractor manufacturer, and with Britain, through Hatzfeld, the German minister at The Hague – in each case, characteristically, with a view to a separate peace, i.e., primarily in order to split the Allies. On July 14, the day before the offensive was due to open, McCormick sent a message that President Wilson was ready to conclude peace and wanted to know what Germany's conditions were. Wilhelm II, however, refused to give them, asking instead what were America's conditions.[1] With the long cherished goal of defeating Britain and establishing Germany's hegemony in Europe now, he thought, within his grasp, the Supreme War Lord was not prepared to consider the possibility of a peace of understanding. The next morning, at 1 a.m., he entered his car, bound for the observation post whence he would watch 8,000 German guns open the barrage and the infantry go over the top on each side of Rheims at 4 a.m.

The turn of the tide in the west, the Black Day and war aims (second Spa Conference)

The offensive of July 15 was a complete failure. The enemy was prepared for it, and it 'failed almost before it started'. After only 24 hours the German command had to give up the hope that it would decide the war in Germany's favour, and when on July 18 a flank

---

[1] Müller, op. cit., p. 393 (entry dated July 14, 1918).

attack by Americans and French from the forest of Cotterêts forced two German armies to retreat behind the Marne to the Vesle positions, the strategic initiative passed definitively to the Allies. Ludendorff wrote:

The attempt to make the Entente peoples ready for peace by defeating them before the arrival of the American reinforcements had failed. The impetus of the army had been insufficient to deal the enemy a decisive blow ... I realised clearly that this made our general situation very serious.[1]

The OHL had only the 'impetus' of the German soldiers to set against the enemy's superiority in material and of man-power reserves. The abrupt reversal of fortune was the more surprising to Germany's leaders because just before launching his last offensive, Ludendorff had answered 'with a definite "yes"'[2] Hintze's 'formal and categorical question whether he was certain of defeating the enemy finally and decisively in the present offensive'. Ludendorff's confidence on the eve of July 15 is confirmed by a later remark of the Emperor's, who on September 2, when the war was lost, wrote bitterly of the OHL:

The campaign is lost. Now our troops have been running back without a stop since July 18. The fact is, we are exhausted. I cannot understand what they have been doing at Avesnes [the G.H.Q.]. When the offensive was opened on the Marne on July 15, I was assured that the French had only 8 divisions left in reserve, and the British perhaps 13. Instead of this, the enemy assembles a crowd of divisions in the forest of Cotterêts, unnoticed by us, attacks our right flank and forces us to retreat. Since then we have received blow after blow. Our armies can simply do no more.[3]

The attack of July 18 was in fact only the prelude to a general Allied offensive on all fronts – and yet even after it the OHL had 'planned further counter-attacks' and had shown themselves 'very confident' to the Chancellor; they had made Radowitz instruct Payer 'to work hard to raise spirits at home ... the opposite of Erzberger's recipe'.[4]

We get a clear picture of how the general judged the situation from the long report drawn up by A. Niemann, a general staff officer not attached to the OHL.[5] The importance of this report is enhanced by the reaction to it of Ludendorff and Colonel Bauer, and by the fact

---

[1] Ludendorff, *Kriegserinnerungen*, p. 545.
[2] Schwertfeger, op. cit., p. 387.
[3] Müller, op. cit., p. 406.
[4] Schwertfeger, op. cit., p. 213.
[5] Id., pp. 215 ff.

that the Emperor sent for its author. Niemann argued, like Kühlmann, that if Germany's armed force 'is not sufficient to break the
enemy's will radically', then success in the field 'can no longer be
used as a means of enforcing political compulsion, but only as a
means of pressure'; in spite of 'the intellectual and moral superiority
of our command', the fact remained 'that in the last instance the war
will be decided by the dwindling of the national forces and the growing shortages of material'. Germany should therefore open negotiations 'while we are still superior in the field', thus using military
power as the means to bring pressure to decide 'the future political
picture of the world'.

Niemann saw this picture in these terms: 'construction of an economic *Raum* taking in the neutrals; link with Japan; compromise
with Britain; creation of a "colonial belt" in Africa to include the
Congo and Nigeria; and final regulation of the question of associated
territories in east and west.'

Niemann suggested, and (as on the question of Japan and trade
relations) Bauer and Ludendorff agreed with him, 'that Britain be
told that we are seeking our future . . . not on the water, but on land.
We must create the pre-conditions for *Germany's position as a World
Power* by a grandiose continental policy'. This position could be
achieved 'by expanding our power position in Asia Minor, which
leads to the vital nerve of the British Empire'. Bauer, however, did
not care for Turkey, 'where there is nothing to be got'. 'Our aims,'
he said – and here we see again how methodically the New Order in
the east was being planned – 'must rather be the economic exploitation of the Ukraine, Caucasia, Great Russia, Turkestan.' That is
where the partners for Mitteleuropa were to be found. Niemann,
still thinking of a compromise with Britain as the price for Germany's
position in Europe, proposed to reduce the 'colonial belt' by dropping Morocco, which would go to France, and East and South-West
Africa, which would go to Britain. Bauer agreed, but would not give
up East Africa. Niemann regarded Wilson's idea of a League of
Nations as offering the best possibility of opening conversations, although 'not with any idea of realising this Utopia'. Bauer, however,
rejected this idea, which might involve 'giving up Alsace-Lorraine,
restoring Poland and letting large parts of Austria-Hungary become
independent'; the 'only correct solution for Poland is a new partition'. Both Bauer and Ludendorff fully supported Niemann's recommendation for stronger, centrally directed press and propaganda
activities to consolidate public opinion.

Niemann was promptly summoned to Avesnes (on August 3) and
appointed the new liaison officer between the OHL and the Em-

peror, in the hope of restoring Wilhelm's confidence in his generals, which had wavered in the critical days of late July and early August. But when Ludendorff said that he hoped to be able to go over again to the offensive, in spite of the previous shortage of reinforcements, Niemann saw how little he could achieve in his position. Both the Emperor and the Chancellor were still optimistic of victory, and agreed with Ludendorff when he wrote as late as August 6: 'During the world war, so far I have had to withdraw my troops five times, only to beat the enemy in the end after all. Why should I not bring this off a sixth time?' But this time he could not do it. The Allied offensive rolled on. There came the Black Day of August 8 and then, in the autumn, Bulgaria, Turkey and Austria-Hungary collapsed in turn and the military defeat of Germany was sealed.

The German leaders were very slow to draw conclusions from the situation which developed after the Black Day. The new military position and its effects on domestic morale were the subject of another Conference of State[1] held at Spa on August 14 under the Emperor's presidency. Here for the first time the leaders of Germany admitted that they must seek peace as soon as might be: 'we have reached the limits of our endurance.' In their analysis of the situation, nevertheless, they involved themselves in almost incomprehensible contradictions. At this conference the political and military leaders of the Reich were once more assembled: besides the Emperor, there were the Crown Prince, Hertling, Helfferich, Stein, von Berg (head of the Civil Cabinet), von Plessen, Freiherr von Marschall, Hindenburg, Ludendorff and Haeften. The proceedings were indeed overshadowed by the grave military crisis, which Hindenburg did not attempt to conceal from Hintze, but the Emperor, the OHL and the Chancellor were still confident and determined to hold out. When Ludendorff told Hintze that the German command had set itself the aim 'of gradually *paralysing* the enemy's will to fight by a strategic defensive', Hintze thought this implied 'solely' a change of strategy; for the military objective, the breaking of the enemy's will to fight, remained unchanged. Hintze stated that Germany's allies were completely exhausted and that her own increasing weakness was becoming obvious in view of the steadily growing stream of American reinforcements; but the OHL replied that 'the aim was the same and could be achieved', and this view reassured the Chancellor and most of those present; only Hintze was, as he said, 'deeply impressed

[1] *Ursachen*, II, pp. 280 ff.; Schwertfeger, op. cit., pp. 386 ff. On the whole complex of questions see also the *Amtliche Urkunden zur Vorgeschichte des Waffenstillstandes, 1918*, issued by the Foreign Ministry and the Reich Interior Office (Berlin, 1924), pp. 3 ff.

by the gravity of the situation' as revealed by Ludendorff's previous 'separate communication'. Thus judgments of the military situation wavered between recognition of defeat and confidence in ultimate victory, and the results of the conference were correspondingly contradictory. Hintze was 'authorised to initiate peace feelers through diplomatic channels', but the value of this concession was reduced by two essential reservations. The feelers were to be put out through Spain and Holland, and both the Emperor and the Chancellor wanted this done only when 'a suitable moment' arrived, the Chancellor expressly understanding this to mean 'after our next successes in the west'. Nor did Hertling, who himself passed no judgment on the military situation, give Hintze the support for which the latter asked in respect of a peace move. The Emperor called in the same breath for peace feelers, a propaganda committee 'to raise the morale of the German people', and unification of the administrative apparatus; but, as Schwertfeger wrote,[1] 'these words did not contain any clear order to the responsible political leaders to take immediate steps for peace'. Germany's war aims carried great weight even at this conference; when Hintze raised the questions of Belgium and Poland, the OHL referred him to the minutes of the earlier Spa conference, and the civilians did not object. Hintze was the only doubter, and Ludendorff in reply expressed most strongly the OHL's conviction 'that it would be able to break the enemy's will to fight and force him to accept peace'. As the conference went on, the Secretary of State found himself increasingly isolated; neither Hertling nor Helfferich nor von Stein supported his views, and the adoption by Hindenburg at the end of the conference of Hertling's slogan of a 'western success' shows once more a unanimity on the question of war aims which, in view of the military situation, can only be called astounding. Hindenburg declared that 'we shall be able to make a stand on French soil and thus in the end to impose our will on the enemy'–the will which had expressed itself at Spa on July 2 and August 14.

As Hintze said later in his account of these days, the OHL 'could not be induced to retreat from the war aims previously agreed'.[2] Any 'diplomatic threads', as Hertling called them, were thus doubly handicapped: first by the war aims, which had to be achieved under all circumstances, and secondly, by the reservation regarding the 'suitable moment' which never arrived. In September the instructions on this point were modified still further: diplomatic action was to be taken when the retreat halted. Hintze had already sent out

[1] Schwertfeger, op. cit., p. 229.
[2] Id., pp. 386 ff.

offers of a separate peace to the U.S.A. on August 15,[1] but he could never feel that he had the support of the real power of thes tate, nor of the Reichstag – whose representatives in the session of the Central Committee of August 21 were 'instructed' by him, characteristically, in most optimistic tones and insisted expressly that the peace must be 'satisfactory and agreeable to us', a demand to which Hintze twice gave his full assent.

The optimism which marked the close of the Spa conference was totally unjustified. Nevertheless it strongly influenced the conduct of German diplomacy in the weeks that followed. The Emperor Charles, Count Burian and Colonel-General von Arz arrived in Spa on the same day,[2] and from that day on the German leaders were engaged for weeks in difficult wranglings with their Austrian allies, who wanted an immediate and direct appeal to all belligerents and were not to be put off with vague references to a 'suitable moment'. If on August 14 the Germans were still clinging to the illusion that they would be able to make the enemy accept peace on Germany's terms by means of a strategic defensive in the west, their attitude was due in part to the exaggerated hopes pinned on a large-scale propaganda campaign. The Emperor favoured a big operation with two objectives: 'weakening the enemy's confidence in victory' abroad, and 'raising the confidence of the German people' at home. His idea was that there should be a 'Propaganda Committee', in which well-known private individuals, as well as statesmen, should deliver fiery speeches on lines to be laid down by the Foreign Ministry. The Chancellor was able to tell him that an 'ample programme' of such measures already existed and was being carried out. Hertling was clearly thinking of Colonel von Haeften's 'political offensive',[3] on which the government was pinning great hopes. In July, 1917, it will be remembered, Erzberger had proposed setting up a sort of 'spiritual food office', and the government was now trying, in exactly the same spirit, to replace through propaganda what was lacking in real political and military strength. Haeften and Deutelmoser, head of the press section in the Foreign Ministry, began by composing a 'convincing proof of our invincibility' and a picture of the 'political, economic and military conditions' which would follow defeat, but they were not able to make good the shortage of real weight. The military balance was already tilted too heavily in favour of the Allies.

[1] Id., p. 235.
[2] Id., p. 234.
[3] *Ursachen*, II, pp. 263 ff.; Schwertfeger, op. cit., p. 356.

'The reserves [of the Central Powers] are running out'; this was stated flatly at the session of the Ministry of State on September 3.[1] Hertling's refusal to take any initiative towards peace, his fixed optimism, reflecting that of Spa, were in crass contradiction with the latest military defeat (of the previous day) and with the attitudes of the Prussian ministers von Stein, von Waldow and von Breitenbach, the Ministers of War, Agriculture and Public Works, none of whom was able to satisfy the demand for more reserves or for the mobilisation of all forces, as agreed between the Chancellor and Ludendorff on August 1. Nevertheless, when Austria pressed for an immediate peace step – 'we are absolutely finished' – it was refused. Hintze was still unable to give Burian any information on Germany's war aims – the German government was still 'not clear' on this point of its policy; nor is this surprising, for on September 8 Hintze had actually returned to Berlin from General Headquarters confirmed in the opinion that there was no reason for anxiety; he had met there with 'only confidence'.

It was only on September 10 that the OHL consented to 'arrange a conversation' with a neutral power – less to put pressure on the politicians than to prevent an Austrian *démarche*. It is thus comprehensible that the publication of the Austrian peace note on September 15 'came like lightning out of a clear sky'. All Hintze's efforts – and they were supported by the Chancellor, the departments and the OHL – were now directed towards reinforcing the Austrian *démarche* by Dutch mediation[2] in the hope of salvaging the western programme which he had drawn up on September 2 on the basis of an exchange of views between Payer and the OHL on August 27: territorial integrity of the Reich, freedom of trade (i.e., no economic war), new regulations for maritime traffic, renunciation of annexations and indemnities (on the eastern pattern), complete restitution of Belgium, on the 'assumption' that no other state was to be better placed politically, militarily or economically, and the possibility of Belgo-German negotiations for a separate peace. No word about the east. Compromise in the west and strengthening of commitments in the east had become the aims which Germany was hoping to achieve by her 'defensive strategy'.

Maintenance of eastern aims and compromise in the west: the policy of September, 1918

As early as June, 1918 the German government had prepared fallback positions from which to justify to the peoples and governments

[1] Schwertfeger, op. cit., pp. 242 ff.
[2] Id., pp. 245 f.

of the west Germany's claim to retain the 'east', should she find herself forced to renounce her war aims in the west. Early in that month Haeften[1] had described the line to be followed in addressing the west in the following eloquent words:

The aim of our eastern policy is not to trample on the border states but to secure their freedom and order.

Defence of the oppressed peoples of eastern Europe against the destructive forces of Bolshevism, safeguarding of the great moral and economic values which have been partly destroyed in eastern Europe and are partly lying fallow. Germany's right and good-neighbourly duty to create order and freedom here in the name of Europe.

Surprisingly, the signal to go over to the new line of anti-Bolshevism as justification for the preservation of Germany's power position in the east came from those who had been the strongest advocates of annexationist policy in both west and east, i.e., heavy industry.

On August 23 and 26 Stinnes conferred with Albert Ballin in Hamburg on the political situation.[2] The two men thought the military position so serious that the Emperor ought to be advised of the necessity of immediately appointing a new Chancellor and concluding an early peace, so that even if the war was liquidated in the west, at least the order in the east could be saved from the wreckage. Stinnes suggested that Ballin, Duisburg, Krupp and he himself should approach the Emperor jointly, but Ballin, who knew the Emperor's mentality intimately, thought that this would not be the best method. With the agreement of the OHL he therefore personally undertook the 'painful mission'. Ballin found the Emperor at Schloss Wilhelmshöhe, near Kassel, on September 5 'again very badly misinformed'.[3] The presence of the ultra-conservative Head of the Civil Cabinet, von Berg, however, prevented the free exchange of opinions for which he had hoped. He was only able to urge on the Emperor the necessity of peace which, he argued, was to be obtained, not through England, but through the 'idealist' Wilson, who was not seeking any territorial advantages in Europe. The Emperor, whose attitude had not changed since the August conference at Spa, agreed in principle, but said that he thought that the peace move could wait ten days until the retreat to the Hindenburg line had been completed; then his plan of using the Queen of Holland to mediate should be tried. Since Ballin had been unable to speak out all that was in his heart owing to continuous interruptions by

[1] *Ursachen*, II, pp. 263 ff.
[2] Id., pp. 290 f. (from Ballin's notes of August 25–26, 1918).
[3] Id., p. 291 (Ballin's notes on his last interview with the Emperor).

von Berg 'as soon as he got a little freer', when he got back to Berlin he left notes on what he had originally meant to say to the Emperor with Admiral von Müller, the Head of the Naval Cabinet.[1] This memorandum, which gives a singularly clear picture of the principles governing Germany's policy in the autumn of 1918, contains the following proposals bearing on war aims:

  (i) Peace in the west through Wilson, using the areas occupied in France and Belgium as pledges;
 (ii) Democratisation of the Reich before the negotiations begin, under the characteristic name of 'modernisation';
(iii) Formation of a front against Bolshevism.

What Haeften in June had described quite generally under the formula of 'safeguarding economic values in the east for Europe', Ballin defined as the common interest of all European economic and financial circles in safeguarding the vast investments and inexhaustible natural resources of Russia against destruction by the Bolshevik revolution.

About the same time, Governor-General von Beseler[2] had reformulated his policy to fit the new line. The Poles were to be won over for an interpretation of the right of self-determination in the 'German-Central European' sense – in other words, Poland was to be made a bulwark of the West against Bolshevism.

This new anti-Bolshevik line in essence only expressed Germany's effort to find a moral justification for retaining her power position in the east in the event of defeat in the west. Payer, speaking at a public meeting in Stuttgart, summarised the internal considerations governing this move, and formulated them as a part of the psychological offensive for home and foreign consumption. This speech, which, like Hintze's war aims programme, was based on a written exchange of views with the OHL of August 27, represents one of the last great expressions of that will to power which animated Germany to the very end. Payer spoke of the general franchise and of a 'peace of understanding'. In his references to domestic affairs his own liberal views found expression in clear advocacy of an early introduction of the general franchise, but what he said on foreign politics agreed exactly with official government policy. It is noteworthy that Payer himself still dismissed the possibility of a 'general military defeat, not to speak of a military collapse' and he fostered illusions about Germany's superiority as based, above all, on her power position in the east, which would more than compensate for the present reverses in

[1] Müller, op. cit., pp. 407 ff.
[2] Conze, op. cit., pp. 368 f.

the west: 'Eastward the world lies open before us again. The occupied territories of Rumania and great parts of the former Russia have been opened up to supply us.' Payer thought popular participation at the conclusion of peace the best guarantee that the peace would result in the *status quo*, without conquests by either side. He made one small exception: he thought a return to the *status quo* possible everywhere 'except only in our east'. Germany must not again withdraw her protection from the border peoples, from Finland to the Ukraine, who had, as he maintained, cut free from Russia of their own initiative, and no one could force her to do so. He therefore sharply forbade the Western Powers to intervene in any way in the regulation of power relationships in the East.

If these states [i.e., the border states], he said, have reached agreement with us, as the nearest interested party and their natural partner . . . that is a question in which . . . we cannot allow anyone to interfere, any more than we propose to submit the treaties concluded by us with the Ukraine, Russia and Rumania to the Entente for their gracious approval or amendment. We have peace in the east and shall go on having it, whether our western enemies like it or not.

For all his verbal acceptance of the *status quo* in the West, Payer did not content himself with claiming domination for Germany in the East. Even now he wanted far-reaching security for Germany's interests in Belgium. Although he was willing to evacuate that country, like Hintze he immediately qualified this concession with an allusion to Germany's Flemish policy, by which he hoped to secure Germany's influence over Belgium even after the peace. Peace should if possible be concluded through separate negotiations, especially as the concurrent economic interests of Belgium and Germany would bring the two countries together.

Payer was criticised by the left for speaking so strongly in the face of the steady deterioration of the general position of the Central Powers. This did not prevent him from rejecting all criticism when he spoke to the Central Committee – which had been convoked to give retrospective approval to the supplementary treaties of Brest – on September 24, and defending more vigorously than ever those treaties and the order established by them. Once again he rejected any intervention by the western allies in the east European settlement. Hintze, following him, also emphasised that he was making the Peace of Brest-Litovsk and the supplementary treaties the basis of his eastern policy. He again expressly described Poland as the 'corner-stone of our policy in the south-east'. A few days earlier, on September 19, Hintze had for the first time officially informed Count Ronikier, the diplomatic representative of the Polish provisional government, of Germany's claim to the Polish Frontier Strip along the Warthe–Narew line, and on September 24 Prince Hatzfeld, Germany's representative in Warsaw, made the same demand in the course of negotiations on the Polish question between Germany and Austria.

September also saw negotiations between Germany and the Ukraine for a new economic agreement[1] which was concluded on September 10 (four days after Wilhelm II had received Hetman Skoropadsky in audience) and gave the Central Powers big economic advantages. Similarly, preparations were going on during that month to link the Baltic provinces and Lithuania closely with Germany. These and other events show that Payer's and Hintze's words continued to reflect the determination of Germany's leaders at least to save the great gains in the east from the wreckage of Germany's defeat, and that Germany was trying to use her 'defensive strategy' to reach a political settlement with the West. Stresemann (who had taken a decisive part in bringing the supplementary treaties into being) expressed himself in the same sense. 'Our policy,' he said, 'aims at retaining what we have achieved in the East, since it is doubtful whether we can realise our Western war aims.' And referring to peace, which he thought 'nearest when the smell of powder is strongest', he said: 'In such a peace we should have to maintain our eastern position, while we must bury our former hopes in the west. Perhaps in the future Germany's whole face will turn rather more to the east. . . .'

On September 27 the Central Committee gave its consent to the supplementary treaties. On September 28 Bulgaria collapsed. On September 29 Hindenburg and Ludendorff brought their Emperor the terrible message that a request for an armistice and peace must go out to President Wilson, and they emphasised that this must be done 'at once, as early as at all possible'; yet even now they did not think of 'giving up the east'. Wilhelm II's reaction was expressed in his succinct remark to his Court: 'The war has ended – quite differently, indeed, from how we expected.'[2] He did not reproach his soldiers, but he did reproach the civilians most vigorously: 'Our politicians have failed us miserably.' The legend of the stab in the back was born.

'Modernisation' from above and mobilisation of Germany's last forces: Germany in October, 1918

When the OHL asked the German government to issue an immediate request for an armistice, Germany had to give up the struggle.

[1] Geiss, *Grenzstreifen*, p. 147.   [2] Müller, op. cit., p. 421.

There could be no more serious talk of German war aims. From this point on, Germany could think herself lucky if she succeeded at least in saving her position as a European great power and emerged from inevitable defeat without too much damage. When the men responsible for the supreme political decisions in Germany met at Spa on September 29 for the last major conference before the request for an armistice,[1] Hintze sketched the political line which Germany would have to follow during the remaining weeks of fighting if she were 'to escape a peace at any price ... with territorial cessions'. She should, he said, 'concentrate all the nation's forces for a final defensive struggle by means either of a dictatorship or of democratisation, 'revolution from above'. The Emperor and the generals rejected dictatorship, which it would need a victory to impose, and decided in favour of 'channelling democratisation', as proposed by Hintze. It was hoped that this mobilisation of the nation's last forces would lead to an armistice and a peace on the basis of Wilson's proposals, and on that day Hintze was still hoping to be able to effect the necessary *démarche* 'when the moment arrived'. The Emperor, the OHL and the civilians were all agreed on 'revolution from above' and the Wilsonian basis. Even then, however, Hindenburg still hoped for the annexation of Longwy–Briey.

From this moment onward all Germany's efforts to obtain peace were concentrated on the U.S.A. The new government of Prince Max of Baden (who protested vainly against such a premature step) accordingly sent Wilson two notes[2] on October 3, asking him 'to undertake the conclusion of peace' and to mediate an immediate armistice, and announced Germany's readiness to conclude peace on the basis of the Fourteen Points.

At the same time 'democratisation' was pushed forward. The victory of parliamentary and democratic institutions in imperial Germany was not, however, the result of a revolutionary upsurge from below, such as had given the Western democracies their inherent strength, but the fruit of a 'revolution from above' consciously planned to take the wind out of the sails of the 'revolution from below' and at the same time to reach a favourable bargaining position *vis-à-vis* the Western Powers. What followed revealed the real purpose of the 'modernisation' of the Reich, as first proposed confidentially by Ballin, and then publicly advocated by Payer, and supported by Hintze in the hour of imminent defeat as the means of concentrating all the nation's forces. The first fruit of this 'modernisation by order' of the political structure of Germany was the appointment

---

[1] *Ursachen*, II, 319 f.; also Schwertfeger, op. cit., pp. 260 ff.
[2] Schwertfeger, op. cit., pp. 305 ff.; *Ursachen*, II, pp. 378 f.

of the liberal south German Prince Max of Baden to succeed Hertling, who resigned on September 30, as Chancellor in what proved to
be the last imperial government. At the same time the entry of important party leaders such as Erzberger and Stresemann into the
cabinet gave it a parliamentary character for the first time in German history.

On October 27 the Reichstag agreed to the constitutional changes
introduced by the government under pressure from Wilson, thus
sanctioning the new development which was to make parliament
thereafter the repository of sovereignty – too late, however, to avert
the revolution which broke out none the less owing to the slowness of
the peace negotiations and the fear that the war would not end.

The defeat of the revolution by the alliance struck between Ebert,
the leader of the Majority Socialists, and Hindenburg, who remained
at the head of the army even after the abdication of the Emperor,
would, it was hoped, commend the young republic to the Western
Powers as an advance guard against Bolshevism and so produce
milder peace terms. The role of the Ebert government as a factor of
stability in the heart of Europe induced the Allies to allow Germany
to keep her troops in the east on guard against red revolution until
replaced by Allied forces. This concession by the Allies fostered an
illusion among many Germans that Germany's power position in the
east could still be saved. The severity of the actual peace terms of the
Treaty of Versailles, announced in the early summer of 1919, consequently produced a violent and nation-wide reaction. Since, however, the idea of resuming the war against the Allies, which had often
figured in the plans of the OHL, had ceased to be practical politics,
a bare majority of the National Assembly sacrificed and ratified the
treaty which, although it imposed territorial losses and heavy financial and economic burdens, yet left Germany a great power in the
centre of Europe.

Germany overtaxed herself in the First World War as the result of
an obstinate underestimate of the strength of others and over-esti-
mate of her own. This permanent misconception of realities forms a
'continuity of error' which goes back far into the world policy of the
reign of Wilhelm II. The best witness is Bethmann Hollweg himself
who, speaking before the Central Committee of the Reichstag at the
beginning of October, 1916, said that this misjudgment of the rest of
the world had been a permanent element in German policy before
and after 1914.

Since war began, he said, we have not escaped the danger of underestimating the strength of our enemies. We inherited this mistake from the years

636

of peace. Our people had developed so amazingly in the last twenty years that wide circles succumbed to the temptation of over-estimating our enormous forces in relation to those of the rest of the world.[1]

But even after the defeat of 1918, many Germans, and especially those who had played leading parts in political and economic life up to 1918, preserved in the two following decades a political and historical image of themselves which was coloured by illusions. Because the German army on the western front had held to the last hour an unbroken defensive front outside the frontiers of the Reich, and had marched home in order, these people failed to understand that Germany had been defeated. Thus the idea took root and spread that the cause of the collapse of Germany was not her own policy or exhaustion in the face of an enemy army made stronger than her own by active American intervention, but a 'stab in the back' behind the front. The accusation was first levelled against the parliamentary government of Prince Max of Baden, then against the socialist parties and the November revolution, and finally against the Weimar democracy which had been forced to accept the 'dictated Treaty of Versailles' owing to 'treachery at home'. This view did not originate in, or become the faith of millions as the result of, the statements made by Hindenburg and Ludendorff to the committee of enquiry of the National Assembly in November, 1919 which attributed the collapse to an alleged 'stab in the back'. It had been propagated by the OHL and the press in contact with it since 1917, and more particularly since November, 1918. The *Evangelische Kirchenzeitung*, for example, wrote on October 20 – before the November revolution: 'Collapse behind the front – not collapse of our heroic front. That is the shattering phenomenon of these last days. . . . The home has not held out.'

And a week later the same paper described the actions of Prince Max's government as an 'organised betrayal of the Reich' and the day of its appointment as 'the Fatherland's blackest hour'.

This false interpretation of defeat was accompanied by another popular illusion: that Germany had been the victim of an organised assault and that her war had been exclusively one of justifiable self-defence. On this assumption contemporaries and later historians either denied the existence of Germany's war aims altogether, or interpreted them as safeguards against a new assault. It came to be believed that the failure at home had prevented this defensive organisation of Germany's power position, and so people were prevented from seeing that in reality Germany had followed for four years aims

[1] See above, p. 92.

the realisation of which would not only have destroyed for ever the European balance of power, but which would have also infringed the liberties of peoples who were either previously independent or had won their independence during the upheavals. Above all, in the years of impotence and humiliation imposed, as the nation felt it, by Versailles the two illusions of the stab in the back and the purely defensive war nurtured a running sore of resentment against the order of 1919 and a faith that Germany would again rise to the rank of a world power.

SELECTIVE BIBLIOGRAPHY

THE German editions of this book contain extensive detailed references to the German and Austrian archives used by the author. Since the student wishing to consult these sources may be expected to use the German editions, these references have been omitted from this edition. The lists of references which follow are those prepared by the author for the first German edition and subsequently revised by him for this edition. Full references to the many other works cited in the text are given in footnotes throughout the book.

1. Published Documents

Die Grosse Politik der Europäischen Kabinette, 1871–1914. Sammlung der Diplomatischen Akten des Auswärtigen Amtes, ed. Johannes Lepsius, Albrecht-Mendelssohn-Bartholdy, Friedrich Thimme, Berlin, 1924 ff. (from vol. 14)

British Documents on the Origin of the War, 1898–1914, ed. G. P. Gooch und Harold Temperley, London, 1926 ff., vols. I, VIII–XI

Documents Diplomatiques Français (1871–1914), ed. Commission de Publication des Documents Relatifs aux Origines de la Guerre de 1914, Paris, 1929 ff., Third Series (1911–14), vols. I–XI

Österreich-Ungarns Aussenpolitik von der bosnischen Krise 1908 bis zum Kreigsausbruch 1914. Diplomatische Aktenstücke des Österreich-Ungarischen Ministeriums des Äussern, bearbeitet von Ludwig Bittner und Hans Übersberger, Vienna and Leipzig, 1930, vols. I–VIII

Die Internationalen Beziehungen im Zeitalter des Imperialismus. Dokument aus den Archiven der Zarischen und Provisorischen Regierung, ed. Kommission beim Zentralexekutivkomitee der Sowjetregierung unter dem Vorsitz von M. N. Prokowski. – German edition ed. von Otto Hoetzsch, Series III, I, II 1911–1914, Berlin, 1933–43.

Die deutschen Dokumente zum Kriegsausbruch 1914, zusammengestellt von Karl Kautsky, ed. Max Graf von Montgelas and Walter Schücking, Berlin, 1919, second expanded impression, Berlin, 1922, vols. 1–4.

Stenographische Berichte der Verhnadlungen des Deutschen Reichstages, 13th legislative period, vols. 306–325.

Stenographische Berichte der Verhandlungen des Preussischen Hauses der Abgeordneten nebst Drucksachen, 20th–22nd legislative period, Berlin, 1904–1918.

Schulthess' Europäischer Geschichtskalender, Neue Folge, vols. 30–33, 1914 to 1918, Munich, 1917–20.

Wippermann-Purlitz, Jhrg. 30–33, 1914–1918 Deutscher Geschichtskalender, Leipzig.

Die Deutsche Nationalversammlung 1919–20. Stenographische Berichte über die öffentlichen Verhandlungen des 15. Untersuchungsausschusses der Verfassunggebenden Nationalversammlung, vols. I and II, Berlin, 1920.

BIBLIOGRAPHY

Das Werk des Untersuchungsausschusses der Verfassunggebenden Nationalversammlung und des Deutschen Reichstags 1919 bis 1928, Dritte Reihe, Völkerrecht im Weltkrieg, 1914–18, 2 Bde, Vierte Reihe, Die Ursachen des deutschen Zusammenbruchs im Jahre 1918, vols. 1, 2, 6, 8, 12

Der Weltkrieg 1914–18, bearbeitet im Reichsarchiv, Bde. I–XII, 1925–1939, Bde. XII und XIV, 1942–44, bearbeitet von der Forschungsanstalt für Kriegs- und Heeresgeschichte im Auftrage des Reichskriegs-ministeriums, ed. Bundesarchiv, 1956

Die Auswirkungen der Grossen Sozialistischen Oktoberrevolution auf Deutschland, ed. Leo Stern, vols. 1–4. Archivalische Forschungen zur Geschichte der deutschen Arbeiterbewegung, vol. IV, 1–4, Berlin, 1959

Ursachen und Folgen. Vom deutschen Zusammenbruch 1918 und 1945 bis zur staatlichen Neuordnung Deutschlands in der Gegenwart, ed. H. Michaelis, E. Schraepler und G. Scheel, vols. 1–2, Berlin, 1958

Ämtliche Urkunden zur Vorgeschichte des Waffenstillstandes 1918, ed. Auswärtiges Amt and Reichsamt des Innern, Berlin, 1924

Ludendorff, Erich, (ed), *Urkunden der Obersten Heeresleitung über ihre Tätigkeit 1916–18*, Berlin, 1920

Tirpitz, A. v., *Politische Dokumente, Aufbau des deutschen Weltmacht*, Stuttgart/Berlin, 1924

Spindler, Arno, *Der Handelskrieg mit U-Booten* (1932–34)

Germany and the Revolution in Russia. Documents from the German Foreign Ministry, ed. Z. A. B. Zeman, London, 1958

Lenins Rückkehr nach Russland 1917. Die deutschen Akten, ed. and with an introduction by Werner Hahlweg, Leiden, 1957

Katkov, G., 'German Foreign Office Documents on financial support to the Bolsheviks in 1917', *International Affairs* 32, 1956

Der Interfraktionelle Ausschuss 1917–18, Bd. 1, I–II. Quellen zur Geschichte des Parlamentarismus und der politischen Parteien. 1. Reihe. Von der konstitutionellen Monarchie zur parlamentarischen Republik. Im Auftrage der Kommission für Geschichte des Parlamentarismus und der politischen Parteien, ed. Werner Conze, Erich Matthias und Georg Winter, Düsseldorf, 1959 (revised by Erich Matthias assisted by Rudolf Morsey)

Gatzke, Hans W., 'Dokumentation zu den deutsch-russischen Beziehungen 1918', *Vierteljahreshefte für Zeitgeschichte* 1955, vol. 1, pp. 67 ff.

Grunewald, Jaques and Scherer, André, *L'Allemagne et les Problèmes de la Paix pendant la Première Guerre Mondiale*, Paris, 1962

G. F. de Martens, *Nouveau Recueil Général de Traités*, Third Series, vol. X. Die deutsche Okkupation der Ukraine, Geheimdokumente. Edition Prométhée, Strasbourg, 1937

Les Archives du Conseil de Flandre, ed. Ligue Nationale pour l'Unité Belge, Bruxelles, 1935

BIBLIOGRAPHY

Glaise-Horstenau, E. v., *Österreich-Ungarns letzter Krieg 1914–1918*, ed. Österreichisches Bundesministerium für Heerwesen und von Kriegsarchiv, vols. 1–7, 1931–38

Bernstorff, Graf Joh. H. v., *Deutschland und Amerika, Erinnerungen aus dem 5järhigen Kriege*, Berlin, 1920

Bethmann Hollweg, Th. v., *Kriegsreden*, ed. F. Thimme, Berlin

Czernin, Ottokar, *Im Weltkriege*, Berlin and Vienna, 1919 (Aktenanhang)

2. Principal Secondary Sources
[Diss. = Dissertation]

Albertini, Luigi, *The Origins of the War of 1914*, 3 vols., London/New York/Toronto, 1952

Barthels, W., *Die Linken in der Sozialdemokratie im Kampf gegen Militarismus und Krieg*, Berlin, 1958

Basler, Werner, *Deutschlands Kriegszielpolitik 1914–1918*, Diss. Kiel, 1951

——, 'Die Politik des deutschen Imperialismus gegenüber Litauen 1914–1918', *Jahrbuch für Geschichte der UdSSR und der Volksdemokratischen Länder Europas*, vol. 4, Berlin, 1960

——, *Deutschlands Annexionspolitik in Polen und im Baltikum*, Veröffentlichungen des Instituts für Geschichte der Völker der UdSSR an der Martin-Luther-Universität Halle-Wittenberg, Berlin, 1962

Bergsträsser, Ludwig, *Die preussische Wahlrechtsfrage im Kriege und die Entstehung der Osterbotschaft 1917*, Tübingen, 1924

Beyer, Hans, *Die Mittelmächte und die Ukraine*, Munich, 1956

Birnbaum, Karl, *Peace Moves and U-Boat Warfare*, Uppsala, 1958

Carlgren, W. M., *Neutralität oder Allianz, Deutschlands Beziehungen zu Schweden in den Anfangsjahren des ersten Weltkrieges*, Stockholm/Göteborg Uppsala, 1962

Colliander, Börje, *Die Beziehungen zwischen Litauen und Deutschland während der Okkupation 1915–18*, Turku, 1935

Conze, Werner, *Polnische Nation und deutsche Politik*, Cologne, 1958

——, 'Nationalstaas oder Mitteleuropa: Die Deutschen des Reiches und die Nationalitätenfragen Ostmitteleuropas im ersten Weltkrieg' in: *Deutschland und Europa; Hist. Stud. zur Völker- und Staatenordnung des Abendlandes*, Düsseldorf 1951, pp. 201–32

Dehio, Ludwig, *Deutschland und die Weltpolitik im 20. Jahrhundert*, Munich, 1955–*Germany and World Politics*, London and New York, 1959

——, 'Gedanken über die deutsche Sendung 1900–1918', *Historische Zeitschrift*, 1952

——, 'Deutschland und die Epoche der Weltkriege', *Historische Zeitschrift* 173

Deuerlein, Ernst, *Der Bundesratsausschuss für auswärtige Angelegenheiten 1870 bis 1918*, Regensburg, 1955

641

BIBLIOGRAPHY

Epstein, Fritz T., 'Ost-Mitteleuropa als Spannungsfeld zwischen Ost und West um die Jahrhundertwende bis zum Ende des Ersten Weltkrieges' in *Die Welt als Geschichte*, 16th year (1956), pp. 64–123

Epstein, Klaus, *Matthias Erzberger and the Dilemma of German Democracy*, Princeton, 1959

——, 'The Development of German-Austrian War Aims in the Spring of 1917', in *Journal of Central European Affairs*, Volume XVII, April, 1957

Fay, S. B., *The Origins of the World War*, New York, 1928

Freund, G., *The Unholy Alliance, Russian–German Relations from the Treaty of Brest-Litovsk to the Treaty of Berlin*, London and New York, 1957

Futrell, Michael, 'Alexander Kesküla', in *St. Antony's Papers*, no. 12, London 1962, pp. 23 ff.

Gatzke, Hans W., *Germany's Drive to the West, a study of Western War Aims during the First World War*, Baltimore, 1950

Gehrke, U., *Persien in der deutschen Orientpolitik während des ersten Weltkrieges*, Diss., Hamburg, 1960

Geiss, Imanuel, *Der polnische Grenzstreifen 1914–1918*, Lübeck/Hamburg, 1960

Gratz, E. and Schüller, R., *Die äussere Wirtschaftspolitik Österreich-Ungarns, Mitteleuropäische Pläne*, 1925

Grebing, Helga, 'Österreich-Ungarn und die ukrainische Aktion 1914–18', in *Jahrbuch für Geschichte des Ostens*, vol. 7

Hahlweg, Werner, *Der Diktatfrieden von Brest-Litowsk*, Münster, 1960

Hallgarten, George W. F., *Imperialismus vor 1914*, 2 vols., Munich, 1951

Hölzle, Erwin, *Der Osten im ersten Weltkrieg*, Leipzig, 1944

——, 'Deutschland und die Wegscheide des ersten Weltkrieges', in *Festschrift für D. Becker, Geschichtliche Kräfte und Entscheidungen*, Wiesbaden, 1954

Hubatsch, Walther, *Der Admiralstab und die obersten Marinebehörden in Deutschland 1848–1945*, Frankfurt, 1958

——, *Die Ära Tirpitz, Studien zur deutschen Marinepolitik 1890–1918* (Göttinger Bausteine, vol. 21), Göttingen/Berlin/Frankfurt, 1955

Janssen, Karl Heintz, *Die Kriegsziele des Bundesstaaten* (1914–18), Diss., Freiburg, 1957

——, 'Der Wechsel in der OHL 1916', *Vierteljahreshefte für Zeitgeschichte*, seventh year 1959, pp. 337 ff.

Katkov, George, 'The Assassination of Count Mirbach', in *St. Antony's Papers*, no. 12, London, 1962 pp. 53 ff.

Kennan, George F., *Soviet–American Relations 1917–20*, 2 vols., Princeton, 1956–58

Klimas, Paul, *Der Werdegang des litauischen Staates von 1915 bis zur Bildung der provisorischen Regierung im November, 1918*, Berlin, 1919

Koschnitzke, R., *Die Innenpolitik des Reichskanzlers Bethmann Hollweg im Weltkrieg*, Diss., Kiel, 1952

BIBLIOGRAPHY

Lewerenz, Lilli, *Die deutsche Politik im Baltikum*, Diss., Hamburg, 1958

Lorenz, Reinhold, *Kaiser Karl und der Untergang der Donaumonarchie*, Graz/Vienna/Cologne, 1959

Lumbroso, Alberto, *Le origini della guerra mondiale*, Milan, 1928

Matthias, Erich, *Die deutsche Sozialdemokratie und der Osten 1914–45*, Tübingen, 1954

May, E. R., *The World War and American Isolation, 1914–1917*, Cambridge U.P., 1959

Mayer, Arnold, *Political Origins of the New Diplomacy*, New Haven, 1959

Meenzen, Johann, *Aussenpolitik und Weltfriedensordnung der deutschen Sozial-demokratie 1914–19*, Diss., Hamburg, 1951

Mehnert, Gottfried, *Evangelische Kirchenpolitik 1917–1919* (Beiträge zur Geschichte des Parlamentarismus und der politischen Parteien), Düsseldorf, 1959

Meinecke, Friedrich, 'Kühlmann und die päpstliche Friedensaktion', in *Sitzungsberichte der Preussischen Akademie der Wissenschaften*, phil.-hist. Klasse, 1928

Meyer, Henry Cord, 'Germans in the Ukraine, 1918', *American Slavonic and East European Review*, April, 1950

——, 'German Economic Relations with South-Eastern Europe 1870–1914', *American Historical Review 57*, 1951–52

——, *Mitteleuropa in German Thought and Action 1815–1945*, The Hague, 1955

Mühlmann, Carl, *Oberste Heeresleitung und Balkan im Weltkrieg 1914–1918*, 1942

——, *Das deutsch-türkische Waffenbündnis im Weltkriege*, Leipzig, 1940

Müller, George Alexander v., *Regierte der Kaiser?* Kriegstagebücher, Aufzeichnungen und Briefe des Chefs des Marine-Kabinets Admiral G. A. v. Müller, ed. Walter Görlitz, Göttingen, 1959

Namier, L. B., 'Richard v. Kühlmann: The Study of a German Diplomatist', *Quarterly Review*, July, 1950

Neck, Rudolf, 'Das Wiener Dokument, von 27 März 1917', in *Mitteilungen des Osterreichischen Staatsarchivs*, vol. 7, Vienna, 1954, p. 294

Nurmio, Yrsö, *Suomen Itsenäistyminen Ja Saksa*, Helsinki, 1957

Pidhaini, Oleg S., *The Ukrainian-Polish Problem in the Dissolution of the Russian Empire, 1914–1917*, Toronto/New York, 1962

Pirenne, Henri, *La Belgique et la guerre mondiale*, New Haven, 1929

Prokopowitsch, Erich, 'Das Ende der österreichischen Herrschaft' in *Der Bukowina, Buchreihe der Südosteuropäischen Kommission*, vol. 2, Munich, 1959

Renouvin, Pierre, *La Crise Européenne et la Grande Guerre*, Paris, 1939

——, 'Les Origines Immediats de la Guerre', *Publications de la société de l'histoire de la Guerre*, Paris, 1927

Reshetar, John S., *The Ukrainian Revolution 1917–1920, A Study in Nationalism*, Princeton, 1952

BIBLIOGRAPHY

Ritter, Gerhard, *Staatskunst und Kriegshandwerk*, vol. II, Munich, 1960

——, 'Die Zusammenarbeit der Generalstäbe Deutschlands und Österreich-Ungarns vor dem ersten Weltkrieg', in *Festschrift für H. Herzfeld*, 1958

——, *Der Schlieffenplan, Kritik eines Mythos*, Munich, 1956

Rosen, Friedrich, *Aus einem diplomatischen Wanderleben*, Wiesbaden, 1959

Rudiger (= A. Wullus), *Flamenpolitik, Suprème Espoir allemand de domination Belgique*, Brussels 1921

Schmitt, Bernadotte E., *The Coming of the War*, New York, 1930

Schüssler, Wilhelm, (ed.) *Weltmachtstreben und Flottenbau*, Witten, 1956

Schwabe, Klaus, *Die deutschen Professoren und die politischen Grundfragen des ersten Weltkrieges*, Diss., Freiburg, 1958

Smith, C. Jay jnr., *Finland and the Russian Revolution 1917–22*, Athens, 1958

Snell, John L., 'Socialist Unions and Socialist Patriotism in Germany, 1914–1918', *American Historical Review*, 59, 1953–4

——, 'Wilson on Germany and the Fourteen Points', *Journal of Modern History*, December, 1954

——, 'Benedict XV, Wilson, Michaelis and German Socialism', *Catholic Historical Review*, July, 1951

Stadelmann, R., 'Friedensversuche in den ersten Jahren des Weltkrieges', *Historische Zeitschrift 1937*, vol. 156

Steglich, Wolfgang, *Bündnissicherung oder Verständigungsfrieden, Untersuchungen zu dem Friedensangebot der Mittelmächte vom 12. Dezember 1916*, Göttingen/Berlin/Frankfurt, 1958. (*Göttinger Bausteine zue Gesch. Wissenschaft*, vol. 28)

Sweet, Paul R., 'Leaders and Policies: Germany in the Winter of 1914–1915', *Journal of Central European Affairs*, vol. 16, October, 1956

——, 'Germany, Austria-Hungary and Mitteleuropa, August 1915 to April 1916', in *Festschrift für Heinrich Benedikt*, ed. H. Hantch und Novotny, Vienn , 1957

Vietsch, Eberhard von, *Wilhelm Solf, Botschafter zwischen den Zeiten*, Tübingen, 1961

Vogts, Alfred, M. M. Warburg & Co., 'Ein Bankhaus in der deutschen Weltpolitik', in *Vierteljahrsschriften für Sozial- u. Wirtschaftsgeschichte*, vol. 45, part 3, September 1958

Wheeler-Bennett, J. W., *Brest-Litovsk, The Forgotten Peace*, London, 1938

Willemsen, A. W., *Het Vlaams-Nationalisme 1914–1940*, Groningen, 1958

Zechlin, Egmont, 'Friedensbestrebungen und Revolutionierungsversuche', in *Aus Politik und Zeitgeschichte*, Beilagen zur Wochenzeitung *Das Parlament*, 17.5.1961, 14.6.61, 21.6.1961

Zmarzlik, Hans Günther, *Bethmann Hollweg als Reichskanzler 1909–1919, Studien zu Möglichkeiten und Grenzen seiner innerpolitischen Machtstellung*, Düsseldorf, 1957

INDEX